Ann Sophia Stephens

Pictorial History of the War for the Union

Vol. 1

Ann Sophia Stephens

Pictorial History of the War for the Union
Vol. 1

ISBN/EAN: 9783337400934

Printed in Europe, USA, Canada, Australia, Japan

Cover: Foto ©ninafisch / pixelio.de

More available books at **www.hansebooks.com**

PICTORIAL HISTORY

OF THE

WAR FOR THE UNION.

A COMPLETE AND RELIABLE

History of the War

FROM ITS

COMMENCEMENT TO ITS CLOSE:

GIVING A GRAPHIC PICTURE OF ITS ENCOUNTERS, THRILLING INCIDENTS, FRIGHTFUL SCENES, HAIR-BREADTH ESCAPES, INDIVIDUAL DARING, DESPERATE CHARGES, PERSONAL ANECDOTES, ETC., GLEANED FROM EYE-WITNESSES OF, AND PARTICIPANTS IN, THE TERRIBLE SCENES DESCRIBED—A TRUTHFUL LIVING REFLEX OF ALL MATTERS OF INTEREST CONNECTED WITH THIS THE MOST GIGANTIC OF HUMAN STRUGGLES.

TOGETHER WITH A COMPLETE CHRONOLOGICAL ANALYSIS OF THE WAR.

By MRS. ANN S. STEPHENS.

EMBELLISHED WITH OVER TWO HUNDRED ILLUSTRATIONS.

TWO VOLUMES.

VOL I.

CINCINNATI:
JAMES R. HAWLEY, 164 VINE STREET,
PUBLISHER OF SUBSCRIPTION BOOKS.
1863.

INTRODUCTION.

THE most difficult task, perhaps, known to literature, is to write a history of events as they transpire—to arrange facts before the hand of time has given them just position and importance. In writing a history of the Civil War which is now raging in the land—the most gigantic and stupendous rebellion yet known to the world—the magnitude of the task, and the difficulties that present themselves, challenge a degree of moral courage almost equal to that physical bravery which has been so conspicuous in the war. But if an honest intention to be just—a thorough desire for truth, and a determination to discard all personal prejudices, can produce a faithful history, this work has a right to claim acceptance.

The political history of a nation, when it merges into armed strife, is generally a record of prejudices and of passion: civil war is the result. In this work the author deals not with causes, but with the terrible events that spring out of them; avoiding so far as possible the threatening clouds of political dissension that preceded and still follow the tempest. Time, which will clear up obscurities and remove passion, and the intellect of a great statesman, are necessary, before the political and military history of this war can be fittingly united.

In this book there is a positive rejection of those partizan dissensions which have burst asunder the sacred ties of the greatest nation on earth, and deluged the soil trodden by millions of happy men with the blood of as brave a soldiery as ever drew breath. This history of the War for the Union is written for no faction—no party—no combination of men, but for the people of every portion of the Union. Political passions die—History lives; and in an enlightened age like this, it must be written in simple truth, or the clear-sighted generations that follow us will detect the sophistry and falsehood. Impartial history demands honest facts. The opinions of an historian are but the assumptions of one mind attempting to control multitudes. The author's duty is to give details, allowing the intelligent reader to draw his own conclusions unembarrassed by obtrusive opinions, which are in all cases liable to be influenced by prejudices.

The History of the War for the Union is a record of stupendous events which have given grandeur to the American arms and sorrow to every good American heart. Taking up the thread of events where the political history of the nation left them on the fourth of March, eighteen hundred and sixty-one, the author has followed the ensanguined track, giving to every battle-field its place, and every heroic act its record. The sources of information in which the work has found its existence, have been authentic reports from the War Department, the official statements of commandants on the battle-field, and the many thrilling and graphic descriptions furnished by eye-witnesses.

In giving due credit to those persons who have aided her in the rapid completion of her first volume, the author acknowledges her great obligation to WM. OLAND BOURNE, Esq., who has devoted much time to the work, and whose ample collection of material for history has been freely used in its preparation; and to J. J. GOLDEN, Esq., whose research and clear judgment in sifting truth from error, arranging facts, and superintending the work in its progress through the press, has enabled her to place it before the public in less than three months from its commencement. To Mr. Golder's critical care the reader is indebted for the compact and excellent Chronology attached to this volume, in which all the historical events of the war are placed in their order of succession.

In the mechanical and artistic execution of the work, the publisher has evinced an enthusiasm which corresponds nobly with the great subject of the history, and has been even lavish in pictorial embellishments. These have been all drawn and engraved expressly for this work, at great cost; and in the truthfulness and beauty of their execution, add to the high reputation already attained by the artists, Messrs. WATERS and SON.

NEW YORK, *October* 1, 1862.   ANN S. STEPHENS.

CONTENTS.

	PAGE
Introduction	7
Inauguration of President Lincoln	17

The coming tempest—The national forbearance—Mustering of rebel troops—Efforts for conciliation—The Border States—South Carolina—Investment of Fort Sumter—The Star of the West—Gen. Beauregard.

Fortifications in Charleston Harbor 25

The iron floating battery—Cummings Point battery—Castle Pinckney.

Bombardment of Fort Sumter 28

Storming of Fort Sumter, viewed from the land—Naval expedition for the relief of Fort Sumter.

The Nation's Response 40

Startling effect of the news of the attack on Sumter—The President's Proclamation—Departure of troops for Washington—Enthusiasm of the people—Their devotion to the national Union—Large contributions to aid the Government.

Reinforcement of Fort Pickens 46

The harbor of Pensacola—Forts McRae and Barrancas—Description of Fort Pickens—Its investment by rebel troops under Gen. Bragg—The Federal fleet in the harbor—Successful landing of troops and supplies.

Burning of Harper's Ferry Arsenal 49

Through Baltimore 50

Arrival of the Massachusetts Sixth, Col. Jones, in Baltimore—Blockade of the streets—Attack by the mob—Defence of the military—Terrible results—The regimental band—The city authorities—Intense excitement of the citizens—Pennsylvania troops—Mayor Brown and Marshal Kane.

Military Occupation of Annapolis, Md. 61

The Eighth Massachusetts and the Seventh New York—Gen. Butler—Gov. Hicks—the frigate Constitution—the Naval Academy—March to the Junction.

Maryland 66

Efforts of secessionists to involve the State in rebellion—Patriotic devotion of loyal citizens—Gov. Hicks—The State Legislature—Gen. Butler in Maryland—Gen. Cadwallader—The *habeas corpus* act—Chief-Justice Taney.

Destruction of Gosport Navy Yard 73

The State of the Nation before its Troops entered Virginia 76

Response of the Governors of Maryland, Delaware, North Carolina, Kentucky, and Missouri, to the President's Proclamation—The position of Virginia—The Confederate Congress, at Montgomery—Jefferson Davis—The Confederate army—Letters of Marque—Postal communication—Tennessee and Arkansas—Border States Convention—Position of Missouri.

Occupation of Alexandria, Va. 83

Assassination of Col. Ellsworth—The Marshall House—J. W. Jackson—Brownell Sketch of Ellsworth—Defection of Gen. Lee—Lieut. Tompkins' scout to Fairfax Court House.

Battle of Great Bethel ....

Death of Major Winthrop and Lieut. Greble.

The Ambuscade at Vienna, Va. 91

CONTENTS.

	PAGE
Review at Washington	93
Advance of the Grand Army	94

Position of the belligerent forces—Gen. McDowell—Gen. Patterson—Gen. Johnston—Gen. Beauregard—Advance to Fairfax and Centreville—Battle of Blackburn's Ford.

The Battle of Bull Run	98

The Federal Commanders and the movements of their forces—The engagement—Arrival of rebel reinforcements—The climax and the retreat—The battle on the left wing—The battle-field at night.

Western Virginia	129
Battle of Phillipi, Va.	131
Destruction of Railroad Property	133
Gen. McClellan in Western Virginia	133
Battle of Scareytown	134
Battle of Rich Mountain	135
Battle of Carrick's Ford	137

Gen. Rosecrans and Col. Lander—Gen. Morris—Capt. Benham—Defeat of the rebel forces and death of Gen. Garnett.

The West	141
Missouri	143
Capture of Camp Jackson	144

Decisive action of Capt. Lyon—Gen. Frost—The Missouri Legislature—Gov. Jackson—Gen. Harney—Gen. Price—Gen. Lyon appointed to command the Department.

Cairo	150
Battle of Booneville	151
Battle of Carthage	152
Battle of Monroe, Mo.	154
Guerrilla Bands in Missouri	155

Gen. Pope in Northern Missouri—State Convention at Jefferson City—Gen. Fremont at St. Louis—Invasion of the State by Gens. Pillow and Jeff. Thompson—Address of the State Convention.

Battle of Dug Springs	156
Skirmish at Athens, Mo.	157
Battle of Wilson's Creek	159

Gen. Lyon at Springfield—Gens. Price and McCulloch—Critical position of the Federal army—The battle—The death of Gen. Lyon—Retreat of the Union army.

Kentucky	164

The neutrality of the State—Position of Gov. Magoffin—Gen. Buckner—Gen. McClellan—The State Legislature—Decisive Union measures.

The Occupation of Paducah	168

Rebel troops ordered to withdraw from Kentucky—Attempt to form a revolutionary government in the State—Military movements of the rebels in Kentucky—The loyal State government.

Naval Operations	175
The Expedition to Cape Hatteras	177
Capture of Forts Hatteras and Clark	180
Western Virginia	182
Surprise at Cross Lanes	183
Battle of Carnifex Ferry	183
Battle of Cheat Mountain Pass	186

CONTENTS.

	PAGE
Engagement at Chapmansville	188
Reconnoissance at Green Brier, Western Virginia	190
Defence of Lexington, Mo.	193

The Federal forces for the defence of the town—Col. Mulligan and the Chicago brigade—Cols. Marshall and Peabody—Advance of Gen. Price's army—The investment—The attack—Bravery of the Federal garrison—Their endurance and privations—The surrender.

Attack on Santa Rosa Island, Fla.	199
Battle of Ball's Bluff, Va.	200

Position of the Federal forces on the Potomac—Gen. Stone—Col. Baker—The proposed reconnoissance—Transportation of the troops—The topography of the Virginia shore—The engagement—Death of Col. Baker—Defeat of the Federal troops—Disastrous retreat—Gens. McClellan and Banks at Edwards Ferry—Sketch of Col. Baker.

Battle at Camp Wild Cat, Ky.	210
Battle of Romney, Va.	212
Battle of Frederickton, Mo.	213
Charge of Fremont's Body-Guard at Springfield, Mo.	217
The Department of Missouri	220

General review of the Department—Gen. Lyon—Gen. Fremont—His proclamation and its modification by the President—Organization of the Federal forces—Their advance—Negotiations with Gen. Price—Gen. Fremont removed—Appointment of Gen. Hunter—Retreat of the Federal army—The disloyal Legislature—Advance of the rebel forces—Recruiting—Gen. Halleck.

The Stone Fleet	225
Battle of Camp Alleghany, Western Virginia	228
Battle of Munfordsville, Ky.	230
Capture of Rebel Recruits at Milford, Mo.	232
Battle of Dranesville, Va.	238
Expedition to Ship Island	241
Engagement at Mount Zion, Mo.	242
Arkansas and the Indians	243
Bombardment at Fort Pickens	245
Rout of Gen. Marshall at Paintsville, Ky.	247
Battle of Middle Creek, Ky.	248
Battle of Silver Creek, Mo.	251
Battle of Mill Spring, Ky.	255
Investment of Fort Pulaski, Ga.	262
New Mexico and Arizona	266
Battle of Valvende, N. M.	267
Battle of Apache Cañon	270
Fight at Blooming Gap, Va.	273
East Tennessee under Confederate rule	275

The loyalty and devotion of the people—Despotism of the rebel leaders—Parson Brownlow—Sufferings of the Unionists—General Zollicoffer—Andrew Johnson—Horace Maynard—Bridge-burning.

Capture of Fort Henry, Tenn.	281

Gen. Grant's army—Gen. C. F. Smith—Com. Foote and the naval flotilla—Sailing of the expedition—Names of the vessels and officers—The attack and surrender—The rebel camp—Advance of the national gunboats up the Tennessee river.

The Burnside Expedition	290

Sailing of the expedition from Hampton Roads—Com. Goldsborough—The naval forces—Gen. Burnside and the troops—Severe storm—The fleet at Hatteras Inlet.

	PAGE
Capture of Roanoke Island	292
Evacuation of Bowling Green, Ky.	296
Capture of Fort Donelson	298

Advance of the Federal land and naval forces from Fort Henry and Cairo—Description of Fort Donelson—The naval attack—Retreat of the gunboats—The army—The land attack—The severity of the engagement—Sufferings of the Federal soldiers—Their courage and endurance—Protracted defence—The surrender.

The Occupation of Nashville	317
Fort Clinch and Fernandina, Fla.	321
The Merrimac and the Monitor	322
Capture of Jacksonville, Fla.	330
Occupation of Columbus, Ky.	332
Battle of Pea Ridge, Ark.	334
Battle of Newbern, N. C.	342
Capture of New Madrid, Mo.	351
Island No. 10	356
Capture of Island No. 10 and the Rebel army	358
Battle of Winchester, Va.	362

Position of Gen. Shield's command—The rebel force under Gen. Jackson—Plans of the Confederate leaders—Strategy of Gen. Shields—Attack by Gen. Jackson—The rebels reinforced—Bravery of the Federal troops—Charge of Gen. Tyler's brigade—Defeat of the rebels.

Battle of Pittsburg Landing	367

Topography of the country—Corinth—Pittsburg—Savannah—Position of the Federal troops—The rebel army and its commanders—The battle of Sunday, March 8—Hurlbut's division—McClernand's division—Desperate hand-to-hand fighting—Perilous position of the national troops—Wallace's division.

Gen. Sherman's Reconnoissance toward Corinth	403
Occupation of Huntsville, Ala.	404
Capture of Fort Pulaski, Ga.	406
Battle of South Mills, N. C.	414
Capture of Fort Macon	418
Siege of Yorktown, Va.	424

Retreat of the rebel army from Centreville and Manassas, toward Richmond—Advance of Gen. McClellan's army—Events of March, 1862—The Federal army at Old Point—Advance toward Yorktown—The Investment—Offensive and defensive operations—Labors and sufferings of. the Federal soldiers.

Battle of Lee's Mills, Va.	427
Capture of New Orleans	429

Bombardment of Forts Jackson and St. Philip—The Federal fleet—The mortar boats—Coms. Farragut, Porter, and Bailey—Stupendous naval engagement—The surrender of the forts—The occupation of New Orleans—Capt. Bailey—Gen. Lovell—J. T. Monroe—Pierre Soulé—Gen. Butler.

The Evacuation of Yorktown	448
The Battle of Williamsburg, Va.	450

Advance of Gen. Stoneman's cavalry from Yorktown—Gen. Hooker's division—Gen. Kearney—Gen. Sumner—Gens. Smith and Couch—Gen. Hooker's attack and protracted contest with superior numbers—Gen. Heintzelman—Gen. Hancock's brilliant charge—Arrival of Gen. McClellan—Retreat of the rebels.

Battle of West Point, Va.	462
Chronology	465

INDEX TO ILLUSTRATIONS.

	PAGE
President Lincoln and his Cabinet	2
Illustrated Title	3
Initial Letter, with Battle Illustrations	7
The Capitol, at Washington	17
Fort Sumter	21
Bombardment of Fort Sumter	29
Attack on the Massachusetts Sixth in Baltimore	53
Assassination of Col. Ellsworth	86
Map of Virginia and Maryland, west of Washington	96
" " " " east "	97
Brilliant Charge on a rebel Battery at Bull Run	108
Closing Engagement at Bull Run	115
Battle of Rich Mountain	136
Map of the Mississippi River, Section 5	148
" " " " " 6	149
Death of Gen. Lyon	162
Map of the Mississippi River, Section 2	166
" " " " " 3	167
Map of Atlantic Coast from Fortress Monroe to Fort Macon	178
The Battle of Lexington, Mo	191
The Death of Col. Baker, at Ball's Bluff	206
Desperate Charge of Fremont's Body-Guard, at Springfield, Mo	219
Map of the Mississippi River, Section 1	221
Battle of Mill Spring	260
Bombardment of Fort Henry	279
Map of the Mississippi River, Section 4	289
Attack on Fort Donelson, by the Gunboats	299
Surrender of Fort Donelson	299
Map of the Cumberland and Tennessee Rivers, &c	305
Birds'-eye View of Hampton Roads, Va	323
Cavalry Charge at the Battle of Pea Ridge	339
Battle of Newbern, N. C	343
Map of the Mississippi River, Section 7	352
" " " " " 8	353
Bombardment of Island No. 10	359
Bayonet Charge at the Battle of Winchester	365
Defence of a Federal Battery at Pittsburg Landing	377
Battle of Pittsburg Landing	387

ILLUSTRATIONS.

	PAGE
MAP OF VIRGINIA, SOUTHERN SECTION	422
" " " "	426
MAP OF THE MISSISSIPPI RIVER, SECTION 21	430
BOMBARDMENT OF FORTS JACKSON AND ST. PHILIP	439
MAP OF THE MISSISSIPPI RIVER, SECTION 20	446
BIRDS'-EYE VIEW OF THE COUNTRY FROM RICHMOND TO YORKTOWN, VA	451
BATTLE OF WILLIAMSBURG, VA	455
REBEL CAVALRY CHARGE AT THE BATTLE OF WILLIAMSBURG, VA	460

PORTRAITS.

Name	PAGE	Name	PAGE
ANDERSON, ROBERT, BRIG.-GEN	253	LYON, NATHANIEL, BRIG.-GEN	315
BANKS, NATHANIEL P., MAJ.-GEN	405	LINCOLN, ABRAHAM, PRES. U. S.	2
BATES, EDWARD, ATTORNEY-GEN	2	MANSFIELD, J. K. F., BRIG.-GEN	15
BLAIR, MONTGOMERY, POSTMASTER-GEN	2	McCOOK, ALEX. McD., BRIG.-GEN	315
BURNSIDE, AMBROSE E., MAJ.-GEN	67	McCLELLAN, GEO. B., MAJ.-GEN	197
BUTTERFIELD, DAN., MAJ.-GEN	15	McDOWELL, IRWIN, MAJ.-GEN	405
BUTLER, BENJ. F., MAJ.-GEN	67	McCALL, GEO. A., MAJ.-GEN	67
BUELL, DON CARLOS, MAJ.-GEN	215	McCLERNAND, JOHN A., MAJ.-GEN	271
CASEY, SILAS, BRIG.-GEN	15	POPE, JOHN, MAJ.-GEN	215
COUCH, DARIUS N., MAJ.-GEN	15	PORTER, D. D., REAR-ADMIRAL	173
CORCORAN, MICHAEL, BRIG.-GEN	253	RENO, JESSE L., MAJ.-GEN	271
CHASE, SALMON P., SEC. OF TREASURY	2	ROSECRANS, W. S., BRIG.-GEN	15
CLAY, CASSIUS M., MAJ.-GEN	315	RICHARDSON, ISRAEL B., BRIG.-GEN	15
DIX, JOHN A., MAJ.-GEN	405	SICKLES, DANIEL E., MAJ.-GEN	405
DOUBLEDAY, ABNER, BRIG.-GEN	253	SEDGWICK, MAJ.-GEN	315
DURYEE, ABRAM, BRIG.-GEN	253	SPRAGUE, WM., GOV. OF R. I	253
DUPONT, S. F., REAR-ADMIRAL	271	STRINGHAM, S. H., REAR-ADMIRAL	173
ELLSWORTH, ELMER E., COL	315	STEVENS, ISAAC I., BRIG.-GEN	15
FARRAGUT, D. G., REAR-ADMIRAL	173	SCHURTZ, CARL, BRIG.-GEN	15
FOOTE, D. G., REAR-ADMIRAL	173	SHIELDS, JAMES, BRIG.-GEN	405
FREMONT, JOHN C., MAJ.-GEN	315	SMITH, CALEB B., SEC. OF THE INTERIOR	2
FRANKLIN, WM. B., MAJ.-GEN	271	SEWARD, WM. H., SEC. OF STATE	2
GOLDSBOROUGH, L. M., REAR-ADMIRAL	173	STANTON, EDWIN M., SEC. OF WAR	2
GRANT, ULYSSES S., MAJ.-GEN	215	SIGEL, FRANZ, MAJ.-GEN	215
HALLECK, HENRY W., MAJ.-GEN	233	SCOTT, WINFIELD, LIEUT.-GEN	127
HANCOCK, WINFIELD S., BRIG.-GEN	15	VIELE, E. L., BRIG.-GEN	253
HAMLIN, HANNIBAL, V. PRES. OF U. S.	2	WALLACE, LEWIS, MAJ.-GEN	215
HOOKER, JOSEPH, MAJ.-GEN	253	WOOL, JOHN E., MAJ.-GEN	67
HEINTZELMAN, SAML. P., MAJ.-GEN	67	WELLES, GIDEON, SEC. OF NAVY	2
HUNTER, DAVID, MAJ.-GEN	315	WINTHROP, THEODORE, MAJ	253
KENLY, J. R., BRIG.-GEN	315	WILKES, CHARLES, COM	271
KELLEY, BRIG.-GEN	15	WEBER, MAX, BRIG.-GEN	313
KEARNEY, PHILIP, MAJ.-GEN	253	WADSWORTH, JAMES S., BRIG.-GEN	315
LANDER, FRED. W., BRIG.-GEN	253		

WAR FOR THE UNION.

On the 4th of March, 1861, when Abraham Lincoln took the inaugural oath in front of the National Capitol, his footprints upon the marble marked the great and terrible epoch in the history of our government. The scene was imbued with a grandeur undiscovered and without acknowledgment from the thousands and thousands of freemen who crowded and surged like an ocean at his feet.

An old man, bowed both by responsibility and years, stood by his side, then and there to render up his august position over a great country, at the very moment struggling with the first throes of civil war. How weary he had become, and how gladly he laid down the burden of his power, no heart save his own can tell. But the darkness and the thunders of coming strife followed alike James Buchanan in his retirement and Abraham Lincoln into the thorny splendors of the White House. Solemn and very sad were these two men as they stood for a brief space before the people. The splendor of power brought no happiness either in the giving or receiving. No two men upon the face of the earth ever stood before a people in an attitude so imposing, so fraught with terrible events. When they shook hands peace veiled her face, and, shuddering, shrunk away into the shadows which have darkened around her closer and thicker, till she is now buried so deep beneath the gathered death-palls that no one can tell where she is hidden. For months and even years she had been threatened by factions, disturbed by reckless speech and still more reckless pens, but now, behind all these, war-cries swelled, and bayonets glistened in the distance, bloodless as yet, but threatening storms of crimson rain.

There, upon the verge of this coming tempest, the two Presidents parted, one for the solitude of a peaceful home, the other outward bound into the wild turmoil of contesting thoughts and heroic deeds. As I have said, no one fully realized the coming terror, or thought how easy a thing it is for a war of passions to verge into a war of blood. Still the signs of the last three months had been painfully ominous. The strife of opinions and clash of factions, which had been waxing deeper and stronger between the North and the South, concentrated after Lincoln's election, and the heart of the nation was almost rent in twain before he took the inaugural oath. When he stood up, the central figure of the imposing picture presented to the nation on the fourth of March, a southern government had already been organized at Montgomery, and Jefferson Davis had been sworn in as its president, while the men who had abandoned their seats in the United States Senate now held place in the Confederate Cabinet.

Between the time of President Lincoln's election and his inauguration, five States had followed the lead of South Carolina and declared themselves out of the Union. One by one the representatives of these States had left Congress, some in sullen silence, others eloquent with passion and sophistry.

The nation saw all this, but would not comprehend the imminence of its danger. At a New England dinner, given in New York, December 22d, 1860, one of the most astute statesmen of the country had prophesied, in words that amounted to a promise, that sixty days would be sufficient time in which to tranquilize all this turbulent discontent, and the people believed him; but the sixty days had long since passed, and instead of peace a Confederate government had planted itself on the Alabama river; secession flags floated over more than one of our forts, and another fort in Charleston harbor had only been preserved by the forethought and bravery of Major Anderson, who was then engirdled by hostile batteries, and half-starving from lack of supplies. In the North also the spirit of sedition was abroad. Southern travellers still lingered in our great cities, and conspiracies grew up like nightshade in the dark—conspiracies that threatened not only the government, but the very life of its elected President.

Even on his way to the Capitol Lincoln had been called from his bed at Harrisburg and hurried forward to Washington in the night, thus, without a shadow of doubt, escaping the assassination that awaited him in Baltimore. Still so blind were the people, and so resolute to believe that nothing serious could result from a rebellion that had been preceded by so much bravado, that even the President's preservation from the death prepared for him was taken up by the press and echoed by the people as a clever joke, calculated to bring out a Scotch cap and long cloak in strong relief, but of doubtful origin. Yet the absolute danger in this case might have been demonstrated to a certainty had any one possessing authority cared to investigate the facts. But the nation had not yet recovered from the excitement of a popular election, and everything was submerged in the wild rush of politicians that always follows close on an inauguration.

In this whirlpool of political turmoil rebellion had time to grow and thrive in its southern strongholds, for its imminence could not be forced upon the cool consideration of a people whose traditions had so long been those of prosperous peace. The idea of a civil war, in which thousands on thousands of brave Americans would redden the soil but just denuded of its primeval timber, was an idea so horrible that the most iron-hearted man failed to recognize it as a possibility. That the revolt of these Southern States would in less than a year fill the whole length and breadth of the land with widows and orphans—that American brothers could ever be brought to stand face to face in mortal strife as they have done—that women, so lately looked on with love and reverence, should grow coarse and fiendish from a scent of kindred blood, mocking at the dead and sending victims into a death-snare by their smiles, alas! alas! who could have foreseen it? The very angels of Heaven must have turned away from the suggestion in unbelief.

Never on the face of the earth has a war so terrible been waged on so little cause. The French Revolution—whose atrocities we have not yet emulated, thank God—was the frenzied outbreak of a nation trodden under foot and writhing in the grasp of tyranny such as no American ever dreamed of. If the people became fiends in their revenge, it was the outgrowth of fearful wrongs. But where is the man North or South in our land who had been subject to tyranny or aggression from its government when this war commenced?

No wonder the government looked upon the rebellion with forbearance. No wonder it waited for the sober second thought which it was hoped would bring its leaders back to the old flag, under which the contending parties might reason together. But no, the first step, which ever counts most fatally, was taken, and every footprint that followed it is now red with American blood.

A month passed. President Lincoln was in the White House, besieged by office-seekers almost as closely as Major Anderson was surrounded in Fort Sumter. Ambassadors, consuls, postmasters, collectors, and all the host of placemen that belong to the machinery of a great nation, made their camping ground in Washington, and their point of attack the White House. But amid all this excitement, great national events would force themselves into consideration. News that Jefferson Davis was mustering troops, and that rebellion was making steady strides in the disaffected States, broke through the turmoil of political struggles.

But the state of the country gave painful apprehension to men who stood aloof from the struggles for place going on at Washington, and those who had time for thought saw that the rebellion was making steady progression. The Border States—Virginia, Kentucky, Tennessee and Missouri—with the non-slaveholding States verging upon them, had made a desperate effort to unite on some plan of pacification, but in vain. The border slave States, being in close neighborhood with the North, hesitated in joining the cotton States already in revolt. But disaffection was strong even there, and no great mind, either in Congress or out of it, had arisen strong enough to check the spirit of revolution. Before Lincoln's inauguration Governor Letcher had declared that any attempt of the United States government to march troops across the State of Virginia, for the purpose of enforcing the Federal authority anywhere, would be considered "an invasion, which must be repelled by force." Never was the government placed in a more humiliating position. President Buchanan was surrounded by advisers, many of whom were secretly implicated in the rebellion, and felt himself powerless to act in this emergency, while leading officers of the Federal government were daily making use of their high powers to consummate the designs of the conspirators.

Immediately after the act of secession of South Carolina, Governor Pickens had commenced the organization of an army. Commissioners had appeared in Washington to demand the surrender of the fortifications in Charleston harbor, and the recognition of the State as a distinct nationality. Castle Pinckney, Forts Moultrie and Sumter were the government fortifications in the harbor. Fort Moultrie was garrisoned by a small force, which had been reduced far below the ordinary peace complement, under the command of Major Anderson, a noble and brave man. On the night of December 26, in order to place his command in a more secure fortification, Major Anderson had removed his men and material to Fort Sumter, where, from its isolated position, he had nothing to fear, for a time at least, from the armed masses that were gathering about him. This movement, peaceable in itself, placed his little band in a position where it could inflict no injury on the inhabitants of Charleston. The city was thus placed beyond the range of his guns. But the movement was received with outbursts of indignation from the people of South Carolina.

The then Secretary of War, John B. Floyd, of Virginia, had promised the South Carolina seceders that everything in the harbor of Charleston should be left undisturbed. But of this promise both President Buchanan and Major Anderson were ignorant. In making a movement of signal importance, that resulted in a terrible inauguration of war, the Major had exercised an undoubted right, conferred by his position as an independent commander.

President Buchanan, when called upon to interfere, repudiated the pledge made by his Secretary, and peremptorily refused to sanction it in any way.

FORT SUMTER.

This threw the people of Charleston into a fever of indignation. The Charleston *Courier* denounced Major Anderson in the most cutting terms. "He has achieved," said that journal, "the unenviable distinction of opening civil war between American citizens, by a gross breach of faith. He has, under counsel of a panic, deserted his post at Fort Moultrie, and by false pretexts has transferred his garrison and military stores to Fort Sumter." The *Mercury*, still more imperative, insisted, "that it was due to South Carolina and good faith, that Major Anderson's act should be repudiated by his government, and himself removed forthwith from Fort Sumter."

Meantime Castle Pinckney and Fort Moultrie were occupied and garrisoned by the troops of South Carolina. The small guard left in charge of these posts by Major Anderson were disarmed and kept by force from joining their commander.

That day the Palmetto flag was hoisted over the Custom House and Post Office of Charleston. That day, also, Captain L. N. Costa, commander of the revenue cutter William Aiken, betrayed his government and delivered his vessel over to the State authorities, carrying with him a majority of his men.

These proceedings at Fort Sumter resulted in the withdrawal of John B. Floyd, of Virginia, from Mr. Buchanan's counsellors, and ultimately in breaking up his cabinet only a few weeks before his term of office expired; for there, as elsewhere, arose a conflict of opinion, northern members taking one side and Southern members another. Howell Cobb, of Georgia, Secretary of the Treasury, and Jacob Thompson, of the Interior, soon followed Floyd, and after them went General Cass, of Michigan. Their places were supplied for the brief time of Buchanan's term by Holt, of Kentucky, Stanton, of Pennsylvania, Dix, of New York, and Horatio King, who had been a leading mind in the Post Office Department for twenty years.

The military authorities of South Carolina, strengthened by volunteers and contributions from other States, commenced the siege of Fort Sumter in earnest. They planted heavy batteries on James Island, Morris Island, and Cummings Point. In every spot where guns could be brought to bear on the fort, powerful earthworks were erected, and an immense floating battery of unexampled construction was planned. This, anchored within short range when the day of attack should arrive, was expected to work terrible execution.

Thus encircled by bristling guns at every point, forbidden all intercourse beyond the walls, and denied the privilege of procuring fresh provisions almost entirely, Major Anderson and his noble band could only wait for the help which was slow in coming.

Thus day by day the isolated fort stood like a solitary rock, against which the angry surges of an ocean were stormfully mustering. Girdled in by an army that grew stronger every moment, its noble commander and his scarcely less heroic men, stood firmly by the flag that floated above its battlements, the only stars and stripes now visible from horizon to horizon.

The God of heaven, and that small handful of men, only know the anxieties that beset them. With no means of intelligence, no certainty of support, if an emergency arose demanding an assumption of prompt responsibility, with nothing but gloom landward or seaward, Anderson and his little forces stood at bay. Every hour, every moment, restricted their privileges and consumed their stores; they began to look forward to a lack of food, and many an anxious eye was turned toward the ocean, in a wistful search after the succor that did not come.

The government in Washington was painfully aware of the peril which hung over these brave men. Still, some hope of an amicable adjustment lingered, and President Buchanan hesitated in taking measures that might inaugurate a civil war. But his obligations to these suffering men were imperative. The heroic band, so faithful to their trust, so true to their national honor, must not be left to starve or fall for lack of food and re-enforcements.

On the 5th of January the Star of the West set sail from New York, laden with stores, ammunition, and two hundred and fifty men. Fort Sumter was at length to be relieved. But the North abounded with secession sympathizers, and in a few hours after the steamer sailed, the people of Charleston were informed of her destination by telegraph. Preparations were promptly made for her reception. Captain McGowan had intended to enter Charleston harbor at night, hoping to veil himself in darkness, and reach Fort Sumter undiscovered. But the buoys, sights and ranges had been removed, and, thus baffled, he was compelled to lie outside the harbor till day-light.

At half-past 7, A.M., January 9th, the Star of the West started for the fort. A shot from Morris Island cut sharply across her bows. She run up the stars and stripes, sending that first aggressive shot a noble answer, in red, white and blue, but keeping steadily on her course.

Again and again the audacious guns on Morris Island ploughed up the waters in her path, and, thus assailed, she slowly changed her course, and left the besieged fort without succor.

The little garrison in Fort Sumter watched these proceedings with keen anxiety; though ignorant of the nature and errand of the steamer, this attack aroused the patriotism in every heart. They saw the stars and stripes deliberately fired upon. Seventeen guns sent their iron messages from Morris Island, and then, ignorant of the cause, ignorant of everything, save that the old flag had been assaulted, the garrison fell to work. The guns of Fort Sumter were run out ready for action, but just then the steamer veered on her course and moved seaward.

Had Major Anderson known that the Star of the West was struggling to give him succor, those seventeen shots would never have been fired with impunity.

While the steamer was yet hovering on the horizon, Anderson sent a flag to Governor Pickens, inquiring if a United States steamer had been fired upon by his authority. Governor Pickens replied that it was by his authority. Immediately on the receipt of this answer, Lieutenant Talbot left Fort Sumter with despatches for Washington, asking for instructions.

From that time the garrison remained in a state of siege, until the 5th of April, one month after the inauguration of Abraham Lincoln as President of the United States.

At this time the fort had become more closely besieged. The little garrison was refused fresh provisions from the city, and its supplies by the Government were almost consumed. Starvation or surrender lay before Major Anderson and his handful of men.

Though cut off from communication with the fort, the Government was not unmindful of its needs. From the 5th to the 11th of April three vessels of war, three transports, and three steamers sailed from New York and Norfolk, with men, horses, and munitions of war. The destination of these vessels was kept secret, and public curiosity became intensely excited. The Confederate Government, now assembled at Montgomery, Alabama, was promptly notified, by its secret emissaries, of these movements. Indeed, it is doubtful if Jefferson Davis was not better informed, regarding the destination of this expedition, than the people of the North. The result was, a formal demand on Major Anderson for the surrender of Fort Sumter by General Beauregard, commander of the Confederate forces investing the fort, which now numbered 7,000 men, protected by batteries mounting 140 siege guns.

President Lincoln had notified Governor Pickens that provisions would be sent to the garrison of Fort Sumpter, peaceably, if possible, if necessary, by force.

General Beauregard, commander of the Confederate forces, knew of the succor at hand, but deeming Anderson ignorant of its coming, hoped that the state of semi-starvation to which the garrison was reduced, might enforce the surrender before help arrived. But the astute rebel found himself matched by a soldier, cautious in negotiation as he afterwards proved himself heroic in battle.

On Thursday, the 11th of April, a boat was seen approaching the work, with Colonel Chesnut, Colonel Chisholm and Captain Lee, aids to General Beauregard. They handed Major Anderson a communication from General Beauregard, which was a summons to evacuate the fort. It was to this effect: that the Confederate authorities had refrained from any hostile act against Fort Sumter in anticipation that the government of the United States would withdraw its troops from that fort; that it appeared probable at one time that this would have been done, but that the authorities of the Confederate States could no longer refrain from taking possession of a fort that commanded the entrance to one of their principal harbors, and that the order to evacuate the fort was now made upon the following terms: The troops to be allowed to carry with them their arms, all personal baggage and company property of every description, and the flag which had been maintained with so much fortitude, might be saluted when hauled down.

Major Anderson replied, that his word of honor, and the duty he owed to his government, forbade his compliance with the demand

These gentlemen then left the fort, displaying a *red* flag.

At half-past 1 A. M., on Friday, a boat containing Colonel Chesnut, Captain Lee and Colonel Roger A. Pryor, approached the work with a communication from General Beauregard, making inquiry as to what day Major Anderson would evacuate the work, and asking if he would agree not to open his batteries unless Fort Sumter was fired upon. Suspecting from the urgency of this midnight negotiation, some strong necessity on the part of his opponent, but convinced that an evacuation would be inevitable, Major Anderson made a written reply, stating that he would evacuate the fort at noon, on the 15th, provided he did not receive supplies or controlling instructions from his government to the contrary. That he would not open his batteries unless the flag of his country was fired upon, or unless some hostile intention on the part of the Confederate forces should be manifested.

Being in hourly expectation of the arrival of a United States fleet with reinforcements off the harbor, and urged to instant action by dispatches from Montgomery, General Beauregard had prepared his messengers for this answer. Anderson's communication was handed to Colonel Chesnut shortly after 3 o'clock, who, after a short consultation with the officers who had accompanied him, handed a communication to Major Anderson, and said,

"General Beauregard will open his batteries in one hour from this time, sir."

Major Anderson looked at his watch, and said,

"It is half-past three. —I understand you, sir, then, that your batteries will open in an hour from this time?"

Colonel Chestnut replied, "Yes, sir, in one hour."

They then retired.

FORTIFICATIONS IN CHARLESTON HAROR.

Fort Sumter is a pentagonal structure, built upon an artificial island at the mouth of Charleston harbor, three and three-eighths miles from the city of Charleston. The island has for its base a sand and mud bank, with a superstructure of the refuse chips from several northern granite quarries. These rocks are firmly embedded in the sand, and upon them the present fortification is reared. The island itself cost half a million dollars, and was ten years in construction. The fortification cost another half million dollars, and at the time of its occupancy by Major Anderson, was so nearly completed as to admit the introduction of its armament. The walls are of solid brick and concrete masonry, built close to the edge of the water, and without a berme. They are sixty feet high, and from eight to twelve feet in thickness, and are pierced for three tiers of guns on the north, east and west exterior sides. Its weakest point is on the south side, of which the masonry is not only weaker than that of the other sides, but it is unprotected from a flank fire. The wharf and entrance to the fort are on this side.

The work is designed for an armament of one hundred and forty pieces of ordnance of all calibres. Two tiers of the guns are under bomb-proof casements, and the third or upper tier is open, or, in military parlance, *en barbette;* the lower tier for forty-two pounder paixhan guns; the second tier for eight and ten-inch columbiads, for throwing solid or hollow shot; and the upper tier for mortars and twenty-four pound guns. The full armament of the fort, however, had not arrived when Major Anderson took possession; but after its occupancy by him, no efforts had been spared to place the work in an efficient state of defence, by mounting all the available guns and placing them at salient points. Only seventy-five of the guns were in position at the time of the attack. Eleven paixhan guns were among that number, nine of them commanding Fort Moultrie, which is within easy range, and the other two pointing towards Castle Pinckney, which is well out of range. Some of the columbiads, the most effective weapon for siege or defensive operations, were not mounted. Four of the thirty-two pounder barbette guns were on pivot carriages, which gave them the entire range of the horizon, and others have a horizontal sweep of fire of one hundred and eighty degrees. The magazine contained seven hundred barrels of gunpowder, and an ample supply of shot, powder and shells for one year's siege, and a large amount of miscellaneous artillery stores. The work was amply supplied with water from artificial wells. In a defensive or strategical point of view, Fort Sumter radiates its fire through all the channels from the sea approach to Charleston, and has a full sweep of range in its rear or city side. The maximum range of the guns from Sumter is three miles; but for accurate firing, sufficient to hull a vessel, the distance would require to be reduced one-half of that figure. The war garrison of the fort is six hundred men, but only seventy-nine were within its walls at the time of the attack, exclusive of laborers.

Fort Sumter is three and three-eighths miles from Charleston, one and one-fourth mile from Fort Moultrie, three-fourths of a mile from Cummings Point, one and three-eighths mile from Fort Johnson, and two and five-eighths miles from Castle Pinckney. The city of Charleston is entirely out of range of the guns of Fort Sumter.

The forts and batteries in the possession of the Confederate forces at this time may be briefly described as follows:

FORT MOULTRIE.

Fort Moultrie, which first opened its batteries upon Major Anderson and his command, is one of the sentinels that guard the principal entrance of Charleston harbor. It is opposite to and distant from Fort Sumter about one and a half miles. Its armament consists of eleven guns of heavy calibre and several mortars. The outer and inner walls are of brick, capped with stone and filled with earth, making a solid wall fifteen or sixteen feet in thickness.

THE IRON FLOATING BATTERY.

This novel war machine, designed for harbor operations, was anchored near Sullivan's Island, commanding the barbette guns of Fort Sumter. It was constructed of Palmetto logs, sheathed with plate iron, and supposed to be impregnable against shot. It was embrasured for and mounted four guns of heavy calibre, requiring sixty men to operate it. The outer or gun side was covered with six plates of iron—two of them of the T railroad pattern, placed horizontally, and the other four bolted one over the other, in the strongest manner, and running vertically. The wall of the gun side was full four feet thick, constructed of that peculiar palmetto wood so full of fibrous material that sixty-four pounders cannot pierce it. The main deck was wide and roomy, and kept in place by four heavy wedges, driven down by a species of ram, which held it fast, preventing any swaying around by the tide.

CUMMINGS POINT IRON BATTERY.

The nearest point of land to Fort Sumter is Cummings Point, distant 1,150 yards. On this point was the celebrated railroad iron battery, having a heavy framework of yellow pine logs. The roof was of the same material, over which dovetailed bars of railroad iron of the T pattern were laid from top to bottom—all of which was riveted down in the most secure manner. On the front it presented an angle of about thirty degrees. There were three portholes, which opened and closed with iron shutters of the heaviest description. When open, the muzzles of the columbiads filled up the space completely. The recoil of the gun enabled the shutters to be closed instantly. The columbiad guns, with which this novel battery was equipped bore on the south wall of Sumter, the line of fire being at an angle of about thirty five degrees.

The Fort Johnson batteries consist of two large sand works, containing mortar and siege-gun batteries.

CASTLE PINCKNEY.

Castle Pinckney is a small work, situated on the southern extremity of "Shute's Folly Island," between the Hog and Folly channels. Though in itself not a very considerable military work, yet, from its position, commanding as it does the whole line of the eastern wharves, it becomes of the utmost importance. The height of the rampart is twenty, and the width thirty-two feet. The width of the outer wall and of the parapet is six feet; the depth of the casemates is twenty feet, height ten; the diameter (east and west) of the castle is one hundred and seventy feet. The entrance is on the northern side, on either side of which are the officers and privates' quarters, mess-room, &c. The armament of this castle consists of about twenty-five pieces, 24 and 32-pounders, a few sea-coast mortars and six columbiads.

BOMBARDMENT OF FORT SUMTER.

Major Anderson made good use of the hour awarded to him, that one solemn hour which stood between a peaceful, happy country, so blessed that it had forgotten to be grateful, and the most terrible war that ever, without cause, deluged a free soil with the blood of its own sons. Were ever sixty minutes, since the creation of time, so portentous with fate?

But that little band of men had no time for such thoughts. No sooner had the deputation withdrawn than each officer and soldier was at his post. They had two flags at the fort, a large garrison flag, which Major Anderson raised when he took up his quarters at Sumter, and a smaller one, called the storm-flag; the former had a slight rip in it, and he ordered the storm-flag to be raised in its stead.

Sentinels were immediately removed from the parapets of Fort Sumter, the posterns closed, the flag drawn up, and an order sent to the troops not to leave the bomb-proofs, on any account, until summoned by the drum. At 4.30 A. M. one bombshell was thrown at Sumter, bursting immediately over the fort.

This was the first gun of the rebellion. How awfully its reverberations have thundered through the land! How little did the prompters of that attack upon the old flag dream of the horrors that were to follow!

After the pause of a few moments the firing became general on the part of the batteries of the secessionists, doing the greatest credit to the artillerists. Battery after battery joined in the murderous attack. The Major took it very calmly—divided his men into companies to relieve each other—had their scanty breakfast prepared, which they partook of in silence, while the iron hail was crashing against their walls—prepared additional cartridges by tearing up the flannel shirts of

BOMBARDMENT OF FORT SUMTER

1. Cummings' Point Iron Battery.
2. Fort Sumter.
3. Sullivan's Island.
4. The Iron Floating Battery.
5. Fort Moultrie.
6. Charleston.

the men, their bed-clothes, etc.,—got out a supply of powder from the magazine—and after nearly four hours' silence, the fort at last opened most vigorously on their assailants. Hot coffee was kept in the boiler in the cook room for the men to partake of whenever they pleased, and they worked the guns with a will. They fired but few shells, for the only guns for that kind of ammunition were the barbette guns on the open rampart, many of which were dismounted by the continuous fire of the enemy, and the serving of which, from the lack of casemate protection, would have rapidly thinned out the Major's little band.

As the number of men was so small, and the garrison so nearly exhausted by the several months of siege which they had gone through, it was necessary to husband their strength. The command was therefore divided into three reliefs, or equal parties, who were to work the different batteries by turns, each four hours.

The first relief opened upon the iron batteries at Cummings Point, at a distance of 1,600 yards, the iron floating battery, distant 1,800 or 2,000 yards at the end of Sullivan's Island, the enfilading battery on Sullivan's Island, and Fort Moultrie. This was at 7 o'clock in the morning, Captain Doubleday firing the first gun, and all the points named above being opened upon simultaneously. For the first four hours the firing was kept up with great rapidity; the enthusiasm of the men, indeed, was so spirited that the second and third reliefs could not be kept from the guns. This accounts for the fact that double the number of guns were at work during the first four hours than at any other time.

Shells burst with the greatest rapidity in every portion of the work, hurling the loose brick and stone in all directions, breaking the windows, and setting fire to whatever woodwork they burst against. The solid shot firing of the enemy's batteries, and particularly of Fort Moultrie, were directed at the barbette guns of Fort Sumter, disabling one ten-inch columbiad, (they had but two,) one eight-inch columbiad, one forty-two pounder, and two eight-inch sea-coast howitzers, and also tearing a large portion of the parapet away. The firing from the batteries on Cummings Point was scattered over the whole of the gorge, or rear, of the fort, riddling it like a sieve. The explosion of shells, and the quantity of deadly missiles that were hurled in every direction and at every instant of time, made it almost certain death to go out of the lower tier of casemates, and also made the working of the barbette, or upper uncovered guns, which contained all of our heaviest metals, and by which alone we could throw shells, quite impossible. During the first day there was hardly an instant of time that there was a cessation of the whizzing of balls, which were sometimes coming half a dozen at once. There was not a portion of the work which was not seen in reverse (that is, exposed by the rear) from mortars.

On Friday, before dinner, several of the vessels of the fleet beyond the bar were seen through the port-holes. They dipped their flags. The commander ordered Sumter's flag to be dipped in return, which was done, while the shells were bursting in every direction. [The flagstaff was located in the parade, which is about the centre of the open space within the fort.] Sergeant Hart saw the flag of Fort Sumter half-way down, and, supposing that it had been cut by the enemy's shot, rushed out through the fire to assist in getting it up. Shortly after it had been re-raised, a shell burst and cut the halyards, but the rope was so intertwined around the halyards, that the flag would not fall.

The cartridges were exhausted about noon, and a party was sent to the magazines to make cartridges of the remaining blankets and shirts, the sleeves of the latter being readily converted into the purpose desired. Another great misfortune was, that there was not an instrument in the fort by which they could weigh powder, which of course destroyed all attempt at accuracy of firing. Nor had they tangent scales, breech sides, or other instruments with which to point a gun.

When it became so dark as to render it impossible to see the effect of their shot, the port-holes were closed for the night, while the batteries of the secessionists continued their fire the whole night.

During Friday, the officers' barracks were three times set on fire by the shells, and three times put out under the most galling and destructive firing. This was the only occasion on which Major Anderson allowed the men to expose themselves without an absolute necessity. The guns on the parapet, which had been pointed the day before, were fired clandestinely by some of the men.

The firing of the rifled guns from the iron battery on Cummings Point became extremely accurate in the afternoon of Friday, cutting out large quantities of the masonry about the embrasures at every shot, throwing concrete among the cannoneers, slightly wounding one man, and stunning others. One piece struck Sergeant Kearnan, an old Mexican war veteran, on the head and knocked him down. Upon being revived, he was asked if he was hurt badly. He replied: "No; I was only knocked down temporarily," and he went to work again.

Meals were served at the guns of the cannoneers, while the guns were being fired and pointed. The fire commenced in the morning as soon as possible.

During Friday night the men endeavored to climb the flag-staff, for the purpose of fastening new halyards, the old ones having been cut by the shot, but found it impossible. The flag remained fast.

For the fourth time the barracks were set on fire early on Saturday morning, and attempts were made to put it out. But it was soon discovered that red-hot shot were being thrown into the fort with the greatest rapidity, and it became evident that it would be impossible to put out the conflagration. The whole garrison was then set at work, or as many as could be spared, to remove the powder from the magazines. It was desperate work, rolling barrels of powder through the fire.

Ninety odd barrels had been rolled out through the flames, when the heat became so great as to make it impossible to get out any more. The doors were then closed and locked, and the fire spread and became general. The wind so directed the smoke as to fill the fort so full that the men could not see each other, and with the hot, stifling air, it was as much as a man could do to breathe. Soon they were obliged to cover their faces with wet cloths in order to breathe at all, so dense was the smoke and so scorching the heat.

But few cartridges were left, and the guns were fired slowly; nor could more cartridges be made, on account of the sparks falling in every part of the works. A gun was fired every now and then only to let the fleet and the people in the town know that the fort had not been silenced. The cannoneers could not see to aim, much less where the shot fell.

After the barracks were well on fire, the batteries directed upon Fort Sumter increased their cannonading to a rapidity greater than had been attained before. About this time, the shells and ammunition in the upper service-magazines exploded, scattering the tower and upper portions of the building in every direction. The crash of the beams, the roar of the flames, the rapid explosion of the shells, and the shower of fragments of the fort, with the blackness of the smoke, made the scene indescribably terrific and grand. This continued for several hours. Meanwhile the main gates were burned down, the chassis of the barbette guns were burned away on the gorge, and the upper portions of the towers had been demolished by shells.

There was not a portion of the fort where a breath of air could be obtained for hours, except through a wet cloth. The fire spread to the men's quarters, on the right hand and on the left, and endangered the powder which had been taken out of the magazines. The men went through the fire and covered the barrels with wet cloths, but the danger of the fort's blowing up became so imminent, that they were obliged to heave the barrels out of the embrasures. While the powder was being thrown overboard, all the guns of Moultrie, of the iron floating battery, of the enfilade battery, and the Dahlgren battery, worked with increased fury.

All but four barrels were thus disposed of, and those remaining were wrapped in many thicknesses of wet woolen blankets. But three cartridges were left, and these were in the guns. About this time the flagstaff of Fort Sumter was shot down, some fifty feet from the truck, this being the ninth time that it had been struck by a shot. A man cried out, "The flag is down; it has been shot away!" In an instant, Lieutenant Hall rushed forward and brought the flag away. But the halyards were so inextricably tangled that it could not be righted; it was, therefore, nailed to the staff, and planted upon the ramparts, while batteries in every direction were playing upon them.

A few moments after, and a man was seen with a white flag tied to his sword, who desired admission. He was admitted through an embrasure. In a great flurry, he said he was General Wigfall, and that he came from General Beauregard, and added that he had seen that Sumter's flag was down. Lieutenant Davis replied, "Oh, sir! but it is up again." The cannonading meanwhile continued. General Wigfall asked that some one might hold his flag outside. Lieutenant Davis replied, "No, sir! we don't raise a white flag. If you want your batteries to stop, you must stop them." General Wigfall then held the flag out of an embrasure. As soon as he had done this, Lieutenant Davis directed a corporal to relieve him, as it was General Wigfall's flag.

Several shots struck immediately around him while he was holding it out, when he started back, and putting the flag in Wigfall's face, said, "D——n it; I won't hold that flag, for they don't respect it. They struck their colors, but we never did." Wigfall replied, "They fired at me three or four times, and I should think you ought to stand it once." Wigfall then placed the white flag on the outside of the embrasure, and presented himself to Major Anderson, and said that General Beauregard was desirous that blood should not be unnecessarily shed, and also stated that he came from General Beauregard, who desired to know if Major Anderson would evacuate the fort, and that if he would do so he might choose his own terms.

After a moment's hesitation Major Anderson replied that he would go out on the same terms that he (Major Anderson) had mentioned on the 11th. General Wigfall then said: "Very well; then it is understood that you will evacuate. This is all I have to do. You military men will arrange everything else on your own terms." He then departed, the white flag still waving where he had placed it, and the stars and stripes streaming from the flag-staff which had become the target of the rebels.

Shortly after his departure Major Lee, the Hon. Porcher Miles, Senator Chesnut, and the Hon. Roger A. Pryor, the staff of General Beauregard, approached the fort with a white flag, and said they had come from General Beauregard, who had observed that the flag had been down and raised again a few minutes afterward. The General had sent over, desiring to know if he could render any assistance, as he had observed the fort was on fire. (This was perhaps a delicate mode of asking for a surrender.) Major Anderson, in reply, requested them to thank General Beauregard for the offer, but it was too late, as he had just agreed with General Beauregard for an evacuation. The three persons comprising the deputation, looked at each other blankly, and asked with whom? Major Anderson, observing that there was something wrong, remarked that General Wigfall, who had just left, had represented himself to be an aid to General Beauregard, and that he had come over to make the proposition.

After some conversation among themselves, they said to Major Anderson that Wigfall had not seen General Beauregard for two days. Major Anderson replied that Wigfall's offer and its acceptance had placed him in a peculiar position. They then requested him to place in writing what General Wigfall had said to him, and they would lay it before General Beauregard.

Before this reached General Beauregard, he sent his Adjutant-General and other members of his staff, including the Hon. Roger A. Pryor and Governor Manning, proposing the same conditions which Major Anderson had offered to go out upon, with the exception only of not saluting the flag. Major Anderson said that he had already informed General Beauregard that he was going out. They asked him if he would not accept of the terms without the salute. Major Anderson told them, No; but that it should be an open point.

General Beauregard sent down to say that the terms had been accepted, and that he would send the Isabel or any other vessel at his command to convey Major Anderson and the troops to any port in the United States which he might elect.

No braver men ever lived than the defenders of Fort Sumter; but the ardor and endurance of musician Hall of Company E was remarked by every man in Sumter, and the company presented him with a testimonial. He was at the firing of the first guns, and fought on all day, and would not accept either of the three reliefs. He was up at the first shot the next day, and worked without cessation till night. His example and words of cheer had great effect. This is the more worthy of remark as he belonged to the musicians, and was not obliged to enter into the engagement at all.

Mr. Hart, a volunteer from New York, particularly distinguished himself in trying to put out the flames in the quarters, with shells and shot crashing around him. He was ordered away by Major Anderson, but begged hard to be permitted to remain and continue his exertions.

Never did famished men work more bravely than those who defended that fortress, knowing, as they did, that if successfully defended and held by them, there was not even a biscuit left to divide among them. They never would have left it while a protecting wall stood around them, had they been provided with provision and ammunition Every man was true and faithful to his post; hunger and want of ammunition alone caused them to leave Fort Sumter. They were exposed to a most terrible fire from all quarters, and it was only by exercising the utmost care that the officers were enabled to preserve the men from a terrible slaughter. Fort Sumter in itself was hardly worth the holding; had there been the full fighting complement of men within its walls, the fort would not have afforded suitable protection for one-half of them. The enemy's shot rained in upon and about them like hail, and more men in Sumter would only have made greater havoc. As it was, the garrison proved fortunate in having escaped without the loss of one of those brave men who were willing to die for the flag which waved over them.

The evacuation took place about 9½ o'clock on Sunday morning, after the burial with military honors of private Daniel Hough, who had been killed by the bursting of a gun. The men had been all the morning preparing cartridges for the purpose of firing a salute of one hundred guns. This done, the embarkation took place, the band meanwhile playing Yankee Doodle.

STORMING OF FORT SUMTER, VIEWED FROM THE LAND.

A person who witnessed the bombardment of Fort Sumter from the harbor, gives this graphic account:

The terrific firing reached an awful climax at ten o'clock at night. The heavens were obscured by rain clouds, and it was as dark as Erebus. The guns were heard distinctly, the wind blowing in shore. Sometimes a shell would burst in mid-air, directly over Fort Sumter. Nearly all night long the streets were thronged with people, full of excitement and enthusiasm. The house-tops, the battery, the wharves, the shipping,—in fact every available place was taken possession of by the multitude.

The discharges of cannon gradually diminished as the sun rose. All the clouds, which rendered the night so dark and dismal, disappeared as day began to break, while the air became most beautiful, balmy, and refreshing. The streets were filled again with persons, male and female, old and young, white and black; some went to the battery, some to the wharves, and some to the steeples of the churches.

A few random shots were fired from the Confederate batteries, to which Fort Sumter only replied occasionally. Soon it became evident that Sumter was on fire, and all eyes were rivetted upon it. The dense smoke that issued from it was seen gradually to rise from the ramparts. Some supposed that this was merely a signal from Major Anderson to call in the fleet to aid him.

At this time the fleet was in the offing quietly riding at anchor, and could clearly be distinguished. Four vessels were ranged in line directly over the bar, apparently blockading the port. Their long, black hulls and smoke-stacks proved them to be Federal steamers. Every one anxiously waited to see what they would do. The suspense was very exciting. On all sides could be heard,

"Will the vessels come in and engage the batteries? If they do not they are cowardly poltroons."

Every person on the battery fully expected that the engagement would become general. By the aid of glasses, it was believed that a movement was being made to this end by two of the war ships, and it was thought that the sand would soon begin to fly from the Morris Island batteries.

At ten o'clock in the morning, attention was again rivetted on Fort Sumter, which was now beyond a doubt on fire. The flames were seen to burst from the roofs of the houses within its walls, and dense columns of smoke shot quickly upward.

At this time Major Anderson scarcely fired a shot. The guns on the ramparts of Fort Sumter had no utterance in them. Burst shells and grape scattered like hail over the doomed fort, and drove the soldiers under cover.

From the Iron Battery at Cummings Point a continuous fire was kept up. Its rifled cannon played sad havoc with that portion of Fort Sumter facing it. The firing from the Floating Battery and from Fort Moultrie continued very regular and accurate. Standing on the Charleston battery, and looking seaward, you have on the right a mortar battery and Fort Johnson, distant from the city two and a half miles. Half a mile from Fort Johnson is the Iron Battery of Cummings Point, mounting three ten-inch columbiads, three sixty-four-pounders, three mortars, and one rifled cannon. Cummings Point is only fifteen hundred yards from Fort Sumter, and so any one can imagine what havoc the regular fire of the Cummings Point battery must have created.

The men working the guns made them terriby effective. The sand redoubt was scarcely injured by the weak fire Major Anderson kept up on the battery. It was commanded by Major Stevens, of the Citadel Cadets. Under his direction each shell that was fired found a destination within Fort Sumter, and during the entire bombardment scarcely one missile of this character missed its mark.

On the other side of the harbor, directly opposite Fort Sumter, is one of the strongest sides of Fort Moultrie. During the last three months it has been strengthened by every appliance that military art could suggest. Its marlons, moats, glaces, and embrasures are perfectly protected. The weak walls of the fort were made perfectly secare for the gunners while at work. From this point throughout the engagement vast numbers of shot and heavy balls were discharged.

Behind this, and near Sullivan's Island, the Floating Battery was stationed, with two sixty-four and two forty-two pounders. Its sides of iron and palmetto logs were impenetrable. Every shot from it told on Fort Sumter, and the men in charge of it were so secure in their position, that some of them indulged in soldiers' pastimes, while others played five cent ante, euchre and bluff.

The Mortar Battery at Mount Pleasant was five hundred yards from the Floating Battery, and was mounted with two mortars within excellent range of Fort Sumter. The shells from this mortar were thrown with great precision. You now have all the positions of the works bearing directly on Fort Sumter.

All through Friday morning the greatest activity at all points was displayed. Three times Major Anderson's barracks were set on fire, and twice he succeeded in putting out the flames, and to do this it was necessary to employ all his force in passing along water. To get water it was necessary for some of his men to go outside the walls, and hand the buckets in through the port-holes, during all which time they were exposed to a most terrific fire from the various batteries.

This last expedient was not resorted to until the fort was on fire for the third time, and the flames had increased to an alarming pitch. Meantime, Major Anderson's guns were silent. He allowed his men to be exposed to the galling fire upon them but for a few moments, and then ordered them in and shut the batteries as the smoke was too thick to work them. At noon the flames burst from every quarter of Fort Sumter, and its destruction appeared inevitable.

NAVAL EXPEDITION FOR THE RELIEF OF SUMTER.

The Government had sent a well-laden fleet to the relief of Fort Sumter, a portion of which arrived in Charleston harbor time enough to witness the bombardment of the fort, without the power to help its heroic garrison.

This fleet left New York and Washington from the 6th to the 9th of April. It consisted of the sloop-of-war, Pawnee, 10 guns, and 200 men; Pocahontas, 5 guns, 110 men; cutter Harriet Lane, 5 guns, 110 men; accompanied by the transport Baltic, and the steam-tugs Yankee and Uncle Ben, with additional men and stores. Owing to stormy weather, the vessels were unable to reach the Charleston coast at the appointed time. The Pawnee, Harriet Lane, and the Baltic arrived at the rendezvous on the morning of the 12th April, but the Pocahontas did not join them until the next day. The steam-tug Yankee lost her smoke-stack in the storm which dispersed the fleet, and did not reach the neighborhood of Charleston till after the departure of her consorts, and eventually returned to New York. Nothing was heard of the Uncle Ben until the 30th of April, when intelligence was received that she had been captured by the insurgents off the coast of North Carolina.

The orders of the expedition were, that unarmed boats should first be sent to the fort with stores only; but if these were fired upon, every effort was to be made to relieve the fort by stratagem or force. The vessels of war and the Baltic proved of too heavy draft for any hopes of passing the bar, and the steam-tugs which were to have been sent in with supplies, failed to make their appearance. The attack on the fort, before any measures of a peaceable character could be adopted for its relief, left no alternative but force, to the commandant of the fleet, if the object of his expedition was to be accomplished. A consultation of officers was held at four o'clock on the afternoon of the 12th, and the following plan was agreed upon: the Pawnee and the Harriet Lane were to remain at anchor during the night; at dawn, on the 13th, the Pawnee was to hoist out her armed launches, and the Baltic was to put her boats alongside, freighted with the provisions and troops designed for the fort. The war vessels were then to tow the boats as far as possible on their perilous journey, when they were to be cast off, and allowed to pursue their course toward the fort, relying upon the guns of the men-of-war, and what aid might be extended from Sumter, to protect them from the batteries and flotilla of armed boats, which were in readiness to dispute their advance. During the night the Baltic went aground on Rattlesnake Shoals, and the plan agreed upon was, from necessity, relinquished. The conflagration of the barracks of the fort having precipitated its evacuation earlier than was anticipated, the officers of the fleet abandoned other plans for its relief.

At two o'clock on the 14th of April, Major Anderson and the garrison of Fort Sumter were received on board the Baltic, and the fleet shortly after sailed for New York. The flag of the fort was borne at the mast-head of the Baltic as she entered the bay of New York, where it was saluted by guns from every fort in the harbor, and hailed by the shouts of more than a hundred thousand people, who lined the wharves of the city. It was also raised over the equestrian statue of Washington in Union Square, in that city, when the great Union meeting was held on the afternoon of Saturday, April 20.

THE NATION'S RESPONSE.

The first gun that boomed against Fort Sumter struck the great American Union with a shock that vibrated from the centre to its outer verge. Every heart, true or false to the great Union, leaped to the sound, either in patriotism or treason, on that momentous day.

The North and South recoiled from each other; the one in amazement at the audacity of this first blow against the Union, the other rushing blindly after a few leaders, who had left them little choice of action, and no power of deliberation. The first news of the attack took the Government at Washington almost by surprise. President Lincoln and his Cabinet had not allowed themselves to believe that a civil war could absolutely break out in the heart of a country so blessed, so wealthy, and so accustomed to peace. True, political strife had waged fearfully; sections had clamored against sections, factions North had battled with factions South; but in a country where free speech and a free press were a crowning glory, a war of words and ideas could hardly have been expected to culminate in one of the most terrible civil wars that will crimson the world's record.

The first boom of the cannon's blackened lips—the first shot hurled against the stars and stripes, aroused the Government from its hopes of security. Scarcely had the telegraph wires ceased to tremble under the startling news, before the Cabinet assembled in President Lincoln's council chamber, and when it broke up, a proclamation, calling for seventy-five thousand troops, had been decided upon, and Congress was to be convened on the Fourth of July.

The startling news, this prompt action, and the defenceless state of Washington, filled the country with wild excitement. It was known that the South had been for months drilling troops; that large portions of Virginia and Maryland were ready for revolt, and many believed that bodies of men were organized and prepared for an attack on the capital. Had this been true, had a considerable number of men marched upon Washington any time within four days after the news from Fort Sumter reached it, nothing could have saved it from capture, and probably, destruction. With only a handful of troops, and exposed at every point, no effectual resistance could have been made The news reached Washington on Sunday; the next day such troops as could be mustered, appeared on parade. Pickets were stationed outside the town; horses were galloped furiously from point to point, and the first faint indication of this most awful civil war dawned upon a people so used to peace, that its import could not be wholly realized.

Smothered alarm prevailed in the city; a military guard was placed each night in the White House, and great anxiety was felt for the arrival of troops, which had been hastily summoned from the North.

That week the near friends of the President were under painful apprehensions for his safety. It was known to a few persons that the very gang of men who had planned his death at Baltimore, were in the neighborhood of the capital, plotting against him there. It was even known that a design existed by which a sudden descent of swift riders was to be made on the White House, with the bold object of killing Lincoln in his cabinet, or carrying him off by force into Virginia. The night-guard in the Presidential mansion was but small, and by day Lincoln had always been imprudently accessible.

The persons believed to be in this plot were brave, reckless men, accustomed to adventures of every kind, and quite capable of carrying out a programme of abduction or bloodshed under more difficult circumstances than surrounded this enterprise. But men of reckless action are seldom prudent in speech; the wild project was too exciting for proper reticence. By a few incautious words, dropped here and there, this treasonable design was fathomed; the friends of President Lincoln warned, and the whole thing quietly defeated, for the gang soon ascertained that their treason had been discovered, and, as its success depended on a surprise of the President's household, the project was abandoned.

Meantime the news of Fort Sumter, and the call for troops, had shot its lightning along every telegraph in the Union; the response was an instantaneous uprising of the people, such as no country on earth ever witnessed before.

The great majesty of the Union had been insulted and set at defiance, and as one man, thousands upon thousands rushed around the worshipped banner of their country, firm in their patriotism, and terrible in their determination that it should never be trailed in the dust, or torn with hostile shot, unavenged.

The proclamation of President Lincoln calling for volunteers, was answered by the voices of freemen from every hill-top and valley, and almost fabulous numbers stood ready and anxious to devote themselves to the vindication of the national honor. Wild indeed was the enthusiasm that ran from heart to heart, linking the great west and the east together. But one sentiment found expression from any lip among the excited populace, and that sentiment was, the Union should be sustained at all hazards. Wealth, life, everything must be counted as dust till the Union had redeemed itself. Who in New York does not remember how the city was ablaze with flags and tri-colored bunting on the memorable day, when, "the Seventh regiment," responded to the call? Never did a finer or braver body of young men pass down

Broadway. Although their arms were not now corded or hands hardened by labor, their prompt action was a living proof that gentle breeding can be associated with hearts of oak, with stern determination, coolness and discretion. Leaping to their arms at the first note of danger, impatient of delay and thrilling with the hope of weaving in their peace-won wreaths laurels earned by hard fighting, this regiment marched from its armory, the very first of the Empire State to obey the call to arms. Their object was war. They hoped ardently that it was no light duty which might fall upon them. They expected to meet hard work and hard fighting too before the capital was reached, for danger menaced them on all sides. Baltimore had risen in revolt even while they were arming for the march and they fully depended on fighting their way through its turbulent streets.

On the 19th of April, at the very time revolt broke out in Baltimore, a very different scene was going on in New York.

Amidst unparalleled enthusiasm the volunteer soldiers of New England and New York struck hands on their march to the rescue of the national capital. And beautiful the streets looked, with bannered parapets, peopled roofs, windows thronged with sympathetic beauty, and sidewalks densely packed with multitudes of excited and applauding citizens.

But it required only a single glance at the faces of this great multitude to become convinced that no mere gala or festive purpose had called out this magnificent demonstration. In every eye burned the unquenchable fire of patriotic ardor, and in every heart was the aspiration to join in defence of one common country. Old men, who must have seen the earlier struggles of our history, came forth to bless the young soldiers on their march to take share in a grander and more noble struggle than any the American continent had yet witnessed.

Mothers, with tears of joyous pride half blinding them, helped to buckle on the accoutrements of their sons, and kissed them as they went forth to battle. Sisters and sweethearts, fathers and wives, friends and relatives, all were represented, and had their individual characteristics in the immense concourse of life which held possession of Broadway.

Perhaps if there could have risen from the dead one of the old Girondists, after being bloodily put away to repose during the great French Revolution, and if he had been dropped down in New York,—by allowing a little for advance in costumes and architecture, he might have seen many curious points of resemblance between the scenes and those of seventy years ago in Paris. Then the inspiration of liberty ran through the people, and the most powerful aristocracy of Europe was destroyed. The result of the struggle which broke out in New York; and in the streets of Baltimore, in one day, time has yet to reveal.

The children of New York, the Seventh regiment, the pets and pride of her society, were going forth to their first war duty. Eight hundred chosen young men, with threads woven to hold them, wherever they went, to the million hearts they left behind—moved down Broadway and started for the capital.

Eight hundred young citizens, each with musket and knapsack, borne along calmly and impassively on a tide of vocal patriotism, making the air resonant with shouts and warm with the breath of prayer.

With that regiment went young Winthrop, on that memorable day, who afterwards passed from the literary fame he had so richly earned, to military glory at the battle of Big Bethel. There also was O'Brien, one of the most promising poets of the age, doomed like Winthrop to reap bloody laurels, and fill a soldier's grave. Let no one say that the Empire State was not nobly represented in these young soldiers. Gentlemen as they were, one and all, no man was heard to complain of hard work, soldiers' fare, or no fare at all, as sometimes happened to them. How cheerful they were in the cedar groves for two days and nights—how they endured the hardships of a bivouac on soft earth—how they digged manfully in the trenches. With what supreme artistic finish their work was achieved—how they cleared the brushwood from the glacis—how they blistered their hands and then hardened them with toil—how they chafed at being obliged to evade Baltimore, and how faithfully they guarded Washington and achieved the object for which they were sent, will be best given in a description of the march from Annapolis of which O'Brien has left a brilliant record.

Nor were their services in protecting the capital all that the Seventh regiment of New York has given to its country. Many a regiment which has since won lasting fame on the battle-field has been officered to some extent from its ranks.

Two days after the departure of the Seventh regiment, the Seventy-first, since-renowned for its bravery at Bull Run, the Sixth, and Twelfth, all city regiments of New York, took the same glorious track, and were hailed with like enthusiasm. In military drill and social position, some of these regiments were not inferior to the Seventh, and their departure was witnessed by a concourse of people equal to that which filled the streets on the 19th.

It was with pride that a city saw her first quota of soldiers departing *en route* for Washington, to take the Empire share with the troops of other loyal states in the contest now inaugurated. The spectacle, instead of being a great pageant, had all the grandeur and solemnity of a step in one of those crises of events which involve individual and national life—engraving new names and new dynasties upon the tablets of history.

As if to make the departure of these troops more memorable, a large American flag, forty feet long by twenty wide, was flung out upon a flagstaff from a window in Trinity steeple, at a height of two hundred and forty feet. The chimes meanwhile played several airs appropriate to the occasion, among which were "Yankee Doodle," "The Red, White and Blue," winding up with "All's Well." A flag-staff with a splendid flag attached, was also run out of a window over the portico in front of St. Paul's Church. Thus under these mighty banners, furling and unfurling in the wind and hedged in by triple walls of human beings, amid the resonant chimes of Trinity, the crash of their own magnificent bands drowning the "God bless you" of many a gentle heart, the city of New York sent its first regiments to the field.

As each regiment passed through New York the concourse of people to see it off increased, till every fresh march was a triumph in advance of the brave deeds the soldiers were expected to perform. In less than a week banners and flags had become so thick across Broadway, that they fairly canopied the departing troops, and shouts loud and deep sent them on the way with many a blessing and hearty God speed.

Nor was this enthusiasm confined to crack regiments or the aristocratic soldiery of our cities. The working men also came forth in masses, claiming a share in the glorious work. Of this class was the Sixth Massachusetts regiment, which had just baptized its colors in the streets of Baltimore, taking lead even of the chivalric regiments of the Empire City. Of this class was the thrice glorious Sixty-ninth, as brave a body of warm-hearted Irishmen as ever trod the earth. Perhaps the greatest crowd that ever gathered to see a regiment off assembled when this body of adopted citizens marched forth under the star-spangled banner and the green flag of old Ireland. On that day human nature acknowledged its own universal kinship. The work-shop and the counting-room, the parlor and the basement met for once on a level of noble enthusiasm. The palace and the tenement house gave forth their inmates alike, for it was a common country which these men went forth to defend with their strength and, alas, their lives.

Proud mothers and wives and sisters, who had watched their beloved ones march off in the ranks of some favorite regiment, looked down from balconies and windows with tearful eyes upon the crowd of women who lined the pavements.

More particularly was this manifest on the departure of the Sixty-ninth. What warm, true hearts crowded the pavements that day! Old women, little children, whole households clung together, sorrowful but O, how proud of the valor that filled their eyes with tears.

If there was weeping on the pavement, it was answered with a feeling of gentle sisterhood from the balcony and window. The same bright eyes that had seen the Seventh, Seventy-first, Twelfth and other regiments pass, through a mist of tears, filled with sympathetic moisture when they saw these poor wives and mothers break through all restraint and rush wildly into the ranks for one more kiss, a hand-clasp, or, if no more, a last glance of loving recognition.

Perhaps some of these highly bred females envied the social freedom which allowed these women of the people to follow their husbands and brothers up to the moment of embarkation, without a thought of the world beyond. Many an embroidered handkerchief was waved, and many a sweet blessing murmured in gentle sympathy with these sister women when those hard-working, hard-fighting, gloriously brave men went forth to earn imperishable renown.

Not only in New York, but all over the North and West these ovations were repeated. Boston Common was one scene of mustering forces, and its streets a panorama of armed men. Every State over which the blessed old star-spangled banner flung its folds, sent forth its sons, only complaining that so few were accepted. Like a prairie fire when the grass is dry, the war spirit leaped from town to town, and from State to State, till the whole North was ablaze with it.

Troops mustered into companies and massed themselves into regiments in the North and the great West so numerous and so fast that a swift pen might fail to keep the record. The uprising was general. Along our water courses, along our railroads, down the broad avenues of our cities, regiment after regiment swept a continued stream of armed men, all bearing toward the capital. For the whole great North rose as one man and sprang to arms. The plough was left in the furrow—the hammer upon the anvil—the saw upon the bench—the reaper in mid prairie—the shuttle in the loom—the pen upon the ledger—the engine untended—the press unfed—the busy sails of commerce unfurled, and the whirring mill unsupplied. A patient people had arisen in its might, with clear steel and the rolling thunder of cannon they were prepared to uphold the sacred majesty of the Union flag, while a splinter remained of the staff, or a shred of the fabric! An electric flash stirred the long-patient and dumb millions to life and speech, and under the red ensign of war they rallied in the common cause.

No one State or town could claim pre-eminence in patriotic fervor over its neighbors, for no where did this wild enthusiasm find check or hindrance. Our great cities could only claim superiority over the smaller towns from the hospitality with which they received troops from the country and cheered them onward to the battle field. Boston, Portland, New Haven, New York, Philadelphia, and the leading Western cities formed a great thoroughfare for the mustering army, for the country around poured their patriotic masses through the streets of these cities, and the press gave eclat to the movements which reflected back upon the cities themselves. But in the great North and the great West there was no nook or corner where this patriotic furor did not exist.

Monster Union meetings were held in every city of the loyal States, and within an incredibly short time, *Three Hundred and Fifty Thousand* men responded to the call of the President. Great as the number was, it proved but small to what would have volunteered had they been needed, or could they have been accepted, for with bonfires blazing upon every hill, and flags waving from every house-top—with the red, white and blue upon every breast, and the long roll beating in every heart—with wives sending their husbands—mothers their sons and girls their lovers, such a battle cry was raised as the earth had never listened to, and nations of the old world heard with astonishment.

REINFORCEMENT OF FORT PICKENS.

April 12, 1861.

The Navy Yard and forts in the harbor of Pensacola, from their extent and importance, were particularly the objects of insurgent ambition. General Bragg and his counsellors had so adroitly arranged their plans that it was confidently expected that the government forts, buildings and property would fall into their peaceable occupation. On the 12th of January, the navy yard and barracks, together with Fort Barrancas, fell into their possession, and shortly afterwards Fort McRae met with the same fate; but Lieutenant Slemmer, the United States officer in command of the forts of Pensacola harbor, courageously threw his small force of eighty-two men into Fort Pickens, and had thus far held at bay the large army of insurgents who were preparing to attack him.

The harbor of Pensacola is probably the largest and finest on the whole coast of the Mexican Gulf. The bay is six miles wide and about twelve long. The Warrington navy yard was seven miles by land from Pensacola and six miles and three-quarters by water. About a mile from the navy yard, west, stood Fort Barrancas, and a mile farther Fort McRae, which commands the bar. Opposite Fort McRae was Fort Pickens, the channel running between them. Near Fort Pickens was a redoubt. On the opposite side of Pensacola, across the bay, Santa Rosa island extends several miles to the bar, at the extremity of which is Fort Pickens. A vessel coming into the harbor must necessarily pass between Fort Pickens and Fort McRae, and in close proximity to Barrancas.

Fort Pickens is a bastioned work of the first class, built of New York granite; its walls forty-five feet in height and twelve in thickness. It is embrasured for two tiers of guns, placed under bomb-proof casemates, besides having one tier *en barbette*. The work was commenced in 1848 and finished in 1853, at a cost of nearly one million dollars. Its war complement of soldiers is 1,260. Its full armament consists of 210 guns, howitzers, and mortars, of all calibres.

Simultaneous with the determination to reinforce Fort Sumter, the government resolved to send relief to Fort Pickens, which was then threatened by a force of 7,000 men under General Bragg, strongly entrenched, and occupying the other forts in the harbor.

A fleet of six United States vessels lay in the harbor, and they had been notified by General Bragg that he would immediately open fire upon them and Fort Pickens also, should they attempt to reinforce the garrison.

Previous to the 10th of April, the steam-frigate Powhatan and the transports Atlantic and Illinois had sailed from New York with troops, ordnance and provisions, for Fort Pickens; but before their arrival at that place, a bearer of dispatches from Washington reached the commander of the naval forces in the bay, with instructions to reinforce the fort. Between the hours of 11 and 12 o'clock on Friday night, April 12th, this was accomplished without bloodshed. "As soon as it became dark," said an officer on board the sloop-of-war Brooklyn, one of the blockading fleet, "we began work with good will and in earnest. At first the marines from the frigate Sabine and the sloop St. Louis, came on board our vessel, and immediately after the accomplishment of this, the anchor was hoisted by the jolly old salts, with the merry chant of—

'General Jackson won the day,
Heave, yeo ho!
At New Orleans, the people say
Yeo, heave yeo!'

We ran as close to the shore as possible, came to anchor, and without a moment's delay, lowered the boats and filled them with troops.

"At 11 o'clock, Lieutenant Albert N. Smith, of Massachusetts, being in command, they started on their mission, uncertain if they would live to see the light of another day. As they left the side of the vessel, many a 'God cause you to succeed,' came from the lips of the loyal men at my side. If I live a thousand years I shall never forget the feelings I experienced when I saw those brave fellows shake hands with their old comrades. A tear would now and then glisten in the gloom, but be instantly wiped away with a clenched hand. These men knew their danger, and with the knowledge, dared to face it with a courage eminently worthy of praise—and may they receive it!

"The party were instructed to send up signals should they be attacked, and I do assure you never were keener eyes than ours on that eventful night, as we pierced into the darkness, momentarily expecting to see a rocket light up the midnight gloom; but none appeared. While we were thus anxiously awaiting some evidence of the success or non-success of their mission, a boat was hailed. A faint answer comes back: 'Lieutenant Smith and the boat's crew!' and in whispers we hear the news, 'they have been successful!' Brother officers shake hands, and give Lieutenant Smith that praise justly deserved by him. They went around inside of the harbor, passed under the guns of Forts McRae and Barrancas without being heard, and safely landed all the troops without molestation.

"This being successfully accomplished, it was almost instantly concluded to make a new attempt, and orders were given that all the marines in the squadron should take to their boats, preparatory to their being put in the fort. This being done, the steamer Wyandotte took them in charge, and towed them as far as she could go, when they left her and pulled into the harbor, taking the same course the first party had, and in good time reached the fort, and safely landed all who were in the boats. Just as the day was breaking, we saw from our deck the boats shoving off from the beach; and when they returned to us, our anchor was instantly 'up,' and we steaming to our old anchorage with very different sensations from those we had when we started for the work. Thus the Brooklyn accomplished what she was sent here for,—the reinforcement of Fort Pickens in spite of General Bragg."

A few days after this fort had been so nobly reinforced, the splendid steamer Atlantic sailed into the Union fleet, laden with troops for the fort. The next day she was joined by the frigate Powhatan, and again by the Illinois, all laden with troops and military stores. Thus a thousand more troops were thrown into the stronghold, which, with the fleet outside, made it impregnable.

There is no doubt that an attack upon Fort Pickens was contemplated the very night these reinforcements arrived. The assaulting party was composed of five hundred picked men, two hundred and fifty of whom were from the Mississippi Ninth, to be led by C. H. Harris of the Home Guard; fifty from the Tenth Mississippi, and the others from other troops at Pensacola. All necessary preparations were made for moving about 11 o'clock at night. The storming party were led down to the Navy Yard, from whence it would probably have embarked in boats.

It is surmised that Colonel Forney would have been the leader. There was no doubt entertained of his success. Before the force arrived it was evident the fort had been reinforced, and all thought of the meditated assault was abandoned. The men picked for this special service lay on their arms all night in the Navy Yard.

BURNING OF HARPER'S FERRY ARSENAL.
April 18, 1861.

The ordinance of secession of the State of Virginia was adopted in secret session on the 17th of April, and the Governor of the State, John Letcher, immediately issued orders for the seizure of the Federal posts and property by the military of the State. A most important post to be first secured comprised the extensive and valuable arsenal, with all its workshops and machinery for the manufacture of arms, at Harper's Ferry, a place which had been rendered familiar as a household word, from its seizure by John Brown and his party, in the autumn of 1859.

Harper's Ferry is situated in Jefferson county, Virginia, at the confluence of the Potomac and Shenandoah rivers, and is 173 miles distant from Richmond, 57 from Washington, and 80 from Baltimore. The population was about 5,000. The arsenal at this place contained 15,000 stand of arms, in addition to other military stores, then in charge of Lieutenant R. Jones, with a detachment of U. S. Rifles, numbering 43 men. Lieutenant Jones had received advice from Washington that his post was in imminent danger. He was directed to be prepared for any emergency that might arise. On the 17th he received information from various sources that an attack would be made on the night of the 18th. Early in the evening of that day, the little garrison commenced preparations to destroy the arsenal and its contents by fire. The windows and doors of the buildings were then thrown open, that the flames might have a full current of air. At nine o'clock authentic information reached Lieutenant Jones that 2000 men were close at hand.

The men worked bravely, cutting up planks and splitting timbers into kindling-wood, which were heaped ready for the flames. They emptied their mattresses, filled them with powder, and carried them thus into the buildings, that no suspicion might be excited among the people. The arms were then placed in the best position to be destroyed by the explosion, and the combustibles deposited in different places in the shops, that all might be ready.

When all was completed, the fires were started in the combustibles heaped in the carpenters' shop. The trains leading to the powder were ignited, and the men were led forth.

All at once a cry of fire rang through the town. The frightened inhabitants rushed from the houses, and as Lieutenant Jones and his men entered the gateway of the bridge, an excited crowd pursued him with menaces and threats of vengeance. He wheeled his men into line, and announced his determination to fire upon the pursuers if they molested him.. The people then fell back, and he escaped by the canal and took refuge in the woods.

A quarter of an hour after, when this band of valiant men were grouped in the darkness of the woods, the first thunders of the explosion echoed through the hills, and flames leaped forth from the burning buildings, illuminating the grand scenery of the place into wonderful beauty. The water, the village, and those glorious mountain passes that surround Harper's Ferry with a grandeur which the whole world recognizes, were illuminated into all their green and crystal depths. After pausing a moment to witness the result of their own noble work, this gallant officer and his brave men turned their faces northward, and left Harper's Ferry, saluted by fresh bursts of explosion, and lighted onward by jets of flame that leaped up from the surging clouds in which the arsenal was enveloped, till the sky glowed above them like a golden canopy.

Leaving the scene of conflagration behind, Lieutenant Jones made a hurried march toward Hagerstown, Maryland, wading through streams and swamps, and reached that place at seven o'clock on the morning of the 19th. There he immediately procured means of conveyance, and started for Chambersburg, Pennsylvania, which he reached in the afternoon in an exhausted condition. The men were covered with mud and dirt, and were overcome with fatigue and hunger, having eaten nothing since leaving Harper's Ferry. They were hospitably entertained by the inhabitants, and departed in the afternoon train for Carlisle barracks. Lieutenant Jones and his men received the approbation and thanks of the Government for their judicious conduct on this occasion, and he was commissioned Assistant Quartermaster-General, U. S. A., with the rank of Captain.

The arsenal buildings were immediately taken possession of by the rebel authorities, and used for the purpose of making and repairing arms, until they again came into possession of the Federal authorities.

THROUGH BALTIMORE.

A terrible civil war, destined to be without parallel for bitter intenseness, was now fully revealed. The curtain that had so long screened the enemies of the Union in their machinations against the Government, had been raised at Fort Sumter; and in the seizure of Harper's

Ferry arsenal, although its usefulness to them had been seriously impaired by the true hearts and hands that applied the torch, and rendered the darkness of night lurid with its conflagration, desolation and ruin had already began their march, leaving their footprints in ashes among the lovely scenes of civilized life, and rioting amid the legendary grandeur and time-honored places of the Old Dominion.

It needed but one act more to encircle us with the thunders of war—to plunge the nation into an almost fathomless ocean of civil hatred and revenge, and leave upon the pages of history the unhappy record of many an ensanguined field. The green sward of a happy, prosperous and free land only remained to be crimsoned with blood! The heart of some martyr freemen needed only to be drained of its life-blood, and the stripes of our old flag dyed a deeper crimson in the precious flood. Soon, too soon, alas! this last fatal act was accomplished. The day after the burning of Harper's Ferry saw the streets of Baltimore red with sacred blood, and a nation shuddered as the lightning spread the fatal news from State to State.

For months threats had been whispered that Washington should be seized; that an armed mob should revel in the capital and drive Lincoln from the White House. These threats were not idle boastings, as the confidence, celerity, and preparation of the insurgents proved. While the country north of the Potomac was solacing itself with dreams of peace—while plenty was filling every coffer to overflowing, great preparations had been making, and that for a very long time, to secure the end they now had in view. Sudden, unexpected, like the deep tolling of a midnight alarm-bell, the news fell upon the country. Fear, amounting almost to panic, seized upon the people, and when the orders were issued for the instant assembling of troops, the rush to arms was proof positive of this deep alarm.

As in the olden days, the sons of Massachusetts—brave, hardy, fearless as their own sea-washed rock—rushed first to arms and responded to the call. In less than twenty-four hours, *seventeen hundred men* were waiting in Boston—armed, ready and anxious to march. The order came, and early in the morning of the nineteenth of April—a day memorable in the history of the country, as the anniversary of the battle of Lexington—the Sixth Regiment of Massachusetts militia, commanded by Col. E. P. Jones, of Pepperell, and accompanied by three companies from another regiment, attached temporarily to his command (comprising, in all, about one thousand men), left Philadelphia for Washington, arriving in Baltimore at ten o'clock, A.M. The same train also contained about twelve hundred men from Philadelphia, under the command of General Small. These were unarmed, provision having been made for their being supplied, in this respect, on their arrival at Washington.

On the arrival of the train at the President-street depot, the locomotives were detached, and horses substituted, occasioning much delay, for there was an inadequate supply. A very large crowd had gathered around, and though the reception was not one of courtesy, yet no one would have anticipated serious trouble.

Six cars passed in safety, before the fast-increasing mob (for it could now be called by no other name), succeeded in obstructing the track, and thus cutting off three companies of the Massachusetts troops from their comrades, besides General Small's command, who had remained at the depot of the Philadelphia road. A hasty consultation was held, and it was determined by the officers to march the Massachusetts companies to their destination; and the detachment, under the command of Captain Follansbee, at once set out.

Then it was that the long-smothered fires burst out openly, and were not to be controlled. In the streets of the Monumental City, in the face of a little band of patriots, and in defiance of the civilized world, a secession flag—a mutilated effigy of the stars and stripes—was flaunted in the face of these Massachusetts men, with taunts and sneers, which they received in grave silence. Hemmed in, surrounded, cut off from assistance, the sons of Massachusetts were forbidden to proceed, and boastfully taunted with their inability to march through the city. Cheer upon cheer rang forth for the South, Jeff. Davis, Secession and South Carolina, and mocking groans for the tried and true friends of the Union.

But the sons of men who fought at Bunker Hill, at Monmouth, and Valley Forge, could not be made to understand the words, "Turn back." The blood of patriots had been transmitted to them, and no shame could fall upon the memories of their revolutionary fathers by their acts. They had started for Washington—started to help form a nation's bulwark around a nation's heart, and were not to be stayed by sneers or threats.

"Forward the Sixth,"—the command given and obeyed in that moment of peril, has rendered the Sixth regiment of Massachusetts immortal! Forward, as at Lexington, with fearless hearts, unblenching lips, and unswerving tread, they marched on boldly, as they would have gone up to the cannon's mouth.

"Forward!" A bridge half destroyed, torn up, difficult of crossing, was passed; then the air was darkened with missiles of every dangerous name and character, showered upon their devoted heads. Stones, brick-backs, clubs, anything savage hands could clutch, were hurled from street and house-top, while the hissing rush of shot and ball played wildly from musket and revolver.

Ah! it was a cruel, cold-blooded murder of innocent men—of brothers. An act of treachery unparalleled in the history of any nation, whether civilized or savage—a rendering of the "Monuments" of Baltimore a mockery for all time.

Struck down by shot and stones, wounded, surrounded, hopeless of help, these brave men yet stood their ground and even questioned *whether it would be right to retaliate.* A question without a parallel and proving the pure gold of those brave hearts.

ATTACK ON THE MASSACHUSETTS SIXTH IN BALTIMORE.

But the time when forbearance ceases to be a virtue, came at last to these heroic men—these tender-hearted, christianized soldiers; when self-preservation, the sternly just primal law of our nature commanded them to defend themselves. With firm front, but with sad hearts they prepared to execute the command, and many a form that would not have trembled amid the shock of battle, trembled now as his musket rang the death peal.

Unable to stand the charge, to face the deadly music their own cowardly hearts had awakened—afraid to listen to the awful tumult of battle, the mob broke and sought also to arm themselves. Save from private sources, stores, gunshops and the like, they failed in securing any, for the armories had been well protected in anticipation of this possible event. An incessant storm of stones, however, answered every musket shot, and while the fearless "Sixth" still pressed on, more than one of their number fell by the way, and was borne off helpless and wounded, by the police.

The fight was a running one, terrific in its results, as it was rapid in its execution, and though the soldiers at length succeeded in reaching the depot, with the loss of only two killed and nine wounded; while their assailants' loss was nine killed and eight severely wounded, yet the streets were stained with American blood, drawn by American hands. The pavement stones were red with the life-tide of brothers. Stained indelibly, for though the marks have long since been effaced by the pure rains of a merciful heaven, and the ceaseless tramp of busy feet, yet they are graven on the records of the age with a pen of fire, carving deeper than steel, and more lasting than marble!

The unarmed Pennsylvania troops, taking the alarm, were sent back, though not without injury from the infuriated mob.

The band of the glorious Sixth, consisting of twenty-four persons, together with their musical instruments, occupied a car by themselves from Philadelphia to Baltimore. By some accident the musicians' car got switched off at the Canton depot, so that, instead of being the first, it was left in the rear of all the others, and after the attack had been made by the mob upon the soldiers, they came upon the car in which the band was still sitting, wholly unarmed, and incapable of making any defence. The infuriated demons approached them, howling and yelling, and poured in upon them a shower of stones, broken iron, and other missiles; wounding some severely, and demolishing their instruments. Some of the miscreants jumped upon the roof of the car, and, with a bar of iron, beat a hole through it, while others were calling for powder to blow them all up in a heap.

Finding that it would be sure destruction to remain longer in the car, the poor fellows jumped out to meet their fiendish assailants hand to hand. They were saluted with a shower of stones, but took to their heels, fighting their way through the crowd, and running at random, without knowing in what direction to go for assistance or shelter.

As they were hurrying along, a rough-looking man suddenly jumped in front of their leader, and exclaimed: "This way, boys! this way!"

It was the first friendly voice they had heard since entering Baltimore; they stopped to ask no questions, but followed their guide, who took them up a narrow court, where they found an open door, into which they rushed, being met inside by a powerful-looking woman, who grasped each one by the hand, and directed them upstairs. The last of their band was knocked senseless just as he was entering the door, by a stone, which struck him on the head; but the woman who had welcomed them, immediately caught up their fallen comrade, and carried him in her arms up the stairs.

"You are perfectly safe here, boys," said the brave woman, who directly proceeded to wash and bind up their wounds.

After having done this, she procured them food, and then told them to strip off their uniforms and put on the clothes she had brought them, a motley assortment of baize jackets, ragged coats, and old trowsers. Thus equipped, they were enabled to go out in search of their companions, without danger of attack from the mob, which had given them so rough a reception.

They then learned the particulars of the attack upon the soldiers, and of their escape, and saw lying at the station the two men who had been killed, and the others who had been wounded. On going back to the house where they had been so humanely treated, they found that their clothes had been carefully tied up, and with their battered instruments, had been sent to the depot of the Philadelphia railroad, where they were advised to go themselves. They did not long hesitate, but started in the next train, and arrived at Philadelphia just in time to meet the Eighth regiment of Massachusetts Volunteers.

Contrast this generous act with that of an old gray-haired man, aged more than sixty-five years, who saw one of the Massachusetts soldiers in the act of levelling his musket, when he rushed in his shirt sleeves from his shop, disarmed the man by main force, and killed him with the bayonet—and you have some idea of the conflicting elements which composed the Baltimore riot.

Increasing by what it had fed on, the lawless spirit ran still more high; its black waves rolled and surged, and no power could be found strong enough to control them. The demon spirit that ran riot during the days of Robespierre, and the fiendish hours of the "Reign of Terror," appeared in the streets of Baltimore, and foul lips sang rebellious songs. Secession and murder mingling together in rude discord.

The rulers were impotent to check the storm, or control the whirlwind. The people were for the time masters—the authorities helpless.

On this memorable 19th of April, the writer of these pages was on her way from Washington to New York. The train in which she travelled was loaded down with persons going northward, for Washington was not considered a safe place to sojourn in that week, especially for ladies.

About ten miles from Baltimore we met the train which bore the Sixth Massachusetts regiment from the scene of its late encounter. Both trains slackened speed, and instantly it flew like wildfire along the cars that there had been riot and bloodshed in Baltimore, and the brave fellows we had passed had been attacked in their passage through the town. The news was received with great excitement, that grew more and more intense until our engine thundered into the depot. The fighting was over, but a mob of morose and cruel-looking men, with a few black women and children, still hung around the building, and we passed out through a lane of scowling faces.

The horse railroad had been torn up and so blockaded that there was no hopes of reaching the Philadelphia cars by that way. With difficulty we procured a carriage and were drawn over the scene of conflict. The railroad was almost obliterated; piles of lumber, fifteen feet high, were heaped upon it. Immense anchors lay across it, forming an iron barricade. Every window along the line was crowded with eager, scared faces, mostly black, and those that were white, evidently of the lowest order.

It became impossible to pass along the railroad, for it was completely blocked up. We turned into a side street, and at last took our places in the Philadelphia train. Here two or three men in uniform entered the cars, and after the train started they were seen talking earnestly with the conductor near our seat. It seemed that the Pennsylvania regiment had been scattered, and while a train had returned toward Philadelphia with the larger portion of the men, some twenty-five or thirty were grouped on the wayside, some miles from the city, hoping that our train would take them in.

The conductor was inexorable. His orders were to proceed direct—besides, he had no room, every seat was crowded. This was true; but all the gentlemen, among whom was Senator Wilkinson, of Minnesota, and several ladies that sat within hearing, pleaded that the men should be taken in, and all offered to surrender their own seats. But it was of no avail—the conductor had his orders.

A few minutes after the officers had retreated we passed a platform on the wayside on which these unlucky soldiers were grouped, in anxious expectation that the train would stop, but it went steadily by, leaving the most disappointed and gloomy faces behind that one often looks upon.

We afterwards learned that these poor fellows wandered around the country for three days, and many of them came back to Philadelphia on foot.

If they were sad at being left, those in the cars were both sorrowful and indignant that they had not been taken up. It seemed to them an act of wanton cruelty; and one of the company, at least, has not yet been able to change her opinion on the subject.

At Wilmington we passed the town in which were the companions of these deserted men. Their train had paused in the town, which we found one blaze of excitement. As the news spread, cheer after cheer arose for the stars and stripes, the soldiers, the government, and everything else around which a patriotic cry could centre, rang up from the streets. The people were fairly wild when they saw that the soldiers were driven back.

In every town and at every depot this wild spirit of indignation increased as we advanced. Philadelphia was full of armed men; regiments were rushing to the arsenals, groups of men talked eagerly in the streets—martial music sounded near the Continental Hotel at intervals all night. The city was one scene of wild commotion. In the morning the Seventh New York regiment came in. The day before they had left the Empire City one blaze of star-spangled flags and in a tumult of patriotic enthusiasm. That morning they were hailed in Philadelphia with like spirit. Expecting to march through Baltimore, they panted for an opportunity of avenging the noble men who had fallen there. The citizens met them with generous hospitality, and their passage through Philadelphia was an ovation.

But their indignation towards the Baltimorians was not to be appeased by fighting their own way through that city. Orders reached them to advance toward Washington through Annapolis, and they obeyed, much against the general inclination of the regiment.

I have said that the authorities in Baltimore were powerless; they had no means of learning how far the secession spirit had spread through the city. It is true the riot of the 19th had been ostensibly the action of a low mob, but how far the same spirit extended among the people no one could guess.

On the 20th the mob became more and more belligerent. It assembled at Canton, fired a pistol at the engineer of the Philadelphia train when it came in, and forcing the passengers to leave the cars, rushed in themselves and compelled the engineer to take them back to Gunpowder bridge. There the train was stopped while the mob set fire to the draw-bridge, then returned to Bush river bridge, burned the draw there, and finished their raid by burning Canton bridge.

While this was going on outside the city, materials for fresh commotion were gathering in the streets.

All through the day the accessions from the country were coming in. Sometimes a squad of infantry, sometimes a troop of horse, and once a small park of artillery. It was nothing extraordinary to see a "solitary horseman" riding in from the country, with shot-gun, powder-horn and flask. Some came with provender lashed to the saddle, prepared to picket off for the night. Boys accompanied their fathers, accoutred apparently with the sword and holster-pistols that had done service a century ago. There appeared strange contrasts between the stern, solemn bearing of the father, and the buoyant, excited, enthusiastic expressions of the boy's face, eloquent with devotion and patriotism; for mistaken and wrong, they were not the less actuated by the most unselfish spirit of loyalty. They hardly knew, any of them, for what they had so suddenly came to Baltimore. They had a vague idea, only, that Maryland had been invaded, and that it was the solemn duty of her sons to protect their soil from the encroachments of a hostile force.

In the streets of the lower part of the city, were gathered immense crowds among whom discussions and the high pitch of excitement which discussion engenders, grew clamorous. The mob—for Baltimore street was one vast mob—was surging to and fro, uncertain in what direction to move, and apparently without any special purpose. Many had small secession cards pinned on their coat collars, and not a few were armed with guns, pistols and knives, of which they made the most display.

Thus the day ended and the night came on. During the darkness the whole city seemed lying in wait for the foe. Every moment the mob expected the descent of some Federal regiment upon them, and the thirst for strife had grown so fierce that terrible bloodshed must have followed if the troops from Philadelphia or Harrisburg had attempted to pass through Baltimore then.

On Sunday, April 21, the city was in a state of unparalleled excitement. Private citizens openly carried arms in the streets. Along the line of the railroad almost every house was supplied with muskets or revolvers and missiles, in some instances even with small cannon. Volunteers were enlisting rapidly, and the streets became more and more crowded. Abundance of arms had sprung to light, as if by magic, in rebellious hands. Troops were continually arriving and placing themselves in readiness for action.

A great crowd was constantly surging around the telegraph office, waiting anxiously for news. The earnest inquiry was as to the whereabouts of the New York troops—the most frequent topic, the probable results of an attempt on the part of the Seventh regiment to force a passage through Baltimore. All agreed that the force could never go through—all agreed that it would make the attempt if ordered to do so, and no one seemed to entertain a doubt that it would leave a winrow of dead bodies from the ranks of those who assailed it in the streets through which it might attempt to pass.

As the wires of the telegraph leading to New York had been cut, there was no news to be had for the crowd from that direction.

The police force were entirely in sympathy with the secessionists, and indisposed to act against the mob. Marshal Kane and the Commissioners made no concealment of their proclivities for the secession movement.

Amid this tumult the Mayor of Baltimore and a committee of citizens started for Washington. Their object was to influence the President against forwarding troops through the city in its present agitated state. But the knowledge of his departure did nothing toward allaying the excitement.

About eight o'clock, the streets began again to be crowded. The barrooms and public resorts were closed, that the incentive to precipitate action might not be too readily accessible. Nevertheless there was much excitement, and among the crowd were many men from the country, who carried shot and duck guns, and old-fashioned horse-pistols, such as the "Maryland line" might have carried from the first to the present war. The best weapons appeared to be in the hands of young men—boys of eighteen—with the physique, dress and style of deportment cultivated by the "Dead Rabbits" of New York.

About ten o'clock, a cry was raised that 3,000 Pennsylvania troops were at the Calvert street depot of the Pennsylvania railroad, and were about to take up their line of march through the city. It was said that the 3,000 were at Pikesville, about fifteen miles from the city, and were going to fight their way around the city. The crowd were not disposed to interfere with a movement that required a preliminary tramp of fifteen miles through a heavy sand. But the city authorities, however, rapidly organized and armed some three or four companies and sent them towards Pikesville. Ten of the Adams' Express wagons passed up Baltimore street, loaded with armed men. In one or two there were a number of mattresses, as if wounded men were anticipated. A company of cavalry also started for Pikesville to sustain the infantry that had been expressed. Almost before the last of the expedition had left the city limits, word was telegraphed to Marshal Kane by Mayor Brown from Washington, that the government had ordered the Pennsylvania troops back to Harrisburgh, from the point they had been expected to move on to Baltimore. It seemed incredible, but, of course, satisfactory to the belligerents.

The moment it was known that the government had abandoned the intention of forcing troops through Baltimore, this intense commotion settled into comparative calm, but the city was forced to feel the effect of its own folly. The regular passenger trains north had been stopped.

Many business men have been utterly ruined by the extraordinary position into which the city was plunged through the action of the mob. Capital has been swept away, and commercial advantages sacrificed, that no time or enterprise can replace. Those engaged in trade, have no part in these troubles except to suffer. The mob had them in complete subjection, and a stain has been cast on the city which no time can efface. Yet the whole of this attack was doubtless the work of those classes who form the bane and dregs of society, in every great city;

after events have proved that it was the uprising of a lawless mob, not the expression of a people. But the Mayor of the city and the Governor of the State were for a few days in which these revolters triumphed alike powerless. In this strait they notified the authorities in Washington that troops could not be passed through that city without bloodshed.

The difficulties and dangers of the 19th of April were speedily removed by President Lincoln's determination to march troops intended for Washington by another route, backed by the determination and efficiency of the government and by the supplies which were sent to the aid of loyal men of the city and State, and thereby Maryland has been saved from anarchy, desolation and ruin. The work of impious hands was stayed—a star preserved to our banner, and the right vindicated without unnecessary loss of life! But nothing save great caution and forbearance almost unparalleled in civil wars, rescued Baltimore from destruction.

When the news of the disaster to the brave Massachusetts regiment reached the old Bay State, a feeling of profound sorrow and deep indignation seized upon the people. Troops gathered to the rescue in battalions, armed men arose at every point, and every railroad verging toward Washington became a great military highway. Not only Massachusetts, but all New England looked upon the outrage with generous indignation, as if each State had seen its own sons stricken down. It seemed to be a strife of patriotism which should get its men first to the field. Directly after the Massachusetts troops, the first regiment of Rhode Island Volunteers passed through New York, on their way to the South. Governor Sprague, who had magnanimously contributed one hundred thousand dollars to the cause, accompanied these troops, as commander-in-chief of the Rhode Island forces. His staff consisted of Colonels Frieze, Goddard, Arnold, and Captain A. W. Chapin, Assistant Adjutant-General. And this was followed by a continued rush of armed men till all the great thoroughfares leading to the capital bristled with steel, and reverberated with the tramp of soldiery.

Governor Andrews sent to Maryland requesting that the martyred soldiers should be reverently sent back to Massachusetts, that the State might give them honored burial. This request was complied with, Governor Hicks responding in a delicate and sympathetic manner, and not only Massachusetts but a whole nation awarded them the glory of first dying for a country that will never forget them. The names of these men were, Sumner H. Needham, of Lawrence; Addison O. Whitney, of Lowell City Guards; and Luther C. Ladd, Lowell City Guards.

MILITARY OCCUPATION OF ANNAPOLIS, Md.
April 21, 1861.

On the 18th of April, the Eighth Massachusetts regiment, under the command of General Butler, left Boston for Washington. On arriving at Philadelphia, he ascertained that all communication with Washington by the ordinary line of travel through Baltimore had been cut off, and telegraphic operations suspended. He proceeded to the Susquehanna river, and at Perryville seized the immense ferry-boat "Maryland," belonging to the railroad company, and steamed with his regiment for Annapolis. Through the supposed treachery of the pilot, the boat was grounded on the bar before that place, and they were detained over night. The arrival of troops at this point proved of vital importance. A conspiracy had been formed by a band of secessionists to seize the old frigate Constitution, which lay moored at the wharf of the Naval Academy at that place, being in service as a school for the cadets. Captain Devereux, with his company, was ordered to take possession of the noble old craft, which was promptly done, and the vessel towed to a safe distance from the landing. Governor Hicks, of Maryland, hearing of their arrival, sent a protest against troops being landed at that place.

On Monday, the 22d, the troops landed at the Naval Academy, followed by the New York Seventh regiment, which had just arrived on board the steamer Boston, from Philadelphia, by the help of which vessel the Maryland was enabled to get off the bar.

In order to insure the ready transportation of troops and provisions which were to follow him by the same route, General Butler seized several vessels in the neighborhood, and promptly entered them into the United States service. Meantime a Pennsylvania regiment had arrived at Havre de Grace, and, anticipating the speedy accession of reinforcements from New York by water, three companies of the Eighth Massachusetts were detached as an engineer corps to repair the road to the Annapolis and Elk Ridge Railroad, of which General Butler had taken military possession.

The Seventy-first New York and other regiments having arrived during the night of April 23d, early on the following morning the Seventh regiment, from New York, took up its line of march on the track to Washington Junction. A member of this regiment, young O'Brien the poet, pays a merited tribute to the brave men who preceded them:

On the morning of the 22d we were in sight of Annapolis, off which the Constitution was lying, and there found the Eighth regiment of Massachusetts volunteers on board the Maryland. They were aground, owing, it is supposed, to the treachery of the captain, whom they put in irons and wanted to hang. I regret to say that they did not do it. During the greater portion of that forenoon we were occupied in trying to get the Maryland off the sand-bar on which she was grounded. From our decks we could see the men in file trying to rock her, so as to facilitate our tugging. These men were without water and without food, were well-conducted and uncomplaining, and behaved in all respects like heroes. They were under the command of Colonel Butler, and I regret that that gentleman did not care more for the comforts of men whose subsequent pluck proved that nothing was too good for them.

On the afternoon of the 22d we landed at the Annapolis dock, after having spent hours in trying to relieve the Maryland. For the first time in his life your correspondent was put to work to roll flour-barrels. He was entrusted with the honorable and onerous duty of transporting stores from the steamer to the dock. Later still he descended to the position of mess servant, when, in company with gentlemen well known in Broadway for immaculate kids, he had the honor of attending on his company with buckets of cooked meat and crackers—the only difference between him and Co. and the ordinary waiter being, that the former were civil.

We were quartered in the buildings belonging to the Naval School at Annapolis. I had a bunking-place in what is there called a fort, which is a rickety structure that a lucifer match would set on fire, but furnished with imposing guns. I suppose it was merely built to practice the cadets, because as a defence it is worthless. The same evening boats were sent off from the yard, and towards nightfall the Massachusetts men landed, fagged, hungry, thirsty, but indomitable.

The two days that we remained at Annapolis were welcome. We had been without a fair night's sleep since we left New York, and even the hard quarters we had there were a luxury compared to the dirty decks of the Boston. Besides, there were natural attractions. The grounds are very prettily laid out, and in the course of my experience I never saw a handsomer or better bred set of young men than the cadets. Twenty had left the school owing to political convictions. The remainder are sound Union fellows, eager to prove their devotion to the flag. After spending a delightful time in the Navy School, resting and amusing ourselves, our repose was disturbed at 9 P. M., April 23, by rockets being thrown up in the bay. The men were scattered all over the grounds; some in bed, others walking or smoking, all more or less undressed. The rockets being of a suspicious character, it was conjectured that a Southern fleet was outside, and our drummer beat the roll-call to arms. From the stroke of the drum until the time that every man, fully equipped and in fighting order, was in the ranks, was exactly, by watch, *seven minutes*. The alarm, however, proved to be false, the vessels in the offing proving to be laden with the Seventy-first and other New York regiments; so that, after an unpremeditated trial of our readiness for action, we were permitted to retire to our couches, which means, permit me to say, a blanket on the floor, with a military overcoat over you, and a nasal concert all around you, that, in noise and number, outvies Musard's *concerts monstres*.

On the morning of the 24th of April we started on what afterwards proved to be one of the hardest marches on record. The secessionists of Annapolis and the surrounding districts had threatened to cut us off in our march, and even went so far as to say that they would attack our quarters. The dawn saw us up. Knapsacks, with our blankets and overcoats strapped on them, were piled on the green. A brief and insufficient breakfast was taken, our canteens filled with vinegar and water, cartridges distributed to each man, and after mustering and loading, we started on our first march through a hostile country.

General Scott has stated, as I have been informed, that the march that we performed from Annapolis to the Junction is one of the most remarkable on record. I know that I felt it the most fatiguing, and some of our officers have told me that it was the most perilous. We marched the first eight miles under a burning sun, in heavy marching order, in less than three hours; and it is well known that, placing all elementary considerations out of the way, marching on a railroad track is the most harassing. We started at about 8 o'clock, A. M., and for the first time saw the town of Annapolis, which, without any disrespect to that place, I may say looked very much as if some celestial schoolboy, with a box of toys under his arm, had dropped a few houses and men as he was going home from school, and that the accidental settlement was called Annapolis. Through the town we marched, the people unsympathizing, but afraid. They saw the Seventh for the first time, and for the first time they realized the men that they had threatened.

The tracks had been torn up between Annapolis and the Junction, and here it was that the wonderful qualities of the Massachusetts Eighth regiment came out. The locomotives had been taken to pieces by the inhabitants, in order to prevent our travel. In steps a Massachusetts volunteer, looks at the piece-meal engine, takes up a flange, and says coolly, "I made this engine, and I can put it together again." Engineers were wanted when the engine was ready. Nineteen stepped out of the ranks. The rails were torn up. Practical railroad makers out of the regiment laid them again, and all this, mind you, without care or food. These brave boys, I say, were starving while they were doing this good work. As we marched along the track that they had laid, they greeted us with ranks of smiling but hungry faces. One boy told me, with a laugh on his young lips, that he had not eaten anything for thirty hours. There was not, thank God, a haversack in our regiment that was not emptied into the hands of these ill-treated heroes, nor a flask that was not at their disposal.

Our march lay through an arid, sandy, tobacco-growing country. The sun poured on our heads like hot lava. The Sixth and Second companies were sent on for skirmishing duty, under the command of Captains Clarke and Nevers, the latter commanding as senior officer. A car, on which was placed a howitzer, loaded with grape and canister, headed the column, manned by the engineer and artillery corps, commanded by Lieutenant Bunting. This was the rallying point of the skirmishing party, on which, in case of difficulty, they could fall back. In the centre of the column came the cars, laden with medical stores, and bearing our sick and wounded, while the extreme rear was brought up with a second howitzer, loaded also with grape and canister. The engineer corps, of course, had to do the forwarding work. New York dandies, sir—but they built bridges, laid rails, and headed the regiment through. After marching about eight miles, during which time several men caved in from exhaustion, and one young gentleman was sunstruck, and sent back to New York, we halted, and instantly, with the divine instinct which characterizes the hungry soldier, proceeded to forage. The worst of it was, there was no foraging to be done. The only house within reach was inhabited by a lethargic person, who, like most Southern men, had no idea of gaining money by labor. We offered him extravagant prices to get us fresh water, and it was with the utmost reluctance that we could get him to obtain us a few pailfuls. Over the mantel-piece of his miserable shanty I saw—a curious coincidence—the portrait of Colonel Duryea, of our regiment.

After a brief rest of about an hour, we again commenced our march; a march which lasted until the next morning—a march than which in history, nothing but those marches in which defeated troops have fled from the enemy, can equal. Our Colonel, it seems, determined to march by railroad, in preference to the common road, inasmuch as he had obtained such secret information as led him to suppose that we were waited for on the latter route. Events justified his judgment. There were cavalry troops posted in defiles to cut us off. They could not have done it, of course, but they could have harassed us severely. As we went along the railroad we threw out skirmishing parties from the Second and Sixth companies, to keep the road clear. I know not if I can describe that night's march. I have dim recollections of deep cuts through which we passed, gloomy and treacherous-looking, with the moon shining full on our muskets, while the banks were wrapped in shade, and each moment expecting to see the flash and hear the crack of the rifle of the Southern guerilla. The tree frogs and lizards made a mournful music as we passed. The soil on which we travelled was soft and heavy. The sleepers, lying at intervals across the track, made the march terribly fatiguing. On all sides dark, lonely pine woods stretched away, and high over the hooting of owls, or the plaintive petition of the whip-poor-will, rose the bass commands of "Halt! Forward, march!"—and when we came to any ticklish spot, the word would run from the head of the column along the lines, "Holes," "Bridge—pass it along," &c.

As the night wore on, the monotony of the march became oppressive. Owing to our having to explore every inch of the way, we did not make more than a mile or a mile and a half an hour. We ran out of stimulants, and almost out of water. Most of us had not slept for four nights, and as the night advanced our march was almost a stagger. This was not so much fatigue as want of excitement. Our fellows were spoiling for a fight, and when a dropping shot was heard in the distance, it was wonderful to see how the languid legs straightened, and the column braced itself for action. If we had had even the smallest kind of a skirmish, the men would have been able to walk to Washington. As it was, we went sleepily on. I myself fell asleep, walking in the ranks. Numbers, I find, followed my example; but never before was there shown such indomitable pluck and perseverance as the Seventh showed in that march of twenty miles. The country that we passed through seemed to have been entirely deserted. The inhabitants, who were going to kill us when they thought we daren't come through, now vamosed their respective ranches, and we saw them not. Houses were empty. The population retired into the interior, burying their money, and carrying their families along with them. They, it seems, were under the impression that we came to ravage and pillage, and they fled, as the Gauls must have fled, when Attila and his Huns came down on them from the North. As we did at Annapolis, we did in Maryland State. We left an impression that cannot be forgotten. Everything was paid for. No discourtesy was offered to any inhabitant, and the sobriety of the regiment should be an example to others. Nothing could have been more effective or energetic than the movements of the Engineer Corps, to whom we were indebted for the rebuilding of a bridge in an incredibly short space of time.

The secret of this forced march, as well as our unexpected descent on Annapolis, was the result of Colonel Lefferts' judgment, which has since been sustained by events. Finding that the line along the Potomac was closed, and the route to Washington, by Baltimore, equally impracticable, he came to the conclusion that Annapolis, commanding, as it did, the route to the Capital, must of necessity be made the basis of military operations. It was important to the government to have a free channel through which to transport troops, and this post presented the readiest means. The fact that since then all the Northern troops have passed through the line that we thus opened, is a sufficient comment on the admirable judgment that decided on the movement. It secured the integrity of the regiment, and saved lives, the loss of which would have plunged New York into mourning. Too much importance cannot be attached to this strategy. To it the Seventh regiment is indebted for being here at present, intact and sound.

On Thursday, April 24, this regiment reached Washington, having taken the cars at the junction. They were followed directly by their noble comrades of the march, the Massachusetts Eighth, and immediately moved into quarters.

While the troops under Butler and Lefferts were lying at Annapolis, great anxiety was felt regarding them at Washington. The lamented Lander was then at the capital, pleading for the privilege of raising a regiment for the defence of the government, but, for some inexplicable cause, General Scott had not yet accepted his services. With Baltimore in open revolt, and Annapolis doubtful in its loyalty, this anxiety about the troops became so urgent, that Lander was sent forward to Annapolis, with general directions to aid the troops with all his ability, and to direct Colonel Butler not to land his men until the kindly feeling of the citizens of Annapolis was ascertained.

Lander started on the mission, as he undertook everything, with heart and soul. He rode from Washington to Annapolis on horseback, without stopping for darkness, or any other cause save the necessary care of his horse, and reached Annapolis an hour after the troops had landed. Bringing his experience, as a frontiersman, who had seen hard service against hostile Indians on the plains, to bear on the position, Lander gave Colonel Butler such aid and advice as assisted greatly in bringing the soldiers forward with less danger and suffering than might otherwise have arisen during their march to the junction.

MARYLAND.

The attack by an armed mob upon the Massachusetts regiment had called the attention of the entire country to the State of Maryland, and her future course was the subject of deep feeling. Indirectly, Washington was, of course, menaced by her movements, and it became a matter of vital importance that she should be retained in the Union and

restored to her fidelity. Not here alone were keen eyes watching her future. England and France, in their eager thirst for dominion and their jealousy of America and her liberal institutions, scrutinized every action, with reference to their own future course. Second only to Washington, therefore, for the time, became the "Monumental City."

From the 19th of April, the day when the banner of the Massachusetts Sixth was baptized in blood, until the 14th of June, all was suspense, and those who still retained their fealty were reluctant to express their loyalty from fear of personal violence. Then an election was held for members of Congress, and every district, save one, returned decisive majorities for unconditional Union men. The majority of the Legislature were unreserved in their expressions of disunion, and were secretly, if not openly, urging on the State to revolt. As early as December, 1860, Governor Hicks had been solicited to call a Convention for that purpose, and emissaries of the rebel government had labored with untiring zeal to spread secession sentiments among the people. The Governor, knowing the heart of the masses to be true, refused, and his decision came like a thunder-clap upon the Southern partizans who hoped to find him a pliant tool in their hands.

The proclamation of the President, of the 15th April, was tortured into a means of exciting popular clamor, and every effort was made to fan the fires of secession, until they should burst forth in fierce flame. Meetings were held for that purpose, and every possible means resorted to for its accomplishment. While very many of the wealthy and commercial classes of Maryland, and particularly of Baltimore, were in favor of disunion, eminent and influential citizens, some of whom were among the most distinguished public men of the State, and whose names are inseparably connected with its civil and political history, were committed irrevocably to the support of the government. In this cause the industrial classes—the working-men and the farmers —were true to the principles they had always professed. Whatever political parties they had sympathized with, it had been ever on the broad basis of the Union and the Constitution.

An illustration of this was given on the 18th of April, the day previous to the attack on the Massachusetts regiment. A party of secessionists had raised a rebel flag in the suburbs of Baltimore, and had a cannon with which they saluted it, but a vast crowd of working-men from the neighboring foundries assembled, tore down the flag, and threw the cannon into the river. His Excellency, Thomas H. Hicks, Governor; John P. Kennedy, Secretary of State under President Fillmore; Reverdy Johnson, John R. Kenley, ex-Governor Francis Thomas, Hon. Henry Winter Davis, Edwin H. Webster, Alexander Evans, and many others boldly stepped forward, and planted themselves in the foreground, to resist the tide of dishonesty, passion, and frenzy, into which the State was plunged by the conspirators. Five thousand citizens of Baltimore addressed a letter to Governor Hicks, on January 2d, approving his course in refusing to call the Legislature together to authorize a Convention, and public meetings were held throughout the State for the same purpose. Notwithstanding this great demonstration of popular opinion, the secessionists were resolved upon making the attempt; and, though foiled in their measures, seized the opportunity afforded by the passage of Northern troops through Baltimore, to enkindle the flames of civil war, hoping, in the confusion, to urge their schemes to a fulfilment.

The pressure upon the Governor after this event became almost insupportable. All the combined influences of political, social and commercial classes were brought to bear upon him, and the wild denunciations and contemptuous and bitter invective and threats hurled incessantly upon Baltimore and Maryland by a large portion of the northern press were persistently used to press the Executive to the commission of the fatal act. Thus urged on all sides, he was compelled, in deference to the sudden and violent appeals of the people, to request the government to send no more troops through Maryland. The proclamation of the President of the 15th of April, and the call for troops, was represented by the secessionists of Maryland, as in other States, as an attempt to "coerce," "invade" and "subjugate" the Southern States. They used this appeal with great effect on the popular mind, and the passions of the people were so inflammable, that many whose convictions were utterly opposed to the disunion measures were determined to resent this attempt to "subdue" them. On the 17th of April an excited disunion meeting had been held in Baltimore, and great efforts were made to commit the citizens to the secession movement. On the following day Governor Hicks and his Honor George Wm. Brown, Mayor of Baltimore, issued proclamations calling upon all citizens to keep the peace. The Governor assured the people that no troops should be sent from Maryland, except to defend the national capital. The arrival of Massachusetts troops and the fatal occurrences of the 19th, caused an almost entire cessation of business, and all commerce was suddenly prostrated.

The secessionists were determined to render it impracticable for any more troops to reach Washington, and for this purpose destroyed the bridges and a considerable portion of the tracks of several railroads both north and south of Baltimore.

The Pennsylvania Northern, Philadelphia, Annapolis Junction, and Baltimore and Ohio roads suffered extensively; and in consequence of these lawless proceedings, the greatest difficulty was apprehended in getting troops to Washington in time to protect the capital from the threatened attack.

On the 21st the government announced that it took possession of the Philadelphia and Baltimore railway as a military road. During the temporary delay and obstruction to the travel, it was almost impossible for travellers to pass either way. Many were molested in Baltimore; some were placed in confinement under false charges by the secessionists, and all were compelled to pay exorbitant prices and resort to the rudest means of conveyance to pursue their journeys, when permitted so to do. On the 22d the Mayor and Police Board of Baltimore laid an embargo on provisions and necessary supplies, as the interruption to transportation threatened a deficiency of food.

The Governor, under these extraordinary circumstances, called a special session of the Legislature, which assembled at Frederick, on the 26th of the month, the capital, Annapolis, being then in possession of General Butler, who threatened to arrest the whole body if an ordinance of secession were passed. The secession members of the Legislature then attempted to procure the organization of a Board of Safety, which should have discretionary power during the crisis, but public meetings were immediately called, which were loud in their denunciations of this covert transfer of the State to its enemies, and it was abandoned. Resolutions protesting against the war, and recommending the President to desist, and resort to arbitration, were adopted, and a committee appointed to visit the President and induce him to promise that no more troops should be passed through Maryland. The President replied that the public necessity must govern him, and that he would consult the wishes of the people to the utmost extent that the national welfare would permit.

The Legislature, after the report of the Committee had been submitted, on May 6, discussed the questions at issue, and on the 10th adopted a preamble and resolution, declaring Maryland sympathized " with the South in the struggle for their rights, solemnly protests against this action, and will take no part in it, denouncing the military occupancy of the State, and transportation of troops, and imploring the President, in the name of God, to cease this unholy war."

The re-organization of the military departments for the war was progressing with all possible dispatch. The Department of Washington was assigned to Colonel Joseph K. F. Mansfield, the Department of Annapolis to Major General Butler, and that of Pennsylvania to Major General Robert Patterson.

On the 5th of May, General Butler took possession of the junction of the Baltimore and Washington and Baltimore and Ohio railroads, at the Relay House, nine miles south of Baltimore. Four days afterwards a body of United States troops landed at Locust Point in that city, and were conveyed by the cars through it without interruption. The Marshal of the city, John K. Kane, was known to be deeply implicated in the work of rebellion, and he was arrested and search was made at the police headquarters for concealed arms and supplies.

The people of Maryland held views which her disloyal legislators had misrepresented. On the 14th of May, a meeting was held at East Baltimore, at which strong Union resolutions were adopted, pledging "lives, fortunes, and sacred honor," to its defence, declaring the right of the government to convey troops through the State, and their own right and duty to aid them in the work.

General Butler the same day occupied Federal Hill, at Baltimore, and issued a proclamation which was scattered in immense numbers among the people, and contributed in a high degree to the restoration of confidence and harmony among all classes. An important step was also taken by Governor Hicks, who, on the same day issued a proclamation calling for the State quota of four regiments of volunteers for three months, to sustain the government and to protect the capital. General Butler had seized various military stores intended for the rebels, and also took possession of arms and powder belonging to loyal parties, to prevent their being removed by enemies to the government.

Brigadier-General Butler, having been appointed Major-General, and placed in command of the military Department of Virginia, North Carolina and Tennessee, a most important position, was transferred to Fortress Monroe, and was succeeded by General Cadwallader on the 20th. Fort McHenry was reinforced, and put into the most effective condition for immediate service, and the conspirators of Baltimore were restrained from further disorders by the apprehension that any attempt at insurrection would be the signal for a bombardment of the city. After Cadwallader came into command, several arrests of prominent persons had been made. Among these was Mr. John Merryman, who applied to Chief-Justice Taney for a writ of *habeas corpus*. This was granted; and General Cadwallader, in answer, said that the prisoner had been arrested on charge of various acts of treason—of holding a command in a company having in possession arms belonging to the United States, and of avowing his purpose of armed hostility to the Government of the United States. In such cases General Cadwallader said he was authorized by the President to suspend the *habeas corpus* act; he therefore requested Judge Taney to suspend further action until instructions could be had from the President.

Judge Taney thereupon issued a writ of attachment against General Cadwallader for contempt of court. The Marshal proceeded to Fort McHenry to execute the writ, but was refused admission. Judge

Taney urged that the President had no authority to suspend the act of *habeas corpus*, or to authorize others to do so. An elaborate opinion to that effect was prepared by the Judge and has since been published.

A sufficient number of troops were also at this time stationed in Baltimore, and the loyal citizens were assured that they would be protected in all their rights and privileges, at every hazard. Thus fortified, protected and encouraged, the loyalty of the people was fully displayed, while the disloyal were held in check. Maryland, glorious in her past history, and her devotion to the Constitution, was saved from destruction, and her loyal citizens will in generations to come receive the plaudits of millions whose gratitude will be deep enough to overwhelm her few days of revolt.

DESTRUCTION OF THE GOSPORT NAVY YARD.
April 21, 1861.

The splendid naval and military establishment at Gosport, Virginia, belonging to the Federal Government, was, at the time Virginia seceded, in the possession of the United States. It was supplied with immense quantities of military and naval stores; and several old vessels which had been withdrawn from service, and others of great value, were either waiting orders to sail or undergoing repairs. The entire establishment, whether on land or water, was indispensable to the conspirators, for the possession of the Navy Yard would give them immediate control of ordnance stores and property worth $30,000,000.

The seizure of this vast establishment having been determined upon, five or six vessels had been sunk by the rebels in the channel of the Elizabeth river, below the Navy Yard, thus effectually preventing the passage of larger vessels.

General Taliaferro was placed in command of the insurgent forces then rapidly concentrating at Norfolk. Commodore McCauley, who commanded at the Navy Yard, had been reluctant to adopt any measures which would bring him into hostility with the State troops, and thus inaugurate the war. The rebels took advantage of this leniency, but for once they were disappointed in their expectations of success. The Commodore determined to destroy the *immediate agencies of the war*, leaving the armories, ship wood, docks and dwellings unharmed, hoping that, although they might for a time be occupied by the insurgents, the stars and stripes would eventually float over them in triumph.

At 8½ o'clock on Saturday evening, the 20th April, the Pawnee, containing 600 Massachusetts troops from Fortress Monroe, arrived at Gosport harbor, the Commodore's flag at its mast-head the white sails, relieved by the dark blue sky, appearing more like the floating wings of the dove of peace than heralds of destruction. The scene that followed is thus graphically described by an eye-witness.

Her coming was not unexpected, and as she glided to her place at the dock, the men on the Pennsylvania and the Cumberland, several hundred in number, greeted her with a volley of cheers that echoed and re-echoed till all Norfolk and Portsmouth must have heard the hail. The men of the Pennsylvania fairly outdid themselves in their enthusiasm on this occasion. They clambered into the shrouds, and not only answered to the "three cheers," but volunteered "three times three," and gave them with a hurricane of heartiness. This intense feeling on their part is easily explained. They had been a long time almost imprisoned on shipboard, on a ship imbedded in the river, motionless and helpless, and subject to *promises* from the secessionists of speedy demolition. In the advent of the Pawnee they saw deliverance from such durance, and they exulted with tremendous emphasis.

All Portsmouth and Norfolk were thoroughly aroused by the arrival of the Pawnee. They did not expect her, and were not prepared for her. They were seized with trepidation, thinking, perhaps, she had come, and along with the Cumberland and Pennsylvania, meant to bombard the towns for having obstructed the channel, and for having, the night before, rifled the United States magazine, just below Norfolk, of about 4,000 kegs of powder. Being utterly defenceless and quite terrified, the secessionists made no protest against the Pawnee's presence, nor did they venture too near the Navy Yard.

The Pawnee made fast to the dock, and Colonel Wardrop marched out his regiment and stationed them at the several gates of the Navy Yard to oppose the entrance of any forces from without, in case an attempt to enter should be made. Having adopted this precaution, the Commodore set the marines on the Pennsylvania, the Cumberland, the Pawnee, and in the yard, to work. All the books and papers, the archives of the establishment, were transferred to the Pawnee.

Everything of interest to the Government on the Pennsylvania was promptly transferred to the Cumberland. On this latter vessel, it was also said, a large amount of gold from the Custom House at Norfolk had been in good time placed. Having made safe everything that was to be brought away, the marines were next set to work to destroy everything on the Pennsylvania, and the other ships, and in the yard, that might be of immediate use in waging war upon the government. Many thousand stands of arms were destroyed. Carbines had their stocks broken from the barrels by a blow, and were thrown overboard. A large lot of revolvers shared the like fate. Shot and shell by thousands went with hurried plunge to the bottom. Most of the cannon had been spiked the day and night before. There were at least 1,500 pieces in the yard—some elegant Dahlgren guns, and Columbiads of all sizes.

It is impossible to describe the scene of destruction that was exhibited. Unweariedly it was continued from 9 o'clock until about 12, during which time the moon gave light to direct the operations. But when the moon sank behind the western horizon, the barracks near the centre of the yard were set on fire, that by its illumination the work might be continued. The crackling flames and the glare of light inspired with new energies the destroying marines, and havoc was carried everywhere within the limits of orders. But time was not left to complete the work. Four o'clock of Sunday morning came, and the Pawnee was passing down from Gosport harbor with the Cumberland, the coveted prize of the secessionists, in tow—every soul from the other ships and the yard being aboard of them, save two. Just as they left their moorings, a rocket was sent up from the deck of the Pawnee. It sped high in air, paused a second, and burst in shivers of many-colored light. As it did so, the well-set trains at the ship-houses, and on the decks of the fated vessels left behind, went off as if lit simultaneously by the rocket. One of the ship-houses contained the old New York, a ship thirty years on the stocks, and yet unfinished. The other was vacant; but both houses and the old New York burnt like tinder. The older and unserviceable vessels, the Pennsylvania, the Raritan, the Columbia, the Dolphin, were fired without compunction; while the Merrimac, Plymouth and Germantown were sunk, and the immense lifting shears used for raising vessels was broken down and rendered useless. The old Delaware and Columbus, worn out and dismantled, seventy-fours, were scuttled and sunk at the upper docks on Friday.

The grand conflagration now burst in judgment on the startled citizens of Norfolk, Portsmouth, and all the surrounding country. The flames leaped from pitchy deck to smoking shrouds, and writhed to their very tops around the masts that stood like martyrs doomed. It was not thirty minutes from the time the trains were fired till the conflagration roared like a hurricane, and the flames from land and water swayed, and met, and mingled together, and darted high, and fell, and leaped up again, and by their very motion showed their sympathy with the crackling, crashing roar of destruction beneath. But in all this magnificent scene, the old ship Pennsylvania was the centre-piece. She was a very giant in death, as she had been in life. She was a sea of flame, and when her bowels were consuming, then did she spout from every port-hole of every deck torrents and cataracts of fire that, to the mind of Milton, would have represented her a frigate of hell pouring out unremitting broadsides of infernal fire. Several of her guns were left loaded, but not shotted, and as the fire reached them, they sent out on the startled morning air minute guns of fearful peal, that added greatly to the alarm that the light of the conflagration had spread through the surrounding country. The Pennsylvania burnt like a volcano for five hours and a half before her mainmast fell. At precisely 9½ o'clock the tall tree that stood in her centre tottered and fell, and crushed deep into her burning sides, whilst a storm of sparks filled the sky.

As soon as the Pawnee and Cumberland had fairly left the waters, and were known to be gone, the gathering crowds of Portsmouth and Norfolk burst open the gates of the Navy Yard and rushed in. They could do nothing, however, but gaze upon the ruin wrought. The Commodore's residence, left locked but unharmed, was burst open, and a pillage commenced, which was summarily stopped. As early as six o'clock a volunteer company had taken possession in the name of Virginia, and run up her flag from the flag-staff. In another hour several companies were on hand, and men were at work unspiking cannon, and by nine o'clock they were moving them to the dock, whence they were begun to be transferred, on keels, to points below, where sand batteries were to be built.

Notwithstanding the splendor of the scene, and the great destruction of property, the result was incomplete, and a large amount of artillery and munitions of war fell into the hands of the Virginians.

THE STATE OF THE NATION BEFORE ITS TROOPS ENTERED VIRGINIA.

President Lincoln, on the 15th of April, issued a proclamation stating that the laws of the United States had been and are opposed in several States, by combinations too powerful to be suppressed by the ordinary course of judicial proceedings; he therefore called for 75,000 troops from the several States. The first service assigned to this force would probably be to repossess the forts and other places and property which had been seized from the Union. An extra session of Congress was also to meet on the 4th of July.

When President Lincoln issued his proclamation on the 15th of April, dispatches were sent from the Secretary of War, addressed to the Governors of the several States, designating the quotas assigned to each State, under this proclamation. The Executives of the slaveholding States, with the exception of Maryland and Delaware, peremptorily refused to comply with this requisition. Governor Ellis, of North Carolina, replied, "I regard the levy of troops made by the Administration for the purpose of subjugating the States of the South as in violation of the Constitution, and a usurpation of power. I can be no party to this wicked violation of the laws of the country, and to this war upon the rights of a free people. You can get no troops from North Carolina." Governor Jackson, of Missouri, answered, "There can be, I apprehend, no doubt but these men are intended to form part of the President's army to make war upon the people of the seceding States. Your requisition, in my judgment, is illegal, unconstitutional and revolutionary in its objects, altogether inhuman and diabolical, and cannot be complied with. Not one man will Missouri furnish to carry on such an unholy crusade." Governor Magoffin, of Kentucky, replied, "In answer, I say emphatically, that Kentucky will furnish no troops for the wicked purpose of subduing her sister Southern States." Governor Letcher, of Virginia, answered, "I have only to say that the militia of Virginia will not be furnished to the powers at Washington for any such use or purpose as they have in view. Your object is to subjugate the Southern States, and a requisition made upon me for such an object—an object, in my judgment, not within the purview of the Constitution, or the Act of 1795—will not be complied with. You have chosen to inaugurate civil war, and having done so, we will meet it in a spirit as determined as the Administration has exhibited toward the South." Governor Harris, of Tennessee, refused, in terms equally explicit, to comply with the requisition of the Government. In his Message to the Legislature, dated April 25, he takes strong ground against the action of the Administration, which he says is designed for the subjugation of the Southern States. He recommended the immediate passage of an Act of Secession, and an Act for the union of Tennessee with the Southern Confederacy, both to be submitted separately to the people at an early day. He also recommended an appropriation for arming the State, and the creation of a large military fund, to be placed under the direction of a special board.

The position of Virginia is of the greatest importance to a thorough understanding of the difficulties in which the country was placed. At the breaking out of hostilities, the State Convention was in session. A resolution was passed, expressing an earnest desire for the re-establishment of the Union in its former integrity: an amendment, declaring that Virginia ought not to accept a form of adjustment which would not be acceptable to the seceding States, was rejected. Commissioners were appointed to wait on the President, and ascertain the policy which he intended to pursue. An amendment, denying the right of the Federal Government to deal with the question of secession, was rejected. A resolution was adopted, expressing a willingness that the independence of the seceding States should be acknowledged. An amendment, declaring that Virginia would secede in case the proposed amendments to the Constitution were rejected by the non-slaveholding

States, was lost. And resolutions were adopted, opposing any action on the part of the Federal Government for retaining or retaking forts in the seceding States, and affirming, that any measures of the Government, tending to produce hostilities with the Confederate States, would leave Virginia free to determine her own future policy. When the proclamation of the President, calling for troops, was issued, the Convention went into secret session, on the 17th of April, passed an ordinance to repeal the ratification of the Constitution of the United States, by the State of Virginia, and to resume all the rights and powers granted under such Constitution.

When the proclamation was received at Montgomery, President Davis issued a proclamation, dated on the 17th of April, inviting all persons to apply for letters of marque and reprisal, to be issued under the seal of the Confederate States. President Lincoln thereupon, on the 19th, issued a proclamation, announcing the blockade of all the ports of the seceding States, and that a competent force would be stationed to prevent the entrance and exit of vessels at these ports. On the 27th, the President issued a proclamation extending the blockade to the ports of North Carolina and Virginia. It was announced that the blockade would be maintained by at least fifty vessels of war, accompanied by a fleet of steam transports, capable of conveying an army of 20,000 men. On the 3d of May the President issued another proclamation, calling into service 42,000 volunteers to serve for a period of three years, unless sooner discharged; ordering that the regular army should be increased by 22,714 men; and directing the enlistment, for the naval force of the United States, of 18,000 seamen, for a period of not less than one or more than three years.

The Congress of the Confederate States met at Montgomery on the 29th of April. The message of President Davis announced that the permanent Constitution had been ratified by a sufficient number of States to render it valid, and that it only remained to elect officers under its provisions. The message of President Lincoln, calling for volunteers, was characterized as a declaration of war, which will render it necessary to adopt measures to replenish the treasury of the Confederation, and provide for the defence of the country. Proposals had been issued, inviting subscriptions for a loan of five millions; more than eight millions was subscribed for, none under par.. The whole amount had been ordered to be accepted; and it was now necessary to raise a much larger sum. The Confederate States had in the field, at Charleston, Pensacola, and different forts, 19,000 men, and 16,000 were *en route* for Virginia. It was proposed to organize and hold in readiness an army of 100,000 men. "We seek no conquest," says Mr. Davis, "no aggrandizement, no concession from the Free States. All that we ask is to be let alone; that none shall attempt our subjugation by arms. This we will, and must, resist to the direst extremity. The moment this pretension is abandoned, the sword will drop from our grasp, and we shall be ready to enter into treaties of amity and commerce mutually beneficial." In the meanwhile warlike and aggressive measures had been pushed forward with all possible activity. The forces besieging Fort Pickens had been augmented, and new batteries had been constructed against it. Vessels belonging to the government and to individuals had been seized. Among these was the steamer Star of the West, which had been dispatched to Indianola, Texas, to bring away the United States troops collected at that port. The vessel was lying at anchor, awaiting the arrival of the troops. At midnight, of the 19th of April, the steamer Rusk approached, and the captain of the Star of the West was informed that she had on board 320 United States troops, which were to be embarked.

Every assistance was given for the reception of the supposed soldiers, who, however, proved to be Texan troops. As soon as they were on board they took possession of the steamer, which was taken to New Orleans, the crew being detained as prisoners of war. Shortly after, 450 of the United States troops attempted to make their escape from Indianola on board of two sailing vessels. They were pursued by two armed steamers, manned by the Texans, overtaken, and made prisoners.

The loyal States had not only been patriotic in sending troops to the capital, but in supplying money also. The Legislature of New York appropriated three millions of dollars for arming and equipping troops; Connecticut appropriated two millions; Vermont one million; New Jersey two millions, and other States in proportion. The Common Council of the city of New York appropriated one million. Besides the public appropriations, in every considerable town and city private subscriptions were made for the same purposes, and to support the families of volunteers. The aggregate of the sums thus furnished was estimated at twenty-five millions—all raised in a few days.

Meantime the Confederate government had adjourned on the 20th of May to meet in Richmond, Virginia, on the 20th of July, or some other convenient place to be selected by the President.

On the 6th of May an act was passed "recognizing the existence of war between the United States and the Confederate States, and concerning letters of marque, prizes, and prize goods." This act gave the President of the Confederate States authority to use the whole land and naval forces of the Confederacy to meet the war thus commenced, and to issue letters of marque and reprisal against the vessels and property of the United States and their citizens, with the exception of the States belonging to the Confederation or expected to join it.

An act was passed prohibiting the export of cotton or cotton yarn from any of the Confederate States except through the sea-ports. It was proposed in Congress that the cotton planters should be invited to put their crops in the hands of the government, receiving bonds for its value, the government to dispose of it in Europe for cash. The Postmaster-General, on the 1st of June, took charge of the transmission of the mails in the Confederate States; and the Postmaster-General of the United States announced that on that day postal communication would close with the seceding States, with the exception of some counties in Western Virginia. All letters for these States were sent to the Dead Letter Office at Washington.

Two more States—Arkansas and North Carolina—had formally seceded from the Union, and joined the Confederate States. In Arkansas the State Convention, on the 18th of April, had passed an ordinance submitting the question of secession to the people, at an election to be held on the 3d of August. When the requisition of President Lincoln was received, Governor Rector, on the 22d of April, replied to the Secretary of War, "In answer to your requisition for troops from Arkansas to subjugate the Southern States, I have to say that none will be furnished. The demand is only adding insult to injury. The people of this Commonwealth are freemen and not slaves, and will defend to the last extremity their honor, lives and property against Northern mendacity and usurpation." On the same day the Governor gave orders for the seizure at Napoleon of a large quantity of military supplies belonging to the United States. On the 6th of May, the Convention, which had re-assembled, unanimously passed an ordinance of secession.

Tennessee also virtually, though not in form, joined the Southern Confederacy. The Legislature passed a Declaration of Independence, which was to be submitted to the people on the 8th of June. Meanwhile a military league had been formed with the Confederate government, in virtue of which the forces of Tennessee were to be employed to aid the Confederate States.

In Kentucky a determined effort was made to preserve a strict neutrality. Governor Magoffin, as before noted, refused peremptorily to comply with the President's requisition for troops. On the 20th of May he issued a proclamation declaring that every indication of public sentiment in Kentucky showed a fixed determination of the people to take neither side, but to maintain a posture of self-defence, forbidding the quartering upon her soil of troops from either section, in the hope that the State might yet become a mediator between the parties. He therefore warned all States, whether separate or united, and especially the Confederate and the United States, against any armed occupation within the State of Kentucky, without the permission of the Legislature and Executive authorities. All citizens of Kentucky were forbidden to make any demonstration against either of the sovereignties, but were directed to make prompt and efficient preparations for the defence of the State. Of similar purport were the proceedings of the "Border States Convention," held at Frankfort. Virginia, North Carolina and Arkansas, having joined the Southern Confederacy, of course sent no delegates; none appeared from Maryland, and only one from Tennessee, and four from Missouri. The remainder were from Kentucky. Senator Crittenden was chosen President. Two addresses, one to the people of the United States, and the other to the people of Kentucky, were adopted. The essential point in the first address is the recommendation that Congress would propose such Constitutional amendments as should secure the legal rights of slaveholders; and if this should fail to bring about a pacification, that a Convention be called composed of delegates from all the States, to devise measures of peaceable adjustment.

The address to the people of Kentucky defended the action of the Executive in refusing troops to the Federal Government, as called for by the peculiar circumstances in which the State was placed. "In all things," says the address, "she is as loyal as ever to the constitutional administration of the government. She will follow the stars and stripes to the utmost regions of the earth, and defend it from foreign insult. She refuses alliance with any who would destroy the Union. All she asks is permission to keep out of this unnatural strife. She has announced her intention to refrain from aggression upon others, and she must protest against her soil being made the theatre of military operations by any belligerent." The address goes on to censure the conduct of the States who have withdrawn from the Union, affirming that there was in the Constitution a remedy for every wrong, and provisions to check every encroachment by the majority upon the minority. In withdrawing the States committed "a great wrong, for which they must answer to posterity. But Kentucky remained true to herself, contending with all her might for what were considered to be the rights of the people, and although one after another of the States that should have been by her side ungenerously deserted her, leaving her almost alone in the field, yet she did not surrender her rights under the Constitution, and never would surrender them. She would appear again in the Congress of the United States, not having conceded the least atom of power to the Government that had not heretofore been granted, and retaining every power she had reserved. She would insist upon her constitutional rights in the Union, and not out of it." The address went on to say that if the war should be transferred to Kentucky, her destruction would be the inevitable result; "and even the institution to preserve or control which the wretched war was undertaken, would be exterminated in the general ruin."

In Virginia the vote upon secession resulted in a large majority in its favor. In the north-western part of the State the vote was largely in favor of the Union. A Convention of the Western Counties convened at Wheeling on the 13th of May, at which resolutions were passed pronouncing the ordinance of secession null and void. The Convention adjourned to meet on the 11th of June.

The position of Missouri was similar to that of Kentucky. The State endeavored to avoid taking part in the war. Troops had been organized with hostile designs against the Government. These were forced to surrender by Captain Lyon, (afterward appointed General). At St. Louis an attack was made by the populace, on the 10th of May, upon the United States volunteers; they returned the fire, killing some twenty; an *émeute* on the next day resulted in the loss of several lives. General Harney, who had been put in command of this district, entered into an agreement with the State authorities, that was disapproved by the Government, and he relieved from the command, which was then given to General Lyon.

The attitude assumed by the great powers of Europe in relation to the American war was important. That of England, indicated by the royal proclamation issued on the 14th of May a determination to maintain a strict neutrality in the contest between the contending parties. The proclamation went on to forbid all British subjects from taking part in any way in the contest, by enlisting in the army or navy of either party; by fitting out or arming any vessel; by breaking any lawfully established blockade, or carrying to either, troops or any articles contraband of war. This proclamation, taken in connection with the explanations of the Ministers and the speeches in Parliament, had an unfriendly aspect toward the United States, recognizing, as it did, the Confederate States as belligerents, and, by implication, entitled equally to the right of carrying prizes into the ports of Great Britain. In the House of Commons, Lord John Russell said that the character of belligerency was not so much a principle as a fact; that a certain amount of force and consistency acquired by any mass of population engaged in war entitled them to be treated as a belligerent. A power or a community which was at war with another, and which covered the sea with its cruizers, must either be acknowledged as a belligerent or dealt with as a pirate. The Government had come to the opinion that the Southern Confederacy, according to those principles which were considered just, must be treated as belligerent. In this critical condition was the country when the Government prepared to advance its armies into Virginia.

OCCUPATION OF ALEXANDRIA, Va.

ASSASSINATION OF COLONEL ELLSWORTH.

May 24, 1861.

The defenders of the Union had been gathering at Washington and in its vicinity for more than a month, in answer to the call for troops, that rang through the land clear as clarion notes. The arduous labor of providing for and disciplining the large number of untrained recruits, collected in such haste, had been met with energy and perseverance by the officers of the government. Very much had been accomplished, notwithstanding all the embarrassments incident to an extensive and untried field of labor.

The heart of the country was beating restively at delay, and popular feeling, as it found its voice through the press, thundered anathemas, and clamored for a forward movement. Nothing but prompt and decisive action would satisfy the people that the government was sturdily bending its whole energies to strangle the monster treason in its youth. The people had not yet learned the first great secret of success—how to wait. They saw the ship of state struggling fiercely amid the rocks of an untried ocean, and worshiping the flag at her mast-head, grew clamorous for its protection. Every newspaper, and almost every household, had its own ideas of how this was to be accomplished. The government, unused to war, and anxious to gratify the spirit of patriotism that had supported it so nobly, was ready to answer the rash clamor; and so this long, loud cry of ignorant impatience became words of fate, and ended in giving us the defeat of Bull Run.

The people, the generous loyal people, ever dissatisfied with anything but lightning speed, in peace or war, clamored for action, and must be appeased. Under this pressure, events forced each other on, culminating in action.

Though an act of secession had been passed by a State Convention, held at Richmond on the 17th of April, it was professedly to be submitted to the people of the State of Virginia for their approval on the 23d of May; and though it had been determined by the United States Government to take possession of, and fortify the Virginia hills, in front of the capital, it was deemed advisable to await that event before making any military movement into that State which could be interpreted into an attempt to influence or control the popular vote. The conspirators, however, without waiting for any ratification of their secession act by the people, immediately made a conveyance of the State to the Confederate government, and claimed its protection;

thus effectually leaving the "mother of States" to associate with the disobedient daughters.

In consequence of the action of Governor Letcher, Confederate troops from Georgia, Mississippi, and other Southern States, were sent rapidly into Virginia, and located at various points, where it was deemed that they could be of the most use, and best serve the interests of the Confederacy. The result of this movement could easily have been foretold. The election was held under military *regime* and terrorism, and loyal men, having been warned of the penalty of voting against secession, either feared to do so, or neglected to vote altogether; a majority was secured for the ordinance, and Virginia, "mother of Presidents," had taken her second grand step in the downward path of disunion.

The people of the city of Alexandria were generally infected with disloyalty, and rebel flags floated boldly from many of the principal buildings. A detachment of Confederate troops was at all times quartered within its limits, and with the hope of capturing them and their supplies, it was determined to occupy the city by a surprise movement. The result of the election clearly foreshadowed, arrangements were made for action—prompt and decisive action—to follow immediately upon the closing of the polls, where disunionists had played a mere farce, and disloyal bayonets had fettered the freedom of the ballot-box.

On the night of May 23d, orders were given for an advance to the troops designed for this expedition, numbering in all about 13,000, and at ten o'clock an advance guard of picked men moved cautiously over the bridge. Sent to reconnoitre, their commands were imperative that if assaulted they were to signalize for reinforcements, which would be speedily furnished by a corps of infantry and a battery. At twelve o'clock the regiment of infantry, the artillery and the cavalry corps began to muster, and as fast as they were prepared, proceeded to the Long Bridge, the portion of the force then in Washington being directed to take that route. The troops quartered at Georgetown, comprising the Fifth, Eighth, Twenty-eighth and Sixty-ninth New York, also proceeded across the Chain Bridge, under the command of General McDowell.

At half-past one o'clock, six companies of District Volunteers, including the National Rifles, and Turners, stepped from the Long Bridge upon Virginia soil. To capture the enemy's patrols by the means of boats had been the original plan, but the bright moonlight prevented it. This vanguard was commanded by Inspector-General Stone, under whom Captain Smead led the centre, Adjutant Abbott the left, and Captain Stewart the right wing. When within half a mile of Alexandria, they halted and awaited the arrival of the main body.

The remainder of the army crossed in the following order: The

Twelfth and Twenty-fifth New York, First Michigan, and First, Second, Third, and Fourth New Jersey; two regular cavalry corps of eighty men each, and Sherman's two batteries; next and last came the New York Seventh. General Mansfield directed the movements of the troops. At a quarter to four the last of the forces left, and fifteen minutes later Major-General Sanford, accompanied by his staff, proceeded to Virginia to assume the command.

The famous Sixty-ninth New York, after crossing the river below Georgetown, took position on the Orange and Manassas Gap railroad, and surrounded and captured the train from Alexandria, with a large number of passengers, of which a few, known to be violent secession partizans, were retained as prisoners.

As the Michigan regiment, accompanied by two guns of Sherman's renowned battery, and a company of regular cavalry, marched into the town, a detachment of thirty-five rebel horsemen were found preparing to mount. The battery came up the street towards them like a whirlwind, and they soon surrendered.

The New York Fire Zouaves, under the command of Colonel E. E. Ellsworth, were conveyed in steamers, and as the day was dawning their dashing uniform and fearless faces flashed upon the citizens of Alexandria. Not until they had landed did the rebel sentinels discover them, and then, after firing their muskets as a signal of warning, they hastened to alarm the sleeping city.

Little need had those brave and untameable "fire fighters" of directions. The master spirit of all their movements had imbued them with feelings akin to his own. They knew their duty, and men trained as they had been in a severe school of danger, could never be backward in performing it. Ellsworth, who, as it might seem, with the shadows of death already gathering around him, could sit calmly down in the dim midnight, after addressing his men in a brief and stirring speech, announcing the orders to march on Alexandria, closing with the well remembered words, "Now boys, go to bed and wake up at two o'clock for a sail and a skirmish;" and after arranging the business of his regiment, pen letters that seemed "as if the mystical gales from the near eternity must have breathed for a moment over his soul, freighted with the odor of amaranths and asphodels"—needed none to tell him of his duty or to urge him to its even rash fulfilment.

In the early light of morning he entered the rebel town. A secession flag waved defiantly from the Marshall House, and with the fiery enthusiasm of his nature, Ellsworth rushed to tear down the hated emblem of enmity to the Union he loved so well. With his own hand he tore the flag from its fastening, and descending the stairs flushed with the pride of success, came upon his fate. A musket in the hands of the proprietor, J. W. Jackson, pealed his death-knell, and he sealed the glories of that too well remembered morning, with his heart's blood.

ASSASSINATION OF COLONEL ELLSWORTH.

BROWNELL, a name now linked with Ellsworth's in all history, was his prompt avenger, and the blood of patriot and assassin ran commingled, a ghastly stream. Both will be long remembered—will stand shadowed forth to the future from the past—one a brave, tender, chivalric heart; and the other, reckless in his courage, vindictive in his passions, and terrible in his cruelty.

And the morning of that day, now lined upon the page of history with letters of blood, that never to be forgotten 24th of May, re-awoke the enthusiasm and stern resolve of Sumter—caused the finest strings of a nation's heart to vibrate with sorrow, and hosts that never before unsheathed a sabre, shouldered a gun or helmeted their brows, had never marched beneath a banner, or given a thought to the glories of war, leaped forth, Minerva-like, fully armed for the strife. Swift vengeance, indeed, followed the death of Ellsworth, but what was that compared to the iron hate of such hearts?

Not here, truly, is the proper place to write the life-history of EPHRAIM ELMER ELLSWORTH, but this much it is fitting—necessary almost to recapitulate. Born in the little village of Mechanicsville, on the banks of the Hudson, on the 23d of April, A.D. 1837, he, after passing through trials that would have utterly discouraged a less ambitious and sanguine man, rendered himself famous by the inauguration, drill, and *marche de triomphe* of the *Chicago Zouaves*. All the country remembers the bloodless march of those young men—the "crimson phantoms" that blazed comet-like before their eyes and secured the championship, without a struggle. When the war broke out, when the knell of Sumter's fall shook the very corner-stone of the nation, Ellsworth sought a place in the army. Jealousy and fear of the youthful aspirant impeded him, and turning his back upon Washington, he hastened to New York, organized the Fire Zouaves, and rushed to his fate.

One who knew him well, and has written a glorious prose-poem to his memory, thus briefly described him. "His person was strikingly prepossessing. His form, though slight, exactly the Napoleonic size, was very compact and commanding: the head statuesquely poised and crowned with a luxuriance of curling black hair; a hazel eye, bright though serene, the eye of a gentleman as well as a soldier; a nose such as you see on Roman medals; a light moustache, just shading the lips, that were continually curving into the sunniest smiles. His voice, deep and musical, instantly attracted attention, and his address, though not without soldierly brusqueness, was sincere and courteous."

And thus, in the very prime of manhood and vigor, with one of the military insignia he sometimes wore—a golden circle, inscribed with the legend "NON NOBIS, SED PRO PATRIA," driven into his heart by the bullet of his assassin, perished a brave spirit—an ambitious follower after the "pride, pomp, and circumstance of glorious war"—a soul devoted to his country and his country's honor—an eagle struck in its high soaring, down—a spirit of fire, fretting at causeless delay, burning against useless restraints, and rushing on to snatch success even from the cannon's mouth.

A nation mourned him long—has not yet forgotten him, and green will ever be the laurel she entwines around the name of the boy-martyr of Alexandria! "Remember Ellsworth" became a watchword with the volunteers, who pledged themselves to avenge his death, and well they redeemed it. His life was stainless and loyal—his death, sealed with his blood the holy bond of his noble faith.

When Lincoln saw this young man lying in his coffin, it is said that he wept over him. It was the first shock and horror of war brought home to the chief magistrate. Alas! if he has wept for all the brave that have since fallen, his days and nights must have been given up to tears.

Alexandria and its neighborhood were occupied by the Federal troops, and a company of Virginia cavalry were captured; after a detention of some days they were released upon taking the oath of allegiance to the

United States. Intrenchments were thrown up around Alexandria, and upon Arlington Heights, which commanded a portion of the capital. Bodies of troops were pushed forward toward Manassus Junction, with the object of interrupting the communication between Richmond and Harper's Ferry.

A detachment took possession of Arlington, the old Curtis Mansion, which had been deserted by its owner, General Lee, when he gave up his flag and took sides with its enemies.

It is said that General Scott held this officer in such high appreciation that he offered him the chance of any position under himself in the Union army. When the letter reached Lee, containing this noble proposition, he was sitting with his family at Arlington. He read the letter in silence, and laying it on the table, covered his face with one hand. When he looked up traces of tears were in his eyes, and he said in a broken voice, "What am I to do? If I take up arms for the Union it must be to turn them on my native State, my own neighbors, dear relations. If I do not, they will brand me as a traitor!"

Again he fell into thought. The result was that he abandoned the home consecrated by Washington, and turned upon the flag that great man had planted.

On the 1st of June, a company of cavalry set out on a scouting expedition to Fairfax Court House, about twenty miles beyond the outposts. Some hundreds of Virginia troops were stationed here, and a sharp skirmish ensued. Several of the Virginians were reported to have been killed; one of the United States troops was killed, and four or five wounded, among whom was the commander, Lieutenant Tompkins. The cavalry withdrew, having made five prisoners, and leaving two of their own number as captives. On the following day the same cavalry company made another dash to Fairfax, and rescued their comrades who had been left behind.

BATTLE OF GREAT BETHEL.

June 10, 1861.

The first engagement on the field occurred at Great Bethel, about ten miles north of Newport News, on the road from Hampton to Yorktown, Virginia, the place having derived its name from a large church, near which the rebels had an entrenched camp.

Under cover of night, the forces, who were under the command of General B. F. Butler, had been repeatedly annoyed by the secession forces, whose rendezvous was Little Bethel, distant about eight miles from Newport News, and the same distance from Hampton, where, also, a church was used as the headquarters of their cavalry, thus literally putting "holy things to an unholy use." The Union-loving, or, at least, Union-respecting citizens, were continually robbed—slaves were impressed to work upon their fortifications, and all that forethought could suggest was recklessly accomplished.

Determined to put a stop to these forays, General Butler organized an expedition for the purpose of surprising the rebels at Little Bethel, giving to the officers commanding discretionary powers, as no positive information could be obtained with regard to their defences or forces.

General Pierce, of Massachusetts, who had the command at Hampton, was instructed to detach Colonels Duryea and Townsend's New York regiments, and Colonel Phelps, commanding at Newport News, was also commanded to start an equal force, about an hour later, to make a demonstration in front. One regiment from each command was directed to repair to a point about one mile from Little Bethel, and there await further orders. Should the design prove successful, they were, when directed, to follow close upon the enemy, drive them into their entrenchments at Big Bethel and attack them.

A naval brigade—a new volunteer organization, stationed at Hampton Roads, had been exercised in the management of scows, with capacity for carrying about one hundred and thirty men, besides those at the oars, and when the night came settling down in darkness, they set out, with muffled oars, passed the mouth of Hampton river, and silently proceeded up the stream. Moored at the hither shore of Hampton, at midnight they awaited the time when the blow was to be struck.

Three companies of Duryea's New York Fifth, under the command of Captain Kilpatrick, crossed and went forward on the Bethel road, followed soon after by the remainder of the regiment, and Colonel Townsend's New York Third. One hour later, five companies, each of the Vermont First and Massachusetts Fourth, under Lieutenant-Colonel Washburne; six companies of the New York Seventh, Colonel Bendix, and a squad of regulars, with three small field pieces under Lieutenant Greble, moved forward from Newport News.

At about one o'clock, A. M., the three companies under Captain Kilpatrick reached New Market Bridge—at about three o'clock they were joined by the main body and started for Little Bethel. The pickets of the enemy were surprised, the officer in command captured, and the Union forces, flushed with success, were pushing forward, when the sound of heavy firing in their rear checked them.

Meantime, the force from Newport News came up the road from that place, and took the road from Hampton to Bethel, not far behind the Fifth; but they left at the junction of the roads, under Colonel Bendix, a rear guard of one hundred and seventy men and one field-piece, with the order to hold this position at all hazards, where they were to be joined by Colonel Townsend's regiment from Hampton. Almost immediately after, the Third New York regiment came up the Hampton road. It was still dark, and their colors could not be seen. Their approach also was over a ridge, and as General Pierce and staff, and Colonel Townsend and staff, in a body, rode in front of their troops, and without any advance guard thrown out, as customary, to reconnoitre, they appeared from Colonel Bendix's position to be a troop of cavalry. It was known that the Federal force had no cavalry, and the fire of this rear guard was poured into the advancing body, at the distance of a quarter of a mile. But the road in which the Third was marching was a little below the level of the land along the edge, and was bordered on either side by fences, forming a partial cover, and rendering the fire comparatively harmless. Fifteen men, however, were wounded and two killed. The Third then fell back and formed upon a hill, and the force again moved in the following order: Colonel Duryea with the New York Fifth; Lieutenant-Colonel Washburne with the companies from Newport News, and Greble's battery; Colonel Townsend, with the New York Third; Colonel Allen, with the New York First; and Colonel Carr, with the New York Second.

The advance was made with great rapidity and fearlessness, and soon the lurid flames of Little Bethel shot upwards in the murky air, and lighted up the country far and wide. Great Bethel was reached next, and our troops received their first intimation of the location of the enemy that was pouring hissing shot upon them from a masked battery. But they were not to be stayed by the iron rain. Steadily, unflinchingly, though death was threatening them every instant, they marched on and gained a position within two hundred yards of the enemy's works. For two hours the whirl and clash and roar of the battle was terrific. Every soldier fought as if upon his individual efforts rested the chances of the day. Charge after charge of the greatest gallantry was made by the infantry against their invisible foemen, and though suffering terribly from the deadly fire, still pouring fiercely upon them, no one thought of retreat. At length, however, General Pierce deemed the exposure too great, and the chances of success too small to warrant a more persistent struggle, and the troops were withdrawn in good order.

Where all fought so nobly, it would be simply invidious to particularize. But one brave heart there was called home from amid the smoke and tumult of battle that cannot be forgotten. THEODORE WINTHROP, Major, and formerly of the New York Seventh, there gave his life for his country—his blood as an offering of sacrifice. A gentleman and scholar as well as a soldier—rich in the rare gifts of genius, he had earned fame in literature before he found that glorious death upon the battle field. He had been one of the foremost to press forward in the hour of his country's need, and breathed his last, nobly struggling for her honor, with wild battle notes ringing in his ear, and the starry flag waving unconquered above him.

Lieutenant Greble, also, an officer of great promise—of coolness, energy and discretion, won for himself a deathless name and a soldier's grave in this battle. Many others, too, of whom fame will not always be silent, men of noble hearts and fearless courage, hallowed the cause with their blood, and when the records of a nation's jewels shall have been perfected, will be found side by side with the hero-author of Great Bethel.

THE AMBUSCADE AT VIENNA, Va.
JUNE 17, 1861.

Information that an attempt would be made to destroy the bridges on the Loudon and Hampshire railway, between Alexandria and Vienna, having been conveyed to General McDowell, he dispatched the First Ohio regiment, Colonel McCook, under the direction of Brigadier-General Schenck, to guard the road.

The train of seven cars, backed out by a locomotive, left Alexandria about noon, and proceeded on its way, dropping detachments all along the road, and meeting with no interruptions until entering a straight line near Vienna. Then a man stepped out upon the road and waved his hand, beckoning the train to stop, and warned them "for God's sake not to go on," as they were dead men if they proceeded; that there was a battery and strong force of the enemy ahead.

The officer in front of the Federal troops paused a moment with his hand on his forehead, as if turning the matter over in his mind, and then beckoned to the engineer to go on.

They proceeded a short distance, when a battery on the high ground, to the right of the road leading to Vienna, opened fire upon the train, and poured well-aimed and rapid discharges into the compact body of Federal soldiery. Some four hundred passengers, troops and laborers, were on the train, and many of them were necessarily on the platforms and the tender. The fire of the enemy, which seemed to be more especially directed in the start to disabling the engine, was particularly destructive amongst the men huddled upon the tender.

A number were killed and wounded here upon the first discharge.

A destructive fire was also poured upon the troops as they leaped from the cars. The engine was struck by a six-pound shot upon a wheel-box, and next upon the cylinder of the engine, which it fractured. The engineer, finding that his engine was in danger, detached it (with one car) from the train, and started back to Alexandria.

Fearful, indeed, was the effect of this deadly storm of fire and iron hail upon the soldiers, helplessly confined, closely packed in the cars. The slaughter intended for them was a species of murder, for, like sheep in the shambles, they were completely in the power of their enemies. Vain was the strong arm, vain was courage and heroism then. Vain the good cause and the longing for victory, or, at least, a soldier's death. Confined within narrow limits, and crowded upon each other, the deadly shot was poured in upon them. It was an hour in which the stoutest heart might have trembled, and yet the men of the North met the iron death manfully. Taken completely by surprise, suffering under every disadvantage, they yet made a good stand. With desperate courage they leaped from the riddled cars and coolly formed into line.

Finding the enemy's batteries strongly posted and supported by cavalry and infantry, they could not hope to carry them until reinforced, and withdrew to the cover of a neighboring wood, carrying with them, however, their dead and wounded.

The enemy's force, estimated at 1,000 to 1,200 strong, had evidently moved down from Fairfax Court-House the preceding night.

Ayre Hill, where the batteries were stationed, is a very commanding point, and is, perhaps, the highest ground in Fairfax County. The purpose of the enemy was evidently to get the cars with the Federal troops on the straight line of the road before opening their murderous fire. There were three six-pound guns in the battery.

The Ohio companies behaved with much credit in their unpleasant position, and General Schenck, particularly, displayed perfect coolness and self-possession. There had been undoubtedly a lack of forethought in neglecting to send scouts in advance, as the country is favorable to such reconnoitering; but when once in the difficulty, both men and officers acted bravely.

They kept undisputed possession of the point where they had posted themselves, the enemy not deeming it prudent to follow up the attack, but contented themselves with burning the cars, although, with greatly superior numbers, they might easily have captured the entire Federal force.

A loss of eight killed and twelve wounded on the part of the Federalists was the sequel to the sad and disastrous transaction, and when the Sixty-ninth New York advanced to Vienna the next day, no trace could be found of the enemy. The place was deserted, and silence reigned where the little band of men had been so nearly sacrificed.

REVIEW AT WASHINGTON.

A few days before the army of the Potomac was to make its advance, thirty thousand new troops passed through Washington, and were reviewed by the President and his Cabinet. A stand had been erected in front of the White House, in full view of Jackson's monument, on which Lincoln, Seward, Chase, and other members of the Cabinet sat while these troops passed them in review. Eloquent speeches were made, and the most unbounded confidence expressed in the soldiers' ability to win a glorious victory over the enemy whenever they should meet him in the open field.

The troops listened with interest, and answered these glowing predictions with enthusiastic shouts, as they passed away from the parade ground and marched in solid columns across the Long Bridge that spans the Potomac, there to share a destiny far different to the promised glory, on the battle field of Manassas.

Another imposing ceremony was witnessed in Washington on the afternoon of the review. A flag was to be raised on a staff near the Treasury Department, and this was a kind of work that Lincoln loved to accomplish with his own hands; so he moved with his Cabinet down to the point of operation.

A platform had been erected at the foot of the flag-staff, and when the President took his place upon it, thousands and thousands of loyal citizens gathered around to see the glorious bunting hoisted in mid air.

It was an imposing sight when the President's tall figure appeared standing in the midst of his councilors, with the halyards in his hands, ready to send the stars and stripes aloft. With his hand uplifted and his face raised toward the sky, he ran the flag up, and saw it catch the wind and float slowly out between him and the blue sky. He stood looking at it a moment, then turned his bright, earnest eyes upon the uplifted faces of the crowd. "My friends," he said, in a clear, full voice, "it is an easy thing for me to run this flag up to the top of the staff, but it will take the whole nation to keep it there."

A shout rang up from the multitude, one of those wild, impulsive echoes of a thousand hearts, which bespeak the enthusiasm of untried strength. It seemed an easy thing to the people, with the tramp of those twenty thousand new troops in their ears, to keep thousands of star-spangled banners skyward; but before many days had passed, the rush of fugitive feet, as they fled along those very pavements, proved how prophetic that simple speech of President Lincoln's was.

But even then the armies on the opposite banks of the Potomac were mustering in force, for it had been decided that an advance should be made and a battle fought, which it was hoped would decide a war which no one expected to be of long duration. Many of these new troops passed from that Washington review, and were swallowed up by the grand army without having been inspected by the commanding General, who afterward considered this fact one cause of his defeat. But the nation was eager for action; a portion of the press fiercely urgent for a forward movement; the two houses of Congress impatient of delay; so, all unprepared, General Scott ordered the advance, against his own judgment, to appease the general clamor.

ADVANCE OF THE GRAND ARMY.

From the time of the President's proclamation calling for troops until the 12th of July, immediately preceding the advance of the Grand Army under General McDowell, to attack the rebel forces at Bull Run, the time had been industriously employed in preparation. Fortifications had been erected on the north side of the Potomac, at eight or ten points within a radius of three miles from Washington and Georgetown. No military force of the rebels was then known to exist on the Maryland shore; but from Mount Vernon to the mouth of the Chesapeake on the south, and from the Chain Bridge to the junction of the Shenandoah at Harpers Ferry on the north, they held undisputed possession.

General Patterson had crossed the Potomac early in July, with a force of thirty thousand men, and was encamped at Martinsburgh, on the 12th, having instructions from the Commander-in-chief to hold the rebel army under General Johnston in check, should he attempt to move forward to Manassas for the purpose of reinforcing Beauregard's command at that point. Johnston was at Winchester, on the direct route to Manassas Gap, twenty-five miles from Martinsburgh, and it was a matter of vital importance that he should be prevented from making a further advance.

The entire marching force of General McDowell was but about fifty-five thousand, while twenty thousand were left as a reserve at Washington and vicinity, under the command of General Mansfield.

And thus the combatants stood, when a day of fearful, bloody ending dawned upon them—a day almost without a parallel in the world's history for deeds of daring and stubborn endurance, unflinching bravery, and wild panic.

Manassas was selected by the Confederates on account of its controlling position. Nature had done very much towards rendering it a second Gibraltar, and art had completed the work. The country around was wild and broken, with but few roads fit for the movements of an army, and those easily guarded. Centreville was twenty-two miles distant from Washington, and Manassas Junction six or seven more. About midway between the two flowed the little rivulet of Bull Run, in a general direction from north-west to south-east. A road led from Centreville to the Junction, crossing the Run three miles from that place, at "Blackburn's Ford," while a turnpike running towards Warrenton, also crossed Bull Run at Stone Bridge, four miles distant. Somewhat east of south, a country road from Centreville crossed Bull Run, and the railroad at "Union Mills."

The Confederate force was distributed along the Run from Union Mills to the Stone Bridge, with reserves and a strongly fortified position near the junction.

The army of General McDowell, when it marched to attack that position, numbered about 30,000 men, consisting, with the exception of 700 or 800 regular troops, of raw volunteers, none of whom had been under military discipline more than two or three months. Added to this must be remembered the fact that, within three days, ten thousand of the number would have a right to claim their dismissal, as their term of enlistment (three months) would then expire. An army, consequently, less prepared to march to the attack of a strongly fortified position it would have been difficult to assemble; and this was rendered more fatal in its effects from the fact that the officers, with the exception of a few who had fought in the Mexican war, were unused to actual fighting, and almost totally unacquainted with their different commands.

Under these unpromising auspices, the army marched from the banks of the Potomac on the afternoon of July 16th. It advanced in four columns, toiling along under the burning sun and over the hot ground. One by the turnpike, one on the right, and one on the left of the railroad, and another between the turnpike and railroad. Expecting to encounter the enemy at Fairfax Court-House, seven miles this side of Centreville, where they had thrown up intrenchments, the three columns were directed to coöperate at that point. But the place was entered about noon on the 17th, only to find the intrenchments abandoned and signs of a hasty retreat visible.

On the morning of the 18th, the different columns commenced their march from Fairfax to Centreville. While General McDowell made a personal reconnoissance to the left, making the forward movement a mere demonstration, Major J. G. Barnard, chief-engineer of the staff, proceeded to examine the enemy's position in front. In this, however, he had been anticipated by General Tyler, who had pushed a brigade on towards Blackburn's Ford. Troops were in motion on the plateau of Manassas, moving up to reinforce the enemy's lines, and though no attack had been intended by the commanding general at that particular

point, they opened upon them with two twenty-pounder guns in hope of ascertaining the position of these batteries. A reply was soon obtained—a battery, invisible except by the smoke, poured forth rapid discharges, and it required the assistance of a battery of rifled six-pounders to enable the Union troops to silence it. The brigade was then filed down to the stream and skirmishing maintained for some time. This battle, though apparently of small importance, was disastrous, inasmuch as it disorganized the arrangements of the commander-in-chief, and was accompanied by great loss of life, when compared with the magnitude of the undertaking and any beneficial result that could have sprung from it. The possibility of charging into Manassas, even under the most fortunate circumstances, was so remote, that the wisdom of an action at that point and at that time has been gravely questioned by the best military authorities. That night the columns of the army united, and encamped about a mile in the rear of Fairfax Court House, upon a broad hill side, and on the extended plain at its base. A stream of water which crossed the grounds rendered the spot peculiarly important to the soldiers.

The next day was spent in reconnoitering, and in determining how and where an attack should be made. The Stone Bridge was guarded by batteries, and the ground beyond obstructed by formidable abattis. The roads leading to fords between Blackburn's and the Stone Bridge were mere by-paths, and the opposite bank of the stream steep, tangled, and obstructed. Two miles above, however, there was a good ford, but slightly guarded, at Sudley's Spring.

On these data the plan of attack was based, as follows: One division, under Colonel Miles, to make, with one of its brigades, a false attack on Blackburn's Ford; another division (Tyler's) to move up the turnpike to the Stone Bridge and threaten that point, and at the proper time carry it, and unite with the principal column, which consisted of Hunter's and Heintzelman's divisions; then by a flank movement reach the Sudley Ford, and descending the right bank of the stream, take the defences in the rear of Stone Bridge, and give battle with the united force, strike at the enemy's railroad communication, or otherwise, as circumstances should dictate.

THE BATTLE OF BULL RUN.

Bull Run, that once unknown name, is marked with great crimson letters upon the scroll of time! Tears wrung from the anguished soul, tears hot and blinding, still fall at the mere mention of its ill-omened name. A nation's *miserere* has been tolled from uncounted steeples over its dead, and a whole nation put on weeds of mourning when its battle cloud spread slowly over the land, filling it with gloom.

With bayonets for pens, and precious human blood for ink, the record of this first great battle of the Union War should be written in the history of the world;—the ensanguined page illuminated with iron hail and leaden sleet—with hissing shot—whirlwinds of death-missiles, and the fire-belching portals of masked batteries. O, day of doom, day of sad errors and illustrious deeds, when blood was poured forth like water, until the reeking earth shuddered as it drank in the crimson deluge! Generations shall hereafter look back on thee with painful wonder, for they will remember that the first pitched battle in which Americans met Americans in mortal strife, was fought on thy soil, beneath "the bloody sun at noon."

On the morning of the 21st, McDowell's forces were encamped in and around Centreville. The divisions were under orders to march at half past two o'clock, that they might reach the ground early and avoid the heat. Before this time the encampments were in motion; but the troops were not yet sufficiently disciplined for the exigencies of a prompt march, and some delay arose with the first division in getting out of camp. Thus the road was obstructed, and other divisions thrown two hours out of time. But there was no lack of energy or zeal; the very want of discipline which caused delay rendered the scenes in the various encampments more grand and imposing. It was indeed a beautiful spectacle. A lovely moonlight flooded the whole country. Soft mists lay in the valleys—the hill-tops were studded for miles around by the camp fires which thirty regiments had left, kindling the landscape with their star-like gleams. In the hollows, along the level grounds, and among the trees, thousands on thousands of armed men moved athwart the fires, harnessing horses to artillery, getting out army wagons, preparing ambulances and filling haversacks with the three days' rations ordered for their subsistence. No man of all that vast host was idle—want of order there might have been, but no lack of energy.

Now, thirty thousand men, horses, ordnance and wagons, were all in place, ready for a march through the beautiful night, and under that serene moon, which many of them would never look upon again.

McDowell and his staff moved with the first—Tyler's—central column, and the advance commenced. The picturesque encampments were soon left behind; the fires grew paler and twinkled out in a glow of mist; the tents dwindled into littleness, till they seemed more like great flocks of white-plumaged birds, nestled in the foliage, than the paraphernalia of war. Nothing could be more quiet and peaceful than the country the troops had left—nothing more solemnly grand than the advance. It was an army of Americans, marching through the still night to meet Americans for the first time in a great pitched battle Nothing but holy patriotism and a stern sense of duty could have led these men into the field. They marched on, with thousands of bayonets gleaming in the moonlight, and casting long-pointed shadows over the path; staff officers formed imposing groups as they moved forward in the moonlight, casting pictures upon the earth that were like broken battle scenes.

In the ranks there was something more than stern courage; generous enthusiasm and honest emulation were eloquent there. Comrade greeted comrade, for the coming danger made friends brothers; and common acquaintances fell into affectionate intimacy. Many a touching message was exchanged between men who had never met out of the ranks, for while they panted for victory, each man prepared to earn it with his life.

These men knew that a terrible day's fighting lay before them; but the previous defeat of Thursday rankled in their proud hearts, and each man felt it as an individual reproach which must be swept away. From the central column to the rear, this feeling prevailed among the men.

The troops of the old Bay State, of Rhode Island, Connecticut, and New York, entered into a spirit of generous rivalry. Ohio, Michigan, Wisconsin and Minnesota entered the list with true Western fervor, while the rich Celtic humor rose in fun and pathos from the Irish troops.

The officers shared this enthusiasm with their men. Tyler moved on, burning to atone for his noble rashness at Blackburn's Ford—Burnside, Corcoran, Keyes, Spidel, Meagher, and many another noble fellow, thought exultingly of the laurels to be gathered on the morrow. General McDowell's carriage halted at the two roads, a spot that he deemed most convenient for receiving despatches from the various points of the battle-field.

Here the column of General Hunter diverged from the main body and went away through the moonlit country on its assigned duty, which led him around the enemy's flank by a long and harassing route. With him went Heintzelman, Porter, Burnside and Sprague with their valiant Rhode Islanders, and Wilcox, that bravest of young men and most brilliant author, who met a fate almost worse than death in the hottest of the coming battle. There, too, was Slocum, Haggerty, and many another valiant fellow, marching forward to a glorious death. Each and all of these, with their regiments or brigades, swept to the right, to meet their comrades again in the hottest of the battle.

A mile from the Cross Roads, and the dawn of a bright July day broke pleasantly on the moving troops—a morning cool with dew, fresh with verdure, and tranquil and peaceful, save for the armed men that made the earth tremble under their solid tread as they moved over it. The mists of a dewy night were slowly uplifted, and beautiful reaches of the country were revealed. On the left was the station assigned to Richardson and Davies; beyond it, the valley which one unfortunate conflict had so lately stained with blood.

When Tyler's division came to the edge of a wooded hill overlooking these scenes, the sun arose, flooding them with rosy splendor. The soldiers knew, but could not realize that this scene, so beautiful and tranquil, had been a field of carnage, and would, before that sun went down, be red with the blood of many a brave heart beating among them then. They knew well that in a brief time the pure atmosphere, which it was now a joy to breathe, would be heavy with stifling smoke; that the noble forests whose leaves trembled so pleasantly in the new-born sunshine, were but a concealment for masked batteries—fearful engines of destruction, and men more ravenous for their lives than the wild animals that civilization had driven away from them.

From the point of view just described, where the road falls gently down to a ravine, the enemy first appeared. A line of infantry was drawn up in a distant meadow, close upon a back-ground of woods.

The second and third regiments of Tyler's brigade, under Schenck, was at once formed into line in the woods on either side, the First Ohio, Second Wisconsin, Seventy-ninth, Thirteenth, and Sixty-ninth New York regiments succeeding each other on the right, and the Second Ohio and Second New York being similarly placed on the left, while the artillery came down the road between.

A great 32-pound rifled Parrott gun—the only one of its calibre in the field service—was brought forward, and made to bear on the point where the bayonets of the enemy had suddenly disappeared in the woods, and a shell was fired at fifteen minutes past six, A. M., which burst in the air; but the report of the piece awoke the country for leagues around to a sense of what that awful day would prove. The reverberation was tremendous, and the roar of the revolving shell indescribable. Throughout the battle that gun, whenever it was fired, seemed to hush and overpower everything else. No answering salute came back, so the 32-pounder sent a second shell at a hill-top, two miles off, where it was suspected that a battery had been planted by the rebels.

The bomb burst close at the intended point, but no answer came. General Tyler ordered Carlisle to cease firing, and bring the rest of his battery to the front of the woods and get the column ready for instant action.

Tyler's position was before the valley of Bull Run, but the descent was gradual, and surrounded by thick woods down almost to the ravine through which the stream flows. The enemy, on the contrary, had cleared away all the obstructing foliage, and bared the earth in every direction over which they could bring their artillery upon the Union forces. Clumps of trees and bushes remained wherever their earthworks and other concealed defences could be advantageously planted among them. The ground on their side was vastly superior to that of the assailants. It rose in gradual slopes to great heights, but was broken into hills and terraces in many places, upon which strong earthworks were planted, some openly, but the greater portion concealed. Nature had supplied positions of defence which needed but little labor to render them desperately formidable. How thoroughly these advantages had been improved was established by the almost superhuman efforts which were required to dislodge their troops, and by the obstinate opposition which they displayed before retiring from one strong point to another. It was now about seven o'clock—for an hour everything was silent. At eight, the deep sullen boom of Richardsons and Davies' batteries at Blackburn's Ford broke the stillness, and from that quarter constant cannonading was kept up for some time.

By this time scouts reported the enemy in some force on the left. Two or three Ohio skirmishers had been killed. Carlisle's battery was sent to the front of the woods on the right, where it could be brought to play when needed. A few shells were thrown into the opposite thicket, and then the Second Ohio and Second New York marched down to rout the enemy from their hiding places. As they rushed toward a thickly-covered abatis on the banks of the Run, the rebels came swarming out like bees, and fled to the next fortification beyond.

General Schenck's brigade was moved forward to the left, but halfway to the Run met the full fire of a masked battery effectually concealed by the bushes.

A few dead and wounded began to be brought in, and the battle of Manassas had commenced. Carlisle's howitzers and the great rifled gun were opened in the direction of the battery, which answered promptly, and a brief but terrific cannonading ensued. In less than half an hour the enemy's guns were silenced, two of Carlisle's howitzers advancing through the woods to gain a closer position, and Schenck's brigade retired to its first lines.

At eleven o'clock, the artillery, which resounded from every portion of the field, extending from Davies and Richardson's position on the extreme left, to the right near Sudley, gave startling evidence that Hunter was making his way around the enemy. The roll and thunder was incessant —great volumes of smoke surged over the vast field, impalling it in the distance, and making the air around the near batteries thick with smoke.

It was true, Hunter's and Heintzelman's columns had taken the field on the extreme right.

McDowell in his plan of battle had calculated that the marching column should diverge from the turnpike by early daylight (a night march being deemed imprudent), and reach Sudley Ford by six or seven, A. M. The Stone Bridge division did not clear the road over which both, for a certain distance, had to pass, so that the column could take up its march, until after the time. The route to Sudley proved far longer and more difficult than was anticipated. The column did not reach the Sudley Ford till near half-past nine, three or four hours "behind time." When it reached the ford, the heads of the enemy's columns were visible on the march to meet it.

The ground between the stream and the road, leading from Sudley south, was for about a mile thickly wooded; on the right, for the same distance, divided between fields and timber. A mile from the ford the country on both sides of the road is open, and for a mile further large, irregular fields extend to the turnpike, which, after crossing Bull Run at the "Stone Bridge," passes what became the field of battle, through the valley of a small tributary of the Run.

But, notwithstanding a fearful march over broken grounds in the hot sun, with his men suffering from heat and thirst, Hunter had reached his point of operation, late it is true, but from no fault of his. The weary soldiers uttered exclamations of joy when they saw the limpid waters of the Run, and plunging into its current bathed their hot hands and burning faces as they waded through, and came out on the other side greatly invigorated. While his thirsty men were refreshing themselves with cool draughts of water, Hunter sent a courier to General McDowell, reporting that he had safely crossed the Run.

The General was lying on the ground, having been ill during the night, but at once mounted his horse and rode on to join the column on which so much depended.

The halt had not lasted two minutes when Col. Burnside led his different regiments into their position on the field. The Second Rhode Island entered first to the extreme right; then the Rhode Island battery of six pieces, and two howitzers of the Seventy-first, and after it on the left, the First Rhode Island and the Second New Hampshire, all formed in line of battle on the top of the hill.

Shortly after the leading regiment of the first brigade reached the open space, and whilst others and the second brigade were crossing to the front and right, the enemy opened his fire, beginning with artillery, and following it up with infantry. The leading brigade (Burnside's) had to sustain this shock for a short time without support, and met it bravely. Gov. Sprague himself directed the movements of the Rhode Island brigade, and was conspicuous through the day for gallantry. The enemy were found in heavy numbers opposite this noble brigade of our army, and greeted it with shell and long volleys of battalion firing as it advanced. But on it went, and a fierce conflict now commenced.

The enemy clung to the protecting wood with tenacity, and the Rhode Island battery became so much endangered as to impel the commander of the second brigade to call for the assistance of the battalion of regulars. At this time news ran through the lines that Colonel Hunter was seriously wounded. Porter took command of his division; and, in reply to the urgent request of Colonel Burnside, detached the battalion of regulars to his assistance, followed shortly afterwards by the New Hampshire regiments. Shortly afterward the other corps of Porter's brigade, and a regiment detached from Heintzelman's division to the left, emerged from the timber, where some hasty disposition of skirmishers had been made at the head of the column, in which Colonel Slocum, of the Second Rhode Island regiment, distinguished himself for great activity.

The rattle of musketry and crash of round shot through the leaves and branches, had warned them when the action commenced, and the column moved forward before these preliminaries were completed, eager for a share in the fight.

The head of Porter's brigade was immediately turned a little to the right, in order to gain time and room for deployment on the right of the second brigade. Griffin's battery found its way through the timber to the fields beyond, followed promptly by the marines, while the Twenty-Seventh took direction more to the left, and the Fourteenth followed upon the trail of the battery—all moving up at a double-quick step. At this time General McDowell with his staff rode through the lines and was loudly cheered as they passed within six hundred feet of the enemy's line.

The enemy appeared drawn up in a long line, extending along the Warrenton turnpike, from a house and haystack upon their extreme right, to a house beyond the left of the division. Behind that house there was a heavy masked battery, which, with three others along his line, on the heights beyond, covered the ground through which the troops were advancing with all sorts of projectiles. A grove, in front of Porter's right wing, afforded it shelter and protection, while the underbrush along the road in the fences, screened to some extent his left wing.

Griffin advanced to within one thousand yards, and opened a deadly fire upon these batteries, which were soon silenced or driven away.

The right was rapidly developed by the marines, Twenty-Seventh, Fourteenth, and Eighth, with the cavalry in rear of the right; the enemy retreating in more precipitation than order as the line advanced. The second brigade (Burnside's) was at this time attacking the enemy's right with great vigor.

The rebels soon came flying from the woods toward the right, and the Twenty-Seventh completed their rout by charging directly upon their centre in face of a scorching fire, while the Fourteenth and Eighth moved down the turnpike to cut off the retiring foe, and to support the Twenty-Seventh, which had lost its gallant Colonel, but was standing the brunt of the action, though its ranks were terribly thinned in the dreadful fire. Now the resistance of the enemy's left was so obstinate that the beaten right retired in safety.

The head of Heintzelman's column at this moment appeared upon the field, and the Eleventh and Fifth Massachusetts regiments moved forward to support the centre, while staff officers could be seen galloping rapidly in every direction, endeavoring to rally the broken Eighth, but with little success.

The Fourteenth, though it had broken, was soon rallied in rear of Griffin's battery, which took up a position further to the front and right, from which his fire was delivered with such precision and rapidity as to compel the batteries of the enemy to retire in consternation far behind the brow of the hill in front.

At this time Porter's brigade occupied a line considerably in advance of that first occupied by the left wing of the rebels. The battery was pouring its withering fire into the batteries and columns of the enemy wherever they exposed themselves. The cavalry were engaged in feeling the left flank of the enemy's position, in doing which some important captures were made, one by Sergeant Socks, of the Second Dragoons, of a General George Stewart, of Baltimore. The cavalry also did brave service.

General Tyler's division was engaged with the enemy's right. The Twenty-Seventh was resting on the edge of the woods in the centre, covered by a hill upon which lay the Eleventh and Fifth Massachusetts, occasionally delivering a scattering fire. The Fourteenth was moving to the right flank, the Eighth had lost its organization, the marines were moving up in fine style in the rear of the Fourteenth, and Captain Arnold was occupying a height in the middle ground with his battery. At this juncture there was a temporary lull in the firing from the rebels, who appeared only now and then on the heights in irregular masses, but to serve as marks for Griffin's guns. The prestige of success had thus far attended the efforts of the inexperienced but gallant Union troops. The lines of the enemy had been forcibly shifted nearly a mile to their left and rear. The flags of eight regiments, though borne somewhat wearily, now pointed toward the hill from which disordered masses of the rebels had been seen hastily retiring.

Rickett's battery, together with Griffith's battery, on the side of the hill, had been objects of the special attention of the enemy, who had succeeded in disabling Rickett's battery, and then attempted to take it. Three times was he repulsed by different corps in succession, and driven back, and the guns taken by hand, the horses being killed, and pulled away. The third time the repulse seemed to be final, for he was driven entirely from the hill, and so far beyond it as not to be in sight. He had before this been driven nearly a mile and a half, and was beyond the Warrenton road, which was entirely in Federal possession, from the Stone Bridge westward. The engineers were just completing the removal of the abatis across the road, to allow reinforcements (Schenck's brigade and Ayers' battery) to join in. The enemy was evidently disheartened and broken.

But at this moment, when everything pointed to a speedy victory, orders came through Major Barry of the Fifth artillery, for Griffin's battery to move from the hill upon which the house stood, to the top of a hill on the right, with the "Fire Zouaves" and marines, while the Fourteenth entered the skirt of wood on their right, to protect that flank, and a column, composed of the Twenty-seventh New York, Eleventh and Fifth Massachusetts, Second Minnesota, and Sixty-Ninth New York, moved up toward the left batteries. It had taken position, but before the flanking supports had reached theirs, a murderous fire of musketry and rifles opened at pistol range, cutting down every cannonier, and a large number of horses. The fire came from some infantry of the enemy, which had been mistaken for Union forces; an officer in the field having stated that it was a regiment sent by Colonel Heintzelman to support the batteries.

As soon as the Zouaves came up, they were led forward against an Alabama regiment, partly concealed in a clump of small pines in an old field.

After a severe fire they broke, and the greatest portion of them fell to the rear, keeping up a desultory firing over the heads of their comrades in front; at the same moment they were charged by a company of rebel cavalry on their rear, who came by a road through two strips of woods on the extreme right. The fire of the Zouaves dispersed them. The discomfiture of this cavalry was completed by a fire from Captain Colburn's company of United States cavalry, which killed and wounded several men. Colonel Farnham, with some of his officers and men, behaved gallantly, and many of his men did good service as skirmishers later in the day. General Heintzelman then led up the Minnesota regiment, which was also repulsed, but retired in tolerably good order. It did good service in the woods on the right flank, and was among the last to retire, moving off the field with the Third United States infantry. Next was led forward the First Michigan, which was also repulsed, and retired in considerable confusion. They were rallied, and helped to hold the woods on the right. The Brooklyn Fourteenth then appeared on the ground, coming forward in gallant style. They were led forward to the left, where the Alabama regiment had been posted in the early part of the action, but had now disappeared, and soon came in sight of the line of the enemy drawn up beyond the clump of trees. Soon after the firing commenced, the regiment broke and retired. It was useless to attempt a rally. The want of discipline in these regiments was so great that the most of the men would run from fifty to several hundred yards in the rear, and continue to fire, compelling those in front to retreat.

During this time Rickett's battery had been captured and retaken three times by Heintzelman's forces, but was finally lost, most of the horses having been killed—Captain Ricketts being wounded, and First Lieutenant D. Ramsay killed. Lieutenant Kirby behaved gallantly, and succeeded in carrying off one caisson. Before this time, heavy reinforcements of the enemy were distinctly seen approaching by two roads, extending and outflanking Heintzelman on the right. General Howard's brigade came on the field at this time, having been detained by the General as a reserve. It took post on a hill on Heintzelman's right and rear, and for some time gallantly held the enemy in check. One company of cavalry attached to Heintzelman's division, was joined, during the engagement, by the cavalry of Colonel Hunter's division, under the command of Major Palmer.

Colonel W. B. Franklin commanded the first brigade of Heintzelman's division. A portion of that brigade rendered distinguished service, and received official commendation from the commanding general.

General Tyler, who kept his position at the Stone Bridge, to menace that point, and at the proper moment to carry it and unite with the turning column, had sent forward the right wing of his command to co-operate with Hunter as soon as he was discovered making his way on the flank.

Two brigades (Sherman's and Keyes') of that division had passed the Run. Colonel Sherman joined himself to the divisions of Hunter and Heintzelman, and was soon engaged in the hottest part of the action.

The famous Irish regiment, 1,600 strong, who have had so much of the hard digging to perform, claimed the honor of a share in the hard fighting, and led the van of Tyler's attack, followed by the Seventy-ninth (Highlanders), and Thirteenth New York, and the Second Wisconsin.

It was a brave sight—that rush of the Sixty-ninth into the death-struggle—with such cheers as proved a hearty love of the work before them! With a quick step at first, and then a double-quick, and at last a run, they dashed forward and along the edge of the extended forest.

Coats and knapsacks were thrown to either side, that nothing might impede their work. It was certain that no guns would slip from the hands of those determined fellows, even if dying agonies were needed to close them with a firmer grasp. As the line swept along, Meagher galloped toward the head, crying, "Come on, boys! you've got your chance at last!"

BRILLIANT CHARGE ON A REBEL BATTERY.

Sherman's brigade thus moved forward for half a mile, describing quite one-fourth of a circle on the right, Colonel Quimby's regiment in front, the other regiments following in line of battle—the Wisconsin Second, New York Seventy-ninth, and New York Sixty-ninth in succession. Quimby's regiment advanced steadily up the hill and opened fire on the enemy, who had made a stand. The regiment continued advancing as the enemy gave way, till the head of his column reached the point where Rickett's battery had been cut up. The other regiments followed under a fearful cannonading. At the point where the road crossed the ridge to the left, the ground was swept by a fire of artillery, rifles, and musketry. Regiment after regiment were driven from it, following the Zouaves and a battalion of marines.

When the Wisconsin Second was abreast of the enemy, it was ordered to leave the roadway and attack him. This regiment ascended the hill, was met with a sharp fire, returned it gallantly, and advanced, delivering its fire. But the response was terrific, and the regiment fled in confusion toward the road. It rallied again, passed the brow of the hill a second time, and was again repulsed in disorder. By this time the New York Seventy-ninth had closed up. It was impossible to get a good view of the ground. In it there was one battery of artillery, which poured an incessant fire upon the advancing column, and the ground was irregular, with small clusters of pines, which afforded shelter to the enemy. The fire of rifles and musketry grew hotter and hotter. The Seventy-ninth, headed by Colonel Cameron, charged across the hill, and for a short time the contest was terrible. They rallied several times under fire, but finally broke and gained the cover of the hill.

This left the field open to the New York Sixty-ninth, Colonel Corcoran, who, in his turn, led his regiment over the crest, and had in full open view the ground so severely contested. The firing was terrific, the roar of cannon, musketry, and rifles, incessant. The enemy was here in immense force. The Sixty-ninth held the ground for some time with desperate courage, but finally fell back in disorder.

At this time Quimby's regiment occupied another ridge to the left, overlooking the same field, fiercely engaged. Colonel Keyes, from Tyler's division, had formed in line with Sherman's brigade, and came into conflict on its right with the enemy's cavalry and infantry, which he drove back. The further march of the brigade was arrested by a severe fire of artillery and infantry, sheltered by Robinson's house, standing on the heights above the road leading to Bull Run. The charge was here ordered, and the Second Maine and Third Connecticut regiments pressed forward to the top of the hill, reached the buildings which were held by the enemy, drove them out, and for a moment had them in possession. At this point, finding the brigade under the fire of a strong force behind breastworks, the order was given to march by the left flank, with a view to turn the battery which the enemy had placed on the hill below the point at which the Warrenton turnpike crosses Bull Run. The march was conducted for a considerable distance below the Stone Bridge, causing the enemy to retire, and giving Captain Alexander an opportunity to pass the bridge, cut out the abatis which had been placed there, and prepare the way for Schenck's brigade and the two batteries to pass over. Before this movement could be made on the enemy's battery, it was placed in a new position; but Colonel Keyes carried his brigade, by a flank movement, around the base of the hill, and was on the point of ascending it in time to get at the battery, when he discovered that the troops were on the retreat, and that, unless a rapid movement to the rear was made, he would be cut off. At this moment, the abatis near the Stone Bridge had been cleared away by Captain Alexander, of the engineers, and Schenck's brigade (the third of Tyler's division) was about to pass over and join Keyes.

But one rash movement had decided the day—that movement the last change of position given to Griffin's battery, throwing it helpless into a murderous fire, which no protecting force could encounter.

When the Zouaves broke on that fatal hill, the Union cause for that day wavered. When hordes of fresh troops poured in upon the Union battalions, beating back as brave regiments as ever trod the battle-field, one after another, overwhelming them with numbers, and driving them headlong into utter confusion, the battle was lost; and after this any description of it must be wild and turbulent as the scene itself—in no other way can a true picture of the tumultuous fighting and more tumultuous retreat be truly given.

THE CLIMAX AND THE RETREAT.

We have described the battle of Manassas, Stone Bridge, or Bull Run, as it is variously called, in its plain details, giving each regiment, so far as possible, its share in the glorious fight; for up to mid-day and after, no braver fighting was ever done than the Union troops performed on that 21st of July. Now a wilder, more difficult, and very painful effort taxes the pen. The heat, turmoil and terrible storm of death rolls up in a tumultuous picture—troops in masses—stormy action—the confused rush of men—all these things have no detail, but hurl the writer forward, excited and unrestrained as the scene to be described.

At high noon the battle raged in its widest circumference. The batteries on the distant hills began to pour their volleys on the Union troops with terrible effect. Carlisle's and Sherman's batteries answered with tremendous emphasis, while the great 32-pounder hurled its iron thunderbolts first into one of the enemy's defences, then into another, tearing up everything as they went. The noise of the cannonading grew deafening, and kept up one incessant roll. Compared to it the sharp volleys of riflemen were like the rattle of hail amid the loud bursts of a thunder tempest. The people of Centreville, Fairfax, Alexandria, and even Washington, heard the fearful reverberations, and trembled at the sound.

Five powerful batteries were in operation at once, joined to the hiss and hurtle of twenty thousand small arms! No wonder the sky turned black, impalled with death-smoke—no wonder the sun shone fierce and red upon the pools of warm human blood that began to gather around those batteries, where the slain were lying in heaps and winrows!

Still amid this roar and carnage, the Federal forces were making sure headway, and driving the enemy before them. Except one brigade of Tyler's division, the entire force of eighteen thousand men was in fierce action. As the Union forces pressed upon the enemy, approaching each moment to the completion of their plan of battle, the rebels grew desperate. The batteries on the western hills poured forth their iron tempest with accumulated fury. The Union guns answered them with fiercer thunder. The roar of the cannonading was deafening, drowning the volleys of riflemen, and sweeping off in one overpowering sound the rattle and crash of musketry. The clamor of the guns was appalling—the rush and tumult of action more appalling still. The whole valley was like a vast volcano, boiling over with dust and smoke. Through this turbid atmosphere battalions charged each other and batteries poured their hot breath on the air, making it denser than before. Now and then the dust would roll away from the plain, and the smoke float off from the hills, revealing a dash of cavalry across some open space, or a charge of infantry up to a fortified point where the struggle, success, or repulse, was lost or vaguely seen through volumes of rolling smoke—columns of ruddy dust trailed after the infantry, broken now and then by the fiery track of a battery masked in foliage. A sullen report, and horrid gaps appeared in what a moment before was a living wall of men. A curl of blue vapor rose gracefully from the trees, and it was only the dead bodies blackening the ground that made the sight so awful.

But the fight gathered fiercest on the westward hill, from which the booming thunder rolled in long incessant peals. Its sides swarmed with armed men, changing positions, charging and retreating. Curtains of smoke, swayed by the wind, revealed the horses around a battery, rearing, plunging and falling headlong, dozens together, in one hideous death. Then in mercy the smoke drifted over the hill again. The enemy were giving ground at every point. The Mississippians had fled in dismay from the batteries, and desperately taken to the field in wavering columns. Other regiments were actually fleeing before the Union troops, but they were generally moving with sullen steadiness to the rear. The entire line which arrayed itself against Tyler in the morning had been relinquished, except one fortified elevation. Still their peculiar mode of warfare was kept up. Masked batteries were constantly opening in unexpected places, leaving heaps of slain in the track of their fiery hail.

On the uplands whole regiments, seen from the distance, seemed to drive against or drift by each other, leaving beautiful curls and clouds of smoke behind; but under this smoke lay so many dead bodies that the soul grew faint in counting them.

Through all this the Federal troops progressed toward a union of their attacking columns. Tyler had already spoken to McDowell, and the two forces were drawing nearer and nearer together. Victory appeared so certain that nothing but a junction of the two columns was wanting to a glorious result, and this now seemed inevitable.

The clamor of the artillery was checked for a little time on both sides. Red-handed death cannot rush panting on the track forever. Black-mouthed guns will get too foul for belching fire, and the swarthy men who feed them must have breathing time. As the fight flagged, and the men paused to draw breath, their terrible suffering was apparent in the parched lips that had tasted water but once through all that hot day, and the bloodshot eyes with which each man seemed to beseech his comrade for drink which no one had to give. Still, with dry lips and throats full of dust, they talked over a thousand details of valor performed on the field. They spoke sadly of the loss of brave Cameron, the wounding of Hunter, the fall of Haggerty and Slocum, the doubtful fate of noble young Wilcox. They discussed the impetuous dash and resolute stand of the Irishmen, the murderous shock sustained by the Rhode Island regiments, how the Highlanders had done justice to their own warlike traditions, and the Connecticut Third had crowned its State with honors. They told how Heintzelman had stooped down from his war-horse to have his wounded wrist bound up, refusing to dismount—of the intrepid Burnside, and of Sprague, the patriotic young Governor, who led on the forces his generosity had raised, to one victorious charge after another, till with his own hands he spiked the Rhode Island guns when compelled to leave them to the enemy.

So tranquil was the field during this short period of rest, that the soldiers who had foreborne to throw their rations away in the march, unslung their haversacks and sat down upon the grass to share the contents with their less prudent companions; those who had been fortunate enough to pick up the enemy's haversacks, cast off in retreat, added their contents to the scanty store.

While a few thus snatched a mouthful of food, others climbed up the tall trees and took a triumphant view of the vast battle-field their valor had conquered. The scene of carnage which it presented was awful. Dead and dying men heaped together on the red earth; crippled horses struggling desperately in their death-throes, wounded men lying helplessly on the grass to which they had been dragged from under the hoofs of the war-chargers—all this grouped where the angry waves of battle had rolled down the beautiful valley, with its back-ground of mountains, looking immovable and grandly tranquil against the sky, was a picture which no man who saw it will ever forget.

The army, far advanced within the enemy's defensive lines, believing itself victorious, was thus falling into quiet. The great struggle of the contending forces, each to outflank the other, had ceased. The prestige of success belonged to the Union, whose stars and stripes shone out triumphantly as the smoke which had engulfed the combatants rolled away.

All at once those in the tree-tops saw a commotion in the far distance. Columns of troops were moving toward them with flashing bayonets, and Southern banners, unfurling the stars and bars to the sun. On they came—rank after rank, column after column, one continuous stream of armed men, pouring down upon the battle-field with bursts of music and wild shouts of enthusiasm.

It was Johnston's reinforcements, marching up from the railroad. On they rushed, fresh, vigorous, and burning with ardor, through masses of wounded soldiers that lay by the road. The infantry broke from the double-quick to a swift run—the cavalry rode in on a sharp gallop—the artillery wagons were encircled with men eager to get their ordnance in place against the thrice-exhausted Union troops. In a continuous stream these columns swarmed into the woods, the greater force centering around the hill about which the storm of battle had raged fiercest.

In an instant the whole battle commenced again. The officers sprang to their guns, anxious but not appalled. The men fell into rank ready for a new onset, tired as they were.

Then it was that Griffin's battery changed position, and the Fire Zouaves coming up under a terrible fire, broke and scattered down the hill-side, but rallied again in broken masses to rescue Rickett's battery, dragging the guns off with their own hands from amid the pile of dying horses that lay around them. Then it was that the Sixty-ninth and Seventy-ninth New York swept through the meadows from the north across the road, and charged up the hill with such daring courage, resisting the shock of battle fifteen minutes, and breaking only when mortal valor could withstand the storm of bullets no longer.

Then the bold Connecticut regiments charged up the hill. Thousands of the impetuous enemy fell upon them, but in spite of all they planted the star-spangled banner and sent its folds sweeping out from the crest of the hill. Not till this was done, and a long last shout sent ringing after the banner, were these heroic regiments driven from their position. But beaten back at last, they retired step by step, fighting as they went.

Then the Zouaves broke into the fight once more, scattered on the ground, some prostrate on their faces, others with limbs huddled together as if dead—while many stood with their eyes to the sun, waiting the onset of the Black Horse cavalry that came galloping upon them from the woods. A few of these eccentric warriors were making a feint of defending themselves while the cavalry stood hesitating on the margin of the wood, but the rest seemed to have been cut down by the sweep of some deadly cannonade, and lay in the grass like a flock of partridge shot down in full flight.

Out from the woody cover the Black Hawks thundered on, their arms flashing and the jetty necks of their horses flinging off the sunshine. The handful of Zouaves now flocked together in front of their prostrate comrades, seeming doubtful whether to fight or flee. On the black chargers came, champing the bit and tossing their heads angrily, the riders ready to trample the scattered Zouaves under hoof, as too easy a conquest for their flashing swords. A sudden, sharp ringing yell, and the dead Zouaves sprang to life, confronting the horsemen in a wall of bristling steel. A sharp volley—the horses reared, plunged, and ran back upon each other, some falling dead with quivering limbs as the fatal bullets rent their vitals, and gushes of blood crimsoned their coal-black chests; others staggering from a dozen wounds, rushed madly through the broken ranks of the terrified cavalry.

Before the chargers could again be brought into line, the Zouaves flung away their rifles, and sprang like tigers upon them. Seizing them by the bit, they wound themselves up over their arched necks—a flash of bowie-knives gleamed like chain-lightning across the ranks, and many a wild black horse plunged on riderless with burning eyes, streaming mane, and ringing empty stirrups, headlong through the already half-disorganized ranks, and scouring over the battle-field, scattering dismay as they went.

A last struggle now ensued, with desperate men and broken forces—then a retreat, so wild, so impetuous and reckless, that all organization was given up. Regiments lost their officers, broke, mingled into others, and rushed across the field a headlong torrent, which no human power could arrest. On they went, plunging through the sea of carnage that surrounded the hill—the surging, angry broken waves of a brave army hurrying tumultuously from what had been a victorious field but an hour before.

Down from the hills, broken into frightened masses, pallid, reeling with exhaustion, they swept onward like a whirlwind, bearing the protesting officers with them, or trampling them under foot; for human life was nothing to them in that hot, mad race. The contagion of retreat spread like a prairie fire, from one point of the battle-field to another, scattering the army in wild confusion.

Still it was not quite a panic; two regiments, the Seventy-first New York and Second Rhode Island, kept their ranks in all this confusion, and were led in order from the field, over the road they had passed in the morning. Other regiments were led off in a wild, scattered way, but most of the great army was broken up, battalions and regiments surging together, and dashing through each other, till they became one mighty scene of confusion.

THE ENEMY LARGELY REINFORCED—DESPERATE FIGHTING OF THE UNION TROOPS AGAINST SUPERIOR NUMBERS.

The enemy pursued them in a broken, hesitating way, like men astonished at their own success; wanting confidence, they did not venture in force to follow the retreating army, but captured many of the scattered bands dispersed over the wide field of conflict. One detachment of cavalry charged on a helpless crowd of wounded, who were gathered near a hospital building; when a handful of unorganized men, mostly civilians, seized upon the first weapons at hand, and repelled it bravely.

Up to this time Schenck's brigade had kept its position at Stone Bridge. Captain Alexander, with his sappers and miners, had just cut through the abatis by the side of the mined bridge, that Schenck might lead his forces after those of Sherman and Keyes, when the torrent of retreat rolled toward him; his protecting battery was taken, and a force of cavalry and infantry came pouring into the road at the very spot where the battle of the morning commenced.

The first battery attacked that day had been silenced, but not taken;

and there, in the woods which protected it, four hundred South Carolinians had been concealed during the entire battle, to swarm out now and fall upon the Union infantry in this most critical moment. A sudden swoop of cavalry completed that unhappy day's work. The Union infantry broke ranks, and plunging into the woods fled up the hill. A crowd of ambulances and army wagons had concentrated close to this spot, and civilians, led to the field by curiosity, blocked up the ground. The panic which had swept the battle-field seized on them. Kellogg of Michigan, Washburne of Illinois, and it is said, Lovejoy of Illinois, flung themselves in the midst of the fugitives, and entreated them to make a stand. Ely, of New York, was taken prisoner in a rash effort to restore confidence to the panic stricken masses of men. But the maddened crowd plunged on. The teamsters urged their frightened horses into a headlong rush for the road; everything and everybody, brave or craven, were swept forward by the irresistible human torrent. It was a stampede which no power could check or resist. From the branch road the trains attached to Hunter's division had caught the contagion, and rushed into the staggering masses, creating fresh dismay and wilder confusion.

It was a frightful scene, more terrible by far than the horrors of the battle-field. Broken regiments, without leaders, filled the road, the open fields, and skirted the fences, in one wild panic. Army wagons, sutler's teams and artillery caissons rushed together, running each other down, and leaving the wrecks upon the road. Hacks were crushed between heavy wagon wheels and their occupants flung to the ground. Horses, wild with fright and maddened with wounds, galloped fiercely through the crowd, rearing and plunging when the worn-out fugitives attempted to seize them and save themselves from the destruction that was threatened at every step.

Wounded men, who had found strength to stagger off the battle-field, fell by the wayside, begging piteously to be taken up. Now and then a kind fellow would mount a wounded soldier behind him, and give the horse he had caught a double load; most of the poor fellows were brought forward in this way. Sometimes a wounded man would be picked up by two passing companions, and carried tenderly forward—for the sweet impulses of humanity were not all lost in that wild retreat.

Then came the artillery—for much was saved—thundering through the panic-stricken crowd, crushing everything as it went, dragged recklessly along by horses wild as the men that urged them on. Rifles, bayonets, pistols, blankets, haversacks and knapsacks were flung singly or in heaps along the way. Devoured by intense thirst, black with powder, famished and halting, these stricken men plunged into the fields, searching for water. If a muddy pool presented itself, they staggered to its brink with a pitiful laugh, and lying down on their faces, drank greedily, then arose with tears in their eyes, thanking God for the great luxury.

As they passed by the few houses on the road, women—God bless them!—would come out, some with curt, but genuine hospitality, others with tears streaming down their cheeks, and gave drink and food to the wounded men as they halted by. Those who fell upon the wayside were taken in and tended kindly till the next day. Boys came from the wells, bearing pailsful of water, which their little sisters distributed to the jaded men in their own tin cups.

But this panic, like all others, was of brief duration. When the fugitives reached Centreville, they found Blenker's brigade stretched across the road ready to guard the retreat. Some of the fugitives rallied and formed into line, but they had flung away their arms, and the highway from Stone Bridge to Centreville was literally covered with these cast-off weapons and munitions of war, hurled from the army wagons by reckless teamsters. In places the road was blocked up by the wagons themselves, from which the drivers had cut their teams loose and fled on the relieved horses.

Blenker, of Miles' division, whose duty up to this time had been one of inaction at Centreville, now did good service at his important post. With three regiments he kept the road, expecting every moment to be assailed by an overpowering and victorious enemy, eager to complete his fatal work. As the darkness increased, the peril of his position became imminent. At eleven o'clock the attack came upon the advance company of Colonel Stahel's rifles, from a body of the enemy's cavalry, which was, however, driven back, and did not return. At this time Richardson and Davies were both in Centreville with their brigades, which composed the entire left wing, all well organized and under perfect command. These troops were put under the command of Colonel Davies, who led them off the field—Blenker's brigade being the last to leave the town it had done so much to protect.

The cause of this stupendous stampede no one ever has or can explain. Cowardice it certainly was not. Those men had fought too bravely, and suffered too patiently for that charge to be brought against them. They were in fact victorious soldiers, for the rout of a single half hour, disastrous as it proved, should have no power to blot out the deeds of heroism that had marked the entire day. Was it excitement, acting on an exhausted frame?

Let those answer who bore the flag of our Union through the long hours of that July day, carried it under the hot sun through the fierce fight, the dust and smoke and carnage, when the sky was one mosaic of flame, and the earth groaned under the vibrations of artillery. They had marched twelve miles fasting, and with but one draught of water; marched without pause straight on to the battle field, and for nearly five hours fought bravely as men ever fought on earth. Many who had food found no time to eat it till the battle was at its close, but in the rash eagerness for the field, these men, new to the necessities of war, had flung their rations away, restive under the weight. They had started not far from midnight, from camps in a tumult of preparation, and therefore lacked sleep as well as food.

To all this was added THIRST—that hot, withering thirst, which burns like lava in the throat, and drives a man mad with craving. Panting for drink, their parched lips were blackened with gunpowder; and exhausted nature, when she clamored for food, was answered by the bitter saltness of cartridges ground between the soldiers' teeth.

Think of these men, famished, sleepless, drinkless, after fighting through the fiery noon of a hot day, suddenly overwhelmed in the midst of a positive victory—called upon to fight another battle, while every breath came pantingly, from thirst, and every nerve quivered with the overtax of its natural strength. Think of them under the hoofs of the Black Horse cavalry, and swept down by the very batteries that had been their protection. Think of all this, and if men of military standing can condemn them, war is a cruel master, and warriors hard critics.

It is very easy for civilians, who sit in luxurious parlors and sip cool ices under the protection of the old flag, to sneer at this panic of Bull Run, but many a brave man—braver than their critics, or they would not have been in the ranks—was found even in the midst of that stampede.

What if all along the road were the marks of hurried flight—abandoned teams, dead horses, wasted ammunition, coats, blankets? Were there not dead and dying men there also? brave and hardy spirits, noble, generous souls, crushed beneath the iron hoof of war—sacrificed and dying bravely in retreat, as they had fought in the advance?

Never on this earth did the proud old American valor burn fiercer or swell higher than on that day and field. And a reproach to the heroes who left the impress of bravery, and gave up their lives on that red valley, should never come from any true American heart.

THE BATTLE ON THE LEFT WING.

On the morning of the 21st, according to McDowell's plan of battle, the left wing, composed of Colonel Miles' division, was stationed at Centreville and at Blackburn's Ford, the scene of Tyler's disaster on the 18th. Thus during the heat and struggle of that awful day the greater portion of the left wing was six miles from the centre of action. But notwithstanding, no better service was rendered to the country on that day than that of this comparatively small handful of men. The first brigade of this command, under Colonel Blenker, occupied the heights of Centreville.

The second brigade, under Colonel Thomas A. Davies, of New York, and Richardson's brigade, were ordered by Colonel Miles to take position before the batteries at Blackburn's Ford, near the battle ground of the 18th, to make demonstrations of attack. In pursuance of General McDowell's order, Colonel Davies, being ranking officer, took command of Richardson's brigade.

On his route from Centreville in the morning, when about half-way to Blackburn's Ford, Colonel Davies, while conversing with the guide who rode by him, saw a country road, apparently little used, leading through the woods to the left. "That road," said the guide, a fine, intelligent fellow, "will give position farther left and nearer the enemy, for it runs directly to Beauregard's headquarters."

Colonel Davies, who had graduated at West Point and served in the Mexican war, was prompt to recognize the importance of a point which might enable the enemy to move upon his rear. He ordered a halt, and detailed the Thirty-first New York regiment, Colonel Pratt, and the Thirty-second, Colonel Mathewson, with a detachment of artillery, to guard the road at its junction, and deployed another regiment with a section of artillery on the road, which was shaded and hedged in on both sides by a heavy growth of timber.

This duty performed, the troops continued their march. Davies took his position in a wheat field with what was left of his brigade, leaving Richardson to make his own arrangements to defend the position in front of the enemy's batteries at Blackburn's Ford, the battle-ground of the 18th. Richardson posted his command in this place, on the road from Centreville heights to Blackburn's Ford.

The wheat field which Davies occupied contained a hill which overlooked a ravine, thickly wooded, on the opposite slope. On this hill Hunt's battery, commanded by Lieutenant Edwards, was placed, having been exchanged from force of circumstances for Green's battery, which belonged to Davies' command, but was now with Richardson. The battery was supported by Davies' own regiment, the Sixteenth New York, and the Eighteenth, Colonel Jackson. This hill commanded a broad view of the country on every side. The battle ground of the right wing, six miles off, was in full sight. Opposite his position, across the stream, was the road which led from Bull Run to Manassas, and also to Beauregard's extreme right. Parallel with the river to his extreme left, it was plainly traced, except where groves and clumps of trees concealed it. This road, with all the high grounds sloping from Manassas, covered with broken ridges, rich pasture lands and splendid groves, lay before the men as they placed their battery.

On their rear the Centreville road stretched along a beautiful tract of country, hidden by a waving sea of luxuriant foliage. Indeed all the converging roads that threaded the vast battle-field were plainly visible from that point.

Posted in this commanding position, Davies opened his demonstration with two twenty-pound rifle guns from Hunt's battery. The first shot hurled a shell into Beauregard's headquarters, which sent the rebels scattering in every direction. Richardson also commenced firing across the Run, producing the desired effect of keeping the enemy at their defences in the neighborhood.

At ten o'clock Colonel Miles visited the command. Finding the two regiments and artillery posted at the country road, he ordered the regiments to move forward one-fourth of a mile, and the artillery to join Davies' command, leaving the road exposed. He then sent two companies to reconnoitre the enemy's position. They had a skirmish on the stream, at Blackburn's Ford, and came back with little damage.

The moment Miles rode back to Centreville, Davies ordered out his brigade pioneer corps, all sturdy lumbermen of the North, with orders to fell trees and block up the country road thus left exposed.

For two hours these sturdy men swung their axes among the heavy timber, answering the distant roar of the battle-field with a wild, crashing music, that broke with a new and more startling expression of war through the familiar roll of cannon. With sharp, crashing groans, the great trees were hurled to the earth, locked their splintered and broken boughs across the road, and covered it with mangled foliage, forming a barricade one-fourth of a mile long, impassable as a thousand cactus hedges. The roar of cannon afar off, and the batteries belching iron close by, failed to drown the groaning rush of these forest monarchs; and when the near guns were silent for a little time, as often happened, the almost human shiver of a tree, in its last poise before it rushed downward with a wail in all its leaves and branches, conveyed an idea of death more thrilling than any noise that battle-field had to give. At twelve o'clock, just after the pioneers had returned to position, a body of the enemy came down this road from Bull Run, intending to march on Centreville and take Miles' division in the rear. Clouds of red dust rising from the trees betrayed them just as they had discovered the barricade, and a storm of shell and shrapnel hastened their backward march.

About this time the road on the other side of Bull Run was one cloud of flying dust. It was Johnston's forces, a close line, going up to snatch victory from the brave army at Stone Bridge. The advance of these forces became visible at first in tiny curls of dust rising from the woods. Then it swelled into clouds, through which jaded horses and tired men seemed struggling onward in a continued stream.

At this time the distant cannonading became louder and more continuous; the far-off woods rolled up vast volumes of smoke, and where the battle raged, a black canopy hung suspended in mid-air. How those brave men, chained to their post by inevitable military law, panted to plunge into that hot contest! The inaction forced upon them when a struggle of life and death was going on in the distance, was worse than torture. They suspected the character of those troops moving forward in the red cloud, and followed them with eager, burning eyes. But they soon had work of their own to do!

The firing on the right slackened between three and four o'clock, growing fainter and fainter. About five, Colonel Davies received a line from Richardson, saying: "*The army is in full retreat;*" but the line was written in the haste and agitation of bad news, and was indistinct. Davies read it: "The *enemy* is in full retreat." But for this providential mistake, the battle of that day would have had a darker record than we are making now; for the retreat, disastrous as it was, would have been cut off, and Washington probably taken.

Believing the army victorious, these brave men bore the restraints of their position more patiently, but still panted for a share in the work.

At this time Beauregard's telegraph, opposite the left of Davies' position, had been working half an hour; and from lines of dust concentrating there and at Davies' front, he anticipated an attack, and made disposition accordingly.

At five o'clock, the enemy appeared on the left, as Davies formed in line parallel to Bull Run, and about eight hundred yards distant. Between the hill which he occupied, and the slope down which they came from the road, was the valley or ravine, about four hundred yards from Hunt's battery.

They filed down the road and formed in the valley, marching four abreast, with their guns at *right shoulder shift*, shining like a ripple of diamonds in the sunshine, and moving forward in splendid style.

At first Davies viewed them in silence, and standing still; but as the column began to fill the valley, he changed front to the left, and ordered the artillery to withhold its fire till the rear of the enemy's column presented itself, and directed the infantry to lie down on their faces, and neither fire nor look up without orders. This was done that the enemy might not learn his strength and charge on the battery.

The rear of the column at last presented itself, an officer on horseback bringing it up. Then an order to fire was given, and Lieutenant Benjamin, a brave young fellow from West Point, fired the first shot from a twenty-pound rifled gun.

A cloud of dust, with a horse rearing, and its rider struggling in the midst, was all the result that could be observed. The rear of the enemy's column then took the double-quick down the valley, and six pieces of artillery opened on them. The effect was terrible; at the distance of only four hundred yards, the enemy took the raking downward fire in all its fury. An awful cry rang up from the valley; the men had been swept down like wheat before a scythe, and their moans filled the air.

This murderous fire was repeated over and over again. There was no waiting to swab the guns, but, fast as powder and ball could be served, the ordnance sent out its volleys. The enemy made a desperate stand, but every shot swept down the men in masses. A vacant space appeared for a moment, then fresh men filed in. Twice they attempted to reform and charge the battery, but the rapidity with which the pieces were served, and the peculiar nature of the ground, rendered every shot effective, and they were swept back, cut down, speedily disorganized, and fled for the woods.

During all this action, Lieutenant-Colonel Marsh, of the Sixteenth, and Colonel Pratt, of the Thirty-first (the former since killed, and the latter wounded before Richmond), controlled their men perfectly. Not an infantry shot was fired during the engagement. Balls from the enemy struck the ground in volleys before the men, filling their eyes with dust. No man gave way; they were compelled to change position three times during the fight. Although so many of the enemy were killed, this spot being named, in the secession reports, as giving the heaviest mortality of the day, only two men of Davies' command were hurt. One man was wounded, and Lieutenant Craig, a brave young officer from West Point, was killed.

This brilliant engagement, so important in its results, sprang out of a singular series of accidents: first, in the mistake made in reading Richardson's dispatch, and again in a failure of orders. When the main army began its retreat past Centreville, at four o'clock, Colonel Miles sent his aid, Captain Vincent, to order Davies and his command back to Centreville, but Vincent, instead of coming first to Davies, stopped to give orders to Richardson, and two regiments of Davies' brigade, stationed to guard his rear. After ordering Richardson back, Vincent came over the ravine to deliver his orders to Davies, when he heard his firing on the extreme left, went back to Centreville, to report, and returned just as the firing ceased, to direct Colonel Davies to retire on Centreville.

Davies, ignorant that Richardson had already fallen back, rode over to order his retreat, but to his astonishment, almost horror, found that the whole brigade, with two regiments of his own force left to guard his rear, had been gone a full hour. Thus it happened that this important engagement had been fought and won with a single battery and two regiments of infantry, utterly alone and unsupported on the deserted battle-field, against a large body of men, endeavoring to sweep to the rear and cut off the army in its retreat.

It was near six o'clock when this contest terminated—two hours after the main army were in full retreat. If ever delay and accident were providential on this earth, it was here; for brave as these men were, no sane leader would have felt justified in exposing them to such peril upon a deserted battle-field, and in the face of a whole victorious army, after all chance of protection had been withdrawn.

When this band of victorious men reached Centreville, a stream of jaded, wounded and heavy-hearted men were pouring through the village, while General McDowell was making a desperate effort to collect all the troops that still kept a show of organization, under his own command. These troops were principally composed of the left wing, which came off the ground in good order. McDowell, about eight o'clock, left Centreville for Fairfax Court House. Before going Colonel Miles was relieved from his command of the left wing, and the following order, written on the back of a visiting card, was handed to Colonel Davies:

Colonel Davies is consigned to the command of the left wing, as the troops are now formed. By command,

J. B. FRY, A. A. G.

July 21.

Under this running order Colonel Davies assumed command of all that was left of the army in Centreville, and marched them in good order to Alexandria and Washington, Blenker's division being the last to leave the field. This gallant officer had been among the bravest and most resolute in protecting the retreat, and had by his firmness held the enemy in check during the afternoon and evening.

THE BATTLE-FIELD AT NIGHT.

At night the calm air, the gently falling dew, visited that blasted earth sweetly as they had done the night before, when the valley was fresh with verdure and beautiful with thrifty crops. But the scene it presented was O, how different! In mercy the deep shadows cast by the woods concealed its worst features, and the smoke had risen so densely between earth and sky that the moon looked down upon it mournfully, through a veil. The battle-field was still, save when the solemn shiver of the leaves came like a painful and mighty sigh, or the troubled waves of the Run continued it in hoarser murmurs. If human moans broke the stillness, they were lost on that vast field, and only heard by the pitying angels.

But solitary lights wandered over the field, like stars dropped by a merciful heaven to light the departing souls through the valley and shadow of death. They were indeed heavenly rays, for all that is divine in human mercy sent them forth. Kind men, and more than one heroic woman carried them from point to point over that dreary battle-field, searching among the dead for those who, breathing yet, might suffer for water or Christian comfort.

There was a house on the hill top where Griffin's battery had stood, and where the Connecticut troops had planted the stars and stripes in their last desperate charge. Through all the fight, a helpless and frightened family had found precarious shelter in their own dwelling. The household was composed of a son, a daughter, and the mother, a gentle Christian woman, who had been confined to her bed for years. There was no hopes of flight for her, poor soul, and neither son nor daughter would abandon her when the storm of battle was at their threshold. Hoping to find a place of safety, the devoted children carried her to a neighboring ravine, sheltering her with their own persons.

But this spot became at last more dangerous than the house. So the harassed children took their parent back to her home, and placing her in bed again, stood to screen her from the bullets that broke like hail through the walls and windows. While her house was riddled with cannon balls and musket shot, and the missiles of death plunged through her chamber and into her bed, three bullets pierced her frail person. Still she outlived the battle tempest that raged around her, a tempest that she had not even dreamed of approaching her dwelling when that fatal day dawned upon it. When the night came on she died peacefully, and the troubled moon looked down on a mournful scene here also. Within the riddled walls and under the torn roof, this gentle woman lay, in a quieter sleep than she had known for many a long night, and by her bed knelt the bereaved children who had dared so much, weeping that a life so peaceful should have met that violent ending. Painful as this was, there lay many poor soldiers on the field that hour, whose children would never have the privilege of weeping over them.

In an orchard of young trees, just forming their fruit, lay many a prostrate Southron, sent to his long account; for the enemy had suffered terribly there. The northern verge of the field was blackened by a fine grove in which a Georgia regiment had fought, and under its black shadows the dead lay thick and numerous. Here Lamar had fallen, and many a brave Northman slept side by side with the foe he had sent into eternity but a moment in advance of himself. The fatal hill, scorched and blackened in every tree and blade of grass, was strewn with the dead of both sections, among them some of the bravest leaders that the enemy boasted.

There have been rumors of great cruelty on the battle-field after the fight was over—of men prowling like fiends among the dead, and murdering the wounded; but these things should be thrice proven before we believe them of American citizens. Rumor is always triple-tongued, and human nature does not become demoniac in a single hour. One thing is certain, many an act of merciful kindness was performed that night, which an honest pen should prefer to record. Certain it is that Southern soldiers in many instances shared their water—the most precious thing they had—with the wounded Union men. A soldier passing over the field found two wounded combatants lying together—one was a New Yorker, the other a Georgian. The poor wounded fellow from New York cried out piteously for water, and the Georgian, gathering up his strength, called out: "For God's sake give him drink; for I called on a New York man for water when his column was in retreat, and he ran to the trench at the risk of his life and brought it to me!"

One brave young enemy lost his life after passing through all the perils of the battle, in attempting to procure drink for his wounded foes.

If there were individual instances of cruelty on either side, and this is possible—let us remember that there was kindness too; and when the day shall come—God grant it may be quickly—when we are one people again, let the cruelty be forgiven and the kindness only remembered.

And now our record of the battle of Bull Run is at an end. It was valiantly contended on both sides, and won only from superior numbers and reinforcements of fresh troops, poured upon the exhausted soldiery of the Union. To gain this contest the South sent her best and very bravest generals. Her forces were led by Beauregard and Johnston, both experienced officers. They were also cheered by the near presence of Jefferson Davis, who came upon the field when the victory was assured, amid the shouts of a soldiery, the more enthusiastic because they had just been rescued from almost certain defeat. They had the choice of position and had fortified it with wonderful skill; a thorough knowledge of the country, and troops unwearied by long marches—indeed, the advantages were altogether on their side. The North, never dreaming that an open rebellion would break out, was utterly dependant on undisciplined troops; while the South, having premeditated resistance to the Government, had been drilling men for months, if not years. There was no one point except in the actual bravery of their leaders and soldiers in which the enemy was not superior to the Union forces. In personal valor the Southerners themselves have never claimed to surpass that exhibited in this battle by their foes.

The smallest estimate of the forces actually engaged on the Southern side is eighteen thousand—while the Union forces which crossed Bull Run did not at any time count more than thirteen thousand. One brigade of McDowell's eighteen thousand was not in the action, except in a vain effort to check the retreat. This brigade, of General Tyler's division, was stationed at Stone Bridge, and never advanced upon the actual battle-field. The attack repulsed by Davies on the left wing, at Blackburn's Ford, took place nearly two hours after the army was in retreat.

In the loss of officers, the enemy was even more unfortunate than the Union army. The fall of General Bee, one of the bravest of their leaders, Bartow, Colonel Thomas, Colonel Hampton, Colonel Johnson, Lamar, and others, shed a gloom upon their victory, and greatly weakened their cause in the future. The Union loss was heavy, for the men who fell or were taken prisoners were among the bravest that marched with the army, but the loss of officers by death was inferior to that of the enemy, and though Corcoran and Wilcox were wounded and taken prisoners, they were not lost to their country. In ordnance and munitions of war the conquest was less important than might have been supposed. Many of the Union guns were rescued from the field during the next day. Of the fine horses attached to the ordnance a large proportion were killed, and others were saved by their drivers, who cut the traces, and rode them from the scene of battle. The loss in killed and wounded on the Union side, was 481 killed, 1,011 wounded, and 1,216 missing: total, 2,708. That of the enemy numbered, by Beauregard's report, 393 killed, 1,200 wounded.

The victory was a very important one to the South, as it gave prestige and force to a rebellion which, had the position of things been reversed, would, it is probable, have expired before the year went out. But in the North it only served to arouse the people to a pitch of excitement hitherto unparalleled; if troops had been sent forth in regiments before, they came in brigades after that defeat.

WESTERN VIRGINIA.

Virginia has three grand divisions, viz.: the Eastern Section, extending from tide-water up to the Blue Ridge Mountains; the Great Valley between the Blue Ridge and the Alleghanies; Western Virginia, stretching from the Great Valley to the Ohio river.

The contest between the people of the eastern and western portions of the State for supremacy had been one of long duration, dating back for many years. Internal improvements appear to have been the cause of this dissension—Western Virginia claiming that the East had enjoyed and been benefitted by them hitherto exclusively. In this jealousy the inhabitants of the Valley sympathized, and the completion of the James River and Kanawha Canal to the Ohio aroused a feeling of such bitter rivalry, that even the Governor favored the project of a division of the State. Added to this was the complaint of unequal taxation. The eastern portion being the large slaveholding district, paid *per capita*, without regard to value, while the wealth of the western, consisting of land and stock, was taxed *ad valorem*. This strife, of necessity, was carried from the people into the Legislature, and stormy debates followed. The feeling of the West on the slavery question, also, added fuel to the flame, and the loyalty of that section was attacked.

In the State Convention which passed the ordinance of secession, the western delegates took a firm and bold stand against it. When the Act was about to be consummated, great excitement prevailed in regard to the action of the western members, both inside and out of the Convention, and some of them were obliged to leave Richmond. In May, when the ordinance was submitted to the people, the northwestern counties voted largely against it.

A Convention assembled at Wheeling, and a committee was appointed, which called a General Convention to convene at the same place on the 11th of June. Forty counties were represented there, and an ordinance was passed for the reorganization of the State Government, every officer to be obliged to swear allegiance anew to the United States, and to repudiate the Richmond Convention. A Governor, Lieutenant-Governor, and other State officers were elected, and the Legislature was summoned "to assemble at the United States District Courtroom in the city of Wheeling, at noon, on the first day of July, 1861." Both houses met and organized. The Governor's Message was sent in together with a document from Washington, officially recognizing the new Government. The message recommended an energetic co-operation with the Federal Government. United States Senators were then elected.

On the 20th of August, the Convention passed an ordinance creating a new State, to be called "Kanawha." It included thirty-nine counties, and provision was made for the admission of other adjoining counties, if a majority of the people of each desired it. The question of forming a separate State was submitted to the popular vote on the 24th of October, and resulted in favor of the proposition by a large majority. Since that time other counties have signified a desire to be admitted.

Western Virginia became the scene of military operations directly after the war broke out, following in close order upon the occupation of Alexandria. On the 30th of May Colonel Kelly took possession of Grafton, and the occupation of Phillipi followed but a few days subsequently. Federal troops also crossed the Ohio and entered Parkersburgh. General McClellan had command of this portion of the State, it being included in the Ohio district, and issued his proclamation to the Union men of Virginia.

A series of offensive and defensive events now followed each other in rapid succession, exhibiting bravery and determination unparalleled in history—individual heroism and uncomplaining endurance of suffering—rapid marches and brilliant charges, that shine in letters of fire upon the pages of our war history, and threw the prestige of early victory about the northern arms. It was here that McClellan won his first laurels—here that chivalric Lander met a soldier's death—here that Kelly was wounded, till for weeks and weeks his life was despaired of. In fact, Western Virginia is covered with victorious Union battle-fields. She has indeed given their greenest laurels to many of our generals.

The military department of Ohio, in which Western Virginia was included, was organized on the tenth of May, and Major-General George B. McClellan appointed to the command. His headquarters were at Cincinnati. On the 26th of the same month he issued his first proclamation, declaring that his mission was one of fraternity, union, and protection, and called upon all patriotic men to aid him in his endeavors to accomplish this holy purpose. The proclamation produced a marked effect. Colonel Kelly, of Wheeling, Virginia, had prior to that date organized a regiment for the defence of the Union, known as the "First Virginia Volunteers."

On Friday, the 24th of May, about twelve hundred rebels had assembled and marched from Harper's Ferry to Grafton, a town on the Baltimore and Ohio railroad, and forced many citizens to abandon their homes and fly for safety, leaving their property to be pillaged by the enemy. About one hundred of the fugitives reached Morgantown. The inhabitants of that place, warned of their danger, immediately flew to arms and prepared for a vigorous defence. Finding that they were not to be molested, and burning for revenge, they marched, 1000 strong—their ranks having been swelled by friends from Pennsylvania—towards Grafton.

The rebels became alarmed and fled to Philippi, in Bourbon county, about 17 miles southward. On Monday, the 27th, detachments of Ohio and Indiana troops crossed the Ohio river at Wheeling and at Marietta, on their way, also, to Grafton. Simultaneously, Colonel Kelly's regiment of Virginians moved forward in the same direction, but the bridges having been destroyed, their march was delayed. At every point, and especially at Mannington and Fairmount, they were received with great enthusiasm and hailed as deliverers.

BATTLE OF PHILLIPI.

Brigadier-General Thomas A. Morris arrived at Grafton on the evening of June 1st, and took command of the Union forces. An expedition was immediately organized to surprise and attack the rebels at Philippi, under the command of Colonel Porterfield. The troops left in two divisions. The First Virginia regiment, part of the Ohio Sixteenth, and the Seventh Indiana, under Colonel Kelly, moved eastward, by rail to Thornton, a distance of five miles, and from there marched on twenty-two miles to Phillipi, reaching the town on the lower side. The second division, consisting of the Sixth and Seventh Indiana, the Fourteenth Ohio, and a section of artillery under Lieutenant-Colonel Sturgis, met by detachments at Webster, on the North-western Virginia railroad, and marched twelve miles to Phillipi. The combined forces were commanded by Colonels Dumont and Lander, and at eight o'clock on the night of the 2d of June marched forward through one of the most overwhelming storms known to our country that year. Lander had been detailed to a special command by General Morris, and in the terrible march that followed, through darkness, mud and rain he led the way, sometimes exploring the route three miles ahead of his forces, in the midst of profound darkness; and through mud so deep and tenacious that every forward step was a struggle. The men followed, bravely toiling through the miry soil, staggering forward in thick darkness, and pelted by the rain so violently that they could not have seen the road had it been daylight. Still, not a murmur was heard. Against the whole force of the elements the brave fellows struggled on, eager for the storm of fire which was soon to follow the deluge that poured upon them. Now and then Lander's majestic form, seated upon his charger, would loom upon them through the darkness, returning from his scouting duty to cheer them with his deep, sympathetic voice, which aroused them like a trumpet. Thus they moved on, supported by one stern purpose, through woods, across valleys, and over hills, the storm drowning their approach till they drew up on the edge of the town overlooking the enemy. But it was not altogether a surprise. Just before they reached the town the troops had passed a farm-house. A woman within that house sprang from her bed as she saw the lines of troops filing slowly by in the misty gray of the dawn, and guessed their object. She instantly aroused her little son and sent him by a short cross-road to give the alarm. The boy was quick of foot, but the hopes of conflict had so aroused the energies of these jaded men that he was but a few minutes in advance of them.

Lander's troops took position on a hill across the river and below the town, commanding it and the encampments around. He at once planted two pieces of artillery, and prepared to open fire at exactly four o'clock, the hour agreed upon for the attack, which was to be made at once by both divisions. Lander was to assault them in front, while Kelly was to attack the rear and cut off all retreat. But Lander found his division alone before the enemy. The terrible night, the almost impassable roads, and a march of twenty-two miles had delayed Kelly's forces, and when he did arrive it was to come in by mistake below the town.

The presence of Lander's troops aroused the town and threw it into terrible commotion. In vain Lander searched the distant hills, impatient for Kelly's appearance. The hour of attack had arrived and passed. The men became impatient as their leader, who, in his indomitable courage commenced the battle with a portion of his forces.

When Lander gave the order his eager men sprang to their posts, and the artillery opened fire. As the first gun awoke its thunder on the encampments, Kelly advanced, but in the wrong direction. He instantly comprehended Lander's action, and with prompt courage charged upon the encampments. The batteries had by this time obtained the range, and were pouring in their messengers of terror and death, tearing through tents and cabins, and scattering the rebels like chaff in every direction. After firing a volley of musketry, Lander advanced.

Colonel Kelly's command was close upon the enemy, the Virginia troops in advance, the Henry Clay Guards in front, and Colonel Kelly and Captain Fordyce leading, while Colonel Lander's force came rushing down the hill to the bridge and joined in an impetuous pursuit of the fugitives. Colonel Kelly, who, with a bravery amounting almost to rashness, had been foremost from the very first, was shot by a concealed foe, the ball entering the left breast and lodging beneath the shoulder blade. As his men conveyed him to a place of safety, this brave man, while in the agony of his pain, exclaimed, "I expect I shall have to die. I would be glad to live, if it might be, that I might do something for my country, but if it cannot be, I shall have at least the consolation of knowing that I fell in a just cause." But he was not destined to be cut off in the zenith of his fame and usefulness. After a few weeks of danger and anguish he was again performing noble duty for the country he loved so well.

In this dashing victory fifteen of the rebels were killed, a large number wounded, and ten taken prisoners, together with a quantity of camp equipage, arms, &c. The organization of the rebels at that point was completely broken up, and the men driven to the mountains.

GREAT DESTRUCTION OF RAILROAD PROPERTY.

The bitter animosity of the rebel army was strikingly illustrated on the 23d July, by the destruction of a large number of locomotives and cars of the Baltimore and Ohio railroad by secession troops under the command of Colonel Thomas J. Jackson. Forty-eight locomotives and three hundred cars were blown up or burned, one of the engines having been previously wrapped in our national ensign. The road had been rendered impassable by the destruction of bridges, and, therefore, the rolling stock could not have been rendered available. The estimated loss was about three-quarters of a million of dollars.

GENERAL M'CLELLAN IN WESTERN VIRGINIA.

General McClellan, during the time that elapsed since his appointment, had been actively engaged in organizing his forces and getting them ready for efficient service. Scouting parties—an important feature of his department—were detailed for service, and raw troops replaced by experienced men. Colonel Kelly, who was now recovering from the wounds received at Phillipi, had been appointed by Governor Pierpont to the command of the Virginia brigade of volunteers. Gens. Morris, Hill, Schenck and Schleich were assigned their respective positions—the telegraph lines were put in order, and new ones for military purposes were constructed where necessary. The arrival of fresh regiments, among which Colonel Rosecranz made his appearance, added great activity to the department. On the side of the enemy were Generals Robert S. Garnett, Henry A. Wise, Ex-Governor, John B. Floyd, Ex-Secretary of War, and Colonel Pegram.

Columns of Federal troops were dispatched to attack the enemy, simultaneously, at three different points, and the first collision between them occurred on the 10th of July.

BATTLE OF SCAREYTOWN.

A brigade of rebels under Governor Wise, crossed the Alleghanies to the head-waters of the Kanawha, with the intention of attacking the rear of McClellan's forces, while General Garnett was prepared to meet him in front. General Cox had been dispatched to this section with a considerable force of Ohio, Indiana and Kentucky troops, and was encamped on the Kanawha about ten miles below its junction with Scarey Creek. Hearing that a portion of the rebel force had taken position at Scareytown, but four miles above his camp, on the other side of the river, and were entrenching themselves there, General Cox dispatched a force of about 1,000 men, consisting of the Twelfth Ohio, a portion of the Twenty-first Ohio, the Cleveland Artillery, and a detachment of cavalry, all under the command of Colonel Lowe, to dislodge the rebels if practicable. The column was ferried across the stream, and moved cautiously onward, the scouts scouring the country as they advanced. The enemy was found to be entrenched on the opposite side of Pocatallico Creek, here intersecting the Kanawha, protected by breastworks, and also sheltered by woods, about half way up a slope of high hills, having two pieces of artillery in position, while a portion of their infantry had possessed themselves of ten or twelve log huts, constituting the village of Scareytown, in which they had improvised loop-holes. The Federal troops were met by a discharge from the rebel battery as soon as they made their appearance; but the artillery of Captain Cotton soon got in position, and returned the fire of the enemy with good effect. The infantry were now ordered to advance, and rushed fearlessly across the stream, which was fordable, in the face of a heavy fire. The left wing, composed of portions of the Twelfth and Twenty-first Ohio, had reached the enemy's entrenchments, but being unsupported by the right, and a fresh regiment of the rebels appearing on the ground, they were compelled to retreat, leaving many of their dead and wounded on the field.

The loss of the Federal forces by this engagement was nine killed, thirty-eight wounded, and three missing. Of the rebel loss we have no record.

A great misfortune of the day, however, was the capture of five of the principal officers of General Cox's command, who were not attached to the expedition.

Colonels Woodruff and De Villers, Lieutenant-Colonel Neff, and Captains Austin and Hurd, prompted by an eager desire to witness the engagement in which they were not assigned a part, rode up the banks of the river to its junction with the creek, and hearing a loud shout, were led to believe that the Federal forces were victorious. They procured a skiff, crossed the creek, and inadvertently strayed within the enemy's lines, where they were all made prisoners.

HOW THE ENEMY WAS TO BE ATTACKED.

General Garnett had at this time nearly 10,000 men under his command, and occupied a position at Beverly, on Tygart's Valley river, Randolph Co., in a valley of the Alleghany Mountains. Two good roads unite at an acute angle at this place, one leading westwardly to Buckhannon, and the other northwest to Phillipi. A mountainous ridge crosses both these roads in front of Beverly, and at each point of intersection General Garnett had an intrenched camp. The first was on the road to Buckhannon, called the Rich Mountain Camp, under command of Colonel Pegram; and the second, on the road to Phillipi, called Laurel Hill Camp, under General Garnett's personal command.

Early on the morning of the 11th of July, General Rosecrans was dispatched to attack Colonel Pegram, and dislodge him from his position. General Morris was to make a simultaneous movement on the position held by General Garnett.

BATTLE AT RICH MOUNTAIN.
JULY 12, 1862.

The rebel entrenchments at Rich Mountain were very strong in their position, and were evidently to be taken only by a great sacrifice of life. They had rolled great trees down the steep sides of the mountain, and banding their branches into a general entanglement, filled the open spaces with earth and stones. The dense forest on all sides made the approach almost impassable. General Rosecranz was accordingly directed to attack them in their rear. For this purpose he took with him the Eighth and Tenth Indiana, and the Nineteenth Ohio, and under the leadership of an experienced guide, started about daylight to ascend the mountain. The path was exceedingly difficult and tedious, most of the distance being through thick laurel underbrush, almost impenetrable woods, and a broken, rocky region, which gave them a toilsome march of nearly nine miles. Meantime a courier from General McClellan with dispatches for General Rosecrans, had been captured by the rebels, who instantly took the alarm, and a body of 2,500 men were sent to the top of the mountain by a short route which they commanded, and on the arrival of the Union forces they stood ready for defence. The rebels had three cannon in place, and awaited the troops, facing that part of the road where they would emerge from the timber. For some time there was skirmishing, the rebels firing their cannon into the woods at random. The Union troops had no cannon, and left the sheltering trees only long enough to deliver a volley at any one time, and then retired back to the bushes. They thus succeeded in drawing the enemy from his earthworks, and leading him into the open fields, where the encounter took place.

BATTLE OF RICH MOUNTAIN.

Colonel Lander called for twenty sharpshooters, who speedily left the cannon without men to work them. Their places were filled by others, when the Nineteenth Ohio, which had gained a position on high ground in the rear, poured in a tremendous volley, and giving loud cheers, rushed forward for a closer struggle. The Eighth and Tenth immediately charged upon the guns and carried them, and then the entire entrenchment. The enemy found it impossible to resist the impetuous and daring onset, and broke up instantly in a total rout. The action was short, but fiercely contested. One hundred and forty rebels were found killed, while the Federal loss was only twenty-five or thirty.

The victors attempted to follow the flying enemy, but after proceeding a short distance were recalled, and formed in line, in anticipation of an attack from the fort, at the foot of the mountain. It appeared, however, that when their cannon ceased firing they gave up all as lost, and deserted their works. General Rosecranz remained on the field burying the dead, and taking care of the wounded, till next morning, when he marched down to the fort with his forces, and took possession. Several hundred prisoners were taken on the field, and Colonel Pegram, after wandering about nearly two days without finding a chance to escape, surrendered unconditionally to General McClellan, with the remnant of his command, numbering six hundred men.

BATTLE OF CARRICK'S FORD.
July 13, 1861.

While these stirring events were transpiring, General Garnett, hearing of the combined movements, and conscious that he would be unable to maintain his position, or make a successful retreat if defeated, withdrew his forces from the Laurel Hill camp, and was proceeding towards Beverly, when he received intelligence of the surrender of Colonel Pegram and the rapid advance of General Rosecranz, accompanied by the intrepid Colonel Lander, towards the spot he was himself approaching. He then struck off on the Leading Creek Pike, half a mile from Leadsville, and commenced a rapid retreat towards St. George, in Tucker county.

General Morris's brigade entered the rebel camp at Beverly at 10 A. M. of Friday, the 12th of July. At 11 o'clock the Federal troops detailed to follow General Garnett started in pursuit, under Captain Benham. The advance comprised Colonel Steedman's Ohio Fourteenth, Colonel Milroy's Ninth and Colonel Dumont's Seventh Indiana, and two pieces of artillery, with forty men—total about eighteen hundred and fifty. At two o'clock on the morning of the 13th they set out in a pitiless storm, guided by the baggage, tents, trunks, blankets, knapsacks, and clothing thrown away by the enemy. The roads had been obstructed by the retreating foe. A guide, however, led them by a cross-road, which enabled them to gain rapidly on the enemy. On reaching the track again, it was found necessary to keep an advance of axe-men to clear the obstructions. This was performed with the greatest zeal and alacrity, while the storm raged furiously around them.

About noon General Garnett had reached and passed Kahler's Ford, twelve miles from St. George. When the advance of the Federal troops emerged from the ford they caught sight of the rear of the enemy, and they were instantly nerved with new life. The retreating Southerners were also excited, and redoubled their speed, if possible, throwing away everything that encumbered their progress. General Garnett had become thoroughly convinced that there was no alternative but to make a stand, and thus test the question of superiority without delay. He continued his course, however, until he came to the fourth ford on the river, known as Carrick's Ford, and prepared to receive his pursuers. On the left bank of the river were level bottom lands, corn-fields, and meadows. On the right high bluffs commanded the fields below, and its bank was thickly hedged in with impenetrable thickets of laurel. Fording the river, and placing his men on the high bluff on the right, they were completely concealed, while the situation gave his artillery every advantage. The wagon train was left standing in the river, evidently to mislead his pursuers with the idea that they were unable to cross the rocky bed of the stream. The Federal troops advanced to seize the train, and were consequently within range of his artillery on the bluff.

The Federal columns pushed rapidly forward, Colonel Steedman's Fourteenth Ohio in front, and as they approached the teams their drivers called out that they would surrender. The position, and the conduct of the teamsters, however, excited the suspicions of the regiment, and the men were disposed in order, with skirmishers thrown out towards the ford, the line moving down after them in the finest order. Just as the advance were approaching the stream, and only about two hundred yards from the steep bluff on the other side, an officer rose from the bushes and gave the order to fire. Immediately a volley of musketry was followed by a discharge of artillery. The Fourteenth Ohio and Seventh Indiana were directly under the fire, and returned it, doing good execution, while that of the enemy flew harmlessly over their heads. The Fourteenth Ohio, being nearest the ford, were almost exclusively aimed at, and for a time the storm of war was frightful. The roar of cannon, the crashing of trees, the bursting of the shells, and quick volleys of musketry made the wild scene of terrible and appalling havoc. Amid it all our men stood undaunted, and returned the fire with great rapidity, and in superior order. Burnett's artillery then came up, and opened, and under cover of their fire the Seventh Indiana was directed to cross the river and climb the bluff on the enemy's left. They made the attempt, and two companies had already reached the top, when they were directed to descend and make the ascent so as to turn the enemy's right. Colonel Dumont led his men down the stream with such dispatch, that the enemy could not turn his pieces upon them until they were concealed from view by the smoke, and beyond the guns on the bluff. During this movement the Fourteenth Ohio, and Colonel Milroy's Ninth Indiana, with our artillery, kept up a brisk fire in front, until suddenly Colonel Dumont's men, having scaled the bluff, appeared on the right, and poured in a volley. The appearance of our troops there was the signal for a retreat, and the enemy instantly broke up in rout and disorder, precipitately flying from the field.

Our regiments and artillery then crossed the river in hot pursuit. At a distance of a quarter of a mile the road again crosses the stream, and General Garnett sought in vain to rally his troops at this point. Major Gordon of the Seventh Indiana led the advance, and soon reached the spot where General Garnett, on the opposite side of the river, was endeavoring to rally his forces around him. Gordon called upon Captain Ferry's company, and ordered them to fire. The rebels greeted Major Gordon with one volley and fled. General Garnett turned to call his men, and motioned them back, but all in vain. At this moment, Sergeant Burlingame, of Captain Ferry's company, raised his piece, took aim, and fired. General Garnett fell backward, his head lying towards our forces, and with open mouth, as though gasping for breath. He uttered not a groan, and when Major Gordon reached him, a few moments afterwards, he was just expiring. The Major stooped down, tenderly closed his eyes, disposed his limbs, and left a guard of loyal soldiers around him to protect all that remained of the chivalrous and honored, but mistaken leader of Western Virginia.

Every Virginian among the followers of this gallant man fled, and left him to fall and expire alone. But a young soldier wearing the Georgia uniform and button, sprang to his side, only to share his fate, for a musket shot answered this devotion with death, and he fell side by side with his commander. The Federal troops, even in the glow of victory, stopped to pay a tribute of respect to this generous youth. They placed a board at his grave and cut rudely upon it, "A brave fellow, who shared his General's fate and fell fighting by his side. Name unknown."

The loss of our troops was killed, two; wounded, twelve. The enemy lost eight on the field, three died in hospital, and ten others were wounded. A large number of prisoners were taken, including six Georgia captains and lieutenants, a surgeon, and a number of non-commissioned officers. Beside prisoners, there were also captured two stands of colors, one rifled cannon, forty loaded wagons, hundreds of muskets and side arms, with other effects of various kinds..

This action is honorable in the highest degree to all engaged in it. They had pursued and overtaken an enemy who had twelve hours advance; they had made a forced march of nearly thirty miles in less than twenty-four hours, over the worst of roads, and with scarcely any food, some of the men having been without nourishment for thirty-six hours. They then fought a battle, cut off the enemy's baggage train, captured their cannon, routed their army, and found themselves in full possession of the field. The day and the event will ever be memorable, and Ohio and Indiana may well be proud of their sons.

The remainder of General Garnett's army effected their escape through the Cheat Mountain Gap, which was seized and fortified by General McClellan. In these two engagements 150 of the enemy were killed, 300 wounded, upwards of 1000 prisoners were taken, and nearly all their war material fell into the hands of the victors.

The loyal troops were too much exhausted by the incessant labors and privations of their three days' struggle to pursue the scattered and dispirited enemy any further through the mountains, and went into camp at Huttonville and Laurel Hill, to await the next call to duty. General McClellan closed his dispatch of July 14th, with the words, "I firmly believe that secession is killed in this section of the country."

During the battle an incident illustrating the coolness, bravery and generosity of Colonel Lander towards a brave foeman occurred, that deserves honorable mention. The horse of the Colonel had been shot from under him, and he, dismounted, had taken his stand upon a rock directly in front of a rebel gun. Discharging musket after musket, as fast as they could be loaded for him, he remained a noted mark for the enemy to shoot at. At a short distance, all the men belonging to a cannon of the Confederates had been shot down or fled, and their Lieutenant was undauntedly serving and firing it, single-handed. Three times had it belched forth flame and ball, when Colonel Lander, noticing the bravery of the man, called out to him—

"If you fire that gun again you are a dead man!"

"Sir, I shall fire it as long as I have life in my body!" was the cool, fearless and curt reply.

This was an instance of noble courage well calculated to be appreciated by a true soldier, and the Union Colonel, leaping from the rock, shouted to his men—

"Boys, that is too brave a man for me to kill."

On the 21st of July the Federal army under General McDowell, having suffered severely, and retreated from Manassas, General McClellan, who by his achievements had earned a brilliant prestige, was ordered, on the 22d, to Washington, to take command of the Department of the Potomac, and General Rosecranz was appointed to succeed him in the Department of the Ohio.

THE WEST.

Comprehended within the boundaries, of that noble portion of our country called "The West," is a people who can justly claim to be not only of the best muscle and nerve of the land, but second to none in intellectual vigor and sterling integrity of character. A single thought tells us how just this claim is. The West was settled by the picked men and women of the old States. When the sloping-roofed farmhouses of New England became too circumscribed for the sons and daughters that filled them, the most enterprising members of a household left the rest to till the homestead acres while they went forth into the wilderness to cut the forest trees away, and let sunshine into the shadowy bosom of the woods, to build their log cabins in the first clearing, and so work out a sure independence for themselves, as they became benefactors to the world.

In the end both position and wealth followed these daring pioneers. As the roving Indian slowly retreated from the frontier which was stretching westward every hour, sweeping the wilderness away with it, he found the rich earth lavish of her returns for his self-sacrifice and his labor. He drank in enlargement of thought and purpose from amid the luxuriant prairies and vast wilderness which spread its untrodden bosom between his home and the Rocky Mountains. He watched the Father of Rivers cleaving the best portions of a continent with his broad waters, and drank in lessons of true freedom which will never lose their value to his descendants. With a rifle for his companion and an axe for his best friend, the backwoodsman of America learned the art of border warfare, and trained himself in a school of hardship that made his sinews firm as iron and capable of resisting any fatigue.

With hearts and minds expanding with the boundless scenes around them, these adventurous men grew so careless of danger that the word fear was blotted from their lexicon long before the present generation came into existence.

Is it strange that the descendants of such men should be open-handed, grand-hearted and brave, as we have found them in this war for our common Union? The enthusiasm of the old men who have dropped quietly away into their western graves, has broken forth anew in this younger generation. Like a spark of fire dropped upon a prairie in the autumn, their enthusiasm is easily enkindled. A single word against the old flag, one sacrilegious touch upon its flag-staff, was enough to rouse them into action. Nowhere on earth is the stars and stripes held more sacred than in the West. The first ball that cut through the flag at Fort Sumter aroused the old pioneer blood into determined and terrible resistance.

The history of the Mexican war is a record of what western men can do on the battle-field—charges at which even their countrymen who knew them wondered—sufferings patiently endured, marches that taxed the strongest—all these things have proved of what true metal the West is made. With war-wreaths dyed in blood at Cerro Gordo, baptized in fire at Chapultepec, and rendered immortal at Buena Vista, these men were not likely to see their own Government turned upon without rising as one man to defend it.

Through the golden grain and the rustling corn-fields of the West, the news of the bombardment of Sumter, the attack at Baltimore, and the call of the President, rushed like one of its own tornadoes from city to village, from farm-house to cabin. The news ran and the answer came thunder-toned. The old man took down his rifle from the antler bracket on the cabin wall. His son left the plow in its furrow, and all classes and conditions of men came forward with brave hearts and ready hands, and laid them on the altar of their country.

The watchfires of freedom were kindled, and on every hill and through the valleys poured a tide of armed men, unconquerable and resistless. These western men took the field, ready at once for the deadly strife. Their entire lives had been one incessant training for the hardships and dangers of war. They had but one regret—that their march was against brothers armed against the nation—all else was merged in the glorious thought that they, the very children of liberty, had the power to yield up everything, even life, and home, that a great country should be maintained in every inch of its soil and every right of its people.

Long had the great West toiled to feed the starving nations of the earth. Long had she poured from her overflowing storehouses countless millions of food into the waiting lap of the needy manufacturing countries. From her great wealth of food she had always been ready to feed the world. When the war-cry aroused her, she was just as strong and just as prompt to fight the world. The national-honor was hers to reverence and avenge. The old flag—its emblem and its glory—who should spring to its rescue if not the West? Did not a chain of crystal lakes crown her at the north, clasped together by the eternal emeralds of Niagara? Was not the Mississippi, her great highway to the gulf, a mighty thoroughfare, which no force should wrest from her while she had power to hold its banks with serried walls of steel? Was this river, the pathway of her greatness, one source of her renown, to be blocked up while she could cleave her own mountains asunder, and force them to give forth iron for gunboats, or gather lead from her bosom to mould into bullets? Not while these people could turn their workshops into manufactories of war-missiles, and their prairie steeds into chargers, should an enemy—brother or stranger—take one right from the West by force. This was the stern resolve of our pioneer men when the war-trumpet rang over the prairies of the West, and quick to act as prompt to resolve, her people arose as one man. There was no cavil about trifles then. Her fertile fields were stripped of their wealth, and her prairies of their cattle to furnish food—not alone to furnish food for themselves, but for the armies of the East. Soon her rivers swarmed with iron-clad gunboats, and her railways became military roads—her cities tented fields, her palaces recruiting offices, her cabins free homes for soldiers when their faces turned toward the war.

The West was impatient of nothing but delay—but she chafed wildly at any obstacle that impeded the progress of her armies.

How well these men have fought, and with what heroism they have suffered, let the record we are about to make of Henry, Donelson, Pittsburgh Landing, and many another bravely contested point, answer. Let the noble hearts stilled in death, and countless graves upon which the tender grass is now springing, answer.

With battle songs on their lips they marched away from their homes, with battle cries upon their lips many of them fell gloriously, never to see those homes again. If the West has been brave in war, so will she prove generous when Peace shall come. The nation they have helped to save, and those in revolt, when true brotherhood comes back, will yet give the West a monument worthy of its fame.

MISSOURI.

The geographical position of Missouri is such, that if thrown into the scale, she would weigh heavily either for or against the Union. When the war broke out her people were divided, though the majority were believed to be loyal to the Constitution; and when the Governor refused to meet the requisition of the President for troops to sustain the national flag, Hon. Frank P. Blair and other prominent citizens of the State, replied, on their personal responsibility, that the quota of four regiments should be raised, without either the aid of the Governor or his consent. In order to give character and legality to their proceedings, and to guard against the power of the State rulers, Captain Nathaniel Lyon, of the United States army, then in command of the Arsenal at St. Louis, was directed by the Government, on the 30th of April, to enrol in the military service of the United States, from the loyal citizens of the city and vicinity, 10,000 men, for the purpose of maintaining the authority of the Government—for the protection of the peaceable inhabitants of Missouri, and to guard against any attempt on the part of the secessionists to gain military possession of the city of St. Louis. Captain Lyon was also instructed that this force should be disbanded when the emergency ceased to exist.

Recruiting offices were opened, under his direction, the loyal citizens were prompt in their response, and on the 2d of May, Colonel F. B. Blair announced that the four regiments called for from that State had been enrolled, equipped, and mustered into service.

The Police Commissioners of St. Louis had called upon Captain Lyon, on the opening of recruiting stations, and demanded the removal of the United States troops from all places and buildings occupied by them in the city outside of the Arsenal grounds, but he declined compliance, and the Commissioners referred the matter to the Governor and the Legislature, alleging that such occupancy was derogatory to the Constitution of the United States—that Missouri had "sovereign and exclusive jurisdiction over her entire territory," and had delegated a portion of that territory only (the Arsenals, etc.,) to the United States for military purposes.

CAPTURE OF CAMP JACKSON.

In response to Governor Jackson's order directing the military in certain districts to go into encampments for the purpose of improvement in the tactics of war, a camp had been formed at Lindell's Grove, in the suburbs of St. Louis, called "Camp Jackson." On the 4th of May it was inaugurated, under the charge of General D. M. Frost, and within a week numbered 800 men. Having received intelligence that it was the purpose of Captain Lyon to break up this encampment, General Frost addressed him a letter, dissuasive in its tone—disclaiming any intention on the part of himself and men of hostility to the Government, and containing an offer to preserve the public peace and guard the property of the United States.

The answer to this, was the surrounding of the camp by 5,000 Federal troops, and the following notice from Captain Lyon:

"SIR,—Your command is regarded as hostile towards the Government of the United States. It is, for the most part, made up of those who have avowed their hostility to the General Government, and have been plotting for the seizure of its property and the overthrow of its authority. You are openly in communication with the so-called Southern Confederacy, which is now at war with the United States, and you are receiving at your camp, from the said Confederacy and under its flag, large supplies of material of war, most of which is known to be the property of the United States. These extraordinary preparations plainly indicate none other than the well-known purpose of the Governor of this State, under whose orders you are acting; and whose purpose, recently communicated to the Legislature, has just been responded to by that body in the most unparalleled legislation, having in direct view hostilities to the General Government and co-operation with its enemies."

Actuated by these considerations, and also by the failure to break up the camp, in obedience to the Presidential Proclamation of April 15th, Captain Lyon demanded its immediate surrender. After a hasty consultation with his officers, General Frost complied, and the place was surrendered unconditionally. But when the result was announced to the troops, it was received with the wildest yells, curses and groans. Some railed out against treachery, but the more loyal were rejoiced at the prospect of escaping from what they denominated a school of secession. Numbers of outsiders, also, when the news became known, rushed into the camp and gave loud voice to their feelings of indignation. The camp had in reality become a vast mob. Hurrahs for Jeff. Davis were given—many of the now disarmed soldiers joining in them. The United States troops were insulted in every possible manner, and rowdyism ruled the hour triumphantly. Officers had broken their swords and privates their guns before surrendering them. The task of marching the men out was a work of great difficulty, but at last it was accomplished, and the prisoners surrounded by two files of loyal troops. This act brought the fury of the mob to a climax, and when most of the troops had left, the few German soldiers that brought up the rear were attacked by the crowd, and showers of stones rattled upon them. The Federals presented their muskets, for the purpose of intimidating the mob, but without avail. The order to fire at length became necessary. It was given and executed with terrible effect, and the swiftly retreating mob left behind them from thirty to forty of their number, either dead or lying on the ground weltering in blood.

Many of the prisoners took the oath of fidelity to the Constitution and the laws, and were set free. A large amount of arms, ammunition, stores, camp equipage and stock was seized.

The event roused the secessionists in the city of St. Louis to the highest fury, and the night was made hideous by bloody encounters, in which several lives were lost.

The Legislature, then in session at Jefferson City, alarmed by these vigorous measures on the part of the Government, passed, the same afternoon, a "Military Bill," authorizing the Governor to call out and equip the State militia, and appropriating all the available funds of the State for that purpose, in addition to the issuing of bonds to the amount of $1,000,000, and authority to borrow $500,000 from the State banks. The bill also gave to the Governor supreme authority in all military matters, and subjected every able-bodied man in the State to such authority, under penalty of $150 fine. The telegraph was seized by order of Governor Jackson, and the bridges on roads leading from St. Louis destroyed, from fear that Federal troops might reach Jefferson City by railroad and arrest the conspirators.

The loyal citizens of St. Louis trembled for their safety—fearful alike of an uprising of the secessionists in ther midst and invasion from without. The "Home Guard" was organized—a reserve of volunteers proceeded to the arsenal for arms, and to take the oath of fealty, and other measures adopted for defence. On the afternoon of the 11th, a body composed mostly of Germans was assailed by a mob on their return from the arsenal. A fierce struggled ensued, and several were killed on either side.

The following day Brigadier-General Harney, of the regular army, reached St. Louis, and assumed command of the Military Department. Being himself a citizen of Missouri, and enjoying the confidence of the people in a very large degree, his presence produced a marked and salutary effect. By proclamation he demonstrated the madness and futility of any attempt to withdraw the State from her allegiance, and gave warning that any disturbance would be promptly suppressed. On the 14th he issued a second proclamation, declaring the "Military Bill" in conflict with the Constitution and laws of the United States, and therefore a nullity—equivalent to an ordinance of secession, and cautioned all good citizens against obeying it. The geographical position of the State, and her best interests, he asserted, rendered it absolutely necessary that she should remain in the Union, no matter what might be the position of the cotton States; and he emphatically declared that the whole power of the United States would be exerted, if necessary, to keep her within the national domain.

But secession influences were exceedingly active in almost all parts of the State, and the fact that the Governor and members of the Legislature were disorganizers, occasioned great apprehension in regard to her future destiny. The neighboring States of Iowa, Illinois, and Kansas made tender of liberal aid to the loyal men of Missouri, whenever required, to maintain their rights and their freedom. The secessionists now threw off their disguise, and resorted to violent aggressions and bitter persecutions of Union men. Many loyal citizens of Potosi, Washington county, seventy miles from St. Louis, were driven from the town, and their property injured or appropriated by the rebels.

Previous to the arrival of General Harney at St. Louis, Captain Nathaniel Lyon was commissioned a brigadier-general, having command of all the troops at St. Louis. On Tuesday, the 14th of May, he sent Captain Cole, of the Fifth Missouri Volunteers, with one hundred and fifty men, to Potosi, who surrounded the town before daylight, and arrested about one hundred and fifty persons. They were marched to the court-house, and fifty of them required to give parole not to take up arms against the Government. Nine of the leaders were taken to the St. Louis arsenal. On his return to St. Louis, Captain Cole led his troop through De Soto, Jefferson county, where a body of secession cavalry was collected, who fled at his approach. Thirty of their horses were captured by Captain Cole, and a large secession flag seized, which they had just raised on a pole in the town, and the stars and stripes elevated in its place.

On the 21st of May, General Harney was induced by Price to enter into an arrangement which was professedly designed to "allay excitement," and "restore peace;" and for this common object, the "general officers of the Federal and State Governments were to be respected." Price was recognized as "having by commission full authority over the militia of the State," to direct the whole power of the State officers, and to maintain order. General Harney admitted that this, faithfully performed, was all he required; and that he had no wish to make any "military movements" on his part. This was all that Price desired. Having by these plausible pretences tied the hands of General Harney, knowing that he would regard his obligations, the secession leaders continued their plots, and took measures for consummating the rebellion in the State. Loyal men in Missouri, as well as in other States, soon perceived the situation of affairs. The General Government became cognizant of the embarrassment in which General Harney was placed, and to release him from his engagements with General Price, as well as to secure the most efficient action at this stage of the rebellion, relieved him and appointed General Lyon to the command. Under his administration, vigorous, all-observant, prompt, and decisive, General Price found himself under a pressure very different from what he had anticipated.

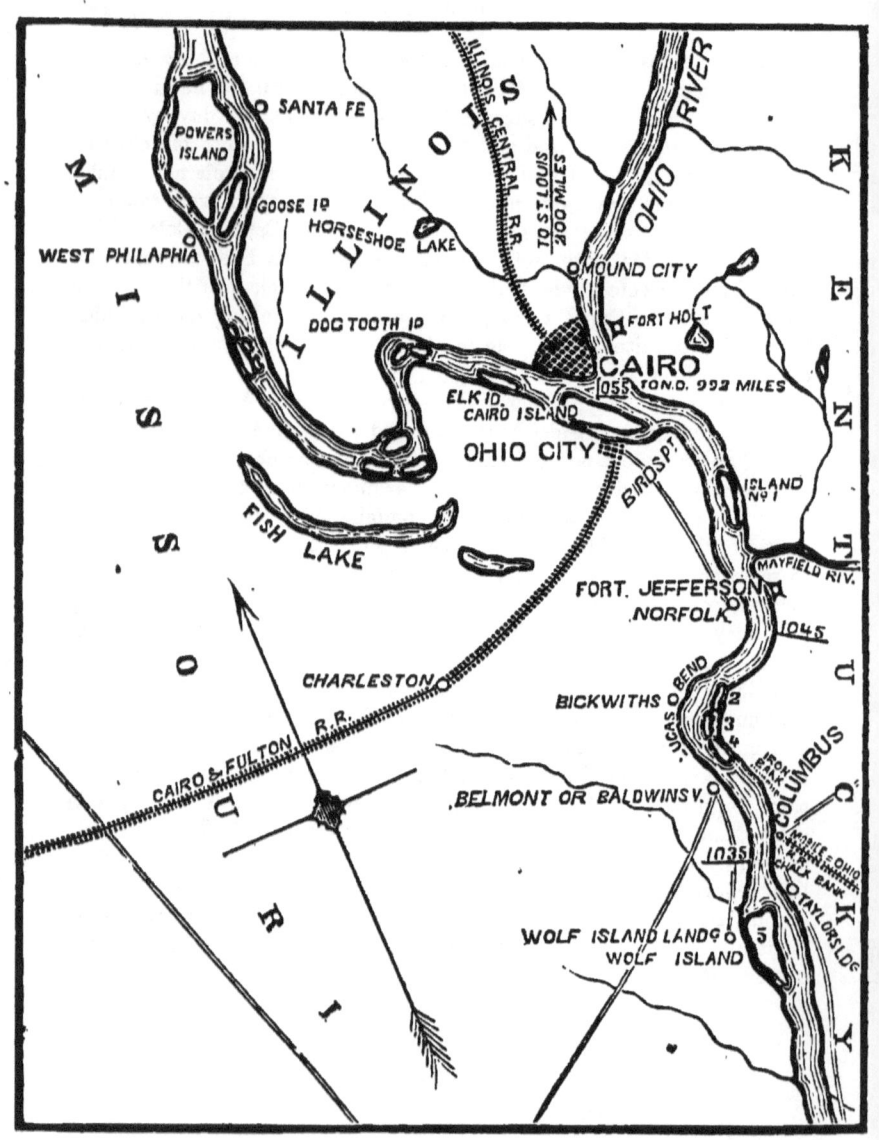

SECTION OF THE MISSISSIPPI RIVER,

SHOWING THE DISTANCES FROM NEW ORLEANS, AND THE ISLANDS BY THEIR NUMBERS.

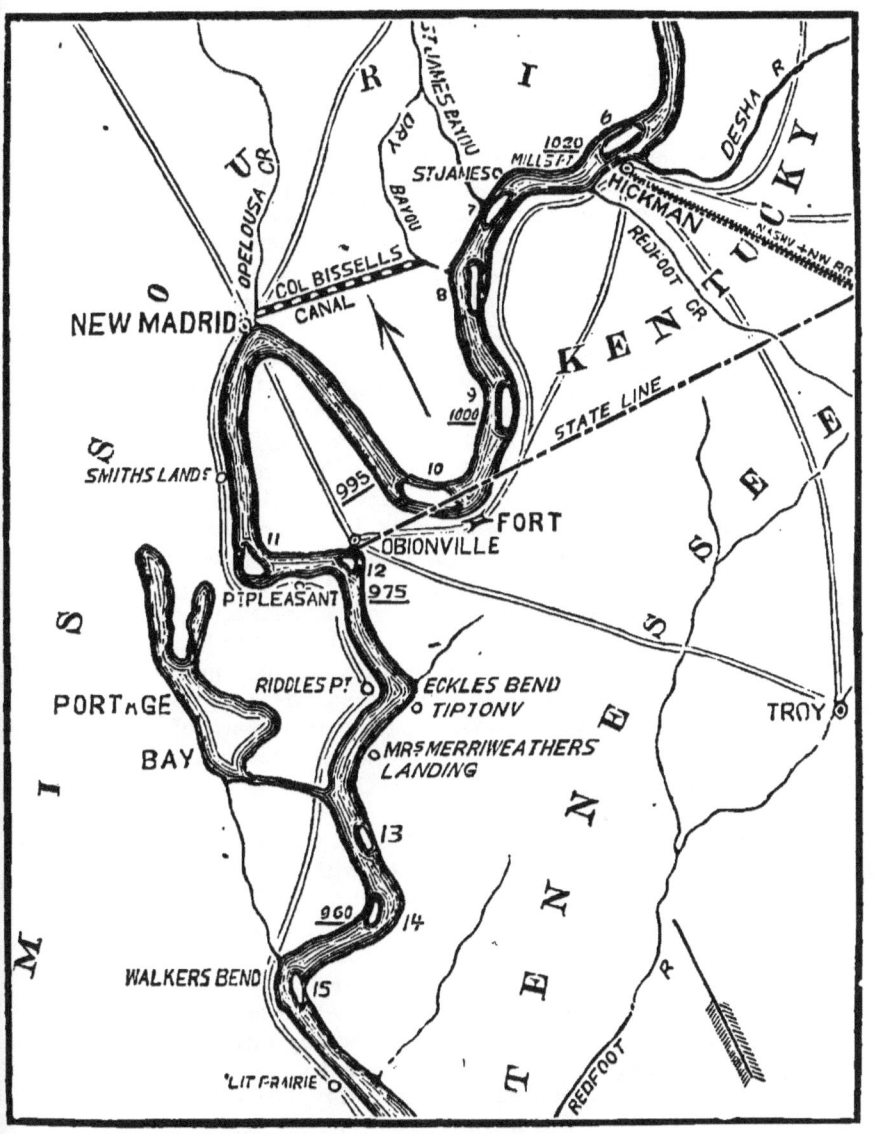

SECTION OF THE MISSISSIPPI RIVER.

SHOWING THE DISTANCES FROM NEW ORLEANS, AND THE ISLANDS BY THEIR NUMBERS.

CAIRO.

The most important strategic point in the West at this time was the city of Cairo, situated at the extreme southern point of the State of Illinois, at the junction of the Ohio and Mississippi rivers, where the latter river separates it from Missouri, and the former from Kentucky. It completely commands both streams, and in a military point of view may be properly considered as the key to what is usually denominated "the Great North-west."

The Illinois Central railroad connects it with Chicago, the greatest grain city of the world—with Lake Michigan, and the chain of lakes, and with the vast net work of railroads that branch from thence eastward. On the Missouri bank of the Mississippi river, two miles distant, is Ohio city, the initial point of the Cairo and Fulton railroad, designed to be extended to the Red river, in Arkansas, and thence to Galveston, in Texas. Twenty miles below, on the Kentucky side of the same giant river, is Columbus, which was soon after occupied and fortified by the rebel troops.

As soon as General Lyon was vested with supreme command in Missouri, one of his first steps was to order a body of Federal troops to take possession of Cairo, under General Prentiss, who immediately proceeded thither, with 6,000 men, and commenced fortifying the place.

On the 28th of May, Bird's Point, on the Missouri side of the river, a commanding position, was also occupied, by direction of General Lyon, by the Fourth Missouri Volunteers, under the command of Colonel Schuttner.

On the 11th of June, Governor Jackson, at his own instance, accompanied by General Price, had an interview with General Lyon and Colonel Blair at St. Louis, when he requested that the United States troops should be withdrawn from the soil of Missouri. General Lyon, as well as Colonel Blair, were equally blind to the advantages of this movement, and could not be made to see how the Government or the State of Missouri could be benefitted by a surrender of the field to the secessionists. Jackson and Price, finding their negotiations altogether vain, and under a previous arrangement that they were not to be arrested or interfered with before the 12th, returned to Jefferson City on the same night, and prepared for an immediate hostile demonstration. General Lyon, convinced that the only effective treatment demanded by the occasion consisted in an instant arrest of the conspirators, if possible, started up the river, and occupied Jefferson City on the 15th, the place having been abandoned by the rebels. On the 16th, he started in pursuit of Price and Jackson, and on the 17th landed about four miles below Boone ville, where their forces were collected, and had resolved to make a stand.

BATTLE OF BOONEVILLE.
June 17, 1861.

The enemy were exceedingly well posted, having had every advantage in the selection of their position. They occupied the summit of the ground, which rises upward from the river in a long slope, and were prepared to give the loyal troops a warm reception. General Lyon opened a heavy cannonade against the rebels, who retreated and dispersed into the adjacent wood, where, hidden by bushes and trees, they opened a brisk fire on his troops.

Arriving at the brow of the ascent, Captain Totten renewed the engagement by throwing a few nine-pounder explosives into their ranks, while the infantry filed oblique right and left and commenced a terrible volley of musketry, which was, for a short time, well replied to. The enemy were posted in a lane running towards the river from the road along which the army of the United States were advancing, and in a brick house on the north-east corner of the junction of the two roads. A couple of bombs were thrown through the east wall of that house, scattering the rebels in all directions. The well-directed fire of the German infantry, Lieutenant-Colonel Schaeffer, on the right, and General Lyon's company of regulars and part of Colonel Blair's regiment on the left of the road, soon compelled the enemy to seek a safer position. They clambered over the fence into a field of wheat, and again formed in line just on the brow of the hill. They then advanced some twenty steps to meet the Federal troops, and for a short time the artillery was worked with great rapidity and effect. Just at this time the enemy opened fire from a grove on the left of Lyon's centre, and from a shed beyond and still further to the left.

General Lyon halted, faced his troops about, and bringing his artillery to bear, opened fire on the rebels, and after a short engagement, killed thirty-five and took thirty prisoners, while the remainder fled in all directions, leaving many of their guns on the field. This accomplished, the General moved forward and took possession of the town. Neither General Price nor Governor Jackson were on the field of battle, though the latter was a spectator, and took an early opportunity to withdraw.

On the 17th of June, Colonel Boernstein was appointed Military Governor at Jefferson City, including Cole and the adjoining counties, the Governor and officers of the State having fled. Colonel Boernstein, on being questioned as to how long he should remain, replied, "I don't know, perhaps a year; so long as the Governor chooses to stay away."

I am Governor now, you see, till he comes back!" His idea of freedom of speech and the press he expressed freely, like this: "All people zall speak vot dey tink, write vot dey pleazhe, and be free to do any tink dey pleazhe—*only dey zall speak and write no treason!*"

The loyal people of the State now entered with zeal into the work of defence. Union Home Guards were organized at Hannibal, Herman, Rolla, Potosi, and many other places, and troops stationed at various points, of which two thousand five hundred kept guard over the Hannibal and St. Joseph, and one thousand over the North Missouri railroad; three thousand took their position also at Rolla, on the southwest branch of the Pacific railroad.

At Booneville, on the 18th, General Lyon issued a proclamation, in which he exposed the misrepresentations of the conspirators. The views they had endeavored to inculcate, that the United States would overrun the State with "military despotism," and "destroy State rights," were pronounced false—the glaring inconsistencies of the secessionists exposed,—and all malcontents solicited to return to their allegiance to the old flag.

On the same day, eight hundred Union Home Guards, under Captain Cooke, at Camp Cole, were surprised and routed by a body of rebels from Warsaw. Twenty-five were killed, fifty-two wounded, and twenty-three taken prisoners. The rebel loss was forty-five killed and wounded. At this time, Colonel Siegel, General Sweeney, and Colonel Brown, with their commands, were in the south-western part of the State, keeping the insurgents at bay.

General Price and Jackson were employed in raising all the turbulent elements of the State, and rallying followers to their standard. They were also greatly inspirited in their labors by the rumor that Ben. McCulloch was approaching with eight or ten thousand men to aid them in the overthrow of the government. On the 3d of July, General Lyon left Booneville with two thousand men, for the south-west. General Sweeney, who was in command of the south-west expedition, at Springfield, published a proclamation to the people, inviting them to remain loyal, and warning all rebels to disperse, take the oath of allegiance, and escape the penalties of their lawless career.

BATTLE OF CARTHAGE.
July 4, 1861.

Colonel Siegel arrived at Springfield on the 23d of June, and there learned that the rebel troops, under Jackson, were making their way southwardly through Cedar county. He immediately proceeded with his command, numbering over a thousand men, and a small field battery, towards Mount Vernon, for the purpose of intercepting him. On arriving at that point, he learned that General Price, in command of one thousand two hundred of the State troops, was encamped at Neosho, the county seat of Newton county, situated in the south-west corner of the State. His object there was to prevent Jackson going south, or Price going north. He appears to have decided to move southwardly and capture Price if possible, and afterwards attend to the Governor.

As he neared Neosho, on the 30th, the reports began to come in of the strength of Price, until his force was swelled to thirty-five hundred men, including Arkansas volunteers. The inhabitants expressed their welcome for Colonel Siegel, and detailed the most pitiable accounts of the oppression of the rebel soldiers.

On the 1st of July, the entire force entered the town without opposition, and encamped there, the enemy having retreated.

On the 2d, Colonel Siegel, learning that the forces of Price, Rains and Jackson had united at Dry Fork Creek, eight miles from Carthage, and having communicated with and received orders from Brig.-Gen. Sweeney, proceeded at once to attack them. He took up his line of march on the 3d, and on the morning of the 4th came upon the enemy, who were in great force.

The Federal command was about one thousand two hundred strong, including part of Colonel Salomon's regiment. They met the enemy in camp on an open prairie, three miles beyond Dry Fork, and after approaching within eight hundred yards, took position. The artillery was placed in the front; two six-pounders on the left, two six and two twelve-pounders in the centre, and two six-pounders on the right.

The fight commenced about half-past nine, the balls and shells of the enemy flying over the Union troops, and exploding in the open prairie.

At eleven o'clock the rebel twelve-pounders were silenced, and much disorder visible. About two o'clock the enemy's cavalry having attempted to outflank the Federal troops, they fell back upon their baggage trains to prevent their capture, Colonel Siegel changing his front. Proceeding in their retreat without serious casualty, they reached Dry Fork Creek, where eight hundred rebel cavalry had concentrated to cut them off; but a cross fire of canister and shrapnell soon broke their ranks, and they fell into wild confusion. Thence the Federal troops proceeded toward Carthage. Just before entering the town, Siegel posted three companies at Buck Creek, while the residue, in two columns, made a circuit around the town, the artillery pouring in a well-directed fire on the pursuing enemy. Night was approaching as the retreating army passed through Carthage, while the rebel horsemen withdrew to the woods on the Mount Vernon road.

Colonel Sigel, notwithstanding the great fatigue of the day—his men having been in action nearly twelve hours, and suffering severely from the heat and from lack of water—ordered his men to press on in retreat from Carthage. A forced march was made to Sarcoxie, in the southeast corner of Jasper county, (Carthage being the county seat,) a distance of twelve or fourteen miles. There they went into camp at three o'clock Saturday morning. In the afternoon of the next day, the retreat was continued to Mount Vernon, in Lawrence county, sixteen or eighteen miles east of Sarcoxie, where Siegel took a stand, and where his headquarters were located.

The Union loss was thirteen killed and thirty-one wounded; while, according to the most reliable accounts, the loss of the enemy could not have been less than three hundred in killed and wounded, and forty-five prisoners.

BATTLE AT MONROE, MO.
July 10, 1861.

Before daylight, on the morning of the 10th, Colonel Smith, with about six hundred men of the Sixteenth Illinois Volunteers, while encamped near Monroe Station, thirty miles west of Hannibal, was attacked by one thousand six hundred rebels under the command of Governor Harris. After a successful skirmish with the enemy, Colonel Smith retired to the Academy buildings for greater security. Here he was again attacked by an increased force of the rebels, and again succeeded in repulsing them. Determined on keeping them at bay, he sent messengers to Hannibal and other places for reinforcements, while the long-range rifles of his men told with fearful effect on his besiegers, and rendered two inferior pieces of artillery which they had brought to bear on him of but little use.

Three companies from Hannibal arrived first to the rescue, with two pieces of cannon of superior power to that of the enemy, and Colonel Smith immediately assumed the offensive. Toward evening, a body of cavalry under the command of Governor Wood, of Illinois, arrived and fell upon the rear of the enemy, when the struggle soon ended, and the rebel besiegers fled, with a loss of thirty killed and wounded, seventy-five prisoners, one gun, and a large number of horses. Of the Union troops, but four or five were severely wounded—none killed.

GUERRILLA BANDS IN MISSOURI.

In consequence of the disorganized condition of society in this State, bands of armed rebels took occasion to commit depredations upon the loyal citizens. Skirmishes became frequent, terror took the place of security, and distrust that of confidence. Men once high in public opinion and the councils of the nation became leaders in revolt, and encouraged by their example, the rabble threw off all restraint, and boldly became banditti.

Brigadier-General Pope was assigned command in northern Missouri, and from his headquarters at St. Charles, issued a proclamation, assuring loyal citizens of protection, and threatening disorganizers and secessionists with severe punishment. The State Convention assembled on the 22d of July, at Jefferson City, and passed an ordinance on the 23d by a vote of sixty-five to twenty-one, declaring the office of President of their body, held by General Sterling Price, to be vacant, and elected General Robert Wilson, a firm Union man, in his place. A committee of seven—one from each Congressional district, was appointed to report what action was necessary for the State to take in the crisis, and prepare an address to the people. The report was made, Union in all its bearings, and the Convention adjourned.

Major-General Fremont arrived at St. Louis on Sunday the 25th, and assumed military command.

The month of July was prolific in proclamations from the commanders of the rebel forces as well as of the Federal troops. On the 30th of July, rebel regiments from Tennessee, Mississippi and Kentucky, occupied New Madrid, on the Mississippi river, in the southern extremity of the State, and fortified it, and General Gideon J. Pillow issued a manifesto, in which he called upon the men of Missouri to enter his ranks. On the 1st of August, Jefferson Thompson, not to be outdone in the declamatory department, also issued a fiery proclamation.

Depredations had become so numerous and troublesome on the line of the Hannibal and St. Joseph's railroad, that General Pope appointed General S. A. Hurlbut to guard it, and divided it into sections, notifying the people that all who had property and interests at stake, would be expected to take an active part in their own protection and security. Citizens were appointed district superintendents.

The Address of the State Convention was published on the 31st of the month, and presented the question before the people in a masterly and able manner. The rebel Lieutenant-Governor, Thomas C. Reynolds, found refuge under the protection of General Pillow, at New Madrid, and on the same day, in the absence of Governor Jackson, issued a treasonable proclamation to the people of the State.

While these events were transpiring in other parts of the State, General Lyon had concentrated his forces at Springfield. Although he had perfect confidence in the bravery and discipline of his troops, he yet felt his inability to cope successfully with the superior numbers that he was warned were marching against him, and appealed to General Fremont to reinforce him. This General Fremont declined to do, alleging as a reason that his best regiments had been withdrawn to Washington and Cairo—to important points in the vicinity of St. Louis and the district under General Pope, that required to be guarded; and General Lyon and his little handful of brave men were left to meet, as best they might, the fast accumulating forces of the enemy who were bent on their destruction.

BATTLE OF DUG SPRINGS.
August 2, 1861.

General Lyon being thus compelled to act, and relying upon the steadiness and efficiency of his army and superior artillery, decided to meet the advancing foe with his small force, rather than retreat and leave a large district of country exposed to secession ravages. In order to meet the enemy on an open field he led his army as far south as Crane Creek, 10 miles below Springfield. The march commenced at 5 o'clock, on the afternoon of August 1st. The weather was intensely hot—the baggage wagons were scattered over a distance of three miles—the march slow, and one of great fatigue; and it was not until 10 o'clock that the camping ground was reached and the march ended, only to be resumed on the following morning, under a burning sun and with but a very scanty supply of water. Slight skirmishes occurred during the day, but the shells of Captain Totten's battery caused a hasty retreat on the part of the rebels. On the arrival at Dug Springs the advance continued on, while the skirmishers maintained a brisk fire with the retreating pickets of the enemy; Captain Steele's regular infantry taking the lead to the left, supported by a company of cavalry, the rest of the column being some distance in the rear. A body of rebel infantry were now seen approaching from the woods with the design of cutting off the Union forces. Captain Stanley drew up his cavalry, and opened upon them with Sharp's carbines. It was a desperate undertaking to keep the rebels in check—scarce one hundred Union cavalry against more than five times that number of the enemy. The rebel infantry kept up the firing for some minutes, when an enthusiastic lieutenant, giving the order to "charge," some twenty-five of the gallant regulars rushed forward upon the enemy's lines, and, dashing aside the threatening bayonets of the sturdy rebels, hewed down the ranks with fearful slaughter. Captain Stanley, who was amazed at the temerity of the little band, was obliged to sustain the order, but before he could reach his company they had broken the ranks of the enemy, who outnumbered them as twenty to one. Some of the rebels who were wounded asked, in utter astonishment, "whether these were men or devils—they fight so?"

The ground was left in possession of the Unionists, strewed with arms, and the men were seizing the horses and mules that had been left, when a large force of the enemy's cavalry were seen approaching—some three hundred or more. At the instant when they had formed, in an angle, Captain Totten, who had mounted a six and twelve-pounder upon the overlooking hill, sent a shell directly over them; in another minute, the second, a twelve-pound shell, landed at their feet, exploding, and scattering the whole body in disorder. The third, fourth, fifth and sixth were sent into their midst. The horsemen could not control their horses, and in a minute not an enemy was to be seen anywhere.

The Union loss was four killed and five wounded, one of whom subsequently died, while that of the enemy was very heavy, fully forty killed and an hundred wounded.

Having routed the enemy, General Lyon continued his march until he arrived at Curran, in Stone county, twenty-six miles from Springfield, where he encamped in order to avail himself of a choice of position. Here, from information that had been obtained of the opposing force and movements, a consultation was held with Generals Sweeney and Sigel, and Majors Schofield, Shepherd, Conant and Sturgis, and Captains Totten and Schaeffer, when it was determined to retire towards Springfield. The enemy was threatening a flank movement, and the necessity of keeping a communication open with Springfield was apparent to all the officers, and induced General Lyon to return to that point. An important consideration was, their provisions had to be transported one hundred miles—the depot being at Rolla—and the men were exhausted with the excessive heat, labors and privations of the campaign.

On the 5th of August they encamped at and near Springfield, and awaited the expected encounter with firm hearts, resolute bearing, and a determination to do or die.

SKIRMISH AT ATHENS, MISSOURI.
August 5, 1861.

While General Lyon and his noble associates were preparing to repel the anticipated attack of the forces of McCullough and Price, another event occurred that demands attention, and we turn to the town of

Athens, situated on the Des Moines river, twenty-five or thirty miles from Keokuk, Iowa.

For three or four weeks that portion of Missouri had been in a state of anarchy. There had been no security for life or property, nor any effectual efforts made to enforce the laws and restore order. Actual force had not as yet been resorted to, but the secessionists, determining to drive the Unionists out of the country, had visited their houses in squads—insulted the women, and threatened death, both by the rifle and rope, unless their orders to leave the country were complied with. Union men and their families, thus kept in a state of perpetual alarm, in many instances abandoned their homes and possessions, and obeying the cruel command, left the State. Some determined men, however, resolved not to be trampled to the earth without resistance, and formed companies of "Home Guards;" but they were powerless to protect themselves or friends from assassination, and being scattered far apart, were almost useless in a sudden emergency. Day by day the rebels became more bold, until finally the Unionists went into camp, at the town of Cahokia, eighteen miles from the Mississippi, in Clarke county, about six hundred strong, with a brave commander who had seen service in Mexico. They soon received two hundred and forty stand of arms from St. Louis, and thus became, in a measure, prepared to protect themselves and sustain their country's honor.

In the mean time, the rebels had formed a camp at Monticello, the county seat of Lewis county, about thirty miles south of Cahokia, under Martin Green, a brother of the ex-Senator.

A few days subsequently the Unionists received word that Green was about to attack them with eight hundred men, and sent to Keokuk and Warsaw for assistance. Keokuk did not respond, but the Warsaw Grays, Captain Coster, fifty in number, went over to the Union camp, though with the intention of acting only on the defensive; but no enemy appearing, Colonel Moore determined to rout the prowling bands of secessionists who were hovering around him, and for three days his men searched in vain to find an enemy to give them battle. Numerous secessionists were arrested, but liberated on taking the required oath, and Moore finally marched his command to Athens. A peace in the vicinity was proposed by the enemy, with the object of lulling the suspicions of the Union men, and inducing them to disperse; and through these influences the Colonel soon found his forces dwindled down to one half their original number.

But Green had not been idle. Constant recruiting had increased his force to nearly fifteen hundred men, and he visited Scotland and Knox counties, driving out the loyal citizens, insulting and abusing their families, and committing fearful depredations upon them. At length it was evident that he was about to attack the Unionists at Athens, and again they sent to Keokuk for assistance. Seventy of the militia from that place went up to Croton, a small town on the Iowa side of the Des Moines river, opposite Athens, but refused to cross. Moore, however, received reinforcements until his command reached four hundred, and encamped in the town, awaiting the moment of action, with his main force stationed on a street parallel to, and his right and left wings extending to the river.

There and in this order the Federalists were attacked by a force of from twelve to fifteen hundred men, with no chance of retreat, except by fording a stream fully three hundred yards in width, and exposed to a murderous fire. They were without artillery, while the enemy had an eight-pounder, which was placed on the brow of the hill, in a position to rake the principal street, while two imitation guns were placed in sight, intended to inspire a fear, which few men of that little band were capable of experiencing. The attack opened between five and six o'clock in the morning. At its very commencement, Lieutenant-Colonel Callahan, who commanded a company of cavalry in the rebel ranks, retired across the river and continued his flight until he reached the Mississippi river at Montrose.

A portion of Moore's infantry were also seized with a momentary panic, and fled across the river; but on seeing their companions stand firm, many returned and took part in the action. About three hundred only of the Unionists bore the brunt, and firm as regulars, delivered their fire with coolness and precision.

The fight, regular and irregular, lasted about an hour and a half, and then Colonel Moore led his centre to a charge, which routed the enemy, and left him and his brave associates undisputed masters of the field. The loss of the Unionists was ten killed and the same number wounded, and that of the rebels fourteen killed and forty wounded.

BATTLE OF WILSON'S CREEK
August 10, 1861.

General Lyon having returned to Springfield after his expedition to Curran, found himself greatly embarrassed by his position, and was forced by circumstances to determine the question whether he should, with his inferior force, give battle to the enemy now pressing upon him, or attempt a retreat to Rolla, encumbered with an immense train, and exposed to the probability of being compelled to defend himself at any point on the route where they might see fit to attack him. Their cavalry force was large, and with this they could by their celerity of movement cut off his communication and flank him whenever disposed. His appeals for reinforcements had not been granted, yet he was daily indulging the hope that he would soon be furnished a sufficient force to enable him to meet the enemy with a reasonable prospect of success. The days were passing on, the enemy was drawing nearer, and General Lyon was compelled to make his decision. The alternative was before him, either to retreat and leave the finest section of the State open to the ravages of the enemy, or make the attempt to expel the foe, even though he might sacrifice his own army in the effort. On the afternoon of the ninth of August, he held a consultation with his officers, when after a full discussion of the question, it was deemed advisable to attack the enemy in his camp at Wilson's Creek, nine miles south of Springfield. The attack was to be made simultaneously by two columns, at daylight on the following morning, Saturday the 10th; the first under command of General Lyon and the second under General Sigel.

The rebel leaders were Generals Sterling Price, Ben McCulloch and Brigadier-General John B. Clark. Somewhat singularly, both parties had planned an attack at the same hour, but the darkness of the night induced the rebels to postpone their movement. Their tents were pitched on either side of Wilson's Creek, extending a mile east and south of the road, crossing to two miles west and north of the same, the creek running nearly in the shape of a horizontal ∞. At the crossing of the Fayette road the hills on each side of the stream are from two to three hundred feet high, sloping gently on the north, and abrupt to the south side. The valley is about half a mile wide.

While on the verge of this, his last engagement, General Lyon was impressed with a sad presentiment—not regarding his own fate—but a fear for his brave command. A terrible responsibility rested upon him. With no adequate strength with which to cope with the enemy, hemmed in and growing weaker every day, his position was both perilous and painful. Unsupported, with his cry for help passed over, he saw nothing before him but the barren satisfaction of dying, bravely performing his duty, and protecting to the last the little army that he felt to be doomed. With these feelings—sadly bitter they must have been—this glorious man entered upon his last battle field.

The following day was one of remarkable quiet, and enlistments in the Springfield regiment went on rapidly. During the afternoon, Captain Woods' Kansas cavalry, with one or two companies of regulars, drove five hundred rebel rangers from the prairie west of the town, capturing eight and killing two men, without loss on their part.

At eight o'clock in the evening, General Sigel, with six pieces of artillery and part of Colonel Salomon's command, moved southward, marching until near two o'clock, and passing around the extreme camp of the enemy, where he halted, ready to press forward as soon as he should be apprised by the roar of General Lyon's artillery that the attack had begun. The main body, under General Lyon, had moved at the same time, and halted about five miles west of the city, from whence, after resting, they proceeded again about four miles in a southwesterly direction, and slept until 4 A. M. on Saturday, the day of battle.

At five o'clock the pickets of the enemy were driven in, and the northern end of the valley, with its thousands of tents and camp fires, became visible, and this most destructive battle, when the numbers engaged are considered, commenced. The roar of the artillery was terrible,—the rattling of the musket-balls was like a storm of great hailstones, and the clash of steel like hammers ringing on countless anvils.

Riding forward in the thick of the fight, his war-horse bearing him more proudly than usual that fatal day, General Lyon performed the work of a dozen heroes. A stern sadness was on his face—a resolute fire burned in the gray depths of his eyes. Twice was he wounded, leading on his men, and his war-steed fell under him, pierced to the heart with a bullet. Those who loved him grew anxious for his safety, for there was something wonderful in the steady courage that made him forget the wounds that would have driven another man from the field.

A member of his staff approached him as he stood by his dead horse, and seeing blood upon his forehead, asked if he was hurt.

"I think not seriously," he answered; and mounting another horse, he plunged again into the terrible melee.

At one time, when the whirlwind of battle was at its height, General Lyon desired his men to prepare for a charge, and the Iowans at once volunteered to go, and asked for a leader. On came the enemy, crushing in their strength, and there was no time for choice.

"I will lead you," exclaimed the impetuous and fearless General. "Come on, brave boys," said he, as he took his position in the van, while General Sweeney prepared to lead on a portion of the Kansas troops, and the serried ranks of glittering deadly steel resistlessly moved on.

In the very act of leading those valiant men, with his hand uplifted in an effort to cheer them on, and his noble face turned partly to his command, but not altogether away from the enemy, a bullet pierced him, and he fell, regretted not only by his devoted little army, but by every man, woman and child who ever heard how bravely he fought for the flag they love.

The battle continued from six until eleven o'clock, with but little cessation; and then the gallant Unionists, overwhelmed by superior numbers, were forced to retreat. In good order they accomplished it, and *the enemy made no attempt to follow,* though their combined forces amounted to about 20,000, while General Lyon's command did not exceed one-quarter of that number.

DEATH OF GENERAL LYON.

The Federal loss was 223 killed, 721 wounded and 292 missing; the rebel loss, (McCulloch's report,) 265 killed, 800 wounded, 30 missing; Price's report of Missouri troops, 156 killed and 517 wounded.

The death of the brave General Lyon was universally deplored. Countless were the tributes to his memory, and deep the sorrow when his body was borne homeward, surrounded with military honors. From amid the murky smoke and fearful glare of battle his soul was called home—the flashing eye dimmed—the good right hand unnerved, and the fiery spirit, that scorned danger and hated treason, was quenched forever.

SKETCH OF GENERAL LYON.

Brigadier-General Nathaniel Lyon was born in the State of Connecticut, in the year 1818, and entered the military academy at West Point in 1837, where he graduated four years afterwards with the rank of Second-Lieutenant of the Second Infantry. In February, 1847, he was made First-Lieutenant, and for gallant conduct in the battles of Contreras and Cherubusco, during the following August, was breveted Captain. On the 13th of September he was severely wounded in a most desperate assault, and in June, 1851, was promoted to a captaincy, which rank he held at the time of the troubles in Kansas. As has been stated, he was in command of the Missouri Volunteers at the capture of Camp Jackson, and was for his well-proven bravery and eminent ability, promoted to the rank which he held at the time of his death. In personal appearance he was about five feet and eight inches in height, his frame wiry and muscular. His hair was long and thick, his whiskers sandy and heavy, and his eyes of a blueish gray. His forehead was high and broad, with a firm expression of the lips, and a countenance that indicated an intellect of no ordinary capacity. He was a strict disciplinarian, endeared to his soldiers, and universally regretted by the whole country which followed him to the grave with deep and mournful affection. In his will, made before he started on his last campaign, he left his entire property to the country for which he gave his life.

RETREAT OF THE UNION ARMY.

The Federal troops remained in Springfield until Monday morning, and then started on their retreat towards Rolla, unmolested by the rebels. The enemy entered the town immediately after its evacuation by the Federal forces, having suffered the loss of a large portion of their tents, baggage and camp stores by the attack of Sigel.

Hundreds of the inhabitants of this section were now compelled to leave their homes, and the exiles were seen every day on the roads leading to St. Louis, fleeing for refuge beyond the lines of the insurgents, plundered of everything and destitute, having been forced to abandon their homes and property to save their lives.

The loyal people who remained were favored with proclamations by McCulloch and Price, which abounded in abuse and misrepresentation of the Federal army, and were filled with professions and promises which strikingly contrasted with their administration and conduct.

This calamity was not merely disastrous by its positive loss, but it gave a prestige of success to the rebel leaders, and afforded an opportunity for them to increase the spirit of rebellion among the people, as well as to nerve themselves to other enterprises. On the 17th, fifteen hundred recruits had assembled in Saline county, and were preparing to join General Price, or to engage in local operations in the surrounding counties. On the 18th, about one thousand men from Chariton county crossed the Missouri at Brunswick, with a large number of horses and wagons, on their march to join Price's division.

The rebels were so much elated with the death of General Lyon and the abandonment of Springfield by the Federal troops, that they became more reckless than ever in their depredations and persecutions of the loyal citizens. In St. Louis, on the 14th, after the retreat became known, they became so bold and defiant that General Fremont proclaimed martial law, and appointed Major J. McKinstry as Provost-Marshal.

On the 20th, a train on the Hannibal and St. Joseph's railroad was fired into, and one soldier killed and six wounded. The train was immediately stopped, and two of the guerrillas were killed and five captured.

Five days afterwards, on the 25th, Governor Gamble issued a proclamation calling for forty-two thousand volunteers to defend the State, restore peace and subdue the insurrection; the term of service to be six months, unless sooner discharged.

KENTUCKY.

Kentucky occupies a central position among the States, and is about four hundred miles in length, by one hundred and seventy in width at the widest point, where the State stretches from the boundary of Tennessee across to Covington, opposite Cincinnati, on the Ohio river. This river, from the Virginia line, follows a circuitous course along the Kentucky border, a distance of six hundred and thirty-seven miles, until it flows into the Mississippi at Cairo. The Cumberland and Tennessee rivers pass through the western part of the State, as they approach their confluence with the Ohio. Big Sandy river, two hundred and fifty miles in length, forms for a considerable distance the boundary between Kentucky and Virginia. The Kentucky river rises in the Cumberland Mountains and falls into the Ohio river fifty miles above Louisville. These geographical facts are necessary to a perfect understanding of the struggles in that State, and are worthy of remembrance.

When the President of the United States, on the 15th of April, 1861, issued his proclamation, in which the Governors of the States that had not already committed themselves to the cause of secession, were called upon to furnish their quota of seventy-five thousand men for the national defence, Beriah Magoffin, Governor of Kentucky, replied by saying, that, "Kentucky will furnish no troops for the wicked purpose of subduing her sister States."

This act was looked upon with both sorrow and surprise by the loyal people of that State, and was hailed with delight by the Confederate Government at Montgomery. The rebel Secretary of War congratulated Governor Magoffin on his "patriotic" response, informed him that Virginia needed aid, and requested him to send forward a regiment of infantry without delay to Harper's Ferry. Though sympathizing with the enemies of the Union, Governor Magoffin was not prepared to set at defiance the wishes of the people of Kentucky, and commit himself unqualifiedly to the work of overthrowing the Federal Government.

Many of the prominent men of Kentucky, including a large number of the wealthy citizens, were zealous in the promotion of the secession interests. The most indefatigable efforts were made by them to force the State into the ranks of the revolted States, and thousands of her young men were induced to enlist, and encamp on the adjoining borders of Tennessee, waiting for the hour when they could sweep Kentucky with the rush of armed battalions, and overwhelm her peace and prosperity with the clash of arms, and the thunders of artillery. The loyal sentiment was, however, in the ascendant, although it was subdued and overawed to a considerable extent. Between the two forces, therefore, it was deemed expedient by her rulers that Kentucky should hold a neutral position, and not ally herself with either the Federal or the Confederate interest.

To render this neutrality more certain, on the 8th of June, General S. B. Buckner, then the acknowledged commander of the State militia, entered into negotiations with General McClellan, at Cincinnati, the terms of which stipulated that Kentucky should protect the United States property, and enforce all the United States laws within her limits—that her neutrality should be respected by the Federal army, *even though the Southern forces should occupy her soil;* " but in the latter case General McClellan should call upon the authorities of the State to remove the said Southern forces from her territory;" if the State were unable to accomplish this, then the Federal forces might be called in.

This negative position was found, however, to be one of positive advantage and aid to the traitors. They desired to secure a "masterly inactivity" on the part of loyal men, of which they might avail themselves by secret organizations. Taking advantage of this confessed neutrality, large numbers of the young men of Kentucky were enticed into Buckner's camp; while bodies of men from Tennessee were thrown into several localities in the southern and western portions of the State, and boldly avowed their determination to march on Frankfort, the capital, and revolutionize the State. Home Guards were organized by the loyal men, and it became apparent, that if the tide were not resisted by active measures, there was no security for Kentucky.

The election for members of the Legislature, however, early in August, the result of which showed an overwhelming majority in favor of the Union, signed the death-warrant of neutrality, and thenceforth Kentucky was regarded as loyal to the Union. The Legislature assembled at Frankfort on the 5th of September, ordered the United States flag to be hoisted on the court-house, and proceeded to adopt various measures calculated to promote the Union cause in the State.

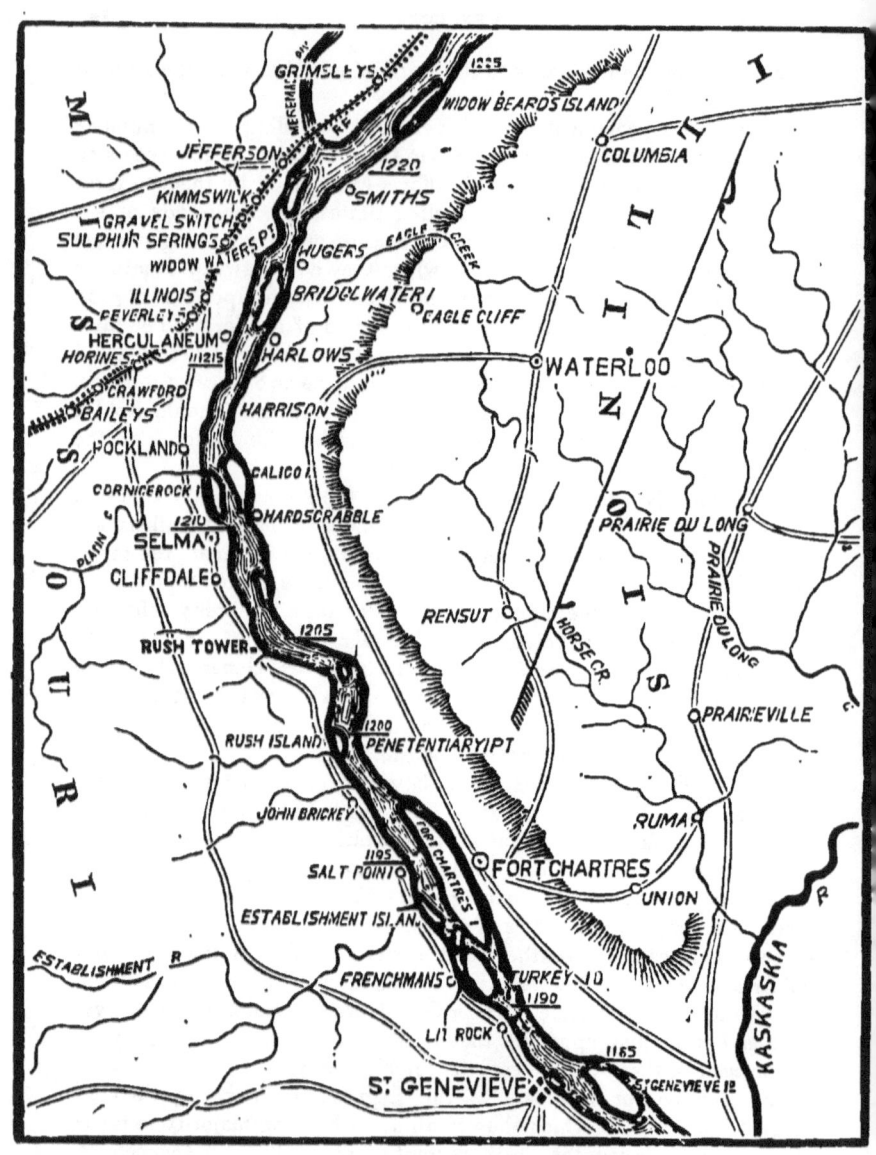

SECTION OF THE MISSISSIPPI RIVER.
SHOWING THE DISTANCES FROM NEW ORLEANS.

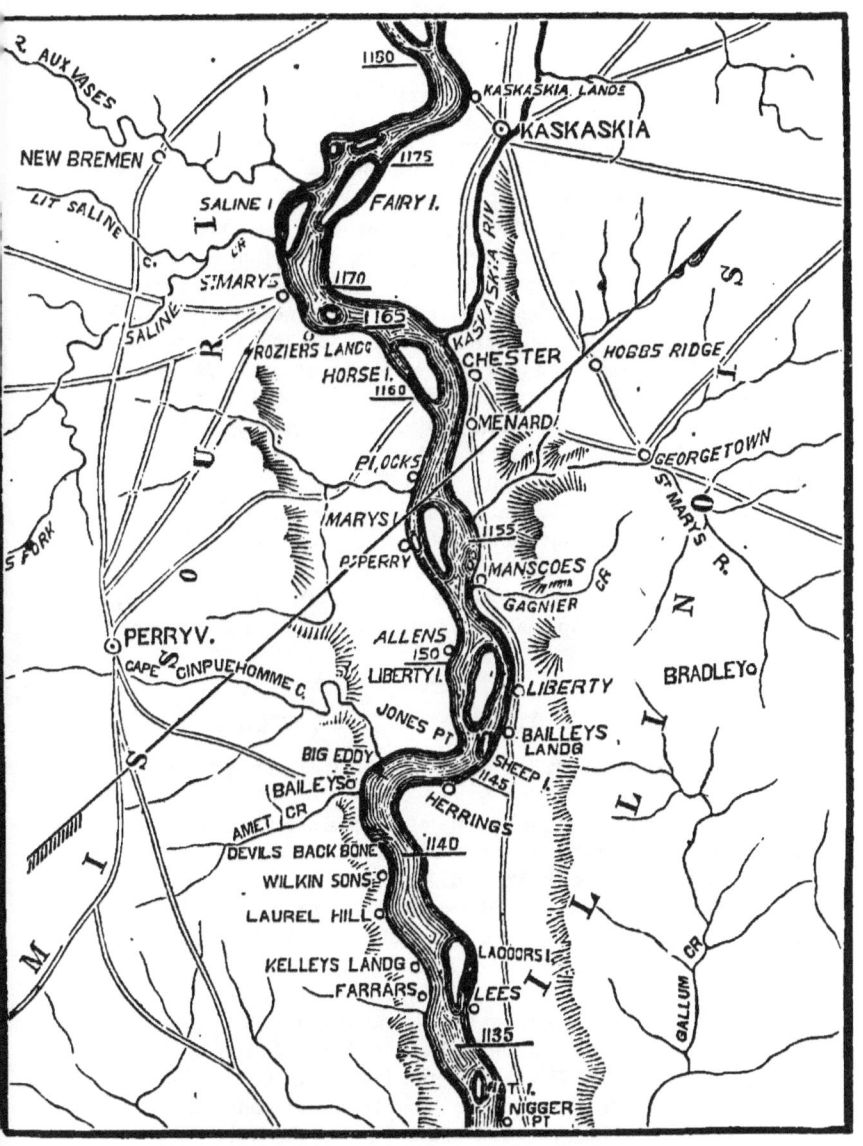

SECTION OF THE MISSISSIPPI RIVER.

SHOWING THE DISTANCES FROM NEW ORLEANS.

The great Union majority now revealed gave such decided evidence that Kentucky was not likely to be seduced from her loyalty, that the secessionists became convinced of the necessity of accomplishing their purpose by other means. The rebel forces were, therefore, ordered to take possession of several important points, which they did on the 4th of September, and commenced fortifying Hickman and Columbus—the former being in the western part of the State, near the line, and the latter some twenty-five miles further north, on the Mississippi river. Generals Pillow and Polk now took command of the rebel troops, and were soon reinforced, their combined forces amounting to thirteen regiments of artillery, six field batteries, a siege battery, three battalions of cavalry, three steamers, and a gunboat. In the mean time, Jefferson Thompson, with two regiments, took possession of Belmont, on the Missouri side, opposite Columbus. The assumed neutrality having thus been broken by this invasion, the Federal commander, General U. S. Grant, then at Cairo, Illinois, lost no time in making a movement to intercept the further progress of the rebels northward. He accordingly sent a sufficient force up the Ohio, to the mouth of the Tennessee river, and effected

THE OCCUPATION OF PADUCAH.

On Thursday evening, the 5th of September, the gunboats Tyler and Conestoga were ordered to convey the troops to Paducah. The Ninth Illinois, under the gallant Major Philips, and the Twelfth Illinois, Colonel John McArthur, with four pieces of Smith's Chicago Artillery, under Lieutenant Charles Willard, embarked on the steamers G. W. Graham and W. H. B., and left Cairo at 11 o'clock, P. M., the gunboat Tyler, Captain Rogers, leading, and the Conestoga, Captain Phelps, in the rear. The fleet pushed out into the stream amid the cheers of thousands of spectators, and steamed grandly up the Ohio.

They reached Paducah about eight o'clock, A. M., on Friday, the 6th. The troops were speedily disembarked. Colonel McArthur's regiment landed at the Marine Hospital, in the lower part of the city, and the Ninth at the foot of Main street. The Twelfth found quarters at the hospital, and the Ninth repaired to the depot of the Ohio and New Orleans railroad. The citizens were sullen and unfriendly, and closed their places of business.

On arriving at the depot the troops found that the rolling stock of the road had all been removed, but a large quantity of stores for the confederate army was discovered, and promptly seized. They were marked for Memphis, New Orleans, and other points south, and were worth about $20,000.

Captain Rogers immediately took possession of the telegraph office. The post-office was next visited, and a large amount of rebel correspondence secured. Five companies of infantry, and a battery of Smith's Light Artillery, Lieutenant Willard, were sent under Major Philips down the railroad about seven miles without meeting any of the rebel troops. Pillow was reported to be advancing, and a large bridge and trestle work were burnt to prevent him from reaching Paducah and falling upon the place by surprise.

A rumor became current that a large force of rebels from Tennessee were on their way down the Tennessee river in steamboats. To ascertain the facts, and to intercept their progress, the gunboat Conestoga was dispatched up the river some thirteen miles to watch the rebel movements, and to capture suspicious vessels. Although no hostile forces were seen, a steamer was discovered on Friday, which, on seeing the Conestoga, turned about, was run ashore, and the officers and crew abandoned her. It was the Jefferson, a small stern-wheel boat, loaded with a cargo of tobacco. On Saturday the Conestoga captured a fine propeller, called the John Gault, and a boat called the Pocahontas, belonging to John Bell, of Tennessee. The prizes were all safely taken to Cairo.

The inhabitants of Paducah were now seized with panic, and large numbers left the town, apprehending an attack from Pillow, in which case they expected the gunboats would freely use shell. On Saturday part of Colonel Oglesby's Eighth regiment, the Forty-first Illinois, and the American Zouave regiment, from Cape Girardeau. entered the town, increasing the forces to about 5,000 men.

THE REBEL TROOPS ORDERED TO WITHDRAW FROM KENTUCKY.

On the 9th of September a dispatch from General Polk to Governor Magoffin was laid before the Legislature, the substance of which was that he had occupied Columbus and Hickman, on account of reliable information that the Federal forces were about to possess those points; that he considered the safety of Western Tennessee and of the rebel army in the vicinity of Hickman and Columbus demanded their occupation, and that, as a corroboration of that information, the Federal troops had been drawn up in line on the river opposite to Columbus prior to its occupation by them, causing many of the citizens of Columbus to flee from their homes for fear of the entrance of the Federal troops. General Polk proposed substantially that the Federal and rebel forces should be simultaneously withdrawn from Kentucky, and to enter into recognizances and stipulations to respect the neutrality of the State.

But it was well known that the cry of neutrality was only an invention of the enemy to work his plans in Kentucky, so that when the appointed time should come Kentucky would swarm with rebels from

Tennessee and Virginia; and two days afterwards both branches of the Legislature, by a vote of 71 to 26, adopted a resolution directing the Governor to issue a proclamation ordering the rebel troops then encamped in the State to evacuate Kentucky. A counter-resolution, ordering both Federal and rebel troops to leave the soil, was negatived under the rules of order. Governor Magoffin accordingly issued a proclamation to the effect that "the government of the Confederate States, the State of Tennessee, and all others concerned, are hereby informed that Kentucky expects the Confederate or Tennessee troops to be withdrawn from her soil unconditionally."

ATTEMPT TO FORM A REVOLUTIONARY GOVERNMENT IN THE STATE.

After this decisive action of the Legislature, which effectually destroyed the hopes entertained by the conspirators of obtaining a semblance of legal authority for their designs, their next expedient was to hold an informal meeting at Russelville, a small town in the southern portion of the State, on the 29th of October. Here they drew up a declaration of grievances, in which they charged the majority of the Legislature with having betrayed their solemn trust, by inviting into the State the "armies of Lincoln," with having abdicated the government in favor of a military despotism, and thrown upon the people and the State the horrors and ravages of war. They recommended the immediate arming of a "Guard" in each county, of not less than one hundred men, to be paid as Confederate troops, subject to the orders of the "Commanding-General." Finally, they called for a Convention to be held at Russelville, on the 18th of November, to be "elected, or appointed in any manner possible," by the people of the several counties, for the purpose of "severing forever our connection with the Federal Government."

John C. Breckinridge, late Vice-President of the United States, was appointed one of the commissioners to carry out the orders of the convention. This Convention met at the time designated, composed of about two hundred persons, professing to represent sixty-five counties, though self-appointed, and without any form of election. On the 20th of November they adopted a "Declaration of Independence, and an Ordinance of Secession," and appointed a "Provisional Government, consisting of a Governor, and a Legislative Council of Ten," and dispatched H. C. Burnett, W. E. Simms, and William Preston, as commissioners to the Confederate States. On the 9th of December, the "Congress" of the Confederate States, in session at Richmond, passed an "Act for the admission of the State of Kentucky into the Confederate States of America," as a member "on equal footing with the other States of the Confederacy."

George W. Johnson, of Scott county, who was chosen as Provisional Governor, by the Convention, in his "Message," declared his willingness to resign "whenever the regularly elected Governor [Magoffin] should escape from his virtual imprisonment at Frankfort."

Governor Magoffin, in a letter, dated December 13, 1861, says of this Convention, "I condemn its action in unqualified terms. Situated as it was, and without authority from the people, it cannot be justified by similar revolutionary acts in other States, by minorities to overthrow the State Governments. My position is, and has been, and will continue to be, to abide by the will of the majority of the people of the State, to stand by the Constitution and laws of the State of Kentucky, as expounded by the Supreme Court of the State, and by the Constitution and laws of the United States, as expounded by the Supreme Court of the United States. To this position I shall cling in this trying hour as the last hope of society and of constitutional liberty."

MILITARY MOVEMENTS OF THE REBELS IN KENTUCKY.

While Pillow and Polk were invading the south-western part of the State, General Zollicoffer was operating in the east. With some six thousand rebels he came to Cumberland Ford—which is situated near the point where the corner of Virginia runs into Kentucky—capturing a company of Home Guards. On the 17th of September the Legislature received a message from Governor Magoffin communicating a telegraphic dispatch from General Zollicoffer, announcing that the safety of Tennessee demanded the occupation of Cumberland and the three long mountains in Kentucky, and that he had occupied them, and should retain his position until the Federal forces were withdrawn and the Federal camp broken up.

That portion of Kentucky lying west of the Cumberland river was then declared under insurrectionary control, and Secretary Chase instructed the Surveyor at Cairo to prevent all commercial intercourse with that section, and to search all baggage and all persons going thither. Just about the same time the gunboat Conestoga captured the rebel steamers Stephenson and Gazelle, on the Cumberland, and one of them was found to contain one hundred tons of iron.

DECISIVE MEASURES OF THE LOYAL STATE GOVERNMENT.

When the seditious plans of General Buckner became too plain for concealment, the Legislature found it necessary to depose him from the command of the State troops, and General Thomas L. Crittenden, a loyal citizen, was appointed to fill that position. Governor Magoffin, in obedience to the resolutions and the enactments of the Legislature, promptly issued a proclamation, authorizing that officer to execute the purposes contemplated by the resolutions of the Legislature in reference to the expulsion of the invaders, and General Crittenden ordered the military to muster forthwith into service. Hamilton Pope, Brigadier-General of the Home Guard (Union), called on the people of each ward in Louisville to meet and organize into companies for the protection of the city.

Great excitement existed at this time in Louisville. The Union Home Guards began to assemble, while other Union forces were arriving and being sent to different portions of the State. At nine o'clock on the morning of the 18th, when the Government troops reached Rolling Fork, five miles north of Muldragh's Hill, they found that the bridge over the fork had been burned by rebels under General Buckner, who were then upon the hill.

The Legislature passed, over the veto of the Governor, a resolution to the effect that, as the rebels had invaded Kentucky and insolently dictated the terms upon which they would retire, General Robert Anderson, the hero of Fort Sumter, one of Kentucky's sons, should be invited to take instant charge of that department, and that the Governor must call out a sufficient force to expel the invaders from her soil. General Anderson, who had been previously appointed by the Government to command in Kentucky, responded to the call, and on the 21st of September issued a proclamation calling upon the people of Kentucky to rally to the support of the Union.

General S. B. Buckner, who had previously acted under neutrality pretences, now gradually assumed an attitude of hostility, and in September was openly arrayed against the Government. On the 12th he issued an inflammatory proclamation to the people of Kentucky, in which he declared that he sought to make no war upon the Union, but only against the tyranny and despotism of the Federal Government, which was about to make the people of Kentucky slaves. By such means as these he aimed to arouse the freemen of that State to arms and to rebellion. The proclamation was dated at Russelville, while he was entrenching a position at Bowling Green, about thirty miles from the Tennessee line, on the Louisville and Nashville railroad.

Very soon the Government formed a new department, consisting of Ohio, Indiana, and that part of Kentucky within a commanding distance of Cincinnati, placing it under the charge of General Mitchell, in order to relieve General Rosecranz in Western Virginia and General Anderson of a part of their responsibility, and enable them to give greater attention to their own specific departments. The department under General Anderson seemed to require similar military discipline to that of Annapolis and Maryland, and, as a commencement, Martin W. Barr, the telegraphic news reporter of the Southern Associated Press, the

medium for the transmission of correspondence from traitors at the North to rebels in the South, was arrested, together with ex-Governor Morehead and Reuben T. Murrett, one of the proprietors of the *Courier*, a rebel sheet.

The State had now become a portion of the ground which was to be so fiercely contested. Rebel journals and leaders made no concealment of their purpose to wrest Kentucky from the Union at every hazard. The Ohio river was to be the boundary of the Southern empire, and notwithstanding the emphatic voice of her people, all the energy of the combined forces of the rebel armies were to be brought to bear upon the work. The fact could be no longer disguised from the people, and the loyal men, finding that their patience and confidence in the disloyal portion, with their previous consent to a negative position of neutralty, were in vain, boldly declared that the time had come to arouse and resist the impending ruin. The attempt of the conspirators of the Cotton States to make Kentucky the battle-field, along with Virginia, was to be defeated at every cost, and the people, rising to a comprehension of their responsibility, hastened to the work of organization and defence.

Among the loyal men of the State to whom the highest honor is due for their bold and stirring advocacy of the Union, and for the most summary measures which patriotism and honor could dictate, were Hon. JOSEPH HOLT, and Hon. LOVELL S. ROUSSEAU, of the State Senate, and the gifted divine, R. J. Breckinridge, D.D.

NAVAL OPERATIONS.

At the commencement of hostilities the Government was unprepared to meet the naval requirements incident to the contest which had so suddenly been forced upon it. The necessity of a stringent blockade of the entire southern coast had become apparent; while the protection and supply of the naval stations in the rebel States still in possession of our forces, and the recapture of those which had been seized, required a a navy vastly greater than that at the command of the Government; and no time was lost in preparing as far as practicable to meet this emergency.

Long before the attack on Fort Sumter, the enemy had given evidence of a determination forcibly to destroy their relations with the Government by seizing the revenue cutters belonging to the United States stationed in the harbors of Charleston, Pensacola and New Orleans, contemporaneously with their appropriation of the forts, arsenals, marine depots and other property belonging to the Government within the limits of the disloyal States.

Immediately upon the opening of hostilities, and to give the pretence of law and authority to the proceedings now determined on, Jefferson Davis, on the 17th of April, 1861, by proclamation, invited men of every class, without regard to nationality, to become privateers under letters of marque, to be issued by the Confederate Government.

A "reward" of twenty dollars was offered by the Confederate Congress for every life taken by these privateers in conflict with a Federal vessel, and twenty-five dollars for each prisoner. In view of the extensive commerce of the United States, the large number of vessels sailing to all parts of the world, and the supposed inefficiency of our navy, confident expectations were entertained by the rebels of a rich harvest of wealth from this source, as well as of the destruction of our commerce. The hope was also indulged that many vessels would be secretly fitted out in northern ports to engage in this enterprise. This hope soon proved to be futile; while the want of proper vessels for the service in their own ports, and the scarcity of able seamen, and, more potent than either, the rigorous blockade that was soon established, presented insurmountable obstacles to their plans. The English Government, by the Queen's proclamation of June 1, decided that privateers should not take prizes to any of her ports; and France and Spain also declared that such vessels should remain but twenty-four hours within their harbors, and prohibited either confiscation or sale during such stay.

The first offensive act of the war on the part of our navy was the attack on Sewall's Point battery, in Virginia, on May 18, 1861. This battery, then not completed, was situated at the mouth of Elizabeth river, commanding also the entrance to James river. On the 18th the United States steamer Star, two guns, and transport Freeborn, of four guns, opened their fire and dislodged the enemy from their entrenchments. During the night, however, the works were repaired and occupied by a larger force. On the following day the steamer Star again opened fire on them, and after exhausting her ammunition retired.

On the 31st of May, the United States steamers Thomas Freeborn, Anacosta and Resolute attacked the rebel batteries at the railroad terminus at Acquia Creek. As the tide was out, the vessels could not approach near enough to accomplish their reduction. On the following day the fire was renewed by the vessels, under command of Captain Ward, and returned by the enemy with spirit from three batteries on the shore, and one on the heights above. They were soon driven from the shore batteries, but that on the hill was at an elevation which could not be reached by shot from the gunboats. The vessels were struck several times, with but little damage, and two men were wounded. The loss of the enemy was not ascertained.

On the 6th of June, while reconnoitering on the James river, the steamer Harriet Lane discovered a heavy battery at Pigs Point, at the mouth of the Nansemond river, opposite Newport News. She opened fire on it to discover its character, and finding from the response that it was too formidable for her guns, she withdrew, having five men wounded in the encounter.

On the 27th of June, Commander J. H. Ward of the steamer Freeborn, accompanied by a party of men from the Pawnee, under Lieutenant Chaplin, who were engaged in erecting a breastwork at Matthias Point, on the Potomac, were attacked by a large force of the enemy. The men on shore were exposed to a galling fire, but made good their retreat in their boats, three only being wounded, taking all their arms and implements with them. Commander Ward immediately opened fire from his vessel on the attacking party, and drove them to cover. While sighting one of the guns of the Freeborn, Commander Ward was struck by a rifle ball, mortally wounded, and died within an hour.

Captain JAMES H. WARD was born in the year 1806, in the city of Hartford, Connecticut. His early days were spent in the usual studies of youth, and on the 4th of March, 1823, he entered the United States service, sailing as midshipman, under Commodore McDonough, in the frigate Constitution. After serving faithfully for four years with McDonough, he was promoted to the position of lieutenant, and was for some time attached to the Mediterranean service. Many years of his life were spent on the coast of Africa, and he was also in the gulf, as commander of the United States steamer Vixen. Nearly all his naval life was spent on the ocean. For some time he had a very responsible professorship in the naval school at Annapolis, and later was in command of the receiving ship North Carolina. His talents were not entirely devoted to naval affairs, for he is well known as an author by his works, entitled "Steam for the Million," "Ordnance and Gunnery," and "Naval Tactics." The news of his death brought sorrow to many, and his memory is safely embalmed in the heart of an appreciating nation.

THE EXPEDITION TO CAPE HATTERAS
August 26-30, 1861.

The first naval achievement of the war which was attended with any important result was the successful attack of the fleet under Commodore Stringham, accompanied by General B. F. Butler, and his land forces, upon Forts Hatteras and Clark, at Hatteras Inlet, North Carolina.

The whole length of the Atlantic coast from Chesapeake Bay to Charleston has a peculiar character. A long line of low, sandy beaches, of variable width and elevation, rise above the surface of the ocean,

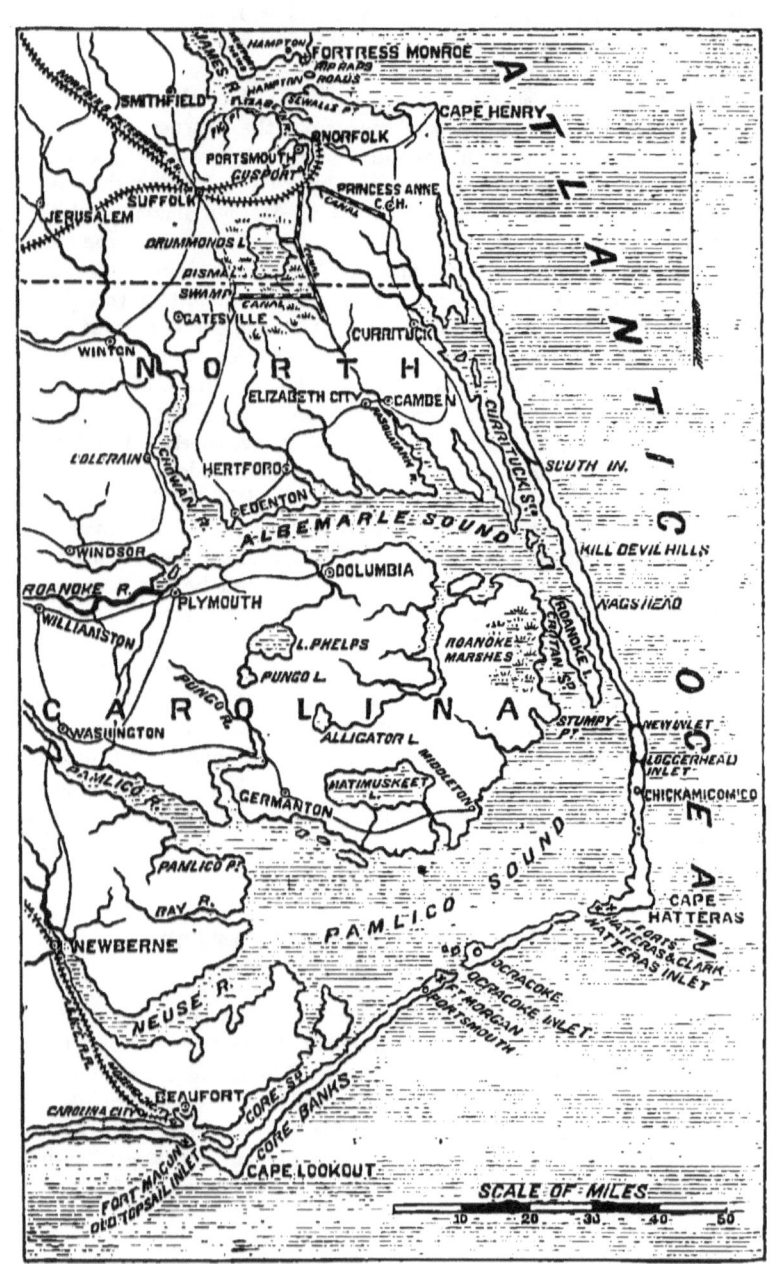

ATLANTIC COAST FROM FORTRESS MONROE TO FORT MACON.

broken at occasional intervals by a passage, ordinarily of shallow depth of water, communicating from the open sea with the lagoons inside. These bodies of water, by the indentations of the main land and the mouths of the rivers, expand into large bays, of which Pamlico and Albemarle Sounds are the principal. These two form capacious highways of safe and easy communication along the coast, and through the Dismal Swamp Canal connect with the Chesapeake Bay, on the north, at Norfolk, Va.

At the south-western extremity of the long, narrow island or beach, the outer angle of which has received the name of Cape Hatteras, and which gives its name to the inlet, the rebels had erected two strong fortifications known as Forts Hatteras and Clark. Captain Samuel Barron, late of the United States navy, was here in command of the naval forces, while Colonel William F. Martin, of the Seventh North Carolina Volunteers, and Major W. S. G. Andrews, commanded the garrisons.

Hatteras Inlet was one of the principal passages through which the vessels of the Confederacy made their way, in defiance of the blockade, and which it was desirable to command with the Federal forces and fleet. An expedition was accordingly planned, and the preparations were far advanced when General Wool reached Fortress Monroe. All things having been made ready, on the 26th of August, the fleet, under Commodore S. H. Stringham, left Hampton Roads for its destination. It consisted of the flag-ship Minnesota, Captain G. A. Van Brune, having in company the United States steamers Wabash, Captain Samuel Mercer; Monticello, Commander John P. Gillis; Pawnee, Commander S. C. Rowan; Harriet Lane, Captain John Faunce; United States chartered steamers Adelaide, Commander Henry S. Stellwagen; George Peabody, Lieutenant R. B. Lowry; and tug Fanny, Lieutenant Pierce Crosby, all of the United States navy. The transports Adelaide and George Peabody, towing schooners with surf-boats on them, and the Monticello and Pawnee surf-boats only.

General Butler embarked his land forces on the two transports Adelaide and George Peabody, having with him five hundred of the Twentieth New York regiment, Colonel Weber; two hundred and twenty of the New York Ninth regiment, Colonel Hawkins; one hundred of the Union Coast Guard, Captain Nixon; and sixty of the United States Second Artillery, Lieutenant Larnéd.

The expedition left Fortress Monroe on Monday, the 26th, at one o'clock, P. M., and the last vessel had arrived at Hatteras Inlet by four o'clock on Tuesday afternoon. Preparations for landing troops were made the same evening, and at daylight the next morning dispositions were made for an attack upon the forts by the fleet, and the landing of the troops.

CAPTURE OF FORTS HATTERAS AND CLARK.

At four o'clock on Wednesday morning, all hands were called, and by five, the whole fleet was in a state of the greatest activity with preparations for the conflict. The Monticello, the Pawnee, and the Harriet Lane were sent to cover and assist generally in landing the troops, and they took up a position about two miles and a half north of the forts. The Cumberland was taken in tow by the Wabash. The iron and flat boats were meanwhile filling with troops from the steamers, and one hundred marines who had been taken from the war vessels to increase the land forces. The Wabash went up to the battery first, drawing the Cumberland after her. The Minnesota followed, and as they drew near the point, the two batteries and the barracks of the rebels were plainly visible. In the sound, beyond the narrow neck of land, several vessels —three steamers, some schooners under sail, and a brig laying at anchor under the guns of the forts—were clearly seen.

Colonel Max Weber, of the Twentieth New York, was appointed to command the land expedition, and about ten o'clock the boats left the transports with the first detachments of the storming forces. They consisted of forty-five men of the New York Twentieth, Captain Larner and Lieutenant Loder; forty-five marines from the Minnesota; sixty-eight men, New York Ninth regiment, Captain Jardine; one hundred and two men of Twentieth New York; twenty-eight men Union Coast Guard, Captain Nixon; and twenty marines, making a total of three hundred and eighteen men.

A heavy surf was breaking on the beach at the time, and the landing was dangerous. The landing was handsomely covered by the Monticello and Harriet Lane. Compelled to wade through the water to the shore from the boats, the men were wet by the surf, and were obliged to march with their ammunition in no better condition than themselves.

The challenge from the Wabash, at a few minutes before ten o'clock, was soon responded to from Fort Clark, the smaller of the two, and for several hours the firing was maintained on both sides with great spirit. The shot from the forts fell short of the vessels, two or three only striking the Monticello, but without doing any damage. After getting the range of the forts from the various vessels of the fleet, the shells that were hurled into the enemy's strongholds were directed with great precision, and almost uniformly reached the points at which they were aimed.

Three hours of cannonading from fifty-seven heavy guns produced a marked effect on the smaller fort, and by half-past one o'clock it became evident that the enemy were becoming discouraged, their firing having been almost abandoned. At this time, the flags of both forts were hauled down, the troops already landed were seen hurrying with their colors towards Fort Clark, and boats laden with men were trying to escape in the sound. General Butler telegraphed from the Harriet Lane a request for the fleet to cease firing, and the proper signal was made, but apparently not fully understood. About thirty of the Federal troops were by this time in and around Fort Clark, and had already raised the Union flag. They were fired upon by the Pawnee and Monticello, under the impression that it was a ruse, and several shells burst in their immediate vicinity. The two vessels were signaled to return, when the latter reported that the inner battery was still in the hands of the enemy; but on again reconnoitering, reported that it was an error.

But the victory was not yet won. The Monticello entered the inlet, and when within six hundred yards of the lower battery, was fired upon, and the real state of affairs became apparent. The gunboat responded, and for fifteen minutes a fire was kept up, which seemed likely to sink the vessel. All hands were called to quarters, and the Federal vessels prepared to resume the attack, the troops having in the mean time withdrawn from Fort Clark to a safer location.

Darkness was gathering thickly around, and the weather became threatening. The order to "cease firing" was reluctantly given, and the fleet withdrew, the Monticello, Pawnee and Lane remaining as near the shore as possible, in order to protect the landed troops, while the larger vessels anchored in the offing.

Early the next morning, all hands were again called. The smaller vessels had been driven ashore during the night by the gale, and the little band of troops were left to protect themselves, as best they might. The smaller steamers were sent in shore to be in readiness to cover the land forces, and to aid in any attempt that might be made to land the remainder. At about eight o'clock, the Wabash and Susquehanna proceeded to take up a position—this time at anchor. Twenty minutes later, the Susquehanna opened fire, followed immediately by the Wabash, and soon the Minnesota found an anchorage ground, and the action commenced in earnest. An hour later, the Cumberland took position near, and did good execution, as did also the Harriet Lane, with her rifled guns.

Thus for an hour a rapid fire had been kept up, but without eliciting any reply from the fort, or without any flag having been shown. Thirty minutes later, their batteries replied, having been mostly aimed at the Cumberland, and the fight continued for half an hour, without intermission, when a white flag was shown from the large fort. Again the order to cease firing was given, the sailors flew to the rigging, and from ship to ship rang the cheers of victory. General Butler sent Lieutenant Crosby ashore to inquire the meaning of the white flag. He soon returned, bringing Mr. Weigel, with a communication from Commodore Barron, offering to surrender, with all the arms and ammunition, the officers to go out with side arms, and the men to retire without arms. General Butler demanded a full capitulation as prisoners of war, which was subsequently complied with.

In three quarters of an hour Lieutenant Crosby returned with Commodore Barron, Major Andrews and Colonel Martin. With these officers General Butler went aboard the flag-ship Minnesota, to make the agreement with Commodore Stringham, on the part of the navy. The articles were signed, and the forts surrendered and occupied by the Union forces. While the terms were under consideration, the Adelaide and Harriet Lane both got aground, and occasioned some fear lest the enemy, taking advantage of this circumstance, might renew the contest. But happily their fears were not realized. In reaching the Minnesota, Commodore Barron was obliged to pass under the guns of the Wabash, the vessel which he had himself commanded a few months before, and which he had just been endeavoring to destroy from his batteries.

The result of this expedition was the capture of seven hundred and fifteen men, including the officers, one thousand stand of arms, seventy-five kegs of powder, five stand of colors, thirty-one pieces of cannon, including a ten-inch columbiad, a brig loaded with cotton, a sloop loaded with provisions and stores, two light-boats, one hundred and fifty bags of coffee and smaller stores.

The prisoners were transferred to the Minnesota, and taken to New York. Their acknowledged loss was forty-nine killed and fifty-one wounded. On the Federal side, not a single life was lost, and only two or three wounded.

WESTERN VIRGINIA.

A series of active events in Western Virginia now claim our attention.

Governor Wise, on hearing of the death of General Garnett, and the defeat and dispersion of his army, commenced a retreat up the Kanawha, cautiously followed by General Cox. He intended to make a stand at Gauley's Bridge, at the junction of Gauley and Kanawha rivers, and had erected defences for that purpose; but in consequence of the demoralization and desertion of his men, and learning that General Rosecranz had dispatched a large force to intercept him, he fled without fighting, on the 28th of July, destroying the bridge to cut off his pursuers. He left behind him a thousand muskets, and a quantity of powder, which were seized by General Cox. Early in the month of August, General Floyd was reinforced by fresh troops from the eastern section of the State, while Jackson was also advancing with a new army to attack the position of Rosecranz at the Cheat Mountain Pass, and General Loring, another rebel commander, was marching towards Huttonsville to act in conjunction with Jackson's forces.

SURPRISE AT CROSS LANES.

On the morning of the 26th of August, the Seventh Ohio regiment, Colonel Tyler, attached to General Cox's brigade, had just encamped at a position in the mountains called Cross Lanes, near Summersville, about twenty-four miles from Gauley Bridge, and eighteen from Twentymile Creek, where the main body of General Cox's forces were.

While at breakfast they were surrounded and attacked in front and on both flanks simultaneously, by a rebel force of three thousand infantry, four hundred cavalry, and ten guns. Colonel Tyler's men were immediately formed for battle, and fought bravely, though in an almost hopeless position. The enemy proving too powerful, the Colonel dispatched an orderly to the baggage train, which was coming up, but three miles distant, and turned it back towards General Cox's camp, where it arrived in safety. The regiment met the advancing foe with desperate valor, and finally succeeded in cutting their way through the superior force by whom they were encompassed, Lieutenant-Colonel Creighton capturing the enemy's colors and two prisoners in their progress. The ranks were much broken, and companies B, C and I suffered severely. The line was soon formed again, and prepared for a renewal of the attack, but they were permitted to make good their retreat without further molestation. Captains Dyer, Shurtleff and Sterling, Adjutant De Forrest, Lieutenant Narrent, and Sergeant-Major King were killed. The total loss is reported at fifteen killed, forty wounded, and thirty prisoners. The loss of the enemy is not known, but could not have been less.

BATTLE OF CARNIFEX FERRY.
September 10, 1861.

More than a month had now elapsed since General Rosecranz had been entrusted with the Federal command in Western Virginia, and the commanders of the hostile forces had been intently watching the movements of the opposing armies, anxious for an opportunity to strike a decisive blow.

From his headquarters at Clarksburg, General Rosecranz moved for-

ward to resume active operations, and at two principal points the enemy
prepared to give him battle. The popular impression was that he intended to attack General Lee, at Cheat Mountain Gap, his nearest and
most accessible opponent, then held in check by General Reynolds.
Floyd had been permitted to cross the mountains at Summersville, and
was known to be then in the Kanawha region, some eighty or a hundred miles distant, where it was the intention of the Federal commander
to seek him. It was not until Monday, the 9th of September, that the
General reached Birch river, where he concentrated his force, drawn
from various encampments, and which had marched in detached bodies
to the rendezvous appointed. After leaving the valley of the Big Birch
the route lay through a mountainous and densely wooded country, in-
fested with guerrillas, who gave them much annoyance; and as no reliable guide accompanied the army, Rosecranz was obliged to rely chiefly
upon the inhabitants for information of the geographical and topographical features of the country. The position of Floyd's forces was also
unknown to him, and it was not until he had reached Cross Lanes,
eight miles from Summersville, that he received reliable information
that the enemy was strongly posted somewhere in the range of hills
that line either side of the Gauley river, immediately facing that village.
Floyd was known to be advised of the approach of the Federal army,
as his scouts and skirmishers had been encountered frequently on the
previous day, and it was the plan of Rosecranz to carefully reconnoitre
the position of the enemy before advancing any considerable force
within range of his guns; but the eager and importunate requests
of various officers, as well as the impetuosity of the men, urged him
forward.

Colonel McCook was first sent with a squadron of Chicago cavalry
to Carnifex ferry, by a road which led through ravines to the Gauley
river. In an attempt to destroy a boat found here he was fired upon
by the enemy, who were out of range of the carbines of the cavalry.
To overcome this opposition, he dispatched a man asking that *ten* infantry should be sent to his aid. By some mistake the whole of Colonel
Lytle's Tenth Ohio, an Irish regiment, came hurrying down, eager for
a fight, and opened fire on the woods on the opposite side that speedily banished the enemy. Colonel Lytle's regiment continued in the
advance, acting as skirmishers, and shortly drove in a detachment of the
rebels from an exposed camp on the left of the road. This road was
very narrow, and shut in to the very wagon tracks with the jungle of
underbrush.

General Rosecranz, who was still ignorant of the precise position of
the enemy, or of the nature of his entrenchments, now sent orders to
General Benham that Lytle should proceed down this road to make a

reconnoissance, to be supported, if necessary, by the remainder of Benham's brigade. Lytle was still a mile in advance of the rest of the brigade, pushing cautiously forward, with companies A, B, C and E, as skirmishers. They suddenly found themselves in front of some kind of fortification, and the enemy discovered them at the same time. At first there was sharp and scattered firing, when suddenly a terrific crash of musketry was followed by a storm of bullets. The enemy had opened along his whole front. The remainder of the Tenth was hurried forward to support the advance, and General Benham sent orders for the Thirteenth, Colonel Smith, and the Twelfth, Colonel Lowe, to come forward. The Federal troops stood their ground with the greatest heroism, in the face of a heavy battery. The firing on either side was not effective; and though the Tenth suffered severely, the loss was not great.

The Thirteenth, Colonel Smith, came in on the left, a little in the rear of the Tenth, and deploying towards Floyd's right, opened in fine style. In the thickest of the firing, Colonel Lytle dashed forward in front of the enemy's works, leading several companies, and as they left the cover of the woods, he received a severe wound. The ball which disabled him also wounded his horse, who dashed his rider to the ground, and in his death agony plunged over the parapet into the enemy's works. Colonel Lytle was carried to a house near by, and lay in great pain, within hearing of the contest he was unable to share. The Tenth, discouraged and embarrassed by the loss of their leader, became somewhat scattered in the woods, but held their position and kept up a steady fire.

Meantime, Colonel Lowe came up with the Twelfth, and was led by Adjutant-General Hartsuff into the woods near the spot where the Tenth first received the enemy's fire. He was leading up his regiment, waving his sword to cheer on his men, when he was struck in the forehead by a musket ball, and fell heavily from his horse. He died bravely, a soldier's death, in front of the foe, and in the presence of his men.

The reconnoissance that was designed, had now grown into a severe and general engagement. But the unknown position of the enemy, and the necessity of calling up other regiments to support the advance, had led to a premature struggle. McMullen's howitzer battery, and Captain Snyder's battery were brought forward as speedily as possible, and rendered efficient service. General Rosecranz dispatched Adjutant-General Hartsuff to order up Colonel McCook's brigade, who rushed forward in a state of wild enthusiasm when they were informed that they would have the honor of storming the batteries. Meantime the General, who had been making a careful survey of the whole field, found that the work would be too hazardous, and cost too many valuable lives, if it were then attempted, and countermanded the order. It was now too dark to distinguish the foe, and it became absolutely necessary to withdraw the troops.

The men had marched seventeen miles and a half, and many of them were exhausted with scouting and skirmishing all day over the hills. They retired slowly, galled with disappointment, and bivouacked, wearied and supperless, within musket-range of the rebel front. Sentinels were posted to prevent any attempt of the enemy to surprise them, and guard against the retreat of Floyd if possible. But total ignorance of the country, and the intense darkness of the night, made it impossible to secure all the avenues of retreat. General Rosecranz himself was up all night long, taking care of his position with jealous and anxious solicitude; but notwithstanding, the foe slipped from his grasp.

The troops expected to storm the position and take it by sunrise, but before that time it was discovered vacant. Floyd began the evacuation as soon as he ascertained that Rosecranz did not intend to storm him, and by three o'clock the next morning the enemy put the deep and turbulent Gauley, and some miles of rugged road, between himself and the disgusted Federal army—sinking the flats and destroying the trestle bridge by which he had secured his retreat.

The Union troops immediately took possession of Floyd's camp, in which he had left his own personal baggage, that of his officers, and their parade stores, the baggage and blankets of private soldiers, large numbers of muskets, squirrel guns, powder, lead, cartridges, forage, large quantities of commissary stores, and some horses and wagons.

He took nothing with him, in fact, excepting his guns, part of his tents, and a small supply of rations. It was also ascertained that he threw at least a portion of his cannon into the Gauley.

The loss of Rosecranz's army in the engagement was 16 killed, and 102 wounded. That of the enemy was probably small, as they were well protected from the Federal fire. Twelve rebel prisoners were taken, and 25 of Colonel Tyler's Seventh Ohio, mostly wounded, who had been captured at Cross Lanes on the 26th of August, were released.

BATTLE OF CHEAT MOUNTAIN PASS.

On the 12th of September, General Reynolds, commanding the Federal brigade on Cheat Mountain, was attacked by General Lee of the Secession army, with a force computed at 9,000 men. The Cheat Mountain Pass lies between the valley of the South branch of the Potomac river and those of Elk and Gauley rivers, tributaries of the Great Kanawha.

The first position held by General Reynolds was at the foot of the mountain, but subsequently two fortifications had been erected on the summit of two adjacent spurs, seven miles apart by a bridle path, which were called Cheat Summit and Elk Water. General Reynolds's headquarters was at Elk Water, while Colonel Kimball of the Fourteenth Indiana, held a subordinate command at Cheat Summit.

The enemy was well informed of the position and strength of these defences, but had no desire to attack General Reynolds in either of his strongholds. Their leader had hopes, however, of escaping the vigilance of the Federal commanders by making a detour and marching on beyond, and was engaged in this enterprise when he met with unexpected reverses.

The two Federal posts were in constant communication by a telegraphic line, and pickets guarded every avenue of approach.

On the 12th, the enemy, five thousand strong, with eight pieces of artillery, under command of General R. E. Lee, advanced on this position by the Huntersville Pike. Our advanced pickets—portions of the Fifteenth Indiana and Sixth Ohio—gradually fell back to our main picket station; two companies of the Seventeenth Indiana, under Colonel Hascall, checking the enemy's advance at the Point Mountain Turnpike, and then falling back on the regiment which occupied a very advanced position on our right front, and which was now ordered in. The enemy threw into the woods on our left front three regiments, who made their way to the right and rear of Cheat Mountain, took a position on the road leading to Huttonville, broke the telegraph wire, and cut off our communication with Colonel Kimball's Fourteenth Indiana Cavalry on Cheat Summit.

At the same time an equal force of the enemy advanced by the Staunton Pike on the front of Cheat Mountain, and threw two regiments to the right and rear of the mountain, thus uniting with his other column. They advanced towards the pass, in order to get to the rear of Elkwater, when three companies of the Thirteenth Indiana, and one from the Fourteenth, met them. The encounter resulted in the rout and retreat of the enemy.

A large portion of the rebel troops were now closing in on Cheat Mountain, when detachments of the Fourteenth Indiana, and Twenty-fourth and Twenty-fifth Ohio, numbering in all about three hundred, held them in check. Affairs rested in this condition till dark. Determined to force a communication between the detached portions of his command, General Reynolds ordered the Thirteenth Indiana, under Colonel Sullivan, to cut their way, if necessary, by the mail road, and the greater part of the Third Ohio and Second Virginia, under Colonels Manon and Moss, respectively, to do the same by the path; the two commands starting at three o'clock, A. M. on the 13th, the former from

Cheat Mountain Pass, and the latter from Elk Water, so as to fall upon the enemy simultaneously, if possible. Early on the 13th, the small force of about three hundred from the summit, engaged the enemy with such effect, that notwithstanding his great superiority in numbers, he retired in great disorder, leaving large quantities of clothing and equipments on the ground. The relieving forces failing to encounter the enemy, marched to the summit, secured the provision train, and reopened the communication. While these events were proceeding on the mountain, General Lee advanced on Elk Water, apparently for a final attack. A rifled Parrot gun from Loomis' battery was run to the front about three-quarters of a mile, and after a few shots, which told with fine effect on their ranks, they retreated to a place beyond its range. On the 14th, the enemy was again in position in front of Elk Water, but were repulsed by the gallant Fifteenth Indiana, who held their ground and fired with the most telling effect. The enemy also made an effort to reach the pass, but they were again repulsed, and withdrew to a point some ten miles distant. On the 15th, the rebels appeared again in much stronger force than before, and attempted a flank movement by the left, but they were driven back and compelled to retire from the field by the vigilant and heroic garrison on the summit.

One hundred of the enemy were killed and wounded, and about twenty were taken prisoners. The Federal forces lost nine killed, and about sixty prisoners. Lieutenant Junod, of the Fourteenth Indiana, was among the killed, and Captain James Bense, and Lieutenants Gillman and Shaffer, of the Ohio Sixth, and Lieutenant Merrill, of the Engineers wounded.

One of the most important incidents of this engagement was the death of Colonel John A. Washington, of the rebel army, aid-de-camp to General Lee.

ENGAGEMENT AT CHAPMANSVILLE.

A brilliant affair took place at Chapmansville, Logan county, Virginia, on the 25th of September, when a body of the enemy under Colonel Davis, numbering about five hundred, was defeated and driven from behind their breastworks by five hundred and fifty men of the Thirty-fourth Ohio, under Colonel Piatt.

The want of men in Western Virginia had induced the Government to call this regiment into the field before its ranks were full, and they had been on duty but one week when the affair at Chapmansville took place. With only six hours notice they marched from Cincinnati, and on the 19th of September arrived at "Camp Enyard," on the Kanawha, occupied by Colonel Enyard with three hundred of the First Kentucky and two hundred of the Home Guards of Virginia.

Three days subsequently they learned that the enemy were in force fifty miles distant, and marched, in company with Colonel Enyard's command to Peytona, where they separated, Colonel Piatt proceeding to Boone Court-house. A march of about sixteen miles the next day brought them in contact with the advance cavalry guard of the enemy, who were quickly driven in. The force was immediately made ready for battle, and proceeded on for two hours, constantly skirmishing with the retreating foe. Though unable to ascertain the position or force of their opposers, they yet marched bravely, with Colonel Piatt in advance, until the dim outline of a breastwork became visible through the dense underbrush, situated on the slope of a hill between two mountain ridges on the right and a small ravine on the left. The brush had been cut down on the right and a force of the enemy, comprising about one hundred men, were stationed there to rake the advancing troops, and their fire was poured in incessantly. The Federals returned the fire and advanced fearlessly, in four columns, with company A, Captain Rathbone, deployed to the right, directly up the side of the mountain, for the purpose of outflanking the enemy on the left; company C, Captain Miller, dispatched for a similar purpose to the left; company I, Captain Anderson, marching up the ravine, and the centre moving directly up the road. When within about twenty yards of the breastworks they were suddenly fired upon from all quarters. The order from Colonel Piatt to storm the entrenchments was responded to with hearty cheers, and the men dashed on, regardless of the storm of bullets that tore up the earth around them.

Captain Anderson was the first to mount the breastworks, his men following steadily and with unflinching courage. Captain Miller on the left, and Captain Rathbone on the right, were impeded by obstructions, but quickly overcoming or dashing through them, joined in the charge. A few minutes sufficed to reach the inside and break the ranks of the enemy, who fled to the mountains. They left twenty-nine dead behind and had fifty wounded, among them Colonel Davis, of North Carolina, who afterwards died. The Federal loss was four killed and eight wounded.

Colonel Piatt marched into Chapmansville, the former headquarters of the enemy, encamped for the night, and then returned to Camp Enyard, almost without provisions, and forced to wade through swollen streams and surmount rugged mountains.

RECONNOISSANCE AT GREEN BRIER, WESTERN VIRGINIA.
October 3, 1861.

General Reynolds, commander of the Federal forces on Cheat Mountain Summit, who had so successfully resisted the attempt of the enemy to flank his position on the 12th of September, having learned that General Jackson had a fortified camp on the Green Brier river, at a point where the Staunton turnpike ascends the Alleghany mountains, about twelve miles distant, determined on a reconnoissance in force, and if possible a surprise of the enemy's encampment. On the night of October 2, at twelve o'clock, he started from his encampment, with the Twenty-fourth, Twenty-fifth and Thirty-second Ohio, and the Seventh, Ninth, Thirteenth, Fourteenth, Fifteenth and Seventeenth Indiana regiments, with Howe's, Loomis' and Daum's batteries, thirteen pieces, and a small force of cavalry, in all about five thousand men.

About daylight they came in contact with the enemy's outposts, at the first Green Brier bridge, which resulted in their being driven within the entrenchments with considerable loss by the Twenty-fourth Ohio and Seventh Indiana.

The rebel camp was located on a steep elevation, known as Buffalo Hill, their entrenchments rising one above another along its terraced sides. Howe's and Loomis' batteries were soon put in position, and were effective in silencing a number of the enemy's pieces, which had opened on the advancing Federal columns. The infantry were impatient for the order to advance to the assault, while for thirty-five minutes every gun of the assaulting batteries were actively engaged.

One after another of the rebel pieces were dismounted, until only one remained, which replied with spirit, while the lower entrenchments were almost wholly evacuated by their defenders. Rockets were thrown up from the enemy's camp at this time, which the General supposed was a signal for reinforcements from another encampment known to exist a few miles distant. It was not long before the surmise was verified. Down the mountains in the rear of the camp came a column of men, estimated at two thousand, bringing with them several pieces of artillery of a superior character. They were received with loud cheers by their hitherto faltering comrades. The fresh pieces were soon mounted on the upper works, and took part in the engagement.

In the mean time the infantry Colonels were clamorous for permission to storm the upper works, but the General opposed this as unnecessarily involving a great sacrifice of life, which would not be justified for the possession of an unimportant position. A flank movement was permitted, however, to gain a more accurate knowledge of the enemy's

SIEGE OF LEXINGTON, MO., SEPT. 12—20, 1861.

entrenchments and force, in which most of the regiments participated. The men were brought under a cross-fire of shell and canister, and the General discovered the works could not be carried without great exposure and loss. As the artillery had nearly exhausted their ammunition, he deemed it prudent to withdraw his force, which was done without any molestation from the enemy.

The entire Federal loss was but eight killed and thirty-two wounded, while that of the enemy was about double this number, principally in the skirmish outside of their entrenchments. Thirteen of the rebels were captured.

DEFENCE OF LEXINGTON, MISSOURI.*
September 12-20, 1861.

One of the most exciting events of the war in the West was the defence of Lexington, Missouri, by Federal troops, commanded by Colonel James B. Mulligan, consisting of the Chicago Irish Brigade, eight hundred strong, four hundred Home Guards, and a part of the Missouri Eighth, under Colonel White; the Missouri Thirteenth, six hundred and fifty men, Colonel Peabody; Illinois First Cavalry, four hundred men, Colonel Marshall. In addition to these, Captain Graham, Lieutenant-Colonel White, Lieutenant-Colonel Given, and Major Wright had also small commands—in all, 2,780 men.

Lexington is the capital of Lafayette county, and contains a population of about five thousand. It is on the right bank of the Missouri river, one hundred and twenty miles west of Jefferson City, and three hundred miles from St. Louis. The heights on which the town is built command the river, and to a considerable extent the back country. Old Lexington, an earlier settlement, is situated east of the new town, back of the river, on the hills, where the main body of Price's army was posted, while the attack was made from different points. Colonel Mulligan's fortifications were between the two towns, and consisted of heavy earthworks, ten feet in height, with a ditch eight feet in width.

On the 1st of September, Colonel Mulligan, whose regiment was then encamped at Jefferson City, received orders to march to the relief of Lexington, then threatened by the enemy, and in six hours the regiment was on its way, and in nine days after entered the town, which they found occupied by Colonel Marshall's cavalry, and a body of Home Guards. On the 10th a letter was received from Colonel Peabody, saying that he was retreating from Warrensburg, twenty-five miles distant, and that Price was pursuing him with ten thousand men. A few hours after, Colonel Peabody, with the Thirteenth Missouri, entered Lexington.

13

On the 12th, as the enemy drew near the city, two companies of the Thirteenth Missouri were ordered out as skirmishers, who recognized General Price (by the aid of glasses), leading on the advance guard of his men. Company I of the Irish Brigade held them in check until Captain Dillon's company of the Thirteenth Missouri drove them back. Subsequently six companies of the Missouri Thirteenth and two companies of the Illinois cavalry were dispatched in search of the retreating enemy.

They engaged them in a cornfield, fought with them gallantly, and harassed them to such an extent as to delay their progress, in order to give time for constructing intrenchments around the camp on College Hill. This had the desired effect, and the Federals succeeded in throwing up earthworks three or four feet in height. This consumed the night, and was continued during the next day, the outposts still opposing the enemy, and keeping them back as far as possible. At three o'clock in the afternoon of the 14th the engagement opened with artillery. A volley of grapeshot was thrown among the officers, who stood in front of the breastworks. The guns within the entrenchments immediately replied with a vigor which converted the scene into one of the wildest excitement. At seven o'clock the enemy withdrew and the engagement ceased for the night.

Next morning General Parsons sent in a flag of truce, asking permission to bury his dead. The request was cheerfully granted, and the Federal troops willingly assisted in burying the fallen foe. On Tuesday the work of throwing up intrenchments went on. It rained all day, and the men stood knee-deep in the mud, building them. Troops were sent out to forage on the three succeeding days, and returned with large quantities of provisions and fodder.

All this time the pickets were constantly engaged with the enemy, well aware that ten thousand men were threatening them, and knowing that the struggle was to be a desperate one. Earthworks had been reared breast-high, enclosing an area of fifteen to eighteen acres, and surrounded by a ditch. Outside of this was a circle of twenty-one mines, and still further down were pits to embarrass the progress of the enemy. During the night of the 17th they were getting ready for the defence, and heard the sounds of preparation in the camp of the enemy for the attack on the morrow. At nine o'clock on the morning of the 18th, the drums beat to arms, and the terrible struggle commenced. The enemy's force had increased to twenty thousand men and thirteen pieces of artillery. They came as one dark moving mass of armed men, as far as the eye could reach. Two batteries were planted by them in front, one on the left, one on the right, and one in the rear, and opened with a terrible fire, which was answered with the utmost bravery and determination. The batteries opened at nine o'clock, and never ceased to pour deadly shot upon the garrison. About noon the hospital was taken. It was situated on the left, outside of the intrenchments. They besieged it, took it, and from the balcony and roof their sharpshooters poured a deadly fire upon the Federal troops. The hospital contained the chaplain and one hundred and twenty wounded men. But it could not be allowed to remain the possession of the enemy. The Montgomery Guard, Captain Gleason, of the Irish Brigade, was brought out, and the word to "charge" given. They stormed up the slope to the hospital, took it, and drove the enemy in wild confusion down the hill. The fire of the rebels was for the time lessened, only to be increased towards evening, and word was sent that if the Federal troops did not surrender before the next morning, the black flag would be hoisted and no quarter given.

The next morning the fire was resumed and continued all day. A fierce bayonet charge was made by the garrison, that served to show the enemy that the Union troops were not yet worn out. All that day the soldiers in that little band stood straining their eyes and searching the distance in hopes that some friendly flag might be coming to their assistance. But no welcome flag came in sight, and with the energy of despair they determined to do their duty at all hazards. It was intensely hot,—the lips of the men were parched and blistering. They were without water, and yet no word of murmuring was heard. That night two wells were dug. The morning of the next day, the 20th, dawned sadly upon them, and still the battle raged furiously. The rebels had constructed moveable breastworks of hemp bales, rolled them up the hill, and advanced their batteries so as to command the fortifications. Heated shot were fired at them but without avail, they having been thoroughly water-soaked. The outer breastworks were soon carried by a charge from the enemy, the Federal lines broken, and the rebels rushed in. At point after point they were repulsed, but the cartridges of the Union troops had given out, and it was evident that the struggle could not be protracted. Of a sudden the firing ceased, and it was subsequently ascertained that the Home Guards had hoisted a white flag. It was taken down, but again raised by the same hands from the centre of the fortifications—when the fire of the enemy slackened and ceased. Under this state of affairs, Colonel Mulligan, calling his officers into council, decided to capitulate, and Captain McDermott went out to the enemy's lines, with a handkerchief tied to a ramrod, and a parley took place. Major Moore, of the brigade, was sent to General Price's headquarters, at New Lexington, to know the terms of capitulation. These were soon made known; the officers to be retained as prisoners of war, the men to be allowed to parole, with their personal property, surrendering their arms and accoutrements.

Reluctantly this was acceded to, and the surrender took place. At four P. M. on Saturday, the Federal forces, having laid down their arms, were marched out of the intrenchments to the tune of "Dixie," played by the rebel bands. They left behind them their arms and accoutrements, reserving only their clothing. Many of the men wept on leaving their colors behind, as each company in the brigade had its own standard presented by its friends. At the surrender, the muster-rolls of the companies were taken to General Price's headquarters, the list of officers made out, and they ordered to report themselves as prisoners of war.

The scenes at the capitulation were extraordinary. Colonel Mulligan shed tears. The men threw themselves upon the ground, raved and stormed; well nigh frenzied, demanding to be led out again and "finish the thing." In Colonel Marshall's Cavalry regiment, the feeling was equally intense. Much havoc had already been done among their horses during the siege, and but little more than half of them remained. Numbers of the privates actually shot their own horses dead on the spot, unwilling that their companions in the campaign should now fall into the enemy's hands.

The privates, numbering some one thousand five hundred strong, were first compelled to take the oath not to serve against the Confederate States, when they were put across the river, and in charge of General Rains marched on Saturday night to Richmond, sixteen miles, whence on Sunday they marched to Hamilton, a station on the Hannibal and St. Joseph railroad, where they were declared free to go where they pleased.

No reliable statement of the casualties at the siege of Lexington seems to have been published. Of the irregular army of General Price, large numbers of whom were not enrolled, but were outside volunteers, many were killed and buried on the spot, no record being made of their loss. One hundred and forty Federals were left in the hospital, many of whom were suffering from sickness, and not from wounds. Colonel Mulligan lost probably two hundred in killed and wounded, while the rebel loss could not have been less, and according to some estimates must have reached three or four times that number. General Price's force was estimated at numbers varying from twenty to thirty thousand, the lowest being probably nearest the actual number, with twenty-one pieces of artillery.

General Price, in his official report to Governor Jackson, inventoried his acquisitions as follow:—"Three thousand five hundred prisoners, including the colonels, and one hundred and eighteen commissioned officers, five pieces of artillery and two mortars, over three thousand stand of infantry arms, a large number of sabres, about seven hundred and fifty horses, many sets of cavalry equipments, wagons, teams, ammu-

nition, more than a hundred thousand dollars' worth of commissary stores, and a large amount of other property."

For daring and patient suffering—fighting day after day without water, the battle of Lexington stands almost without a rival in history. It was stubbornly contested, and evinced in the most striking manner the devotion and faithfulness of the adopted citizens of our country.

ATTACK ON SANTA ROSA ISLAND.
October 9, 1861.

Santa Rosa Island is a long, narrow strip of low land, partially covered with bushes and stunted trees, lying opposite Escambia and Santa Rosa counties, on the western coast of Florida. The Bay of Pensacola is separated from the Gulf of Mexico by this island, which varies in width from one hundred yards to five-eighths of a mile. At the western extremity of the island Fort Pickens stands, commanding the channel, and on the mainland, a short distance west of the Navy Yard, is Fort San Carlos de Barrancas.

General Bragg, commanding at Pensacola, had matured a well-devised plan by which he designed to surprise and capture Fort Pickens, but in which he was signally defeated by the watchfulness and bravery of the troops at the fort, and on the island. The Federal force encamped on the island was a part of the New York Sixth Volunteers, known as Wilson's Zouaves, numbering about three hundred men; and the destruction or capture of this force, was the first design of the leaders of the expedition, who confidently hoped, in the confusion arising from a night attack and rout, to obtain possession or destroy the batteries on the island, if not to capture Fort Pickens itself.

On the morning of Wednesday, the 9th of October, at two o'clock, the enemy silently commenced their advance upon the camp from a point about four miles distant, where they had landed during the night, about fifteen hundred strong, under General Anderson. The night was extremely dark, and it was almost impossible to distinguish any object at a distance of twenty yards. The Zouaves, numbering about three hundred, were encamped a mile from the fort, on the shore, but between the fort and the approaching foe, with their pickets thrown out a mile in advance. About three o'clock, the rebels, having driven in the pickets, who made a gallant resistance, reached the camp of Colonel Wilson, and owing to the confusion and darkness, before he had time to form his men, they were driven from their tents, many of which were burnt or destroyed by the enemy.

On the first alarm, Colonel Harvey Brown, commandant of the fort, dispatched Major Vogdes, with two companies of regulars, to the scene of conflict. The men soon became intermingled with the enemy, who succeeded in taking the Major prisoner. Major Arnold, with two additional companies, was soon after sent out from the fort, and favored by the light of the burning tents, they were enabled to ascertain the position and force of the enemy, and gallantly rushed to the attack. Captain Hildt, now in command of the two companies which had been led on by Major Vogdes, extricated his men from their perilous position, and opened a well-directed fire on the enemy, compelling them reluctantly to give way. Colonel Wilson, who had succeeded in bringing a body of his men together after their sudden surprise, formed them into line, and now joined in the battle, when the insurgents were very soon thrown into confusion, and made a rapid retreat to their boats, pursued by a victorious force of only one-fourth their number.

Colonel Brown, in his report, says that "the plan of the enemy's attack was judicious; and, if executed with ordinary ability, might have been attended with serious loss to the Unionists. But he failed in all save the burning of one-half of the tents of the Sixth regiment, which, being covered with. bushes, were very combustible, and in rifling the trunks of the officers. He did not reach within five hundred yards of either of the batteries, the guns of which he was to spike; nor within a mile of the fort he was to enter with the fugitives retreating before his victorious arms!"

Many of the rebels were wounded by the sharp firing continued by the Federal troops during their re-embarkation. One of their flat-boats sunk, and many bodies were found floating in the water on the following day. The Federal loss was fifteen killed, forty-one wounded, and eighteen prisoners; that of the rebels in killed and wounded was over one hundred, and thirty-five of them remained prisoners in the hands of the Federal forces.

BATTLE OF BALL'S BLUFF.
October 21, 1861.

Perhaps no event in the course of the war thus far produced a more profound sensation than the news of the Battle of Ball's Bluff, which occurred on the 21st of October. The loss of life was heavy on the part of the Federals. Several accomplished and valuable officers were killed, among whom was the distinguished and eloquent Senator from Oregon, General Baker. The fatality attending this battle caused it to be regarded with peculiar interest, and remembered as fruitful in daring deeds and memorials of terrible bloodshed.

BATTLE OF BALL'S BLUFF.

The north and south banks of the Potomac river, from the Great Falls, a few miles above Washington, to Harper's Ferry, were held by the Federal and secession troops respectively. Great care was taken by the Government to defend the north bank, in order to prevent the threatened incursion of the enemy into Maryland, from whence, aided by the disunion sympathizers of that State, they designed to make the long contemplated attack upon the capital. Among the troops stationed on the Potomac, extending from Great Falls to Edwards Ferry, was the division of General Banks; from Edwards Ferry to Conrad's Ferry, a division under General Stone; while Colonels Lander, Geary, and others held the line thence to Harper's Ferry.

On the south side of the river, two strong positions were held by the enemy—Dranesville and Leesburg. The latter is the terminus of the Loudon and Hampshire railroad, about five miles from the Potomac, and opposite Edwards Ferry. The Southern commanders having determined to abandon their design of crossing the Potomac, had commenced the withdrawal of their troops from various points towards Manassas.

General McClellan, anxious to ascertain whether any movement of the forces at Leesburg and Dranesville had been made, directed General McCall, on the 18th, to push a reconnoissance in force in the direction of Dranesville. General McCall penetrated to that town, found that the enemy had evacuated the place, and was informed that Leesburg had also been abandoned.

While this reconnoissance was progressing, General McClellan informed General Stone of the fact, and directed him to make careful observations of the movements of the enemy, to ascertain what effect was produced by the expedition of General McCall. He also suggested that a slight demonstration on his own part might be successful in expediting their removal.

In obedience to these orders, General Stone, on the 20th, made a feint of crossing the river at Edwards Ferry, while four companies of the Fifteenth Massachusetts were sent to Harrison's Island, in the Potomac, situated between Edwards and Conrad's Ferries. At ten o'clock, P. M., Lieutenant Howe, Quartermaster of the Fifteenth Massachusetts, reported that Lieutenant Philbrick had returned to the island from his reconnoissance to Leesburg, and that he had been within one mile of that place, discovering only a small encampment of thirty tents, and without encountering any of the enemy—no pickets being out at any distance from their camp.

The Federal forces in that vicinity were then posted as follows:— General Stone, with General Gorman's brigade, Seventh Michigan, two troops of Van Alen cavalry, and the Putnam Rangers, at Edwards Ferry; five companies of Massachusetts Volunteers, under Colonel

Devens, at Harrison's Island; and Colonel Lee, with a battalion of the Massachusetts Twentieth, a section of the Rhode Island battery, and the Tammany regiment, were sent to Conrad's Ferry. A section of Bunting's New York battery was planted at Edwards and a section of Rickett's battery at Conrad's Ferry.

When the report of the scouts was received, orders were sent to Colonel Devens to march four companies to the Virginia shore, from Harrison's Island, and under cover of the night, take up a position near the camp referred to, and attack it at daybreak, drive out the enemy, pursue them as far as prudent, and return to the island. Orders were also sent to Colonel Baker, to march the First California regiment to Conrad's Ferry, to arrive there at sunrise, and to have the remainder of his brigade ready to move at an early hour.

Lieutenant-Colonel Wood, of the Fifteenth Massachusetts, was also ordered to move with a battalion to the river bank opposite Harrison's Island by daybreak. Two mounted howitzers in charge of Lieutenant Trench, of Rickett's battery, were ordered to the tow-path of the canal opposite Harrison's Island.

This disposition of the troops having been made for the commencement of the movement, it was necessary to provide the means for their transportation across the river, which is quite rapid at this point. Edwards Ferry is below the island, which is about three miles in length, and Conrad's Ferry is a short distance beyond the upper end. The island lies about a third of the distance from the Virginia shore, while a swift current of three hundred yards separates it from the Maryland banks, traversed by a tow-path of the Chesapeake and Ohio canal. The Virginia bank opposite the island is steep, and is backed by a precipitous bluff, varying in height from eighty to one hundred and fifty feet, covered with brush, trees and undergrowth.

There was no adequate preparation to effect the passage of troops at these points. The means were scanty either for reinforcement, or for retreat, if that should become necessary. On the Maryland side of Harrison's Island were two scows, capable of carrying thirty persons each, which could make two trips hourly, thus conveying one hundred and twenty men. On the Virginia side was one scow and a small boat. At Edwards Ferry there were two scows and a ship's yawl. With these insufficient means of transportation an attempt was made to land the forces on the opposite shore.

The landings at both of the ferries are good, but stretching almost the entire distance between them is the high and steep bank known as Ball's Bluff, where the crossing was attempted, and which has given its name to this bloody struggle.

Passing along and up the steep and difficult way from the landing below the bluff until it turns at the top, the road enters an open field of some six acres, surrounded on all sides by a forest. In this field the battle took place, the rebel forces being posted in the woods. .

At daybreak, four companies of the Massachusetts Fifteenth, under Colonel Devens, had reached the opposite shore, and after reconnoitering had formed their line on Ball's Bluff, on the edge of the corn-field. While in this position they were attacked by a considerable body of the enemy, with whom an irregular skirmish was kept up. Colonel Baker had during the morning been transferred from Conrad's Ferry to Harrison's Island, and appointed to the command. About noon the reinforcements began to come up, consisting of three companies of the Massachusetts Twentieth, six hundred of the California regiment, two companies of the Tammany regiment, with two howitzers and one rifled gun, in charge of Lieutenant Bramhall of the New York Ninth.

In the mean time the rebels, well informed of the difficulties of the Federal position, and only awaiting the arrival of a larger number that they might add to the magnitude of the victory which was within their grasp at any moment, having engaged the Federals by a series of irregular skirmishes during the earlier part of the day, concentrated their forces on General Baker's command at half past two o'clock. With a force of three thousand men they commenced a vigorous attack from the woods on three sides of the Federal position. A portion of Colonel Gorman's command at Edwards Ferry crossed over, but from want of means of transportation could not make either their numbers or presence of effective service.

The real battle, however, commenced on the left. Baker threw the whole responsibility of that wing upon Wistar. The latter did not like the appearance of the adjacent wood region, and threw forward companies A and D of his battalion to test them. Captains Markoe and Wade, the former well ahead, accordingly advanced on their hazardous duty; passed through the forest to the horn-like projection of the field, crossed it, and had arrived within ten paces of the further thicket, when a murderous fire blazed out upon them.

The poor fellows gallantly sprang through it upon their assailants, and were in a moment fighting in the woods. Not half of this noble band ever came back. The rebels, taking this as a signal for the commencement of the action, now bestirred themselves in force, and fired a terrific volley along their whole front. Only the sheeted flash showed itself from those frowning forests; the foe still clung to cover; but the hail of bullets rattled against the Union lines, and many brave souls were sent into eternity by that first fiery revelation of the enemy's strength. The reply was instant and extended. In a second both ends of the field were clouded with smoke, the day's skirmishing was over, and the contest that was to rage so hotly for an hour had commenced its fury.

The battle on the part of the Federals was fought heroically, and in a true sacrificial spirit. The enemy was in force in front; he began to creep down the treacherous sides of the enclosure; his sharpshooters climbed the trees everywhere, picking out the stateliest and most gallant forms for the death they so unerringly dealt. The lines thus received a scathing fire from the front, from above, and a cross-fire at angles right and left. All they could do in reply was to aim steadily and swiftly at the places whence the loudest yells and deadliest volleys proceeded. But the men dropped everywhere, and were borne by dozens to the gory skiffs below. On the right the Massachusetts men were more than decimated by the regular, unavoidable shower of bullets. But against the left, where Wistar commanded, the rebels, confident of their force and the effect of their deadly fire in front, began to make venturesome charges, each one repelled by the gallant fire of the Californians, but each one getting nearer the Federal lines than the last. On the fourth charge they actually flanked the left, and sprang forth, savage and eager, from the thicket beyond the ravine. Down this they were about to plunge. "Hold!" cried Wistar to his men; "not a man of you must fire;" and he dashed at the piece of one; "wait till they reach the bottom of the ravine; then we'll have them."

So they charged down the hill, only to meet the most effective volley fired on the Union side during that day. When the smoke rose their front ranks lay fallen in the hollow of the valley of death, and the rear had broken and fled in disorder through the forest.

Lieutenant Bramhall had posted his gun near the centre of the line, and opened fire to the best advantage possible. When he mounted the piece, he had eight artillerists, three riders, a corporal and sergeant. In ten minutes, five of these were shot down; in the end, all but two were killed, wounded or missing. Lieutenant Bramhall himself was severely wounded, but stood by his gun. Colonel Coggswell saw the necessity of the case, informed Colonels Wistar and Lee, Adjutant Harvey (of Baker's brigade), and Stewart (of General Stone's staff, present on the field); and those five distinguished officers and determined men manned the piece themselves. Coggswell and Harvey, understanding the business, would load, while Lee and Wistar were giving orders to their commands, and spurring them into the fight; then Wistar and Stewart would wheel the gun forward to position; Coggswell would take aim and give the word to Harvey, who held the percussion lanyard. In this way and by these men a dozen of the twenty rounds used were fired, doing more effect than all the musketry volleys. When the enemy was making his fifth charge on the left, the cannon had just been loaded and was pointed at the woods in front. Captain Beiral, of the Californians, who was with his company supporting the piece, exclaimed to Coggswell,

"Look to the left! look to the left!"

Coggswell saw the dark column of the rebels sweeping across the spur of the field, wheeled the terrible gun around, and discharged it square at their centre. The shell opened a lane through the charging force, a score or more falling never to fight again, and the column retreated upon the main body behind.

But the end was fast approaching. The thinning Union forces were assailed by four times their number. From every side death stormed upon their unsheltered bodies. Half their line officers were wounded or killed. The undaunted leaders were also falling. Ward, Lieutenant-Colonel of the Fifteenth, had received a frightful wound; Coggswell was shot through the wrist; Lee, Devens, Harvey and Stewart, were still fighting sadly and in vain; a ball shattered Wistar's sword arm—he dropped the weapon, picked it up with his left hand, and General Baker himself restored it to the scabbard. The shouting enemy began to break from the wood and through the smoke upon the confused lines. The crisis had come. There was some hand-to-hand fighting; a few of the gray-coats got entangled with the Federal forces, who took a prisoner and passed him to the rear: the enemy took a dozen, and made charge after charge. Just then a body of men appeared, pressing down from the left. The General ordered the troops around him to stand firm, and cried, "Who are those men?" "Confederate troops!" was the reply; and they rushed almost within bayonet distance. One of them drew a revolver, came close to Baker, and fired four balls at the General, every one of which took effect, and a glorious soul fled through their ghastly openings. Captain Beiral seized the slayer by the throat, and blew out his brains—the hero and the traitor falling within the same minute, and face to face. In a second the enemy swarmed over the spot. "For God's sake, boys," cried Adjutant Harvey, in his hot English way, "are you going to let them have the General's body!"

An angry howl was the answer, and a dozen charged, with set teeth and bayonets fixed, upon the rebels, who recoiled from the shock, and surrendered their priceless trophy. The body of this thrice-heroic man was passed down the bluff, and safely conveyed to the island. But now the Union lines were hopelessly disordered. The rebels came through both the field and woods in final force. Coggswell saw that the day was lost, and that the desperate, impossible retreat had come. So he ordered his scattered men to retire for embarkation, and the field was given up to the foe.

Large numbers of the Union troops had anticipated the order to retreat; for an hour the shore had been lined with stragglers and wearied men. Still, the reinforcing business had not ceased from the island, and during the fiercest of the action the two boats, which were bringing away the dead and wounded, returned from each trip laden with the residue of the Tammany and Massachusetts regiments. The life-boat proved a death-boat, for it swamped, from some cause, while conveying to the battle-field the last of the Tammany companies.

DEATH OF COLONEL BAKER.

Down the hill they came, in every direction and without order, hotly followed by the rebels to the very edge of the descent. Then the pursuers paused, too cautious to meet the chance of volleys from Harrison's Island, but throwing a plunging fire upon the retiring loyalists, and aiming ruthlessly at the hundreds trying to swim the rapid river channel. The tumult and agony of that headlong descent, the clamor and crowd along the shore, the rush into one wretched skiff, already over-laden with wounded men, which forced it beneath the surface and brought the horror of death by water upon men who had already so fairly faced the battle-field are beyond description. Who can depict the wild struggle with those turbid waters, and the desperate calmness with which each wretched soldier went down at last? Who can tell of those who, struck down by the fire from above, slipped in their own blood upon the clayey river bank; of those who wasted too feeble strength in swimming half way across the cruel stream; of the shouts for help where no help came. A few, more fiercely courageous than the rest, dragged the cannon to the edge of the hill and plunged them over, thus rendering them useless to the enemy. The colonels who had fought so steadily still refused to surrender, but guarded the retreat, so far as desperate courage could do it, to the end. Led by Coggswell and Lee, several organized companies charged up at their tormentors, once and again returning dangerous volleys. They kept the enemy at bay till long after nightfall closed upon the scene. All who could pass over to the island had escaped, and midnight was close upon them before the two colonels and the other field officers still on the shore saw that their duty was accomplished, and surrendered themselves and the remnant of their commands to the enemy.

A most painful scene transpired at the sinking of the launch, in which were some sixty wounded men, and twenty or thirty members of the California First. The launch had been safely taken half way across the river, when, to their utter consternation, it was discovered that it was leaking, and the water gradually, but surely, gaining upon them. The wounded were lying at the bottom, suffering intolerably from their various dislocations, wounds and injuries, and all soaking in water, which at the very start was fully four inches deep. As the water grew deeper and rose above the prostrate forms of the wounded, their comrades lifted them into sitting postures that they might not be strangled by the fast rising stream. But the groans and cries, screams and moanings of the poor fellows who were thus tortured, were most distressing and indescribable. Despite all that could be done, the fate of the launch, and all that were in it, with the exception of a few expert swimmers, was sealed; suddenly, and like a flash of lightning, the fragile craft sunk, carrying with it at least fifty dying sufferers, and some twenty or thirty others, who had trusted their lives to its treacherous hold.

The very skies were pitiless that evening. O the misery of the black, tempestuous night, when the rain poured down upon that narrow island where those who escaped the flood and field were bivouacked, huddled together and bereft of their comrades-in-arms! Scores of the dead were guarded by sullen watchers; the wounded were tended in every possible shelter. The river swelled in a kind of savage triumph over the havoc it had made, its current darkling and murmuring on the east and west, while on the opposite shore lay their dead comrades, whose white faces the rain beat in merciless fury, but all unfelt, and far more harmless than it fell upon the living victims.

Next morning boat loads of dead and wounded were brought from the battle-field under a flag of truce; and a dispatch had been published in Washington stating that General Stone had successfully thrown his force across the Potomac, and held his position secure against any hostile force.

The statistics of this conflict show that the total number of Federal troops that crossed the Virginia channel was about 1,853 officers and men. Of these 653 belonged to the Massachusetts Fifteenth, 340 to the Massachusetts Twentieth, about 360 to the Tammany regiment, and 570 to the first battalion of the First California. The Massachusetts Fifteenth lost in killed, wounded, and missing 322, including a lieutenant-colonel (wounded), and 14 out of 28 line officers who crossed. The Massachusetts Twentieth lost in all 159, including a colonel, major, surgeon, and adjutant (prisoners), and 8 out of 17 line officers who crossed. The Tammany companies lost 163, including a colonel, and 7 out of 12 line officers who crossed. The Californians lost 300, including their colonel (the general commanding), lieutenant-colonel (wounded), adjutant, and 15 line officers out of 17 who crossed. Total engaged in the fight, 1,853; total losses, 953; field officers crossing, 11; returning uninjured, 3; line officers crossing, 74; returning uninjured, 30.

The troops that were successful in reaching Harrison's Island remained there during the night of the 21st, and on the morning of the 22d were all passed over in safety to the Maryland shore, no attempt being made by the rebels to interfere with the movement. The condition of many of the men was pitiful. Some of them in their encounters with the enemy, and in struggling through the trees and thorny undergrowth, or plunging down the rocky steep, having been almost stripped of clothing. In a short time they were encamped in comforable quarters, and the wounded were provided for with the greatest care.

Large bodies of rebel troops had been brought up to Leesburg after the battle, to defend that point, and to make an offensive movement, if deemed expedient. About four thousand Federals, under the command of General Stone, occupied the Virginia shore immediately opposite Edwards Ferry, and were in imminent danger of attack from the now rapidly increasing force of rebels threatening their front. Generals McClellan and Banks, who had repaired to Edwards Ferry, on the Maryland shore, and were ready to furnish large reinforcements in the event of a general engagement, watched with anxiety the rebel movements on the opposite side of the river. Becoming convinced that the means of transportation were entirely inadequate to properly reinforce General Stone's command, the commander-in-chief ordered a withdrawal of all the Federal forces to the Maryland shore, which was safely accomplished on the night of the 23d.

Colonel E. D. Baker, whose death will make this battle-field immortal, was born in England, early left an orphan, and emigrated to this country. Few men have had a more eventful career, and few men have done so much to win the admiration of the people. He was, without question, one of the ablest speakers in the country; when he addressed public audiences he thrilled them with the electricity of his eloquence, and kindled them by his earnestness as a storm of fire sweeps over the prairie. For many years, whether at the bar, in the Congress of the nation, or before wild wood caucuses; in speaking to citizens, jurors, statesmen or soldiers; on the slope of the Atlantic, in the valley of the Mississippi, at the head of legions in Mexico, before the miners of California, or upon the banks of the Columbia, he held a place with the best men and finest orators in the land.

At the age of nineteen he was admitted to the bar in the State of Illinois. Subsequently he twice represented that State in the lower house of Congress. In 1846 he resigned in order to lead the Fourth Illinois regiment to Mexico. At Cerro Gordo, after the fall of General Shields, as senior Colonel he took command of the brigade, and fought through the desperate battle in a manner that drew an especial compliment from General Twiggs.

Returning home, he was, after his recovery from a severe wound received on the Rio Grande, again elected to Congress. Later in life he was connected with the Panama railroad; still later, in 1852, he removed with his family to Oregon, where he was elected United States Senator.

The struggle for the Union came, and he hastened to New York, where his fiery eloquence stirred the heart of its people. When they rushed impetuously to arms, he warned the country of the magnitude of the struggle, and was foremost in support of the Government. He was not, however, a speaker only, but a worker as well. In a little time he had gathered about him an effective regiment. Men from all States rushed to fill up the ranks. Refusing to resign his position in the Senate and be promoted to a Major-Generalship, he retained his simple title of Colonel, and died with no higher rank.

He was killed at the head of his brigade, and with his life's blood sealed the vow he had made to see America a free and united people or die in the struggle. Courageous, upright, earnest, indomitable spirits like his can never be forgotten; they are the jewels of a nation, which brighten as they pass into eternity. In his own words, the words that from his eloquent lips rung over the grave of Broderick, let us give him to immortality.

"True friend and hero, hail and farewell!"

BATTLE AT CAMP WILD CAT, KY.
October 21, 1861.

On the same day that the disastrous battle at Ball's Bluff, Va., was fought, and also the successful engagement of Colonel Plummer's command at Frederickton, Mo., a spirited fight was maintained by a small force of Federal troops in Kentucky. They were successful in resisting the attack of a large body of the enemy under General Zollicoffer, who had made advances into that State from Tennessee, by the Cumberland Gap. The engagement was unimportant when viewed in reference to the numbers engaged, or the loss of life, but its moral effects were significant. It was the first battle thus far that had taken place upon the soil of Kentucky, and it was bravely fought by her own loyal sons.

To oppose the advance of the rebels, a single Kentucky regiment, under Colonel Garrard, was stationed at Rock-castle creek, at an encampment known by the name of "Wild Cat." General Zollicoffer conceived the design of cutting off this isolated regiment, and for that purpose was moving rapidly forward with six regiments of infantry and one of cavalry, sacking the towns of Barbourville and Loudon in his progress. General Albin Schoepf, who commanded the Federal troops in this district, hearing of the advance of the rebel forces, dispatched the Thirty-third Indiana, Colonel J. Coburn, from the camp at Big Hill, nineteen miles south of Richmond, with instructions to occupy an eminence half a mile to the east of Camp Wild Cat, while directions were also given to the Fourteenth Ohio to proceed to the same place; and two regiments of Tennessee Federalists, then at Camp Dick Robinson, forty-four miles from the scene of action, hastened to participate in the expected fight, and marched the whole distance on the day of the 21st, arriving just after the last feint by the enemy. Colonel Woolford's Kentucky cavalry had also arrived, and General Schoepf and staff reached the scene of action in the course of the day.

At eight o'clock on the morning of the 21st, before the arrival of Colonel Coburn's forces at the point designated, the advance of the enemy, with wild and exultant shouts, attacked Colonel Garrard's camp, and anticipated an easy victory over an inferior force, much reduced by sickness. But the brave Kentuckians met them with an undaunted front, and poured into their ranks a deadly fire. Having been taught to despise the little band they were now attacking, the rebels advanced again gallantly to the assault, but the cool and determined resistance they met with soon put them to flight, and they retired discomfited, to await the arrival of the main body of their forces.

Meantime Colonel Coburn, with four companies of the Thirty-third

Indiana, had started at seven o'clock, to reach the hill designated. The command consisted of Company D, Captain McCrea; Company I, Captain Hauser; Company E, Captain Hendricks; and Company G, Captain Dille—in all about three hundred and fifty men. Their arrival was most opportune, as the rebel forces were on the point of seizing the same position. The companies were immediately deployed as skirmishers. In about twenty minutes, the rebels, who were concealed in the woods, commenced firing. Soon after they appeared in front, half a mile to the south, and below in the valley. They were in large numbers, and formed in line, near an open space, and then approached the Federal force under cover of a wood which concealed them from view, and opened fire. At this moment the Kentucky cavalry (Colonel Garrard,) came up, and reinforced the Thirty-third. The enemy charged, but were repulsed under a galling fire. The front of the rebels approached within a few rods of Colonel Coburn, with their caps on their bayonets, saying that they were "Union men," and were "all right;" and having thus attempted to disarm the suspicion of the loyal troops, suddenly poured a murderous fire upon them. After an hour of severe struggle, the enemy were compelled to retreat, leaving part of their dead and wounded behind them.

At about the close of this attack, another detachment of the forces under General Schoepf came upon the ground. It consisted of four companies of the Seventeenth Ohio. Company E, Captain Fox; company C, Captain Haines; company K, Captain Rea; and company H, Captain Whisson, all of whom, under Major Ward, promptly formed in line ready for their part in the contest. But the enemy had retreated only to return with an increased force. At about two o'clock, P. M., the attack was renewed, and at the same time, company C, Fourteenth Ohio, Captain J. W. Brown, appeared on the field. The position was fiercely contested, the Federal troops rendering the most gallant and effective service in the face of the largely superior force brought against them. A few discharges of cannon, three pieces of which were in use, aided by the well-directed infantry fire, resulted in the total rout and dispersion of the enemy, who again retreated, and during the night were finally removed by General Zollicoffer. Captain Stannard's Ohio battery earned for itself high commendations in this contest.

The Federal loss was four killed and twenty-one wounded. We have no record of Zollicoffer's loss.

While the battle was raging, General Schoepf, who had just arrived, and had tied his horse to a tree at a short distance, desired a soldier to go and get him. The man hesitating, the General went himself, and just as he was unfastening the reins he was greeted with a storm of bullets. One of them passed through his boot-top, and several struck the tree to which the horse was tied. With the most perfect coolness the General mounted his horse, and rode off to his post, as leisurely as if he were an unconcerned spectator of the scene.

Zollicoffer subsequently had large reinforcements, which he put into a condition for the best possible service, and commenced fortifying the strong positions at Cumberland Gap.

BATTLE AT ROMNEY, VA.
October 26, 1861.

The town of Romney is located in Hampshire county, Virginia, on the south branch of the Potomac, one hundred and ninety miles northwest from Richmond. It had been the theatre of previous military adventures between the loyal troops and their enemies, who were on several occasions compelled to retire from the place, but afterwards took advantage of the absence of the Federal forces to return. Brigadier-General B. F. Kelley, who commanded a portion of the forces in the encounter at Phillipi, where he was wounded, was encamped with part of his command at New Creek. He resolved to dislodge the rebels from Romney, and ordered his forces to unite in a march on the town on the morning of the 26th of October. The Fourth and Eighth Ohio, and Seventh Virginia, were in the brigade, with the addition of the Ringgold Cavalry.

The forces, after a march along their various routes of from twenty to twenty-five miles, united, and about half-past two o'clock in the afternoon, encountered the outposts of the enemy at Mill Creek, five miles from Romney. These they drove in, and advanced to the Indian Mound Cemetery, west of the town, where the rebels made a stand, and opened fire with a twelve-pound rifled gun, placed in a commanding position in the cemetery, and with a mountain howitzer from the high grounds on the east bank of the river, at a point which commanded the road for half a mile. At the east end of the bridge the enemy had thrown up intrenchments, from which they kept up a constant fire of musketry upon the head of the column. They were responded to by a twelve-pounder and two six-pounders, until in about half an hour the General understood the position, when he gave the command to charge upon the enemy's entrenchments. The cavalry, led by Captains Keys and McGhee, dashed across the river at the ford, with enthusiastic shouts, while the infantry, under the command of Colonels Mason and De Puy, Lieutenant-Colonel Kelley, and Major Swearingen, rushed over the bridge to encounter the enemy at the mouth of his guns. As soon as they saw this movement, they immediately abandoned their positions, and retreated precipitately through the town, flying in the direction of Winchester.

General Kelley captured a considerable number of the enemy, among whom was Colonel Angus McDonald; two hundred horses, three wagon loads of new rifles, three cannon, a large quantity of corn, wagons, tents, and, in fact, everything they had.

Colonel Johns, with seven hundred men of the Second Potomac Home Brigade, under orders from General Kelley, started from North Branch bridge early in the morning, passing through Frankfort, having been instructed to make a diversion with his force toward Springfield to withdraw the attention of a portion of the enemy stationed there from General Kelley's movements. When within a mile and a half of Springfield the rear of his column was fired upon by the rebels, occasioning a delay of nearly an hour. The march was then renewed through Springfield, disclosing evidences of the retreat of the enemy on the way. On arriving at the bridge crossing the south branch of the Potomac, they were discovered on the opposite side of the river, when a brisk fire was commenced. After skirmishing half an hour, Colonel Johns determined to cross the bridge, but found that a portion of the planking had been torn up and removed. The enemy at the same time kept up a sharp fire, killing one, and wounding six of his men. The passage of the bridge being impracticable, and the firing having ceased in the direction of Romney, Colonel Johns inferred that General Kelley was in possession of the town. His own purpose having been accomplished in producing a diversion of the rebel forces, and the necessity of joining Kelley no longer existing, he withdrew his command to Oldtown, in Maryland, about nine P. M., after a march of twenty-five miles.

BATTLE OF FREDERICKTON, MO.
October 21, 1861.

Brigadier-General U. S. Grant commanding at Cairo, Illinois, being informed that the rebel recruits under Colonel Jeff. Thompson and Colonel Lowe, were congregating in Madison county, Missouri, ordered Colonel J. B. Plummer, of the Eleventh Missouri Volunteers, to proceed to Frederickton. Colonel Plummer was in command at Cape Girardeau, and on the 18th, the day following the receipt of the order, he marched with about fifteen hundred men, composed of the Seventeenth and Twentieth Illinois Volunteers, Colonels Ross and Marsh, the Eleventh Missouri, under the immediate command of Lieutenant-Colonel Pennabaker, Lieutenant White's section of Taylor's battery, and Captains Steward and Lansden's companies of cavalry.

On arriving at Frederickton, Colonel Plummer found that the rebels had evacuated the town the evening before, and that Colonel Carlin, with about three thousand Federals from Pilot Knob, had occupied the place a few hours before him. The enemy had retired in the direction of Greenville, and Colonel Carlin having reinforced Colonel Plummer with the Twenty-first and Thirty-third Illinois Volunteers, under Colonels Alexander and Hovey, six companies of the First Indiana Cavalry, Colonel Baker, and one section of Major Schofield's battery, under Lieutenant Hascock, they started in pursuit. The column, thus reinforced, was put in motion at about one o'clock, P. M., but had not proceeded more than three-quarters of a mile when the enemy was discovered a short distance in advance.

Colonel Ross, whose regiment was the leading one of the column, immediately deployed it to the left into a lane, and threw forward two companies as skirmishers, to feel the enemy, whose exact position and strength it was difficult to determine. Colonel Plummer directed Colonel Ross to move forward his regiment into the cornfield in support of his skirmishers, and ordered up Lieutenant White's section of Taylor's battery, which immediately opened fire, and by its effectiveness soon caused the enemy to respond. Their artillery consisted of four pieces, masked, upon the slope of a hill about six hundred yards distant. The principal body of their infantry, under Colonel Lowe, was posted in the cornfield to the left of the road. With them the Seventeenth Illinois was soon engaged. The other regiments of the column were deployed to the right and left of the road as they came up. Colonel Plummer then ordered forward the Thirty-eighth Illinois from the town, which promptly came upon the field under one of its field officers, leaving there the Eighth Wisconsin, under Colonel Murphy, and one section of Major Schofield's battery in reserve—a post of honor, though one disagreeable to them, as all were eager to participate in the engagement.

As soon as it was practicable, Major Schofield, of the First Missouri Volunteer Light Artillery, brought upon the field two sections of his battery under Captain Matter and Lieutenant Hascock, which were placed in position, and did efficient service. Major Schofield rendered valuable aid in bringing the regiments on the right of the road into line of battle, and in directing their movements.

In the mean time the enemy were falling back before the steady advance and deadly fire of the Seventeenth and Twentieth Illinois, and a portion of the Eleventh Missouri. Their retreat soon became a rout, and they fled in every direction, pursued by the Union troops.

At this time the enemy's infantry on the right, where Thompson commanded in person, being in retreat, the Indiana Cavalry charged and pursued them. Thompson, however, had rallied a portion of his

troops, about half a mile in the rear of his first position, and brought one gun into battery on the road, supported by infantry on either side. The cavalry charged and took the gun, being exposed at the same time to a deadly fire from the enemy's infantry; but as the column that had been ordered forward to their support did not reach the point in time, the enemy were enabled to carry the piece from the field. It was here that Major Gavitt and Captain Highman fell.

The rout now became general, and the enemy were pursued by the Union troops several miles, until the approach of night induced Colonel Plummer to recall them to town. Captain Stewart, however, with his squadron of cavalry followed them until late in the night, and brought in several prisoners.

Jeff. Thompson had left Fredrickton on the previous evening, marching ten miles on the Greenville road, and then turning to meet Colonel Plummer at a point where he had intended to make the attack in the morning. On learning that the national troops had taken a different road, he led his force back to the point near Fredrickton where the encounter took place. The rebel force was about two thousand five hundred. Colonel Lowe, his colleague, was killed, and one hundred and twenty-five dead were left on the field; the number of their wounded is not definitely known. Four of their guns and eighty prisoners were taken. The loss of the Federal army was seven killed, and sixty wounded.

CHARGE OF FREMONT'S BODY-GUARD AT SPRINGFIELD, MO.
October 25, 1861.

Subsequent to the death of General Lyon, Springfield had been made a rebel stronghold, and General Price, when the advancing army of General Fremont compelled him to retreat from the central part of the State, had established his headquarters there. During the month of October, however, being warned by approaching columns of the Federal troops, he had commenced the withdrawal of his forces and the immense train and supplies he had accumulated in case he should be compelled to retreat to Arkansas.

On the 20th of October, General Sigel, who commanded the Federal advance, was near Bolivar, and General Sturgis' command was one day behind. General Lane was at Osceola; Hunter's and McKinstry's divisions, as well as General Ashboth, were at or near Warsaw; General Pope was near Louisville; while General Fremont and his staff were at Pomme de Terre river, *en route* for Quincy.

Having obtained information from his scouts that only about three hundred of the enemy were at Springfield, General Fremont dispatched Major Zagonyi, with 150 of his Body-guard, and also an equal force of Prairie Scouts under Major F. J. White, who was then attached to Sigel's command, to combine their forces before reaching Springfield, and attack the rebel camp by surprise.

The distance from the camp on the Pomme de Terre river to Springfield was fifty-one miles. The Body-guard started on Thursday, the 24 at 8½ P. M., and reached the neighborhood of Springfield, at 3 P. M. on the 25th, having overtaken the command of Major White, dispatched from the camp of General Sigel to take part in this enterprise. Major White, who was suffering from severe illness, was obliged to stop for an hour or two to rest, and when he again started to join his command, expecting to find them in the direct road from Bolivar to Springfield, he was captured by the rebel scouts, who had been informed of the approach of the Federal cavalry. Zagonyi had deemed it necessary to change his plan of attack, and to approach the rear of the rebel camp, of which fact Major White had not been informed. The change was occasioned by unexpectedly meeting a small body of the enemy, who thus became aware of the designed attack.

Major Zagonyi, on approaching within about eight miles of Springfield, came upon a small foraging party, five of whom he captured, and the remainder returned to the city and gave the alarm. Proceeding further on, the Major gained additional information from Union citizens and learned that the place was held by a force at least five or six times as large as was supposed. Notwithstanding this he resolved to press on and examine for himself, but the farther he proceeded the more positive was the information that the town was held by a large force.

The first that was seen of the enemy was a short distance from the town, where the advance discovered a full regiment drawn up on selected ground, near the road, and prepared to receive them. The ground being unfavorable for offensive operations, Major Zagonyi resolved not to attack them, but to cross the prairie to the westward and approach the city by the Mount Vernon road.

This was successfully accomplished, and upon arriving within about a mile, the citizens notified him that the enemy, two thousand strong, were awaiting his coming a quarter of a mile distant. Major Zagonyi was entreated not to risk his little band in the encounter; but he had not made a forced march of fifty miles to gain possession of a town without at least making an attempt to fulfil his instructions; and placing the Body-guard in front, and himself leading, he gave the order to advance.

As the Major was to approach from the west, the rebels had scattered skirmishers throughout the dense woods or chaparral on either side, who greeted his approach with a scathing fire which emptied several saddles. The woods and rough bushy ground to the south of the road, was also full of their skirmishers, hidden in the branches and behind bushes and trees. The main body of the force, however, was drawn up in the form of a hollow square, in a large open field to the north of the road, the infantry bordering along a high Virginia rail fence, nearly to the brook, and also at the head of the field bordering on the woods, and the cavalry on the other side of the field also supported by the for

DESPERATE CHARGE OF FREMONT'S BODY-GUARD.

Upon reaching the vicinity of this place, Major Zagonyi ordered an advance at a trot, and when fairly in the woods, the pace was increased to a gallop. When the fire opened, the two companies of the First Missouri Cavalry, and the Irish Dragoons, composing Major White's battalion, countermarched to the left. Major Zagonyi's command alone proceeded down the road through the fire of the enemy. Upon reaching the open field, an attempt was made to tear down the fence and charge upon the enemy. It was soon discovered, however, that this would be impossible without a heavy loss, and they immediately made a rush down the road, over a brook, where, in a measure shielded from the enemy's fire, they levelled the rails and effected an entrance. Here, in the midst of the briars and stubble bordering the brook, he succeeded in forming his men, and with the Major at their head, they gallantly charged up the hill of the open field, right into the midst of their foes. As they charged, the command spread out fan-like, some to the right, some to the left, and others straight up to the woods in front.

The cavalry to the right were scattered almost instantaneously; the infantry made a somewhat firmer stand, but it was only for a moment. The charge was so furious, so well directed, and so compact, that the rebel ranks were quickly scattered. Under the well-directed fire of the enemy's sharpshooters, the little band of one hundred and sixty-two rank and file, contending against one thousand eight hundred, necessarily suffered severely.

Pursuing a portion of the rebels into town, the Major here assembled his command, or such portions of it as were at hand, raised the stars and stripes upon the court-house, detailed a guard to attend to his wounded, and then fearful that the enemy might become cognizant of his small force, and rally, determined to retrace his steps toward Bolivar, where he could meet reinforcements, the more especially as they had ridden over eighty miles and been over twenty-four hours without food.

In the mean time Major White's command had made a detour through the cornfield, and after making a successful charge and defeating the rebel forces stationed there, he reached the town a little while after Zagonyi had left, and took possession of it.

The loss of the enemy, as nearly as could be ascertained, was one hundred and six killed, wounded not known; that of the Federals but fifteen killed, twenty-seven wounded and ten missing.

THE DEPARTMENT OF MISSOURI.

The death of General Lyon and the defeat of the Federal army at Wilson's Creek, on the 10th of August, and the disastrous consequences— followed on the 20th of September by the loss of Lexington and its noble band of defenders, filled the whole land with discontent. The commanding officer of the Department at this time was Major-General Fremont. The public, asking for success, and confident that it could be achieved, were impatient of the delays and heavy expenditure of money that seemed at least to fetter the Missouri Department. From General Fremont the public had expected the most vigorous and brilliant campaign. The difficulties and obstacles with which a commander must contend in organizing a military force sufficient to encounter a large army of dashing and lawless insurgents, are not always properly under-

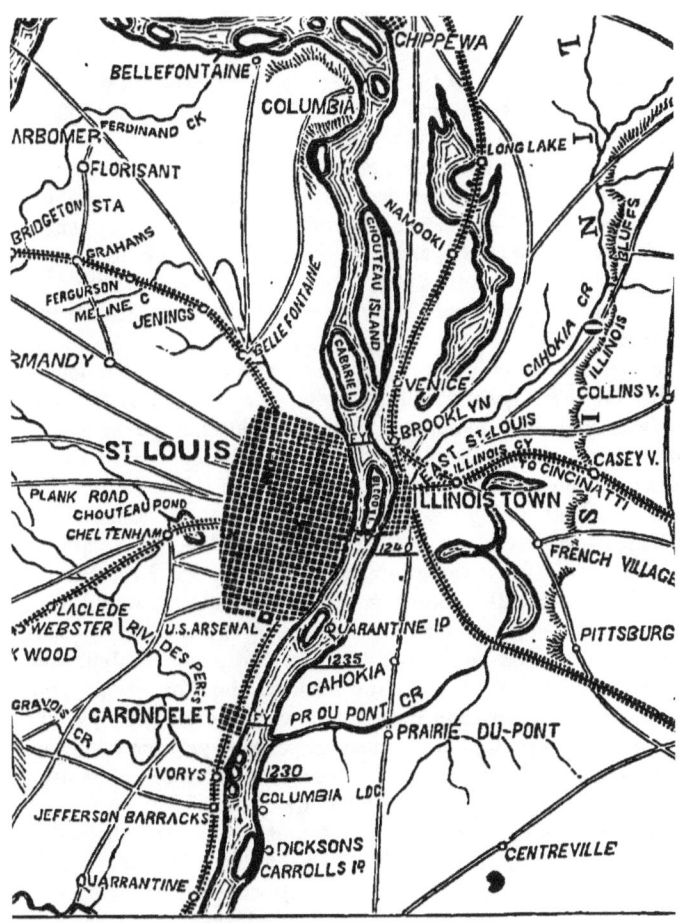

SECTION OF THE MISSISSIPPI RIVER.

SHOWING THE DISTANCES FROM NEW ORLEANS.

stood and considered by the public; and their expectations, no doubt, led far in advance of the possibilities of the situation. Occupying a field which had just been made the scene of open hostilities, and where the Governor and the Legislature, as a body, were hostile to the General Government, the entire work was to be done after General Fremont had entered upon it. The difficulty of supplying reinforcements where needed, with no reserves upon which he could draw, left no alternative to Lyon and Mulligan but that of retreat or collision with an overpowering enemy. In these reverses they suffered a cruel defeat, but won imperishable fame.

The loss of General Lyon, and the reverses to the national army, afforded cause for great exultation to the secessionists of St. Louis and its vicinity, and their demonstrations of hostility became so marked that General Fremont, on the 14th of August, was compelled to resort to the extreme measure of declaring martial law in that city. This had the effect of restraining the rebel sympathizers in immediate proximity with the headquarters of the Commander, but was not regarded in the State at large. Under these circumstances General Fremont followed this proclamation with another on the 30th of August, establishing martial law in the State, and fixing the lines of the army of occupation as extending from Leavenworth by way of the posts of Jefferson City, Rolla and Ironton, to Cape Girardeau, on the Mississippi river. All persons taken with arms in their hands were to be tried by courts-martial, and if found guilty, shot. The property of persons taking up arms against the United States was declared confiscated to public use, "and their slaves, if any they have, are hereby declared free men."

This proclamation produced a profound excitement throughout the country, and was received by the people with varied emotions—enthusiastically applauded by some, and bitterly condemned by others.

The President, on the 2d of September, addressed a letter to General Fremont, recommending him to modify his proclamation. General Fremont desired the President to make an order for the modification in his own name, a request with which the Chief Magistrate complied, and under date of September 11th, communicated to General Fremont, that the proclamation in question should be made to conform to the act of Congress of August 6th, which confiscated only property *used* in rebellion; and referred the question regarding slaves to the determination of the courts, or to subsequent legislation.

While in St. Louis, General Fremont was actively engaged in the organization of his forces, and making preparations for his approaching campaign. To protect the city he had extensive fortifications constructed. He also projected and ordered the building of the gunboats, which have since rendered such signal service. The necessity of massing a large army near Washington, after the defeat at Bull Run, compelled the withdrawal of many regiments which had been assigned to the Missouri Department. It was not until the 27th of September that Fremont was prepared to enter upon an offensive campaign. Accordingly on that day he left St. Louis, and with fifteen steamers and fifteen thousand men, sailed up the Missouri to Jefferson City. Here he halted several days to collect additional material necessary for his march into the interior.

On the 29th, two days after General Fremont's departure from St. Louis, General Price commenced the evacuation of Lexington, leaving a small force as a guard. On the 7th of October, General Fremont left Jefferson City, marching in the direction of Sedalia, for the purpose of attacking the rebel commander at the earliest opportunity.

On the 16th, two hundred and twenty men of the First Missouri Scouts, under Major F. J. White, surprised the rebel garrison at Lexington, and recaptured the place, with the Federal sick and wounded there, together with two pieces of cannon, a quantity of guns, pistols and other articles which the rebels threw away in their flight. The garrison numbered three hundred men. The victorious troops found the inhabitants in a deplorable condition. Some portions of the town had been plundered of everything that could be appropriated, and many persons were suffering for the necessaries of life. It was a painful scene, and formed one of those early pictures of the war which have since been multiplied so fearfully in the border States.

On the 1st of November, General Fremont, then at Springfield, entered into an arrangement with General Price, to facilitate the exchange of prisoners, agreeing to release any who had been made prisoners "for the mere expression of political opinions;" and providing also that "the war in future be confined exclusively to the armies in the field." Armed bodies, unauthorized by the commanders, were to be disbanded, and persons guilty of violence and lawless acts were to be subject to trial by courts-martial. This agreement was signed by Major Henry W. Williams and D. Robert Barclay, Esq., for General Price, and J. H. Eaton, Assistant-Adjutant-General, for General Fremont. A proclamation, announcing this negotiation, was accordingly published on the first of November.

The next day, General Fremont received from the Department at Washington, an order relieving him from his command. General David Hunter was appointed to the Department of Missouri, temporarily as his successor. General Fremont returned to St. Louis, and soon afterwards reached New York city, where he awaited the orders of the Government.

The Federal army was now withdrawn from the south-western portion of the State, and the whole of that vast field was reoccupied by the insurgent forces, and thousands of recruits were gathered into their ranks.

On the 4th of November, the antagonist forces were commanded as follows:—General Hunter, 5,000; General Sigel, 4,000; General Ashboth, 4,500; General McKinstry, 5,500; General Pope, 4,000; General Lane, 2,500; General Sturgis, 1,000. The rebels under General Price numbered 15,000; under General McCulloch, 7,000.

The disloyal members of the Legislature held a session at Neosho, Newton county, in the extreme south-western portion of the State, and on the 19th of November passed an ordinance of secession, and sent their Commissioners to the Confederate Congress at Richmond. Missouri, as represented by them, was admitted to the Confederacy on the 27th of November.

On the 30th of November, General Price, then at Neosho, issued a proclamation to the people of Missouri, calling upon them in the most earnest manner for recruits to the rebel army. He called for fifty thousand men, who might rendezvous at headquarters with anything in the shape of arms that they could find; and if unarmed, to enroll themselves, and they would be supplied. He represented the hopelessness of the cause, and the certain defeat of the rebel army unless immediately reinforced. His appeals had some effect in promoting sedition, and in securing enlistments, but they fell far short of the number he demanded.

On the 1st of December, Gen. Price was at Osceola, with 18,000 men.

On the 6th of December, Independence was entered by a band of rebels, who seized several citizens and compelled them to take an oath not to bear arms against the Southern Confederacy.

On the 13th of the same month, Governor Jackson, at New Madrid, issued a proclamation to the insurgent army, in which he attempted a defence of the rebellion, and asserted that the people of Missouri were in favor of secession. Unfortunately for the veracity or the knowledge of Governor Jackson, wherever the people of the State were delivered from the terrorism of the rebels and marauders, they adhered to the Union, as was verified by the fact, that up to the 20th of January, 1862, no less than 33,882 Missourians had entered the Federal service for three years, and 6,000 had volunteered for three months.

Major-General Henry W. Halleck was now in command of the Department. He was compelled to adopt rigorous measures in some cases in consequence of the pertinacious conduct of the secessionists. A memorable event of the month of January was the annual election for officers of the Mercantile Library Association, in which loyalty and secession were antagonistic elements. General Halleck officially announced that each officer of the Association would be expected to take the oath of allegiance within ten days from the date of his order, and in default thereof the officers failing should be deemed to have resigned their offices. Any officer refusing to take the oath of allegiance, who should exercise or attempt to exercise the functions of his office, should be arrested and dealt with under the laws of war.

He also ordered that all carriages bearing the enemy's flag should be seized and confiscated; and that women resorting to the neighborhood of the military prison and insulting the Federal troops, or communicating with prisoners by exhibiting and waving secession flags, should be imprisoned. Disloyal persons who, under the military rules, were liable to assessment for the support of loyal fugitives from their homes, should be compelled to pay their assessment. All persons of every rank or position, violating the laws, or interfering with their execution, should be dealt with under strict penalties.

This energetic administration had the desired effect; and the violent minority who were determined, at every hazard, to plunge the State into war, were restrained, and order and peace assured and restored.

THE STONE FLEET.

Notwithstanding all the activity and watchfulness of the blockading vessels off the Southern coast, many instances were exultingly heralded by the Southern press, as well as in Europe, of the successful running of the blockade by vessels bound both outward and inward. The logic of these occurrences was very simple on the part of the secessionists and their sympathizers. The frequent evasion of the blockade proved that it was "inefficient" on the part of the Federal government, and therefore not only to be disregarded, but officially declared by foreign governments to be incomplete, and practically null and void. This declaration was expected to be sufficient to warrant the free movements of commerce, and any attempt to interfere on the part of the United States would be a challenge for the intervention of England and France.

The repeated instances of vessels escaping rendered it an imperative necessity for the government to adopt some measure that would, if possible, prevent their recurrence at the principal ports of the South. For this purpose it was determined to close several of the harbors by placing obstructions in the channels. Most of the harbors of the Southern coast, in consequence of the deltas, and numerous islands at their entrances, have several channels, through which vessels of light draft may pass, while those of the heaviest draft are confined to one principal channel. This is the case in the approach to both Charleston and

Savannah. The obstructing of these two principal channels was therefore assigned for the month of December.

For this purpose a number of old whaling vessels were purchased at New Bedford and New London, freighted with granite from the Bay State, and taken to Port Royal as a rendezvous, whence they were to be convoyed to their destination. The people of Savannah, after the capture of Port Royal and Beaufort, anticipating the approach of the Federal fleet, volunteered the work on their own behalf and blockaded their own port by similar means. The fleet was therefore at liberty to repair to Charleston, and within sight of the walls of Sumter, to shut out the rebellious people of that city from the ocean.

The "Stone Fleet" sailed from Port Royal on the 18th of December, accompanied by the steamers Cahawba, Philadelphia and Ericsson, to tow and assist, the whole convoyed by the Mohican, Captain Gordon, the Ottawa, Captain Stevens, and Pocahontas, Captain Balch.

The fleet arrived off Charleston harbor the next day and preparations were made for sinking them in their places. Each of the weather-beaten and storm-tossed old vessels that had so long borne the stars and stripes in every latitude, were now to make a stubborn protest against treason by keeping watch at the very door of its birth-place. They were furnished with ingenious contrivances and plugs, the withdrawal of which would allow the water to flow in and sink them on the floor of the channel.

The sinking of the fleet was intrusted to Captain Charles H. Davis, formerly on the Coast Survey, and ever since more or less intimately connected with it. It is remarkable that when, in 1851, an appropriation was made by the Federal Government for the improvement of Charleston harbor, and, at the request of South Carolina, a commission of army and navy officers was appointed to superintend the work, Captain Davis was one of the commission, and for three or four years was engaged in these operations. The present attempt was of somewhat different character. The entrance by the main ship channel runs from the bar to Fort Sumter, six miles, nearly south and north. The city is three miles beyond, bearing about N. W. The other channels are Sanford's, Swash, the North, and Maffit's, or Sullivan's Island, which need not to be particularly described. Only the latter is practicable for vessels of any draught, but all serve more or less to empty the waters discharged by the Ashley and Cooper rivers. Over the bar, at the entrance of the main ship channel, is a narrow passage, through which vessels may carry eleven feet at low water; about seventeen at high water. The plan of Captain Davis for closing the harbor proceeded on the following principles:

The obstructions were to be placed on both sides of the crest of the bar, so that the same forces which created the bar might be relied on to keep them in their places.

The bar was not to be obstructed entirely; for natural forces would soon open a new passage, since the rivers must discharge themselves by some outlet; but to be only partially obstructed, so that, while this channel was ruined, no old one, like Swash or Sanford, should be improved, or a new one formed.

The vessels were so placed that on the channel course it would be difficult to draw a line through any part of it that would not be intercepted by one of them. A ship, therefore, endeavoring to make her way out or in could not, by taking the bearings of any point of departure, as she could not sail on any straight line.

The vessels were placed checkerwise, at some distance from each other, so as to create an artificial unevenness of the bottom, remotely resembling Hell Gate and Holmes's Hole, which unevenness would give rise to eddies, counter-currents and whirlpools, adding so seriously to the difficulties of navigation that it could only be practicable by steamers, or with a very commanding breeze.

The execution of this plan was begun by buoying out the channel and circumscribing within four points the space where the vessels were all to be sunk, as follows:

*
S. W. * THE BAR. * N. E.
*

The distance between the points from s. w. to n. e. is about an eighth of a mile; the breadth perhaps half as much. It was no part of the plan to build a wall of ships across, but to drop them at a little distance from each other, on the principles above stated, closing the channel to navigation, but leaving it open to the water.

Work was resumed on Friday morning, the 20th, the Ottawa and Pocahontas bringing the ships to their stations. The placing of them was an operation of considerable nicety, especially as some of the vessels were so deep as to be with difficulty dragged on the bar, except at high water. A graver hindrance to their exact location was found in the imperfection of the arrangement for sinking, several of the ships remaining afloat so long after the plug was knocked out, that they swung out of position. They were, nevertheless, finally placed very nearly according to the plan. Great credit was earned by Mr. Bradbury and Mr. Godfrey for the successful execution of so difficult an undertaking. The last ship, the Archer, closed the only remaining gap, and the manner in which Mr. Bradbury took her in with the Pocahontas and then extricated the latter from her perilous position, filled the fleet with admiration for his skillful seamanship and cool daring. By half past ten the last plug was drawn, and every ship of the sixteen was either sunk or sinking.

One of the vessels, the Robin Hood, with upright masts, stood erect, in water too shallow to submerge her. As evening drew near she was set on fire, and in a little time the evening sky was lighted up with the pyrotechnic display, while the inhabitants of Charleston, the garrison of Fort Moultrie, and the surroundings, were compelled to look on and see the temporary completion of the blockade they had so long derided and defied.

This event provoked loud and vindictive complaints and assaults in France and England, and the measure was denounced as an outrage on civilization, and a sufficient warrant for interference in the war. But an examination of the historical precedents afforded by British practice closed the mouths of the declaimers in Parliament as well as through the press, and once more American practice was permitted to pass, justified by the verdict of opinion as well as of illustrious example.

BATTLE OF CAMP ALLEGHANY, W. VIRGINIA.
December 13, 1861.

On Thursday morning, December 12th, Brigadier-General R. H. Milroy started from his headquarters on Cheat Mountain Summit, with fifteen hundred men, with the design of attacking a rebel camp on the Alleghany mountains, twenty-five miles distant. The column started at eight o'clock, and after a fatiguing day's march arrived, at eight P. M., at the old Camp Bartow, on the Greenbrier river, the scene of General Reynolds' rencontre on the 3d of October previous. Here the troops rested until eleven P. M., when the General divided his force into two columns, with the intention of reaching the enemy's camp on the summit of the mountain, about eight and a half miles distant, from two opposite points, at four o'clock, A. M., of the 13th.

The first division, consisting of detachments from the Ninth Indiana, Colonel Moody, and Second Virginia, Major Owens, about one thousand strong, took up its march on the old Greenbank road to attack the enemy on the left.

The second division consisted of detachments from the Thirteenth Indiana, Twenty-fifth and Thirty-second Ohio, and Bracken Cavalry, under Major Dobbs, Colonel J. A. Jones, Captain Hamilton and Captain Bracken. Brigadier-General Reynolds and his staff conducted this division, numerically about the same as the first division. This column took the Staunton pike, and marched cautiously until they came in sight of the enemy's camp, where, after throwing out more skirmishers, the division left the road and commenced to ascend the mountain to the enemy's right. After driving in some of the hostile pickets they reached the summit in good order. The enemy were fully prepared to receive them. The fight on the enemy's right commenced about twenty minutes after daylight.

Lieutenant McDonald, of General Reynolds' staff, with one company of the Thirteenth Indiana, formed the line of battle, placing the Twenty-fifth Ohio on his left, part of the Thirteenth Indiana on their left, and part of the Thirty-second Ohio on their left. The enemy immediately advanced to attack the Federal troops, but after a few rounds retreated in great confusion, leaving their dead and wounded. Colonel Moody's division not appearing to attack the enemy on the left, the rebels seeing the inferior force opposed to them, were again encouraged to advance toward their assailants, which they did with a far superior force, pouring in their fire with vigor. Some of the Federals now commenced falling to the rear, all along the line; but Captains Charlesworth and Crowe, of the Twenty-fifth Ohio, Lieutenant McDonald, Captains Myers and Newland, of the Thirteenth Indiana, and Hamilton, of the Thirty-second Ohio, rallied them, and brought them into line in a few moments. The enemy again fell back and attempted to turn their right flank, but was immediately met and repulsed. The fortunes of the day appeared to alternate between the respective armies for three hours, the Federals holding out bravely against the superior numbers of the enemy, who were enabled to concentrate their entire army of two thousand men and four or five pieces of artillery against this comparatively small force.

Colonel Moody's force not having then been heard from, Colonel Jones, who had charge of the division now in action, after exhausting his ammunition, withdrew his men from the field.

Almost at this juncture, Colonel Moody's command, which had been detained by obstructions placed in the road over which they were compelled to pass, arrived, and attacked the enemy vigorously on his left, and in turn maintained an obstinate contest, unaided, against the entire rebel command, which they did with much courage and skill, until three o'clock, P. M., when they too were compelled to retire before the superior force of their opponents.

Though thwarted in his plan of attack by the unexpected obstructions which Colonel Moody's division had to encounter, General Milroy was far from being disconcerted by the result. The men had evinced a high order of courage, and the divisions had alternately maintained an obstinate fight against an army of nearly three times their number.

The official report of the casualties on the Federal side gives the number of killed, twenty; wounded, one hundred and seven; missing, ten. The rebel loss is acknowledged by the Richmond *Enquirer* to have been about the same.

BATTLE AT MUNFORDSVILLE, KY.
December 17, 1861.

Colonel Willich, with the Thirty-second Indiana, a regiment composed of Germans, occupying an advance post of General McCook's division of the Federal army in Kentucky, was attacked on the 17th of December, by three regiments of Arkansas infantry, Colonel Terry's Texan Rangers, and Major Phifer's cavalry, and also an artillery company, with four pieces, the whole under the command of General T. C. Hindman.

Colonel Willich's regiment was guarding a new bridge built by the Federal troops over Green river, at Rowlett's Station, on the Louisville and Nashville railroad, a temporary substitute for the handsome iron structure which had been destroyed by the rebels, in front of Mumfordsville. A picket guard of two companies had been thrown across the river on the south side, occupying a wide area of cleared ground, which was skirted by forests, from whence the rebels attempted to surprise and capture them.

The second company, Captain Glass, was acting in detached squads as pickets in the woods on the right flank, and were attacked in detail by the enemy's skirmishers. The pickets made a gallant defence, and fell back slowly and in good order on their supports. The alarm in the mean time having been given to the other companies on the north side of the river, they started in "double-quick" over the bridge, crossed the hill on the opposite side, and rushed with fierce haste into the woods whence the firing proceeded, led on by Lieutenant-Colonel Treba, Colonel Willich at the time being necessarily at headquarters. A portion of the third company, under Lieutenant Sachs, occupied a covered position on the left flank, where they were now attacked by the advancing enemy. Unable to restrain the ardor of his men, the Lieutenant boldly left his sheltered position and attacked the rebels in the open field; but fierce as his onset was, the disparity of numbers proved too greatly against him, and his little band would have inevitably been cut to pieces but for the timely arrival of Lieutenant-Colonel Treba, with the main body of the regiment. He sent the sixth, seventh and tenth companies to support the second company on the right, and the first, fifth, eighth and ninth companies to support the third company on the left flank. At the very first rush of the skirmishers, the enemy were thrown into confusion, and driven back at all points.

Then the most severe and bloody part of the battle commenced. With terrible ferocity Colonel Terry's regiment of Texas Rangers poured in black masses of cavalry upon the Union skirmishers along the whole line. They rode up within fifteen or twenty yards, some even in the very midst of the men, and commenced a terrible fire from their carbines and revolvers. At their first onset, it seemed as if every one of the men would be destroyed. But here it was that the veteran coolness and bravery of the Union troops shone forth. They allowed the enemy to come almost as near as he chose, and then poured a deadly fire upon him, which shook the entire line. Upon the right flank of the third company's position, by order of Adjutant Schmidt, the eighth company was led forth by Lieutenants Kappel and Levy; upon the left, Lieutenant-Colonel Treba advanced with the ninth company; both attacked the enemy in close skirmishers' line, drove him back, and rescued the rest of the heroic little band under Lieutenant Sachs. He himself and a number of his men were, however, already killed, though they had made the enemy pay dearly for their lives.

Now the artillery of the enemy was brought to bear upon the Union men. Their fire, balls and shrapnell, was well directed, but fortunately not very fatal. Only a few of the men were wounded by splinters of balls.

While this was going on upon the left wing, the conflict on the right was no less severe. The second, sixth and tenth companies were scattered as skirmishers, while the seventh was drawn up in company column for their support. The sixth company had taken position behind a fence. The Rangers galloped up to them in close line, and commenced firing from rifles and revolvers. Their fire was steadily returned by the sixth, which held them in check till a part of them got behind the fence, when the skirmishers fell back behind the seventh, drawn up in a square. Now a fearful conflict ensued. A whole battalion of Rangers, fully two hundred strong, bore down upon the little band of not more than fifty. Upon the front and left flank of the square they rushed, with a fierce attempt to trample down the squad before them.

Captain Welschbellich allowed them to come within a distance of seventy yards, then fired a volley, which staggered and sent them back. But immediately afterward they reformed and again rushed fiercely upon the front and both flanks of the square. They seemed frantic with rage over the successful resistance offered to them, and this time many of their band rode up to the points of the bayonets. But another well-aimed volley emptied a number of saddles, and sent back the whole mass which a moment before had threatened certain destruction to Captain Welschbellich's company. A few bayonet thrusts and scattering shots brought down those who had ventured to the front. This second repulse had a marked effect. Yet a third attack was made, much less determined and fierce than the two first, though it was more disastrous to the enemy. During this third attack it was that Colonel Terry, the commander of the Rangers, was killed. Upon his fall, the whole column broke and fled in wild dismay.

But in place of the Rangers, a whole regiment of infantry, accompanied by their band of music, now marched against the "invincible square." Before this overpowering force Captain Welschbellich deemed it prudent to retire, and united with the second, sixth and tenth companies again.

About this time it was that Colonel Willich, with his battle horse in a foam, arrived upon the field. He saw the right wing retiring, and the entire infantry of the enemy, two regiments, coming on, thus endangering the retreat of the left wing. He therefore ordered the signal for "retiring slowly" to be given, and collected the companies. The second company, under Captain Glass, and the seventh, under Captain Welschbellich, were the first who took their places in the line of battle of the regiment.

About this time a manœuvre was executed by the first company, under Captain Erdemeyer, which decided the day. When the battle commenced, and the impression prevailed that the Unionists were fighting cavalry alone, Lieutenant-Colonel Treba had detached this company to take a position and attack the flank of the enemy. When the first company arrived at the place of destination, Captain Erdemeyer found that the enemy had likewise a large force of infantry and artillery, to attack which would have been certain destruction to his company. He therefore kept his covered position until the time mentioned. Then, finding the larger part of the infantry drawn to another part of the field, he ordered an advance. His appearance was the signal of a general retreat of the enemy. The rest of the cavalry fled, the artillery retired in haste, and the infantry followed as quickly.

The Union loss was eleven killed, twenty wounded, and five missing. The enemy left a large number of killed on the field, and among their dead was the body of Colonel Terry. The rebel loss was thirty-three killed and sixty wounded.

CAPTURE OF REBEL RECRUITS AT MILFORD, MO.

On the eighteenth of December, Brigadier-General Pope, commanding the Federal troops in the central district of Missouri, made a brilliant and successful movement, which resulted in the capture of a considerable number of the enemy.

It will be recollected that the withdrawal of the Federal troops from Springfield and the leading points of both central and southern Missouri, had given free scope to the action of the enemy. Seditious proclama-

tions been had issued by Ex-Governor Jackson and General Price, and had been thoroughly circulated. Enlisting agents, also, had been very active, and some two thousand recruits, mostly drawn from the northern counties, were proceeding by slow stages southward, to unite with the main body under General Price.

A well laid plan was matured by Generals Halleck and Pope to capture these reinforcements; and two brigades of General Pope's division were dispatched without exciting any suspicion as to their destination, to intercept the enemy on their march. The brigades were constituted as follows:

First Brigade, Acting Brigadier-General Steele.—Twenty-seventh regiment Ohio Volunteers, Colonel Kennett; Twenty-second regiment Indiana Volunteers, Colonel Hendricks; First regiment Kansas Volunteers, Colonel Thayer; one battery First Missouri Volunteers, Lieutenant Marr; four companies regular cavalry, Colonel Amory.

Second Brigade, Acting Brigadier-General Jeff. C. Davis.—Eighteenth regiment Indiana Volunteers, Colonel Patterson; Eighth regiment Indiana Volunteers, Colonel Benton; Twenty-fourth regiment Indiana Volunteers, Lieutenant ——; one battery First Missouri Artillery, Lieutenant Klaus; one squadron First Iowa Cavalry, Major Torrence.

The whole was under the immediate command of General Pope. The four companies of regular cavalry were the fragments of the original companies, B, C, D, and E, and numbered but a little over a hundred men. They were under the command of Captain Crittenden, of the regular army, son of Hon. John J. Crittenden.

The command started from Sedalia on Sunday, the 15th, and encamped at night eleven miles distant on the road to Clinton. The next day they marched twenty-six miles, and at sunset arrived at Shawnee Mound, in Henry county. Here reports of various companies of rebels began to come in from residents and from Union scouts. One company of near five hundred was heard of at a point about twelve miles northwest, and several smaller bodies directly south, from Clinton to Butler. General Pope then dispatched his whole available force of cavalry, nearly seven hundred, before they had secured three hours' rest, after the five hundred near Morristown. The cavalry under Lieutenant-Colonel Brown, of the Seventh Missouri Volunteers, pushed on all night, and arriving at the rebel camp they found it vacated. The enemy had received warning and fled precipitately, leaving numerous evidences of haste. The cavalry, notwithstanding their forty miles' continuous march, pushed on after the fleeing rebels till they reached Rose Hill, picking up some twenty or thirty stragglers on the road. At Rose Hill the rebels separated into several squads, some taking the road west, others taking the south route to Butler, and Colonel Brown had no other alternative than to rest his exhausted horses, and finally to make his way back to the main column next day, near Warrensburg. He brought in nearly one hundred prisoners.

General Pope in the meantime kept advancing in a direction west of north to Chilhowee, a most important point, being the centre of numerous cross-roads. This was near the site of the rebel camp just referred to, and here the pickets brought in some few straggling men who were bound for Price's army. At Chilhowee they heard of a rebel force of 1,800 from the north, and of the scouring of the country south of Clinton by Major Hubbard, of the First Missouri Cavalry. The direction of the Union forces was at once east, toward Warrenburg. That night (Wednesday) they encamped two and a half miles west of Warrenburg. The reports were confirmed by a loyal man, who was on his way to give the information. He gave their location as at Kilpatrick's mill, on the Clear fork of Blackwater Creek. (Milford is the post-office name.) Early on Thursday morning they started in the direction of Knob Noster, being directly south of the enemy. Colonel Merrill's Horse was ordered to take the direct road running parallel with the course of the Blackwater, so as to intercept them in case they took a western course.

The brigade of Colonel Davis was placed in the advance, with orders to keep well up to the cavalry, a section of artillery being ready to support the cavalry upon a minute's warning. General Pope, with the main body, kept due west for Knob Noster, ready to come up if necessary. Colonel Davis, finding that the enemy was still in camp at Milford, diverged to the left, and put the regular cavalry, under Lieutenant Amory, in the advance, the four companies of the First Iowa Cavalry, under Major Torrence, being next. On approaching the mill, the men discovered that the rebels were posted on the opposite side of the bridge, across the dam. Finding that it would be dangerous to charge the bridge mounted, Lieutenant Amory ordered the men to dismount and skirmish with pistols and sabres, as infantry, the fourth man holding the horses of the other three. This they instantly did, and advanced under the lead of Lieutenant Gordon, of Company D. Some ineffectual skirmishing took place between the regulars, who were sheltered behind a barn on the south of the creek, and the rebels, who were on the north side. During this interval the Iowa Cavalry filed off to the left, in the attempt to cross the stream higher up, but after vainly traversing its steep sides and muddy bottom for a mile, returned to find Lieutenant Amory charging across the bridge, the rebels having deserted it upon seeing Colonel Davis, with the artillery advancing. Lieutenant Amory followed the road, thinking that the rebels might flee to the north. Lieutenant Gordon immediately dashed after some of the scattering fugitives through the wood, and after penetrating a few rods, received a volley from the enemy, whom he just then discovered formed in line. He instantly formed in line, and ordered his men to fire.

The cavalry, under Major Torrence, and the regulars, under Lieutenant Amory, had in the mean time reached the flank and rear of another body of the enemy, who was thus enclosed on one side by a long marsh, on the other by a deep and muddy mill-pond, and on the third by our cavalry. Colonel Davis had by this time come up in the rear. A white flag was displayed, and Colonel Alexander, a young man, came forward and asked if thirty minutes would be allowed them for consultation. Colonel Davis's answer was "that as night was closing in, that was too long." Colonel A. then asked if he would be allowed to go to head-quarters and bring back the answer of the commander of the corps, Colonel Robinson. Permission being granted, he returned in about five minutes, with the response that "they would be obliged to surrender as prisoners of war." The arms were stacked, and the men formed in line and marched between two files of infantry, the Eighteenth and Twenty-fourth Illinois, with all the honors of war. Colonel Davis immediately sent dispatches to General Pope announcing his success, and as night was closing around, the arms were hastily stowed in wagons, and the Federal troops commenced the march for camp. One thousand guns of all kinds were captured, with a full supply of clothing and provision. One of the enemy was killed, and several wounded. Two Federals were killed and eight wounded.

Dispatches were received Thursday evening from General Halleck ordering the Union troops to fall back to Sedalia. General Pope, therefore, accompanied with the victors as an escort, and the wounded men, started and made the journey (twenty miles) by two o'clock.

Following close upon them was the brigade of Colonel Hovey, of the Twenty-fourth Indiana, who had been dispatched with two regiments, a battery, and two squadrons of the First Missouri Cavalry, on the Clinton road some twelve miles from Sedalia, where the cavalry, under Major Hubbard, some two hundred and fifty in number, made a reconnoissance of the country extending westward and southward, as far as the Grand river, beyond Clinton. Here they came upon the pickets of General Rains, who, with an advanced cavalry force was guarding the Grand river. The pickets were driven in, one shot, about sixty prisoners taken within the lines of General Rains, and a mill near Clinton burned.

The detachment of cavalry under Lieutenant-Colonel Brown also burned a mill near Johnstown, on the borders of Bates county. His force travelled two hundred and fifty miles in six days.

Colonel Hovey, of the Twenty-fourth Indiana, effected a successful ruse, whereby he succeeded in making a capture of six prisoners and two hundred bushels of corn meal. He was ordered by General Turner to reconnoitre with about a hundred men on the road to Clinton. He left on Monday morning, taking Fairview and Sisconville on his route. Learning on Tuesday that a party of the enemy was encamped at a mill near Chapel Hill, he adopted a scheme for capturing the whole of them next day.

He ordered his men into the wagons, and had them drawn, with the exception of a small guard, resembling a provision train. As they approached Hall's store the rebels appeared in the brush ready to seize the train. One of his officers rode around a hill to see the whereabouts of the party, when he encountered a mounted rebel, who raised his shot-gun, when he was brought to the ground by a revolver. Colonel Hovey then ordered his men to emerge from their concealment, and a search was made for the enemy. One of them was wounded in the fray, and one killed, two balls lodging in his neck. A few horses and mules were captured, some of which were branded U. S. The mill was afterward burned, and the meal put in Hovey's wagons.

The total number of prisoners taken exceeded sixteen hundred. The march was accomplished in exceeding cold weather, and many of the troops suffered severely.

BATTLE OF DRANESVILLE, VA.
December 20, 1861.

In the month of December, the Pennsylvania reserve regiments, under the command of Major-General McCall, constituted the right wing of the great Potomac army. The division occupied an extensive range of country, beyond Langley's church and tavern, the encampments stretching toward Lewinsville. Beyond this, north-westwardly, an open country extended, in the direction of Leesburg, some twelve or fifteen miles, unoccupied by hostile forces. Midway was the village of Dranesville, a small town, almost deserted.

It having been determined to send a foraging party to take possession of a quantity of hay, oats and provender known to be in this neighborhood, the brigade of General E. O. C. Ord, the third of McCall's division, was assigned to the duty.

The force consisted of the Sixth regiment, Colonel W. W. Rickets; Ninth, Colonel C. F. Jackson; Tenth, Colonel John S. McCalmont; Twelfth, Colonel John H. Taggart. The regiment of riflemen known as the Bucktails, Lieutenant-Colonel Thomas L. Kane; a battery of two twenty-four-pounders and two twelve-pounders, commanded by Captain

Easton, and a detachment of cavalry from Colonel Bayard's regiment, also accompanied the expedition. Each regiment was strongly represented, and there were about four thousand men in the expedition. The order for march was received on Thursday evening, the men being directed to take with them one day's rations. The morning was clear, and rather cold, with a slight mist around the sun, and a thin layer of frost whitening the road and coating the grass. The Bucktails were assigned the advance of the infantry column, the cavalry preceding as scouts, and battery being in reserve. Colonel Taggart's regiment brought up the rear. A number of teams were also in company. Each regiment had two companies of flankers thrown out, on either side of the column, to scour the woods, search the thickets, and prevent the column from falling into an ambuscade. They halted at Difficult Creek, a narrow stream, with a heavy stone bridge. The stream is fordable, the average width being thirty feet.

The march continued. The day became warm, the sky soft and clear, as the soldiers approached Dranesville. About noon the flanking companies of the Twelfth regiment came in and reported that a large body of rebels could be seen from a neighboring hill. At another part of the line shots were exchanged between the hidden enemy and the Union flanking companies. Instantly a line of battle was formed, but no enemy appeared, and the firing ceased.

The delay was that of a few minutes. The Union men were anxious, expectant, and enthusiastic. Suddenly a fire was opened upon our line from a wood or thicket nearly a mile distant. The enemy's battery contained six guns, and was placed in a road skirting the wood, and sheltered by it. Their guns were of large calibre, and they fired shells. At first they passed over the column and exploded beyond. The rebel artillerymen discovered this, altered their range, and their shells fell short. In the mean time, Easton's battery was brought into position on the side of an elevation in front of the Twelfth regiment, which was in line of battle. General Ord himself sighted the guns, and a sharp fire was opened upon the enemy.

The Union infantry laid down on their arms, awaiting the orders of their superior officers. At length the fire of the enemy began to be irregular and uncertain, proving that they either intended to retreat or change position. At this time Colonel Kane, who was on the right of the column, discovered the infantry of the enemy passing through an open clearing near the wood, evidently intending a flank movement, or designing to occupy a brick house within a hundred yards of his regiment. He sent a detachment of twenty men, under command of Lieutenant Rice, to take the house, which they did, and, under shelter of its walls, opened fire upon the advancing regiments. Having bestowed the family found in this house safely in the cellar, the small garrison demolished the windows and attacked the enemy, which was afterwards discovered to be an Alabama regiment, under command of Colonel John H. Forney; a Kentucky regiment, commanded by Colonel Tom Taylor; and a South Carolina regiment. They took the shelter of underbrush, and, under the supposition that the house was filled by Union troops, opened a heavy fire upon it, supported by two small guns, which threw shot and shell upon it. They advanced nearer and nearer every volley, the brave Union riflemen firing rapidly and with great effect. Colonel Kane was among them all the time, inspiring them with his example. They fell on the ground, they loaded their pieces, rising suddenly, taking deliberate aim, and lying down to load again. The burden of the enemy's fire was directed at the house, and it was shattered and pierced, the roof being broken, and some of the walls giving way.

The Federal fire was so terrific that the enemy fell back from the advanced position they had assumed, abandoned their flanking manœuvre, and retreated to the woods under cover of their battery, which kept up an irregular and uncertain fire. The Bucktails advanced in pursuit. As they rose to follow, Colonel Kane, who was leading them, was wounded. He fell, but instantly arose, and continued to advance. In the mean time General Ord ordered the line to charge and take the battery. The order was given to the Twelfth regiment, Colonel John H. Taggart commanding. It was received with a cheer by the men, and they advanced in the direction of the unseen battery. They proceeded to the edge of the wood and entered, keeping the line as straight and precise as on dress parade. The wood was dense, and so impenetrable that the men found it difficult to proceed. Colonel Taggart threw his scabbard away and preceded his men with his drawn sword in one hand and his pistol in the other.

They came into an open clearing, only to find that the rebels had retreated in the most precipitate manner. While the Union troops were crowding through the woods, the enemy had started along the Leesburg road, taking their cannon, but leaving their dead and wounded, and large quantities of arms and ammunition. A single caisson remained. Their magazine had been struck by a shell, and exploded with appalling effect. Around it the dead and dying were heaped in masses—fifteen men and five horses being killed. The Union men were wild with the enthusiasm of victory, and having placed the wounded in the houses near by, and chopped the gun-carriages to splinters, they started in pursuit of the retreating foe.

This was about three o'clock. General McCall, with his staff, had arrived on the ground only to hear of a victory won. Knowing that an advance would be fatal, he ordered a recall, and with the wounded and dead, and the trophies of war, the troops returned from the field.

The brave and victorious band arrived at Langley's about nine o'clock in the evening, where they were met by thousands of their shouting and exultant comrades.

The rebel troops engaged in this battle were on the same errand. Two hundred wagons had been sent out by General Stuart, their commander, under the care of a foraging party, escorted by the Eleventh Virginia, Colonel Garland; the Sixth South Carolina, under Lieutenant-Colonel A. J. Secrest; the Tenth Alabama, Colonel John H. Forney; the First Kentucky, Colonel Sam. Taylor; the Sumter Flying Artillery, Captain Cutts, and detachments from Ransom's and Radford's Cavalry. The rebel troops fought well, and did honor to themselves as soldiers, whose nerve and bravery would have been worthy of triumph in a sacred cause. Their loss was seventy-five killed, one hundred and fifty wounded, and thirty prisoners. Of the Federals, seven were killed and sixty-one wounded.

EXPEDITION TO SHIP ISLAND.
December, 1861.

General B. F. Butler, after having been stationed for a short time at Fortress Monroe, was assigned to the North-Eastern Department, and located his headquarters at Boston, where he superintended the organization of the New England troops, and the fitting out of an expedition intended to make a demonstration at some point on the Southern coast. A portion of his troops sailed from Boston on the 23d of November, in the steam transport Constitution, which arrived at Fortress Monroe on the 26th, with the Twenty-sixth Massachusetts, and the Ninth Connecticut regiments, and Captain Manning's battery—making a total of one thousand nine hundred men. Brigadier-General J. W. Phelps here took the command, and reached Ship Island harbor, in Mississippi Sound, December 3.

On the west end of this island there was a partly-finished fort, occupied by Lieutenant Buchanan and one hundred and seventy sailors and marines, with several ship guns in position. The rebels had evacuated the island in September, destroying what they could not carry away with them.

General Phelps, on assuming the command of Ship Island, published a proclamation "To the loyal citizens of the South-west," in which he defined the political "motives and principles" by which his command would be governed. He then at the very opening of his address, declared that every slave State admitted into the Union since the adoption of the Constitution, had been admitted in direct violation of that instrument. That every slave State that existed as such at the adoption of the Constitution, was by that act placed under the "highest obligation of honor and morality to abolish slavery." The rest of the "proclamation" was in harmony with these statements. General Phelps made an official report of his expedition to General Butler, who reported the facts to the Adjutant-General of the United States. General Phelps was commended for the successful manner in which he had performed his military duties, but his proclamation was pronounced superfluous and uncalled for.

The occupancy of Ship Island being secured, the forces remained in undisturbed possession, awaiting the future movements of the commander of the expedition.

ENGAGEMENT AT MOUNT ZION.
December 28, 1861.

On the 23d of December, General Prentiss, commanding the army of Northern Missouri, having his headquarters at Palmyra, received orders to disperse a body of the enemy's forces that had concentrated in Boone County. In pursuance of his instructions he started on the following morning with two hundred of the Third Missouri Cavalry, Colonel John Glover, and five companies of Sharpshooters, under Colonel Birge, and arrived at Sturgeon on the evening of the 26th.

During the following day, having learned that there was a concentration of rebels near the village of Hallsville, in Boone County, General Prentiss sent forward one company of cavalry, commanded by Captain Howland, to reconnoitre in that vicinity. Captain Howland proceeded to Hallsville, but found no rebels. After proceeding about two miles beyond, his advance guard encountered the rebels in force, commanded by Colonel Dorsey. Captain Howland endeavored to draw off his company, having taken nine prisoners, but was overpowered. Being wounded, and having lost his horse, he was taken prisoner, with one private of his company. The remainder of his men made good their retreat, arriving at Sturgeon at nine o'clock, P. M.

Having learned the position of the enemy, General Prentiss ordered his command, numbering in all four hundred and seventy, to march at two o'clock, A. M., at which hour he started, and after marching a distance of sixteen miles, at eight o'clock A. M. of the 28th inst. found one company of rebels, commanded by Captain Johnson, in position to the left of the road leading from Hallsville to Mount Zion. General Prentiss ordered two companies of sharpshooters to pass to the rear of the enemy, and one of cavalry to dismount and engage them in the front.

Colonel Glover opened fire, and succeeded in killing five and capturing seven prisoners, from whom was ascertained the number and position of the main force—the enemy being posted at a church, known as Mount Zion, in Boone County, one mile and a half in advance, numbering near nine hundred men. General Prentiss ordered the cavalry under Colonel Glover forward, accompanied by two companies of Birge's sharpshooters. Colonel Birge, arriving near the encampment, ordered one troop of cavalry to dismount and engage the enemy. The sharpshooters were afterward ordered through a field on the right to skirmish with the enemy's left, and if possible drive them from the woods.

The firing being heavy, and these three companies proving unable to drive the enemy from his cover, Colonel Glover, with his available force, moved in double-quick to their aid, and for half an hour longer the battle raged and became a hand-to-hand fight. Captain Boyd's company of sharpshooters were in the midst of the rebel camp. Also, Major Carrick, with Company C of the Cavalry. When Colonel Glover arrived, the enemy retreated, leaving in the Federal hands 90 horses and 105 stand of arms. The battle was brought to a close about 11 A. M.

The reserve of two companies coming into action at the moment the enemy gave way, the victory was complete. After collecting the wounded, the Federals proceeded to care for those of the enemy, placing them in the church, and sent for farmers and friends in the vicinity to render assistance, when they returned to Sturgeon, where they arrived at 9, P. M. The loss in the battle of Mount Zion, and in the engagement of the evening previous, was: Killed, 3; slightly wounded, 46; severely wounded, 17. Rebel loss: Killed, 25; wounded, 150.

ARKANSAS, AND THE INDIANS.

The prominent and active men in the State of Arkansas, and particularly all who held official positions, were allied politically with the South Carolina conspirators, while the majority of the people, in the early stages of the insurrection, were loyal. Hence, the leaders were slow in their movements to carry the State out of the Union; but when the Confederate government had become organized, and transferred to Richmond, and the rebellion had been fully inaugurated by the attack on Fort Sumter, followed by the proclamation of President Lincoln, they deemed that the time had come for the development of their plans.

The Governor of the State, Henry M. Rector, on the 22d of April, 1861, directed the seizure by State troops of the United States stores at Napoleon; followed on the 24th by the capture of Fort Smith by the forces under Colonel Borland.

The Legislature being convened at Little Rock, an unconditional ordinance of Secession was passed on the 6th of May, and on the 18th the Confederate Congress at Richmond declared the admission of Arkansas to the Southern Confederacy.

It was the misfortune of the loyal men of the State that they did not number in their ranks any citizens of power and influence, who had energy sufficient to organize the Unionists, and oppose a barrier to the acts of the enemies of the Federal Government. Unarmed and unorganized, while the conspirators were in a state of preparation for any resistance that might be made, protest and opposition were of no avail, and the loyal men of the State were compelled to submit, and endure the persecutions and depredations of the more numerous secessonists.

A great deal of excitement was occasioned during the month of November by the discovery that the Union men of Izard, Fulton, Independent and Searcey counties had secret organizations and societies for mutual protection and co-operation. This accidental disclosure exasperated the conspirators, who adopted the most violent measures to disperse the Unionists, and break up their associations. Many were taken to Little Rock and hanged, while others were arrested in the woods, attempting to escape beyond the State, and shared the same fate. Large numbers of refugees, however, succeeded in reaching Missouri, where they remained, and subsequently, under Captain Ware, a member of the Arkansas Legislature, organized as a military body at Rolla, Missouri, and entered the service under General Curtis, receiving large accessions on the marching of Curtis' expedition into the State.

Impressed with the importance of securing the services of the Indian tribes within the limits of Arkansas, as well as the adjoining territory, the agents of the Richmond government were instructed to negotiate with the Cherokees and Creeks on the borders of Arkansas, promising the payment of the United States annuities by the Confederacy in case of their allegiance. On the 24th of August an agreement was entered into by some of the Cherokee chiefs, and the two tribes raised 2,000 men for the war. The nations were divided on the question, the most intelligent being convinced that loyalty to the Federal Government was their true policy not less than their duty. The Choctaws, Chickasaws, and other tribes were treated in a similar manner, and with the same results—secession having the effect of dividing the Red Men of the forest as it had divided the pale faces of the east.

From authentic sources it was learned from the Seminole agency that Opothleyoholo, a loyal chief, had collected together four or five thousand Indians, and about thirteen hundred negroes, who had gone to him with the hope of being rendered free. When General Cooper (rebel,) at the head of the Creek, Choctaw and Chickasaw regiments, with other Indians, amounting to near five thousand, advanced upon Opothleyoholo's camp, his followers fled, leaving all behind. Opothleyoholo left with a few adherents for the south-west. Most of his followers were reported to be with Colonel Cooper, who was said to have a very large Indian force with him.

BOMBARDMENT AT FORT PICKENS.

On the 1st of January, 1862, Fort Pickens with the rebel forts and batteries on the Bay of Pensacola again awoke the thunders of their heavy artillery, whose tremendous explosions reverberated for thirty miles along the Florida coast.

The loyal garrison at the fort had been long chafing under the restraints of continued inaction. The commander, Colonel Harvey Brown, Fifth United States Artillery, had been anxiously awaiting the time when a sufficient force would be at his command to drive the unwelcome foe from his position near the fort.

Lieutenant Adam J. Slemmer, of Pennsylvania, of the First United States Artillery, the former brave commander, who saved the fort by his courage and loyalty, on the 12th of January, 1861, had been relieved, on account of ill-health. He received a Major's commission in the Sixteenth United States Infantry, May 14th, 1861.

On the first day of the year a small steamer was seen from Fort Pickens making her way toward the Navy Yard. She was a saucy, defiant looking craft, and some one on board waved a secession flag ostentatiously in sight, as if challenging a fire. This was an exasperating insult to the restive men shut up in the fort. Colonel Brown had frequently warned General Bragg against forcing the presence of these insolent steamers upon him, and when this presumptuous little craft approached Fort Pickens, with its flag in commotion, he opened fire upon her. She drew in her flag and retreated instantly with a crestfallen, retrograde movement, in amusing contrast with her first approach.

The fire from Fort Pickens was directly answered by all the rebel batteries, and in a brief time the engagement became general. The firing on both sides was kept up through the entire day, and at night Pickens maintained a slow fire from her thirteen-inch mortars, which was promptly returned by the rebels.

About midnight a conflagration broke out in the Navy Yard. It flamed up furiously, consuming the buildings of the Yard, and spreading to the town of Woolsey, adjoining the Navy Yard on the north, where it raged all night.

The scene during the night was wonderfully magnificent. Every shell could be tracked in its course through the air from the moment it left the gun until it exploded, scattering destruction all around. These shells, rising up against a cloud of surging flame, which sent its red light in a continued glare landward and seaward, formed an appalling spectacle. The minutest outline of the grim fort seemed sketched on a background of fire, rendering the light which Colonel Brown hung out from its walls, in scornful bravado, offering a sure mark to the enemy, scarcely more than one of the ten thousand sparks that filled the atmosphere with gleams of gold. Far off over the beautiful land the light of that conflagration spread, filling the inhabitants with alarm; and so brightly did it flame over the ocean, that the United States steamer Mercedita floated in the glow of its ruddy light when over twenty miles at sea.

Through the heat of this conflagration the guns kept up their slow booming thunder, adding to the sublime interest of the scene. The firing on both sides was remarkable for its extreme accuracy. Shells in countless numbers fell inside of Fort Pickens, and were returned with double vigor by its guns.

All the batteries were engaged, and did their work admirably. Fort McRae, which had been so roughly handled by the Federal squadron at the last engagement, resumed its accustomed vigor, and Battery Scott kept up a constant fire throughout the engagement.

Several ships of the squadron were present, but took no part in the fight. It was well they did not, for nothing could have been gained, and probably much would have been lost had they attempted to oppose their wooden sides to stone walls and earthworks.

The bombardment was the old story of fort against fort, at a distance too great for any decisive result. The Unionists gained nothing, yet expended a large amount of powder, shot and shell, and the enemy had no greater advantage. Apart from the burning of Warrington, the Navy Yard and Woolsey, no injury worth speaking of was sustained. The next day Fort Pickens stood out against the sky grim and strong as it was before the bombardment. There were but few if any casualties worth recording during this affair. Even Colonel Brown's lantern, hung out to guide the rebel shot, failed to invite any real injury; and except that it left a wide field of devastation behind, the bombardment of Fort Pickens had few important results.

ROUT OF GENERAL MARSHALL AT PAINTSVILLE, KY.
January 7, 1862.

On the 7th of January, Colonel Garfield, who had his encampment on Muddy Creek, in Eastern Kentucky, marched to attack the rebel General Marshall, who with a large force of men and a battery of four pieces, was known to have an entrenched camp at Paintsville, the capital of Johnson county. Colonel Garfield's command, composed of the Forty-second Ohio, the Fourteenth Kentucky, and Major McLaughlin's squadron of Ohio cavalry, making an effective force of about fifteen hundred men, broke up their camp on Muddy Creek, and moved toward Paintsville. While on the march they were reinforced by a battalion of the First Virginia cavalry, under Colonel Bolles, and by three hundred of the Twenty-second Kentucky, raising the force to about twenty-two hundred men. The enemy, under Humphrey Marshall, numbering three thousand five hundred men, and having a battery of four pieces, learned of the approach, and also that of the Fortieth Ohio and of four hundred of Colonel Wolford's cavalry by the way of Mount Sterling and the valley of the Paint Creek. They had, two days previously, after burning large quantities of grain, broken up their intrenched camp, and effected a retreat to the heights on Middle Creek, two miles distant from Prestonburg. They had left a corps of observation at the mouth of Jennie Creek, three miles west from Paintsville, of three hundred cavalry, and a large force of infantry about seven miles up Jennie Creek, to protect and facilitate the passage of their trains.

Immediately on arriving Colonel Garfield, learning the position of this cavalry, but unaware of the whereabouts of the other divisions of the rebel force, immediately commenced the erection of a pontoon or floating bridge across the Paint Lick Creek, at Paintsville. At four P. M. he crossed with eight companies of the Forty-second Ohio, and two companies of the Fourteenth Kentucky, with a view of making an armed reconnoissance, and if possible of cutting off and capturing the cavalry. At two P. M. he had dispatched Colonel Bolles' cavalry and one company of the Forty-second, under the command of Captain S. M. Barber, with orders to give a good account of the cavalry. But later in the day, on learning the possibility of cutting them off, he had sent orders to Colonel Bolles not to attack them until he had obtained time to get in their rear. Not receiving the last orders, and indeed before they were issued, Colonel Bolles, in obedience to his first directions, crossed the Paint by fording, and vigorously assaulting the enemy, soon put them to flight up the valley of Jennie. In their haste, followed as they were by the cavalry, they strewed the road with their equipments, while here and there a dead or wounded soldier gave proof that they were losing men also. The pursuit was kept up for seven miles, right into the infantry division which was guarding the train. Stationed on either side of the road, that did not permit more than two to ride abreast, it opened a heavy cross-fire on the Union cavalry, compelling them to fall back, and finally to retreat, which they did in good order, having inflicted a loss of twenty-five in killed and wounded, according to rebel account, and losing but two killed and one wounded. Fifteen rebels were taken prisoners. Meanwhile Colonel Garfield, with his command, having remained a short time to fully explore the enemy's deserted fortifications, (consisting of lunettes, breastworks, rifle-pits and a fort situated on the top of a conical hill,) and wholly unaware of what had taken place, pressed forward to the hoped for consummation of the march. But few miles had been traversed, however, when the evidences of a hasty retreat became so apparent that all were convinced that the enemy had flown. The object of the march having been thus thwarted, an early return to Paintsville became desirable, and it was accomplished at the dawn.

BATTLE OF MIDDLE CREEK, KY.
January 10, 1862.

Having recruited his men by a night's rest at Paintsville, Colonel Garfield was preparing to start in immediate pursuit on the morning of the 8th, but receiving information of the superior force of the enemy, he awaited the arrival of the Fortieth Ohio regiment, and Wolford's Kentucky cavalry, by way of Mount Sterling. These troops joined him on that day, raising his effective force to about two thousand four hundred men, after deducting Colonel Bolle's Virginia cavalry, which, in obedience to orders, had returned to Guyandotte in that State. On the 9th, Colonel Garfield detailed from the Forty-second and Fortieth Ohio, and Fourteenth Kentucky each three hundred men, and from the Twenty-second Kentucky two hundred men, and taking the immediate command, supported, however, by Colonel Craner of the Fortieth, and Major Burke of the Fourteenth. After detaching Colonel Wolford's and Major McLaughlin's cavalry up Jennie's Creek, he marched up the river road leading to Prestonburg. Early on the morning of the 10th, Colonel Sheldon of the Forty-second Ohio, in command at the camp, received a dispatch from Colonel Garfield, stating that he had found the enemy, and asking reinforcements. In compliance with the order, at six A. M. on the tenth, Colonel Sheldon marched with eight hundred men, who eagerly pressed forward on their way to the scene of action. As Colonel Garfield had stated, he had found the enemy two miles from Prestonburg, on Middle Creek, in a chosen position among the hills, with between four and five thousand men and four pieces of artillery. The Fifth Virginia regiment, Colonel Trigg, Colonel John S. Williams' Kentucky regiment, Colonel Moore's Kentucky regiment, Markham and Wicher's cavalry, and the Fourth Virginia infantry, lay in full strength on the hills at the forks of the creek, while their battery seemed to forbid all approach. Nothing deterred by the formidable position and number of the enemy, Colonel Garfield, not fully aware of their exact locality, sent skirmishers forward with a view of drawing the enemy's fire, and thus ascertaining his whereabouts. Not succeeding in this, about noon he sent forward his escort of cavalry, some twenty strong, in a headlong charge. This accomplished the object, for the enemy, thinking the whole Union force upon them, opened with musketry, shot and shell upon the cavalry, and a small party of the skirmishers under Adjutant Olds of the Forty-second, then in a corn-field immediately in front of the position of Colonel Williams' Kentucky regiment, and flanked on the left by the artillery and Trigg's Virginia regiment. The cavalry made a hasty retreat, and the enemy concentrated their whole fire on Adjutant Olds and his party, but without effect. After replying with some fifteen rounds of musketry, and observing a large force thrown out on his right, with intent to cut him off, he fell back upon the main body. The position of the enemy thus disclosed was as follows: Colonel Williams' regiment was behind a ridge at the head of the gorge, and on the right of the road, so that his fire commanded the gorge and road for a half-mile. Colonel Trigg's regiment, the Fourth Virginia, was on the crest of the crescent-shaped hill on the left of the road, commanding it by their flanking fire. The artillery was between the two at the forks of the creek and the turn in the road and gorge. The evident design of the enemy was to draw the Unionists up the road in front of their cannon and between the cross-fire of the three regiments, but this well-formed plan failed in its execution, as in their impotence or nervousness they neglected to reserve their fire for the approach of the main body. The remainder of their force were in the rear of their cannon, in a strong supporting position. Occupying Graveyard Point, the end of a high ridge on the right of the creek north of his main body, Colonel Garfield dispatched a hundred men across the creek to ascend the horn of the crescent farthest up the gorge. The ascent was most difficult, the men being compelled to creep on their hands and knees most of the way. On attaining the summit, they were greeted with the whole fire of Trigg's regiment, stationed at the base, and deployed along the other horn; also by a fire from the artillery and the reserve in the rear. On the top of the ridge, and at points nearly equi-distant from each other, were three piles of stone, the possession of which was eagerly sought for by the contending parties.

The small band on the summit of the ridge were now reinforced by two hundred men, and assisted by the reserve at Graveyard Point, who poured a galling fire on the deployed right flank of the enemy, they soon drove him from the first stone pile, and took possession of it.

A force of two hundred men was then thrown out by Colonel Garfield for the ascent of the lower horn of the crescent. These soon reached the summit, where being reinforced by Colonel Craner of the Fortieth with three hundred men, they captured the third stone pile, while the rebels were thus confined to the second or central one. The fire was now exceedingly heavy. Both parties betook themselves to the shelter of the rocks and trees, and the battle raged furiously, the shots tearing through the branches and surging up the defiles of the mountains in a wild tumult of sounds.

About half-past four a burst of loud cheering heralded in reinforcements for the Union troops. A detachment of brave soldiers came in simultaneously with the shouts that welcomed them, panting, and almost breathless from the fatigue of a long march; for fifteen miles they had struggled through the mud of a broken road without breakfast, and at a tiresome pace. Excited by the sound of the conflict, they had marched the last two miles on the double-quick, and came in bathed with perspiration, bespattered with mud, and half the men carrying their coats on their arms.

Though fatigued with the forced march, and faint with hunger, these noble fellows demanded only to be led at once into battle. After a short rest, they were thrown across the creek to ascend the right horn of the crescent, but were finally ordered back, as it had now become too dark to advance with safety, and the storm of battle, by mutual consent, ceased. Resting upon their arms, determined to renew the battle in the morning, the Union troops spent the night; but when morning dawned, the enemy, it was found, had vanished. Under cover of the darkness he had burned his heavy baggage and retreated. He left twenty-seven dead on the field, and it is definitely ascertained had some one hundred and twenty-five wounded, of whom forty-two subsequently died. The Federals lost two killed and twenty-five wounded.

The Richmond papers claimed a brilliant Confederate victory on this occasion, estimating the Federal forces at 8,000 men, and their loss at 400 killed and wounded.

BATTLE OF SILVER CREEK. MO.
JANUARY 8, 1862.

It was the misfortune of Missouri, more than any other State, to be a battle-ground for the guerrilla forces of the rebels, and for the skirmishing engagements of the war. These minor battles, while they had but little effect on the great result, inflicted untold horrors on the people dwelling there.

At the opening of the year 1862, General Pope had command of the North-western District of the State, with his headquarters at Otterville, Cooper county.

Having heard that the enemy was busily engaged in recruiting men in Roanoke and adjoining counties, Major W. M. G. Torrence of the First Iowa Cavalry was ordered to concentrate and take command of several small bodies of Federal troops, then guarding important points in the district, and to break up the rebel encampments.

From Booneville, Major Torrence proceeded to Fayette, Howard county, and for several days was actively engaged in scouring the country and endeavoring to ascertain the position and strength of the rebel forces. He found that Colonel Poindexter was recruiting in various places in the county, and that he was encamped with his principal force, of from five to seven hundred men, on Silver Creek, and had other camps to reinforce him when ready to move, to the number of from twelve to fifteen hundred men.

They further reported that he had pledged himself to his men that he would *clean out* the Federals in the county of Howard in a very few days. Night after night was selected to surprise the Union camp with his whole force, but through some mishap they never appeared. On the morning of January 8th, all was in motion in the Federal camp, under orders from Major Torrence to hold themselves in readiness to move with all their able-bodied men at an early hour. They took up their line of march for Roanoke, and, after moving a few miles, were joined by Major Hubbard's command. The forces now comprised a portion of Merrill's horse, under Major Hunt, one company of the Fourth Ohio, under Captain Foster, a part of the Missouri First, under Major Hubbard, and four companies of the First Iowa, under Major Torrence. After passing the town of Roanoke, the whole column moved rapidly about five miles, and halted to have position and duties assigned to the several commands. Learning that the enemy were in a strong position on the Creek, where it probably would be impossible to charge them with mounted men, it was determined to dismount and fight as infantry.

Captain Foster was assigned the advance, followed by Merrill's Horse and the Missouri First, all armed with carbines. The First Iowa were to make a descent upon the camp with drawn sabers, and if impossible to make a charge mounted, they were to dismount and move on foot. Lieutenant Dustin, of the First Iowa, with ten men, formed the advance guard. All being in readiness, they moved forward very rapidly, and followed the tortuous windings of a road leading through narrow lanes and thick timber, till the sharp crack of a rifle warned them that they were upon the rebel pickets. This was the signal to rush forward, which was done. On, on they pushed, through underbrush and defiles, till the advanced guard rushed to the entrance of their camp, and found the enemy drawn up in line of battle. It was now found that the thick timber and underbrush forbade a charge upon the camp. The order to dismount passed along the lines, and a column of armed infantry emerged from the lines on the roadside, ready for the onset. The battle now commenced in earnest, and volley after volley of musketry told that the work of death had begun.

The enemy rushed from their line of battle, after their second volley, into the intrenchment formed by the creek, and behind trees, logs, etc., opened fire upon the Union lines, which was promptly answered by their forces, armed with carbines, by a continued fire. Major Torrence now ordered his men forward with revolver and sabre, to make a charge on the camp; and with a yell running wildly along their lines they advanced, in the face of the enemy's fire, and rushed into their camp. So great was the eagerness to move forward, that three companies claimed the honor of being first in camp.

The enemy now gave way tumultuously, and ran from their camp, leaving guns, horses, camp equipage, powder, and a large quantity of new clothing for men in Price's army. It was a complete rout, as the appearance of the camp fully attested. It was now nearly dark, with a heavy fog, and fearing that the enemy had only retired as a ruse to rally and come to the attack again, the order was given to destroy the whole camp and equipage. The work of destruction was soon complete—wagons, saddles, tents, blankets, clothing, etc., were gathered up, flung on the fires, and soon became one heap of burning ruins. The Federals now looked up their dead and wounded, and cared for them. The enemy's dead lay in all portions of the camp, and the groans of their dying mingled with the exultant shouts of the victors. It was a fearful struggle, as the soldiers all knew that they never could retreat, and it was victory or death to them. The cool courage and gallant bearing of the officers in command, were worthy of Americans.

The loss of the enemy was 12 killed, 22 wounded and 15 prisoners. That of the Federals 3 killed and 10 wounded.

BATTLE OF MILL SPRING, AT LOGAN'S CROSS-ROADS, KY.
SUNDAY, JANUARY 19, 1862.

This battle was the first of the series of splendid triumphs that occurred early in the year 1862, which resulted in severe losses to the rebel armies of the West, both in men and material. It was the first breach in their well-planned line of defence, by which the right wing of the Confederate army of the West was broken, and their great stronghold at Bowling Green, the centre of their operations, laid open to the advancing army of the Union.

After the discomfiture of Zollicoffer in his attack on the camp of General Schoepf, at Camp Wildcat, on the 21st of October, he left two regiments to defend the post at Cumberland Gap, and occupied a position on the Cumberland river, opposite Mill Spring, at the mouth of White Oak Creek. Here he was engaged in fortifying this most advantageous natural position, and in recruiting and organizing an army, which was now formidable in numbers, and whose frequent forays had rendered his name a terror to the loyal inhabitants of that region.

The rebel stronghold was familiarly known among the inhabitants as "Zollicoffer's Den." It was situated on the north bank of the Cumberland, where it is intersected by White Oak Creek. The country for two miles from the river is entirely clear, and broken into hills of imposing altitude. Six of these hills, forming a picturesque range, commanded each other and the entire approach to the camp for miles around. On these hills Zollicoffer had raised breastworks and redoubts. The south side of the river, commanding the entire camp, was also well fortified.

On the 6th of January the rebel Major-General George B. Crittenden, commanding the division to which Zollicoffer's brigade was attached, arrived at Mill Spring, and established his headquarters. He brought to his position three Tennessee and one Mississippi regiment, and was afterwards reinforced by three regiments from Bowling Green, and still more recently by some fifteen hundred Virginia troops from Knoxville. This gave him, all told, over ten thousand men. A very effective portion of his force was a body of cavalry, from two thousand to three thousand strong, in which he was superior to General Thomas, but which was of no service to him in the engagement.

General Buell, the Federal commander in Kentucky, having now at his disposal a competent army to commence offensive operations, ordered General Thomas to advance with his division against General Crittenden's position at Mill Spring. With two brigades under his command General Thomas broke up camp near Lebanon and marched, by way of Columbia, toward the rebel stronghold. On Thursday, the 16th of January, the Ninth Ohio (German), Colonel McCook, brother of the General in command at Mumfordsville, the Second Minnesota, Colonel Van Clear; Tenth Indiana, Colonel Manson; Fourth Kentucky, Colonel (formerly Judge) Fry of Danville, and Colonel Wolford's Kentucky Cavalry, and one battery, with General Thomas and staff, arrived after a most fatiguing march of many days. They came in incessant rain, over horrid roads, via Jamestown, at a point about eight miles south-west of Somerset, on the road leading to Hart's Ford, and the rebel intrenchments, and pitched their tents near a fork of country roads, upon what is known all through that section as "Logan's place," a very extensive plantation of several thousand acres. On Friday, the Fourteenth Ohio, Colonel Stedman, and the Tenth Kentucky, Colonel Harlan, three detached companies of the First regiment of Michigan Engineers and Mechanics, and an Ohio battery, reached within eight miles north-west of the position of General Thomas. After undergoing indescribable hardships in making their way on a direct line, through the wild, rugged, heavily-timbered, and almost untravelled country intervening between that point and Columbia—(they had to construct a road as they went)—they encamped there.

General Schoepf's command was stationed at the time the above seven and a half regiments arrived at a short distance south-west of Somerset. It comprised the Seventeenth, Thirty-first, Thirty-fifth and Thirty-eighth Ohio, the Twelfth Kentucky, Colonel Haskins, the First and Second Tennessee regiments, some companies of cavalry, and two batteries. On Saturday morning, in accordance with orders received the previous evening, that part of General Schoepf's command constituting General Carter's brigade, consisting of the Twelfth Kentucky, the First and Second Tennessee, and Captain W. E. Standart's battery, left their camps, with twenty-four hours' rations, and proceeded five miles on the Columbia road to Fishing Creek, where they halted, awaiting further orders. At five o'clock they were ordered to join General Thomas' main body at Logan's Place. In crossing the swollen creek the water reached to the waists of the men. Owing to the wretched condition of the road, they did not reach their point of destination until midnight.

Simultaneously with the above, three regiments and a battery, the balance of General Schoepf's command, with the exception of the Thirty-eighth Ohio, advanced over another road leading out from Somerset in a south-easterly direction to Fishing Creek, which they found risen so high as to render it almost impossible to cross. After much exertion, a rope was finally stretched across, holding on to which the men slowly managed to get over. At nightfall only one regiment, however, had landed on the other side, and while the remainder were crossing on the morning of the battle, orders came from General Thomas that their assistance was no longer needed, and the brigade retraced their steps to Somerset.

During this time a heavy storm came on, and torrents of rain continued to pour upon the devoted troops. General Thomas' immediate command was tolerably well protected; but General Carter's brigade had started without tents, and hence were completely exposed to the drenching rain and chilling wind. Every man in the brigade was soaked to the skin before Logan's Place was reached, and during the remainder of Saturday night the poor fellows lay on the wet ground sheltered only by the dripping woods.

On the morning of the fight the regiments posted on Logan's farm were distributed as follows: on the right of the road to Hart's Ford, facing toward the river, were the Ninth Ohio and Second Minnesota; directly opposite them, on the left, lay General Carter's brigade; three-quarters of a mile south-east of it were the Fourth Kentucky, Tenth Indiana, and two batteries—the Tenth Indiana occupying the most advanced position. In front of the last mentioned regiment were encamped about one hundred and twenty of Wolford's Cavalry, the balance of the regiment being off on escort duty; about two and a half miles further south was the outmost Union picket—twenty of Wolford's cavalry, the Fourteenth Ohio and Tenth Kentucky being still encamped eight miles to the north-east. It is thus seen that the Federal force advanced upon by the rebels included no more than seven infantry regiments, the detached Michigan companies, one hundred and forty cavalry, and two batteries.

The main characteristics of the battle-ground are steep, bluff-like hills, and abrupt narrow ravines. The only comparative levels are formed by the undulating ridges of the former. Logan's Place extends over one of the most extensive of these, and, with its large cleared fields, afforded the best field for a battle that could have been found in many miles around. The whole country is covered with a thick growth of timber, except where the husbandman had cleared it away. The roads were but a succession of rugged little hills, tiring to the footman and taxing the wagoner's skill to the utmost in the best weather.

According to the statements of persons subsequently captured, Zollicoffer's original force did not exceed six thousand in number, which had been increased to ten thousand, comprising ten regiments of infantry, about three thousand cavalry, and fifteen pieces of artillery. On Saturday morning information was brought to General Crittenden by secession sympathizers, living near Somerset, of the proposed movement of General Carter's brigade. The rebel commander had learned that General Thomas' division was on the march to Somerset, but was not aware that it had already arrived; and supposing that General Carter's command was merely setting out for scouting purposes, conceived a plan of falling upon it with his whole force. The plan being communicated to Zollicoffer, he strenuously objected to any demonstration outside of their intrenchments. His superior, however, insisted upon the project—bold and creditable enough, if not based upon wrong premises—and hence the whole rebel army moved out of the fortifications shortly after dark. Owing to the difficulty of working their artillery ahead, it took them until 3 A. M. to come within one mile of the Union pickets. Here they halted and rested, in a deluge of rain. At six o'clock they renewed their march, and their cavalry advance guard came up with Wolford's men. Supposing them to be only a foraging party, the Union dragoons attacked and drove them back. Perceiving, however, masses of infantry down the road, they sent word to General Thomas, and then retreated to their camp. The squadron was quickly mounted and rode towards the enemy; but, discovering his overwhelming strength, fell back, dismounted, and joined the Tenth Indiana, and afterwards actively participated in the fight.

Companies K and I, of the Tenth Indiana, Captains Shorter and Perkins, were detailed as pickets in advance of their regiment, and were first attacked by the advancing rebels at half past six o'clock, and with the assistance of Company A, Captain Hamilton, all under Major Miller, gallantly held the enemy in check, until supported by the remainder of the regiment.

In twenty minutes after General Thomas was apprised of the approach of the enemy, his whole force was under arms, and eagerly awaiting the onset. The Tenth Indiana, Second Minnesota and the dismounted cavalry pushed forward a short distance from their encampment in an open field to a piece of timber, and the Fourth Kentucky took a position in the woods on the left. The Tenth Indiana having the lead, was within musket range of the rebels just before eight o'clock, and now the battle fairly commenced.

At least six regiments formed the rebel right, and pressed first on the Tenth Indiana; but this brave regiment had learned the fighting metal of the enemy at Rich Mountain, in Western Virginia, and could not be made to yield an inch even to such fearful odds. Fortunately protected somewhat by the trees from the hostile fire, they stood steadily, pouring volley after volley into the rebels; responding to their yells with defiant cheers; fighting four times their number for nearly an hour and a half, and never yielding an inch, in spite of a constant and fearful hail of lead, until their ammunition became exhausted; when they were ordered to give way to the Second Minnesota. This they did with composed and unbroken ranks, bringing off their dead and wounded, whose number was a mournful proof of the fearful trial they had undergone.

Some thirty minutes after the Tenth Indiana had opened the contest, the Fourth Kentucky engaged the rebels on the left of the former, and displayed coolness and firmness most remarkable, in view of the fact that it had never before been under fire. It also had to contend against superior numbers, but maintained its formation, and did not allow the rebels to gain a foot of ground. The men cheered each other, and in their ardor came within short range of the enemy, to whose irregular fire they replied with great vigor and effect. Colonel Fry inspired all under him by his courageous conduct. Up and down the line of his command he moved, urging his Kentuckians on under a shower of bullets.

Meantime, the Second Minnesota fulfilled the trust left to it by the Tenth Indiana. The stalwart farmers and lumbermen that composed it performed the duty allotted to them deliberately and with perfect success. They loaded and fired with ease and calmness, and seemed to think no more of the work they were doing than of handling a plow or plying an axe.

The widely-renowned Ninth Ohio did not join in the bloody strife in its earliest stages. At about half-past eight, however, its impatience for the fray was at last gratified, and it appeared upon the stage in solid line of battle, moving measuredly, and with the confident and determined air of veterans, through a broad, open field on the right of the road, to within two hundred yards, and began a fire upon some rebel regiments that were firing from behind a fence, with regularity and precision. It held the right alone while the action continued.

The rebels succeeded in bringing a battery of their artillery in position about nine o'clock, and opened upon the Federal troops shortly afterward with solid and hollow shot. Their balls and shells all went high over the Union soldiers, not one of whom owed his death or wound to the rebel artillery.

Captains Kinney's, Standart's, and Whetmore's Ohio batteries were brought into position, and rendered effective service whenever an opportunity offered. In the heat of the engagement Captain Kinney ordered one section of his battery within sixty yards of the enemy's line, and opened a deadly fire upon them, which added greatly to the success of the day.

The battle was now at its height, and the effect of the artillery, roaring through the conflict, with the crash of shells and sharp whistle of bullets, was increased by a storm that had broken out in the morning, and now poured a deluge of rain on the combatants. For a time, the lightning of heaven vied in sharpness with the flash of artillery, and rolling bursts of thunder went booming over the mountains, giving terrible effect to the whole scene.

BATTLE OF MILL SPRING.

Amid this storm, the opposing lines of battle were several times carried so close to each other that the fight was urged on with a hand-to-hand encounter, and the commanders on both sides came in dangerous contiguity with the foe.

Up to eleven o'clock, the fighting was confined almost entirely to an exchange of lead and iron. The Union right and left would advance on the enemy, fire, and fall back. Then the Secession forces would advance, exchange shots, each side holding its own ground and no more.

The Fourteenth Ohio and Tenth Kentucky, sent for as soon as the alarm had been given, being reported to General Thomas coming up with their battery from their encampment on the Columbus road, on a full run, he at last determined to bring matters to an issue. He directed General Carter to flank the enemy's right with his regiments, which had been restive all the morning under the necessity of remaining idle spectators.

But before this movement could be made, the heroes of the Ninth Ohio had already decided the battle. Colonel McCook (by the way the only American in the regiment) had his horse shot under him, and was himself wounded, but nevertheless continued in command. About eleven the patience of the regiment became exhausted, and the Colonel gave the order to advance. It was received with a hurrah. Steadily and compactly the column moved over the two hundred yards separating it from the enemy. When within thirty yards of the foe the order was given to "charge bayonets," and in an instant the moving human wall bristled with bayonets and pressed forward in quick step. The rebels looked aghast at a sight they had never witnessed before. A Tennessee regiment on their extreme left fired a random volley and broke. A Mississippi regiment—the same that held the fence already mentioned—hesitated a few moments longer. But the triumphant shout from the Germans, and the bristling array of pointed steel was too much for them. In an instant, those of the enemy between the fence and the Federals, with the exception of a few, who were bayoneted, had scrambled over and fled in wild disorder.

Colonel S. S. Fry, of the Fourth Kentucky, was in the act of leading his regiment into a charge upon the Mississippians, when General Zollicoffer, accompanied by his aid, rode up to him and said, "You are not going to fight your friends, are you? These men (pointing to the Mississippians) are all your friends." In the mean time Zollicoffer's aid fired upon Colonel Fry, wounding his horse, from which wound the animal died. Colonel Fry then turned and fired upon Zollicoffer, with fatal effect. General Z. evidently labored under the impression that Colonel Fry was a rebel officer. They had never met before, nor did Colonel Fry know the position of the officer upon whom he fired, as the evidences of his rank were covered by a cloak which General Zollicoffer wore in battle.

From this moment the battle was won. The rebels in front of the Union left had grown dispirited by the news of Zollicoffer's fall, and their fire was slackening. When they saw the breaking of their left wing, they faltered and commenced retreating. The Tenth Kentucky, Fourteenth Indiana, and two batteries were immediately pushed after them. But the speed of the enemy increased, and although the Union troops followed in quick step, they could only manage to come within range of his rear, to which they gave from time to time parting salutes with rifle balls and shells. The pursuit was continued to within a mile of the intrenchments, when owing to the close approach of night, the victors stopped and made themselves as comfortable as possible on the northern declivity of a hill overlooking the fortifications.

Rain was still falling, and although all were greatly fatigued from the labors of the day, but few sought repose on the soaked ground. The excitement of the battle kept the majority awake, and the uncomfortable night was spent in the discussion of the stirring events of the preceding hours, by the immense camp-fires, which burned brightly in defiance of the drifting rain.

With daybreak some of the Federal guns were got into a position commanding the rebel intrenchments, and were soon hurling shells upon them. Crowds of the enemy were seen hurrying down the hill toward the landing, and the little ferry-boat was rapidly steaming to and fro, carrying bodies of men, the last of the Confederates on the right bank of the river. No response being elicited, the infantry was ordered forward, the Tenth Kentucky in the advance. With lusty cheers the troops rushed down the road and up the hills crowned by fortifications, and climbing over the barricades of logs, obstructing the approaches on all sides, the Kentuckians were in a few minutes on the parapet, shouting, jumping, and waving their hats and muskets. Hardly five minutes more elapsed when the rebel camp teemed with thousands of soldiers, frantic with excitement.

The rebels literally saved nothing but what they wore on their persons. Eight of their guns, including two Parrot 20-pounders, with caissons and ammunition, were left behind, together with nearly a thousand stand of arms, and hundreds of boxes of cartridges, 1,700 horses and mules, a drove of cattle, 100 wagons, with harness, vast quantities of commissary and quartermasters' stores, some twenty bales of blankets and quilts, and the personal effects of officers and men.

The enemy left all their dead and many of their wounded behind them, five of their surgeons, however, remaining. One hundred and fifteen of their killed, including Zollicoffer, and about 120 of their wounded were found on the field, and 150 prisoners taken. Their entire loss must have been much greater. The Federal loss was 39 killed and 207 wounded.

Taken as a whole it was one of the fairest contested battles and most glorious victories of the war—one in which the Western troops fully sustained their reputation for unflinching courage and stern determination never to yield, no matter how great the force opposed to them.

INVESTMENT OF FORT PULASKI, GA.
January 27, 1862.

Tybee Island, lying at the mouth of Savannah river, immediately below Fort Pulaski, on Cockspur Island, was occupied by Federal troops very shortly after the capture of Port Royal by Commodore Dupont, the Flag-officer of the South Atlantic blockading squadron. It was late in December, however, before a garrison was established there. This was the first step toward the investment of Fort Pulaski, whose heavy embrasures frowned in stern defiance at the Federal fleet investing the harbor.

Late in December, from his headquarters at Tybee Island, an island forming the eastern shore of Calibogue Sound, and lying north of Savannah harbor, General Sherman, commanding the army in this district, had dispatched several reconnoitering parties to explore the small rivers, creeks and inlets which intersect each other at various points on the left of the Savannah river, forming the series of islands which dot the map of the harbor. A well grounded hope was entertained that an inside channel would be discovered, connecting with the Savannah river, of sufficient depth to float the gunboats to a point on that river far above Fort Pulaski.

In order to understand the nature of the reconnoissance, it will be necessary to have a clear apprehension of the geography of the country. Savannah is about fifteen miles from the mouth of the river, and on the right or southern bank. Approach to it by water is defended by Fort Pulaski, a casemated fort on Cockspur Island, at the mouth of the river, and Fort Jackson, a barbette fort on the mainland, only four miles below the city. The left bank is formed by a succession of islands, and the channel also is interrupted by large and numerous islands, the most important of which is Elba, whose upper extremity is immediately opposite Fort Jackson. Lower down in the stream is Long Island. The network of creeks and bays that surrounds Hilton Head terminates southward in Calibogue sound, which is divided from the Savannah river at its mouth by Turtle and Jones Island. The waters that form two sides of Jones Island, which is triangular in shape, are called Mud and Wright rivers; the latter is the southernmost, and separates Jones from Turtle Island, which lies next to Dawfuskie Island, the western shore of Calibogue sound. The islands on the Savannah are all very low and marshy, overgrown by high grass, and frequently without a solitary shrub or tree; they are all liable to be submerged by a very high tide. Jones Island is a broad, marshy, uninhabited island, five miles above the fort, not more than five miles long, by two or three broad. About half way between its upper and lower angles, and fronting on the Savannah, is Venus Point.

This first reconnoissance was undertaken by Lieutenant J. H. Wilson, of the topographical engineers. Taking with him two boats and a company of Rhode Island soldiers, together with his negro oarsmen and pilots, he started on the dangerous expedition, making all the necessary explorations by night, while his boats were hidden by the tall grass on the marshy and swampy shores he traversed. To the rear of Jones Island he discovered a canal called Wall's Cut, connecting the Mud and Wright rivers, the former emptying into the Savannah six, and the latter two miles above Fort Pulaski. The navigation of Wall's Cut had been obstructed by three rows of piles, driven across its entire width by the rebels, but at high tide the boats were got over these obstructions, and soon after floated on the waters of the Savannah, at night, unobserved by the rebels. The feasibility of traversing this route with the gunboats had been demonstrated, but the movement was betrayed to the rebels before the plan could be consummated.

A reconnoissance in force, through a corresponding series of channels on the right of the Savannah river, was then determined on, and Captain C. H. Davis was dispatched with the gunboats Ottawa, Lieutenant-Commanding Stevens; Seneca, Ammen; and the steamers Isaac Smith, Nicholson; Potomska, Watmough; Ellen, Budd; Western World, Gregory; in company with the transports Cosmopolitan, Delaware and Boston, having on board the Sixth Connecticut, Fourth New Hampshire, Ninety-seventh Pennsylvania; in all twenty-four hundred men, commanded by Brigadier-General H. G. Wright. Commander C. R. P. Rodgers accompanied the expedition.

Captain Davis sailed from Port Royal harbor on the 26th of January, and anchored in Warsaw Sound the same evening. The next morning he entered the Little Tybee river, or Freeborn Cut, and at half past one passed up that river above Fort Pulaski, and within long range of the rebel guns, but was unmolested, as they were not prepared for an enemy on that side. After passing the high land on Wilmington Island, the principal one on their route, they were arrested by a heavy double row of piles, driven across the channel. The island was now carefully explored, and found to have been deserted. The launches were also dispatched to examine the numerous creeks leading to the river, and to explore the main stream. At five o'clock five rebel steamers made their appearance in the Savannah river to reconnoitre the proceedings of the Federal fleet. At this hour Captain Ammen made his way through the marsh and cut the telegraph wire communicating with Fort Pulaski.

Captain John Wright, who had been dispatched by Flag-officer Dupont with a number of gunboats up the Wright river on the left of the Savannah, by the route previously explored, made his appearance on Tuesday, the 28th, and by means of the new army signals communication was opened between the two fleets. At eleven o'clock, the rebel steamers again made their appearance in the Savannah, and attempted to pass below the fort, when a spirited engagement commenced between them and the two Federal fleets. Three of the rebel steamers succeeded in passing, but the other two were driven back disabled.

The attempt to reach the Savannah river with the gunboats having been abandoned, measures were undertaken to blockade the river, and interrupt communication between Fort Pulaski and Savannah, by land approaches, and the establishment of batteries on the banks of the river. It was resolved to erect a battery on Jones' Island, the rear of which could be reached by the national flotilla. The first attempt was made on the night of February 7th, but owing to storms and other causes, it was not successful. A few days after, General Sherman issued orders for a second expedition to Jones' Island, and, if practicable, erect a battery there, so as to command the Savannah river. This was to be done without the assistance of the naval forces.

The expedition was placed under the command of Brigadier-General Viele, and consisted of the Forty-eighth New York Volunteers, Colonel Perry, two companies of volunteer engineers, and two companies of the Third Rhode Island artillery. The troops, with six large guns, (thirty-two pounders,) were embarked in flatboats at Dawfuskie Island, and in tow of light-draught steamboats. The expedition reached Jones Island, a preliminary reconnoissance was made of all the points on the island, and a site at Venus Point was selected for the erection of a fortification. The swampy character of the soil seemed to forbid the landing of troops on the island, much more to erect batteries and mount heavy guns thereon. It was determined, however, to erect the battery at the point already designated, and to carry the guns a distance of a mile through the swamp. To facilitate matters, Colonel Perry undertook the construction of a corduroy road from the place where the troops landed on the Mud river side of Jones Island to Venus Point. The road was constructed, and by the untiring labor of the troops, the guns were at last placed in battery.

While the construction of the road was going on, another detachment of Colonel Perry's regiment attempted to erect breastworks to cover the guns. The mud, as fast as it was piled up for the battery, slipped and sunk away; but the platforms were laid and the guns mounted. The guns were landed on a wharf made of bags filled with sand, and long planks laid across them. Tramways were laid along the marsh, constructed of planks thirty feet long, placed in parallel lines; two sets of these parallels were used for each gun, and as fast as the pieces were taken over one set, it was taken up and placed still further in advance. Holes were drilled in the planks, and ropes looped through the holes, so that the planks might be more easily dragged by the troops. In this manner the guns were conveyed across Jones Island to the chosen position. Colonel Perry, Lieutenant J. H. Wilson, of the United States Engineers, and Lieutenant Horace Porter, of the Ordnance Department, superintended the removal of the guns. On the first night the heavy guns were dragged two hundred yards. The second night the work proceeded, and the guns were dragged the remainder of the route, and before morning all were in position. The work of tugging the guns was performed entirely by the Forty-eighth New York regiment, commanded by Colonel Perry. In the morning a rebel gunboat came down the river to reconnoitre, and doubtless was amazed to find the Federal fort confronting her; but by hugging the western shore she was enabled to pass the guns on Jones Island without serious injury. This demonstrated the necessity of another battery on the west end of Bird Island, in the middle of the river opposite, which was subsequently erected, and the river thus effectually blockaded. On the 15th, four rebel gunboats attacked the batteries on Venus Point, Jones Island, but were all driven back, and one of them disabled.

By the erection of these batteries Fort Pulaski was cut off from all supplies and reinforcements; and General Hunter now commenced the erection of batteries for the reduction of the fort.

NEW MEXICO AND ARIZONA.

The comprehensive scheme of the rebel leaders was not confined to the mere occupancy of the Cotton States, or the entire section of the Union south of the Ohio river, but included within its future all the vast domain west of the Mississippi and south of Kansas. The restoration of peace, and the independence of the Southern Confederacy, would then enable it to carry its victorious arms into Mexico, and a vast empire would be erected, subject to the control of the Confederate government. In order to accomplish these purposes with the greatest promptitude, it was determined to take possession of New Mexico and Arizona at an early day, and bodies of armed men were dispatched from Texas upon this errand.

They reached the Territories during the month of July, 1861; one portion of the invading force entering Arizona, and the other took their line of march toward Santa Fé, in New Mexico, under the command of Brigadier-General H. H. Sibley. There was no military organization of the *inhabitants* of either New Mexico or Arizona to favor the rebel cause, excepting, perhaps a very few recent emigrants from Texas or other Southern States, who joined the invading forces—the *natives* were for the most part loyal.

Fort Fillmore, then under command of Major Lynde, of the United States army, who had seven hundred regulars for its defence, was surrendered, or betrayed on August 2d, to a force of Texan troops inferior to his own. The men were paroled, and finally brought to the east, where they were stationed by the Government at various posts on the northern lakes. Subsequently Forts Davis, Bliss and Stanton were easily captured by the rebel chieftains. The want of military organization among the people, their unprotected towns, and the scarcity of arms, prevented any effective resistance, and they were compelled to submit to the invasion, while waiting anxiously for the relief which they felt assured the Government would send.

At length the Governor of New Mexico, Henry Connelly, issued a vigorous and stirring proclamation, on the 9th of September, calling upon the citizens to enrol themselves for the defence of their homes against the invaders, who were coming to subdue them to the rule of the Texan authorities. He ordered an organization of the militia in the several counties of the State, and the Adjutant-General was instructed to carry the orders into effect.

On the 9th of November, New Mexico was constituted a military department, and Colonel E. R. S. Canby, of the United States army, was appointed to the command. Colonel Canby immediately entered upon his duties, and pushed his work with so much energy, that by the end of December he had retaken Forts Craig and Stanton. Federal forces also held Fort Massachusetts to the north, and Fort Union, on the southeast of Santa Fé, the capital of the Territory.

On the 2d of December, the Legislature assembled, and the Governor recommended the adoption of measures to secure the loyal adhesion of such of the Indian tribes as had not been betrayed into the hands of the Confederate agents. While loyal to the Government in their sentiments, they found themselves apparently cut off from its protection and support, under the circumstances in which they were placed; and pressed on all sides, they were somewhat divided. While some remained loyal, and were willing to enlist in the Federal service, others joined the Confederates; but the great body desired to pursue a course which would be entirely neutral.

On the 30th of December, General Sibley, the rebel commander, issued a proclamation from his head-quarters, notifying the people that he took possession of New Mexico in behalf of, and for the benefit of the Confederate States. He declared, that "by geographical position, by similarity of institutions, by commercial interests, and by future destinies, New Mexico pertains to the Confederacy." General Sibley also declared the United States tax laws abolished.

BATTLE OF VALVENDE.
February 21, 1862.

Colonel Canby had no intention of remaining inactive while the rebel leader was thus earnestly endeavoring to persuade the people into willing submission to Confederate power, or of permitting him by an apparent triumph to exercise his authority for the subversion of the legitimate government. He accordingly prepared for the important business of expelling him from the territory, determined to accomplish this, whatever effort it might involve. The rebels, on their way through the territory, followed the valley of the Rio Grande, and consequently would be obliged to pass Fort Craig. At this place Colonel Canby resolved to dispute their advance. His force was composed in part of United States regulars, and in part of New Mexican volunteers. With these he descended the river to meet the invaders. They were informed of his approach, and on the 10th crossed the river in order to take a position on the other side, from which they could shell the fort, and obtain command of the stream above it, by which movement they could cut off his communications. On the afternoon of the 19th, Colonel Canby ordered the detachments of the Fifth, Seventh and Tenth United States Infantry, under Captains Selden and Wingate, and Colonels Carson's and Pino's regiments of volunteers to cross the river and occupy an elevation opposite the fort, which would otherwise be appropriated by the rebels. On the afternoon of the 20th, Captain McRae's battery and the cavalry under Major Duncan were ordered to cross the river, and were brought into position. The enemy were thus cut off from the river, and suffered from want of water. Their mules were so much exhausted that it was found necessary to double the teams in order to draw the wagons; but this resort at last failed, and the animals gave out entirely. The rebels finding the desperate strait to which they were reduced, opened a heavy cannonade upon the Federal troops. Being protected by the elevations between them and the enemy, the Union troops suffered no injury, except one man, who was wounded by a fragment from a ball, which struck a rock, and was shattered by the blow. The night closed on the antagonists. About two hundred mules were captured by the Union scouts, and a number of wagons burned.

On the morning of the 21st, at about eight o'clock, Colonel Canby ordered Colonel Roberts, with his cavalry, Colonel Valdez's cavalry, Colonel Carson's volunteers, the regular infantry, and Captain McRae's and Lieutenant Hall's batteries to proceed up the west bank of the Rio Grande, and prevent the Texans from reaching the water, at the only point where the river was fordable by the sloping banks. This position was seven miles north of the fort, and when Colonel Roberts' command reached it, he found that the enemy had gained the water first. Colonel Roberts immediately opened his batteries upon them, on which they retreated with a loss of twenty-five or thirty killed, and one cannon. The gun was dismounted, spiked, and rendered unfit for use. Colonel Roberts then crossed the river, and held his position until the issue of the battle was decided.

After one o'clock Colonel Canby came upon the ground with his staff, followed by Colonel Pino's regiment of volunteers, and took the command in person. Up to this time the fighting had been principally with the batteries. Captain McRae's battery occupied the left, and Lieutenant Hall's battery the right of the line. On the left flank, and within about a hundred yards of McRae's battery, was a piece of woods, where bodies of the enemy were seen to collect, but out of range of the guns. Two companies of regulars and two companies of volunteers were assigned to support this battery. Lieutenant Hall's guns were to be supported by the cavalry and Colonel Carson's volunteers.

Thus disposed, Colonel Canby intended to make an advance, when suddenly a brisk fire of musketry was opened towards the right of the field. This was entirely unexpected, but the object was soon discovered to be a ruse to divert attention from an attempt which was immediately made to take the batteries. Advancing to the front, in two divisions, the enemy rushed on and made their charges against the batteries in the most determined and gallant manner. The charge against Lieutenant Hall's battery was made by the cavalry, who dashed forward with an unbroken front, in the face of the destructive fire to which they were exposed. Standing true to their posts, the experienced gunners worked their pieces with such deadly effect, that the enemy was appalled by the carnage, and compelled to retire from the field.

The charge upon McRae's battery was made on foot, and was never surpassed for the cool and deliberate determination with which the rebel infantry pressed forward undismayed to their work. The iron hail belched forth from the guns swept through their ranks, opening a pathway through the columns, which closed up and moved onward, apparently heedless of the losses they sustained. Volley after volley from the batteries poured destruction on the advancing foe. But still they came on steadily under the fire, pouring forth in return volley upon volley, and closing with their revolvers and bayonets, until the last brave man was shot down while standing faithfully by his gun. During all this time the New Mexicans remained inactive, and when once convinced of the danger they were in, fled in haste, leaving the thrice heroic McRae alone with his gunners, who fell one by one till he stood alone before the enemy. When this fearless man saw that he was utterly abandoned, he sat down, with sublime coolness, on one of his useless guns, with his face to the enemy, waiting for the glorious death which soon came to his relief. A ball struck him on the forehead, and he fell by the gun his courage had defended to the last.

Captain Plimpton's regulars stood their ground and fought until one-half their number were wounded, or dead and dying on the field, when they were compelled to retire.

When the battery was lost, the day was decided in favor of the enemy, and the Federal forces retreated to Fort Craig.

Colonel Canby had in the engagment about 1,500 men, consisting of regulars and volunteers. The force of the enemy, under Colonel Steele, was from 1,500 to 2,000. Our loss, according to the best information, was 50 or 60 killed, and about 140 wounded. The loss of the enemy was estimated at from 100 to 200 killed and wounded. Captain Rossel, of the regulars, was taken by the Texans, his horse having been drowned in crossing the river.

THE BATTLE OF APACHE CANON.
MARCH 28, 1862.

The immediate consequence of the battle of Valvende was that the insurgents marched directly past Fort Craig, which for want of men and provisions they were powerless to invest or capture, direct on Albuquerque and Santa Fé, which fell into their power without resistance. Albuquerque was the depot of United States Government stores, most of which was removed on the advance of the insurgents, and the rest destroyed. The occupation of Santa Fé was followed by the proclamation of a provisional government, which however never entered into practical operation. Fort Craig still remained in the rebel rear, and Fort Union in the possession of the national troops, on the northeast, from which direction reinforcements might be expected. The policy of the insurgents was therefore either to capture Fort Union before relief could arrive, or maintain their position, isolating Fort Craig until that post should be compelled to surrender for want of supplies.

Meantime, news of the critical condition of affairs having reached the Colorado territory and Kansas, troops were at once organized to go to the relief of the threatened positions. By forced marches, scarcely paralleled in history, a Colorado regiment 950 strong, under Colonel Hough, reached Fort Union on the 13th of March. Here he gathered around him all the troops available, or possible to obtain, and marched for Santa Fé, to give battle to the invaders. The latter moved their forces forward to meet him. The numbers on both sides were nearly equal—between 1,200 and 1,500. They met at a point called Apache Pass.

The main fight took place at Apache Cañon, eighty miles from Fort Union, and twenty miles from Santa Fé. Three battalions, one under Major Chivington, one under Captain Lewis, and one under Captain Wynkoop, advanced to the cañon, on the 28th, when the pickets reported no enemy in sight. The command then advanced, when shots

were fired at them by the Texans, who were in ambush and succeeded in killing four privates. The Union men, under Hough, rushed on them, killing 20 or 30 Texans, wounding many of them, and taking seven prisoners, four officers and three privates. Major Chivington's command, which went ahead and surprised the Texan pickets, taking 67 prisoners, and 64 provision wagons, now arrived, and a plan of action was determined upon. It was to meet the enemy in front and flank them at the same time.

About 12 o'clock they advanced, and the action became general, the Coloradans doing wonders. The battery under Captain Ritter, and also the howitzer battery under Lieutenant Cláflin, swept the Texans from the field. The fight lasted until four o'clock, when flags of truce were interchanged to bury the dead and care for the wounded. The enemy had about 2,000 men and one 6-pounder. The Unionists had 1,300 men, one six and one 12-pounder, and four howitzers. The enemy lost their entire train (64 wagons and provisions), 230 mules, about 150 killed, 200 wounded and 93 taken prisoners, among whom were 13 officers.

The Texans, when surprised, supposed it was Colonel Canby's force that was coming. The Texan officer in command, with two of his companies, made several attempts to charge on the Union men and seize their batteries, but they were each time repulsed, with tremendous loss, while daring, noble deeds were performed by the Federal soldiers. At one time, the Texan companies charged within a few yards of the Union batteries.

The defeat at Apache Pass proved an effectual check on the invaders, and so far weakened their forces as to compel their abandonment of the territory, and its complete restoration under the national authority.

The enemy fled into Arizona, where they found it useless to remain, and applied to the authorities of Mexico for permission to cross their territory on their return home, but were refused; they however succeeded in reaching Texas. A reinforcement of Federal troops soon after arrived in New Mexico.

FIGHT AT BLOOMING GAP, VA.
February 14, 1862.

To General F. W. Lander's brigade had been assigned the perilous duty of protecting the Baltimore and Ohio railroad at Cumberland, Md., and the various towns and strategic points in Virginia within a radius of forty or fifty miles from that centre, at several of which his troops were quartered.

On the 13th of February, Lander received information that a brigade of rebels under General Carson had occupied Blooming Gap, a strong pass in the mountains seven miles beyond the Cacapon river, whose turbid waters, swollen by the storms of winter, were deemed an impassable barrier to the advance of the Federal forces. No bridge spanned the torrent, and the blackened buttress and crumbled pier gave evidence that the incendiary torch had been at work.

Lander was then at Pawpaw Tunnels, on the Maryland shore of the Potomac, a station on the Baltimore and Ohio railroad, midway between Hancock and Cumberland, with a small force. He immediately marched to New Creek, in Hampshire county, Va., to join the detachment of troops at that point, where he also hastily concentrated all his available command. Taking twenty wagons loaded with lumber, he proceeded to a point on the Cacapon river, seven miles south of the railroad, and between the hours of nine and one o'clock at night he improvised a bridge one hundred and eighty feet long, by placing the wagons in the river as a foundation, over which he marched his force of four thousand men, and advanced upon the enemy's pickets before the dawn of day.

With five hundred of the First Virginia cavalry, under Colonel Anastanzel, he had designed to charge through the rebel camp at the Gap, and then form immediately in his rear, cut off the retreat, and capture the whole force, after the Federal infantry, following up the cavalry charge, should have completed the discomfiture of the enemy. But the rebels had retired before Lander's approach; and when led by the General and his staff, the cavalry flew through the Gap and beyond it, they met with no opposition. Colonel Anastauzel was at once ordered to push forward on the Winchester road with the cavalry, reconnoitre, and, if possible, overtake and capture the baggage of the enemy.

General Lander meantime brought up Colonel Carroll with the Eighth Ohio regiment, and the Seventh Virginia, Colonel Evans, for a support. Colonel Anastanzel encountered the enemy at the head of the pass, two miles from Blooming. He was met by a sharp fire, and halted his command. On hearing the firing, General Lander came up and led the charge, followed by Major Armstrong, Assistant Adjutant-General; Lieutenants Fitz-James O'Brien, the well-known poet of his staff, and Major Bannister, Paymaster U. S. A., who had volunteered for the expedition. A group of rebel officers were distant about three hundred yards, encouraging their men. General Lander being the best mounted, outran the rest of the party, and cut off the retreat of the rebel officers.

"Surrender, gentlemen," he said, coolly dismounting, and extending his hand to receive the sword of Colonel Baldwin, over whom an instant before he had appeared to be riding.

Five of the rebel officers surrendered to General Lander, and four others immediately afterward, to the officers of his staff, among them the Assistant Adjutant-General of General Carson.

By this time the rebel infantry, perceiving the small number of their adversaries, commenced a heavy fire from the woods, but the cavalry had recovered from its panic, and now rushed up the hill. General Lander ordered Anastanzel to charge up the road, and capture the baggage of the enemy. The cavalry dashed forward, and the advance guard soon overtook and turned fifteen wagons and horses out of the road. Colonel Evans now came up with his regiment of infantry, and captured many more of the rebels. Colonel Carroll cleared the road as he went, both infantry regiments behaving admirably, following and engaging the enemy to the last, until ordered back. The pursuit was continued eight miles.

The result of this affair was the capture of eighteen commissioned officers, and forty-five non-commissioned officers and privates. Thirty-three of the rebels were killed and wounded, with a loss on the Union side of seven killed and wounded.

During this engagement Lieutenant Fitz-James O'Brien was shot mortally while in advance of his comrades, and like the author-soldier Winthrop, immortalized his name with the sword, as he had before proved himself great with the pen.

General Dunning, of Lander's command, returned to New Creek the same day from an expedition to Moorfield, forty miles south of Romney, having captured 225 beef cattle and 4,000 bushels of corn. In a skirmish two of his men were wounded, and several rebels killed.

EAST TENNESSEE UNDER CONFEDERATE RULE.

The history of the world has never exhibited more exalted devotion to an idea, nor a more splendid patriotism than that of the people of East Tennessee. We may almost challenge the records of religious history to produce anything more like holy enthusiasm, than the lofty inspiration which has characterized these people. In no country, and among no class can be found more heroic persistence or unfaltering adherence to principle than has exalted the patriotism of this region. With many inhabitants of the eastern portion of the State, loyalty and devotion to the Union became in truth a part of their religion.

The rebel leaders knew that they had very little sympathy in East Tennessee, and took measures to crush out all Union sentiment with the iron heel of military despotism. Any expression of sympathy with the Union cause, any co-operation of its inhabitants with the loyalists, either for their own protection or for the aid of the Government, was punished as a crime. The presses of that part of the State had all been silenced or converted to their own use by the Secessionists, with one exception.

The Knoxville Whig remained true to the Union. Its vigorous defence of the Government, its exposures and denunciations of the rebel leaders, its unsparing invective against the rebellion, and its bold, defiant appeals to the people, rang like a clarion through the hills and valleys of East Tennessee, and as the echo gathered from thousands of loyal voices, it made itself heard through all the valleys and mountain passes of that noble border State.

The heroic editor of this paper was not to be silenced either in his voice or his press without a vigorous struggle. The Rev. Wm. G. Brownlow had learned how to denounce and how to endure, for that is a lesson most Methodist clergymen are called upon to learn; and being brave in deeds as well as words, he stood forth in defence of the country he loved, when she greatly needed the power of his eloquence and the strength of his arm. The popularity which this man had won by his uprightness, his courage, and firm adherence to the Constitution, gave his opinions a force that made him an object of peculiar importance to the enemy—yet they hesitated to lay violent hands upon a man whose words were more potent than their bayonets.

He was frequently threatened by soldiers passing through Knoxville from other States, yet none dared to execute their threats. His family were inspired with the same lofty heroism, and on one occasion when a company of rebels came to his house to haul down the Stars and Stripes, which was kept floating over his domicil, one of his daughters stepped out to meet them, and by her courage and decision protected the flag.

The suppression of this undaunted advocate of the Union, and faithful and fearless witness against secession, became an inevitable necessity; and at last, in the hope that he would at least become silent on political affairs, it was resolved to offer him the alternative of the oath of allegiance or the cell of a prison. He chose the latter, and in a valedictory to his readers, published October 26, which must ever be memorable for its heroic defence of the Union, its bold denunciation of the rebels and their course, he announced to his readers the suspension of his paper. This remarkable address, which, under the circumstances, rises to the sublime in its moral courage, closed with these words:

"Exchanging, with proud satisfaction, the editorial chair and the sweet endearments of home for a cell in the prison, or the lot of an exile, I have the honor to be, &c. WILLIAM G. BROWNLOW."

Mr. Brownlow was sent to prison, and for months occupied a room with several other patriots who preferred imprisonment to denial of the government they loved. Here he was in daily expectation of being led forth to execution. Though suffering from ill-health he was no way daunted by the dark fate that threatened him. Nor were these anticipations groundless, for during his stay there, many a brave man left that prison to meet a violent death, and he had no reason to expect a happier destiny.

During the closing months of the summer and fall the hopes of the people were excited by promises of aid from the government. Loud and earnest appeals were made, for help, and with the energy of despair the people clung to their principles, through every species of persecution, robbery, arson, and imprisonment. Hundreds were hung or assassinated, and the records of Tennessee are among the most heart-rending that this war for the Union will leave to posterity.

The position of the rebel armies in western Tennessee was at that time very strong, but the importance of keeping their lines of communication open with the Atlantic States was great, and thoroughly understood by the loyalists. To cut these lines was to the Federals a work of pressing necessity; and in view of the probable redemption of East Tennessee, the loyalists organized, and on the night of November 8 they destroyed several bridges, and broke the lines. Two of these were on the Georgia State road, two on Chickamanye Creek, Hamilton county, and one on the East Tennessee and Georgia railroad, on Hiawassee river, Bradley county. Besides these, two bridges on the East Tennessee and Georgia railroad on Lick Creek, Green County, and another on Holstein river, were also burned. The rebels were thrown into consternation by these events, and their leaders took the most active measures to arrest and punish the perpetrators. A correspondence between some of the prominent men ensued, and a large portion of the letters was discovered among other papers and effects captured after the battle of Mill Spring, which took place on the 19th of January, 1862. This correspondence, in which the names Colonel William B. Wood and General F. K. Zollicoffer appear, prove that the majority of the people were unalterably for the Union, and that they could only be restrained by the most oppressive and cruel measures. Colonel Wood wrote to J. P. Benjamin, the Secretary of War, asking what disposition should be made of the bridge-burners, to which Mr. Benjamin replied— "All such as can be identified as having been engaged in bridge-burning are to be tried summarily by drum-head court-martial, and if found guilty, executed on the spot by hanging. It would be well to leave their bodies hanging in the vicinity of the burnt bridges."

The loyalists were encouraged in their cause by the devotion of Hon. Andrew Johnson, U. S. Senator, and Hon. Horace Maynard, M. C., for Tennessee, whose eloquent and powerful appeals, and confident assurances of aid, cheered the hearts of the people.

Thousands of East Tennesseeans escaped by night, wandering along unfrequented roads, until they reached Kentucky, where they organized regiments, under the direction of the Federal commanders. Their cherished desire was to return to their own State, with a powerful army, and redeem their soil. The atrocity of the rebel guerrillas drove them almost to a passion of revenge, and when disappointed at the announcement that their time had not come, and that they must await a more favorable condition of the army, hundreds of them, when ordered to retreat from the border lines of their State, strayed from the ranks, despairing and heart-sick, and falling down by the way, wept bitterly. Several of them, exhausted by hard labor and forced marches, never rose again, but were afterwards found dead on the road to Mount Vernon.

On the 26th of November the house of a gentleman named Bell was attacked by an armed party of the enemy and set on fire. The inmates, a large family of nine persons, were consigned to the flames. Two alone of the whole household escaped this horrible fate.

On the 29th a band of twenty-one Union prisoners at Nashville were compelled to take the oath of allegiance, and enter a company in the rebel army.

Leadbetter, the secession commander in East Tennessee, had his headquarters at Greenville, and on the 30th of November issued a proclamation promising protection and pardon to all who would lay down their arms and submit to the Confederate government. From this clemency he excepted bridge-burners and destroyers of railroad tracks. He closed his proclamation with the assurance that "they will be tried by drumhead court-martial, and be hung on the spot." This terrible order was put into execution a few days afterward. Jacob M. Hemslier and Henry Fry, two Unionists, being tried and pronounced guilty of these offences, were hung.

The days of hope for the Unionists were weary and prolonged, but deliverance was drawing nigh. The loyal men of the western part of the State organized to oppose the measures of the leaders, and early in January a bold resistance was made in Carroll, Weakly, McNairy, and other counties, against the conscription act. Rebel troops were sent into these counties to compel submission, and enforce obedience.

The defeat and death of Zollicoffer, the breaking up of his army, and the destruction of his stronghold, at last gave a brilliant promise to these persecuted people that their deliverance was drawing nigh. This event, succeeded in a few weeks by the capture of Fort Henry, Fort Donelson, the evacuation of Bowling Green and Columbus, and the occupation of Nashville, filled every true heart with rejoicing, and the good old flag once more swept its folds freely over the houses of East Tennessee.

The appointment of Hon. Andrew Johnson as military governor of

BOMBARDMENT OF FORT HENRY, FEB. 6, 1862.

Tennessee was greeted with enthusiasm by the people. His reputation and conservative, principles were a guarantee for the character of his administration, and he soon began to rally to his support the wavering and timid of the people who were still apprehensive that the Confederates would return and restore their rule.

Parson Brownlow, after having borne a long and severe confinement in prison, in which his health suffered terribly, was released, and sent beyond the military lines of the Confederates. His reception by the Federal guards was enthusiastic and joyous in the extreme. As soon as his health permitted he visited several cities in the West, where he was greeted with overwhelming demonstrations of popular admiration and respect. On his arrival at New York, May 17th, he was honored with a public reception at the Academy of Music, which was densely filled with a brilliant audience, eager to welcome him.

CAPTURE OF FORT HENRY, TENN.
February 6, 1862.

The brilliant victory obtained by General Thomas' army over the Confederate forces at Mill Spring, on the 19th of January, laid open the rebel lines to the successful advance of the Federal arms, and served to stimulate the commanders of the land and naval forces to avail themselves of the opportunity thus afforded.

Previous to the battle of Mill Spring, General Grant, with a large force, had left Cairo and marched toward Columbus, for the purpose of reconnoitering the country, and to prevent rebel reinforcements moving from that point to the assistance of General Buckner, at Bowling Green, Ky., who was then threatened by the approach of General Buell's army. Upon the return of General Grant's division to Cairo, a combined movement of the land and naval forces was determined on for the purpose of capturing Fort Henry, on the Tennessee river, in Henry county, Tenn., just beyond the Kentucky State line.

Fort Henry and its approaches were reconnoitered on the 21st January by the United States gunboat Lexington, with a view to ascertain its strength and the position of the rebels. She went within two miles of the fort, and flung a number of shells into it without eliciting any reply. At first it was thought the rebels had evacuated the work, but on approaching it still nearer pickets were discovered at various points. The heavy guns on the work were seen distinctly; also a number of field-pieces. In addition to the fort proper, numerous earthworks had been thrown up on a high bluff above the fort, on the west bank of the river. This additional work, named Fort Hieman, commanded Fort Henry.

On the 22d January, Brigadier-General C. F. Smith, commanding the second division of General Grant's army, was at Crown Point, Ky., where he had arrived with 6,000 men after a fatiguing march of over 100 miles from Paducah. He proceeded thence on a personal reconnoissance, on the gunboat Lexington, in the direction of Fort Henry. The gunboat advanced up the west channel of the river to a point within one mile and a half from the fort. General Smith obtained an excellent view of the rebel fort, camp and garrison, and sent his report to headquarters. He then marched his division back to Paducah.

The flotilla of gunboats, which had been so long in course of preparation on the Ohio and Mississippi, was now ready to take part in the impending battles of the nation, and to assume that prominence in the momentous events which were to follow to which they have proved themselves justly entitled.

Flag-officer Andrew H. Foote was appointed by the Government to command the naval forces on the Upper Mississippi and the Western waters, and now led forth his gallant fleet to attack the enemy, in conjunction with the land forces under General Ulysses S. Grant. The fleet consisted of

Fleet Officers.—Flag-Officer Andrew H. Foote; Fleet Captain, Commodore A. M. Pennock; Ordnance Officer, Lieutenant J. F. Sanford; Ordnance Lieutenant, Byron Wilson; Flag Lieutenant, James M. Prickett. *Essex*, 9 *guns*, Commander William D. Porter. *St. Louis*, 13 *guns*, Lieutenant-Commanding Leonard Paulding. *Cincinnati*, 13 *guns*, Commander R. N. Stembel. *Carondelet*, 13 *guns*, Commander Henry Walke. *Conestoga*, 9 *guns*, Lieutenant-Commanding —— Phelps. *Tyler*, 9 *guns*, Lieutenant-Commanding W. Gwin.

For several days, at Paducah, the utmost vigilance was exercised at the headquarters of the Provost Marshal, in issuing passes, and on Sunday and Monday, the 3d February, no persons were allowed in or out of the lines. Half a dozen gunboats steamed leisurely into port and brought their black forms to anchor opposite the levee, in the centre of the river.

Monday afternoon, steamers commenced coming up from Cairo, laden with troops and stores, and by night the whole landing in front of the town was crowded with the arrivals. The fleet which came up brought General Grant and Staff, and the first division, under command of Brigadier-General McClernand. The steamers were under command of Commodore G. W. Graham, and consisted of the following boats: City of Memphis, Iatan, D. A. January, Chancellor, Alp, "W. H. B," New Uncle Sam, Rob Roy, Alex. Scott, Minnehaha, Illinois, Emerald, and Fanny Bullett.

The first division, on these boats, was made up of two brigades,

composed as follows, and commanded by General John A. McClernand:
—*First Brigade, Colonel Oglesby, Commanding.*—Seventh Illinois, Colonel Cook: Eighth Illinois, Lieutenant-Colonel Rhoades; Eighteenth Illinois, Lieutenant-Colonel Lawler; Twenty-ninth Illinois, Colonel Reardon; Thirtieth Illinois, Lieutenant-Colonel Dennis; Thirty-first Illinois, Colonel John A. Logan; Swartz's and Dresser's Batteries; Stewart's, Dollins', O. Harnett's and Carmichael's Cavalry.

Second Brigade, W. H. L. Wallace, Commanding.—Eleventh Illinois, Lieutenant-Colonel Hart; Twentieth Illinois, Colonel Marsh; Forty-fifth Illinois, Colonel Smith; Forty-eighth Illinois, Colonel Harney; Taylor's and McAllister's Batteries—in the latter four siege guns; Fourth Illinois Cavalry, Colonel Kellogg; Seventh Illinois Cavalry, Colonel Dickey.

Soon after arriving, General Grant and staff paid a visit to General Smith, and had a conference, in which it was determined to forward the division of General McClernand that night, and after landing them at some point below Fort Henry, out of range of its guns, send the boats back after General Smith's division at Paducah. It was nearly midnight before the boats took their departure.

The point at which the troops were landed is about four or five miles below Fort Henry, opposite a small town in Kentucky, called Buffalo. Immediately at the place is a clearing of about one hundred acres, surrounded on three sides by high bluffs densely timbered, and reaching down to the river. The troops, on landing, immediately took possession of these eminences, and planted batteries which commanded the country in every direction, and then awaited the arrival of the remaining forces, under General Smith.

Tuesday afternoon, while the troops were disembarking, the Osband Cavalry, with Carson's and Carpenter's scouts thoroughly examined the country in every direction, even up to within two miles of Fort Henry. Tuesday night was beautiful; a thousand camp-fires flashed through the shadows that lay upon the amphitheatre of wooded hills. The sky was warm and serenely purple, as if brooding over the first sweet blossoms of May. The silver crescent of a new moon glittered in the western sky, shedding a faint radiance over the tree-tops and sloping hill sides. All at once the music of half a dozen bands broke through the stillness of this lovely scene, and the "Star-Spangled Banner," "Red, White and Blue," and "Columbia the Gem of the Ocean," filled the night with bursts of patriotic music. Then some dreamy strain followed, hushing the soldier's heart with thoughts of "Home, Sweet Home."

On Wednesday, parties were out reconnoitering near the enemy's works, and in one case a squad of cavalry went within a mile of the fort and encountered two hundred rebel horsemen. Both sides fired, when the rebels ran, leaving one of their number dead, and carrying off three severely wounded. One man on the Union side was shot through the brain, and killed instantly. He was the first man who gave up his life in the vicinity of Fort Henry.

It had been noticed that a steamer belonging to the rebels was busily engaged in running from the fortifications to some point up or across the river, which was doubtless bringing in reinforcements. Two of the gunboats—the Taylor and Conestoga, ran up to nearly the centre of the island, and dropped a few shells in the direction of the fort and the steamer, with what result was not known. They effected a thorough reconnoissance on both sides, and discovered two ugly torpedoes sunk in the west channel, which they carefully hauled out and towed down to the shore below.

During the day and night the division of General Smith, from Paducah, arrived, and was landed on the west shore of the river, with a view of operating against batteries supposed to be on that side, and also to counteract a large body of troops, which scouts reported to be concentrating opposite the fort.

Wednesday night was cold and most disagreeable. About eight o'clock a heavy storm set in, which speedily quenched the camp-fires, and sent the troops wet and disconsolate under any shelter that could be found. All over the southern horizon, in the direction of Fort Henry, a tremendous thunder-storm swept its way, filling the hills with flashes of fiery blue lightning, and shaking the forests with loud reverberations of thunder. Hailing this burst of heaven's artillery, rolling southward toward the enemy, as a good omen, the Union soldiers pulled the wet blankets closer around them, turned drearily in the yielding mud, and fell asleep.

Thursday dawned cloudily, but towards nine o'clock it cleared up and the sun came out warm and gloriously. Nature nowhere seemed to anticipate the bloody event which gives the day prominence. A few more troops arrived, among whom were the Ohio Seventh, Colonel Lauman, and the Ohio Twelfth, Colonel Wood, both from Smithland, and which, together with the Seventh Illinois, Lieutenant-Colonel Bancock; Thirteenth Missouri, Colonel Wright; the Fifteenth Illinois, Colonel ———, and Company D, First Missouri Artillery, made the Third Brigade, Colonel John Cook commanding, assigned the right wing of the advance up the Tennessee shore.

About ten o'clock the gunboats started slowly up the river, four iron clad steamers leading abreast—the Essex, Captain Porter, on the right, and the Cincinnati, Commodore Foote, on the left. The three wooden gunboats ranged themselves abreast and followed, half a mile or so to the rear.

The iron-clad boats moved up abreast, keeping up the west or high water channel. Almost immediately on passing the lower end of the island, the boats and the forts were in each others' range, but on both sides an ominous silence was preserved—a silence that betokened deadly intent on the part of the belligerents. On swept the boats, coming in full view of the long line of breastworks that broke the east shore—in full view of the black muzzles of the heavy guns which seemed watching the approach of the gallant little fleet in ominous silence—in full view of the flag waving defiantly from a high staff in the centre of the works, until one could almost see down the huge bore of the guns, the bright straps of the shells, which seemed like leashes to prevent the deadly missiles from springing forth upon their work of destruction—and yet not a trigger was pulled on either side.

Less than a mile separated the fleet and the fort, and yet not a word was said. The insurgents appeared to be confidently anticipating the conflict; and grouped like statues around their guns, with lanyards stretched, they waited for the onset.

When about six hundred yards from the fort, the bow-guns of the flag-ship poured their contents into it, and so close after, that the reports seemed almost one, the other three poured in their fire. Scarcely had the smoke cleared from the muzzles of the pieces, ere the whole ten guns of the rebels belched forth their contents, sending a terrific iron shower in, above and around the gunboats. Taking their cue from the others, the three wooden gunboats, which were about a mile below, opened from their bow-guns, and then the contest was fairly begun. For one hour the roar was so incessant that the successive reports of the guns could, not in many cases, be distinguished. Occasionally there would be a momentary lull—then a single reverberating roar would give the key-note, and an instant after all the voices would swell together in one tremendous chorus.

A thick cloud of smoke enveloped the boats, hiding them completely from view. Over them hovered a dense white vapor, from which quick flashes of flame leaped and quivered, incessantly followed by delicate balloon-like forms of smoke, which burst like ghostly shadows from the enemy's shells.

From the very first, the fire of the rebel guns seemed directed at the Essex. In their first volley two thirty-two pound shots struck the Essex on the starboard bow, indenting deeply the iron sheathing, and then glanced off, down the river, while a perfect storm of the iron missiles whistled over her decks, and plowed into the water on either side. She received in all eleven shots—one of which carried death through the whole length of the vessel. It entered a larboard port, carried off the head of the master's mate, and passing on, entered the boiler. The steam and water poured out, filling the whole space between decks, and causing more destruction than all the enemy's missiles put together—four men were instantly suffocated, and some twenty-five severely scalded, among whom was the gallant Commander Porter. The two pilots, who were in the pilot-house above, had no escape except through a passage from below, and up this the steam rushed, as if coming from a safety-valve, and of course with fatal effect. Both these poor men perished.

Of course the Essex was thenceforth unmanageable. She slowly drifted down the main channel, and was soon after met by a steamer, which towed her down to the place occupied by the boats before starting. Soon after the Essex became disabled, the pelting of the iron storm proved too hot for endurance, and the rebel flag came rapidly down. The firing on the part of the gunboats immediately ceased, and messengers were sent off from the flag-boat, which found, upon landing, that the rebels were disposed to an unconditional surrender. In scarcely more than an hour after the first attack, the flag of Fort Henry was in the dust.

The fort was soon after taken possession of, and it was found that the sum total of rebel prisoners was between seventy and one hundred, the balance having left the night before on the steamer Dunbar.

Among those who surrendered were Brigadier-General Tilghman, Major Corrico, Colonel Carmichael, Captain Hayden, of the Engineers, and Captain Miller, with several other commissioned officers.

Ten of the rebels were found killed, and some twelve or fifteen wounded. Three hundred and six tents were found on the west side of the river, and about as many near the fort, all of which bore evidences of the haste with which the rebels had evacuated their quarters. Several hundred stands of arms were found, chiefly squirrel rifles and double-barrelled shot-guns, also a large amount of clothing, forage, provisions, wagons, mules and horses.

There was a large supply of ammunition, and when the Union forces entered the fort there was beside each gun an abundance unexpended. The tents were new and of excellent make, sufficient to shelter five or six thousand men. The enemy had flour, corn, bacon and sugar in large quantities, but no salt, and not a large supply of beef.

There were nineteen guns in position, of the following calibre: two 128-pounders, one 80-pounder, two 42-pounders, rifled, ten 32-pounders, two 24-pound howitzers, two 12-pound howitzers. Three 6-pound smooth bores, five 6-pound rifles, found outside the intrenchments.

A twenty-four-pound rifled gun exploded on the fourth round, and near the close of the fight a shell from one of the Union boats entered the eighty-pounder and burst, disabling it. Several caissons were captured in the redan upon the west side of the river, but no guns were in position.

Evidences abounded on all sides of the deadly accuracy of the Federal gunners. Every one of the eleven log buildings within the ramparts was perforated with shot, the roof of one of the small magazines was torn open, hurdle-work scattered in all direction, half the guns knocked out of place, and great gulleys cut in the parapet and the ground. A thirty-two pounder bearing upon the gunboats had been struck by a Union shell, completely shattering the muzzle. The ground beside the embrasure was stained with blood, which lay in pools on the uneven surface. Beside one of the buildings, with gray blankets thrown hastily over them, lay six dead soldiers, all fearfully mutilated. Inside, ten wounded men were stretched upon cots, or on the ground, some insensible, and others rending the air with groans, while the surgeons of the garrison were attending upon them. Just above, on the river, was the hospital ship of the rebels, the stern-wheel steamer R. M. Patten, which had been captured with the fort. The ensign of disease, the yellow flag, was flying from the staff, waving off destruction from sixty invalids.

THE REBEL CAMP.

Upon a high plateau, the heavy trees had all been cut away over a large area. They were designed for the construction of an abattis, and though nothing had been done beyond chopping down the heavy timber, the large trunks and limbs, lying in all directions, would have presented almost insurmountable obstacles to the approach of cavalry or artillery, had the rifle-pits, just beyond, been filled with men.

Crossing the rifle-pits, the Unionists were in the enemy's camp, though still more than half a mile from the fort. Here were the wall tents of a regiment, all standing in complete order, with the camp-fires still blazing, the copper pots of soup for dinner boiling over them, and the half-made biscuits in the pans. Inside the tents everything was just as the enemy had left it—pistols, shot-guns, muskets, bowie-knives, clothing, tables partially set for dinner, letters half-written, with the ink scarcely dry upon the open page, cards thrown down in the midst of the game, overcoats, blankets, trunks, carpet sacks, and so on through all the articles of camp life. It seemed as if the men were out at guard-mounting, and expected to return in ten minutes.

Along the river bank were long rows of log barracks, enough to accommodate two or three thousand men, and finished comfortably. Inside they bore the same indications that the inmates had decamped without a moment's warning.

ADVANCE OF NATIONAL GUNBOATS UP THE TENNESSEE RIVER.

In accordance with the instructions of Commodore Foote, given before the attack on Fort Henry, immediately after the capture of the fort, February 6, the gunboats Conestoga, Lexington and Tyler, under the command of Lieutenant Phelps, advanced up the river twenty-five miles, to the crossing of the Bowling Green and Memphis railway, breaking up a portion of the railway bridge, and rendering it impassable. They next proceeded to destroy the rebel gunboats and transports, capturing large quantities of munitions of war and supplies, and advanced up the river for upwards of two hundred miles to Eastport, in Mississippi, and Florence, at the foot of Muscle Shoals, in Alabama, annihilating the rebel flotilla in the Tennessee river. The expedition was welcomed at every point by the inhabitants. Twenty-five Tennesseans enlisted at Cerro Gordo, where also three steamers were seized, containing 250,000 feet of valuable ship timber.

Toward the latter part of February, intelligence reached Fort Henry that the rebels were fortifying a point on the Tennessee river, near the Mississippi State line, whereupon Lieutenant-Commanding William Gwin, with the gunboats Tyler and Lexington, were sent forward to reconnoitre the position.

Having learned that the rebels had occupied and were fortifying a place called Pittsburgh, nine miles above, on the right bank of the river, he determined to attack them.

At twelve M. the Taylor, followed by the Lexington, Lieutenant-Commanding Shirk, proceeded up the river. When within twelve hundred yards of Pittsburgh, they were opened upon by the rebel batteries, consisting of six or eight field pieces, some rifled. Getting within one thousand yards, the Taylor and Lexington opened a well-directed fire, and had the satisfaction of silencing the batteries.

They then proceeded abreast of the place, and, under the cover of grape and canister, landed two armed boats from each vessel, containing, besides their crews, a portion of company C, Captain Thaddeus Phillips, and company K, First-Lieutenant John C. Rider, of the Thirty-second regiment, Illinois Volunteers (sharpshooters). Second-master Jason Gondy, commanded the boats of the Taylor, and Second-master Martin Dunn, commanded the boats of the Lexington. The landing was successfully accomplished. This small force drove back the rebels, and held them in check until they had accomplished their difficult object, which was to discover the real strength and purpose of the enemy, and to destroy a house in close proximity to the batteries. In addition to their artillery, the enemy had a force of not less than two regiments of infantry, and a regiment of cavalry.

SECTION OF THE MISSISSIPPI RIVER.

SHOWING THE DISTANCES FROM NEW ORLEANS.

THE BURNSIDE EXPEDITION.*

SAILING OF THE FLEET FOR HATTERAS INLET.

January 12–20, 1862.

Immediately after the departure of the expedition to operate against Port Royal and the adjacent territory, the organization of another armament, to proceed to the North Carolina coast, was commenced, and like its predecessor, was mainly fitted out at Annapolis, Md., and gradually concentrated at Fortress Monroe. After many delays, it sailed from that place for its destination on the 12th of January, 1862. The expedition consisted of a large naval force of light-draught boats, taken from the commercial marine, fitted up and armed, and a numerous retinue of transports and supply vessels, all under the command of Commodore L. M. Goldsborough. There were thirty-one gunboats in the expedition, exclusive of transports, carrying an aggregate of ninety-four guns. Five of these, called "floating batteries," were vessels of strong hulls, heavily braced, and cut down so as to present but a small surface when in action, and designed to be anchored during an engagement. The entire number of vessels of all classes was one hundred and twenty-five.

The land force consisted of about fourteen thousand men, under the command of Brigadier-General Ambrose E. Burnside, who was also Commander-in-chief of the expedition. It consisted of fifteen regiments, divided into three brigades, commanded in their order by Generals John G. Foster, Jesse L. Reno, and John G. Parke.

The vessels encountered adverse weather immediately after starting from Fortress Monroe, and a number of the transports were obliged to put back, having experienced one of those severe storms which have rendered the coast of Cape Hatteras a terror and a proverb to the mariner. For a time the expedition was in deadly peril. Communication between the vessels of the fleet was rendered impossible, and wreck and disaster appeared to be their inevitable fate. Several gunboats and vessels were driven ashore and lost, and a number of valuable lives sacrificed to the fury of the elements, in a vain endeavor to succor some of the disabled vessels.

Along the whole coast of North Carolina there are many desolate sand-bars or islands, varying from half a mile to two miles in width, intersected by numerous inlets, which with few exceptions, are not navigable. A principal one of these, known as Hatteras Inlet, opening into the waters of Albemarle Sound, was the point where Commodore Goldsborough's fleet was now endeavoring to concentrate.

On Monday morning, January 13, they were off Hatteras Inlet. Day broke with a leaden sky, against which the angry, white-crested waves raced their mad career along the reefs of Cape Hatteras, that threw its headland oceanward but eight miles distant. Fourteen steamers were laboring to weather the storm point. Bravely they breasted on, staggering beneath the giant blows of each successive sea, the decks swept fore and aft, and all on board reeling from side to side like drunken men. One figure stood immovable, grasping the bits and scanning the horizon for traces of ships as they rose on the glittering mass of foam. It was the square, manly form of General Burnside, whose anxiety for the fate of his army was intense. Many of the vessels on which the troops were embarked were nothing more than huge top-hampered river steamers, with projecting guards, that would break up like cardboard if fairly struck by a sea.

At dark, all hands on the flag-ship were startled by the report of a gun, and on reaching the hurricane deck they saw a large brig drifting rapidly on to the bar. As it grew darker, and her outline became less defined, the excitement became intense. She was evidently in a most critical position, and every moment might be her last. Slowly the black hull rose and fell, each time gliding nearer and nearer to the vortex of white breakers, which, once reached, nothing could save her. Suddenly a fringe of musketry fire surrounded her bulwarks, and blue-lights were burnt in her tops. Volley after volley succeeded each other in rapid succession, yet apparently no one could help her; no human power dared face the tempest, and, perhaps, share her doom. General Burnside boarded every steamtug in the harbor; offered any reward, and also to go himself in aid of the brig, but all held back. Were three hundred men to be launched into eternity, and no effort made to save them? At last one brave seaman volunteered to take his little steamer out—General Burnside jumped aboard her—but by the earnest entreaties of the officers he delegated the honorable position to one of his staff, for his heroic conduct had nerved every brave heart in his command.

BURNSIDE'S FLEET AT HATTERAS INLET.

From the 13th of January until the 4th of February, the fleet at Hatteras Inlet experienced an almost uninterrupted series of gales, and the two dykes which reach the east and west boundaries of the inlet, were fringed with perpetual spray and foam from the breakers. The lighter vessels, comprising the propeller gunboats, the side-wheel steamers, and most of the schooner transports, had gone safely through the

"Swash," and were securely anchored some two miles from the throat of the inlet, while the larger ships and barks were still riding outside, with colors continually flying for a pilot.

Many of these vessels were crowded with men suffering for the want of necessary supplies, especially water, and the largest of the transports had a draught of from two to four feet more than the specifications of the guarantee should have allowed. The consequence was, that they grounded in attempting the passage. An occasional cessation of a few hours in the storm afforded opportunity that could be taken advantage of by vessels to try the dangerous passage, aided by the tugs, that responded but shyly to the signals for aid. And thus for days the severity of the gale defied all communication between the vessels outside of the bar, as they battled with a fiercer foe than that upon the land—fighting a very hand-to-hand fight with storm and ocean.

Nearly three weeks passed before all the vessels of the expedition were brought in safety through the swash to anchorage within the inlet. Though the severity of the storm had threatened the destruction of the entire armada, and occasioned the deepest gloom and anxiety in the minds of thousands of loyal friends at home, the brave and skillful commanders were never despondent, and met the new dangers of each day with hopeful energy and perseverance. Eight vessels of various sizes were cast away or foundered in the storm, though but few lives were lost.

Colonel J. W. Allen and Surgeon T. S. Weller, of the Ninth New Jersey, were drowned from a small boat while on a noble mission to relieve a suffering crew.

Many of the large transports were grounded in attempting to pass inside the inlet. From the necessity of lightening them, vast quantities of property were lost or thrown overboard. An expedition beset with such difficulties, all overcome by indomitable perseverance, has seldom been recorded in the history of any country.

CAPTURE OF ROANOKE ISLAND.

February 8, 1862.

After a detention of three weeks in sight of Hatteras Inlet, occasioned by the severity of the storm, and the difficulty of piloting the heavily-laden vessels through the inlet, the expedition received sailing orders on the 4th of February, and proceeded on the next day to the point of attack. The fleet anchored on the night of February 5, about ten miles below the southern point of Roanoke Island, from whence they again weighed anchor at eight o'clock on the morning of the 6th. A storm retarded their progress, and they remained over night without passing through Roanoke Inlet to Croatan Sound.

At ten o'clock on the morning of the 7th, the gunboats, under the lead of the Flag-officer's ship, moved forward, and were soon inside the narrow passage leading into Croatan Sound, known as Roanoke Inlet. The mainland juts eastward, forming a point of marshy land at the southern extremity of Croatan Sound, which is the only navigable water leading past Roanoke Island. A small island forms the eastern boundary of the channel, while the western shore is a low marshy point. Following Commodore Goldsborough's squadron were the gunboats of the coast division, all of which passed through without interruption.

The S. R. Spaulding, with General Burnside on board, next passed through, but the remainder of the transports were detained about two hours. The rebel gunboats could now be seen close in shore, evidently under the guns of batteries on shore. As the fleet passed into the sound, a signal was fired from one of the rebel gunboats, to announce its approach. This was about half-past ten o'clock. At half-past eleven the first gun was fired from the flag-ship, and was replied to by the rebels. The Flag-officer hoisted the signal: "This day our country expects that every man will do his duty." The effect was electric. The men worked their guns with unflagging energy, determined that their country should have nothing to complain of in relation to them. As the Federal vessels came within shorter range, the fire became more rapid, but the regular fire did not commence until noon, when the flag-ship displayed the signal for close action.

The number of the rebel gunboats visible in the early part of the engagement was seven. As the vessels came into closer action, they moved to the northward, with the design of drawing the Union fleet after them, and bring them under the guns of their batteries on the island. At twelve o'clock the engagement became general, between the retreating gunboats of the rebels and the Union fleet, varied by an occasional shot from a battery on shore. The firing was exceedingly brisk for some time, but the distance was evidently too great for destructive effect. The one hundred-pound Parrott gun on board the Southfield, to which the Flag-Officer transferred his flag, boomed forth terrific explosions, followed by the roar and crash of flying shells. The puff of smoke in the air was almost simultaneous with the splash of fragments in the water. The rebel gunboats kept up a steady fire in reply. Their fire was varied at times by the louder report of a hundred-pound Parrott gun on board one of their vessels. The Sawyer gun on board the Fanny, which was captured by the enemy at Hatteras Inlet, was the most annoying in its effects, as the range was long and very accurate.

The fire from the fort indicated a weak force working the guns. The rebel gunboats retired steadily a considerable distance up the sound. A line of piles driven into the bed across the principal channel, obstructed the progress of the Union vessels in the pursuit of the retreating rebels, who occupied an inner channel under the guns of their battery. The Union fleet now turned their attention to the fort, which kept up a steady and rapid fire.

On the afternoon of the 7th, the transports, with the land forces, were all brought safely through Roanoke Inlet, and clustered securely in rear of the bombarding fleet. General Burnside gave immediate orders for landing the forces, which was done at a small cove, known as Ashby's Harbor. In less than an hour four thousand men were landed, and by eleven at night, the entire force, excepting one regiment, were on the island, and their bivouac-fires lighted up the shore and the woods for the distance of a mile.

At nine o'clock on the morning of the 8th, a few shots were exchanged between the Federal gunboats and the battery, which ceased after fifteen minutes' duration, and was not renewed during the day. The rebel gunboats had retreated, and all interest now centered in the movements of the land forces.

From definite information received by General Burnside, the position of all the works on the island was clearly known, and his movements were based on this knowledge. The plan of attack consisted of a central attacking column, led by Brigadier-General Foster; a left flanking column to attack the right of the enemy's work, under Brigadier-General Reno, and a right flank column to attack the left of the enemy's position, under the command of Brigadier-General Parke.

The approach to the enemy's position was through a swampy wood, with a dense undergrowth, rendering it almost impenetrable. An ordinary cart-road leading through this wood from the shore to the field-work, a distance of about a mile, was the only mode of communication. The woods in front of the battery had been cut down a distance of three hundred yards, forming an open space to be played on by the rebel guns, about two hundred feet wide. The woods immediately in rear of the work were also cut down to permit the manœuvreing of their own forces.

Their battery consisted of an earth-work with three faces covering the open space before, and the woods at each side of the open space, but with a general direction of fire to the front. The guns were mounted in embrasure, and consisted of a twenty-four-pounder brass Dahlgren howitzer, a long eighteen-pounder brass field-gun, and a twelve-pounder brass field-piece. In front of the work was a ditch eight feet wide and about three feet deep, filled with water. The earth-work was about thirty-five yards wide, and was erected across the road. The ground in front of the work was a deep marsh, on which the trees which were felled still lay. The difficult nature of this ground was increased by the pits from which the turf and earth for the field-work had been taken. Branches were strewn over the front of the work, making it impossible to discover it from the wood in front.

The defending force consisted of about three hundred men, within the breastwork, and about two thousand as a reserve, partly deployed as skirmishers on the left of the battery. The rebels relied chiefly for the defence of their flanks on the almost impenetrable nature of the wood on each side. Their entire force, with the exception of the force working the battery, was scattered in front and in the woods on the left as skirmishers.

The Federal army advanced from the bivouac-ground of the evening previous, where they had spent the night with nothing but thin overcoats to protect them from a cold, driving rain. They had left their knapsacks and blankets on the transports, each man carrying nothing but his haversack, with three days' provisions, and his cartridge-box, with forty rounds of ball-cartridge. The centre, under the command of General Foster, was composed of the Twenty-fifth Massachusetts, Colonel Upton; Twenty-third Massachusetts, Colonel Kurtz; Twenty-seventh Massachusetts, Colonel Lee, and the Tenth Connecticut, Colonel Russell, and moved forward about eight o'clock. They were followed by the second column, under General Reno, consisting of the Twenty-first Massachusetts, Lieutenant-Colonel Maggi; the Fifty-first New York, (Shepard Rifles,) Colonel Ferrero; Ninth New Jersey, and the Fifty first Pennsylvania, Colonel Hartraaf. The third column, led by General Parke, was formed of the Fourth Rhode Island, Colonel Rodman; First battalion, Fifth Rhode Island, Major Wright; and Ninth New York, Colonel Hawkins.

A brilliant, well-contested fight of two hours' duration put the Federal forces in possession of Roanoke Island, with all the batteries, mounting thirty guns, and Fort Forrest, on the mainland, mounting eight guns. It resulted in the unconditional surrender of the rebel army on the island, numbering 2,500 men, with all their arms and munitions of war. Captain O. Jennings Wise, son of ex-Governor Wise of Virginia, lost his life in this engagement. The Governor himself, being absent from his command on the day of battle, escaped.

Colonel Russell, of the Tenth Connecticut, and Lieutenant-Colonel De Monteuil, of the New York Fifty-third, were killed.

The Federal loss was fifty killed and one hundred and fifty wounded. That of the rebels was about twenty killed, and sixty wounded.

EVACUATION OF BOWLING GREEN, KY.
February 14–16, 1862.

Before the commencement of hostilities in the State of Kentucky, the rebel General Buckner, Commander-in-Chief of the State militia, seized upon the town of Bowling Green, in Warren county, in the southern section of the State, and occupied it as the grand centre and depot of future military operations. The position was well chosen. It was situated on the line of the Louisville and Nashville railway, and connected also by rail with Memphis and Nashville; while water communication through the Barren river was open to the Green river, the Ohio, and Mississippi, and thus to all important points.

As a military post, its means of defence were also of the first importance. The town lies on the south bank of Barren river, at a point where the channel makes a bend not unlike a horse-shoe. The buildings are situated a distance of five hundred yards from the banks, which rise by jutted rocky sides fifty feet from the water level. A series of nine swelling hills, or knolls, completely encompass the town on the land side, and on these Buckner had erected a cordon of forts; some of stone, and others of earth, twenty feet in thickness—all of great magnitude. Forty-nine guns were mounted on the various fortifications, and great engineering skill had been displayed in their construction.

On learning the defeat of Zollicoffer's troops at Mill Spring, on the 19th of January, General A. S. Johnson, on the 25th, ordered the evacuation of Bowling Green, and General Floyd's brigade immediately marched from thence to Fort Donelson. Active measures were then taken to carry out the order further, by shipping heavy ordnance to Columbus, which place General Grant's reconnoissance at that time had induced the Confederates to believe would be the first point of attack from the Federal army.

After the capture of Fort Henry, on the 6th of February, by which the enemy's communication with Columbus was intercepted, the remaining troops were distributed, some to Fort Donelson, some to Nashville and other points; and a work of indiscriminate destruction of the buildings and property in the town commenced. The beautiful iron railway bridge, and the wooden turnpike bridge over the Barren river were first destroyed. The railway bridge over the Green river, some forty miles to the northeast, had long since been burned, and the forces of General Buell had been deterred from crossing that stream up to the present time.

On the 11th of February, however, General Mitchell's division, encamped on Bacon creek, seven miles north of the Green river, were ordered to advance on Bowling Green, and on that day marched to Camp Madison, one mile north of the river; where receiving confirmatory information of the retreat of the rebel forces, they hastened forward.

Thursday morning, February 13th, the division—infantry, cavalry, and artillery, left Camp Madison for Bowling Green, forty-two miles distant, and made twenty miles the first day. The railroad appeared to be but little injured, but all the buildings were destroyed. The roads the first day were in splendid order, but much obstructed by trees, which were, however, speedily removed by two companies of mechanics and engineers, who swung their axes with energy, and were never delayed over fifteen minutes by any impediment. The ponds along the road were filled with dead horses and cattle, so long as any cattle were to be found to fill them. The troops rested at noon at Cave City, which was very nearly destroyed. On the second day they started again for Bowling Green. The next morning was cold, with about an inch and a half of snow, but they were up betimes and on their way, the Nineteenth Illinois ahead as usual, with her blue flag waving triumphantly. The road was obstructed, and filled with signs of the rapid retreat of Hindman's forces.

Hearing repeatedly that the railroad bridge over Barren river was destroyed, and that the Confederates would not stand this side of the river, Colonel Turchin ordered the cavalry and one battery ahead. The ranks opened to the right and left, and Captain Loomis' battery dashed by in fine style toward Bowling Green. The men hearing the cannon roar, hurried on, and reached the banks of the river opposite Bowling Green, about two o'clock, making the forty-two miles in about thirty-seven hours. After the firing commenced they seized every team along the road, and had the knapsacks drawn by horses the rest of the way, much to the relief of tired shoulders. General Turchin fired the first shell into the town, and immediately three regiments were seen scampering to the cars, and putting off in great confusion.

But though within a mile of Bowling Green, they were powerless to interfere, for there was Barren river, wide and unfordable, between them, and both bridges destroyed. The Texan Rangers soon began to fire all the public buildings. Fifty men under Captain Scott, got ready to cross in a little skiff by parties, and try to drive out the few who remained to perform this work, but the General would not allow it. They then pitched their tents and prepared to wait until a bridge could be erected. When snugly tucked in their blankets, the assembly beat to arms, and the brigade was soon in ranks. They expected to march to town, but were put on the back track some three miles.

They left the main road, and soon came to the river, where they built fires and rested as well as possible. Here the repairs of an old wherry were completed, and they crossed the river, protected by artillery. There was a slight snow falling, and it was uncomfortably cold. The Nineteenth and Twenty-fourth, Hecker's Illinois, crossed first. The men suffered intensely from cold, but declared that they had rather be shot than frozen, and pushed on. But no enemy appeared, and the tired soldiers soon surrounded the fires, some of which had been burning for several days. All the public buildings and several warehouses, filled with pork, beef, coffee, etc., were destroyed. A pile of grain thirty feet by twenty, was burning when the Federal troops arrived. Four engines and several cars were also burnt. The cars had been carrying away provision for a week, but still immense quantities were destroyed. Boxes of guns, large numbers of bowie-knives roughly fashioned of iron, every conceivable kind of shooting apparatus, and all sorts of hardware for cooking and other uses were found in immense quantities.

Bowling Green is a town of considerable commercial importance, and possesses many large stores and warehouses. The majority of the inhabitants were loyal in their sentiments, though many influential citizens sympathized with the rebellion; but when the work of destruction commenced, no discrimination was allowed, and all were made sufferers. The unexpected arrival of General Mitchell's army, and the terror of his artillery, drove the rebels from the town before their incendiary intentions were fully consummated, and much private property was saved which would else have been consumed by the flames.

When General Buckner was exercising military sovereignty in southern Kentucky, one of his proclamations demanded that every man in Wright county should deliver to him at his headquarters, one gun, or twenty dollars in money, under the penalty of fifty dollars' fine, or ninety days' imprisonment. In response to this edict, a motley collection of old squirrel and shot guns were added to the Confederate stores, and with other treasures were packed in buildings at Bowling Green. A hasty evacuation of that stronghold having become a "military necessity," these buildings were fired by the retreating rebels, and among the ruins which met the curious gaze of General Mitchell's men when they entered the town, were scattered piles of the iron parts of these guns, in several places a foot thick.

CAPTURE OF FORT DONELSON.
February 13–16, 1862.

Bravely as the army of the West had sustained the honor of the Union, the crowning glory of taking Fort Donelson remained to be accomplished. To attack a strongly-defended fort, formidable by nature

ATTACK ON FORT DONELSON BY THE FEDERAL GUNBOATS.

THE SURRENDER OF FORT DONELSON.

and rendered almost impregnable by military art, was a work of extreme danger, nay, of impossibility to less resolute men.

The relative positions of Fort Henry and Donelson, the former on the Tennessee river and the latter on the Cumberland, should be clearly understood, in order to comprehend the difficulties of this undertaking.

Fort Henry had been occupied by Federal troops, and it became necessary to effect the reduction of Fort Donelson, in order to open the river to the navigation of the national flotilla, and to reach Nashville, the capital of Tennessee.

The surrender of Fort Henry took place on the 6th of February. One of the gunboats, the Essex, being disabled, was obliged to return to Cairo for repairs, while the Lexington, Conestoga and Tyler, returned to the Ohio, in order to reach the Cumberland river to make the ascent to Fort Donelson. Commodore Foote having completed his preparations, left Cairo on the 11th of February for the scene of action—the Carondelet having previously been sent forward to reconnoitre the position.

On the same day General Grant issued his orders for the movement of the land forces in two divisions, on the following morning. The distance from Fort Henry to Fort Donelson across the land lying between the two rivers, is fourteen miles. There are several roads running from Fort Henry to Dover, near which Fort Donelson was situated. The divisions were disposed by brigades, one of which was to be thrown into Dover to cut off the retreat of the enemy, if attempted by that route.

Fort Donelson takes its name from Andrew Jackson Donelson, a citizen of Tennessee, and its construction was commenced as early as May, 1861. It occupied the best position for defence on the Cumberland river, standing on the summit of a fine slope, rising to the height of one hundred and fifty feet from the river, on its right bank, and mounted sixteen guns. There were two water-batteries, one of which was about twenty or thirty feet above the river, and defended by nine pieces, eight thirty-two-pound guns, and one ten-inch columbiad. The second was some sixty feet above, and was mounted with one ten-inch columbiad, and two thirty-two pound carronades.

Both these batteries were sunken or excavated in the hill-side. In the lower one, strong traverses were left between the guns, to secure them against an enfilading fire. The elevation above the water at the time of the gunboat attack, gave them a fine command of the river, and made the task of attacking them in front an arduous one. The range of the guns in arc, was, however, quite limited.

The third occupied the summit of the hill, and mounted four 128-pound guns. The camp was behind the fort on the hill, but within range of gunboats on the river.

THE NAVAL ATTACK.

On the night of February 11th, the St. Louis, (the flag-ship,) Louisville, and Pittsburg, sailed from Cairo. The Carondelet, as already stated, had been dispatched a day or two in advance, and at Paducah, on the noon of the 12th, the fleet was joined by the Conestoga and Tyler. Of these the three first were iron-clad vessels. From Paducah the fleet was accompanied by sixteen transports, carrying six thousand infantry, and cavalry and artillery.

The fleet followed the flag-ship of Commodore Foote, as they turned out of the Ohio, and began the ascent of the Cumberland. Passing onward from the Ohio, sweeping through Kentucky and Tennessee up to the western boundaries of Virginia, the fleet carried the national ensign, which was met with continual cheers and responses from the people on the banks.

About four o'clock in the afternoon, a messenger steamer, the Alps, met the fleet, with a dispatch from General Grant, requesting all haste to be made, as the gunboats were anxiously expected. Putting on steam, the Alps took the St. Louis and Louisville in tow, leaving the transports to hasten as rapidly as they could be urged. The former arrived within two miles of the fort at twelve o'clock, on the night of Thursday, the 13th.

On the morning of that day, the Carondelet, by order of General Grant, had bombarded the fort, and single-handed, commenced the attack on the works. On the previous day she had advanced and fired eight shots, but without drawing out any reply. The attack of the 13th was differently met by the fort, as the shells were briskly responded to, and a vigorous fire was maintained for two hours. The Carondelet kept her bows hard on the fort, carefully guarding against presenting her broadside to the enemy. She fired one hundred and twenty-eight shots in ninety-five minutes. At the end of that time, a ball from one of the 128-pound guns entered her port-bow, and struck a portion of her machinery. Six men were slightly wounded by the splinters which flew from the ship's timbers. She retired beyond the range of the guns, to ascertain the amount of damage, and in the afternoon, after repairing, was again ordered to the charge, and fired a number of shots, but without sensible effect.

The morning of the 14th found the flotilla lying in the wake of the flag-ship. The transports had arrived, and the troops, with the artillery, were landed about two miles from the fort. The arrival of the fleet, and the thousands of determined soldiers, inspired the troops already at the scene of action with new vigor; long and tumultuous cheers came down the hills from the army under General Grant, which could be seen in the distance, watching the movements of the fleet. General Grant and his staff had gone on board the St. Louis, before daylight, and an attack by the land forces was agreed upon, to be made as soon as the signal gun should be given from the river. Accordingly, at two o'clock, P. M., all the vessels comprising the flotilla, the iron-clad boats St. Louis, Carondelet, Pittsburg, and Louisville, and the two wooden boats, Conestoga and Tyler, got under way. They were then about two miles from the fort. The line of battle was immediately formed, the flag-ship taking the extreme right, with the Louisville, Pittsburg, and Carondelet at the left, four abreast; the Conestoga and Tyler, not being iron clad, remained in the rear, about a quarter of a mile. The fleet proceeded at a speed of about three miles an hour, up the river. At twenty-five minutes to three o'clock they reached the termination of a long range of woods to the right, and came in full view of the fort.

The fortifications were distinctly visible, consisting of three tiers of frowning batteries, on the slope of a steep hill, one hundred and fifty feet in height. About half-past two o'clock, the enemy opened fire from a battery about twenty feet above water level, by discharging a 32-pounder, but the shot fell far short. This was followed by another ball of larger dimensions, which also fell short. The Union men were anxious to show the enemy a specimen of their fighting power, but the Commodore would not permit them to fire a gun for fifteen minutes, until they got within certain range of the fort. At a few minutes before three o'clock, the St. Louis opened the battle on the national side, and the other boats quickly followed. For a while all the shot fell short of the mark.

The boats kept advancing slowly and steadily for about half an hour, when the order was given to slack the engines, so as to prevent them from coming in too close range. The firing then increased to a terrific rate on both sides. The enemy poured 32 and 64-pound balls into the vessels with great effect, and the gunners returned their 8-inch shell and 64-pound rifle balls with unusual skill. In the heat of the action, a shot from the enemy's water battery carried away the flagstaff of the St. Louis; almost the next shot took the chimney guys of the same boat. A well sent ball from the St. Louis soon struck the flagstaff of the enemy, which was on the top of the hill behind the batteries. This terrible fire lasted about half an hour, when a 64-pound ball from the middle battery cut the tiller ropes of the gunboat Louisville, rendering her steering apparatus unmanageable. About the same time a shot entered one of the windows of the pilot-house of the Carondelet, mortally wounding the pilot. Thus the control of two Union boats was in a great degree lost. Shortly after this, a 32-pound ball penetrated the pilot-house of the St. Louis, mortally wounding one of the pilots, injuring two other pilots, and severely wounding Flag-officer Foote. There were five men in the pilot-house at the time, only one of whom escaped injury. The room was filled with pieces of the broken wheel, chains, room furniture and rubbish of every sort; there was no one there to take the helm save the Commodore—no chance to call another to his aid—so, equal to the emergency, the gallant old Commodore seized the remaining handles of the wheel, and for a quarter of an hour acted the double part of commander and pilot, and at last, when compelled to fall back, he kept bow to the foe, and gave his orders as calmly and coolly as when first entering the action.

At about the middle of the engagement, a 32-pound rifle shot took away the flagstaff and Commodore's pennant. In a moment half a dozen men sprang out of the ports, caught the mutilated staff upon their shoulders, hoisted the "blue flag" to its place, where they stood and held it for several minutes, in the face of a most murderous fire.

Thus three powerful vessels were disabled by accidents that do not happen twice in a hundred times. The men on board were unwilling to give up the fight. The enemy had been driven from the lower battery, and their fire had slackened perceptibly. What remained to be done? To fight in such a current, with unmanageable boats, would, the Commodore knew, be worse than folly. Reluctantly, therefore, he ordered them to fall back.

The vessels then stopped their engines and floated slowly from their positions. They had been within two hundred yards of the fort. The enemy soon saw the condition of the fleet, and redoubled their fire. They ran to the lower batteries and opened them on the retiring vessels with terrific force. One of the guns of the Carondelet had burst in the middle of the action, and the Pittsburg had received two balls below water-mark, causing her to leak rapidly. But they replied well to the reinvigorated foe, and fired the last shot.

The fleet retired in good order, and anchored two miles below the fort. The injuries to the gunboats were not very great. The principal damage to the St. Louis was that sustained by the shot entering her pilot-house. She was struck 61 times; the Pittsburg 47; the Carondelet 54; and the Louisville about 40. The enemy fired about 500 shots.

The fleet fired a little more than 300, about 75 of which were 8-inch shells.

The demeanor of Commodore Foote during the engagement was the subject of admiration with every man in the fleet. His countenance was as placid and his voice as mild in the heat of the action as if he had been engaged in social conversation. He stood in the pilot-house for a long time, watching the effect of every shot. When he saw a shell burst inside of the fort, he instantly commended the deliberate aim of

the marksman, by a message through his speaking tube. When the balls fell short, he expressed his dissatisfaction in such words as "A little further, man; you are falling too short." During a part of the action he was on the gun-deck, superintending the care of the wounded. In the end, nothing but the pilot's assurance that his vessel could not be managed with her broken wheel, induced him to consent to a withdrawal.

Incidents on board the Louisville were not wanting. Captain Dove had just complimented one of the gunners on a splendid shot, when the shot that played such havoc entered his port, and completely severed the gunner in twain, scattering his blood and brains over Captain Dove's person. But the Captain never blanched; he only wiped his face, and in an instant was superintending the replacement of another gun as if nothing had happened. Cool, brave and determined, he was throughout the action a support to his men and an honor to his country.

THE LAND ATTACK.

In addition to the two water batteries already described, a third had been commenced, but was not at the time completed. The fort stood on a hill, and within its ample lines nearly a hundred large and substantial log-houses had been erected for quarters. In order to prevent any lodgment of an opposing force on the hills back of the fort, it was necessary to construct a line of defenses around the fort, at the distance of a mile, and in some places more than a mile, from the principal work. These outworks extended from a creek on the north side of the works to another which entered a quarter of a mile below. Both of these streams were filled with backwater from the swollen river, for the distance of three-quarters of a mile from their mouths. This chain of breastworks and the miry bed of the creeks formed a most complete impediment to the marching of an artillery force within sight of the main fort. This line of works was not less than three miles in length, breast high, and formed from a ditch on either side, so as to answer the purpose of rifle pits and parapets. At intervals on every elevation platforms had been constructed and mounted with howitzers and light field pieces. Such were the works, defended by from 20,000 to 25,000 men, that the national troops were determined to take by assault.

Early on the morning of the 12th of February, the national troops left Fort Henry with two days' rations in their haversacks, without tents or wagons, except such as were necessary to convey a surplus of commissary stores and ammunition, and ambulances for the sick.

The expedition under the command of Brigadier-General U. S. Grant, was divided into three columns—the division under Brigadier-General McClernand, taking the road from Fort Henry to Dover, running to the

CAPTURE OF FORT DONELSON.

south of the enemy's position; the second division, under command of Brigadier-General C. F. Smith, taking the direct or telegraph road to the fort; the third division, subsequently placed under the lead of Brigadier-General L. Wallace, being sent round by Paducah and Smithland, ascending the Cumberland, under the escort of the gunboats. Each of these divisions consisted of about ten regiments of infantry, batteries, and cavalry.

First Division, Brigadier-General McClernand.—1st *Brigade*, Col. Oglesby, acting.—8th Illinois, Lieut. Col. Rhodes; 18th Illinois, Col. Lawler; 29th Illinois, Col. Reardon; 13th Illinois, Col. Dennis; 31st Illinois, Col. J. A. Logan; Schwartz's battery; Dresser's battery; 4 battalions Illinois cavalry. 2d *Brigade*, Col. W. H. L. Wallace, acting.—11th Illinois, Lieut. Col. Hart; 20th Illinois, Col. Marsh; 48th Illinois, Col. Smith; 49th Illinois, Col. Hainey; Taylor's battery; McAllister's battery; 4th and 7th Illinois cavalry, Cols. Kellogg and Dickey.

Second Division, Brigadier-General C. F. Smith.—1st *Brigade*, Col. Cook, acting.—7th Illinois, 50th Illinois, 12th Iowa; 13th Missouri, Col. Wright; 52d Indiana; 3 batteries Missouri 1st artillery, Maj. Cavender commanding; Capts. Richardson, Stone, and Walker. 2d *Brigade*, Col. Lauman, acting.—7th Iowa, Lieut.-Col. Parrott; 2d Iowa, Col. Tuttle; 14th Iowa, Col. Shaw; 25th Indiana, Col. Veatch; 56th Indiana.

Third Division, Brigadier-General Lewis Wallace.—1st *Brigade*, Col. Croft, acting.—17th Kentucky, 25th Kentucky, 31st Indiana, 44th Indiana, Col. Hugh B. Reed. 2d *Brigade*, Col. Thayer, acting.—1st Nebraska, Lieut. Col. McCord; 13th Missouri, Col. Wright; 48th Ohio, Col. Sullivan; 58th Ohio, Col. Bousenwein; Willett's Chicago battery.

By nine o'clock all the forces were on the march. The division of General McClernand took the upper or southern road to Dover. The division of General Smith proceeded by the northern or telegraph road, running directly to the fort. The route lay through broken and undulating lands. Small streams of the purest water were crossed at every ravine. The hills were in places covered with green pines and tall, heavy timber. The weather was mild and spring-like; the men in admirable spirits, marching in regular order, and the surrounding scenery almost tropical in its luxuriance. At about two o'clock in the afternoon the advanced skirmishers of McClernand's division came in sight of the enemy's tents stretching between the hill upon which the fort was situated, and the next, on Dover ledge.

Word was passed back to General Grant that the enemy and his camp had been sighted. General Grant at once ordered up the rear of the column. Dresser's battery was posted on an eminence overlooking the tents, and a few shells sent into the camp. There was a general and promiscuous scattering of men from the camps into the earthworks to right and left. General Grant immediately ordered the division of General Smith into line of battle on the ravine back of the main elevation. A column of men was pushed up on the left of the fort. Scouts returned saying that the breastworks could be discovered on the extreme left. An hour or two was then spent in reconnoitering along the various hills surrounding the enemy's position.

This preliminary skirmish was soon over, and the enemy had fallen back within his intrenchments, when the shades of night fell upon the two armies. Many of the Federal soldiers, in anticipation of an engagement had relieved themselves of their overcoats, blankets, and haversacks, and were altogether unprepared for the experience of the night. But cheerfully kindling their camp-fires, under a mild and genial temperature, they gathered around the cheerful blaze and gradually fell into slumberous dreams of home, of conquest, or of love.

During the night the enemy made a sortie on the extreme right of the Federal lines, which by its suddenness created some confusion for the time, but he was repulsed and compelled to retire.

On Thursday, the 13th, the attack commenced. The morning sun rose brightly on the scene. The men were soon engaged in cooking what provisions could be obtained. Several hogs running at large in the woods had been shot for breakfast, and a sumptuous meal was made from their flesh. At sunrise the firing of riflemen commenced. The enemy could be descried behind his breastworks. The most available positions were selected for batteries, and by eight o'clock a regular exchange of shot and shell had commenced across the ravine which separated the combatants. Taylor's battery was on the extreme right, next came Schwartz's, further to the left. Further still was a section of an Illinois battery. Across a deep ravine and in the centre of the position was Captain Richardson's First Missouri Light Artillery, on the point of a ridge provokingly near the enemy's lines. Higher upon the same rise was McAlister's battery of twenty-four pound howitzers, and on the left could be heard at intervals an Iowa battery.

The long established form of opening the fight by a contest of sharpshooters and artillery was observed. For two hours nothing was to be heard but the loud thuds of cannon, with the relief of a sharp crack of rifles, and an occasional report of a musket, which in the distance could hardly be distinguished from a field piece. Major Cavender, of the Missouri First, sighted his twenty pound Parrott rifle guns. Two or three shots had been sent whizzing through the trees, when "clash" came a shot in front of the piece. Without moving a muscle the major completed his task, and bang! went a response. Bang went another from the sister-piece under the intrepid captain. A second was received from the fort, passing over the hill, exploding just in the rear, a third burst directly over head, and the combat was kept up with spirit. Dresser's battery poured out shell from his large howitzers in splendid style. The enemy held a slight advantage in position, and had the range with accuracy. The shells were falling fast around the batteries, doing however but little injury. A few minutes and a round shot passed over the gun, and carried away the shoulder and part of the breast of artilleryman Bernhard of Richardson's battery, killing him almost instantly. The captain shifted his position three times during the morning, whenever the enemy got his range with too much accuracy.

On the extreme right Schwartz and Taylor were blazing away fearlessly. The ground between them and the intrenchments was nearly cleared of trees, and they could observe by the smoke the position of each other with accuracy. The firing from the batteries in McClernand's division was continuous. An attempt had been made by the enemy to capture Taylor's battery, which had been gallantly repulsed. The rebels had reached close upon the battery, and only an incessant shower of canister saved it from capture, the infantry not being formed in position to support it effectually. The Twentieth Illinois came up in time to drive the enemy into their works.

In the afternoon General McClernand determined to make a formidable assault of a redoubt of the enemy, fronting the centre of his right. The redoubt was the only one which could be distinctly seen, owing to timber and undergrowth. At this point the ground was for the most part void of large timber, the barren extending even beyond the road on the ridge which the Union troops passed. The batteries of this redoubt had a very perfect range, and gave the troops considerable uneasiness, by blazing away at them whenever they passed over the brow of the hill. Three regiments were detailed for the work—the Forty-eighth, Seventeeth and Forty-ninth Illinois. They advanced in line of battle order, the Forty-ninth, Colonel Morrison, on the right, the Seventeenth, under command of Major Smith, in the centre, and the Forty-eighth, Colonel Hainley, on the left. Colonel Morrison, as senior Colonel, led the attack. The advance was a most beautiful one. With skirmishers arrayed in front, the three regiments swept down the hill, over a knoll, down a ravine, and up the high hill on which the redoubt was situated, some two hundred and fifty or three hundred feet in height, covered with brush and stumps, all the time receiving a galling fire of grape, shell and musketry, with a precision which would have done them credit on the parade ground. The breastworks were nearly reached, when Colonel Morrison, while gallantly leading his men, was struck by a musket ball. The captain of the company on his right was also killed, while the Forty-ninth fell into some confusion; but unappalled the

Seventeenth still gallantly pressed forward and penetrated even to the very foot of the works. But it was not in the power of man to scale the abattis before them. Brush piled upon brush, with sharp points, fronted them wherever they turned; so, after a few interchanges of musketry with the swarming regiments concentrated there, the word for retiring was given. It was done in good order, by filing off to the left and obliqueing into the woods below; but many a gallant soldier was left behind underneath the intrenchments he had vainly sought to mount. They were not, however, destined to die unavenged. Scarcely had their retiring columns got out of range, ere Taylor's Chicago battery opened on the swarming rebel masses with shell and shrapnell. The effect was fearful. Each gun was aimed by the captain himself, and when its black mouth belched out sudden thunder, winrows of dead men fell in its track.

While this heavy firing had been heard on the right, General Smith, had ordered the enemy to be engaged on the left. The Twenty-fifth Indiana, at the head of a brigade, led the way. They had reached a position on the brow of a hill where the successful assault was afterwards made, and were met by the enemy in force, who swarmed behind the works, pouring a deadly hail of bullets and grape into them. The leading regiment broke in disorder after sustaining a hot fire, and the whole line fell back out of range. The object of the sortie had been accomplished, and the enemy's forces drawn from the other side, but the advantage did not result, as might have been anticipated, in the occupation of the fort on the right by General McClernand.

Six companies of the famous regiment of riflemen, raised by Colonel Berge, accompanied the expedition from Fort Henry, and two companies afterwards arrived by the transports. This was a corps of picked men skilled in the use of the rifle, drawn from the Northwest.

These hardy pioneers started out in the morning, with a hard biscuit in their pocket and a rifle on their shoulder, for the rebel earthworks, where they remained until relieved by a fresh gang. So adventurous were they, that many of them crept within fifty yards of the rifle-pits and exchanged words as well as shots with the enemy.

One piece in front of Dresser's battery was kept in silence during the morning by the sharpshooters picking off their gunners. At last a shell from a Union battery, falling short, drove them away. One valiant southerner, to prove his bravery, jumped into the rampart to take aim; in an instant he was pierced by three balls, and fell out of the intrenchment, where he lay till nightfall.

The firing for the rest of the day was slow, and appeared by general consent to be abandoned. The Unionists seemed to have failed in every attempt on the fort. Wounded men were being brought in on stretchers; some limped along, supported by comrades, others staggered forward with bleeding hands and battered heads tied in handkerchiefs. The ambulances had brought in the maimed and seriously wounded. In the gray dusk of evening men came forth with spades to dig the graves of their fellow-soldiers, whose remains, stiffened in death, were lying under the pale stars.

Hardly had the camp-fires been kindled for the night when a drizzling shower set in, which soon turned into a steady fall of rain. The wind grew suddenly colder. The weather, hitherto so pleasant, was chilled in an hour to a wintry blast. Snow began to fall, and the mercury sank below freezing point.

Many of the soldiers had lost their overcoats and blankets during the day. Not a tent, except hospital tents, in the command. Provisions growing very scarce—the muddy, wet clothing freezing upon the chilled limbs of the hungry soldiers. It was a most comfortless night. Not five houses could be found within as many miles, and these were used as hospitals. Various expedients were devised to ward off the cold. Saplings were bent down and twigs interwoven into a shelter; leaves piled up made a kind of roof to keep off the snow. Large fires were kindled, and the men lay with their feet to the fire. The victims who perished of cold, exposure, hunger and neglect, on this night, will fill up a long page in the mortality record of that eventful siege.

On Friday, the conflict was maintained only by the pickets and sharpshooters, General Grant having concluded to await the arrival of additional forces, before assaulting the works.

Hitherto the investment had been made by the divisions of Generals McClernand and Smith, about ten thousand men each, including the cavalry and artillery. A third division had been sent up the Cumberland, and should, by reasonable calculation, have been opposite Fort Henry on Wednesday night. Here was Friday morning and no transports arrived. What could have befallen them? General L. Wallace, who had been left in command at Fort Henry, was summoned over, and arrived on Friday evening with two regiments of his brigade. Couriers were seen dashing along from the headquarters to the point where the boats were expected to land. About ten o'clock came the joyful intelligence that the gunboat fleet, with fifteen transports, had landed five miles below the fort. The troops from Fort Henry were pouring in, and close upon them came the troops from the boats. The men had heard something of the fighting, and moved up in splendid order, expecting to be marched directly into battle.

At about half past two o'clock the sound as of thunder, with long reverberations, in the distance, told that the river guns had at last opened their mouths, and were paying their compliments grandly to the rebel batteries. Now and then could be seen in the distance, high up in the air, a sudden puff of white smoke, which sprang as if from nothing, slowly curling in graceful folds, and melting away in a snow-white cloud; it was a bursting shell, instantly followed by the rumble of the gun from which it had been sent. The loud roar of the cannon kept growing thicker and faster. The heavy columbiads and Dahlgrens in the fort were returning the fire. One, two, three, and then half a dozen at once! The terrible game of death becomes wildly exciting!

The gunboats were advancing—the bombardment had fairly begun. The cheers went up in ten thousand voices. The death-dealing bolts of Fort Henry were falling thick and fast into Fort Donelson. But little did the besiegers know what protection and defence nature had laid against the ingenuity of art, which the insurgents had seized upon to accomplish their purpose! No one considered the importance of those great natural traverses and curtains of rock which had been thrown up by the primeval subterranean fires, nor what bomb-proofs and lunettes the waters of a thousand years had worn into the sides of those hills. The area of the place was so large that nearly the whole force could be removed from the water front, and thus leave the shells to explode against the bleak hill-sides, or crush through the deserted huts of the enemy.

Meantime an occasional shot from the batteries surrounding the outer lines of defence must have told upon the enemy on the other side. The enemy replied but feebly. The entire morning had been in anxious expectancy, neither party being willing to risk the chances of another trial of valor. The weather was keen and frosty, the roads slippery and clogged with stiff mud.

Saturday, which was destined to witness the grand *denouement* of the painful tragedies enacted about Donelson, was cold, damp and cheerless. The enemy, during the night, had transferred several of their batteries to portions of their works, within a few hundred feet of which the extreme right wing of the Federals was resting. Upon the first coming of dawn, these batteries suddenly opened on the Ninth, Eighteenth, Twenty-ninth, Thirtieth and Thirty-first regiments, comprising Oglesby's brigade, which had the advance. Simultaneously with the opening of the batteries, a force of about twelve thousand infantry and a regiment of cavalry was hurled against the brigade with a vigor which, made against less steady and well-disciplined troops, must surely have resulted in their entire demolition.

Sudden and unexpected as was this sally on the part of the enemy, it did not find the gallant Illinoisans unprepared to meet them. The attack was made in columns of regiments, which poured in upon the little band from no less than three different directions. Every regiment of the brigade found itself opposed to two, and in many cases to no less than four different regiments. Undismayed, however, by the greatly superior force of the enemy, and unsupported by adequate artillery, the brigade not only held their own, but upon two occasions actually drove the rebels fairly into their intrenchments, but only to be pressed back again into their former position. At last having expended every round of their ammunition, they were obliged to retire and give way to advancing regiments of Colonel W. H. L. Wallace's brigade, the Eleventh, Twentieth, Seventeenth, Forty-fifth, Forty-eighth Illinois, and Forty-ninth Indiana regiments.

By rapid firing from the two batteries of Taylor and Schwartz, the enemy was driven back. The Union regiments which had suffered so much were withdrawn. The enemy had by this time concentrated their broken troops for another attack. General McClernand had already prepared for the emergency. Anticipating that an attempt would be made to force a passage through, he ordered a brigade to the rear and extreme right to form behind the regiments then in front.

An hour had elapsed when the enemy returned in a dense mass, renewing the fight. The battery of Captain Schwartz seemed to be the object of their attack. On they came, pell-mell, with deafening volleys of fire. The Union batteries, well nigh exhausted of canister, poured a storm of shell into their ranks. Ammunition caissons were sent back in haste to get a fresh supply of canister. The Ninth, Eighteenth, Thirtieth and Forty-first were the next regiments to be brought up. The crest of the hill was contested with variable success for a full hour, when the enemy was finally driven back. The line of battle was so much confused that no connected account of the movements can be detailed. The utmost bravery was displayed on both sides, until the struggle degenerated into a wild fierce skirmish. The rebels finally retired a third time.

The Union men had expended their ammunition. It was during this lull, and before the men could realize the fact that they had driven the enemy before them, that the fourth and last attempt was made to seize the battery. The horses being shot, the enemy succeeded in gaining possession of the battery of Captain Schwartz, and were on the point of turning the guns on the Federal troops, when Captain Willett's Chicago battery, which had just toiled up fresh from Fort Henry, arrived on the ground and poured in a perfect storm of canister, just in time to save the day. The rebels fell back in disorder, dragging the guns of Schwartz with them down the hill, and gained entrance to the fort before the Federals could overtake them. Some eager regiments followed them to the embankments, a few men climbing over, who were driven back for want of support.

The regiments which suffered most in this morning's engagement were the Eighteenth and Eleventh Illinois; next them, the Thirty-first and Eighth. The expenditure of ammunition must have been excessive, on the hypothesis that each man had his cartridge box full on going into action. Forty rounds of the standard cartridge is enough to fight with, and more than enough to carry with other accoutrements of battle.

There were many instances of men who displayed the utmost heroism in this action—some refused to be called off the field, fighting to the last moment; others returned after having their wounds dressed. One of the artillerymen, who received a wound, walked to the hospital, a mile or more, had the ball extracted, and then insisted on going back to his battery. The surgeon refused, when he quaintly said: "Come, come, put on some of your glue and let me go back."

General McClernand, who had been a conspicuous mark during the whole of this fight, bore himself with firmness, exhibiting great decision and calmness in the most arduous situation. The tumult on the left having subsided, he sent a messenger back to General Grant to know if the left wing of General Smith was secure; if so he was ready to advance. As the day waned, an occasional shot was to be heard from the gunboats, but no satisfactory account could be received of their operations. A lull followed the storm. Both armies were preparing for the grand *coup de main*, by which Fort Donelson was to be taken.

It was resolved to storm the fort. The honor of accomplishing this difficult and perilous exploit on the left wing was given to General Smith. When Colonel Lauman led his brigade in solid columns up the steep sides of the hill, he drove the enemy from his entrenchments, pouring a fearful volley into their disorganized and broken ranks. The national ensign was immediately flung out from the earthworks, and greeted with deafening cheers from ten thousand loyal voices.

The shades of night cast their canopy over the contending hosts, and compelled the Federal commander to delay the completion of his victory till morning. Soon after daylight, the Federal columns advanced in battle array, prepared to storm the works at all points, when their eyes were greeted with innumerable white flags, thrown out by the enemy at every threatened position.

What followed may be told in few words. The enemy seeing that the Unionists had gained one of his strongest positions, and successfully repulsed him in his most daring attempts to raise the siege, took advantage of the darkness, and called a council of war, in which it was determined to surrender. With all possible haste some 7,000 troops were dispatched up the river by night. The rebel Generals Floyd and Pillow made their escape. The fort, with all its contents, fell into the conquer-

ors' hands. More than 13,000 prisoners, Brigadier-General Buckner, with twenty Colonels and other officers in proportion; sixty-five cannon, forty-eight field and seventeen siege guns, a million and a half dollars in stores, provisions, and equipage, twenty thousand stand of arms— was glorious result, purchased at comparatively small loss. The Federal loss in killed and wounded was 2,200; that of the rebels 1,275.

At the storming of Fort Donelson many acts of personal valor might be recorded. An instance of reckless gallantry, and fortitude under a most painful surgical operation, that of Hamilton, a son of Professor Leiber, is worthy of record. This young man was twice wounded in the battle of Fort Donelson. The first was a flesh wound, of which he made nothing. Presently, however, he was struck by a Minie ball in the same arm; this shattered his elbow, with the bones above and below, and he sank to the ground, fainting with loss of blood. He was picked up towards night, carried to a house, and thence, over a rough road, in an army wagon, to the river bank, a distance of three miles, which necessarily caused the greatest suffering. Arrived at the river bank, he was put on board a boat and conveyed with other wounded to an hospital, where his arm was amputated. When the operation was over, the brave young fellow's first words were, "How long will it be before I can rejoin my company?" At that time young Leiber was a Lieutenant of the Ninth Illinois regiment. He was appointed aid-de-camp by General Halleck soon after the battle of Donelson as a reward for his great bravery.

THE OCCUPATION OF NASHVILLE.

February 25, 1862.

After the surrender of Fort Donelson, on the 16th of February, it became evident to the Confederate leaders that the cities of Nashville and Memphis, and other important positions must soon fall into the hands of the victorious Federal army. Public meetings were held at both these cities, in which it was recommended to defend them to the last extremity, and if necessary to prevent their occupancy by the Union troops, many of the more violent and reckless of the military determined that they should be burned, and every description of property destroyed. At Nashville, the Governor, Isham G. Harris, pledged himself to "shed his blood, fight like a lion, and die like a martyr," rather than submit to the enemy; and at the same time efforts were made, but with little success, to organize additional forces for defence.

During the progress of the siege at Fort Donelson, dispatches were sent to Nashville, announcing a series of rebel successes, and on Saturday night information was conveyed that the Federals had again been defeated both on land and water, but they had been reinforced and might renew the attack in the morning. With these hopeful and exulting assurances, the city rested in peace, confident that the light of the morning would open upon a glorious victory for the rebel arms.

Early on the morning of Sunday the first rumors of this heavy calamity to the rebel cause had been conveyed to the leaders in Nashville. At first, suppressed whispers and grave countenances indicated that something important had transpired. But the people generally were confident and hopeful as on the evening before, and anticipated that any hour of the day would give the signal for a grand jubilee and rejoicing. The time for public service in the churches drew near, and the people repaired to their several places of worship. The churches were partly filled and the streets crowded with the passing multitude, when a startling rumor broke the peaceful stillness of the day. The Federals were victorious! Fort Donelson had surrendered! Fifteen thousand Confederate prisoners had laid down their arms to the invaders! Fear, added to imagination, ran riot in the town.

It was said that the Federal troops had already reached Robertson, a place about twenty-five miles from Nashville, connected by railroad, and that the gunboats were at Clarksville, on the river, on their way to the city. Governor Harris, taking advantage of his early information, had hastily convened the members of the Legislature, then in session at Nashville, which had met, and adjourned to convene at Memphis. These circumstances becoming known, gave plausibility to the exciting rumors of the celerity of the Federal movements, and the people were panic stricken.

Before nightfall hundreds of citizens, singly and in families, were making their way South, many of them having no idea why they were thus recklessly abandoning comfortable homes, or where they were going. Toward night it was announced that the military authorities would throw open the public stores to all who would carry the property away.

This excitement continued throughout Sunday night, constantly gaining strength, aided by the destruction of two gunboats which were in process of construction—two fine New Orleans packets, the James Woods and James Johnson, having been taken for that purpose. The army of General Johnston commenced its retreat, encamping by regiments at convenient points outside of the city. On Monday morning, great excitement prevailed; the public stores were distributed to some extent among the people, while the army and hospitals were making heavy requisitions, and pressing all the vehicles and men that could be obtained to carry supplies to their camp. At the same time, considerable quantities of stores were removed to the depots for transportation south.

Evening came, and no gunboats—no Federal army from Kentucky. General Johnston left for the South, placing General Floyd in command, assisted by Generals Pillow and Hardee. The apprehensions of the near approach of the enemy having been found groundless, it was determined by General Floyd that the distribution of the stores was premature. An order was sent to close the warehouses, and a force detailed to collect what had been given out. This was done, so far as practicable—but on Tuesday the distribution commenced again, and continued with slight restrictions, under the eyes of the most judicious citizens, until Saturday morning. Tuesday night the iron and railroad bridges across the Cumberland were destroyed, in spite of the most earnest and persistent remonstrances of leading citizens. The iron-bridge cost about one hundred and fifty thousand dollars, and the railroad bridge two hundred and fifty thousand dollars. It was one of the finest drawbridges in the country.

The scenes which were enacted during the following days, up to Monday morning the 24th, were still more exciting. The untiring energy of the Mayor and city authorities, who throughout this whole affair acted with prudence and zeal, was inadequate to keep the excited people under control.

On Sunday morning, twenty-five Federal pickets breakfasted in Edgefield, opposite the city, and during the morning eight of them seized a little stern-wheeled steamer that had been used as a ferry, and refused to permit it to continue its trips. Mayor Cheatham immediately crossed in a skiff, but found no officer with whom he could negotiate. In the evening, Colonel Emmet, of the Fourth Ohio Cavalry arrived, and sent a message to the Mayor, requesting his presence. The interview was satisfactory on both sides, though the formal surrender of the city was deferred until the arrival of General Mitchell, who was expected on Sunday night or Monday morning.

On Monday morning the city became comparatively quiet. In the evening Generals Buell and Mitchell arrived in Edgefield, and understanding that the authorities had appointed a committee, consisting of the Mayor and several of the leading citizens, he sent a message requesting an interview. The hour of the interview was fixed at eleven o'clock, A. M. on Tuesday. In the mean time General Nelson arrived in the city about eight o'clock, A. M., in command of a fleet, consisting of one gunboat, the Cairo, and eight transports. Transports continued to arrive during the day, and at night the number reached eighteen or twenty. A large portion of this army disembarked during the morning, and occupied the public square, encamping in the vicinity at night. At eleven o'clock, the committee of citizens were conveyed by order of General Buell to Edgefield, on the steamer Hillman. They were met at the landing by Generals Nelson and Mitchell, and escorted to General Buell's headquarters. The interview was an amicable one, General Buell giving assurance that the personal liberty and property of all citizens would be fully protected, and no State institutions of any kind interfered with.

The first business of General Buell, after having thus established a cordial understanding with the officers of the city, was to inaugurate his military authority by the appointment of a Provost-Marshal, to preserve order, and regulate the intercourse of the Union troops with the citizens. Colonel Stanley Matthews, a highly respected and well-known gentleman, conservative in politics, was selected for this responsible position, an appointment which was greeted with satisfaction by the citizens. The post-office was continued in the hands of Colonel J. H. Markland, a native Kentuckian, and a gentleman of high character and social standing.

General Buell immediately restored the mail facilities, which had so long been denied the people by the rebellion, and adopted every measure to ensure and restore confidence among the citizens. Many of them had fled their homes during the panic, the stores and places of business were closed, and the whole community were perfectly paralyzed during the week that had intervened between the fall of Fort Donelson and the occupation of the city. Eight days of terror afforded them a fearful illustration of lawlessness and violence: and when the Federal troops took possession, their sobriety, decorum and uprightness, amazed the people with the contrast. The loss of many of their relatives, the deep hostility that had been engendered in their breasts, and the doubts as to the ultimate restoration of the Federal authority, made the development of loyal sentiments a work of time and patience. The retreat of the national forces from Nashville, and the withdrawal of the protection of the Government, would be the death-warrant of any person committing himself too openly for the Union cause; and many citizens allowed these contending motives to restrain their welcome to the flag under which they had so long enjoyed peace, prosperity and repose.

The government at Washington took an early opportunity to appoint a military governor for the State of Tennessee, in the person of Hon. ANDREW JOHNSON, a man who had long represented its people as Governor and United States Senator.

Some of the ladies of Nashville were peculiarly ardent in their dislike of the Union occupation, and took especial pains to avoid or sneer at the glorious old flag which was directly hoisted in the most prominent parts of the town.

Over the large gate at the Provost-Marshal's splendid headquarters—Elliott's female school—a Union flag was hoisted. A very ardent secesh lady, who wished to see Colonel Matthews, was about to pass through the gate, when looking up she beheld the proud flag streaming on the breeze. Starting back horror-struck, she held up her hands and exclaimed to the guard:

"Dear! I can't go under that dreadful Lincoln flag. Is there no other way for me to enter?"

"Yes, madam," promptly replied the soldier, and turning to his comrade, he said:

"Here, orderly, bring out that rebel flag and lay it on the ground at the little gate, and let this lady walk over it!"

The lady looked bewildered, and after hesitating a moment, concluded to bow her head to the flag which had so long protected her, and passed under it with submissive grace.

FORT CLINCH AND FERNANDINA, FLA.

On the 28th of February, 1862, Commodore S. F. Dupont, commanding the South Atlantic Blockading Squadron, set sail from Port Royal, S. C., the headquarters of General Sherman, for the purpose of taking military possession of the forts and towns on the coasts of Georgia and Florida. Brigadier-General Wright accompanied him, as commander of the land forces. The squadron consisted of twenty vessels of war, seven transports, and a few schooners and smaller vessels.

The first point of attack was to be Fernandina, Fla., an important sea-port near the entrance of St. Mary's river, the boundary between Georgia and Florida. The main channel is between Cumberland and Amelia islands, with fourteen feet of water on the bar.

Fort Clinch, a regular bastioned work of brick, with heavy casemates, and guns mounted *en barbette*, commanded the entrance. This place had been strongly fortified by the rebels and mounted with guns of the heaviest calibre. Commodore Dupont anticipated a stubborn resistance, but the garrison, on learning the approach of the formidable expedition, deemed their position indefensible, and evacuated the fort, leaving twelve of their heaviest guns behind.

The town of Fernandina was also occupied by the Federal forces without any resistance. Many of the inhabitants had fled, and those remaining were terrified on the approach of the vessels, having been assured by the rebels that the national forces would subject them to unrestrained pillage and abuse. The kind and conciliatory government instituted by General Wright soon restored confidence, and the people returned to their homes and occupations.

THE MERRIMAC AND THE MONITOR.
March 9, 1862.

The most remarkable naval battle which has ever taken place in the history of the world was the encounter between the two iron-clad steam batteries, Merrimac and Monitor, in Hampton Roads, Va.

The Merrimac was one of five war-steamers authorized to be constructed by an act of Congress, passed at the session of 1844–5, and was built at Charlestown, Mass. The spar deck was 281 feet long, and 52 broad, in her original condition. The vessel was completed and launched in 1856. She was soon put in commission, and continued in the service until April, 1861, when she was lying at Norfolk Navy Yard for repairs.

When the Government property at the Navy Yard and in the neighborhood of Norfolk was destroyed or rendered unserviceable, to secure it from seizure by the Confederates, the Merrimac was scuttled.

Not long after the rebels had taken possession of the Navy Yard the Merrimac was raised, and placed in the floating-dock. Here she was remodeled, and covered by a sloping roof of iron plates, four inches thick, which bore her down so heavily, that it became almost impossible to launch her. When launched she drew four feet of water over the calculated draught, and was again placed upon the dry-dock, and underwent material changes in her construction. Her bow and stern were steel-clad, and the bow furnished with a projecting ram for the purpose of piercing an antagonist. The armament consisted of four eleven-inch navy guns, broadside, and two one hundred-pounder rifled guns, at the bow and at the stern.

The Monitor was built by contract, under the act of Congress of July, 1861, appropriating $1,500,000 for iron-clad vessels. Captain Ericsson presented proposals for a battery to be launched within one hundred working days from the date of the contract. The contract was awarded to him in October, and on the one hundred and first working day the Monitor was launched from the Continental Iron Works at Greenpoint, New York.

The Monitor is low, wide, and flat-bottomed, with vertical sides, and pointed ends, requiring but shallow water to float in. The sides of the vessel are formed of plate-iron, half an inch thick, outside of which is attached solid white oak twenty-six inches thick: outside this again is rolled iron armor five inches thick. The inclination of the lower hull is such that a ball to strike it in any part must pass through at least twenty-five feet of water, and then strike an inclined iron surface at an angle of about ten degrees. In the event of an enemy boarding the

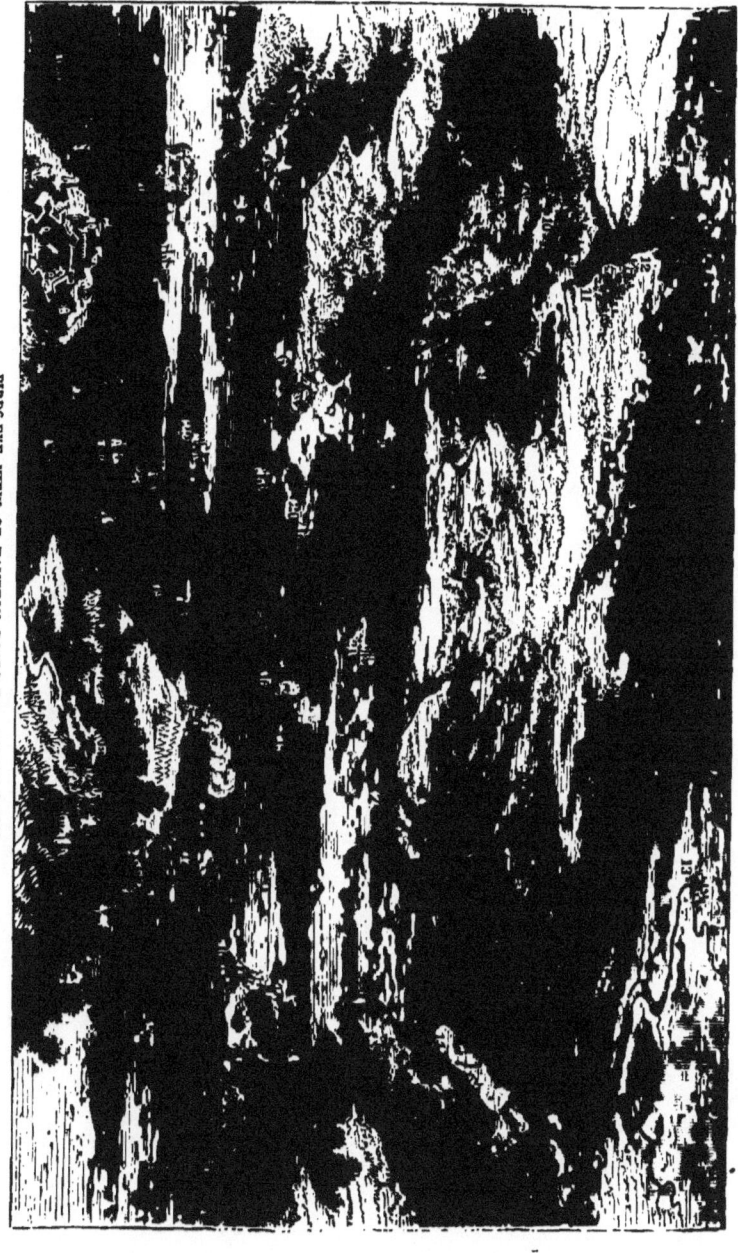

BIRDS-EYE VIEW OF HAMPTON ROADS, VA., MARCH 8, 1862.

1. Hampton Roads.—2. Fortress Monroe.—3. Rip Raps.—4. Newport News Point.—5. James River.—6. Sewall's Point.—7. Pigs Point.—8. Craney Island.—9. Elizabeth River.—10. Norfolk.—11. Portsmouth.—12. Gosport.—13. Suffolk.—'4. Nansemond River.—15. Merrimac.—16. Monitor.—17. Cumberland.—18. Congress.—19. Minnesota.—20. Yorktown.—21. Jamestown.—22. St. Lawrence.—23. Roanoke.

battery they can do no harm, as the only entrance is at the top of the turret or citadel, which cannot easily be scaled, and even then only one man at a time can descend into the hull.

The principal novelty of this vessel is the cylindrical revolving turret, rising from its exact centre, in which the guns are placed. This is formed of rolled one-inch iron plates bolted together to the thickness of eight inches; its internal diameter is twenty feet, and it is nine feet high. It rests at its lower edge on a smooth, flat ring of composition metal, but when in action the principal portion of its weight is sustained by a central shaft, about which it revolves; a massive wedge being driven below the steps of the shaft on such occasion to raise it, and thus cause it to bear up the turret. A large spur wheel upon the shaft is connected by a train of gearing with a small steam-engine, which supplies the power for turning the turret.

Two eleven-inch guns are placed within the turret, in position precisely parallel with each other, on smooth ways, or slides; a clamp being arranged upon the sides of the ways for adjusting the friction and taking up the recoil in such distance as may be desired.

The turret is pierced in different places with four holes for the insertion of telescopes, and just outside of the holes reflectors are fixed to bend the rays of light which come in a direction parallel with the guns through the axis of the telescope, which is crossed by a vertical thread of spider's web through the line of collimation. The sailing-master takes his position in the turret, with his eye to the telescope, and his hand upon the wheel that governs the motion of the small engine, and turns the turret so as to keep the guns always directed with absolute precision to the object against which the fire is directed. A scale is also arranged for adjusting the elevation of the guns with similar engineering precision.

Upon the sides of the turret that have the port-holes through which the guns are discharged, the massiveness is increased by an additional plating three inches in thickness; making the sides of the turret presented to the enemy eleven inches.

In preparing for action, the awning over the turret is removed, and the square smoke stacks as well as the shorter pipes, through which air is drawn into the vessel, are taken down. A small, square tower at the bow is the wheelhouse, in which the steersman stands. It is made of bars or beams of iron nine by twelve inches, interlocked at the corners.

After a preliminary trial trip, the Monitor sailed from the Brooklyn Navy Yard for Fortress Monroe, on the 6th of March, and at five o'clock on the afternoon of that day, discharged her pilot off Sandy Hook. Her officers at this time were as follows:

Lieutenant-commanding John S. Worden; Lieutenant and Executive Officer, S. D. Green; Acting Masters, I. N. Stoddard, J. W. Webber; Acting Assistant-Paymaster, Wm. E. Keeler; Acting Assistant-Surgeon, D. C. Logue; Government Inspector, Alban C. Stimers; First Assistant-Engineer, Isaac Newton; Second Assistant-Engineer, Albert S. Campbell; Third Assistant-Engineers, R. W. Sands, M. T. Sunstron; Acting Masters'-Mate, George Frederickson.

The voyage to Fortress Monroe was safely terminated by the arrival of the vessel with her consort about eight o'clock on the evening of the eighth. Important events had transpired in Hampton Roads on that day. The Merrimac had steamed down towards the sloop-of-war Cumberland, blockading James river, and demanded a surrender. This was refused, when the monster turned ponderously, and bringing her bow to bear on the Cumberland, dashed into her side, rending the timbers as she went. She then drew her iron prow from the shattered vessel, scattering a storm of splintered wood on the water, and receding to a safe distance, poured a broadside in from her guns. The crippled Cumberland, still vibrating in all her timbers, returned the broadside. This was answered and returned without intermission for fifteen minutes. During this time shot and shell boomed over the water, crashed into the doomed vessel, and fell like mighty hail on the iron coat of the Merrimac. But while every shot told on the quivering wood-work of the Cumberland, the Merrimac threw off the iron missiles as a rock beats back the tempest, sending in her volleys more triumphantly each moment. The brave old man-of-war stood up to the slaughter much as a blinded horse, forced among the wild bulls of a Spanish arena falls, gored to the heart, but fighting desperately. Half full of water, which still came pouring in through her wounded side, recoiling like a living thing from each outburst of shot and shell, she at last settled slowly to the waters' edge, and sunk, pouring out a defiant broadside as she went down, with the stars and stripes floating at her mast-head.

The Merrimac then challenged the Congress, a Federal sailing frigate, of 1,867 tons, but was also refused a surrender. This refusal was replied to by the guns of the rebel vessel, and after a short contest, when it became hopeless to continue resistance, the Congress surrendered, and was fired and abandoned. The evening was clear, the air still, the water without a ripple, and the scene was magnificent, as the noble vessel became wrapped in its fiery shroud. When entirely enveloped in flame, the fire reached the magazine, and an explosion took place which scattered the burning wreck in one vast upheaving of fragments and cinders, kindling up the sky with its glare, and throwing portions of the wreck the distance of a mile. The Merrimac having succeeded in sinking the Cumberland and compelling the Congress to surrender, withdrew for the night, evidently confident that in the morning she would sweep away the rest of the fleet.

As the day closed, sadness and gloom filled the hearts of the Federal officers in the fleet and Fortress. They felt assured that the powerful enemy that had just made such murderous work had only retired for the night to recruit, and then return to complete the destruction she had commenced, having the sailing vessels at her mercy. While despondency settled on many brows, and conjectures were rife as to where the Merrimac would direct her attention the next day, a gleam of hope arose. At eight o'clock in the evening a bright, movable light was discovered seaward, coming from the direction of Cape Charles beacon. It being known that the Ericsson Battery had left New York two days previous, surmises were rife that this light might proceed from her deck. The best night telescopes were brought into requisition, and in less than half an hour after it first hove in sight, the fact was circulated that the Ericsson Battery was coming up the Roads. The news spread like wildfire, and the ramparts in the fort were soon lined with troops. At nine o'clock the Monitor anchored off Fortress Monroe.

The next day, (Sunday, the 9th,) dawned fair and calm. The sun rose with almost cloudless splendor, a soft haze alone hung upon the water, so silvery and transparent that it hardly intercepted the view.

At half-past six o'clock, A. M., this haze cleared away. Looking towards Sewall's Point there appeared the Merrimac and the rebel steamers Yorktown and Patrick Henry. They were stationary—the Merrimac to the right of the others, blowing off steam. Their appearance was the cause for a second alarm. The rebel craft seemed deliberating what to do—whether to move on and attempt the destruction of the Minnesota, which was aground, or to attack the Union fleet anchored near the Rip-Raps. The appearance of the Merrimac on this second visit caused great precipitation in the removal of the Federal transport fleet to a safe harbor a mile or two up the Chesapeake. At seven A. M., a plan seemed to have been adopted, and the Merrimac steamed in the direction of the Minnesota, which was still aground. The Yorktown and Jamestown were crowded with troops, and steamed slowly after the Merrimac. The plan of the latter seemed to be to destroy the Minnesota, and then proceed to shell out the Union camp at Newport News, land and take possession of the camp with their own troops.

The Merrimac steamed along with boldness until she was within three miles of the Minnesota, when the Monitor emerged from behind the latter, and proceeded towards the Merrimac. At first the rebel craft seemed nonplussed, and hesitated, no doubt, in astonishment at the strange-looking vessel approaching her. The Merrimac then closed the distance between her and the Monitor until they were within a mile of each other. Both batteries stopped. The Merrimac fired a shot at the Minnesota, to which no reply was made. The rebel craft then fired at the Monitor; the latter replied, hitting the Merrimac near the water line. The Merrimac then commenced firing very rapidly, first from her stern gun at the Monitor, and then her broadside guns, occasionally firing a shot at the Minnesota. The fight went on in this way for an hour or two, both vessels exchanging shots pretty freely. Sometimes the Merrimac would retire, followed by the Monitor, and *vice versa*.

While the fight between the batteries was going on, one hundred solid nine-inch shot were sent up from Fortress Monroe on the steamer Rancocas to the Minnesota. At a quarter past ten o'clock the Merrimac and Monitor had come into pretty close quarters, the former giving the latter two broadsides in succession. They were promptly replied to by the Monitor. The firing was so rapid that both craft were obscured in columns of white smoke. The ramparts of the fort, the rigging of the vessels in port, the houses and the bend were all crowded with sailors, soldiers and civilians. When the rapid firing alluded to took place, these spectators were singularly silent, anxious and doubtful of the result. Their impatience was soon removed by the full figure of the Monitor, with the stars and stripes flying at her stern, steaming around the Merrimac, moving with the ease of a duck on the water. The distance between the vessels was forty feet. In this circuit the Monitor's guns were not idle, as she fired shot after shot at her formidable antagonist.

At eleven A. M., the Minnesota opened fire, and assisted the Monitor in engaging the Merrimac. She fired nine-inch solid shot with good accuracy, but with apparently little effect. The Merrimac returned the fire with shell, one of which struck and exploded the boiler of the gunboat Dragon, which was alongside the Minnesota, endeavoring to get her off. For the next hour the battle raged fiercely between the Merrimac on the rebel side and the Union vessels, the Monitor, Minnesota and Whitehall, but with no particular result. The Minnesota presenting the best mark, the Merrimac fired at her frequently, alternately giving the Monitor a powerful shot. The Merrimac made several attempts to run at full speed past the Monitor to attack and run down the Minnesota. All these attempts were parried, as it were, by the Monitor. In one of these desperate efforts the Merrimac ran her plow or ram with terrible force against the side of the Monitor; but it only had the effect of careening the latter vessel in the slightest degree.

The rebel boats Yorktown and Patrick Henry kept at a safe distance from the Monitor. The former vessel, at the beginning of the fight, had the temerity to come within range of the Monitor. The latter fired one shot at her which entered her pilot-house, carrying it away, when she retired out of range.

The fire raged hotly on both sides, the opposing batteries moving around each other with the skill, ease and dexterity of knights in a tournament. The Merrimac, though the strongest, did not move with the freedom of her antagonist; hence the Monitor had the advantage, taking choice of position. At a quarter before twelve o'clock, the Merrimac was in full retreat, heading for Sewall's Point, and chased for a few minutes by the Monitor. The Merrimac had evidently suffered to some extent, and it was thought at one time that she was sinking. After she got safely under the guns of the rebel battery at Sewall's Point, she stopped and signalled for help from her consorts, who were beating a retreat. Subsequently two tug-boats or gunboats went alongside, took her in tow, and proceeded to Norfolk. This ended the combat.

Toward the close of the engagement, Lieutenant Worden was standing in the pilot-house, when a percussion shell struck the turret, and exploded. The openings for sighting outside objects, through one of which Lieutenant Worden was looking, allowed the fine dust and splinters to enter, injuring his eyes. Almost immediately afterward the same thing occurred, and this second injury rendered him completely blind, and he was compelled to retire below. It was feared that he was permanently injured in this gallant encounter, but after careful treatment his sight was restored, and he was again ready for duty.

This remarkable encounter between two iron-clad vessels was regarded with the greatest interest throughout Europe, where its importance to the questions of naval architecture and warfare was fully appreciated and understood. It had not only a direct bearing upon the construction and working of floating batteries, but it demonstrated that a new engine of war had been introduced that might render valueless for effective defence all the land batteries against which these iron antagonists might be brought to bear.

The destruction of the Cumberland and Congress on the first day of the engagement, and the triumphant condition in which the Merrimac had retired from the heavy broadsides of the Federal frigates, which would almost have destroyed an ordinary vessel, created intense excitement in all the seaport cities of the North. The loud boasts of the rebels over the strength, sailing qualities, and impregnable character of their vessel, apparently justified by the events of March 8th, led to an apprehension that she might be successful in running out to sea, and visiting Philadelphia, New York, Boston, and other cities, which were entirely unprepared for a sudden attack.

The appearance of the Monitor alongside of the Minnesota, on the morning of the 9th, was altogether unexpected, and the rebel commander evidently knew that he had no common foe with which to deal.

CAPTURE OF JACKSONVILLE, FLA.
March 12, 1862.

Jacksonville, the principal town in East Florida, is situated on the St. John's river, twenty miles from the sea. Vessels drawing twelve feet of water can cross the bar. An important commercial city of Florida, it was desirable to restore it to the protection of the government, and after the capture of Fernandina, the commanders of the expedition turned their attention to the accomplishment of this object. The United States gunboat Ottawa, in company with the Pembina and Seneca, succeeded in crossing the bar off Jacksonville, on the 11th of March. Commodore Rogers found to his great satisfaction, as already at Fernandina and St. Mary's, no attempt to dispute his progress or resist the restoration of the city to its allegiance to the government.

Contrary to expectation on both sides, the approaches to this place by the river were not defended, and no resistance was offered to the Union forces by land or water. As at Fernandina, the batteries were evacuated, and the guns for the most part left behind. This was by order of General Trapier, who is said to have acted upon orders from General Lee, commanding the Confederate troops on the South Carolina, Georgia and Florida coast. There were some five thousand rebel troops in this part of Florida—at Fernandina, and on the line of the railroads to Tallahassee and Cedar Keys.

When it was ascertained by the Mayor of the city that the troops were to be withdrawn, he held a consultation with General Pyles, in company with a portion of the city council, in which the question of resistance was freely discussed. The retirement of the troops, and the entirely defenceless condition in which the people had been left, allowed them no choice had they been ever so much determined to dispute the entry of the Federal forces. The Mayor, H. H. Hoeg, issued a proclamation, informing the citizens that no opposition would be made, and calling upon all the inhabitants to treat their expected visitors with proper decorum, and to do nothing that would provoke any ill-feeling between citizens and soldiers.

On the arrival of the vessels Lieutenant Stevens was politely received by the authorities, who came on board his vessel, the Ottawa, and through S. L. Burritt, Esq., gave up the town. Many of the inhabitants had abandoned their homes, fearing to trust the Federal troops. Others, however, remained, and testified their gratification at the arrival of the fleet.

Unfortunately, however, they did not reach Jacksonville in time to save that beautiful town from the flames, as a part of it was laid in ruins. On the afternoon of the 11th, some five or six hundred armed men, claiming to be a part of the force which had been stationed at Fernandina, arrived by railroad, and announced that they had come, by order of General Trapier, to burn the steam saw-mills, lumber, etc., which might be of value to the Federal authorities. No time was given to save property of any description. At dusk the torch was applied, and in a brief space eight of these immense establishments, forming nearly a circle on both sides of the river, were in a blaze. Immediately afterwards, the spacious and elegant hotel, well known to Northern invalids as the Judson House, was fired by unknown persons, together with warehouses, the railroad freight depot, etc., etc. All this property was a total loss to the owners, as no attempt was made to save or rescue any portion of it. The loss was estimated at half a million of dollars.

The population of Jacksonville, before the war broke out, was about four thousand. It had a large trade, as the St. John's river is settled with plantations, and is navigable for two hundred miles above the town for large vessels, and there were a dozen steamers running on it. The lumber trade was very extensive and prosperous. About fifty million feet of Florida pitch pine were sawed there annually. This business was ruined by the incendiaries. The exports of rosin, turpentine, etc., amounted to $100,000 annually; cotton, $250,000; cedar, $100,000, etc. The arrivals of vessels were about 400 yearly. The town was built mainly of brick, lighted with gas, and was a great resort for invalids, for its mild and balmy climate. The Florida, Atlantic and Gulf rail road, starting here, intersects with the road from Fernandina to Cedar Keys, twelve miles from Jacksonville, and then goes on to Tallahassee, the capital, one hundred and sixty miles, and thence eighteen miles to St. Mark's, on the Gulf.

General Sherman and staff arrived on the 20th, in the steamer Cosmopolitan. He immediately issued a proclamation to the people, assuring them of protection and peace, and calling upon them to continue their accustomed business. On the same day a meeting of the citizens was held, at which the most loyal sentiments were avowed, and a series of very strong resolutions adopted in favor of the Union, and denouncing the acts of the secession convention and the State authorities in a most emphatic manner. The resolutions also called for the holding of a Convention of the State to organize a State government for Florida, and called upon the chief of the military department of the United States to retain at Jacksonville a sufficient force to maintain order and protect the citizens and their property and persons.

The loyal men of the town, after being thus assured of the continued protection of the government, gave evidence of their patriotism and devotion to the constitution; and for a time they enjoyed the peace and protection they so much desired. But it was of short duration, and the result was more disastrous to them than the uninterrupted occupancy of the place by the rebel force would have been. Not only had the most important business establishments been sacrificed to the flames, but the principal hotels and other buildings had also been destroyed by the retiring enemy. In a short time General Hunter, the new commander in that department, ordered the evacuation of the city by the Federal troops, and they accordingly withdrew. Immediately the rebel forces returned, the secession authorities renewed their administration, and the active Unionists were arrested, imprisoned, their property confiscated, and in many cases their lives were sacrificed. Some of them were fortunate enough to escape with their families and some personal effects, and obtain passage on vessels bound to New York, where they arrived, and narrated a painful history of their sufferings. Jacksonville occupied and speedily evacuated by Federal troops, makes a gloomy chapter in the history of loyal adversities during the rebellion.

OCCUPATION OF COLUMBUS, KY.
March 3, 1862.

The city of Columbus stands on the Kentucky shore of the Mississippi, twenty-five miles below Cairo, which is at the junction of the Ohio and Mississippi rivers. It is a place of great natural strength, from the high and precipitous bluffs upon which the city is built. This important position had been early seized as a stronghold by the enemy, and herculean labors had been performed in the erection of batteries and fortifications, and the mounting of immense guns of the heaviest calibre. The necessity of holding Columbus against the Federal approach, in order to protect Nashville, Memphis, Vicksburg and New Orleans, was one of the great incentives to the rebel commanders in expending so much labor and time in its defence. But all their calculations had been shaken by the capture of Forts Henry and Donelson, and the evacuation of Bowling Green. Their line of defence was broken by these brilliant movements, their flank was exposed, and they were in danger of having their retreat cut off by a vigorous movement of the Federal army flushed by brilliant successes. There was no alternative but to risk a similar defeat and capture, or to evacuate their works. The latter course was adopted, and on February 27th, the army commenced its retreat from the apprehended foe. They carried away with them large quantities of commissary stores, ammunition, guns, and war material of every description, and by March 2d, had abandoned their works and the city.

On the same night, Lieutenant-Colonel Hogg, of the Second Illinois Cavalry, left Paducah to reconnoitre in the direction of Columbus. At the same time, the flotilla at Cairo was being put in a state of complete readiness for a movement, which was kept a profound secret from all but the commander and his advisory officers. Commodore Foote, himself, was not acquainted with the movement of Lieutenant-Colonel Hogg.

On the morning of the 4th, at daylight, the flotilla left Cairo, and dropped down the river. Commodore Foote and General Collum were on board the flag-ship Cincinnati, accompanied by the gunboats St. Louis, Louisville, Carondelet, Pittsburgh, Lexington, and four mortar boats. General Sherman commanded the transports Aleck Scott, I. L. McGill and Illinois, with the following troops aboard: Twenty-seventh Illinois, Colonel Buford, Forty-second Illinois, and two batteries.

On reaching that part of the river which makes a curving sweep toward Columbus, the vessels took up various positions, the mortar-boats being placed at a favorable point on the Missouri shore, where they could shell the rebel works, and be out of sight and range of their guns. While the gunboats were gradually nearing the fortifications, a flag was discovered flying from the summit of the bluffs. It was at too great a distance to be distinctly discerned, but the possibility of the Federal flag flying on that spot was not to be entertained. General Sherman, on a tug-boat, advanced and turned the bend in the river, out of sight of the fleet. No shot was fired, and the gunboats followed in time to discover the General and some of his men scaling the summit of the bluff. The stars and stripes were floating magnificently where only a few hours before the flag of the enemy asserted dominion. The General soon ascertained that Lieutenant-Colonel Hogg had arrived on the afternoon of the 3d, and quietly occupied the abandoned fortifications, and raised the national colors on their walls.

The works were extensive, of massive strength, capable of resisting a protracted siege, and supplied with guns, of which 128-pounders formed a part. The natural position, as well as the immense defensive preparations which had been made, seemed to render them impregnable to an attacking force. Yet with all these advantages the enemy had spiked many of their guns, rolled them down the bluff into the river, destroyed large amounts of stores, burnt their buildings and retired.

The Federal forces, jubilant with their easy conquest, and spared the horrors of bloodshed, took possession of the place in a spirit of cheerful triumph. There was no drawback to the rejoicing—no dead to bury, no wounded to send their groans through the cheering shouts that rang far and wide from under the stars and stripes when they were once more flung to the wind. Columbus was drawn back to the Union almost without an effort.

BATTLE OF PEA RIDGE, ARK.
March 6–8, 1862.

One of the most brilliant events of the war west of the Mississippi, was the battle of Pea Ridge, which lasted from the 6th to the 8th of March, and crowned the national army with a splendid victory, after a long and toilsome pursuit of the rebels.

After the removal of General Fremont from the command in Missouri, the army which he had led from Jefferson City to Springfield, made a retrograde movement, falling back on Rolla, St. Louis and the towns on the line of the Missouri river. As was to be anticipated, the consequence of this retreat was the return of General Price, with his forces, and the reoccupation of the whole of Southern Missouri by the insurgents. They remained in possession of the field until February, when a new national force, under Generals Curtis, Sigel and Ashboth entered the field and advanced rapidly in pursuit of the retreating enemy. The rebels fell back, to avoid a general engagement, and evacuated Springfield, on the 12th of February, near which, in a brief skirmish, General Curtis' army encountered and defeated them. On the morning of the 13th General Curtis entered the town, and restored the national flag to its place. Price left about six hundred sick men behind him, and large quantities of forage and wagons. He expected that the Federal army would remain several days at least in Springfield, to give the troops rest, satisfied with the re-occupation of this valuable position.

But General Curtis was not a man to sleep upon his arms. On the morning of the 14th, he resumed his pursuit, and continued his march to Crane's Creek, about twenty-two miles from Springfield. He pressed closely upon the enemy, and on the 17th had another encounter with them at Sugar Creek. This protracted pursuit of three weeks, at an average rate of twenty miles a day, is remarkable in the history of warfare. But like most western men, General Curtis had learned the art of war, and the expediency of energetic action to some purpose. He had given up his seat in Congress when the war broke out, and took the field, forgetting politics and every thing else in a burning love of his country. With such men long marches and hard fighting is the business of war. They shrink from nothing but inaction.

Both armies had now reached the soil of Arkansas. The rebels being rapidly reinforced by regiments which had been stationed in that State and the Indian Territory, General Price was in a better position to give battle. Upon mature deliberation, General Curtis selected Sugar Creek as the best position he could take to withstand any attack which might be made upon him. The enemy had, in the mean time, taken up his position in the locality of Cross Hollow, which was peculiarly adapted to his mode of warfare. But this was not long permitted, for on learning that the Union troops were turning their flank by way of Osage Spring, Price's followers again decamped in hot haste, leaving behind a considerable quantity of supplies and munitions of war. By this time the lines of the Union army extended nearly ten miles. The right was under General Sigel, resting at the Osage Springs, and the left under Colonel Carr, extending to Cape Benjamin. Colonel Carr's headquarters were at Cross Hollows.

Having abandoned Cross Hollows, General Price took up a fresh position in the Boston Mountains, a high range that divides the waters of the White Mountains and Arkansas, where every effort was made to rally the dispirited rebels and augment the ranks of his command. Here it was that he was reinforced by Generals McCullough, Pike and Van Dorn. These combined armies were estimated at thirty-five thousand men.

Matters remained comparatively quiet until the 5th of March, when General Curtis received information that the rebels were advancing to give battle. The information proved correct, and the 6th, 7th and 8th will long be held in remembrance as the anniversary of one of the bloodiest conflicts of the war.

Pea Ridge is in the extreme northwest part of Arkansas, situated in Benton, the corner county of the State. A range of hills—a spur of the Ozark Mountains—sweeps from Missouri into this corner of the State, and from thence branches into the Indian Territory, where the section known as the Boston Mountains is found. Sugar Creek, where the battle commenced, is situated close to Bentonville, the capital of the county on the north. Pea Ridge is also adjacent to the same town, and forms a part of the mountain range just described.

At this time it became evident to the several commanders that a general contest was inevitable. A decisive combat was, in fact, desired by both of the opposing forces. General McIntosh, confident of success with his large army, under the leadership of Price, McCulloch, Pike and Van Dorn, believed that he could strike a fatal blow at the Union cause west of the Mississippi, by the annihilation of the Federal army. General Curtis, on the other hand, was not less anxious for a contest, even at the fearful disadvantage offered him. With his keen discrimination, he saw the glorious results of a defeat of the four rebel chieftains united against him. Should he prove successful in the almost desperate encounter, it would prove the destruction of the rebel forces in the two States, and leave a clear field for future operation. Should he fail—but no true general even thinks of that after he has made up his mind to fight.

At this time his force was divided into three divisions, as follows:
GENERAL SIGEL'S DIVISION.—*First Brigade, Colonel Gruesel.*—36th Illinois, Col. Gruesel; 25th Illinois, Col. Coler; 44th Illinois, Col. Knoblesdorf *Second Brigade, Col. Osterhaus.*—12th Missouri, Col. Osterhaus; 17th Missouri, Col. Hassendeufel; 2d Missouri Col. Schaeffer. *Third Brigade, Col. Asboth.*—3d Missouri, Col. Friala; Illinois Cavalry, (one battalion,) Capt's. Jenks and Smith; 3d Iowa Cavalry.

GENERAL DAVIS'S DIVISION.—*First Brigade, Col. Benton.*—8th Indiana, Col. Benton; 18th Indiana, Col. Patterson; 22d Indiana, Col. Hendricks. *Second Brigade, Col. Julius White.*—59th Illinois, Col. Fredericks; 37th Illinois, Col. Burnes; Missouri Cavalry, (battalion,) Maj. Broen; 2d Ohio, Battery, Col. Catin; 1st Missouri Light Artillery, one battery.

GENERAL CARR'S DIVISION.—*First Brigade, Col. Dodge.*—4th Iowa, Lieut.-Col. Galighan; 35th Illinois, Col. G. A. Smith; 24th Missouri, (battalion,) Maj. Weston. *Second Brigade, Col. Vandenier.*—9th Iowa, Lieut.-Col. Herron; 25th Missouri, Col. Phelps; 9th Iowa, battery, Capt. Hayden; 1st Iowa, battery, Lieut. David. *Third Brigade, Col. Ellis*—1st Missouri Cavalry, Col. Ellis; 3d Illinois, ———; 6th Missouri, battalion, Maj. Wright.

Opposed to the forces of General Curtis, just enumerated, the rebel army had fully ten thousand Missouri State troops under Major-General Price; six to eight regiments of Arkansas troops under General McCulloch; six regiments of Texans under General Earl Van Dorn; three thousand Cherokee, Choctaw and Seminole Indians under Colonel Albert Pike, all under command of Major-General McIntosh. Besides those mentioned, there were two or three regiments of Louisiana troops and companies of Mississippi and Alabama regiments under the command of their respective colonels, majors and captains.

Upon this occasion the Union troops were well armed and equipped, while the weapons of the rebels varied in character and effectiveness. Many of them were excellent, embracing Minie rifles, Enfield muskets, and good United States muskets. The larger portion, however, were hunting rifles and shot-guns. The rebels had eighty-two field pieces, twenty of which were rifled, while General Curtis' forces had but forty-nine; nearly all, however, were of superior manufacture and destructive power.

On the evening of the 5th of March, the scouts of General Sigel brought in word, that large forces of the rebel cavalry were on the Pineville road at Osage Spring. Sigel was evidently in a bad position, and on the following day he commenced moving back, his pickets being driven in before he could get his wagon train in motion. His route lay a few miles to the north, when he struck the bed of Sugar creek, along which he travelled six miles. It was there the battle first began. General Sigel with two battalions of Missouri infantry and a squadron of cavalry formed the rear guard of his division, and were delayed by the train which moved slowly along the rough roads. He determined not to desert a single wagon to the rebels, although by so doing, he could have easily reached the main body of the Union forces.

The enemy made his appearance with 4,000 cavalry, at about 10 o'clock in the morning, a few miles out of Bentonville, and immediately commenced the attack by a desperate charge. Sigel had with him nearly 1,000 men. He sent forward two hundred infantry to prevent the enemy cutting him off, and with the remainder he received the whole of the vast army. He ordered his men to stand firm and take good aim. The teams were put upon good pace, and the enemy came rushing on in several lines. The horsemen on the flanks and infantry in the rear awaited their approach until within about 200 yards, when they delivered a terrible volley of Minie balls into the rebel ranks, which had the effect of throwing them into temporary confusion. In a few minutes the leaders succeeded in getting them into something like order. This time they came up to close quarters. The same volley, succeeded by a second and a third, greeted them. The enemy came on in crowds, and their cavalry closed all around the little band, notwithstanding horses and riders were falling thick and fast before its steady fire. General Sigel rode undismayed along the whole line, inspiring his men. Some of the cavalry on the flank had succeeded in getting across the road so cutting the train in two. Here the enemy set up a shout of triumph.

It was short lived. In a minute more the bayonets of the Union men had done their work, leaving hundreds of dead and wounded in their tracks. The enemy was driven off, broken and dismayed. Galled and maddened at the repulse, his scattered ranks could be seen re-forming to renew the attack.

The column was yet seven miles from the encampment. A dispatch had been sent forward to General Curtis, explaining the position and asking for assistance. It was hardly possible that the messenger could have been captured. The enemy was advancing on the road and along the ridges enclosing the stream. At about two o'clock a second attack was made and desperately carried forward. The rebel cavalry spurred their horses right on to the irresistible bayonets, delivering their load of buckshot from their miscellaneous guns, and then brandishing huge knives, which every one of them carried in place of sabres.

They surrounded the rear guard a second time, and for a few minutes friend could hardly be distinguished from foe. The dense smoke enveloped the whole of the combatants, and for some time it was doubtful whether any of the Union band survived. The faithful Germans never faltered for a moment. Their gallant leader struck down a dozen who clamored for his life, and hewed his way through a line of enemies to rejoin his command. The bayonets proved the invincibility of the Union infantry against horsemen. The foe retired a second time, and for an hour could not be induced to return. By this time the advance, which had been constantly skirmishing with the rebel cavalry, announced reinforcements in sight, and a faint cheer went up, which was re-echoed by the troops from the camp. A third and last attempt was made to capture the train. It failed, and the enemy withdrew about 3½ o'clock.

General Sigel reached camp at 4½ o'clock, to receive the congratulations of the whole army. His loss in the entire march was estimated at 60 killed and 200 wounded, many of whom fell into the hands of the rebels, it being impossible to bring them off.

The night of the 6th of March was passed in a state of suspense. The houses in the valley had been appropriated as hospitals, and a strong force posted on the hill on the south bank of the creek under Colonel Carr, with General Sigel occupying the ridge on the north side, while Colonel Davis occupied the centre, near the crossing. The enemy, it was supposed, would naturally make the attack from the Fayetteville road, and the baggage trains and hospitals had been placed to the rear of the lines. During the night the manifestations showed conclusively that he was approaching in great strength by the road leading from Bentonville to Keatsville, thus getting to the flank and rear. This road lies, after crossing Sugar creek, over a high table land, called Pea Ridge. It extends from the stage road westwardly some eight miles along the right bank of Sugar creek.

The ridge is covered with a growth of stunted oaks, and a sprinkling of larger growth, called post-oaks. Three or four farms were located upon the ridge two miles west of the road, to which the name of Leetown has been given. It was near these farms that the principal part of the fighting took place.

Thursday night, March 6th, was clear and cold; the reflection of the enemy's camp fires could be seen stretching along for miles to the right. On the Fayetteville road the Union pickets reported nothing unusual. Several Union field pieces had been placed in position, sweeping that road. The men slept on their arms, that is each man lay on the ground in line of battle with his musket by him, ready for action at a moment's notice. A strong picket guard was extended for a quarter of a mile beyond the lines, and the Federal soldiers awaited the break of day with premonitions that the morrow's sun would be the last which would rise for many of them.

The evidences were very clear on the morning, that a strong force had been posted on the Fayetteville road, thus standing directly between the Union forces and their next line at Cassville, completely cutting off communication with the outer world. The line of battle was changed. Colonel Carr was sent back along the Fayetteville road, two miles, with his right resting on Cross Timber Hollows at the head of Beaver Creek, a tributary of Big Sugar Creek, immediately facing the rebel batteries on the side of Elkhorn tavern. General Davis, with the central division, was posted on the top of Pea Ridge, leaving Sigel to cover the camp with his left wing resting on Sugar Creek. In this position things stood when the rebels opened the fight with artillery on the extreme right, from a very advantageous position at the distance of a mile. The Federal batteries soon replied. The fight raged in front of Colonel Carr's division from 10 to 11 o'clock, when another battery was ordered up to his support, for he was hotly pressed. The left, as yet, had not been menaced. General Sigel felt confident that the enemy might be expected to make a descent from the south side, and it was deemed indispensable to keep the men ready for action in that direction.

ATTACK OF COLONEL OSTERHAUS' MISSOURI CAVALRY ON THE TEXAS RANGERS.

Colonel Osterhaus was sent with his brigade in the morning along the high land in the direction of Leestown, where he intercepted the reinforcements of the enemy. This was one of the most spirited and successful attacks of the battle, and resulted in a complete diversion of the enemy from the overpowered forces of Colonel Carr, on the Fayetteville road.

The Union cavalry penetrated along the main ridge beyond the road by which the enemy had advanced, and were on the point of seizing some of his wagons when a brigade of rebel cavalry and infantry attacked them. Then followed one of the most sanguinary contests that ever has been recorded between cavalry. Most of the fighting was done at close quarters. Pistols and carbines having been exhausted, sabres were brought into requisition. The rattle of steel against steel, sabres against muskets and cutlasses, was terrific. The rebels were Texas Rangers, and fought like demons. The slaughter was awful. The Missouri cavalry cleaving right and left, left winrows of dead and wounded in front of their horses. The enemy fell back in dismay, the valorous Federals pursued them along the road for a mile, when they opened a battery upon the mass of friends and foes, plowing through them with solid shot and shell. Colonel Osterhaus had succeeded in his attempt, and retired, bringing off his dead and wounded in safety.

Meantime the contest was raging furiously on the extreme right on both sides of the Fayetteville road. The First and Second Iowa batteries, planted at an eminence overlooking the declivity in the road, were plying shrapnel and canister into the ranks of the enemy, who appeared in immense numbers on all sides, as if to surround the right of the Union line, and thus completely environ them. In order to defeat this object, a severe struggle took place for the occupancy of a rising knoll on the east side of the road. The enemy gained upon the Federals, and it was not until the men were half stricken down that they yielded the point. Word had been passed back to General Curtis that the enemy was pressing severely on the right flank, and the Union forces were sent back. The section of a battery had been left on the hill, and the enemy was now turning it upon the Union lines. Colonel Carr, fearing that no reinforcements would arrive, collected his strength, and mustered his entire force for a last desperate charge, resolved to retake the position or perish in the attempt. A heavy firing on the centre, and a cheer from the advancing division of General Davis favored the effort. The troops marched up to the battery amid a storm of shot from their own guns, and, after a desperate hand-to-hand struggle, finally drove the enemy down the ravine, in hopeless confusion. Colonel Carr received a wound in the arm, but remained on the field.

During the night a sharp fire of artillery had been kept up upon the left, and from two Missouri batteries on the centre, under Colonels Patterson and Fiala. The enemy had made frequent attempts to gain a position nearer the Union lines, and succeeded in getting so near that the balls from their guns would strike near the tents and baggage wagons. Towards night the enemy made an attempt to break the Federal centre, but the timely support of a brigade of General Sigel and a section of artillery promptly repulsed them. The night closed with skirmishing and sharpshooting.

Occasionally the report of a musket could be heard during the night, then a second, and an interval of silence. But few of the soldiers slept. The communication with Springfield was cut off, and Union messengers were falling into the enemy's hands. As yet the Federals had gained little advantage, and with desperate fighting had only succeeded in repelling equally desperate attacks. Nothing but hard fighting could avail them. Filled with these thoughts, the soldiers solemnly gave their wives and children into each others' charge, no one being aware who the survivor would be. Young men talked in low voices of the loved ones at home, fathers, mothers, sisters, sweethearts—and messages full of tender pathos were left to be given after death. It was indeed, an anxious, mournful night.

The fight on the morning of the 8th, commenced by a salute from the Union batteries on the extreme right. General Asboth, with a regiment of infantry and a battalion of cavalry, had been sent to the support of Colonel Carr, while General Sigel was moving up to a fresh position on the ridge near Leestown. The enemy was unprepared for this sudden and vigorous assault, and fled after a short and spiritless resistance. They ran, leaving four pieces of artillery behind them, and a fifth was afterwards taken in the pursuit. The enemy was being turned by the left flank, General Sigel pushing boldly after him. An hour or more was spent in contesting the possession of a spot on Cox's farm, when the rebels fell back to the hollow.

A pause ensued, when the right, under General Davis, moved along, and after a sharp contest of half an hour, in which the rebel General McIntosh, was killed, the enemy began to retreat to Cross Timber Hollow. The whole line was then ordered forward. The rebels attempted to make a stand on the next hill, but the Union artillery played upon them with disastrous effect. The enemy on the road near the tavern refused to be moved. General Asboth, with a large column of cavalry, was sent round to outflank them, when another desperate conflict ensued between the Union cavalry and the Texas and Louisiana troops. The Indians also took part in it, but beyond shrieks and yells their influence was not felt. The batteries of the enemy fired chains, spikes, pieces of bar-iron, and solid shot. It was evident that his canister and shell were exhausted. Now the Federal batteries on the right were ordered to the front. Taking a position within five hundred yards, they poured in an incessant shower of grape, canister and shell for twenty minutes. A general bayonet charge was then ordered, and the Union line rushed down the valley and ascended the opposite hill. A cheer went up from them as they delivered volley after volley into the enemy's ranks. The rebels cheered also; and it was evident that they doubled the Union forces, from the overwhelming shout that rang up from their lines.

At this time General Sigel was carrying everything before him on the extreme left. The foe was running, and the Union men catching the inspiration of the moment rushed on in pursuit. Before one o'clock the rout was complete.

To the westward of Pea Ridge there was a wide strip of timber which had been blown down by a hurricane the previous summer. Across this swarth of uprooted trees, which were larger and denser in the low lands, the enemy's cavalry and artillery attempted to retreat, and were mercilessly pelted with shell. The panic was overwhelming, and their defeat decided. Muskets, clothing, and shot-guns were strewn along the woods. Horses roamed about in wild droves. The cries of the cavalry men and the yells of the Indians, with the groans of the wounded, surpassed all description. Caissons overturned, wagons broken down, and horses dying and dead strewed the whole road. Thirteen cannon, 6 and 12-pounders, were taken in all, besides thousands of shot-guns and loads of provisions.

It was in this position of affairs that General Price with a detachment of his army had, in his attempt to make a stand on the Keatsville road, caught the contagion of his fleeing comrades, and betook himself to the northward, Colonel Carr and General Asboth keeping closely after him.

This was probably one of the most hotly contested battles of the war, when every thing is taken into consideration, and it is worthy of remark that few officers were wounded, although at all times exposed even to recklessness. For three days the fighting continued, the men only resting during the darkness, to renew the attack with the first light, and even then were but partially allowed to slumber. Pea Ridge will never be forgotten while we have a history.

The Federal loss in killed, wounded and missing, was 1,351. That of the rebels about 2,000. Generals McIntosh and McCulloch were killed.

BATTLE OF NEWBERN, N. C.
March 14, 1862.

Newbern, in Craven county, N. C., is situated at the confluence of the Trent and Neuse rivers, which flow into Pamlico Sound, from whence, through Ocrakoke Inlet, communication is had with the Atlan-

BATTLE OF NEWBERN, N. C., MARCH 14, 1862

tia. It is eighty-miles N. E. of Wilmington, and one hundred from Raleigh; has a population of six thousand, and considerable commerce.

The importance of Newbern was early appreciated by the rebels, who adopted vigorous means for its defence. The approaches to the city on the south bank of the Neuse, the only available route of an assailant, were defended by formidable earthworks, and, as a protection against gunboats, a line of vessels, backed by a *chevaux-de-frise*, was placed in the channel, commanded by heavy batteries.

The expedition designed to operate against Newbern sailed from Hatteras Inlet on the 12th of March, the land forces under General Burnside, and the naval forces under Commander Rowan. The land forces consisted of the brigades of Generals Foster, Reno and Parke, much reduced, however, by regiments left behind at Roanoke Island and Hatteras Inlet, and not exceeding eight thousand men. They were supported by McCook's battery of boat howitzers, three companies of marines, and a detachment of the Union Coast Guard. The distance from Hatteras Inlet to the entrance of Pamlico Sound is twenty-three miles; thence, through the sound and up the river to Newbern, about fifty miles.

Early on the morning of the 12th the entire force started for Newbern, and that night anchored off the mouth of Slocum's Creek, some eighteen miles from Newbern, where General Burnside decided to make a landing. The landing commenced by seven o'clock the next morning, under cover of the naval fleet, and was effected with the greatest enthusiasm by the troops. Many, too impatient for the boats, leaped into the water, and waded waist deep to the shore; then, after a toilsome march through the mud, the head of the column moved within a mile and a half of the enemy's stronghold, at eight P. M., a distance of twelve miles from the point of landing, where they bivouacked for the night, the rear of the column coming up with the boat howitzers about three o'clock next morning. This detention was caused by the shocking condition of the roads, consequent upon the heavy rain that had fallen during the day and the whole of the night. It required a whole regiment to drag the eight pieces which had been landed from the navy and the vessels of General Burnside.

By signals agreed upon, the naval vessels, with the armed vessels carrying the land forces, were informed of each others' progress, and were thereby enabled to assist the march by shelling the road in advance.

At daylight on the morning of the 14th, an advance of the entire division was ordered. General Foster's brigade marched up the main country road to attack the enemy's left; General Reno up the railroad, to attack their right, and General Parke was to follow General Foster and attack the enemy in front, with instructions to support either or both brigades.

On the morning of the 14th, at seven o'clock, the column of General Reno, on the railroad, was the first to move, the Twenty-first Massachusetts, as the right flank regiment, leading the advance. The regiment had not proceeded far before it saw a train of cars standing on the track. In front of the locomotive, on a platform car, a large rifled gun was placed in position to rake the road. The men advanced at the double-quick and poured in a volley with such accuracy of aim that the enemy, who had already rolled the gun and caisson off the car, did not stop to unload the carriage, but ran into the intrenchments, and the train was backed towards Newbern, leaving the platform-car standing on the track. The Twenty-first had got within short range of the enemy's earthworks, but now fell back, and, forming line of battle in the woods, opened fire. The Fifty-first New York was moved to the left and ordered forward to engage a series of redans, the Ninth New Jersey occupying the left of the line, and the Fifty-first Pennsylvania held in reserve, in rear of the Ninth, a little to the left.

Meanwhile General Foster's brigade had advanced up the main road to the clearing, when the Twenty-fourth Massachusetts was sent into the woods to the right of the road, and opening a heavy fire on the enemy commenced the action of the first brigade. The Twenty-seventh was sent to their left to support them, and, news being received that the enemy were trying to outflank the Federals on the right, the Twenty-fifth was sent to resist the movement. The Twenty-third being moved to the front next in line of battle, opened fire upon the enemy, which was replied to by very heavy volleys, and a cannonade from a park of field-pieces behind the breastwork. The very first cannon-shot killed Lieutenant-Colonel Henry Merritt of the Twenty-third. General Foster's line of battle was completed by moving the Tenth Connecticut to the extreme left, a position which they were compelled to maintain under the most discouraging disadvantages. The ground was very wet, swampy, and cut up into gulleys and ravines, which opened toward the enemy, offering no protection from his fire.

General Parke's brigade, which had followed the first brigade up the main road, was placed in line between the Tenth Connecticut and Twenty-first Massachusetts, the Fourth Rhode Island holding the right of line, the Eighth Connecticut the next place, the Fifth Rhode Island, next, and the Eleventh Connecticut on the left. The line of battle was now complete, the Twenty-fourth Massachusetts on the extreme right, and the Fifty-first Pennsylvania at the extreme left, and extended more than a mile. The naval battery was in position at the centre, with Captain Bennett's and Captain Dayton's rifles alongside, and were all worked with the greatest gallantry throughout the day.

The fire of the enemy was now telling so severely upon the Twenty-first that Colonel Clark ordered the regiment forward on a double quick, and at the head of four companies entered the breastworks from the railroad track in company with General Reno, and the colors were taken into a frame house which stood near, and waved from the roof. The men at the nearest guns seeing the movement, abandoned their pieces and fled, and the four companies being formed again in line of battle, charged down the line upon the battery. Colonel Clark mounted the first gun, waved the colors, and had nearly reached the second when two full regiments of the enemy emerged from a grove of young pines and advanced upon his men, who, seeing that they were likely to be captured or cut to pieces, leaped over the parapet and retired to their position in the woods.

On being driven from the battery, Colonel Clark informed Colonel Rodman of the Fourth Rhode Island of the state of affairs inside, and that officer decided upon a charge with the bayonet. His regiment had been firing, like the rest of the line, by companies and otherwise. When the command was given to charge, they advanced at the double-quick directly up to the battery, firing as they ran, and entered at the right flank, between a brick-yard and the end of the parapet. With a steady line of cold, sharp steel, the Rhode Islanders bore down upon the enemy, and, routing them, captured the whole battery, with its two flags, and planted the stars and stripes upon the parapet. The Eighth Connecticut, Fifth Rhode Island and Eleventh Connecticut, coming up to their support, the rebels fled with precipitation, and left the Union troops in undisputed possession.

General Reno's brigade were still attacking the redans and small battery on the right of the railroad, and the firing was very heavy. The Twenty-first was engaging the battery of five small pieces, the Fifty-first New York the first of the redans, and the Ninth New Jersey the next two. The Fifty-first Pennsylvania was still in reserve, drawn up in a hollow or ravine, from which they would move up to the top of the eminence, discharge their volleys, and retire to such cover as the inequalities of ground might furnish. General Reno, becoming impatient at the loss of life which his regiments, particularly that of Colonel Ferrero, was suffering, urged that regiment to advance as soon as possible; so Lieutenant-Colonel Potter took a color over the brow of the hill into another hollow, and from thence charged up an acclivity and over brushwood and abattis into the redan. The Fifty-first Pennsylvania was ordered up to participate in the decisive charge of the whole brigade upon the line of redans, and passing through the Fifty-first New York, as it was lying on the ground after having exhausted all its ammunition, came under the heaviest fire, and without flinching or wavering moved to its place, and rushed, with the other regiments, upon the defences of the enemy.

The movement of Colonel Hartranft's regiment was executed splendidly, and proved a complete success.

The movement of the Third brigade was supported by a charge of the Fourth Rhode Island from the captured main battery upon the works which were being assailed, and the enemy, already demoralized by the breaking of their centre, fell back before the grand charge upon the left and front of their position, and fled in confusion. On the extreme right the brave Twenty-fourth and its supporting regiments had been advancing inch by inch, standing up against the enemy's musketry and cannonade without faltering, and almost at the time when the Fourth Rhode Island charged in at the right flank, the colors of the Twenty-fourth were planted on the parapet at the left, and the whole of the First brigade poured into the fortification. The whole line of earthworks was now in Union hands, and the cheers of the Federal men, from one end of it to the other, broke out with fresh spirit as each new regimental color was unfurled on the parapet.

The approaches to Newbern were defended by a line of water batteries or forts communicating with extensive field fortifications. The lower fort is about six miles from the city; the next communicates with the unfinished batteries and breastworks; the others were distributed about equal distances along the shore. The line of fortifications attacked and stormed was some three miles in extent. At the river bank a hexagonal fort, or water battery, with a large bomb-proof and thirteen heavy guns, commanded in addition, the river approach. By means of pivot carriages the cannon could be turned upon an advancing land force, and even sweep the line of breastworks itself in case the garrison should be driven out. From the fort to the centre of the line a well-made breastwork extended, with a deep moat in front. At the centre was a bastion and sallyport, after which the breastwork was continued to the railroad embankment, which was used as a means of defence. Beyond the railroad, but completely protecting the right flank of the main battery, was a small battery, of irregular shape, communicating with a system of thirteen redans, or rifle-pits, each pair of which were constructed on a knoll rising between ravines, the conformation of the ground furnishing in itself a most admirable basis for field-works. The locality was chosen with rare judgment, and all that engineering skill could accomplish was done to make these fortifications an impassable barrier to hostile troops. From the railroad westward, a swift, deep brook, with muddy bottom, and a wide border of swamp on both sides, ran in front of the redans; and on the side of approach, the timber was so very heavy, that, when felled, it presented a barricade which would seem enough of itself to stop any army of French Zouaves. On the brow of each mound, brushwood had been piled with regularity to the height of four feet in front of the redans, rendering it extremely difficult to take them by assault from the front. The redans were constructed of heavy timbers, covered with at least five feet thickness of earth, while an interior ditch say three feet in depth gave complete protection to the garrison from volleys of musketry, or discharges of grape and canister shot.

Inside, the battery presented a most revolting appearance. Beneath the parapet, in the ditch, on the open ground under the gun-carriages, lay the dead and mangled bodies of rebels. On every side lay heaped the bleeding carcasses of artillery horses, killed by musket or rifle balls. Here and there a broken gun-carriage, or caisson, lay tilted into the mud. Stores of all kinds were scattered over the ground or trampled in the black mire. Muskets with broken stocks or bent barrels were thrown about in every direction. It was a scene of wild confusion on all sides.

It was not known with certainty that there was no other battery erected formidable as this still further up the road; but thinking it best to increase the panic which had seized upon the enemy, General Burnside ordered an advance. General Foster immediately sent forward the Twenty-fourth, Twenty-fifth, Twenty-seventh, and the whole brigade by the straight road. In the charge on the rifle-pit about one hundred rebels, among them the Colonel of the Thirty-third North Carolina and a number of commissioned officers, were captured. When these were secured in an old brick-kiln and placed under guard, Generals Reno and Parke moved their brigades after General Foster's, the former going before up the railroad track and the latter by the country road. The march to Newbern was unobstructed, the enemy having apparently all he could do to get away on any terms, and early in the afternoon the Union forces reached the bank of the river immediately opposite the city. Long before they came in sight of it, however, dense volumes of smoke were seen rising in that direction, and the suspicion that the place had been fired by the enemy was fully realized when its steeples and houses came in view. Newbern had been fired in seven different places, and if the wind had not mercifully subsided there would hardly have been a house left standing by nightfall. The splendid railroad bridge, seven hundred yards long, had been set on fire by a scow load of turpentine which had drifted against it, and the great structure was wrapped in one grand sheet of flame. Preparations were made by General Foster to move his forces across the river. This was accomplished by the assistance of a light draft stern-wheel steamer which had been captured with four or five small side-wheel boats by the naval gunboats, which by this time were quite up to the city wharves.

To the eastward of the city a very large rebel camp, with barracks and tents, was found deserted and taken possession of. Stragglers from different regiments wandered through the city and committed some acts of depredation; but were speedily checked by a strong Provost-Guard appointed by the commanding General.

The forts taken were Fort Dixie, 4 guns; 1 100-pound rifle and 3 32-pounders. Fort Thompson, 12 guns; 2 100-pound rifle and 10 32 pounders. Fort Ellis, 8 guns; 1 8-inch columbiad, 1 100-pounder, under casemate, and 6 32-pounders. Fort Lane, 4 guns; 2 100-pounders and 2 32-pounders. Two forts, at the foot of the city, mounting 2 guns each. Three guns on a car and two lying on the wharf.

The Federal loss was about 100 killed and 450 wounded. That of the rebels, who were protected by their fortifications, about 220 in killed and wounded. About 300 prisoners were taken by Lieutenant Hammond of the gunboat Hetzel, who was serving one of the guns of McCook's battery.

NAVAL OPERATIONS.

The naval operations under Commander Rowan, were conducted with great skill and success. The navigation was impeded in every possible way by the rebels. Sunken vessels closed the main channels at all accessible points, while torpedoes, chevaux-de-frise and fire-rafts threatened destruction on every side. Captain Rowan hoisted his pennant on Thursday morning on board the steamer Delaware. At half-past eight A. M., the gunboats commenced shelling the woods in the vicinity of the proposed place of landing, taking stations at intervals along the shore to protect the advance of the troops. At half-past nine A. M., the troops commenced landing, and at the same time six naval boat howitzers with their crews, under the command of Lieutenant R. S. McCook, of the Stars and Stripes, were put on shore to assist the attacks. The army commenced to move up the beach at half-past eleven A. M., the debarkation of troops still continuing. In the mean time the vessels were slowly moving up, throwing shell in the woods beyond. At a quarter-past four, P. M., the first of the enemy's batteries opened fire on the foremost of the gunboats, which was promptly returned at long range. The troops were now all disembarked, and steadily advancing without resistance. At sundown the firing was discontinued, and the fleet came to anchor in position to cover the troops on shore. At half-past six, A. M., Friday, 14th instant, there was heard a continuous firing of heavy guns and musketry inland, and immediately the fleet commenced throwing shells in advance of the position supposed to be held by the Union troops. The fleet steadily moved up, and gradually closed in towards the batteries. The lower fortifications were discovered to have been abandoned by the enemy.

A boat was dispatched to it and the stars and stripes planted on the ramparts. As they advanced, the upper batteries opened fire. The fire was returned with effect, the magazine of one exploding. Having proceeded in an extended line as far as the obstructions in the river would permit, the signal was made to follow the movements of the flagship, and the whole fleet advanced in order, concentrating their fire on Fort Thompson, mounting thirteen guns, on which rested the enemy's land defences. The army, having driven them out of these defences, the forts were abandond. Several of the vessels were slightly injured in passing the barricades of piles and torpedoes which had been placed in the river. The upper battery having been evacuated on the appearance of the combined forces, it was abandoned and subsequently blew up. They now steamed rapidly up to the city. Upon the approach of the Federals, several points of the city were fired by the enemy, where stores had been accumulated. Two small batteries, constructed of cotton bales, and mounting two guns each, were also fired by them. Two small steamers were captured, another having been burned. A large raft, composed of barrels of pitch and bales of cotton, which had been prepared to send down upon the fleet, was fired, and floating against the railroad bridge, set it on fire and destroyed it. In addition to the prizes, a quantity of pitch, tar, and a gunboat, and another vessel on the stooks, several vessels afloat, and an immense quantity of arms and munitions of war, fell into their hands.

Washington, Morehead City and Beaufort were in turn occupied by General Burnside's forces without resistance, and the inhabitants generally evinced a friendly spirit. The commandant of Fort Macon having refused to surrender, preparations were immediately made to invest and capture that place.

THE CAPTURE OF NEW MADRID, MO.
March 14, 1862.

Shortly before the evacuation of Columbus, General Pope, with a large force, was dispatched by the commander of the Department to besiege the town of New Madrid, on the Mississippi river, in the extreme southeastern section of Missouri. This place had been strongly fortified by the rebels, and garrisoned by five regiments of infantry and several companies of artillery. The town is about seven miles below Island No. 10, but owing to a bend in the river, lies nearly west. Its possession was deemed important, in order to advance the Union forces down the Mississippi.

The enemy had one bastioned earthwork, mounting fourteen heavy guns, about half a mile below the town, and another irregular work at

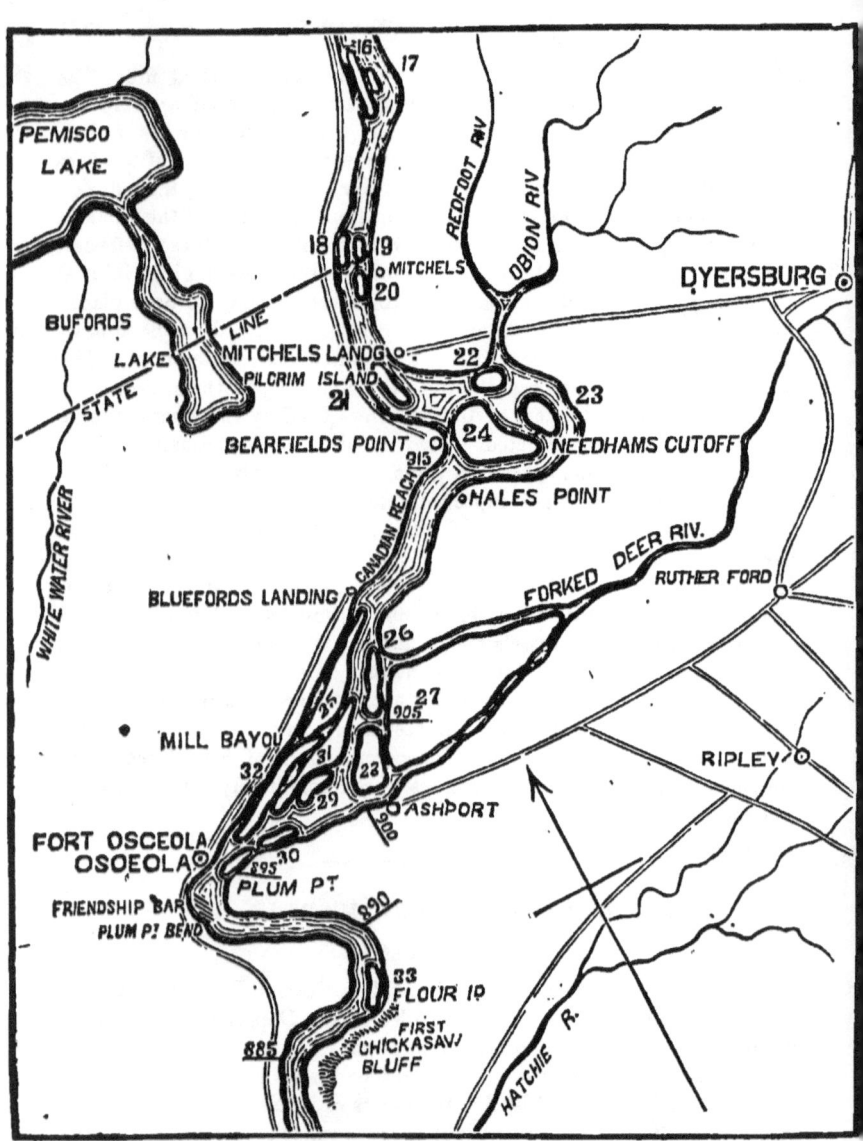

SECTION OF THE MISSISSIPPI RIVER.

SHOWING THE DISTANCES FROM NEW ORLEANS, AND THE ISLANDS BY THEIR NUMBERS.

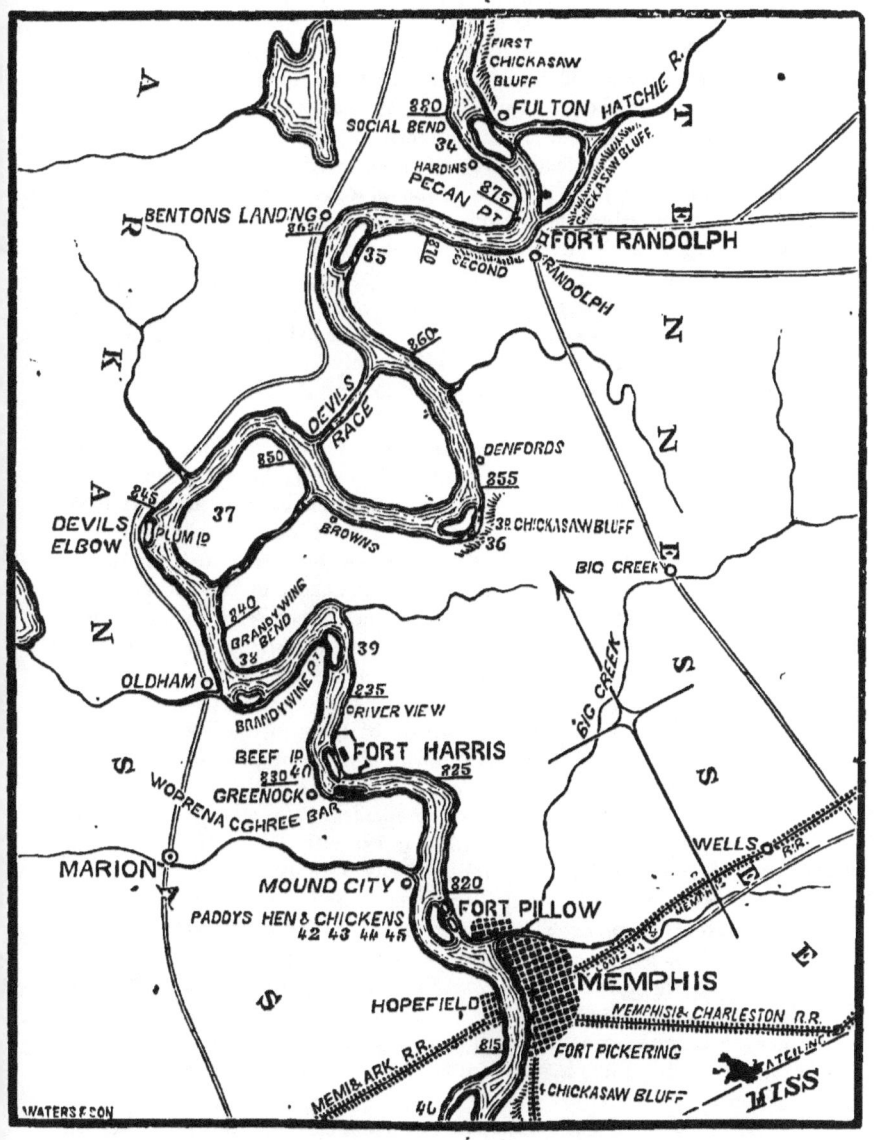

SECTION OF THE MISSISSIPPI RIVER.

SHOWING THE DISTANCES FROM NEW ORLEANS, AND THE ISLANDS BY THEIR NUMBERS.

the upper end of the town, mounting seven pieces of heavy artillery, together with lines of intrenchments between them. Six gunboats carrying from four to eight heavy guns each, were anchored along the shore, between the upper and lower redoubts.

The country is perfectly level for miles around the place, and the river was so high just then, that the gunboats looked directly over the banks; and the approaches to the town for seven miles were commanded by direct and cross fire from at least sixty guns of heavy calibre.

The column under General Pope left Commerce, Mo., on the 27th of February, and, after six days of hard marches through and over the interminable jungles of the great Mingo or Nigger Wool swamp, sat down before the town. They had scarcely been in camp a day before the river batteries opened upon them, forcing the right wing back a few hundred yards further from the river.

Trials and dangers now beset the Federal army, which would have discouraged less brave men. It would not have been difficult to carry the intrenchments, but it must have been attended with heavy loss, and they could not have been held half an hour exposed to the destructive fire of the gunboats. It therefore became necessary to bring down a few heavy guns by land to operate against those of the enemy. They were accordingly sent for; and meantime, forced reconnoissances were pushed over the whole ground, and into several parts of the town. Some brisk skirmishes resulted, in which the enemy invariably retreated precipitately. It was found impossible to induce them to trust any considerable force of their infantry outside of their intrenchments. While awaiting the arrival of the heavy guns, Colonel Plummer, of the Eleventh Missouri, was dispatched to Point Pleasant, eight miles below, with three regiments of infantry, three companies of cavalry, and a field battery of 10-pound Parrott and rifled guns, with orders to make a lodgment on the river bank; to line the bank with rifle-pits for a thousand men, and to establish his artillery in sunk batteries of single pieces between the rifle-pits. This arrangement was made in order to present the smallest possible marks to the shells of the gunboats, and to render futile the use of round shot from their heavy guns. Colonel Plummer, after some cannonading from the gunboats which he found there, succeeded in making a lodgment, constructing his batteries and rifle-pits, and occupying them in sufficient force to maintain them against any open assault.

After repeated and persistent cannonading from the gunboats, the enemy found it impossible to dislodge him. He maintained his position, and effectually blockaded the river to transports, during the whole siege. Meantime, the enemy continued every day to reinforce New Madrid, until, on the 12th, they had nine thousand infantry, besides a considerable force of artillery and nine gunboats. The fleet was commanded by Commodore Hollins, the land forces by Generals McCown, Stewart and Gantt. On the 11th, the Federal siege guns were delivered to Colonel Bissell for his engineer regiment, who had been sent to Cairo. They were at once shipped to Sykestown, reached New Madrid at sunset on the 12th, and were placed in battery during the same night, within eight hundred yards of the enemy's main work, commanding the river above it. They opened fire at daylight on the 13th, just thirty-four hours after they were received at Cairo.

A brigade, consisting of the Tenth and Sixteenth Illinois, under Colonel Morgan, of the Tenth, was detailed to cover the construction of the battery, and to work in the trenches. It was supported by Stanley's division, consisting of the Twenty-seventh and and Thirty-ninth Ohio, under Colonel Groesbeck, and the Forty-third and Sixty-third Ohio, under Colonel Smith. Captain Mower, First United States infantry, with companies A and H of his regiment, was placed in charge of the siege guns.

The enemy's pickets and grand guards were driven in by Colonel Morgan, from the ground selected for the battery. The work was prosecuted in silence, and with the utmost rapidity, until at three o'clock, A. M., two small redoubts connected by a curtain, and mounting four heavy guns were completed, together with rifle-pits in front and on the flanks for two regiments of infantry. The batteries opened as soon as the day dawned, and were replied to in front and on the flanks by the whole of the enemy's heavy artillery on land and water.

The Union guns were served by Captain Mower with vigor and skill. In a few hours they disabled several of the gunboats, and dismounted three of the heavy guns in the enemy's main work. Shortly after the Union batteries opened, one of the 24-pound guns was struck in the muzzle by a round shot from the enemy's batteries and disabled.

The cannonading was continued furiously all day by the gunboats and land batteries of the enemy, but without producing any impression. Meantime the Union trenches were being extended and advanced toward the bank of the river. General Paine now made a demonstration against the rebel intrenchments on the left, supported by Palmer's division. The enemy's pickets and grand guards were driven in, and the skirmishers forced their way close to the main ditch.

A furious thunder storm began about eleven o'clock that night, and continued almost without interruption until morning. Just before daylight, General Stanley was relieved in his trenches with his division by General Hamilton. A few minutes after daylight, a flag of truce approached the batteries, bearing information that the enemy had evacuated his works. Small parties were at once advanced by General

Hamilton to ascertain the truth of this report; and Captain Mower, First United States infantry, with companies A and H of that regiment, were sent forward to plant the United States flag over the abandoned works.

The enemy had made a hasty and precipitate flight. Their dead were found unburied, their suppers stood untouched on the tables—candles were burning in the tents. Private baggage of officers and knapsacks of the men were left behind. Neither provisions nor ammunition were carried off—everything gave evidence of a panic. Artillery, field batteries and siege-guns, amounting to thirty-three pieces; magazines full of fixed ammunition of the best character; several thousand stands of inferior small arms, with hundreds of boxes of musket cartridges; tents for an army of ten thousand men; horses, mules, wagons, intrenching tools, etc., were among the spoils.

Their flight was so sudden that they abandoned their pickets, and gave no intimation to the forces at Island No. 10.

The Union loss was fifty-one killed and wounded. The enemy's loss could not be ascertained. A number of his dead were left unburied, and over a hundred new graves were found.

ISLAND No. 10.

When the necessity of an early evacuation of Columbus became apparent to the rebel leaders, they commenced the fortification of Island No. 10, in the Mississippi river, forty-five miles below Columbus and twenty-six from Hickman. It is located 250 miles below St. Louis and 997 from New Orleans; and when chosen by the secessionists it was deemed impregnable. The earthworks were constructed with great skill, and well calculated to resist any assault which could be made from the river above, while they held undisputed control of the navigation below, and had at their command a formidable fleet of gunboats. New Madrid, on the Missouri shore of the river, a few miles below, was fortified and garrisoned by rebel troops, and they had easy communication and abundant facilities for supplies and reinforcements, if needed.

The energy and perseverance of General Pope, which enabled him, despite the most serious obstacles, to invest and capture the town of New Madrid, was the first note of warning received by the rebels at Island No. 10 that their position was no longer tenable.

The topography of the peninsula on the Tennessee shore, immediately back of the island, where most of the rebel forces were located, is very peculiar; and if the disadvantages of position which the course of events gradually unfolded could have been foreseen, the site would never have been selected. Commencing at a point about a mile and a half above the island is a range of high land, which extends back south-eastwardly to Reelfoot Lake, a distance of four miles. This lake, in the rear of the peninsula, is fifteen miles in length, and terminates in a swamp, which extends south of Tiptonville, a town on the river bank, below the peninsula. The swamp at that time varied in width from one and a half to eight miles, its narrowest point being four miles above Tiptonville, where the rebels had prepared a corduroy road and bridge, as a means of escape from their position, should retreat by land become necessary.

On the 15th of March, the gun and mortar-boats comprising the fleet of Commodore Foote commenced the investment and bombardment of Island No. 10, and the rebel batteries and camps at the adjacent peninsula on the Tennessee shore.

The fleet consisted of eleven gunboats, and twelve mortar-boats, each of the latter carrying one immense mortar, throwing a shell of two hundred and twenty pounds weight a distance of from two to three miles. The Commodore engaged the rebel batteries almost daily for three weeks, deeming it imprudent to risk the destruction of his vessels by close action, as any misfortune to them would have placed all the towns on the Upper Mississippi at the mercy of the armed steamers of the enemy.

The rebels had eighty guns of heavy calibre in the batteries on the island and the adjacent peninsula, while the iron-clad ram Manassas, and a fleet of twenty vessels—gunboats, steamers and transports, were moored under their guns, prepared to act as opportunity or emergency might require.

One or more gunboats would advance to attack a shore battery from the right hand of the river—or engage the water battery on the island, approaching from the left bank. The mortars kept continually changing positions, generally hugging the shore on the left bank where the rebel batteries could not reach them, as they were covered by a promontory, or neck of land, made by the bend of the river; and their fire was kept up so unceasingly, that frequently a mortar-shell was thrown every hour during the night.

At two o'clock on the morning of April 1, a most daring enterprise on the part of Colonel Roberts, of the Forty-second Illinois regiment, was crowned with success. Taking advantage of a severe storm while the elements were raging furiously, and a dreadful hurricane, accompanied with thunder and lightning, was sweeping the earth and driving the vessels from their moorings, he started with forty picked men, in six yawl boats, and with muffled oars rowed towards the upper water battery on Island No. 10, keeping close to the edge of the river bank. The boats, favored by the intense darkness, approached within a few rods of the battery, when a blinding sheet of lightning flashed across the water, revealing the adventurous party to the enemy's sentinels. The dark object looming out from the storm alarmed the sentinels, who fired wildly and at random, fleeing with the first discharge. The Union boats made no reply. A few minutes more brought them to the slope of the earthworks, and the men at once sprung over the parapet. In less than five minutes the huge guns on the battery were securely spiked. They were all of large calibre, consisting of two 64, two 80-pounders and one splendid 9-inch pivot gun. Their desperate work accomplished, the boats returned safely to the fleet, having performed a perilous exploit with wonderful success.

CAPTURE OF ISLAND No. 10 AND THE REBEL ARMY.

After the surrender of the forts at New Madrid, Colonel Bissell's engineer regiment was engaged for four days unspiking guns, changing batteries, and establishing new works. Then they were sent over by General Pope to ascertain whether it would be practicable to establish batteries opposite Island No. 10, and enfilade the rebel works on the Tennessee shore. They spent three days in the swamps, living in their canoes with negroes, but found the project impracticable. Colonel Bissell, however, stated that he could by hard labor get steamboats and flatboats through the woods and bayous, and by that means avoid the batteries on the island, and bring the vessels to New Madrid, whence General Pope's army could be transported to a point nearly opposite, and take all the enemy's works in the rear.

General Pope at once gave him a *carte blanche*, and he sent to Cairo for four steamboats, six flats, and such guns as could be spared. They sent the steamers W. B. Terry, John Trio, Gilmore, and Emma, with the barges, a quantity of lumber, etc., and one eight-inch columbiad and three thirty-two pounders. Tools were not needed, for the regiment carried everything, from the heaviest ropes and screws down to fine steel drills for unspiking guns.

The route was about twelve miles long, of which two traversed were through thick timber, and the remaining ten narrow, crooked bayous, choked up with brush and small trees. They cut their way through, the track being fifty feet wide, of which thirty feet was required for the hulls of the boats. The timber was cut four feet below the surface of the water. In one short stretch they cut seventy-five trees, not one less than two feet through. The machines were rigged from rafts and flats, and each worked by about twenty men. In the first place three large launches went ahead to cut out and clear away the underbrush

BOMBARDMENT OF ISLAND NO. 10.

1. Rebel Floating Battery.—2. Rebel Gunboats and Rams.—3. Federal Gunboats.—4.—Point Pleasant.—5. Island No. 10.—6. Smith's Landing.—7. Mortar Boats.

and driftwood; then three rafts followed, on which were the axe-men, followed by the saws, two large barges, and one of the steamboats. Very large lines were provided to run from the capstan of the steamboat and haul out by snatchblocks what the men could not handle. Men were engaged all the time in the fleet which followed, converting the flatboats into floating batteries.

From the starting point on the river to the levee the distance is about five hundred feet; here the water was shallow and the route full of stumps. It took one whole day to pass this point. Then they cut in the levee. Here the fall was over two feet, and the rush of water tremendous. The largest boat was dropped through with five lines out ahead. Then a corn field, overflowed from a cut in the levee, where a channel was cut by the swift water, and floated them onward nearly a quarter of a mile to the woods. Here was great labor—two straight and long miles to the nearest point in the bayou. It took eight days to get through this distance. Then came Wilson's Bayou, East Bayou, and St. John's Bayou, which empties into the Mississippi at New Madrid. It sometimes took twenty men a whole day to get out a half sunken tree across the bayou; and as none of the rafts or flats could get by, this always detained the whole fleet. The water, after they got in the woods, was about six feet deep, with a gentle current setting across the peninsula. In the East Bayou the current was tremendous, and the boats had to be checked down with heavy head lines. Here they found some obstructions, caused by heaps of driftwood, but a few sturdy blows dislodged some of the logs and sent the whole mass floating down the current.

While the engineers were engaged in this herculean enterprise, the gunboat Carondelet ran safely by the rebel batteries on the island, and reached New Madrid on the night of April 4th. On the succeeding night another boat, the Pittsburg, ran the gauntlet of the enemy's fire unscathed, in time to convoy the transports as they entered the river.

On the 6th of April the two gunboats attacked and destroyed four batteries erected by the rebels on the Tennessee shore. On the 7th, by daylight, the divisions of Generals Paine and Stanley were marched to Tiptonville, fifteen miles down the river from New Madrid. The rebels had retreated in that direction the afternoon before, and it was thought that they were endeavoring to cross over Reelfoot lake. The troops were pushed forward with all possible speed, and at night encamped at Tiptonville and Merriwether's, while a strong force was posted at the only point where by any possibility the rebels could cross the lake, some four miles from the town. Squads of rebel soldiers kept in sight of the Union pickets during the night, and at times would come boldly up and surrender themselves as prisoners of war. At daylight General Pope and staff, and Assistant Secretary-of-War Scott, went down to the locality, and General Pope assumed the full command. It was expected that some resistance would be made, and no one surmised that the enemy, who it was learned had marched over from Island No. 10, had concluded to give himself up. But shortly after sunrise General Pope received a message from the General commanding the Confederates, stating that he had surrendered the island and fortifications to Commodore Foote the night before, and that the forces under his command were ready to follow the "fortunes of war;" and he requested General Pope to receive and march them into camp. General Pope gave directions for the Confederate troops to come into camp and go through the formula. Accordingly about four thousand rebels were marched in and stacked their arms.

On the same day Island No. 10 was surrendered to Commodore Foote, with all its war material; and all the gunboats and transports fell into the hands of the victors.

BATTLE OF WINCHESTER, VA.
March 22, 23, 1862.

On the 21st of March, General Shields, commanding a division of the Fifth Army Corps of the Potomac, under General Banks, was stationed at Winchester, with a force of about seven thousand men. General Jackson, with a rebel force of ten thousand men, and twenty-eight pieces of artillery, was then at Strasburg, ten miles distant, closely scrutinizing the movements of the Federal army, and only awaiting the arrival of General Johnston, his superior, who was daily expected with a much larger force. With these united, they expected to strike a telling blow on the army of General Banks, and thus prevent any combined action on his part with General McClellan.

Not anticipating an immediate attack from General Jackson, General Banks had just left Winchester for Harper's Ferry, and General Williams' division had marched the same day towards Centreville. Of these movements the rebel General was duly notified, as his numerous spies within the Federal lines lost no opportunity of supplying the enemy with full details of all the actions of the Federal commanders.

Though looking for reinforcements from Generals Longstreet and Smith, Jackson determined to attack Shields' troops;—but his attempt to surprise them was frustrated by the vigilance of that officer. Apprehensive that the enemy designed an early advance, General Shields had just completed a hasty reconnoissance to Strasburg, by which he obtained important information of Jackson's numbers and intentions.

This induced him to withdraw most of his men to a position two miles north-east of Winchester, while his pickets extended five miles beyond, on the Strasburg road. The enemy were led to believe that the town was open to their occupation, and that the greater portion of the Federal troops had been withdrawn from the vicinity.

On Saturday afternoon, March 22, about a quarter-past two o'clock, the Federal advanced pickets on the Strasburg road discovered the rebel cavalry, under Colonel Ashby, about half a mile beyond them, reconnoitering the woods on both sides of the turnpike, and steadily advancing. The pickets consisted of a few men of the Fourteenth Indiana infantry at that point, and they fell back half a mile to the hamlet of Kernstown, four miles from Winchester. Steadily did the troopers advance as the Union men wheeled to aim and fire. The first volley sent many rebels reeling from their saddles, and threw the rest into confusion. Before they could be again rallied for a charge, the gallant little band of infantry was beyond their power, without having lost a man killed or wounded. General Shields hearing of the advance of the rebel cavalry, ordered four advanced companies of infantry to rally to the support of the pickets, and hold the rebels in check till he could move down the division. These companies were one from the Maryland First, one from the Twenty-eighth Pennsylvania, one from the Forty-sixth Pennsylvania, and one from the Twenty-eighth New York. Their regiments had marched away under General Williams.

A battery of artillery was also sent forward, and General Shields, after ordering out the division, rode to the front, accompanied by his staff. While engaged in directing the fire of the artillery, a shell from the rebel battery of four guns, which now began to play on them, burst near him, and a splinter from it struck him in the left arm, just above the elbow, fracturing the bone and creating a painful wound. But without heeding it he gave a fresh order to the artillery, and continued on the field till satisfied that all was right.

The Federal division began to arrive in force on the field towards dark; the rebels, perceiving this, did not push their advance, but halted about three miles from Winchester for the night, lighted their camp fires and bivouacked, while the opposing army lay between them and the town.

About ten o'clock on Sunday, reinforcements of five regiments of infantry and two batteries of artillery having arrived from Strasburg, under General Garnett, were welcomed by vociferous and prolonged cheers from their lines. The attack was not long delayed. The enemy advanced his army, which now consisted of sixteen regiments of infantry, numbering eleven thousand men; five batteries of artillery, with a total of twenty-eight field pieces, and three battalions of horse, under Ashby and Stewart. His line of battle extended about a mile on the right of the village of Kernstown, and a mile, and three-quarters on the left of it. The village lay on the road between the rebel right and centre. There is a mud road branching from the turnpike a mile or so from Winchester to the right of the road going towards Strasburg. This road passed through the left of the enemy's centre, and was one of their points of defence. Beyond that is a grove of trees, and farther on, a ridge of hills with a stone wall about breast-high running along its summit. This was the rebel line of offence and defence on the right of the Union line.

The most advanced regiment on the Union side was the Eighth Ohio, of General Tyler's brigade. The rebels made a furious onslaught about half-past ten o'clock, A. M., on Thursday, with the intention of turning the right flank. The Ohio Eighth met them with a deadly fire of rifles. Five times did the enemy emerge from the woods and from behind their stone parapet with vastly superior numbers, and strive in vain to accomplish their object. The Union left wing, consisting of the Thirteenth Indiana, Seventh Ohio and a battery of the Fourth regular artillery, under Captain Jenks, had a feint made on it, while the real attack of the enemy was being directed against the Union right wing. The feint on the left was a heavy fire of artillery posted on both sides of the village and the turnpike, which, however, did trifling damage. The Union battery replied, silencing those of the enemy, though the firing was well maintained for a long time on both sides. The Union centre consisted of the Fourteenth Indiana, the Eighth and Sixty-seventh Ohio, and the Eighty-fourth Pennsylvania. Two artillery batteries belonging to the First Ohio artillery, and the cavalry, consisting of the First Michigan and First Ohio, were drawn up in the rear. The Union right wing was made up of the Fifth and Eighth Ohio regiments and a battery of the First Virginia regiment. The reserves consisted of the Twelfth Indiana, the Thirty-ninth Illinois and a squadron of the Michigan cavalry. General Shields was unable to appear on the field in person, and the command consequently devolved upon Acting-Brigadier Kimble, who led the centre. The right was commanded by Acting-Brigadier General Tyler, while Colonel Sullivan directed the operations on the left.

The battle raged along the whole line with great fury from eleven A. M. till half-past two P. M., when General Shields, who received accounts of the progress of the fight on his couch, ordered the right, where the contest raged the hottest, to charge upon the enemy. That was an awful charge. The left of the enemy prepared desperately to repel the gallant troops, but their rush was irresistible. Previous to this the Union line of battle had been somewhat changed. The Eighty-fourth

Pennsylvania reinforced its right, and also a battery of artillery. The whole Union force now engaged was about six thousand men, while that of the enemy was at the lowest estimate eight thousand. The rebels had also changed their line, and extending both their wings, presented a concave front. They had reinforced their left wing, and the charge to be made by the Union right was all important in its consequences. On it, at three o'clock, depended the fate of the entire battle. Tyler led the charge, sword in hand. The rebels fired from the woods with artillery and small arms, while the Federals advanced against their murderous showers of lead and iron, returning few shots and reserving their fire.

SPLENDID CHARGE OF THE RIGHT WING, UNDER GENERAL TYLER.

Up to this time the armies had not been much nearer to each other than three hundred yards, unless in some few instances. The wood was soon cleared at the point of the bayonet, the Unionists discharging their pieces at twenty and even five yards distance from the rebels, and then dashing at them with the bayonet.

The rebels fought well. They contested the ground foot by foot, and marked every yard of their retreat with blood. They retired behind the stone wall, on the ridge, but the Unionists jumped over, and drove them in the greatest confusion and with fearful slaughter upon their centre. The panic was contagious. Kimble ordered a charge along the whole line, and for a short time the fighting was desperate. The roar of the cannon was no longer heard, unless in occasional bursts, but the rattle of musketry was more deafening than ever.

The rout of the rebels had fairly commenced; two of their guns and four caissons were taken, and though many of them turned and fired again and again at the pursuing host, many more threw away muskets and bayonets without hesitation. Darkness and the extreme fatigue of the Union troops, however, saved them for the time, and the Federals retired about two miles and bivouacked.

At daybreak General Shields ordered the rebel position to be attacked, and the enemy, after replying by a few shots from his artillery, continued his retreat. Meantime General Banks, who had been at Harper's Ferry, arrived, and taking command of the troops in person, continued the pursuit with about ten thousand men, and pressed the rebels beyond Middleburg, cutting off many stragglers. The object was to capture his whole force, if possible. General Williams, with his forces, arrived on the field, too late to participate in the action. They joined in the chase.

The loss of the enemy in killed and wounded was six hundred. The number of prisoners taken was three hundred.

The Union loss in killed was one hundred, and about four hundred wounded. Though the enemy had a much larger force, four pieces of cannon more than the Federals, the selection of fighting ground, and every other advantage, yet all the trophies of the occasion belong to the Union army.

The rebels had an Irish battalion of one hundred and fifty men, of whom forty were killed on the field, and many of the rest wounded. Their commander, Captain Jones, was captured, having lost both eyes by a bullet.

The loss on the Union side was heaviest in the Eighty-fourth Pennsylvania regiment. Of the five companies of three hundred men, in all, engaged, they lost Colonel Murray, a brave officer; one captain, one lieutenant, twenty-three privates and non-commissioned officers killed, and sixty-three wounded. The loss in the Eighth and Fifth Ohio regiments was about seventy-five and sixty, respectively, killed and wounded.

Lieutenant-Colonel Thorburn, of the Third Virginia, was among the wounded. These were the only field-officers killed or wounded in the Union forces.

The battle-field after the struggle was a terrible sight. The night was dark and cold. After the battle the ambulances were busily engaged removing the wounded. The enemy carried off most of their wounded and some of their dead. The wounded were intermingled with the dead, and their sufferings before they were removed to the hospitals were heart-rending. The next day was spent in burying the dead. The ghastly aspect of the field after the wounded were removed, and before the dead were interred, was appalling.

BATTLE OF PITTSBURG LANDING.
April 6–7, 1862.

When the surrender of Forts Henry and Donelson reached Washington and Richmond there was depression among the secessionists and great rejoicing at the North. The news of these events was followed directly by the capture of Nashville and New Madrid, and it became certain to the Confederate leaders that Island No. 10 must soon surrender. Under these untoward events it became imperative that a new strategic point should be at once established beyond reach of the gunboats, that had already produced so much mischief. Beauregard, then in command, selected Corinth as the most promising point for his operations, and a position which would render any attempt of the Federals to cut him off from western Tennessee, or the eastern and southern States, extremely difficult of success. He called on the Governors of Tennessee, Mississippi and Alabama for help, and a prompt response was made. First came Polk from Columbus, then Bragg from Mobile and Pensacola, followed by General A. S. Johnston from Murfreesborough, who took command. After selecting their new line of defence, they commenced fortifying it and diligently concentrated their forces. Generals Hardee, Breckinridge, Sterling Price and Hindman soon came in, and the fortifications made rapid progress.

Corinth is a very important strategical point. It is situated in a branch of the Apalachian range, which diverges from the Alleghany mountains, and forms the uplands and gold-bearing regions of Georgia and Alabama. The village is nearly surrounded by an irregular circle of hills, rising in the north, about four miles distant, with the State line between Tennessee and Mississippi crossing their summit. The Mobile and Ohio railway intersects this ridge through a cut seventy-five feet in depth. Similar cuts, of lesser depth, penetrate the hills on the east, west and south, where the railways enter. Beyond these hills, in the direction of Pittsburg and Savannah, the ground becomes more level, and is generally low and swampy. The topography of the region renders Corinth susceptible of strong defences. The village was formerly called Farmington, and is so mentioned in the gazetteers. It is a post village of Tishomingo county, Mississippi, distant two hundred and sixty-two miles north-east from Jackson, the capital of the State. There were not half a dozen stores in the village, and its population was relatively small. Tishomingo county forms the north-eastern extremity of Mississippi, bordering on Tennessee and Alabama. The Tombigbee river rises in the county; the Tennessee flows along the north-east border, and it is drained by Tuscumbia creek. A large portion of the county is covered with forests of oak, hickory, walnut and pine.

The principal military value of this place consists in the fact that the railroads from Memphis on the west, Columbus, on the north, and Mobile on the south, cross at this point.

About the middle of March Grant's victorious army at Nashville was sent by Halleck to occupy first Savannah, and then Pittsburg Landing, preparatory to the arrival of Buell's Kentucky army, when Halleck intended himself to take the field and move on Corinth.

Pittsburg Landing is situated in Hardin county, Tenn., on the west side of the Tennessee river. It is in itself of little importance, being close to Savannah, which is a flourishing post village of Hardin county, situated on the eastern side of the river. The Landing is about one hundred and twenty miles from Nashville; nearly one hundred miles from Columbia, on the Nashville and Decatur railroad; by a turnpike road, crossing the river at a ferry, about twenty-five miles from Corinth. The country is very wild, the surface rising on both sides of the river in a gradual ascent.

Savannah is the capital of Hardin county. Previous to the rebellion it had been a place of considerable business note. The population in 1853 was only eight hundred, but it had been greatly increased. The area of the county is about six hundred and fifty miles. The Tennessee river flows through it, dividing it into nearly equal parts. The river is navigable for steamboats through the entire county, which has a population of over ten thousand persons, nine-tenths of whom are free.

General Grant proceeded at once to Savannah, where his headquarters were established. The divisions of his army were sent gradually to Pittsburg, and had not all arrived when the assault was made. No defences had been erected, and the possibility of an attack from the Confederates had not been for a moment entertained. On the 5th of April Buell left Nashville and arrived at Savannah the same day. The division of his army under Nelson was on the battle field on the sixth, at five P. M.

The Confederates had for some time intended to attack Grant before Buell could join him, and on hearing of his near approach they hastened the action, without waiting for their own reinforcements. This bold movement was made just one day too late.

POSITION OF THE FEDERAL TROOPS.

Pittsburg Landing is simply a narrow ravine, down which a road passes to the river bank, between high bluffs on either side. There is no town whatever. Two log huts comprise all the signs of habitation visible. Back from the river is a rolling country, cut up with numerous ravines, partially under cultivation, but the greater portion is thickly wooded with large patches of underbrush. From the Landing a road leads directly to Corinth, twenty miles distant. A mile or two out, this road forks; one branch is known as the lower Corinth road; the other, the Corinth ridge road. A short distance out, another road curves off to the left, crosses Lick Creek, and leads back to the river at Hamburg, some miles up the stream. On the right, two separate roads lead off to Purdy, and another, a new one, runs across Snake Creek to Crump's Landing on the river below. Besides these, the whole country that composed the battle-field was cut up with roads leading to different camps.

On and between these roads, at distances of from two to five miles from Pittsburg Landing, lay several divisions of Major-General Grant's army on Sunday morning. The advance line was formed by three divisions—Brigadier-General Sherman's, Brigadier-General Prentiss' and Major-General McClernand's. Between these and the Landing lay the forces of Brigadier-General Hurlbut and Major-General Smith, who, being absent from severe illness, left his command to Brigadier-General W. H. L. Wallace.

The Union advance line, beginning at the extreme left, was thus formed:—On the Hamburg road, just north of the crossing of Lick creek, and under bluffs on the opposite bank that commanded the position, lay Colonel D. Stuart's brigade of General Sherman's division. Some three or four miles distant from this brigade, on the lower Corinth road, between that and the road to Purdy, lay the remaining brigades of Sherman's division, McDowell's forming the extreme right of the whole advance line. Hildebrand's came next to it, and Buckland's following. Next to Buckland's brigade, though rather behind a portion of Sherman's, lay Major-General McClernand's division, and between it and Stuart's brigade, already mentioned as forming the extreme left, Brigadier-General Prentiss' division completed the line.

Back of this line, within a mile of the Landing, lay Hurlbut's division, stretching across the Corinth road, with W. H. L. Wallace's to his right. Such was the position of the Union troops at Pittsburg Landing at daybreak on Sunday morning. Major-General Lew. Wallace's division arrived at about half-past seven o'clock that day.

Nearly four miles intervened between the different parts of Sherman's division. McClernand's lay partially behind Sherman, and there was a gap between him and Prentiss, which the rebels did not fail speedily to find. The extreme left was commanded by unguarded heights, easily approached from Corinth.

The secession army was commanded by General Johnston; Beauregard was second in command. The three army corps were led by Hardee, Polk, and Bragg. Breckinridge commanded the reserve.

On the evening of Friday, April 4, there had been a preliminary skirmish with the enemy's advance. Rumors reached the Union camp that some officers had been taken prisoners by a considerable rebel force, near the lines, and that pickets had been firing. A brigade, the Seventieth, Seventy-second and Forty-eighth Ohio regiments, was sent out to ascertain the facts. They came upon a party of rebels, perhaps a thousand strong, and after a sharp action drove them off, losing Major Crocket, of the Seventy-second Ohio, and two lieutenants from the Seventieth were taken prisoners. In return the Union party took sixteen prisoners, and drove the rebels back to a battery which they had placed undiscovered at no great distance from the Federal lines. General Lew. Wallace's troops, at Crump's Landing, were ordered out under arms; they marched to Adamsville, half way between the river and Purdy, to hold position there and resist any attack in that direction. The long rainy night passed drearily and uncomfortably, but no further hostile demonstrations were made, and it was generally supposed that the affair had been an ordinary picket fight, presaging nothing more. On Saturday there was more skirmishing along the advanced lines.

The secession leaders at Corinth knew that they largely outnumbered Grant, and that no measures had been taken to strengthen the position at Pittsburg landing; they knew equally well, that when Buell's entire Kentucky army was added to Grant's forces, they could not possibly expect to hold their important position at Corinth. Their only hope lay in attacking Grant before Buell arrived, and defeating his troops in detail.

During Friday and Saturday the enemy had marched out of Corinth, about seventy thousand strong, in three lines of battle; the first and second extending from Owl Creek on the left to Lick Creek on the right—a distance of about three miles, supported by the third and the reserve. The first line, under Major-General Hardee, was constituted of his corps, augmented on his right by Gladden's brigade, of Major-General Bragg's corps, deployed in line of battle, with their respective artillery, following immediately by the main road to Pittsburg, and the cavalry in rear of the wings. The second line, composed of the other troop of Bragg's corps, followed Hardee at a distance of five hundred yards, in the same order as the first. The army corps under General Polk followed the second line, at the distance of about eight hundred yards, in lines of brigades, deployed with their batteries in rear of each brigade, moving by the Pittsburg road, the left wing supported by cavalry. The reserve, under Brigadier-General Breckinridge, followed closely the third line, in the same order, its right wing supported by cavalry.

THE BATTLE ON SUNDAY.

As if in beautiful contrast with the terrible scenes that were soon to follow, the holy Sabbath-day which dawned on the sixth of April was one of unusual loveliness. The soft spring sunshine lay upon the green slopes, breaking up their, delicate green with a thousand fleeting shadows flung downward by the young leaves. A gentle, pleasant wind shook the budding branches, and happy birds were singing their love-tunes in the underbrush, a touching prelude to the stern battle music that soon put them to flight. A few fleecy clouds wreathed themselves along the serene blue of the sky, and floated idly over the battle field, casting transparent shadows now in some green hollow, then upon a hill slope, till the whole field smiled like an Eden—smiled even after the cannon belched their thunders over it. While the morning dew was yet on the grass, the enemy began pouring the fire and smoke of a most deadly strife over this lovely scene.

The attack commenced so suddenly and with such bitter violence, that the enemy's artillery was brought to bear on the outer camps almost simultaneously with the arrival of the pickets they had driven in.

The divisions of Sherman and Prentiss, composed in a great part of inexperienced troops, were selected and compelled to meet the first shock of the enemy's onset. Much confusion and panic was occasioned by the sudden and unexpected attack, from which neither corps was able fully to recover during the day. Both commanders exerted themselves with bravery and skill in the trying crisis, and were soon enabled to bring the greater part of their troops into line of battle, and check the advance of the Confederate forces, which were then devastating the Federal camps.

It is impossible to describe the fearful scenes that followed the first wild onset of the enemy. Many of the sick and wounded, and the more tardy officers and men were shot in their tents and left for dead, lying through the whole of this fearful struggle, gasping in their agony. On Monday evening some of these poor fellows were found in the riddled tents, scarcely able to ask for the drink for which they were perishing.

But the Union forces were not long held at this terrible disadvantage. As the enemy advanced in force on Sherman's centre, and a battery opened fire in the woods, shelling the Federal camp, the Unionists were in a condition to respond with emphasis. Taylor's and Waterhouse's batteries met this first regular attack.

Under cover of their artillery, the rebel advance, by heavy battalions of infantry, was made obliquely to the left, across the open field in front of the Fifty-third Ohio, while solid columns came in, direct upon

Sherman's front. Immediately the entire line opened fire, and the battle became general. The enemy's design was to left-flank Sherman. To this end he flung himself with terrific force upon Prentiss. Directly the sound of musketry and artillery announced that Prentiss was engaged, and at nine A. M. he was falling back. About this time Appler's regiment broke, followed by Munger's regiment, and the enemy pressed forward on Waterhouse's battery, exposed by the disordered retreat. The three Illinois regiments in immediate support of this battery stood for some time, but the enemy's advance was so impetuous and his fire so terrific that they began to waver. While the Forty-third Illinois was in the thickest of the iron storm, Colonel Raith received a severe wound and fell from his horse. This threw his regiment into some disorder, and the enemy got possession of three guns of Waterhouse's battery.

Although the left was thus turned, and the enemy pressing the whole line, Colonels McDowell and Buckland held their ground until ten o'clock, A. M., when the enemy had got his artillery to the rear of the Union left flank, and some changes became absolutely necessary. Two regiments of Hildebrand's brigade—Appler's and Munger's—had already disappeared to the rear, and Hildebrand's own regiment was in disorder. Taylor's battery—still at Shiloh—received orders to fall back as far as the Purdy and Hamburg road; and McDowell and Buckland were directed to adopt that road as their new line. Behr's battery at the cross-roads, was ordered immediately to come into battery action right. As Captain Behr gave the order, he was shot from his horse, when the drivers and gunners fled in confusion, carrying off the caissons, and abandoning five out of the six guns. The enemy pressed on after gaining this battery, and the Unionists were again forced to choose a line of defence. Hildebrand's brigade had substantially disappeared from the field, though he himself bravely remained. McDowell's and Buckland's brigades still maintained their organizations, and joined McClernand's right, thus abandoning the original camps and line.

General Prentiss, too, brave, eager, and resolute to retrieve lost ground, reformed his lines under the hot fire of the enemy, without a choice of position, and in the full raking fire of the foe, hid in the scrub oak jungles, which gave them secure covert. If his troops had cowered at first, the remainder of his division held their position and braved the galling fire it was impossible to return with the heroism of old veterans. Hildebrand and McDowell were compelled to withdraw their brigades from their camps to a ravine behind them, but they made a gallant defence, while Buckland's men fell back, and McClernand threw forward his left, supporting them.

It is hardly to be wondered that the raw regiments broke under this appalling fire, before which veteran troops were powerless to stand. Yet it must be said that Hildebrand's brigade gave way with unreasonable panic. Colonel Hildebrand himself was cool and self-possessed as any man that ever led a hostile force. He made a powerful effort to keep his troops in place when he saw them giving way; but the power of a single man is unavailing when panic seizes the masses. Still this brave hero kept his individual regiment in force a full hour after Appler's and Munger's regiments had retired from their proper field of action, and thus a larger portion of his forces were scattered and drifted away from the contest.

Prentiss still fought valiantly, but down on either flank came the enemy in an overwhelming rush, and a wall of bayonets closed him in on either side. It was an appalling situation. The enemy made vigorous use of his advantage. They had driven two divisions from their camps and nearly opened a passage to the river. Here it was, between nine and ten o'clock, that McArthur's brigade of W. H. L. Wallace's division came up to give assistance to Stuart's brigade, of Sherman's division, now in imminent danger of being cut off. Mistaking the way, McArthur marched far to the right, and instead of reaching Stuart, came in on the other side of the rebels, now closely pushing Prentiss. His men at once opened vigorously on the enemy, and for a time they seemed likely to save the imperilled division. But coming unawares upon the enemy, their positions were not well chosen, and the whole force was compelled to fall back together.

HURLBUT'S DIVISION.

Hurlbut's division, in reserve, saved the first repulse from proving an absolute defeat, by offering a line behind which the discomfited divisions of Sherman and Prentiss could re-form, while his solid ranks were a wall of steel against which the enemy could not prevail. The General, in his report, says of their five hours' service:

"Receiving from General Prentiss a pressing request for aid, I took command in person of the first and third brigades, respectively commanded by Colonel N. G. Williams, of the Third Iowa, and Brigadier-General Lauman. The first brigade consisted of the Third Iowa, Forty-first Illinois, Twenty-eighth Illinois and Thirty-second Illinois. The third brigade was composed of the Thirty-first and Forty-fourth Indiana, the Seventeenth and Twenty-fifth Kentucky.

"In addition, I took with me the first and second battalions of the Fifth Ohio cavalry; Mann's light battery of four pieces commanded by first Lieutenant E. Brotzmann; Ross' battery of the Second Michigan; and Meyer's battery of the Thirteenth Ohio.

"I formed my line of battle—the first brigade thrown to the front on the southerly side of a large open field—the third brigade continuing the line with an obtuse angle around the other side of the field, and extending some distance into the brush and timber. Mann's battery was placed in the angle of the lines, Ross' battery some distance to the left, and the Thirteenth Ohio battery on the right, and somewhat advanced in cover of the timber, so as to concentrate the fire upon the open ground in front, and waited for the attack."

At half-past seven o'clock, when Brigadier-General Sherman was attacked in force and heavily upon his left, Colonel I. C. Veatch, commanding the second brigade of General Hurlbut's division, was ordered to proceed to the left of General Sherman. This brigade, consisting of the Twenty-fifth Indiana, Fourteenth, Fifteenth, and Forty-sixth Illinois, was in march in ten minutes, arrived on General Sherman's left and went into action rapidly. In a few minutes they were in line of battle, and moving forward to the attack. But the brigade had hardly left the camp before it found the roads full of flying Unionists, and the route for two miles was strewn with guns, knapsacks, and blankets. The front had been completely surprised; nearly a whole division was scattered and retreating in utter confusion, and the enemy in force was already a mile within the Federal camps. The brigade, under command of Colonel Veatch, was drawn up in line of battle in a skirt of timber, bordering a large field, on the outer edge of which the Federal troops were engaging the enemy. But the enemy pressed on in overwhelming force, and just as the troops in front began to waver, they discovered that he had flanked Veatch on the right and was rapidly advancing to attack the brigade on the right and rear.

The Fifteenth Illinois was on the right, the Fourteenth Illinois in the centre, and the Twenty-fifth Indiana on the left—the other regiment, the Forty-sixth Illinois, by the rapid flanking of the enemy became detached from the brigade, and was not with it again during the action. This brought the first fire upon the Fifteenth Illinois, which stood it nobly, but was soon overpowered; the Fourteenth followed with a like result. In the mean time the troops in front and on the left were completely routed by the enemy, and came pell mell through the Union lines, causing some little confusion. Hardly had they passed through to the rear before the enemy came rushing on, and the fire of musketry became terrific. There was no resisting this fiery onset short of annihilation; so with a few well directed volleys the brigade left the field. The loss was very heavy. All the field officers of the Twenty-fifth Illinois were killed instantly; two lieutenants were killed and three wounded.

M'CLERNAND'S DIVISION.

McClernand's division lay a short distance in the rear, and with one brigade stretching out to the left of Sherman's line. Properly speaking, merely from the location of the camp, he did not belong to the front line. Two-thirds of his division were entirely behind Sherman. But as the latter fell back, McClernand was compelled to bear the shock of battle.

His division was composed as follows:—First brigade, Colonel Hare commanding, Eighth and Eighteenth Illinois, Eleventh and Thirteenth Iowa; Second brigade, Colonel C. C. Marsh commanding, Eleventh, Twentieth, Forty-eighth and Forty-fifth Illinois, Colonels Ransom, Marsh, Haynie and Smith (the latter was the "Lead Mine regiment"); Third brigade, Colonel Raith commanding, Seventeenth, Twenty-ninth and Forty-ninth Illinois, Lieutenant-Colonels Wood, Farrell and Pease, and Forty-third Illinois, Colonel Marsh. Besides this fine show of experienced troops, they had Schwartz's, Dresser's, McAllister's and Waterhouse's batteries.

McClernand was at once in the hottest of the fight. As Buckner's brigade fell back, the protecting woods grew thinner and storms of grape swept over them like the blasts of a tornado. Lieutenant-Colonel Canfield, commanding the Seventy-second Ohio, was mortally wounded, and borne dying from the field. Colonel Sullivan, of the Forty-eighth Ohio, was wounded, but continued at the head of his men. Company officers fell in numbers and were carried away from the field. The rebels, by a sudden dash, had taken part of Waterhouse's battery, which McClernand had sent over. Behr's battery, too, was taken, and Taylor's Chicago Light Artillery was terribly exposed, and compelled to retire with heavy loss. As the troops gave way they came out from the open woods into old fields, completely raked by the enemy's fire. For them all was lost, and away went Buckner's and Hildebrand's brigades, Ohioans and Illinoisans together, to the rear and right.

McDowell's brigade had fallen back less slowly than its two companions of the same division. It was now left entirely alone. Having formed the extreme right, it had no support there; its supporting brigades on the left had gone; and through the space they had occupied the rebels were pouring furiously. In imminent danger of being entirely cut off, they fell back among the ravines that border Snake creek.

Sherman was indefatigable in collecting and reorganizing his men, and a contest was kept up along portions of his new lines. The General bore with him one token of the danger to which he had so recklessly exposed himself—a musket ball through the hand. It was a miracle that he escaped so slightly, for his courage had been conspicuous. He had dared death fifty times since the attack was made on his raw division that memorable Sunday morning.

Now the great force of the enemy fell on McClernand's right. As

Sherman fell back, McClernand was compelled to bring in his brigades to protect his left against the onset of the rebels, who, seeing how he had weakened himself, hurled themselves against him with tremendous force. A couple of new regiments, the Fifteenth and Sixteenth Iowa, were brought up; but taking utterly raw troops on the field, under heavy fire, was too severe a trial, and they gave way in confusion. Then the whole division made a change of front, and faced along the Corinth road. Here the batteries were placed in position, and till ten o'clock the rebels were foiled in every attempt to gain the road.

But Sherman having now fallen back there was nothing to prevent the enemy from coming in further out on the road, and turning McClernand's right. Prompt to seize the advantage, a rebel brigade dashed audaciously through the abandoned camp of the division, pushing up the road in order to come in above McClernand. Where Sherman had been, a battery of rifled guns was turned upon them, hurling fearful slaughter in their midst and driving them back.

But the enemy managed his reserves with great skill. A constant advance of fresh regiments proved overwhelming, and the storm of death swept many a brave Union officer away. Death after death was proclaimed, disaster followed disaster with disheartening quickness.

This was about half-past ten A. M., at which time the enemy had made a furious attack on General McClernand's whole front. He struggled determinedly; but finding him severely pressed, Sherman moved McDowell's brigade directly against the left flank of the enemy, forced him back some distance, and then directed the men to avail themselves of every cover—trees, fallen timber, and a wooded valley to the right. The brigade held this position for four long hours, sometimes gaining and at others losing ground, Generals McClernand and Sherman acting in perfect concert, and struggling to maintain this line.

By eleven o'clock, many of the commanders of regiments had fallen, and in some cases not a single field officer remained; yet the fighting continued with desperate earnestness—the fearful contest on both sides was for death or victory. The almost deafening sound of artillery, and the rattle of the musketry, were all that could be heard. The men stood and bravely delivered their fire, regardless of the thunders of artillery and the storm of iron missiles that raked through them. Foot by foot the ground was contested. The wounded fell in heaps on the battle field. There was no easy transportation at hand, but such means as the soldiers could invent were adopted, and their wounded comrades carried to the rear. Many who were hurt fell back without help, while others fought in the ranks until they were actually forced back by their company officers.

Major Eaton, commanding the Eighteenth Illinois, was killed; Colonel Haynie was severely wounded; Colonel Raith, commanding a brigade, had his leg so shattered that amputation was necessary; Major Nevins, of the Eleventh Illinois, was wounded; Lieutenant-Colonel Ransom, of the same regiment, was wounded; three of General McClernand's staff—Major Schwartz, Major Stewart and Lieutenant Freeman—were wounded, and carried from the field. Line officers had suffered heavily. The batteries were broken up—Schwartz had lost half his guns and sixteen horses. Dresser had lost several of his rifled pieces, three caissons and eighteen horses. McAllister had lost half his twenty-four pound howitzers.

DESPERATE HAND-TO-HAND FIGHT OVER SCHWARTZ'S BATTERY.

The soldiers fought bravely to the last—bravely as ever men fought—but they were at a terrible disadvantage. Gradually they began falling back, making a determined resistance; occasionally they rallied and repulsed the enemy for a hundred yards, then were beaten back again, renewing the retreat to some new position for fresh defence.

By eleven o'clock the division was back in a line with Hurlbut's. It still did some gallant fighting; once its right swept round and drove the enemy before it for a considerable distance, but again fell back; at last it brought up near the position of W. H. L. Wallace's division.

Now Prentiss, Sherman and McClernand were driven back, and their camps were all in the hands of the enemy. The whole front line, for which Hurlbut and Wallace were but the reserves, was gone.

Sherman's brigade, on the extreme left, was doubly left alone by the

Generals. General Grant did not arrive on the field until each division General had been in action, and the respective Generals had in the best manner they could, carried on the battle; but this brigade was even left by its division General, who was four miles away, doing his utmost to rally his panic-stricken regiments there.

It was commanded by Colonel David Stuart, and was composed of the Fifty-fifth Illinois, Lieutenant-Colonel Malmbourg, commanding; Seventy-first Ohio, Colonel Rodney Mason; the Fifty-fourth Ohio (Zouaves), Colonel T. K. Smith. It was posted along the circuitous road from Pittsburg Landing, up the river to Hamburg, some two miles from the Landing, and near the crossing of Lick Creek, the bluffs on the opposite side of which commanded the position, and stretching on down to join Prentiss' division on its right.

When the rebels marched out from Corinth, a couple of brigades (rumored to be under the command of Breckinridge), had without molestation reached the bluffs of Lick Creek, commanding Stuart's position.

During the attack on Prentiss, Stuart's brigade was formed along the road, the left resting near the Lick Creek ford, the right, Seventy-first Ohio, Colonel Rodney Mason, being nearest Prentiss. The first intimation they had of disaster to their right was the partial cessation of firing. An instant afterwards, muskets were seen glimmering among the leaves, and presently a rebel column emerged from a bend in the road, with banners flying, and moving at double-quick toward them. Their supports to the left were more remote than the rebels, and it was evident that, with but one piece of artillery, a single regiment could do nothing there. They accordingly fell back toward the ford, and were reinforced in an orchard near the other regiments.

The rebel column veered on further to the right, and for a brief space, though utterly isolated, they remained unmolested.

Before ten, however, the brigade, which stood listening to the wild roar of battle on the left, was startled by a shell that hurtled directly over their heads. In an instant the rebel batteries that had gained the commanding bluffs opposite, by approaching on the Corinth and Hamburg road, were in fiery play. The orchards and open fields in which they were posted, looking only for an attack in the opposite direction, were swept with the exploding shells and a hail-storm of grape.

Under cover of this fire from the bluffs, the rebels rushed down, crossed the ford, and in a moment were seen forming on the creek, in open fields, and within close musket range. Their color-bearers stepped defiantly to the front, as the engagement opened. The storm came in sharp and quick volleys of musketry, the batteries above supporting them with a destructive fire. The Union sharpshooters panted to pick off the audacious rebel color-bearers, but Colonel Stuart interposed,—

crying out, "No, no, they are too brave fellows to be killed." Almost at the first fire, Lieutenant-Colonel Barton S. Kyle, of the Seventy-first, was shot through the breast. The brigade stood firmly at least ten minutes, when it became evident that its position was untenable, and it fell rapidly back, perhaps a quarter of a mile, to the next ridge; a few of Stuart's men, at great personal risk, carrying Lieutenant-Colonel Kyle, in a dying condition, from the field they were abandoning. Ohio lost no braver, truer man that day.

When they reached the next woody ridge, rebel cavalry, that had crossed the creek lower down, were seen coming up on the left; and the line of battle was formed fronting in that direction, to resist this new attack. For three-quarters of an hour the brigade kept this position. The cavalry, finding it prepared, did not come within range. In front they were hard pressed, and the rebels began to come in on their right. Colonel Stuart had sent across to Brigadier-General W. H. L. Wallace, then not engaged, for support. Brigadier-General McArthur's brigade was promptly started across, but mistaking the way, and bearing too much to the right, found itself in the midst of the rebel forces. He vigorously engaged the rebels to his front and flanks, fell back to a good position and held these troops in bay till the rest of his division came up. General McArthur was himself disabled by a wound in the foot, but he rode to a hospital, had it dressed, and returned to the brigade, which meantime held its position stoutly.

But this brought Stuart's isolated brigade little assistance. They were soon forced to fall back to another ridge, then to another, and, finally, about twelve o'clock, shattered and broken, they retreated to the right and rear, falling in behind General McArthur's brigade to reorganize. Colonel Stuart was himself wounded by a ball through his right shoulder, and the loss of field and company officers greatly disheartened the troops.

DESPERATE CONDITION OF THE NATIONAL TROOPS.

Now the entire front was cleared. The enemy had full possession of Sherman's, Prentiss' and McClernand's camps. By ten o'clock the whole front, except Stuart's brigade, had given way, and the burden of the fight was resting on Hurlbut and W. H. L. Wallace. Before twelve, Stuart, too, had come back, and for the time, those two divisions stood absolutely alone between the Union army and destruction.

But truly brave men are bravest when driven to extremities. Hurlbut and Wallace made a most gallant stand; and most of the troops from the three scattered divisions were still to some extent available. Many of them had wandered down the river, some to Crump's Landing, and others even to Savannah, to be brought back on transports. Brigades could not be collected again, much less divisions, but the regiments were gathered together from the loose squads wandering about, and officered, often by men who could find scarcely a soldier of their own commands. These were hurried to the front, and many of them did good service.

According to general understanding, in the event of an attack at Pittsburg Landing, Major-General Lew. Wallace was to come in on the Union right, and flank the rebels by marching across from Crump's Landing below.

But, as has been stated, Wallace, with his division, though all drawn up and ready to march anywhere at a moment's notice, was not ordered to Pittsburg Landing till nearly twelve o'clock. Then, by mistake, he got on the new road, four miles of marching were lost, and the circuitous route made it a march of twelve miles before he could reach the scene of battle. Meantime the right was almost wholly unprotected.

Fortunately, however, the rebels did not seem to have discovered the full extent of this weakness, and their heaviest fighting was done on the centre and left, where the Union lines were still preserved.

HURLBUT'S DIVISION.

Hurlbut's division stretched across the Corinth road, facing to the left. W. H. L. Wallace's other brigades had gone over to assist McArthur, and the divisions thus reunited, steadily closed the line. To Hurlbut's right the lines were united by the reorganized regiments that had been re-sent to the field. McClernand and Sherman were both there.

Hurlbut had been encamped in the edge of a stretch of open fields, backed with heavy timber, which lay nearest the river.

Three times during those long hours the heavy rebel masses on the left charged upon the division, and three times were they repulsed with terrible slaughter. Close, sharp, continuous musketry filled the air with fire and smoke—whole lines belched their furious fire on the rebels, and a leaden storm swept the fields over which they attempted to advance with terrible fury. No troops could have withstood this deadly fire. Rebel discipline gave way under it, though dead bodies left scattered over the field, even on Monday evening, bore ghastly testimony to the daring with which they had been precipitated towards the Federal lines.

The rebel generals handled their forces with a skill that extorted admiration even from their enemies. Repulse was nothing to them; if a rush on the Union lines failed, they took their disordered troops to the rear, and sent up fresh forces, who ignorant of the deadly reception that awaited them, were ready to make a new trial. Hurlbut's jaded division was compelled to yield at last, and after six hours' magnificent fighting, it fell back of its camps to a point within half a mile of the landing.

WALLACE'S DIVISION.

Hurlbut's companion division—that of Brigadier-General W. H. L. Wallace, included the Second and Seventh Iowa, Ninth and Twenty-eighth Illinois, and several of the other regiments composing Major-General Smith's old division. Wallace had also three excellent batteries—Stone's, Richardson's and Weber's, all from Missouri.

With him, too, the fight began about ten o'clock, as already described. From that time till four in the afternoon his troops bore up manfully. The musketry fire was absolutely continuous; there was scarcely a moment that some part of the line was not pouring in their rattling volleys, and the artillery sent forth its death-thunders with but little intermission through the entire time.

Once or twice the infantry advanced, attempting to drive back the continually increasing enemy; but though they could hold their own ground, their numbers were unequal to the task of conquering more.

Four separate times in turn the rebels attempted to charge on them. Each time the infantry poured in its quickest volleys, the artillery redoubled its exertions, and the rebels retreated with heavy slaughter. The division was eager to remain, even when Hurlbut fell back, and the noble fellows serving the guns were particularly indignant when compelled to silence their own batteries. But their supports were gone on both sides. It was madness to remain in isolated advance. Just as the necessity for retreating was becoming apparent, General Wallace, whose cool, collected bravery had commanded universal admiration, was, as it was believed, mortally wounded, and borne away from the field. At last, the division fell back. Its soldiers claim the proud distinction of being the last to yield, in the general breaking up of the lines that gloomy Sunday afternoon.

Captain Stone could not resist the temptation of stopping, as he passed what had been Hurlbut's headquarters, to try a few parting shots. He did fine execution, but his wheel horses were shot down, and he narrowly escaped losing his guns.

With the first dash of the enemy on the left wing, it became evident that a stupendous effort would be put forth to break through it. For two hours sheets of fire blazed from both columns, and clouds of smoke surged up between them with the rush and stifling effect of a prairie fire. The Mississippi riflemen in the enemy's ranks fought with terrible valor, which was met with steady heroism by those who stood firmly under their unerring fire. Three different times the enemy seemed on the verge of a victory. They drove the Union forces slowly before them until they came in sight of the river, but up to three o'clock the desperate attempt to break the Federal lines proved unavailing. Having failed to drive in the main columns, they had turned with furious strength on the right wing; baffled there, they made another onset on the left wing, fighting more desperately than ever. But the Union lines were prepared for the assault, fierce as it was, and met it with wonderful steadiness.

The whole army was crowded into Wallace's camps, and confined in a circuit of from half to two-thirds of a mile around the Landing. The Union army fighting bravely, had been falling back inch by inch all day. The next repulse threatened to drive them into the river.

Brigadier-General Prentiss and three regiments with him—the Twenty-third Missouri, of his own division, and the Twelfth and Fourteenth Iowa, of those that had come to his assistance—delayed their retreat too long, having relied too confidently on their supporting division to check a flank movement of the enemy. Almost before they saw their danger, the flanking forces rushed in from either side behind them, and they stood, perhaps two thousand strong, in the midst of thrice their number. Hedged in with battalions, with a forest of steel bristling on every side, these brave men yielded to the force of numbers, and were taken prisoners, after fighting bravely till further contest would have been self-murder.

Meantime Sherman's brigades had maintained a confused fight. Buckland's were almost gone, Hildebrand's and McDowell's were holding their ground more tenaciously.

General Hurlbut gives a clear statement of the retreat and final position of the Federal forces on Sunday afternoon:

"When, about three o'clock, Colonel Stewart, on my left, sent me word that he was driven in, and that I would be flanked in a few moments, it was necessary for me to decide at once to abandon either the right or left. I considered that General Prentiss could, with the left of General McClernand's troops, probably hold the right, and sent him notice to reach out toward the right, and drop back steadily parallel with my first brigade, while I rapidly moved General Lauman from the right to the left, and called up two twenty-pound pieces of Major Cavender's battalion to check the advance of the enemy upon the first brigade. These pieces were taken into action by Dr. Corvine, the surgeon of the battalion, and Lieutenant Edwards, and effectually checked the enemy for half an hour, giving me time to draw off my crippled artillery, and to form a new front with the third brigade. In a few minutes, two Texas regiments crossed the ridge separating my line from Stuart's former one, while other troops also advanced.

"Willard's battery was thrown into position, under command of

Lieutenant Wood, and opened with great effect on the Lone Star flags, until their line of fire was obstructed by the charge of the third brigade, which, after delivering its fire with great steadiness, charged up the hill, and drove the enemy back three or four hundred yards. Perceiving that a heavy force was closing on the left, between my line and the river, while heavy firing continued on the right and front, I ordered the line to fall back. The retreat was made steadily, and in good order. I had hoped to make a stand on the line of my camp, but masses of the enemy were pressing on each flank, while their light artillery was closing rapidly in the rear. On reaching the twenty-four-pounder siege guns in battery, near the river, I again succeeded in forming line of battle in rear of the guns, and, by direction of Major-General Grant, I assumed command of all troops that came up. Broken regiments and disordered battalions came into line gradually upon my division.

"Major Cavender posted six of his twenty-pound pieces on my right, and I sent my aid to establish the light artillery, all that could be found, on my left. Many officers and men, unknown to me, fled in confusion through the line. Many gallant soldiers and brave officers rallied steadily on the new line. I passed to the right and found myself in communication with General Sherman, and received his instructions. In a short time the enemy appeared on the crest of the ridge, led by the Thirteenth Louisiana, but were cut to pieces by the steady and murderous fire of our artillery."

The enemy were in possession of nearly all the Union camps and camp equipage. Half the field artillery had fallen into his hands; a division general had been captured—many officers had followed him, and more than one regiment of soldiers had been made prisoners. The battle field was cumbered at every step with killed and wounded; the hospital tents were overflowing and crowded with human agony. A long ridge bluff set apart for surgical purposes swarmed with the maimed, the dead and the dying, whose cries and groans broke fearfully through the pauses of the artillery. A dogged, stubborn resolution took possession of the men; regiments had lost their favorite officers; companies had been bereft of their captains. Still they continued to fight desperately, but with little hope.

At three o'clock the gunboat Tyler opened fire on the enemy, and at four the Lexington came up, taking position half a mile above the landing, and opened fire, striking terror into the ranks of the enemy.

General Grant was confident that his troops could hold the enemy off till morning, and said this while standing with his staff in a group by the old log post-office on the landing, which was then crowded with surgeons and the wounded; but still the men fought with a despairing light in their eyes.

In a time like this, minutes count for years. General Grant used them to a golden purpose. Colonel Webster, chief of staff, and an artillery officer of ability, had arranged all the guns he could collect in a sort of semi-circle, protecting the Landing, and bearing chiefly on the Union centre and left, by which the rebels were pretty sure to advance. Corps of artillerists to man them were improvised from all the batteries that could be found. Twenty-two guns in all were placed in position. Two of them were very heavy siege guns, long thirty-two's. Where they came from, what battery they belonged to, no man questioned. It was quite unimportant. Enough that they were there, in the right place, half a mile back from the bluff, sweeping the approaches by the left, and by the ridge Corinth road, but with few to work them. Dr. Corvine, surgeon of Frank Blair's First Missouri Artillery, proffered his services, which were gladly accepted, and he worked them with terrible effect.

It was half-past four o'clock—perhaps later still. Every division of the Union army on the field had been repulsed. The enemy occupied almost all their camps. The struggling remnant of Federal troops had been driven to within little over half a mile of the Landing. Behind was a deep, rapid river. In front was a victorious enemy. Still there was an hour for fighting. O, that night or Lew. Wallace would come! Nelson's division of Buell's army evidently could not cross in time to save the day. No one could tell why Lew. Wallace was not on the ground. In the justice of a righteous cause, and in that semi-circle of twenty-two guns in position, lay all the hope these beleaguered men could see.

At five o'clock the artillery which had been thundering so stormily, held its fire a little; the flash of muskets from the enemy's lines died away, and his columns fell back on the centre for nearly a mile. With a sudden swoop they wheeled and again threw their entire force on the left wing, determined to end the fearful contest of the day then and there.

Suddenly a broad, sulphurous flash of light leaped out from the darkening woods, and through the glare and smoke came whistling leaden hail. The rebels were making their crowning effort for the day, and as was expected, they came from the left and centre. They had wasted their fire at one thousand yards. Instantaneously a new tempest from the black-mouthed Union guns flung out its thunderous response. The rebel artillery opened, and shell and round shot came tearing across the open space back of the bluff. The Union infantry poured in a glorious response from their broken battalions, invigorated by the announcement that the advance of Buell's army was in sight. Just then a body of cavalry appeared across the Tennessee river, waiting transportation.

In their extremity the soldiers turned their eyes anxiously that way. Was it Buell—was it Nelson coming to the rescue?

ARRIVAL OF GENERAL BUELL.

The eyes of those weary soldiers brighten. Their courage revived. Help was near. Even in that lurid atmosphere they could see the gleaming of the gun-barrels amid the leaves and undergrowth down the opposite side of the river. They caught hopeful glimpses of the steady, swinging tramp of trained soldiers. A division of Buell's army was coming up.

Then came a boat across with a lieutenant and two or three privates of the Signal Corps. Some orders were given the officer, and as instantly telegraphed to the other side by the mysterious wavings and raisings and droppings of the flags. A steamer came up with pontoons on board, with which a bridge could be speedily thrown across the river.

She quietly reconnoitered a few moments, and steamed back again. Perhaps, after all, it was better to have no bridge there. It made escape impossible, and left nothing but victory or death to the struggling Union troops. Preparations were rapidly made for crossing General Nelson's division, (for he had the advance of Buell's army,) on the dozen transports that had been tied up along the bank.

The division of W. H. L. Wallace held the enemy at bay in his last desperate effort to break the Union lines. While forcing through a cross fire, General Wallace fell mortally wounded. Brigadier-General McArthur took the command, but he too was wounded, and Colonel Tuttle, as senior in rank, rallied the shattered brigades. He was joined by the Thirteenth Iowa, Colonel Crooker; Ninth Illinois, Colonel Mersy; Twelfth Illinois, Lieutenant-Colonel Chatlain, and several other fragments of regiments, and forming them in line on the road, held the enemy in check until that noble line was formed that breasted that last desperate charge.

At this critical moment a long, loud shout from the Union forces welcomed in the reinforcements. Eight thousand strong had at length crossed the river, and swept down upon the battle-field. Buell and Nelson, by forced marches, made within sound of the booming thunders of artillery, reached the battle-field just as the fate of war trembled in the balance. There was no pause for rest or council. So eager were they for the strife, they scarcely paused for breath before a line of battle was formed which decided that stormy day's fight.

The men, weary from the long march, and panting from the speed which had marked its last stages, ranged themselves in advance of the exhausted, but unfaltering troops of Sherman, McClernand, Hurlbut and of W. H. L. Wallace, who lay dying on the battle-field, while Colonel Tuttle led his brigades to their noble work.

The gunboats Tyler, Lieutenant Gwinn commanding, and Lexington, James W. Shirk commanding, now steamed up to the mouth of the little creek, near which Stuart's brigade had lain in the morning, and where the rebels were attacking the Union left. When they reached the mouth of the stream the boats rounded to, commanding a ravine cut through the bluff, as if for the passage of their shells, which poured destruction into the ranks of the enemy. This movement was made under the direction of General Hurlbut, and it soon swept the enemy's ranks, carrying terror with every burst of deadly iron the guns belched forth.

Eager to avenge the death of their commanding General (now known to have been killed a couple of hours before), and to complete the victory they believed to be within their grasp, the rebels had incautiously ventured within reach of their most dreaded antagonists, as broadside after broadside of seven-inch shells and sixty-four-pound-shot soon taught them. This was a foe they had hardly counted on, and the unexpected fire in flank and rear produced a startling effect. The boats fired admirably, and with a rapidity that was astonishing. The twenty-two land guns kept up their stormy thunder; and thus, amid the crash and roar, the scream of shells and demon-like hiss of minie balls, that Sabbath evening wore away.

Startled by the accumulated force, and disheartened by the fearful combinations against them, the rebels fell slowly back, fighting as they went, until they reached an advantageous position, somewhat in the rear, yet occupying the main road to Corinth. The gunboats kept pouring a storm of shell on their track, until they retired completely out of reach, and the battle of the first day ended.

As the sounds of battle died away, and division generals drew off their men, a council of war was held, and it was decided that as soon as possible after daybreak the enemy should be attacked and driven from their snug quarters in the Union camps. Lew. Wallace, who was coming in on the new road from Crump's Landing, and crossing Snake Creek just above the Illinois Wallace's (W. H. L.) camps, was to take the right and sweep back toward the position from which Sherman had been driven on Sunday morning. Nelson was to take the extreme left. Buell promised to place Crittenden next to Nelson, and McCook next to him, by a seasonable hour in the morning. The gap between McCook and Lew. Wallace was to be filled with the reorganized divisions of Grant's army; Hurlbut coming next to McCook, then McClernand, and Sherman closing the gap between McClernand and Lew. Wallace.

From the first fearful onslaught upon Buckland's brigade, which, gathering up its shattered regiments, and firing as they ran, to form in

BATTLE OF PITTSBURG LANDING, APRIL 6, 1862.

the heavy woods, leaving winrows of slain on their track, to the last outburst of shot and shell from the gunboats, the contest of that day had been a fearful one. Most of the troops which received the first shock of battle were raw recruits, just from the camp of instruction. Hundred and hundreds of them had never seen a gun fired save in sport in their lives. With officers equally inexperienced, admitting brilliant exceptions, it is not wonderful that the ranks were broken and driven back when the terrific roar of cannon burst in their midst, and bombshells scattered fire and death among the tents, in which they were quietly sleeping but an hour before. Springing to arms, half prepared only to rush through the blinding smoke to meet the serried columns of the rebels' impetuous advance—truly it is not strange that they fell into confusion, fighting blindly and at random. But it was a grand sight when Sherman dashed along the lines, shouting encouragement to the men, exposing his own life a hundred times, and rallying his forces with a wonderful power of voice and action. The herculean exertions of this brave man no doubt saved the division from utter destruction.

From the first tranquil opening of that beautiful day to its lurid and bloody close more desperate bravery has seldom been exhibited. When Americans meet Americans, all that is heroic and daring in the national character springs to action, and deeds are done on both sides that thrill the nation as it stands breathlessly listening, North and South, to know how her sons have fought.

NIGHT BETWEEN THE TWO BATTLES.

In dead silence the troops took their new position, and lay down on their arms in line of battle. All night long the remainder of Buell's men were marching up from Savannah to a point opposite Pittsburg Landing, whence they were brought over in transports. An hour after dark Wallace came in with his division. There had been delay in getting the right road, which made him late on the field. But once there he fell to work with energy. He ascertained the position of certain rebel batteries which lay in front of him on the right, and threatened to bar his advance in the morning, and selected positions for a couple of his batteries from which they could silence the enemy. In placing his guns and arranging his brigades for support, he was occupied till one o'clock in the morning. His wearied men had lain down to snatch a few hours of sleep, with the shadows of death all around them.

At nine o'clock all was hushed near the landing. Men still panting from the hot contest of the day, threw themselves on the earth to sleep or die as they chanced to be unhurt or wounded unto death. The bright stars looked down upon the ranks of sleeping, dying and dead men, with sweet Sabbath-like calm, and never did the stars of heaven brood over a spectacle more appalling. The sound of marching troops from the far distance alone broke the solemn stillness, save when the moans of the wounded, and the agonizing cries for water thrilled the night with sounds of anguish. Now a flash shed a flood of sheet-lightning over the river, turning its waters to lurid fire, and the roar of heavy naval guns reverberated on the bluffs, breaking up the sublime silence of the night. Again and again the guns boomed great volumes of sound. By the flashes, the gunboats could be seen receding back into the fiery blue of the waters with each graceful recoil produced by the discharge. A thin veil of smoke settled around them, floating drowsily between their black hulls and the beautiful stars. Far away in the distant woods came the muffled explosion of shells thus let loose on the tranquil air.

Thus the night wore on. The soldiers, far too weary for the boom of cannon to awake them, slept quietly almost as the dead were sleeping. The wounded answered back the dismal sound with more dismal groans. At midnight a thunder-storm broke over the battle field, and the artillery of heaven swept its fires through the sky, while the guns from the river boomed a sullen answer. Torrents of rain fell, drenching the sleepers, but falling cool as balm on the parched lips of the wounded, assuaging their burning thirst and moistening their wounds.

The vigilant officers knew that half a mile off lay a victorious army, commanded by splendid Generals, rendered ardent by a half-won conquest which might be a victory on the morrow. For them there was little rest. When the day broke it found these men watching. When the brain is active men do not sleep, and the General who has divisions to command and protect must earn success by vigilance.

THE BATTLE ON MONDAY.

The line of battle agreed upon for the Union forces on Monday was this:—Right wing, Major-General Lew. Wallace; left wing, Brigadier-General Nelson. Between these, beginning at the left, Brigadier-Generals T. Crittenden, A. McD. McCook, Hurlbut, McClernand and W. T. Sherman. In the divisions of the three latter were to be included also the remains of Prentiss' and W. H. L. Wallace's commands—shattered and left without commanders, through the capture of one, and the mortal wound of the other.

Buell's three divisions were not full when the battle opened on Monday morning, but the lacking regiments were gradually brought into the rear. The different divisions were composed of the following forces:

BRIGADIER-GENERAL NELSON'S DIVISION.—*First Brigade*—Col. Ammon, 24th Ohio, commanding; 36th Indiana, Col. Gross; 6th Ohio, Lieut.-Col. Anderson; 24th Ohio, Lieut.-Col. Fred. C. Jones. *Second Brigade*—Saunders D. Bruce, 20th Kentucky, commanding; 1st Kentucky, Col. Enyart; 2d Kentucky, Col. Sedgwick; 20th Kentucky, Lieut.-Col. ———, commanding. *Third Brigade* — Col. Hazen, 41st Ohio, commanding; 41st Ohio, 6th Kentucky, and 9th Indiana.

BRIGADIER-GENERAL T. CRITTENDEN'S DIVISION.— *First Brigade*— Gen. Boyle; 19th Ohio, Col. Beatty; 59th Ohio, Col. Pfyffe; 13th Kentucky, Col. Hobson; 9th Kentucky, Col. Grider. *Second Brigade*—Col. Wm. S. Smith, 13th Ohio, commanding; 13th Ohio, Lieut.-Col. Hawkins; 26th Kentucky, Lieut.-Col. Maxwell; 11th Kentucky, Col. P. P. Hawkins; with Mendenhall's regular and Bartlett's Ohio batteries.

BRIGADIER-GENERAL McCOOK'S DIVISION. — *First Brigade* — Brig.-Gen. Lovell H. Rousseau; 1st Ohio, Col. Ed. A. Parrott; 6th Indiana, Col. Crittenden; 3d Kentucky (Louisville Legion); battalions 15th, 16th and 19th regulars. *Second Brigade*—Brig.-Gen. Johnston; 32d Indiana, Col. Willich; 39th Indiana, Col. Harrison; 49th Ohio, Col. Gibson. *Third Brigade*—Colonel Kirk, 34th Illinois, commanding; 34th Illinois, Lieut.-Col. Badsworth; 29th Indiana, Lieut.-Col. Drum; 30th Indiana, Col. Bass; 77th Pennsylvania, Col. Stambaugh.

MAJOR-GENERAL LEW. WALLACE'S DIVISION — RIGHT OF ARMY.— *First Brigade*—Col. Morgan L. Smith, commanding; 8th Missouri, Col. Morgan L. Smith, Lieut.-Col.-James Peckham, commanding; 11th Indiana, Col. George F. McGinnis; 24th Indiana, Col. Alvin P. Hovey; Thurber's Missouri battery. *Second Brigade*—Col. Thayer (1st Nebraska) commanding; 1st Nebraska, Lieut.-Col. McCord, commanding; 23d Indiana, Col. Sanderson; 58th Ohio, Col. Bausenwein; 68th Ohio, Col. Steadman; Thompson's Indiana battery. *Third Brigade*—Col. Chas. Whittlesey (20th Ohio) commanding; 20th Ohio, Lieut.-Col. ——— commanding; 56th Ohio, Col. Peter Kinney; 76th Ohio, Col. Chas. R. Woods; 78th Ohio, Col. Leggett.

At daylight it became evident that the gunboat bombardment through the night had not been without a most important effect. It had changed the position of the rebel army. The sun had gone down with the enemy's lines encircling the Union forces closely on the centre and left, pushing them to the river, and leaving them little over half a mile of all the broad space they had held in the morning. The gunboats had cut the coils and loosened the anaconda-like constriction. Their shells had made the old position on the extreme Union left, which the rebels had been occupying, utterly untenable. Instead of stealing upon their foe in the night, which was doubtless their intention, they were compelled to fall back from point to point out of range of the shells which came dropping in ;. go where they would within range, the troublesome visitors would find them out, and they fell back beyond the inner Union camps, and thus lost more than half the ground they had gained the afternoon before.

Less easily accounted for was a movement of theirs on the right. Here they had held a steep bluff, covered with underbrush, as their advanced line. Through the night they abandoned this, the best possible position for opposing Lew. Wallace, and had fallen back across some open fields to the scrub oak woods beyond.

To those who had looked despairingly at the prospects on Sunday evening, it seemed unaccountable that the rebels did not open the contest by daybreak. Their retreat before the bombshells of the gunboats, however, explained the delay. The Union divisions were put in motion almost simultaneously. By seven o'clock Lew. Wallace opened the day by shelling the rebel battery, of which mention has been made, from the positions he had selected the night before. A brisk artillery duel was followed by a rapid movement of infantry across a shallow ravine, as if to storm; and the rebels, enfiladed and menaced in front, limbered up and made the opening of their Monday's retreating.

NELSON'S ADVANCE.

Nelson, who was assigned the left wing, moved his division about the same time Wallace opened on the rebel battery, forming in line of battle, Ammon's brigade on the extreme left, Bruce's in the centre, and Hazen's to the right. Skirmishers were thrown out, and for nearly a mile the division thus swept the country, pushing a few outlying rebels before it, till it came upon them in force. Then a general engagement broke out along the line, and again the rattle of musketry and thunder of artillery echoed over the late silent fields. There was no straggling this morning. These men were well drilled, and strict measures were taken to prevent miscellaneous thronging back out of harm's way. They stood up to their work and did their duty manfully.

It soon became evident that, whether from change of commanders or some other cause, the rebels were pursuing a new policy in massing their forces. On Sunday the heaviest fighting had been done on the left. In the morning they seemed to make a less determined resistance here, while toward the centre and right the ground was more obstinately contested, and the struggle fiercely prolonged.

Until half-past ten o'clock Nelson advanced slowly but steadily, sweeping his long lines over the ground of defeat on Sunday morning, moving over scores of dead rebels, and resistlessly pressing back the jaded and wearied enemy. The rebels had received but few reinforcements during the night. Their men were exhausted with the desperate contest of the day before, and manifestly dispirited by the fact that they were fighting Grant and Buell combined.

Gradually, as Nelson pushed forward his lines under heavy musketry, the enemy fell back, till about half-past ten, when, under cover of the heavy timber and a furious cannonading, they made a general rally. The Union forces, flushed with their easy success, were scarcely prepared for the sudden onset, when the rebel masses were hurled against them with tremendous force. The men halted, wavered, and were driven back. At this critical juncture Captain Terry's regular battery came dashing up. Scarcely taking time to unlimber, he was loading and sighting his pieces before the caissons had turned, and in an instant was tossing in shell from twenty-four-pound howitzers in to the compact and advancing rebel ranks.

Here was the turning point of the battle on the left. The rebels were checked, not halted. On they came. Horse after horse from the batteries was picked off. Every private at one of the howitzers was shot down, and the gun was worked by Captain Terry himself and a corporal. A regiment dashed up from the Union line, and saved the disabled piece. Then for two hours artillery and musketry raged at close range. At last the enemy began to waver. The Federals pressed on, pouring in deadly volleys. Just then Buell, who assumed the general direction of his troops in the field, came up. At a glance he saw the position of things, and gave a prompt order. "Forward at double quick by brigades." The men leaped forward with the eagerness of unleashed hounds. For a quarter of a mile the rebels fell back. Faster and faster they ran; less and less resistance was made to the advance. At last the front camps on the left were reached, and by half-past two that point was cleared. The rebels had been steadily swept back over the ground they had won, with heavy loss, and fell into confusion. The Unionists had retaken all their own guns lost here the day before, and one or two from the rebels were left to attest how bravely that great victory in Tennessee was won.

ADVANCE OF CRITTENDEN'S DIVISION.

Next to Nelson came Crittenden. He, too, swept forward over his ground to the front some distance before finding the foe. Between eight and nine o'clock, however, while keeping Smith's brigade on his left even with Nelson's flank, and joining Boyle's brigade to McCook on the right, in the grand advance, he came upon the enemy with a battery in position, and, well supported, Smith dashed his brigade forward. There was sharp, close work with musketry, and the rebels fled. He took three pieces—a twelve-pound howitzer and two brass six-pounders. But they cost the gallant Thirteenth Ohio dear. Major Ben. Piatt Runkle fell, mortally wounded.

For half an hour, perhaps, the storm raged around these captured guns. Then came the recoiling rebel wave that had hurled Nelson back. Crittenden, too, caught its full force. The rebels swept up to the bat teries—around them, and down after the retreating Union column. But the two brigades, like those of Nelson's to their left, took a fresh position, faced the foe, and held their ground. Mendenhall's and Bartlett's batteries now began shelling the infantry that alone opposed them. Before abandoning the guns so briefly held, they had spiked them with mud, and this novel expedient was perfectly successful. From that time till after one o'clock, while the fight raged back and forth over the same ground, the rebels did not succeed in firing a shot from their mud-spiked artillery.

At last the Union brigades began to gain the advantage. Crittenden drove the enemy steadily forward. Captain Mendenhall, with First-Lieutenant Parsons, a Western Reserve West Pointer, with Bartlett, poured in their shell. A rush for the contested battery, and it was taken again. The rebels retreated towards the left. Smith and Boyle holding the infantry well in hand, Mendenhall again got their range and poured in shell on the new position. The fortune of the day was against them, as against their comrades in Nelson's front, and they were soon in full retreat.

Just then Brigadier-General Thomas J. Woods' advance brigade from his approaching division came up. It was too late for the fight, but it relieved Crittenden's weary fellows, and pushed on after the rebels until they were found to have left the most advanced Union camps.

M'COOK'S ADVANCE.

Thus the left was saved. Meanwhile McCook, with his magnificent regiments, was doing equally well toward the centre. His division was handled in a way to save great effusion of blood, while equally important results were attained. The reserves were kept as much as possible from under fire, while the troops in front were engaged. Thus the lists of killed and wounded will show that while as heavy fighting was done here as any where on the right or centre, the casualties were remarkably few.

An Illinois battery, serving in the division, was in imminent danger. The Sixth Indiana was ordered to its relief. A rapid rush, close musketry firing—no need of bayonets here—the battery was safe. The enemy were to the front and right. Advancing and firing the Sixth pushed on. The rebel colors dropped. Another volley; yet once more the fated colors fell. Was there fatality in this? The rebels seemed to think so, for they wheeled and disappeared.

Rousseau's brigade was drawn off in splendid style. The rebel General saw the brigade filing back, and pushed his forces onward again. Kirk's brigade advanced to meet him, coming out of the woods into an open field. It was met by a tremendous fire, which threw a battalion of regulars in its front into some confusion. They retired to reform, and meanwhile down dropped the brigade on the ground. As the front was cleared the men sprang up and charged across the open field, straight to the woods, under cover, driving the enemy back with their impetuous advance. He rallied promptly, Fierce musketry firing swept the woods. They advanced thirty rods, perhaps, when the Twenty-ninth Indiana got into a marsh and fell partially to the rear. Heavier came the leaden hail. The Twenty-ninth and Thirtieth both fell back fifteen or twenty rods; they rallied and advanced again. They were repulsed, started impetuously forward, and this time came in on the vulnerable points. Colonel Waggoner's Fifteenth Indiana come up to the support and the enemy disappeared. Fresh troops took their places, and for them the fight ended.

Beginning at the left the waves of success swept forward from point to point over the lost fields of Sunday. Pæans of victory, and the wild cheers of successful soldiers sounded the requiem of the fallen rebels, who had atoned for their treason by the brave man's death. Nelson, Crittenden, McCook, Hurlbut, McClernand, led their divisions bravely through the fray. The contest lasted longer on the right, and was even more fiercely contested.

LEW. WALLACE'S MOVEMENTS.

When Major-General Lew. Wallace opened the battle at seven o'clock by shelling with enfilading fires a rebel battery, a few shots demonstrated to the rebels that their position was untenable. The instant Sherman came in to protect his left, Wallace advanced his infantry. The rebel battery at once limbered up and got out of the way. The advance had withdrawn the division from Sherman, making a left half wheel, to get back into the neighborhood of the Federal line; they advanced some two hundred yards, which brought them to a little elevation, with a broad open stretch to the front. As the division halted on the crest of the swell, through the edge of the timber, skirting the fields, the head of a rebel column appeared, marching past in splendid style on the double-quick. Banner after banner flashed out through the foliage; the "Stars and Bars" forming a long line, stretching parallel with Wallace's line of battle. Regiment after regiment swept forward, the line lengthened, and doubled and trebled; the head of the column was out of sight and still they came. Twenty regiments were counted passing through the woods. Their design was plain. The rebels had abandoned the idea of forcing their way through the Union left, and the manifest attempt was to turn the right.

Thompson's and Thurber's batteries were now ordered up, and the whole column was shelled as it passed. The rebels threw their artillery into position rapidly, and a brisk cannonading began. After a time, while the fight still rested with the artillery, the rebels opened a new and destructive battery to the right, which the Union men soon ascertained was "Watson's Louisiana battery," from the marks on the ammunition boxes the enemy were forced from time to time to leave behind.

Batteries, with a brigade of supporting infantry, were now moved forward over open fields, under heavy fire, to contend against this new assailant. The batteries opened, the sharpshooters were thrown out to the front to pick off the rebel artillerists, and the brigade was ordered down on its face to protect it from the flying shell and grape. For an hour and a half the contest lasted, while the body of the division was still delayed, waiting for Sherman.

SHERMAN'S DIVISION.

Sherman had received orders from Grant to advance and recapture his camps. His division was composed of odds and ends, as it came out of the conflict on Sunday evening.

His command was of a mixed character. Buckland's brigade was the only one that retained its organization. Colonel Hildebrand was personally there, but his brigade was not. Colonel McDowell had been severely injured by a fall of his horse, had gone to the river, and the regiments of his brigade were not in line. The Thirteenth Missouri, Colonel Crafts J. Wright, had reported itself on the field, and fought well, retaining its regimental organization, and it formed a part of Sherman's line during Sunday night and all Monday. Other fragments of regiments and companies had also fallen into his division, and acted with it during the remainder of the battle.

This was not a very promising host with which to "advance and recapture his camps." Sherman, full of ardor, moved forward and reoccupied the ground on the extreme right of General McClernand's camp, where he attracted the fire of a battery located near Colonel McDowell's headquarters. Here he remained, patiently awaiting the sound of General Buell's advance upon the main Corinth road. It was this independent action of Sherman which caused Wallace to halt—he evidently not understanding that General's design.

By ten o'clock Sherman's right, under Colonel Marsh, came up. He started to move across the field, but the storm of musketry and grape was too much for him, and he fell back in good order. Again he started on the double-quick and gained the woods. The Louisiana battery was turned; Marsh's position left it subject to fire in flank and in front, and it then fled. The other rebel batteries at once followed, and Wallace's division, in an instant, now that a master move had swept the board, pushed forward. Before them were broad fallow fields, then a woody little ravine, succeeded by corn-fields and woods.

The left brigade was sent forward. It crossed the fallow fields, under fire, gained the ravine, and was rushing across the corn-fields, when the same Louisiana steel rifled guns opened on them. Dashing forward they reached a little ground swell, behind which they dropped like dead men, while skirmishers were sent forward to silence the troublesome battery. The skirmishers crept forward till they gained a little knoll, not more than seventy-five yards from the battery. Of course the guns opened on them. They replied to some purpose. In a few minutes the battery was driven off, the artillerists killed, the horses shot down, and badly crippled every way. But the affair cost the Union cause a brave man—Lieutenant-Colonel Garber, who could not control his enthusiasm at the conduct of the skirmishers, and in his excitement incautiously exposed himself. All this time rebel regiments were pouring on to attack the audacious brigade that was supporting the skirmishers, but fresh regiments from Wallace's division came up in time to defeat their purpose.

The battery was silenced. "Forward" was the division order. Rushing across the corn-fields under a heavy fire, they now met the rebels face to face in the woods. The contest was quick and decisive. Close, sharp, continuous musketry drove the rebels back.

Here unfortunately Sherman's right gave way. Wallace's flank was exposed. He instantly formed Colonel Wood's Seventy-sixth Ohio in a new line of battle, in right angles with the real one, with orders to protect the flank. The Eleventh Indiana was likewise contesting a sharp engagement with the enemy, who made a desperate attempt to flank it, and for a time the contest waxed furious. But Sherman soon filled the place of his broken regiments. Wallace's division came forward, and again the enemy gave way.

By two o'clock the division was in the woods again, and for three-quarters of a mile it advanced under a murderous storm of shot. Then another contest, and another with the batteries, always met with skirmishers and sharpshooting—then by four o'clock, two hours later than on the right, a general rebel retreat—a sharp pursuit—from which the triumphant Union soldiers were recalled to encamp on the old ground of Sherman's division, in the very tents from which those regiments were driven that hapless Sunday morning.

With great thanksgiving and shouts of triumph the Union army took possession of the camps. They had repulsed the enemy in one of the most hardly contested battles of the war, under many disadvantages, and with a heroism that fills a glorious page in the history of nations. The enemy was near, yet retreating—his columns broken and altogether defeated. His cavalry still hovered within half a mile of the camps, but it was allowed to depart, and the battle of Pittsburg Landing, written by more than a hundred thousand bayonets, was at an end.

AFTER THE BATTLE.

The sight of that battle field was horrible. The first approaches, occupying the further range of the enemy's guns, bore fearful witness of the wild devastation made by the ball and shell which had over-shot the mark. Large trees were entirely splintered off within ten feet of the ground; heavy branches lay in every direction, and pieces of exploded missiles were scattered over the forest sward. The carcasses of horses and the wrecks of wagons strewed all the woods and marked every step of the way.

Half a mile further on, and the most terrible results of the struggle were brought to view. Lifeless bodies lay thickly in the woods; the dead and dying lay close together in the fields, some in heaps on their backs, some with clenched hands half raised in air—others with their guns held in a fixed grip, as if in the act of loading when the fatal shaft struck them dead. Others still had crawled away from further danger, and, sheltering themselves behind old logs, had sunk into an eternal sleep. Here were the bodies of men who had fallen the day before, mingled with those from whose wounds the blood was yet warmly trickling.

Around the open space known as "The battalion drill ground," the scene was still more appalling. This spot had been desperately contested on both sides; but the dead on the rebel side were four to one compared to the Union losses. It was horrible to see in what wild attitudes they had fallen. Here a poor creature appeared in a sitting posture, propped up by logs, on which the green moss had been drenched with blood, and with his hands rigidly locked over his knees, sat still as marble, with his ashen face drooping on his breast. One poor wretch had crept away to the woods, and ensconcing himself between two logs, spread his blanket above him as a shield from the rain of the previous night. He was a wounded rebel, and asked pitifully of those who searched among the dead if nothing could be done for him.

In the track of the larger guns terrible havoc had been made, and scenes of revolting mutilation presented themselves. The field of battle extended over a distance of five miles in length, and three-quarters of a mile in width. This space was fought over twice in regular battle array, and many times in the charges and retreats of the different divisions of the two armies. Every tree and sapling in that whole space was pierced through and through with cannon-shot and musket-balls, and it is reported that there was scarcely a rod of ground on the five miles which did not have a dead or wounded man upon it.

On Sunday, especially, several portions of the ground were fought over three and four times, and the two lines swayed backward and forward like advancing and retreating waves. In repeated instances, rebel and Union soldiers, protected by the trees, were within thirty feet of each other. Many of the camps, as they were lost and retaken, received showers of balls. At the close of the fight, General McClernand's tent contained twenty-seven bullet-holes, and his Adjutant's thirty-two. In the Adjutant's tent, when the Union forces recaptured it, the body of a rebel was found in a sitting position. He had evidently stopped for a moment's rest, when a ball struck and killed him. A tree, not more than eighteen inches in diameter, which was in front of General Lew. Wallace's division, bore the marks of more than ninety balls within ten feet of the ground.

THE ARTILLERY AND REGIMENTS ENGAGED.

A record of the dead, wounded and missing in that fearful battle, bears sure evidence of the almost superhuman bravery with which it was contested.

The Illinois men, already famous at Donelson, fought like tigers to sustain their well-earned reputation. Missouri, Ohio, Indiana, Wisconsin, and some of the Iowa regiments, won imperishable laurels. The First and Second Kentucky were gloriously brave in the fight. They, as well as the Sixth, were under fire more than five hours, yet when the enemy turned their faces toward Mississippi, they were ready and eager to follow. The Ohio Fifty-fourth, Zouave regiment, were at their post in the thickest of the fight. Also the Fifty-seventh, who remembered well that Ohio expected her buckeye sons to do their duty.

Taylor's and Waterhouse's batteries were first in the fight. Two regiments that should have supported the last broke and ran. Waterhouse was wounded in the thigh by a minie ball. Taylor's battery continued to fight, supported splendidly by the Twenty-third Illinois, until he and his support were outflanked on both sides.

Waterhouse, with his three guns, took up a second position, supported by the second brigade of McClernand's division, Colonel Marsh commanding. During the forenoon they were compelled to retire through their own encampment, with heavy loss, into the woods. There a second line of battle was formed, when McClernand ordered an advance. A hundred rods brought the solid columns within sight of the rebels, and then followed one of the most fiercely contested and sanguinary engagements of that desperate field. It resulted in the repulse of the rebels, who were driven back through the Union encampments. Then the enemy was reinforced, and Colonel Marsh, finding his ammunition nearly expended, was compelled to retreat before the overwhelming forces of the enemy.

On Monday a fine Michigan battery, captured by the enemy the day before, was retaken by the Sixteenth Wisconsin, at the point of the bayonet. The fight, after taking this battery, was conducted by General Beauregard in person. In his efforts to recover it he was wounded in the arm. He was successful in taking it, but it was again wrested from him. This battery was retaken and recaptured no less than six times.

Company A of the Chicago Light Artillery, so severely handled on the first day, was only able to man three guns on Monday; but with these, after a desperate contest, they succeeded in silencing and capturing a rebel battery of six guns. They were, however, compelled to abandon it from want of horses.

The report of General Lew. Wallace especially commended the Nebraska First, the Twentieth, Fifty-eighth, Seventy-sixth and Seventy-eighth Ohio, and the Twenty-third Indiana. The Indiana Twenty-fifth literally covered itself with glory. The Indiana Sixth, Ninth, Eleventh, Thirty-first, Thirty-second, Twenty-fourth, Forty-third and Fifty-seventh all performed most honorable parts in the terrible drama.

Of the United States regulars, there was a fine representation. They were used at those points where the utmost steadiness was demanded, and fought with consummate skill and determination.

The losses of the Illinois regiments in McClernand's division were very heavy, in officers and men. On Sunday, company A, of the Forty-ninth Illinois, lost from one volley twenty-nine men, including three officers; and on Monday morning the company appeared on the ground commanded by a second sergeant. General McClernand's third brigade, which was led by Colonel Raith until he was mortally wounded, changed commanders three times during the battle. On Monday morning, one of General Hurlbut's regiments (the Third Iowa) was commanded by a first lieutenant.

General Grant is an illustration of the fortune through which some men, in the thickest showers of bullets, always escape. He has participated in skirmishes and fourteen pitched battles, and is universally pronounced, by those who have seen him on the field, daring even to rashness; but he has never received a scratch. At four o'clock on Sunday evening, he was sitting upon his horse, just in the rear of the Union line of batteries, when Carson, the scout, who had reported to him a moment before, had fallen back, and was holding his horse by the bridle, about seven feet behind him. A six-pound shot, which flew very near General Grant, carried away Carson's head, passed just behind Lieutenant Graves, volunteer aid to General Wilson, tearing away the cantle of his saddle and cutting his clothing, but leaving him uninjured. It then took off the legs of a soldier in one of General Nelson's regiments, which was just ascending the bluff.

About the same hour, further up to the right, General Sherman who had been standing for a moment, while Major Hammond, his chief of staff, was holding his bridle, remounted. By the prancing of his horse, General Sherman's reins were thrown over his neck, and he was leaning forward in the saddle, with his head lowered, while Major Hammond was bringing them back over his head, when a rifle-ball struck the line in Major Hammond's hand, severing it within two inches of his fingers, and passed through the top and back of General Sherman's hat. Had he been sitting upright it would have struck his head. At another time a ball struck General Sherman on the shoulder, but his metallic shoulder-strap warded it off. With a third ball he was less fortunate, for it passed through his hand. General Sherman had three horses shot under him, and ranks high among the heroes of that nobly won battle.

General Hurlbut had a six-pound shot pass between his horse's head and his arm; a bullet hurtled through the animal's mane, and one of his horses was killed under him.

The statement has gone forth that General Prentiss was made prisoner at the first early onslaught of the enemy, when his division was driven in upon Sherman's lines. But this is an error. Prentiss' men fought well even in retiring. They retired to re-form, and pursued the conflict up to late in the afternoon, under Prentiss' personal lead. They maintained a stand on McClernand's left and Hurlbut's right. In the thick underbrush where they made their last stand, almost every shrub and bush was struck by bullets; no spot on the entire field evidenced more desperate fighting. The last time General Prentiss met General Hurlbut, he asked him: "Can you hold your line?" General Hurlbut replied, "I think I can." Not long after he sent a messenger to General Prentiss, to inform him that he was forced back, but the man was probably killed, as he never returned or delivered the message. About the same time, McClernand was forced back on his right, and Prentiss, without knowing that his supports on each side were gone, held his line. The enemy, both on his right and left, was half a mile in his rear before he discovered it, and his capture was inevitable.

Of General Buell's conduct in battle, one of his men wrote, "I wish you could have seen the gallantry, the bravery, the dauntless daring, the coolness of General Buell. He seemed to be omnipresent. If ever man was qualified to command an army, it is he. He is a great, a *very* great General, and has proved himself so; not only in organizing and disciplining an army, but in handling it. He had his horse shot under him." -

LOSSES.

The official reports of losses are given in the following tabular statement:

GRANT'S ARMY.

DIVISIONS.	KILLED.	WOUNDED.	MISSING.	TOTAL.
1—General McClernand	251	1,351	236	1,848
2—General W. H. L. Wallace,	228	1,033	1,163	2,424
3—General Lew. Wallace,	43	257	5	305
4—General Hurlbut,	313	1,449	223	1,985
5—General Sherman,	318	1,275	441	2,034
6—General Prentiss,	196	562	1,802	2,760
Total	1,349	5,927	3,870	11,356

BUELL'S ARMY.

2—General McCook,	95	793	8	896
4—General Nelson,	90	591	58	739
5—General Crittenden,	80	410	27	517
Total,	265	1,794	93	2,152
Grand Total,	1,614	7,721	3,963	13,508

The official report of General Beauregard states the rebel loss to be 1,728 killed, 8,012 wounded, and 959 missing; which is far below the estimated losses of the enemy given by the Federal officers, who buried the dead on the field.

Bravely was that battle contested on both sides. We have described the way in which the Federal Generals fought and won a victory. But the South was gallantly represented—so gallantly, that a victory over such men was worth a double conquest over a meaner foe.

Beauregard seemed omnipresent along his lines throughout that memorable day, striving by expostulation, entreaties, command, exposure of his own person, to stem the tide of defeat; but it was in vain. The steady flank advances of the Federal wings—the solidity of their centre, rendered it necessary to "retreat," if he would not be cut off entirely. His baffled and somewhat dispirited brigades fell back slowly upon the Corinth road, which, in all the fortunes of the two days' fight, had been carefully guarded from any approach of the Unionists. The retreat was neither a panic nor a rout. Some regiments threw away their arms, blankets, etc., from exhaustion; great numbers of killed and wounded crowded the army wagons, and much camp equipage was necessarily left behind.

The pursuit was kept up with but little energy. The nature of the woods rendered cavalry movements extremely difficult, and though three thousand mounted fellows had waited two days for an order to ride into the fray, it came too late for much service. The infantry pushed onward only a mile or two, for being unacquainted with the topography of the country, General Buell considered it dangerous to pursue his advantages any farther.

In giving a record of this contest, one thing is assured—the Union victory was won by the heroic fortitude of men, many of whom never before had been under fire; and the field is written all over with the records of soldiers whose unfaltering heroism gave the name of Pittsburg Landing to the hardest fought and noblest won battle of the American continent.

GENERAL SHERMAN'S RECONNOISSANCE TOWARD CORINTH.
April 8, 1862.

The fatigue and suffering experienced by the victorious army at Pittsburg were too severe for an immediate pursuit of Beauregard's forces on their retreat from the battle field on the 7th of April. On the morning of the 8th, however, General W. T. Sherman was ordered by General Grant to follow up the enemy, with a small force. With two brigades of infantry, and Colonel Dickey's Illinois cavalry, he advanced on the Corinth road, to the forks, several miles beyond the battle field. The abandoned camps of the enemy lined the road, in all of which were found more or less of their wounded with hospital flags thrown out for their protection. At that point, reconnoitering parties were sent out on both roads, which reported the enemy's cavalry in force in either direction. A Federal brigade under General Wood, which had been stationed in that vicinity, was ordered to advance on the left hand road, while General Sherman led the third brigade of his division up the right. About half a mile from the forks was a clear field, through which the highway passed, and immediately beyond it a space of two hundred yards of fallen timber; beyond that an extensive camp of the enemy's cavalry could be seen. After a reconnoissance, the two advanced companies of the Ohio Seventy-seventh, Colonel Hildebrand, were ordered to deploy as skirmishers, and the regiment itself to move forward into line, with intervals of one hundred yards. In this order they advanced cautiously until the skirmishers were engaged.

Taking it for granted that this disposition would clear the camp, Gen. Sherman held Colonel Dickey's Fourth Illinois cavalry ready to charge. The enemy's cavalry came down boldly, breaking through the line of skirmishers, when the regiment of infantry wavered, threw away its guns and fled. The ground was admirably adapted to a defence of infantry against cavalry, it being miry and covered with fallen timber.

As the regiment of infantry broke, Colonel Dickey's cavalry began to charge with their carbines, and fell into disorder. General Sherman instantly sent orders to the rear for the brigade to form in line of battle, which was promptly executed. The broken infantry and cavalry rallied on this line, and as the enemy's cavalry came up to it, the Union cavalry in turn charged and drove them from the field. General Sherman then advanced the entire brigade upon the same ground, and sent Colonel Dickey's cavalry a mile further on the road. On the ground which had been occupied by the Seventy-seventh Ohio, were fifteen dead and about twenty-five wounded. Two hundred and eighty Confederate wounded and fifty of the Federals were found in the camp from which the enemy were driven.

General Halleck attributed the victory at Pittsburg greatly to the bravery and skill of General Sherman, and recommended that he should be promoted to a Major-Generalship, which rank was conferred upon him by the President.

OCCUPATION OF HUNTSVILLE, ALA.
April 10, 1862.

On the same day that General Buell left Nashville for Pittsburg, he dispatched General Mitchell's division on a hazardous expedition through Tennessee, to Huntsville, Ala.

Leaving Murfreesborough, Tenn., on the 5th of April, they marched to Shelbyville, twenty-six miles, in twelve hours, amid a cold, drizzling rain. They experienced a warm welcome from the inhabitants of that beautiful city. Here they were obliged to remain two days, awaiting the arrival of their supply train; and on the 8th, after a march of twenty-seven miles, they reached Fayetteville, Lincoln Co., a town where the secession sentiment was almost universal. Fifteen miles beyond they crossed the State line and entered Alabama, continuing their course due south. A Northern journal says:

"It stirs the blood with enthusiasm to read the exploits of General Mitchell, in Alabama—so full are they of dash, enterprise and daring. When the General was on his way to Bridgeport, he met a 'native,' whom he asked to show him a point where a certain stream could be forded. The Alabamian declined to furnish the information. 'Bind him and march him to the head of the column,' said the General. Then every man of three thousand in the ranks was ordered to take a rail from the adjacent fences, and these were thrown into the river, extemporizing a bridge on which the troops crossed. At another place, they came upon a stream three hundred feet wide, and twenty feet deep.

'Never mind,' said the General, 'I have a pontoon bridge;' and he ordered his men to roll down the bales from a load of abandoned cotton near by. Some of the officers laughed at the idea of making a bridge of such materials, but he told them he had calculated the buoyancy of cotton, and found it to be four hundred and eighty-six pounds to a bale. The bridge was made, and the calculation proved correct.

"On reaching a bridge near Sunrise, it was found to be on fire, with a piece of rebel artillery stationed to command it. General Mitchell entered the bridge and asked who would volunteer to save it. A sergeant of the Thirty-third Ohio sprang after him. 'You are my man!' said the General. In a moment the bridge was thronged with volunteers, and they saved it. At another place the General himself was found in the mud with his coat off, working at a bridge on which his command crossed a swamp."

As the army advanced, an eager curiosity became manifest to know the point of destination. On the way, the General met a man travelling on foot. He asked him how far it was to Huntsville.

"Eleven miles."

"Do they know we are coming?"

"No; they have not the least idea of it."

Huntsville, then, was the desired haven. Ten miles from the place the General called a halt, to wait for the artillery and infantry to come up. No tents were pitched, but for miles away the impatient invaders could be seen around their camp fires. The General flung himself down by an old log, overrun with moss, and on this novel bed snatched two hours' rest. Just as the moon was going down, the bugle call was sounded. The soldiers sprang to their feet, and in a few minutes they were ready to move.

The Simonson battery led the way, supported by Kennett's and Colonel Turchin's brigade. The army passed a magnificent plantation, with many negroes, owned by the rebel ex-Secretary Walker. Four miles from Huntsville, the shrill whistle of a locomotive was heard. In a few moments the train hove in sight, and was stopped by the outbreak of Simonson's brass guns. The train was captured, together with one hundred and fifty-nine prisoners.

On to the town was the cry. Daylight was dawning, and the citizens quietly sleeping as the foe entered the silent streets. The clattering noise of the cavalry aroused them from their slumbers, and they flocked to the doors and windows, exclaiming, with blanched cheeks and sinking hearts, "They have come—the Yankees have come!" Never in the history of any military movement was a surprise so complete. Men rushed into the street half dressed, women fainted, children screamed, the negroes laughed, and for a short time a scene of perfect terror reigned.

This state of affairs soon subsided, when these startled people realized that the Union soldiers were disposed to treat them kindly.

Colonel Gazley, of the Thirty-seventh Indiana, was appointed Provost-Marshal, and his regiment occupied the city as Provost-Guard.

At the extensive depot was found seventeen first-class locomotives, and a great number of passenger and freight cars. At the foundry, two or three cannon with several small arms. The General soon made good use of the engines. Ere the close of the night, one hundred miles of the Memphis and Charleston railroad was in his possession, stretching in one direction as far as Stevenson, in the other as far as Decatur, capturing at the latter place the entire camp equipage of a regiment, which left very hastily on the approach of the Union troops.

Making Huntsville his headquarters, where he remained for six weeks, General Mitchell rendered essential service by intercepting the enemy's communications, and capturing or destroying his supplies. He evinced marked ability, and met with uniform success in fitting out many smaller expeditions through that region of country. He extemporized a gunboat on the Tennessee, which aided him materially when visiting the eastern side of the river.

CAPTURE OF FORT PULASKI, GA.
April 11, 1862.

Fort Pulaski, the key to the city of Savannah, stands on Cockspur Island, at the mouth of the Savannah river, about fourteen miles below the city. It was built by the United States Government at a cost of nearly one million of dollars. It is of a pentagonal form, and covers several acres of ground. The walls are forty feet high, presenting two faces towards the sea, the ranges of fire radiating at opposite angles. It was a position of immense strength, being constructed for a full armament, on the lower tier, of sixty-five 32-pounders, and the upper tier for fifty-three 24-pounders, four 18-pound flanking howitzers, one 13-inch mortar, twelve 8-inch columbiads, and seven 10-inch mortars—altogether, one hundred and fifty guns. The interior of the fort was well supplied with large furnaces for heating shot, quarters, barracks, ammunition, etc.

Tybee Island, and the lighthouse, had been previously evacuated by the rebels. The investment of Fort Pulaski was a work of great magnitude, and long and careful preparations for its reduction were necessary. Batteries were erected at several points, after severe labor on the part of the Federal forces, and at the end of the month of March the final arrangements were drawing to completion.

Cockspur Island, on which Fort Pulaski stands, is low and marshy, and the nearest solid land is Tybee Island, lying to the seaward, and within three-quarters of a mile distant. Tybee Island stretches out from a point known as Goat Point, two or three miles to the sea—the nearest point to the fort being that just named. General Q. A. Gillmore took command at Tybee Island on February 20th, which had been previously evacuated by the rebels, and here were built the heaviest breaching batteries; but others were erected at intervals along the shore for a distance of nearly two miles. The subjoined table gives their strength and armament:

BATTERY.	NO. OF GUNS.	SIZE.	KIND.	WEIGHT. LBS.	RANGE.	COMMANDER.
Stanton	3	13 inch.	Mortar.	17,120	3,476	Captain Skinner.
Grant	3	13 "	"	17,120	3,256	" Palmer.
Lyon	4	10 "	Columb'd	15,059	3,256	" Pelouze.
Lincoln	3	8 "	"	9,240	3,045	" Pelouze.
Burnside	1	13 "	Mortar.	17,120	2,760	Sergeant Wilson.
Sherman	3	13 "	"	17,120	2,677	Captain Francis.
Halleck	2	13 "	" .	17,120	2,407	" Sanford.
Scott	2	10 "	Columb'd	15,059	1,777	" Mason.
	1	8 "	"	9,240	....	"
Sigel	5	30 lbs.	Part's s.c'r	....	....	" Seldenkirk.
	1	24 "	James	....	....	"
McClellan	2	42 "	"	....	....	" Rogers.
	3	32 "	"	....	....	"
Totten	4	10 inch.	Mortar.	1,852	1,643	" Rodman.

These works were erected wholly at night, as they were all within range of Fort Pulaski. Their faces were bomb-proof, while in the rear of those most exposed lay a long wide swamp, into which it was supposed that a great portion of the shot and shells from Fort Pulaski would fall. The supposition proved correct. The magazines were bomb-proof, and trenches connected the batteries on Goat's Point; besides this, splinter-proofs were provided for the reliefs, so that every protection possible was secured to the men. The result proved with how great success these preparations were made; during the bombardment of thirty hours the gunners lost but one man killed or wounded. The work occupied six weeks, and was chiefly performed by the Seventh Connecticut, Colonel Terry, the Forty-fifth New York, Colonel Ross, and a detachment of Volunteer Engineers, under Lieutenant-Colonel Hall. When the guns were nearly all in position, a battalion of the Third Rhode Island Volunteer Artillery was sent to Tybee to assist in manning the guns, and later the Eighth Maine regiment, Colonel Rust.

The mounting of ordnance was executed under the direction of Lieutenant Porter, of the U. S. army; he also assumed the entire charge of all duties connected with the ordnance department on the island, supervised the landing of ammunition and implements, and directed the transportation of all the guns. This was a task of infinite labor. The transportation of heavy guns, always difficult, was here rendered peculiarly so. They had to be landed through a bad surf on an open beach, and thence dragged by the soldiers for nearly two miles through a yielding sand. The works were placed so as to be hidden from the enemy until they opened fire. Battery Totten was nearly 1,700 yards from the fort; Batteries Sigel and McClellan 1,620; Battery Scott nearly 1,677; Battery Halleck 2,400; Battery Burnside and others were all more than 3,000; Battery Grant 3,500 yards away. Breaching casemated forts at this distance had never been supposed practicable in modern warfare; indeed, 800 yards is the greatest distance at which it was ever attempted.

On the 9th of April the batteries were completed, the guns placed, and the magazines filled. General Viele had constructed a co-operating battery on the southern extremity of Long Island, in the Savannah, and not more than two miles, if so far, from the fort. The purpose of this was to obtain a reverse fire during the bombardment, which otherwise would proceed entirely from Tybee Island. This battery was not completed in time to engage in the first day's action, but opened fire on the second.

A day or two before the bombardment actually commenced, General Hunter (who had superseded General Sherman in command of the land forces at Hilton Head) and his aids, and General Benham with his staff, came down on steamers from Hilton Head to be present during the engagement, though the command was left with General Gillmore.

On the 9th of April General Gillmore issued orders when the bombardment should be opened, and the part which each of the batteries should take in the work. General Hunter sent a letter to Colonel Charles H. Olmstead, First Regiment Georgia Volunteers, demanding an unconditional surrender of the fort to the United States; and representing the loss of life which would occur if resistance were made to the numerous batteries with which he was surrounded. Colonel Olmstead replied briefly, saying in language worthy of a more sacred cause, "I am here to defend the fort, not to surrender it." When Lieutenant J. H. Wilson returned with this reply, orders were given to open fire from the batteries, and at half-past seven A. M., the first shot was fired from Battery Halleck. The other batteries followed, and Fort Pulaski promptly responded.

The guns for some time not obtaining the proper range, were ineffective. The Federal gunners after a little time learned to distinguish the various shot fired by the enemy, and the range they had. When a gun was fired, and the shot was seen approaching, the cry of "casemate" or "barbette" was given, and they sheltered themselves accordingly. Still later in the engagement they distinguished the shot by the cry "barbette" and "rifle," and when the latter was fired they protected themselves under cover, as far as possible. The same skill was attained by the rebels in the fort.

The bombardment had continued several hours, when two mortar batteries along the shore outside of the fort, on Goat's Point, opened, and to them the enemy directed his hottest fire.

About one o'clock the halyards attached to the flagstaff were shot away, and the flag came down, but was immediately raised in a less conspicuous place. During the afternoon an embrasure in the *pancoupe*, on the southeast angle of the fort, was struck repeatedly, and pieces of the brick work gave way. This angle was the nearest point to the batteries, and in a direct line with the magazine of Fort Pulaski—a fact well known to the Federals from plans of the work in their possession. Afterwards all efforts to effect a breach were directed to this spot. Several of the most important guns, however, were out of order; the mortar shells were observed to fall mostly wide of the mark; and no great result could be noticed even when one fell within the fort. Numerous marks, however, all along both faces of the work which were exposed, told the force and accuracy of the firing. By nightfall, the breach was so far effected that it was evident it could eventually be converted into a practicable one. The bombardment was discontinued at dark, three mortar batteries firing one shell each at intervals of five minutes all night long, worrying the enemy, and preventing any attempt to stop the breach, but without any idea of doing material harm. Several of his guns had evidently been dismounted, and others silenced, during the day. The breach had been commenced, but on the whole the result did not seem especially encouraging. The men and officers were very thoroughly tired with the severe work they had undergone, and the still more fatiguing excitement; few had found time to eat or drink. Many, however, had night duties to perform. Strong infantry pickets were placed, and still stronger supports, in expectation an attempt would be made to relieve the garrison.

Shortly after daybreak all the batteries were opened again. The reply was more vigorous than on the day before. On the Federal side every gun was in readiness, and did good service. The great columbiads under Captain Pelouze were especially effective; they certainly shook the walls of old Pulaski, and damaged them to a considerable extent. All along the line the firing was more rapid and more accurate, five shots striking the walls within as many seconds. Rebel officers said that, on an average, one out of three shots that were fired took effect, and that during all of the second day one shot or shell every minute was the average they received. Early in the morning Captain Seldenkirk, of Battery Sigel, was relieved, and Captain C. P. R. Rodgers, of the frigate Wabash, with a portion of her crew, worked several of the guns of this battery during the remainder of the fight. At the same time Captain Turner, Chief of Commissary on General Hunter's staff, and Lieutenant Wilson, undertook to drill a detachment of the Eighth Maine Volunteers (Colonel Rust). These men went to work, were drilled under fire, and in ten minutes were able to serve their guns with more than tolerable accuracy, and did some of the most effective service rendered that day. This same regiment lay not more than half a mile in the rear of Battery Halleck, for more than half of the entire engagement, covered only by some brushwood, but perfectly content with their exposed position.

Early on the second day, especial attention was directed to the breach. Every gun that could be brought to bear upon the *pancoupe* was trained that way, and directly the aperture began to show the effects. In an hour it became large enough for two men to enter abreast, and the nearest embrasure on its left was also considerably enlarged. Meanwhile, all the other effects of the day before were enhanced; shots struck all over the two exposed faces of the fort; the mortar batteries on the shore of Cockspur Island were silenced, and several of the casemate guns were struck through the embrasures. The battery put up by General Viele, on Long Island, opened fire that morning, and received repeated replies, rendering good service by the destruction it occasioned. The gunboat Norwich, laying on the right of the fort, also became engaged—the distance, however, was too great for her to render any special assistance,—still she got an occasional answer from the garrison. On this day clouds of red dust were seen to rise more frequently from the fort, indicating that the brickwork of which it is constructed was breaking up, and after a while, the great breach became so large that the propriety of a storming party was discussed. The lower part of the aperture was partly filled by the *debris* that fell from above; the arch of the casemate was laid bare, while evidently shaken, a gun in barbette, immediately over the breach, was tottering and ready to tumble below. The breach by its side was also momentarily becoming wider, and just as General Benham was questioning whether a messenger should not be sent to demand a surrender, before risking so great a loss of human life as must be incurred in an assault, the rebel flag on old Pulaski was lowered half way, and a final shot fired from a casemate in the fort. As the flag was not completely hauled down, the Unionists were for a moment uncertain of its import, but all firing was ordered to cease. In a minute more the white flag was raised, and with cheer after cheer all along the batteries on Tybee, came down the stars and bars. It was on the 11th of April, a year to a day from the time when the stars and stripes were first dishonored by Americans at Fort Sumter.

General Hunter was aboard the McClellan with his aids, watching the engagement. Generals Gillmore and Benham were active, and rode rapidly out to Goat's Point. On arriving at this place, General Gillmore, with his aid, Mr. Badeau, and Colonel Rust, entered a boat and put off for the fort. The passage was rough, the channel unknown, and the skiff got aground, and was nearly upset; but at last, soaked and dripping, the party landed on Cockspur Island.

They were met near the landing-place by Captain Sims, of the Georgia Volunteers, who conducted them to the fort. Colonel Olmstead, the commandant, stood at the entrance, and received them courteously. He invited General Gillmore into his own quarters, for a private interview. The terms of capitulation were arranged, and General Gillmore was then conducted over the fort by the Colonel, and took his leave, accompanied by Colonel Rust. General Hunter, in the mean time, had sent messengers to the fort. Colonel Olmstead showed them around the works, and conducted them to the interior, when the swords were delivered. This took place in the Colonel's headquarters, all standing. Major Halpine represented General Hunter. As soon as this ceremony was over, the American flag was raised, and the stars and stripes floated again on the walls of Fort Pulaski. In giving up his sword, Colonel Olmstead said, "I yield my sword, but I trust I have not disgraced it."

The arms of the privates had been previously stacked on the parade, and the men marched to quarters. Both officers and men were allowed to remain all night in their usual quarters. The interior of the fort presented a sorry picture. Blindages had been put up extending on all the rampart, and a part rendered bomb-proof; but shot and shell had burst through many of the sides—knocked in walls, broken down stairways, entered casemates, upset guns, and piled up masses of rubbish and *debris* all around. Seven guns on the parapet were dismounted; nearly every traverse had been struck and partly torn to pieces; all the passageways were obstructed by piles of stones and fallen timber; the magazine had been struck, and part of its outer casing of brick torn away, while at the breach, the havoc was, of course, greatest of all. The breach was entirely practicable; the ditch, sixty feet across, was more than half filled up by the fragments that had fallen, and half a dozen men abreast could have entered the aperture. The Colonel declared, however, that he should have held out until nightfall, had the magazine not been struck. This, of course, settled his fate, and rendered any prolonged resistance a useless risk of human life. Forty thousand pounds of powder, seven thousand shot and shell, and forty-seven guns were captured. The prisoners were three hundred and sixty in number, and belonged to the Georgia Volunteers, the Oglethorpe Light Infantry, and to a German regiment. The Colonel excited the sympathies of his captors by a bearing at once soldierly and subdued. The officers invited the Unionists to their quarters, where several took supper, and some even slept with the rebels whom they had been fighting a few hours before. There was no apparent bitterness on either side; no desire to introduce personal animosities.

This long and severely contested siege resulted in the loss of only two lives, while the number of wounded was very small. This fact is remarkable, in view of the immense amount of shot and shell exchanged during the bombardment.

On Sunday, the 13th, the men were divided into two parties—the officers and about two-thirds of the men forming the first, who were placed on the Ben de Ford—the remainder on the Honduras, and taken to Bay Point. Here they were transferred to the McClellan and Star of the South, to be sent to Fort Columbus, in the harbor of New York.

BATTLE OF SOUTH MILLS, CAMDEN, N. C.
April 20, 1862.

A short but severely contested engagement took place on the 20th of April, between the command of General J. L. Reno, and a body of rebels posted in a strong position to intercept the supposed advance of the Federal troops on Norfolk. General Burnside directed General Reno to make a demonstration on that city, and the latter, taking with him from Newbern the Twenty-first Massachusetts and Fifty-first Pennsylvania, proceeded to Roanoke, where he was joined by detachments of the Eighty-ninth New York and Sixth New Hampshire. With these forces he started for Elizabeth City, and commenced disembarking at midnight, on the 19th, at a point about three miles below the city, on the east side.

By three A. M. Colonel Hawkins' brigade, consisting of the Ninth and Eighty-ninth New York, and Sixth New Hampshire, were landed and ready to move. Colonel Hawkins proceeded with his brigade toward South Mills. General Reno remained to bring up the other two regiments, which had been delayed by the grounding of their vessels at the mouth of the river. They came up at daylight, and were landed by seven A. M. General Reno marched directly toward South Mills, and about twelve miles out met Colonel Hawkins, with his brigade, who, either by the treachery or incompetency of his guide, had been led some miles out of his way. As his men were very much jaded by the long march, they were ordered to follow the Second brigade, about four miles further, to within a mile and a half of South Mills.

The rebels were posted here, and opened a fire of artillery, before the advanced guard discovered them. General Reno reconnoitered their position, and found that they were posted strongly in a line perpendicular to the road, their infantry in ditches, their artillery commanding all the direct approaches, and their rear protected by a dense forest. He ordered the Fifty-first Pennsylvania immediately to file to the right, and pass over to the edge of the woods, to turn their left—the Twenty-first Massachusetts pursuing the same course; and when Colonel Hawkins came up with his brigade, he was sent with the Ninth and Eighty-ninth New York to their support.

The Sixth New Hampshire was formed in line to the left of the road, and its commander ordered to support the four pieces of artillery. Owing to the excessive fatigue of the men, they met with some delay in reaching their position. Meanwhile the enemy kept up a brisk artillery fire, which was gallantly responded to by the small pieces under charge of Colonel Howard, of the Coast Guard. As soon as the Fifty-first Pennsylvania and Twenty-first Massachusetts had succeeded in turning their left, they opened a brisk musketry fire, and, about the same time, the Ninth New York, also coming in range, eager to engage, unfortunately charged upon the enemy's artillery. It was a most gallant charge, but they were exposed to a deadly fire of grape and musketry, and forced to retire, but rallied immediately upon the Eighty-ninth New York. General Reno then ordered both regiments to form a junction with the Twenty-first Massachusetts. In the meantime, the Fifty-first Pennsylvania and Twenty-first Massachusetts kept up an incessant fire upon the rebels, who had withdrawn their artillery, and commenced to retreat in good order. The Sixth New Hampshire had steadily advanced in line to the left of the road, and when within about two hundred yards poured in a deadly volley, which completely demoralized the enemy and ended the battle.

The men rested under arms in line of battle, until about ten o'clock, P. M., when they were ordered to return to the boats, having accomplished the principal object of the expedition, that of conveying the idea that the entire Burnside Expedition was marching upon Norfolk. Owing to a want of transportation, sixteen of the most severely wounded were left behind. Assistant-Surgeon Warren was left with them. Only about ten or fifteen prisoners were taken. Most of them belonged to the Third Georgia regiment. The Ninth New York suffered most severely, owing to their premature charge. The total loss of the Federal troops in killed and wounded was about ninety, some sixty of the number belonging to that regiment.

Just as the decisive volley of the Sixth New Hampshire had compelled the rebels to abandon their position, a terrific thunder-storm broke upon the scene of conflict, and a heavy rain rendered the hope of pursuit futile. After burying the dead, and taking a brief rest, General Reno and his command took up their march for headquarters, at Newbern. On the advance the sun beat fiercely upon his exhausted men, the weather was intensely hot, and they were almost prostrated with the fatigue of the battle and the labor of the march, before they reached a place of rest.

CAPTURE OF FORT MACON, N. C.
April 26, 1862.

The occupation of the town of Beaufort and Morehead City by the Federal troops, on the 24th of March, was followed by active preparations for the reduction of Fort Macon, which commanded the entrance to the harbor. It was anticipated that on the retreat of the rebel troops from Beaufort the overwhelming numbers and equipment of the national forces would demonstrate to the commander of the fort the hopelessness of any attempt to resist the armament that would be brought against him in the event of his refusal to surrender. This hope was not realized. Colonel M. J. White, the commander, resolved to meet the Union forces with every possible resistance; and if the fort was captured by the Federal arms, the doughty rebel determined that it should be purchased at no slight cost.

Fort Macon is situated on a bluff on Bogue's Bank, nearly two miles from the town of Beaufort. It commands the entrance to the harbor, and no vessel can enter the main channel without coming within range of its guns. Opposite the fort, at the entrance of the harbor, is Shackelford Banks, distant about one mile and a half. Fort Macon is of a hexagonal form, and has two tiers of guns—one in casemated bomb-proof, and the other *en barbette*. Its armament consisted of twenty 32-pounders, thirty 24-pounders, two 18-pounders, three field-pieces for flank defence, twelve flank howitzers, eight 8-inch howitzers (heavy), eight 8-inch howitzers (light), one 13-inch mortar, three 10-inch mortars, and two Cohorn mortars—total, 89 guns. The war garrison of the fort was 300 men. There are large furnaces in the fort for heating shot, and before the investment there was a considerable quantity of powder in the magazine. The construction of Fort Macon was commenced in 1826, by Captain Eliason, of the United States Engineer Corps, and was finished in 1860, by Captain, afterwards Brigadier-General John G. Foster.

This fort, like most others in the Southern States, at the opening of the rebellion, was in an almost defenceless condition. Ordnance Sergeant Alexander was the sole guardian of this important position in April, 1861.

CAPTURE OF FORT MACON. 417

In March, the vote on the question of calling a State Convention was taken in North Carolina, and a majority was given against the Convention. Governor Ellis assured the officer in command that the fort would not be taken from under the control of the government, but on the 11th of April, a citizen of Beaufort, in the interest of the secessionists, collected a body of fifty men, with whom he crossed over to the fort and demanded its surrender. Sergeant Alexander delivered up the keys, and the rebel flag was hoisted on its walls. Subsequently stores and supplies for a garrison of 500 men were collected and placed within it, and an efficient body of troops took possession, under Colonel White.

On March 25th, 1862, Morehead City, on the mainland, opposite Bogue Island, was occupied by a portion of General Parke's division of Burnside's army. A few days subsequently a landing had been effected on Bogue Island, and a camp established for the force selected to operate against Fort Macon. On the 11th of April the enemy's pickets were driven in by the Fifth Rhode Island regiment and one company of the Fourth Rhode Island, and eligible localities for the batteries were selected by Captain Williamson, Topographical Engineer on General Burnside's staff. On the next day a working party commenced the erection of the main battery, and from that time the labor proceeded night and day. The troops employed in this service were the Fourth and Fifth Rhode Island and the Eighth Connecticut regiments. The labor was most severe. The men were often on duty twenty-four hours at a time, and labored zealously to accomplish their task in the shortest possible period. What rest they got when on duty was obtained by sleeping on the sands, as no tents or barracks could be erected, since these would have informed the rebels of the location of the troops, and indicated the position of the batteries. The picket duty performed by the men was also very severe. All their work had to be done under a continuous and often severe fire from the fort. From this, however, they were protected by the peculiar formation of the ground, which consisted of a succession of sand-hills up to within about half a mile of the fort.

Previous to the bombardment the garrison were allowed to send letters to their friends at Beaufort.

Three batteries were erected for the reduction of the fort. The first was mounted with four ten-inch mortars, and was built under cover of a large sand-hill, near the edge of the marshes which line the northern shore of the island, at a distance of about 1,400 yards from the fort. This battery was allotted to Lieutenant Flagler, and manned by a portion of battery I, New York Third artillery. The second was in advance 100 yards, built and worked by Captains Lewis O. Morris, and Lieutenants Gowan and Pollock. Three long thirty-pound siege Parrott guns, rifled, composed its armament. The last battery consisted of four eight-inch mortars. It stood 100 yards in advance of the second battery, and was placed in charge of Lieutenant Prouty, and manned by a detachment of battery I, Third New York artillery. Rifle-pits and trenches were also excavated.

On the 24th of April, the preparations having been completed, General Burnside arrived from Newbern, on the steamer Alice Price, having in tow two barges, the Schrapnel and Grenade, fitted up as floating batteries, each armed with two thirty-pound Parrott guns. The Schrapnel had in addition a twelve-pounder rifled Ward gun. They anchored about three miles below the fort.

During the afternoon a flag of truce was sent to the fort, in charge of Captain Biggs, of General Burnside's staff, with a demand for its surrender. Colonel White refused to yield to the demand, and announced his purpose to defend the fort to the last extremity. An understanding was obtained, however, that the commander should have a personal interview with General Burnside on the following morning.

Accordingly, at an early hour on the 25th, the steamer Alice Price, under a flag of truce, proceeded down the bay to a point previously indicated, where General Burnside was soon joined by Colonel White. The meeting was courteous. Colonel White said that he had been placed in command of the fort for the purpose of holding it, and should defend it to the best of his ability.

On the following morning, the 26th, the Federal forces took their respective posts at an early hour. The morning mists had not yet disappeared, when orders were given for the opening of the siege, and before six o'clock the loud thunder of the guns and the deep boom of the heavy mortars broke on the ears of the sleeping citizens of Beaufort, and roused the slumbering garrison of the belligerent fort. Booming loudly over the waters, and rolling away in the distance, the explosions followed in rapid succession for half an hour before the garrison was ready to respond. When prepared, the rebels bravely assumed their allotted positions, manned their guns, and Fort Macon opened upon the national flag.

During the forenoon the eight-inch mortar battery of Lieutenant Prouty sent its shells with regularity and precision into the fort, and at each explosion the red dirt and sand of the glacis' slopes, ramparts, parapets and terrepleins were dashed in a cloud many feet into the air. The flagstaff, with its defiant colors floating at the top, was at times completely obscured in the smoke and dust which rose with the bursting of the missiles. The ten-inch mortar battery was not so successful in the morning. The shells from it burst beyond or high in air over the fort, scattering the fragments of iron far and wide into the water;

but in the afternoon the battery played with an effect that was evidenced in the decreased fire from the fort.

The battery of Parrott guns under command of Captain Morris, in the mean time, kept up an incessant fire upon the ramparts. The difficulty of obtaining accurate range was for some time experienced, and the shots either went over the fort, ricocheting across the water towards Shackleford Banks, or fell short and buried themselves in the sand and glacis on its westerly side. But the range grew more accurate with every shot, and from twelve o'clock until the close of the fight Captain Morris seldom failed to plant his terrible conical balls among the guns, on the edges of the ramparts, and against the walls. The latter were pierced in two places, the balls passing through into the casemates, from which their unceremonious visit hastily expelled the occupants. Wherever these shots struck they tore through all obstacles with a force that hurled fragments of iron and brick, stones, grass-sods and sands bags about in every direction. Many of the rebels were knocked down senseless by the flying sods. When it is considered that the walls of the fort were protected by the slopes of the glacis, the accuracy of the firing from the Parrott battery will be perceived. That part of the walls just protruding above the ramparts of the glacis was the only target presented whereat to aim for the purpose of penetrating the casemates.

About two o'clock, P. M., Major Allen went out with a flag of truce to carry letters written to the garrison from their friends in Beaufort. Many of these entreated the officers to prevail upon Colonel White to surrender the fort. Some ladies in Beaufort set on foot a petition to that effect.

The precision attained by the practice of the forenoon, and the facility of loading and firing, which even the experience of a few hours had given, were now evidenced in the successful results of each shot from the Union batteries. The scene assumed its grandest aspect after two o'clock. A flash and a puff of smoke betokened a discharge; an interval elapsed, which terminated with the report of the piece; then came the sonorous hum of the shell as it flew through the air; another puff of smoke soon followed by a second report, and the deadly missile had exploded.

With glasses every manœuvre in the fort could be distinctly seen. The look out was esconced behind a pile of sand bags upon the ramparts, and spectators fancied they could hear him ejaculate the word "Down!" as he marked the approach of every shot. Its effect was like magic. As he himself disappeared, down out of sight went the crowd of men around the guns, to reappear again when the shot had accomplished its errand.

Little remains to tell of the bombardment. The garrison had at first responded with some seven or eight guns, exclusive of carronades, which were made to serve the purpose of mortars. The squads of gunners could be observed passing about, alternating with the pieces as they became hot under the discharges. Gradually the fire slackened to four, then to three, and then to two guns. . The Federal shot and shell were doing their duty, and subsequent examination showed that fifteen guns were dismounted or disabled on the fort.

To those who worked the mortars of the Federal batteries, the matter was entirely new, and to Captain Ammon's men, of the Third New York artillery, the greatest praise is deserved for their cool and unflinching conduct in this their first experience under fire. The exposed nature of Captain Morris' battery of siege guns drew upon it almost the concentrated fire of the fort, and shot and shell rained around it. The only injury sustained by the battery was the temporary dismounting of one of the guns by a thirty-two-pound solid shot, which came through the embrasure and carried off a wheel. Another carriage was in readiness, and the gun was soon remounted. One of the guns was slightly dented by a solid shot, which struck the reinforce or band around the breech, and then glanced off. The sand bags in all the batteries were disturbed more or less by the concussions, and the embrasures of the three-gun battery were begrimed and black with powder. Eleven hundred shots in all were fired on the Federal side, and of these five hundred and sixty struck the fort.

The firing from the fort gradually slackened as the guns one after another became disabled, until at last the iron thunderers ceased to respond to the continuous peals of the Federal batteries. About half-past four o'clock a white flag was run up over one of the guns, dimly seen through the smoke that had just before issued from it in a heavy cloud. Not long after two officers left the fort, bearing a flag of truce. They advanced towards the batteries, and Captain Pell, of General Burnside's staff, and Lieutenant Hill, of General Parke's staff went out to meet them. They were Captains Pool and Guion, with a message from Col. White, asking the terms of surrender. General Parke replied that the only terms were unconditional surrender, but that he would communicate with General Burnside, who might make different arrangements. The inquiry was telegraphed to Beaufort, and a messenger was sent off to General Burnside, who was on board the Alice Price, some distance up the river. In the morning General Burnside returned to the harbor, and had an interview with Colonel White, on board the Alice Price, when the terms of capitulation were agreed upon. The fort, armament and garrison were to be surrendered to the United States, the officers and men being released on parol, until properly exchanged, returning to their homes with their private effects, such as clothing, bedding, books, etc.

Immediately after the return of Colonel White to his quarters, preparations for the surrender commenced. After a little interval the gates were thrown open and a train of soldiers marched out, and forming a square on the green, just outside, stood a few moments in impressive stillness. Then they formed into line, where they stacked their arms, and returned to their quarters.

General Burnside, General Parke, and Captains Biggs and King directly after this ceremony, returned from the fort, and the Fifth Rhode Island being ordered into line, came up. General Burnside unfolded the new colors presented by the State of Rhode Island, inscribed with the words "Roanoke" and "Newbern," which had been just received, and returned them to the color-bearer, who took his place at the head of the column. The regiment then moved forward in order, to take formal possession of the fort.

The time had at last come for the great event. The wharves and houses of Beaufort were crowded with spectators. The surrounding waters were covered with small craft, hovering near the scene. The squadron of gunboats, with steam up and colors flying, lay off and on outside the bar. At half-past ten o'clock a squad of men from the garrison, detailed by Colonel White for the purpose, cut loose the halliards and hauled down the rebel flag. Ten minutes later four of the Rhode Island boys hoisted the American ensign, the glorious stars and stripes, and a loud cheer broke from the men, which was caught up and echoed by the sailors on ship-board, and even by the citizens over the harbor, in Beaufort, whose shout came cheerily on the breeze.

The Federal fleet, consisting of the steamers State of Georgia, Chippewa, Daylight, and bark Gemsbok, under command of Flag-officer S. Lockwood, took an active part in the bombardment in the forenoon.

The destruction effected by the bombardment was like that at Fort Pulaski. The works outside as well as inside, gave incontestible proof of the execution of the heavy projectiles hurled at the fort. They also showed as clearly the bravery of the men who defended it, and proved that though they were engaged in rebellion, they had the courage and energy of heroic soldiers.

The garrison consisted of about four hundred and fifty men, exclusive of the officers. There were found in the fort nearly twenty thousand pounds of powder, shot and shell in proportion, and a large quantity of provisions.

The rebel loss was 7 killed, 18 wounded; Federal, 1 killed and 3 wounded.

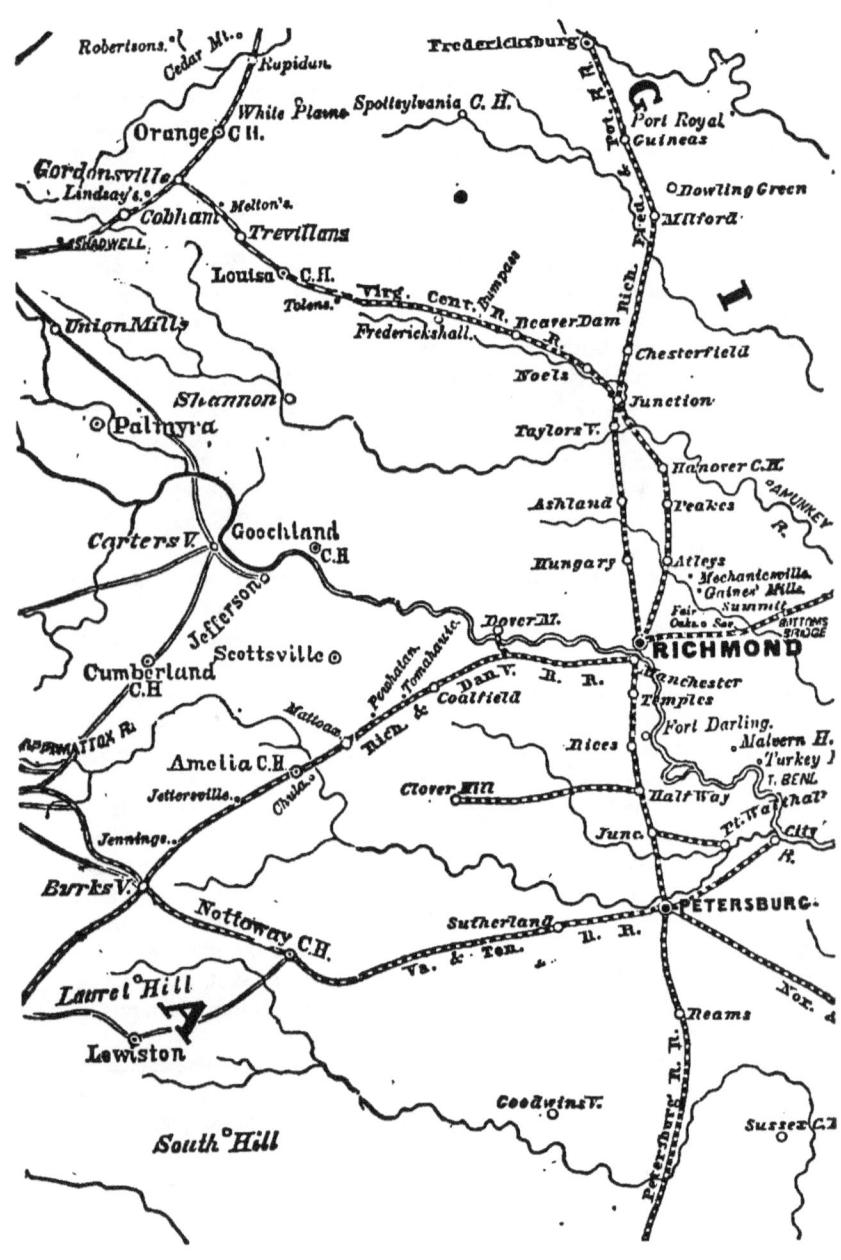

SIEGE OF YORKTOWN, VA.

On Sunday, the 9th of March, the rebel camps at Centreville, Manassas and vicinity were evacuated, and on the 10th, the army of General McClellan commenced a forward movement from the vicinity of Washington toward the abandoned works of the enemy. On the same day a portion of General Kearney's forces reached Centreville, and Federal scouts had explored the deserted works at Manassas Junction. The enemy continued their retreat on the line of the Orange railroad, burning the bridges, and destroying the railroad property on their route.

On the 14th, General McClellan issued an address to the army from his headquarters at Fairfax Court-House, complimenting the men on their discipline, equipment, and patience during the long delay incident to the work of preparation. They were now to be brought face to face with the enemy, and he besought the army to place perfect trust in him, though his plans of action might seem at times unaccountable.

The cheering news of the capture of New Madrid, the evacuation of Columbus, and the victory at Pea Ridge, now filled all loyal hearts with enthusiasm; and it was fully believed that the army of the Potomac was on the direct route to Richmond, destined to give the death-blow to the rebellion before the month of April should open. Will the rebels make a stand? asked many a confident Unionist, hopeful that the prestige of McClellan's splendid army would compel the enemy to retire from point to point without risking a battle.

The month of March passed;—and while the public mind was animated with the most cheering details of the western victories—the capture of Newbern, and the defeat of the enemy at Winchester, the great army of the Potomac appeared for the time to have passed from recollection. The Government censorship restrained the publication of any reports of McClellan's movements, and the people, left entirely to hope and conjecture, were sanguine in anticipation of the speedy possession of the Confederate capital.

Late in the month, rumors reached the northern cities of the arrival of forces at Old Point, on the James river, twenty miles from Norfolk, which were supposed by the Richmond papers to be reinforcements for Burnside. Again curiosity was awakened by the immense number of transports called for and chartered by the Government, daily arriving at the mouth of the Chesapeake. On the 26th, Great Bethel was taken possession of by the Federal troops, and on the 29th a reconnoissance in force was made toward Yorktown It was now generally known that the large army under General McClellan had been conveyed by transports to Old Point, and was marching to attack the rebel entrenchments at Yorktown, the key of the Peninsula.

On the 5th of April, General McClellan's dispatch to the Secretary of War, announced that his army had that day arrived in front of the enemy's works, having met with but slight opposition on its route.

During this period the weather was unfavorable for military operations. Heavy storm-clouds frowned inauspiciously on the approaching army, rain fell almost daily in torrents, and this at a time when there could be no adequate provision for shelter.

The Federal army was now destined to undergo an experience of toil and privations calculated to try its endurance to the utmost.

Solid roads were absolutely necessary for transportation from the landings to the various encampments, as it was impossible to draw the immense siege and supply trains over or through the soft alluvial mire formed by the unremitting rains, while the creeks and water courses were swollen into torrents. Skirmishing was of daily occurrence—for the enemy neglected no opportunity to annoy their formidable opponents, while the Federal army found it necessary to push its advances within commanding reach of the rebel entrenchments, which stretched from the York to the James rivers, a distance of six miles. The rebel earthworks were ponderously built—some of them of a height and thickness hitherto unparalleled in any war.

The Union soldiery toiled incessantly in the trenches, while covering parties, with efficient batteries, stood guard in their defence, and daily sacrificed some of their brave numbers while protecting their toiling comrades.

The labors of the Federal army soon became apparent. Formidable earthworks began to show their heads, and artillery of the largest calibre was put in position. The rebel generals were struck with astonishment and dismay when the evidences of engineering skill hitherto unsuspected, stood revealed before them.

On the other hand, every day more fully revealed the extensive and intricate line of the rebel defences. Their strength in forts, lunettes and rifle pits—their constantly increasing numbers, and untiring activity, with their accurate knowledge of the topography of the country, increased the magnitude of the work before the Federal army. The natural obstacles to its progress were by no means few or trifling. The sinuous windings of the line of attack they were obliged to assume—the innumerable swamps and pools of water confronting them on every side, the almost impenetrable forests and tangled undergrowth added to their labors and their sufferings. Cold and shivering under garments saturated anew by the rains of to-day, ere those of yesterday had been vaporized, the soldiers endured the pangs of hunger and fatigue unappalled. In view of the terrific struggle before them, human suffering counted for nothing with these brave men. No signs of discontent were manifest. Even in their hardest trials the utmost cheerfulness prevailed; and in more remote positions, where a less rigid discipline was enforced, the patriotic strains of "The Star Spangled Banner" and the "Red, White and Blue," were heard ringing up through the storm. Not unfrequently, with faces turned toward the patriot homes from whence they came, would they sing "Do they Miss me at Home?" or "Let me Kiss him for his Mother"—while they breathed the silent prayer that, through the uncertainties of war, they might be permitted again to mingle with their friends in the enjoyment of a bravely won peace.

Daily would some adventurous band of Federal soldiers explore the intricacies of the rebel defences, coming constantly in collision with the enemy. In these adventures the new and efficient regiments of sharp-shooters, just introduced into the United States army, rendered valuable service.

A month before the Union army invested Yorktown, the iron battery Merrimac had made her advent in Hampton Roads, and after destroying the noble old frigates Cumberland and Congress—the pride of a past era—she met the Monitor, her conqueror and the nation's champion. The combat that ensued has stamped a glorious page on the world's history for all time. Like Lucifer in his fall, the rebel monster shrank with "despairing, cursing rage" behind the batteries at Yorktown, while the terrors of her exploits, and rejoicings at her defeat, quickened the nation's heart-pulses from Maine to Maryland.

The noble Minnesota, resting in calm and majestic repose, on the waters of the Chesapeake, hitherto would have acknowledged no superior in a naval combat. An exposure for two hours to the heavy guns of the Merrimac, which pierced her wooden walls with shot and shell, while her own missiles were ineffective as pebbles on the scales of the leviathan, destroyed her prestige and her pride of strength.

An efficient fleet of gunboats had been ordered to act in conjunction with McClellan's forces in the reduction of Yorktown; but the presence of the Merrimac no doubt frustrated their plans. On the 15th of April several of the gunboats commenced shelling the woods below Gloucester. One boat approaching within two miles of Yorktown, brought her guns to bear on that place, until driven off by the rebel batteries.

About the same time a portion of the Potomac flotilla ascended the Rappahannock, meeting with but slight opposition, visiting the towns of Urbana and Tappahannock, and destroying the enemy's batteries and huts at Lowry's Point

BATTLE OF LEE'S MILLS, VA.
April 16, 1862.

The defence of Yorktown prompted the rebel chiefs to project a line of batteries and earthworks across the peninsula which has been rendered so prominent in historic interest by the series of important events that have occurred between Richmond and Fortress Monroe. In the course of completing this line, a battery was commenced at a point on the Warwick road, on the estate of Mrs. Garrow, between Lee's Mills and Winn's Mills. There is here an extensive field, with woods to the right and left, and in the rear of the road. In front, at the foot of a gradually descending slope, is a branch of the Warwick river. The stream had been dammed up between these mills, the water covering a breadth of from thirty to forty rods, and in the deepest parts about four and a half feet deep. On the bank was a rifle-pit, and above it, on the hill, breastworks, with their embrasures for guns, frowned upon the water.

The arrest of this work, and the expulsion of the rebels, became necessary, in order to prevent the completion of what might have become a formidable obstacle. Accordingly, on the morning of the 16th, a party of skirmishers from the Fourth Vermont was thrown out, and took a position near the enemy's one gun battery, at the point named, a New York battery being also advanced at the same time. Opposite the enemy's works at that place there was a considerable space clear of large wood, overgrown with low shrubs and young pine, and surrounded in every direction except towards the enemy by a dense forest. Warwick Creek—from four to five feet deep and about twenty rods wide—separated this field from the rebel battery. Through the low shrubs and young pine the Vermonters made their way up to the edge of the stream, and poured upon the enemy a storm of rifle shot that he soon found it impossible to withstand. After a few moments of this fire not a man was to be seen within the enemy's lines.

Two pieces of the battery—ten-pound Parrots, under Lieutenant Flynn—then took up a position in the edge of the wood, at one thousand yards from the enemy's line, and opened fire. Then the enemy came bravely up to the business, and responded with the large gun in his one gun battery, and with two others in a battery behind it. Lieutenant Stewart, with the second section of the same battery—two twelve-pound Napoleon guns—was ordered up, with the left section, under Lieutenant O'Donald. With this reinforcement the fire became heavy between the artillery on both sides; the Union skirmishers and numbers of the enemy's skirmishers also pouring in their fire whenever they saw an opportunity.

At about ten A. M., after nearly two hours' sharp firing, the enemy ceased to respond, not, it was thought, because his guns had been disabled, but because the Union riflemen held his position so entirely under fire that it was almost certain death for his men to be seen.

It was now deemed necessary to ascertain the enemy's force at this point and his disposition to fight. Upon consultation between General McClellan and two division commanders, it was determined to make a more decided demonstration of attack, and, accordingly, between three and four P. M., three batteries were ordered forward into the exposed field, and opened fire at about five hundred yards. This woke the enemy up; he responded warmly for twenty minutes, and once more relapsed into silence. In no way deceived by this, the three batteries continued to play upon his position for some minutes longer, when word was brought to the General of the Vermont brigade that the creek was easily fordable, at some distance to the right, and Colonel Hyde, in command of four companies of the Vermont Third, who had skirmished in advance, was ordered to send two of his companies across the creek at the point where it was said to be only knee-deep, advance them to the enemy's left, and charge the work in rear. He accordingly sent across companies D and F, and supported them very closely with companies E and K. Meanwhile the Federal batteries became silent. No sooner were the Vermonters in the stream than the water was found to be much deeper than had been stated; the men went up to their arm-pits, and every charge of their ammunition, was, of course, thoroughly soaked. This attempt was made below the dam, and the enemy, when he saw their intention to cross, let in more water upon them by a floodgate.

While the men were in the stream, a large body of the enemy, estimated at three regiments, opened upon them from a rifle-pit on the bank, and this terrible fire cut down nearly half their number. Never was a fire received with greater steadiness or more glorious intrepidity. Except the poor fellows who had been killed or wounded, not a man of the magnificent Vermonters wavered, but all pushed on, and with one shout leaped to the bank, rushed upon the enemy with their bayonets, and fairly drove them in utter rout and confusion. But the contest was too unequal. No supports were within proper distance; and though the enemy was driven away from the first line of pits, and the other two companies of the Third were in the water to cross, those on the other side were ordered to retreat.

After the remnant of these companies returned, the Union batteries, which had in the mean time ceased firing, opened in full force again. Then the Sixth Vermont regiment was ordered to storm the work by the left flank.

Led by their gallant Colonel Lord, they rushed into the water. Seven companies had entered, and some had reached within three yards of the breastwork, when they were met by the fire of a long line of rebel rifles, which appeared above the parapets. A running fire from a thousand small arms was poured upon the Union men, who stood three feet deep in water. It was returned as gallantly as the circumstances would warrant. The breastwork was lighted up with a continuous sheet of flame, the artillery belched away at the enemy, shells were bursting over their breastworks, the smoke of the battle was ascending, and for a few moments the scene was one of appalling grandeur. Not a man flinched, and the fire of the enemy was returned with deadly effect. Wherever a head appeared above the parapet it became the mark for a hundred guns. Finding that rebel reinforcements were still advancing, and despairing of a successful assault with the bayonet, Colonel Lord retired with his men, who brought most of their wounded comrades away with them.

The loss of the Federals in this engagement was between thirty and forty killed, and one hundred and thirty-two wounded and missing. The object of the demonstration was fully accomplished, the rebels being compelled to relinquish their work, and abandon it as a defensive position. Their loss was not ascertained, but it must have been very considerable, their number being large, and the firing of the Federal gunners fatally precise. Captain Wheeler reported that he fired 313 shots, 126 of which were case shot, the remainder shell. Ayers' and Kennedy's batteries threw about 450, and Captain Mott reported 954, making more than 1,700 shot and shell hurled upon the rebels. The behavior of the Federal troops was excellent, and the event of the day successful, although the object was dearly purchased.

CAPTURE OF NEW ORLEANS.
BOMBARDMENT OF FORTS JACKSON AND ST. PHILIP.
April 18-26, 1862.

The work of opening the Mississippi river, which had been so magnificently commenced and prosecuted by that portion of the army and fleet above Memphis, was destined to find an equally imposing, if not more brilliant counterpart, in the naval operations near the city of New Orleans, once more to open that important commercial point to the world, and restore its citizens to the protection of the national flag. As an important auxiliary to this grand enterprise, a fleet of mortar-boats was fitted out in Brooklyn, N. Y., and other places, which formed a rendezvous at Ship Island, awaiting orders. Commodore DAVID D. PORTER was assigned to the command of the mortar fleet. The entire fleet,

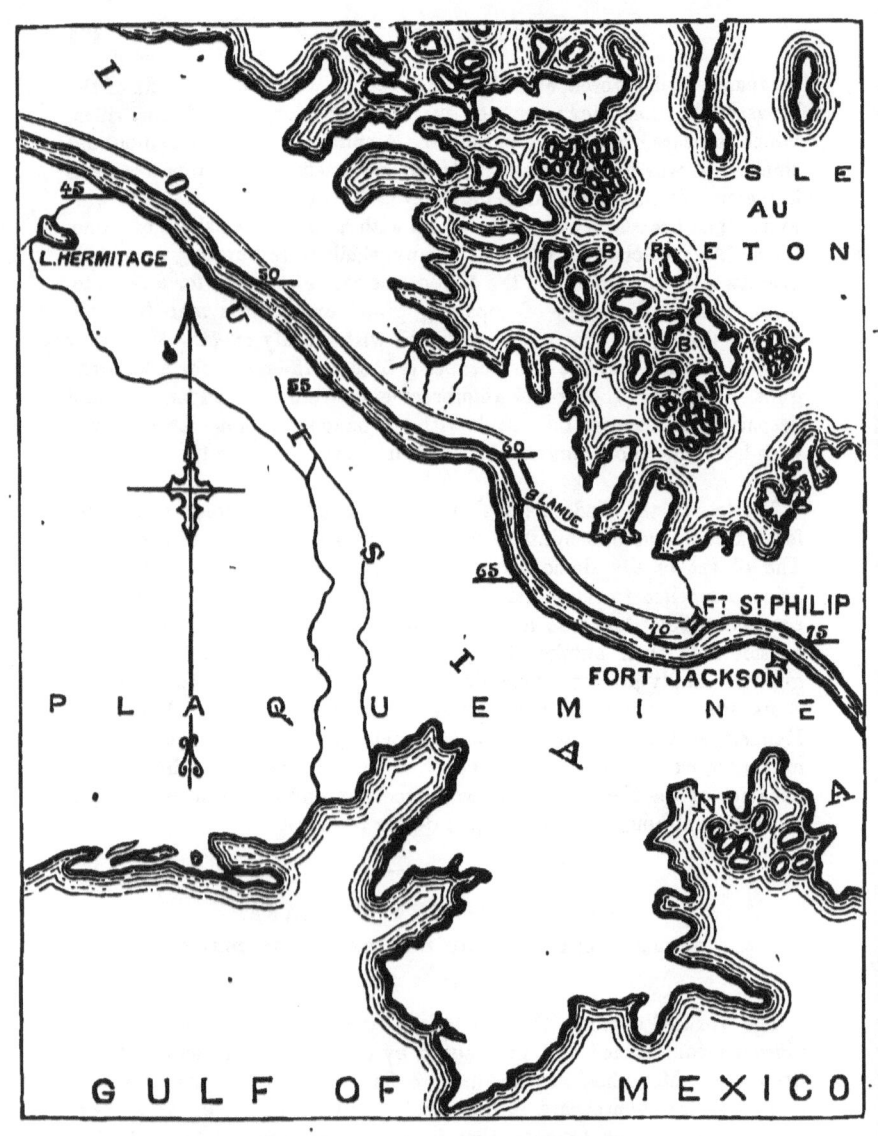

SECTION OF THE MISSISSIPPI RIVER.

SHOWING THE DISTANCES BELOW NEW ORLEANS.

under the command of Commodore D. G. Farragut, was composed as follows:

First Division of Ships, Flag-officer D. G. FARRAGUT, commanding—Hartford, R. Wainright; Brooklyn, Craven; Richmond, Alden.

Second Division of Ships—Pensacola, Morris; Portsmouth, Swartwout; Mississippi, Smith.

First Division of Gunboats, Captain T. Bailey—Oneida, Lee; Varuna, Boggs; Katahdin, Preble; Kineo, Ransom; Wissahickon, Smith; Cayuga, Harrison.

Second Division of Gunboats, H. H. Bell—Iroquis, De Camp; Sciota, Donaldson; Kennebeck, Russell; Pinola, Crosby; Itasca, Cauldwell; Winona, Nichols. Total, 18.

The mortar flotilla consisted of twenty-one brigs and schooners, and was divided into three squadrons of seven each. Besides these, five steamers, the Harriet Lane, (flag-ship,) Miami, Owasco, Westfield, and Clifton, were connected with the mortar flotilla, and these were afterwards joined by the Octorora, a new boat, commanded by Captain George Brown, of Indiana, which afterwards became Porter's flag-ship.

The entire fleet, thus constituted, numbered forty-six vessels, carrying two hundred and eighty-six guns. On the morning of April 16th, it made a rendezvous in the river, at a distance of about four miles below Forts Jackson and St. Philip, the two formidable fortifications on the river, which it was necessary to pass before reaching the city of New Orleans. On the morning of the 16th, Commodore Porter brought up several schooners, and stationed them about two miles and a half from the forts, in order to ascertain the range of the mortars before opening the bombardment. After several hours of practice, in which the range was admirably obtained, and the execution on the works was plainly visible, Commodore Porter expressed himself fully satisfied, and suspended operations for the night.

Fort Jackson, which is by far the stronger work, is a regular pentagonal bastioned fortification, having two fronts bearing on the river, and three on the land side. The land fronts have each a glacis and covered way, and the channel is commanded by a battery of twenty-five guns. A wet ditch, from forty to seventy feet wide, and six feet deep, surrounds the main work on the river, and a similar ditch, one hundred and fifty feet wide, the land fronts. There is also a wet ditch, six feet deep, and thirty feet wide, around the channel-bearing battery. The two channel-bearing fronts have each eight casemated guns, which are the only casemated ones in the work. The ditches are defended by twenty-four-pounder howitzers at either flank. The parapet is carried across the gorge of the bastion, so that there is no flank parapet defence. The bastions are only arranged for musketry fire from the walls. The main work of the lower battery mounts in the aggregate one hundred and twenty-five guns, of which one hundred bear on the channel. There was a one-story brick citadel within the fort, having two tiers of loop-holes for musketry defence, the walls of which are five feet thick. The entrance to the work is by a wooden bridge on the west side, connected with a draw bridge ten feet wide.

Fort St. Philip consists of a main work and two attached batteries, which bear respectively up and down the river. The principal work is irregular in form, having seventeen faces. It is surrounded by a wet ditch six feet deep, and from twenty to thirty feet wide. At the foot of the glacis is a ditch from seventy to one hundred and forty feet wide. There is a glacis and covered way entirely around the fort. Outside of the principal ditch is another, which was dug to furnish earth for the levee, and this is twenty feet wide, and four feet deep. Fort St. Philip mounts one hundred guns, of which seventy-five bear on the channel. All the guns were mounted *en barbette*. The scarp works were strengthened by relief arches, which were pierced with loop-holes for musketry.

Both forts are built of brick. The guns of Fort Jackson are twenty five feet above the level of the river, and those of St. Philip nineteen feet. The guns of the outer batteries of both forts are fourteen feet above the river. When the rebels took possession of these forts there were only thirty-six guns mounted, none of which were of larger cali-bre than thirty-two-pounders. All the carriages were poor. The plans for completing these forts were taken from the Custom-house at New Orleans, just after the rebellion broke out, and the works were finished in accordance with the original intention. From centre to centre of the forts the distance is three-quarters of a mile, and the river between them half a mile in width.

On the 17th the rebels commenced their defence against the Federal fleet, by sending down the stream a fire-raft. This incendiary messenger was a common flat-boat, about one hundred and fifty feet long, fifty broad and eight deep, filled with pine knots and other combustible matter, which burned fiercely, and sent a dense column of black smoke rolling heavily upwards as it was borne along by a fresh breeze that blew up the river. As soon as the raft floated near enough it was fired into and destroyed, without damage to the fleet, and then ran ashore. It was a timely warning to the squadron, for during the day the vessels were fitted up with grapnel-ropes, fire-buckets, axes and other appliances with which to attack other of these fiery islands that might be set adrift by the enemy.

The arrangements were scarcely completed, and the review made, when, about ten o'clock at night, a brilliant fire appeared on the river, flaming out from a heavy dense column of smoke, which rolled up and displayed another of the fiery pioneers of the rebel flotilla lying near the forts. It burned magnificently, and made a splendid pyrotechnic display for the sailors, who were waiting impatiently to reach the grand magazine whence it issued. Signals were made, and in a few moments a vast crowd of boats were launched upon the waters and moved rapidly toward the island of fire. The Westfield came plowing her way up and plunged her prow into the blazing mass, at the same moment opening her steam-pipes and pouring a heavy force of water into the hottest of the conflagration. Amid the steam and smoke and seething struggle of the flames, the men leaped upon the raft with their buckets, and completely extinguished the fire. Then the blackened and smoking mass of logs was sent contemptuously adrift to follow its companion.

The sailors of the mortar fleet enjoyed this amusement with the greatest zest, and pursued their work among the logs with laughter and enthusiastic cheering. When the floating monster had been sent blackened and smoking down the river, they retired to their various boats and slept soundly in preparation for the contest of the following day.

On the mortar fleet a portion of the day was given to the very singular duty of disguising the vessels. Large quantities of branches were cut from the forest trees on the banks of the river, which were bound with all their fresh leaves to the masts, rigging, and around the hulls. This was so adroitly done that from the distance it was impossible to distinguish the fleet from the groups of trees on the banks, thus concealing the position of the vessels entirely from the enemy.

On the following morning, Good Friday, April 18th, at early dawn, the towing vessels of Commodore Porter's fleet took each five mortar boats, and proceeded up the river to their fighting station. The fleet thus in motion presented a splendid spectacle—the noble steamers leading a group of vessels, each embowered in green, as though some oasis of lofty trees had migrated from their forest home and were on an excursion to a distant shore. The larger number were anchored on the right bank of the river, while five were put in position on the left bank.

At nine o'clock precisely, and before all the mortar boats had taken their position, the rebels opened fire. It was instantly returned by the mortars, and the grandest naval engagement of the war, and one of the most memorable bombardments in the history of the world commenced.

For some time the fire of the forts fell short of the range, but after about an hour their shot passed over the vessels and fell harmless beyond the fleet. The mortar practice for the first half hour exhibited a similar defect, but the range was then obtained, and the bombs fell thick and fast over and around the entrenched foe. At ten o'clock the

Iroquois, Cayuga, Sciota and Wissahickon opened upon the forts with their 11-inch shells and fifteen-second fuses.

The scene now became one of thrilling grandeur. The loud roar of the mortars as they hurled their immense projectiles into the air, the quick succession of guns from the war-ships, and the rapid discharges from the forts in reply; the flashes of fire, the clouds of smoke, as they rolled blackly together, filling the air, and the shells flying up to a great altitude, then pencilling their arching line against the blue sky as they sped to their mark, passing and repassing in almost momentary rapidity, presented a spectacle awfully sublime. At times eight or ten of the destructive missiles were to be seen rushing away on their errands of death and destruction at the same moment, sometimes exploding and scattering the fragments in wide circles over the water, throwing it up in vast silver columns, or on the shore plowing up the earth and sending soil and foliage in thick masses high in the air.

The rebels diversified their operations during the day by again sending two immense fire-rafts down the river, which would have occasioned much confusion among the fleet, but for the precautions already taken, and the previous experience of the sailors in the reception of these pyrotechnic visitors. The sailors not employed at the guns were allowed to witness the contest from the yards and rigging of the vessels. As soon as the rafts appeared they were called down from their places, manned the boats, and soon piloted these burning islands to the shore, where they were left to smoulder away for the entertainment of the fleet. These rafts were now regarded as a side-play. At six o'clock Fort Jackson was reported to be on fire, and at half-past six the Harriet Lane signalled the mortar boats to cease firing. Two of these boats were struck during the day. The cabin of one was destroyed by a shot, and a ball plunged through the magazine of another which sent her out of the action for an hour in order to make repairs. The men on board had been exhausted by their heavy labors, and when the night came they were heartily glad to rest.

A morning of serene beauty dawned upon the fleet, with a light southeast wind, that gradually increased in volume till about ten o'clock. Notwithstanding the breeze, the sun was warm, and the heat sometimes oppressive. At half-past six the mortar boats opened the bombardment. The fire at first was slow, and the vessels which were on the left bank of the river the day before, were placed in position on the other bank near the anchorage. At seven o'clock the gunboats Oneida, Pinola and Sciota were sent up to support and cover the mortar vessels, while the Wissahickon and Cayuga were relieved—having been on duty twenty-four hours. As soon as these vessels had opened fire, Fort Jackson replied from her casemate guns, and kept up a very heavy fire.

At half-past eleven o'clock a rifle shot went through the schooner Maria J. Carlton, and she sunk in about twenty minutes. Everything was saved from her except the mortar, and only two or three men were injured slightly by splinters.

Just after the sinking of the M. J. Carlton the gunboats Itasca and Kineo were ordered into close action, the Owasco being sent up by Captain Porter to assist. The firing now was frequent and terrific. Each moment it seemed as if some one of the boats must be sunk. The Oneida attracted much attention by her coolness and her heavy fire. At two o'clock she was struck twice, one ten-inch solid shot from a Columbiad striking a thirty-two pounder gun carriage and knocking off one of the trucks, and passing out of the ship on the port side. Shortly afterwards another shot of the same description hit the forward part of the starboard after port, striking the carriage of an eleven-inch pivot gun and then lodging on deck. This shot wounded nine men, but none mortally. One poor fellow lost his left hand. The pivot gun of the Oneida was not injured, but the pivot rail was slightly damaged, and to repair it she hauled out of action.

At about half-past three o'clock the firing from the forts began to slacken. At four o'clock Fort Jackson was silent, and only the water battery and Fort St. Philip were at work. The mortar shells were falling all around the fort. One appeared to fall into the water battery soon afterward, and silenced it. The gunboats were throwing shells with fine effect, the Kineo in particular. At five o'clock General Butler and his staff went on board the Hartford to confer with Commodore Farragut, and at half-past six the signal was given to discontinue the firing.

A number of men were wounded during the day, and were placed on board of the Katahdin, to be conveyed to the hospital at Pilot Town, down the river.

Night closed around the fleet as it lay at its moorings. The mortar-boats kept up the firing during the night at stated intervals, by divisions, and so continued until the morning of Sunday, the 20th, when the contest was renewed on both sides, with the same zeal and industry as had marked the bombardment of the first two days. During the forenoon a deserter from Fort Jackson came to the shore, and hailed one of the mortar vessels. A boat was immediately dispatched to him, and he was taken on board the Harriet Lane, where he had an interview with Commodore Porter. He was a citizen of Pennsylvania, and reported that great execution had been done by the well-directed fire of the fleet.

Commodore Farragut began to fear, from the protracted resistance of the forts, that they would hold out so long that the supply of shells and material of the fleet would become exhausted, and the enterprise result in a simple blockade. He therefore issued orders for running the forts, at an early opportunity, and arranged the vessels in several divisions for this important undertaking, when the signal should be given to move. While passing the forts, Commodore Porter's mortar fleet were to engage the batteries, in order to distract and divide the fire of the forts.

During the afternoon, Fort Jackson suspended its fire, but Fort St. Philip sent its iron messengers about the fleet in a perfect hail, without, however, doing much injury. After continuing this work for a short time the fire was slackened, and gradually fell off, a shot only being sent at long intervals.

During the afternoon preparations were made for removing the obstructions which the rebels had placed in the river. The principal of these was a strong and heavy iron chain thrown across the stream, supported by six or eight vessels, which formed a line across from shore to shore. Beyond this battery, and above the forts, lay a fleet of eighteen gunboats, and a monster ram, called the *Manassas*, a massive and heavily mailed vessel, built expressly for running down and destroying any vessel that it might attack.

About two o'clock the expedition to accomplish this work started on its errand. The night was as dark as could be desired, and, closely watched by the fleet, the Itasca and Pinola left their moorings to cut the chain, and, if possible, destroy some of the vessels supporting it. At a given signal the mortar vessels, which had been keeping up a slow fire, opened a tremendous volley of shell, presenting a spectacle which has seldom been witnessed in naval warfare. The sky was like a vast arch in conflagration from the explosions of the shells, which vaulted upwards, and fell in a meteoric shower upon the forts. From three to eight or ten were in the air almost all the time, and the beauty and grandeur of this vast pyrotechnic display was heightened by the use of the Caston signal lights. Dimly in the distance could be seen the Iroquois, Winona, and Kennebec, who were in the advance of the mortar fleet. A signal light was sent up from Fort Jackson, and both forts opened fire with all their heavy guns.

An hour was spent in this manner, when the Pinola sent a boat down to report that the chain was cut, and that the Itasca was ashore. The forts had slackened their fire, and there was good cause to fear that if she were not rescued before the moon rose, she would be captured by the rebels. Orders were immediately sent to the picket boats, which repaired to her aid, and although the project of blowing up some of the supporting schooners was not accomplished, the vessels all returned in safety, having cleared the river of its barrier. The mortar fleet then subsided into the accustomed routine of a bomb-shell at regular intervals, to prove to the rebels at the forts that their visitors were at the post of duty.

At two o'clock on Monday morning, the 21st, the moon rose clear and beautiful, lighting up the entire scene. It was the fourth day of the bombardment, and with accustomed promptitude the entertainment of the day commenced with a fire raft, sent down the river from Fort Jackson, larger and more formidable than any that had preceded it. The current was running swiftly, the wind was fresh, and the blazing mass sped fiercely over its watery pathway. It burned with terrific fury, a high wind sweeping its flames back in fiery banners; while the pine knots, crackling and roaring, sent their forked flames leaping like tongues of fire through the dense column of smoke which rolled its huge black pall against the azure of the sky, as it floated past the fleet, scattering a storm of harmless fire on the water. The mortar boats took it in charge, and the men fell to work extinguishing the flames. When this was done it was towed ashore to keep company with its forerunners, a harmless, charred mass of timbers.

During the day the bombardment was continued. The forts for a time responded with more determination even than they had previously exhibited. Attempts were made by the rebels to repair the massive fragments of the chain, and to destroy one of the Federal vessels by a submarine torpedo, but without success. The fifth day proved like the others, but it became apparent that the crisis of the contest was approaching. The mortar boats continued their usual practice during the night, and on the return of day, (Wednesday, the 23d,) renewed the severer labors of the bombardment.

There was an ominous silence on the part of the forts. The look-outs at the mast-heads reported that the shells were doing their work at Fort St. Philip, and that there were twelve steamers in sight. The forts maintained profound silence during the day, and this circumstance occasioned much discussion on the Federal vessels. On consideration, it was deemed that the time had come to hazard an attempt to run the forts, destroy the rebel fleet, and ascend to New Orleans. The Itasca was selected as the picket boat, to advance and ascertain whether the chain had been repaired; and the fleet of ships and gunboats was alive with enthusiasm and excitement, at the prospect of running the gauntlet of fire which would be opened on either side when their desperate attempt became known. Not only were the two forts to be passed, but the rebel fleet, with its monster of destruction, the Manassas, and the fire-rafts which would be let loose upon them, to spread conflagration and death in their most fearful forms: while a foe desperate with energy and hate, was working the formidable engines of destruction.

At eleven o'clock, P. M., the Itasca signalled that the chain was clear.

Everything was quiet around the fleet, save the hissing of the steam as it escaped from the boilers. The night was moderately dark, and a gentle southerly wind made the weather rather hazy. The mortar vessels kept up an incessant roar, and bright globes ascended high aloft to curve downward in fury at the forts. The second division, under Captain Bailey (of the Colorado), formed on the left bank of the river, while the third division was in the centre of the lines—the first division lying on the right bank of the river.

The fleet was to sail in the following order:—

First Division—Flag-officer Farragut commanding: Hartford, Brooklyn, Richmond.

Second Division—Captain Bailey commanding: Cayuga, Pensacola, Mississippi, Oneida, Varuna, Katahdin, Kineo, Wissahickon, Portsmouth, towed by J. P. Jackson.

Third Division—Captain Bell commanding: Sciota, Iroquois, Pinola, Itasca, Winona, Kennebec.

At one o'clock all hands were called, hammocks stowed, and everything put in readiness to weigh.

At two o'clock on the morning of the 24th, red lights at the peak of the Hartford announced the time to get underweigh. At three o'clock the moon rose, and a silvery path was marked out on the swift waters of the river, so soon to be the scene of one of the grandest naval fights known to history. The moon had lifted itself above the horizon just thirty minutes, when the fleet sailed in order for the battle-ground. In the dim distance could be seen the signal fires of the enemy, built to light up the river, and reveal the position of the fleet.

At precisely twenty minutes of four o'clock the enemy opened fire from Fort St. Philip. At that moment the star-spangled banner was hoisted at the peak of the Hartford. Full speed was given to the ship, the engineers performed their duty nobly, and on she went, as it were, into the jaws of death. At the time the enemy opened fire the mortar vessels went to work, and the rapidity with which they threw shells at the enemy was terrific.

At five minutes to four o'clock the bow gun of the Hartford belched forth fire and smoke, and a messenger, in the shape of a nine-inch shell, was sent to Fort Jackson. In a few minutes more the broadside firing was commenced. Both forts were replying as fast as they could. Broadside after broadside was delivered to them in rapid succession, while the mortar vessels lent their aid to make the scene one of wonderful grandeur.

A scene like this has probably never before been witnessed. Steadily the vessels steamed on, the forts firing rifle shot and shell, ten-inch columbiads, forty-two, thirty-two and twenty-four pounder balls, while the

BOMBARDMENT OF FORTS JACKSON AND ST. PHILIP, APRIL 24, 1862.

1. Fort Jackson.   2. Fort St. Philip.   3. Federal Ships-of-War and Gunboats.   4. Rebel Gunboats and Rams.

thirteen steamers of the enemy, and the floating battery Louisiana, were pouring into and around the fleet a storm of iron perfectly indescribable. Not satisfied with this, one fire raft after another was kindled, and set adrift to do their fiery work. The ram was busy trying to force them under the bows of the Federal vessels. One of them approached the Hartford, when Captain Broome opened on her with two nine-inch guns. An explosion—a loud burst of terrific cries and wails,—a careen, and the rebel steamer, with its wretched multitude of victims, plunged beneath the waters, and disappeared from view. The rebel vessels were crowded with troops, who fired volleys of rifle balls, most of which did no harm. Their steamers were bold and fearless; but no sooner did they come in sight of our gunners than they were sunk. The Varuna sunk six of them one after another.

In the midst of this awful scene a tremendous fire raft came down the river, and the ram shoved her under the port-quarter of the Hartford. The flames caught her rigging and side, and for a moment it seemed as though the flag-ship must fall a prey to the flames. A fire was also burning on the berth-deck. The fire hose was on hand, and the crew soon subdued the flames, and gave the ram a return of rifle shell. She, however, returned to the onset, when some other vessel assaulted her, and she hauled off. During this stage of affairs the Hartford grounded, and her fate seemed to be sealed; but the men worked splendidly, and the engineers soon got the ship astern and afloat. The scene of the engagement at this time almost defies the power of description. The river and its banks were one sheet of flame, and the messengers of death were moving with lightning swiftness in all directions. Steadily the Federal fleet poured upon the enemy their shell and grape, interspersed with shrapnel. The rebel boats were fast being riddled by well directed broadsides, and their commanders who were able made for the shore to run them on the bank and save their lives. Some were on fire and others were sinking. The crews of the Union fleet broke out in frequent cheers as they saw the havoc that was made, and the retreat of the rebel vessels. The flag-ship had been on fire three times, and was riddled from stem to stern. The cabin was completely shattered, the starboard steerage torn up, and the armory severely damaged.

After being under a terrific fire for one hour and twenty minutes, the Federal vessels passed the forts. The flag-ship was badly cut up with a shot through the mainmast, two in the stern, and several through her. Language cannot give an adequate idea of the engagement. Wrapped up in smoke, shot and shell were whistling around, above, before and in the rear; flames from fire rafts encircling the ships, splinters flying in all directions, shells bursting overhead; while the roar and booming of the guns rolled almost incessantly, and made the contest as destructive as it was terrible.

So effective had been the work of the fleet, that at half-past five o'clock no less than eleven rebel steamers were in flames along each side of the river. The Federal vessels steamed up to the Quarantine to anchor, when the Manassas made her appearance, and saucily fired at the Richmond.

The Mississippi being near at hand, put about for the ram, with the intention of running her down. The Manassas endeavored to elude the attack, but finding the Mississippi gaining on her, ran into the bank of the river, and immediately about thirty men came up out of the hatch and went on shore. The Mississippi fired two or three broadsides into her, and boarded her, but finding that she was of no importance, again fired into her, and she drifted down the river, sinking very fast.

Besides the ram, the rebels had a heavy floating battery, called the Louisiana, which carried eight large guns, and which occasioned a good deal of annoyance, although, to use the language of the Charleston *Mercury*, it was a complete failure. In addition to this, they had an immense steam-ram, called the Mississippi, which had just been launched, but which was then unfinished. She was a propeller, with three screws and six engines, and to be mounted with twenty guns of the largest calibre. She was twice as large and powerful as the Merrimac, and without a gun would have been almost sufficient to have run down the Federal fleet. There was, however, about forty days' work required to complete her, and to prevent her falling into the hands of the victors, she was scuttled, set on fire and sunk.

At six A. M., the Varuna, Commander Boggs, was attacked by the Morgan, iron-clad about the bow, commanded by Beverly Kennion, an ex-naval officer. This vessel raked her along the port gangway, killing four and wounding nine of the crew, butting the Varuna on the quarter, and again on the starboard side. Three three-inch shells were fired into her abaft her armor, also several shot from the after rifled gun, when she dropped out of action, partially disabled.

While still engaged with her, another rebel steamer, iron-clad, with a prow under water, struck the Varuna in the port gangway, doing considerable damage. The Varuna's shot glanced from her bow. She backed off for another blow, and struck again in the same place, crushing in the side; but by going ahead fast, the concussion drew her bow around, and the Varuna was able with the port guns to give her, while close alongside, five eight-inch shells abaft her armor. This settled her and drove her ashore in flames. Finding the Varuna sinking, she was run into the bank, when they let go her anchor, and tied her up to the trees. During all this time the guns were actively at work, crippling the Morgan, which was making feeble efforts to get up steam.

The fire was kept up until the water was over the gun-trucks, when attention was turned to getting the wounded and the crew out of the vessel. The Oneida, Captain Lee, seeing the condition of the Varuna, had rushed to her assistance, but was not needed, and the Morgan surrendered to her, having over fifty of her crew killed and wounded. She was set on fire by her commander.

In fifteen minutes from the time the Varuna was struck, she was on the bottom, with only her topgallant forecastle out of water. The officers and crew lost everything they possessed, no one thinking of leaving his station until driven thence by water.

The Federal vessels made their rendezvous at the Quarantine, some miles above the forts, and took possession of the camp of the Chalmette regiment of rebel sharpshooters, some of whom escaped, while the others surrendered, and were paroled. The officers were taken to the flag-ship and paroled. The wounded men of the various ships were now carefully attended to. The heroic dead who had fallen in defence of their flag were taken ashore, and laid in their last resting-place, in a manner worthy of the cause in which they had shed their blood, and the national flag was left floating over their graves. The Federal loss was 30 killed and 120 wounded. The loss of the rebels was very severe, some of the estimates making it as high as 800 or 1,000 in killed and wounded.

THE SURRENDER OF THE FORTS.

When the fleet started in its attempt to pass the forts, the mortar-vessels opened a tremendous fire, which was continued until five o'clock, when they were signalled to cease. During the forenoon, Commodore Porter dispatched Captain Grant, in the Owasco, with a flag of truce, to demand the surrender of the forts. The vessel approached Fort St. Philip to within about a mile, when the batteries were opened upon her and five shots were fired, upon which she withdrew. The flag of truce was hauled down, but soon afterwards a boat flying a flag of truce at her bows, and the secession flag at her stern, approached, and Captain Grant went out and held a conference with the rebel officer. He offered an apology in behalf of his superior officer for the unintentional firing upon the flag of truce, declaring that its color had not been seen, and could not be distinguished in the distance. He then returned to the fort, and the bombs again commenced their thunders, which lasted until Commodore Porter ordered the fleet down the river.

On the 25th, Commodore Porter sent six of the mortar vessels to guard the bayous in the rear of Fort Jackson, when three of them, the Henry Janes, Kittatinny and Geo. W. Maryham, on the 26th, drifted off to Fort Livingston, a stronghold of the rebels, guarding one of the passages. There was a flag of truce flying on the fort, and on boats being sent ashore, they found the place deserted by all except several men, women and children, who resided on the island. The Federals found eleven 32-pounders, three 12-pound howitzers, two 24-pounders, one 8-inch columbiad, one 80-pound rifled cannon, one thousand 32-pound shot, and other articles of minor importance. The fort was in good condition, with all its property. It was left in charge of Acting-master Tamsen, of the U. S. navy.

On the 28th, Lieutenant-Colonel Higgins, commanding the forts, sent a communication to the Commodore, offering to surrender. The Harriet Lane (flag-ship) accordingly steamed up to the forts, and received the commander on board, when the articles of capitulation were drawn up and signed. Not to prolong the contest by very exacting terms, Commodore Porter received the forts and property, and allowed Brigadier-General Duncan, commander of coast defences, and Lieutenant-Colonel Higgins, commanding the forts, to retain their side arms, under parole. The other officers and privates were to retire on parole, giving up all arms and accoutrements, the United States to transport the men from the forts.

Three steamers of the rebel fleet remained, and were under the direction of Commander J. K. Mitchell. Lieutenant-Colonel Higgins said he had no command over them, and was not responsible for their conduct. While the flag of truce was up, and the capitulation was under conference, they towed the iron floating battery, Louisiana, to a place above the forts, set it on fire, and turned it adrift upon the Federal fleet. The guns soon becoming heated, began to discharge, throwing their shot around the river, and in a little while the battery itself exploded with a terrific report, scattering the fragments all over the river, and wounding one of their own men in Fort St. Philip.

As soon as the terms of capitulation were concluded and signed, Commodore Porter started for the rebel fleet. One vessel had been sunk by the Federal guns during the consultation, and another was taken by the Commodore. He immediately put the officers in close confinement, for the attempt to blow up the Federal vessels while under the flag of truce.

While the reduction and surrender of the forts was effected apparently by the fleet, it was evident that they could have held out in defiance of the bombardment for an indefinite period. The successful passage of the gunboat fleet threw an immense force above the forts, while a competent force remained below. In addition to this, General Butler had succeeded in finding a passage for a portion of his land forces through the channels in the rear of Fort St. Philip, and thus threatened the forts in a direction where they were easily vulnerable. Under these circumstances, a considerable part of the garrison revolted, on the night of the 27th, refused to serve, and demanded a surrender, because defence was no longer of the least service to their main purpose, that of defending the approach to the city. The discontented part of the troops, about two hundred in number, were permitted to leave the fort, and they proceeded to the quarantine and gave themselves up to General Butler. This timely co-operation of General Butler led to the decision of the commander, and on the following morning the capitulation was completed, and the national flag was restored to the walls of Forts Jackson and St. Philip.

The forts were placed in command of General Phelps. Fort Jackson suffered most from the bombardment, the chief object being to compel its surrender, Commodore Porter knowing that the other would inevitably follow. Nearly 8,000 shells and round shot were thrown from the Federal fleet, of which more than 2,000 fell into or exploded over the forts. More than 1,100 were counted on the ground near the forts, lying around after the capture.

THE OCCUPATION OF NEW ORLEANS.

At eleven o'clock, A. M., on the 24th, the flag-ship raised her anchor, and led the way up the river towards New Orleans. Commander Farragut had been apprised of the obstacles which he would meet, and was therefore prepared to encounter them. There was no occurrences of moment on the way up the river, except the demonstrations of joy or of opposition made by the people, according to their loyal or disloyal sympathies. Boats loaded with cotton were burnt or burning along the river as they passed, and fragments of the Mississippi battery floated down the stream.

At about the same hour of the next day, the fleet reached two forts, one on either side of the river, about two miles below the city, known as the Chalmette batteries, which had no flags flying. At eleven o'clock they opened on the Cayuga, which was then in the advance. After a short time spent in firing the bow guns, the Hartford poured in a terrific broadside, which appeared to be very destructive. Other discharges followed from other vessels, and the garrison abandoned the works without hoisting a flag. The guns being silenced, and the forts evacuated, the fleet passed on and came to anchor opposite the city about one o'clock. The river was filled with vessels on fire, and along the levee cotton, stores, and other property were wantonly burned, filling the atmosphere with suffocating smoke, and adding to the heat of the day. Vast amounts of property were thus destroyed. On shore and on the wharves the people hastened to and fro, some cheering for Jeff. Davis and the Confederacy, Beauregard, and others, while some of the more exulting loyalists cheered for the Union and the old flag.

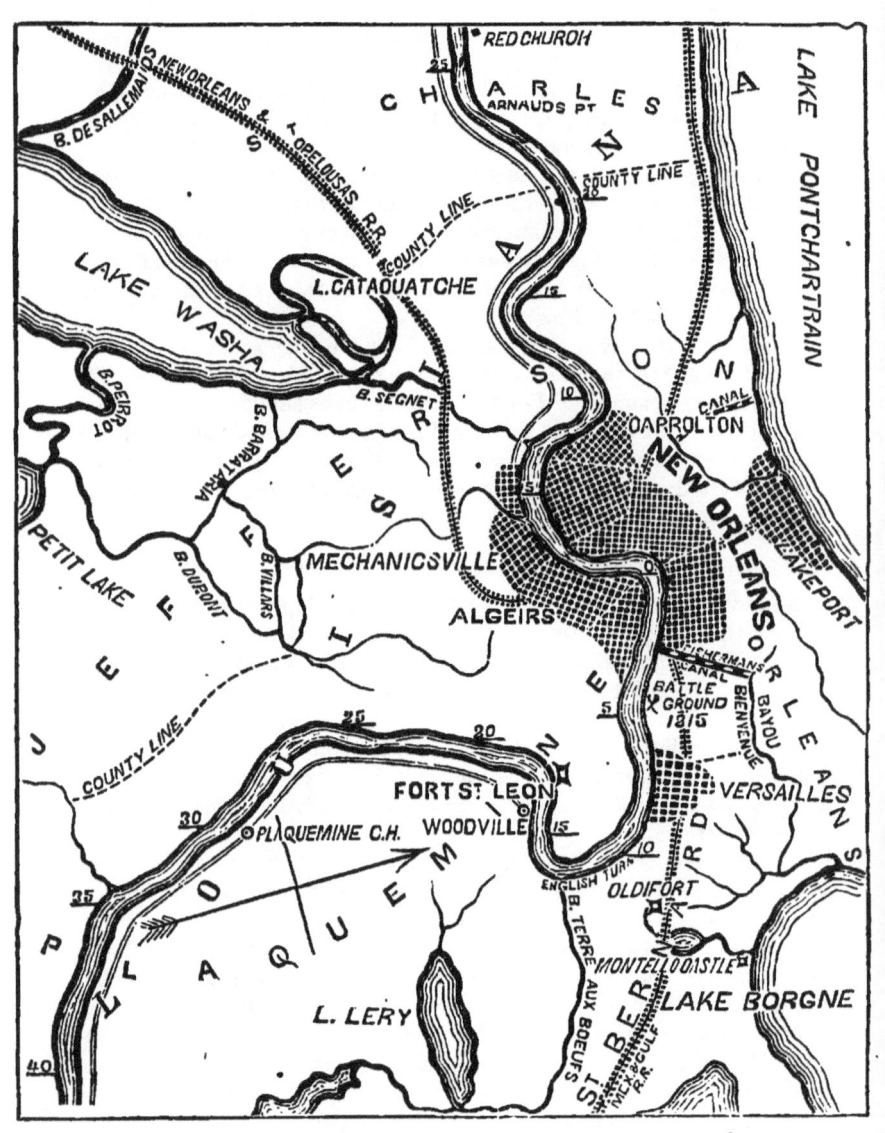

NEW ORLEANS AND VICINITY.

SHOWING THE DISTANCES ON THE MISSISSIPPI, AND THE ISLANDS BY THEIR NUMBERS.

At two o'clock Commodore Farragut sent Captain Bailey on shore to communicate with the authorities, and demand a surrender of the city. He started with a flag of truce, and on reaching the levee was greeted with curses by the mob. With some difficulty he reached the City Hall, with the officer who accompanied him, and there found the Mayor, City Council, and General Lovell, the commander of the rebel forces in the city. New Orleans being under martial law, the civil authorities could do nothing, and General Lovell declared he would never surrender it. He was informed that the city was then in the power of the Federal fleet, and the responsibility of any suffering or destruction that might follow his obstinate determination must rest with him. If no resistance were made, nothing would be injured. General Lovell then agreed to evacuate the city, and restore it to the control of the civil authorities. Captain Bailey and Lieutenant Perkins entered a carriage and returned to their boats. Just before they reached the levee, the new ram Mississippi, already mentioned, floated down the river wrapt in flames. The rebels had attempted to tow her up the river, but finding some of the Federal vessels on the alert in pursuit, they set her on fire. Two or three other similar vessels, partly built, were in the shipyards of the city and Algiers, on the other side of the river, which were also destroyed.

When the news of the passage of the forts by the Federal fleet had been telegraphed to the city, the popular excitement was unbounded. Under apprehension that the city would be pillaged, and given up to the violence of a body of Northern desperadoes, the mob, led on by some of the most bitter secessionists, were anxious to fire the public buildings, and reduce the city to ruin in advance. But other counsels prevailed, and they were fortunately restrained from the commission of these atrocities.

On the following morning, the 26th, at half-past six o'clock, the Mayor sent his secretary and chief of police to see the Commodore, informing him that he would call a meeting of the Council at ten o'clock. Commodore Farragut replied to the message of the Mayor, and sent him a formal demand for the unqualified surrender of the city. The Council met, and on hearing a message from the Mayor, John T. Monroe, that body adopted resolutions in accordance with the message, and the Mayor made a reply to the Commodore, stating that the city was subject to his power. Both the message of the Mayor, and his reply to Commodore Farragut, breathed a spirit of bold defiance to the Federal authority, declaring that they submitted only to stern necessity, and that they still maintained their allegiance to the Confederate States.

At ten o'clock two officers were sent on shore, with a body of marines, to raise the flag on the Custom House; but the protest of the Mayor was so urgent, under the apprehension that the mob would resist this attempt to plant the old flag in its rightful place, that the Commodore deemed it advisable to recall the order. About the same time the Pensacola sent a boat to raise the flag on the mint. A general order for a thanksgiving service at eleven o'clock, on shipboard, had been issued, for the success of the expedition, and while thus engaged, the stars and stripes were torn down by a mob. The Pensacola fired a howitzer, killing one man, which occasioned intense excitement.

On the surrender of the forts, General Butler hastened with his forces to the city, where he arrived, with his transports, on the afternoon of the 28th.

On the morning of the 29th, Pierre Soulé, one of the most prominent men of New Orleans, visited the Commodore for the purpose of a private interview. Soon after he left the ship, the marines of the fleet went ashore in the small boats to raise the flag on the Custom House and Post Office. Two howitzers were in the company, to assist, if necessary, in maintaining order. The duty of hauling down the State flag of Louisiana, and replacing it with the national emblem, was assigned to Commander H. H. Bell. When the boats reached the levee, the men formed in line of march, and proceeded to the Custom House, where the stars and stripes were once more flung to the southern breeze. After leaving the Custom House, they proceeded to the City Hall, where Captain Bell generously yielded the distinction of raising the flag to George Russell, boatswain's mate of the Hartford, who had won general approbation by his heroic conduct.

General Butler established his headquarters in the city, proclaimed martial law, and commenced his administration without opposition. With this peaceful and successful result was crowned one of the most brilliant achievements in naval history.

THE EVACUATION OF YORKTOWN.

May 4, 1862.

As the month of April was passing away, dispatches from the peninsula gave assurances that the two great armies now confronting each other before Yorktown would in a few days be compelled to test their relative strength in a general engagement, should neither, meantime, voluntarily abandon the position. The daily bulletin of casualties gave evidence of closer and more sanguinary contests among the working or reconnoitering parties, or from the batteries erected on new parallels of rugged embankments springing up daily in closer proximity. A most arduous portion of the soldiers' labor during the siege is thus graphically described:

WORKING IN THE TRENCHES.—A working party is detailed for night duty. With muskets slung on their backs and shovels and picks on their shoulders, they proceed to the selected ground. The white tape marks the line of excavation—the dark lanterns are "faced to the rear"—the muskets are carefully laid aside—the shovels are in hand, and each man silently commences to dig. Not a word is spoken—not one spade clicks against another. Each man first digs a hole large enough to cover himself—he then turns and digs to his right-hand neighbor. Then the ditch deepens and widens, and the parapet rises. Yet all is silent—the relief comes and the weary ones retire. The words and jests of the enemy are often heard, while no noise from the men disturbs the stillness save the dull rattle of the earth as each spadeful is thrown to the top. At daylight a long line of earthworks, affording complete protection, greets the astonished eyes of the enemy, while the sharpshooters' bullets whisper terror to his ears.

On the 2d of May the rebels opened fire from an immense gun mounted on a pivot at a corner of the main fort on the heights of Yorktown, which inflicted serious injury on the Federals, who replied with much spirit from their No. 1 battery, mounting one and two hundred-pounder Parrot guns. On the twenty-third discharge of the enemy's gun it burst into a thousand pieces, tearing up the parapet, and making fearful havoc among the immense crowd surrounding it. The Federal guns on No. 1 battery were then brought to bear on the rebel works at Yorktown and Gloucester, and on their shipping, with marked effect, to which they were unable to reply.

From the 1st to the 4th of May the Confederate army evacuated Yorktown, without awaking the suspicions of the besiegers, making a safe retreat with all their field artillery and most of their stores. Eighty heavy guns at Yorktown and Gloucester, with large quantities of ordnance stores, fell into possession of the Federals, who occupied the rebel ramparts on the morning of the fourth.

On the same day the iron battery Merrimac made her appearance off Sewall's Point, and the Federal gunboats availed themselves of the opportunity to go up the York river, convoying a portion of the army transports, with the design of intercepting the retreating enemy, while most of the cavalry and horse artillery, followed by the infantry, started in immediate pursuit by land.

When within two and a half miles of Williamsburg, at two o'clock on May 4th, General Stoneman's advance came up with the enemy, who threw out a body of cavalry to check the pursuit. Captain Gibbon's battery was brought to bear on the horsemen, who on their approach were met by a charge of the First and Sixth regular cavalry, who drove them back, capturing twenty-five of their number. Two of the Federals were killed, and about twenty wounded; and twenty of Captain Gibbon's horses were killed.

THE BATTLE OF WILLIAMSBURG.
May 5, 1862.

The evacuation of Yorktown, which occupied several days, was completed on the morning of Sunday, the 4th of May, the main body of the retreating rebels taking the principal road through Williamsburg, and smaller portions of the army passing along the road near the banks of the York river. A line of entrenchments had been run about two and a half miles from Williamsburg, and became the scene of a fiercely contested engagement on May 5th.

The rebel forces had succeeded in passing through the city, and left a force of about five thousand men to engage and retard the advance of the Union army.

The approach to Williamsburg from the lower part of the peninsula is by two roads, one on the James river side, from Warwick courthouse, and the other from Yorktown, on the York river side. Both these roads lead through a dense forest, broken only by occasional openings, and over alternate soils of sand, reddish clay and swamp. The heavy rains had saturated the soil, and the retreat of the rebels, with their ponderous trains, had cut the roads up to an extent that made them almost impassable. In very many places where they led over swampy ground, horses and wagons would sink together, and other teams were necessary to draw them out and place them upon soil that was firm only by comparison. This was the general character of both these roads. They gradually approach each other through the forest, and meet at a sharp angle about forty rods beyond the edge of the forest, in a large open plain, which stretches away on either side, and lies directly in front of the village of Williamsburg, at a distance of about two miles. Beyond this intersection of the two roads, and directly ahead, was a long earthwork, some hundred rods in advance, called Fort Page, (also called Fort Magruder,) commanding with its guns and the infantry who were concealed behind its walls both these converging roads. Looking to the right, the eye ranges over a broad open field, stretching a mile or more away, with a rolling surface, backed by a swamp, and dotted with five separate earthworks, placed to command the plain in advance and concentrate their cross-fire upon the troops approaching by the roads. Looking to the left, there are three

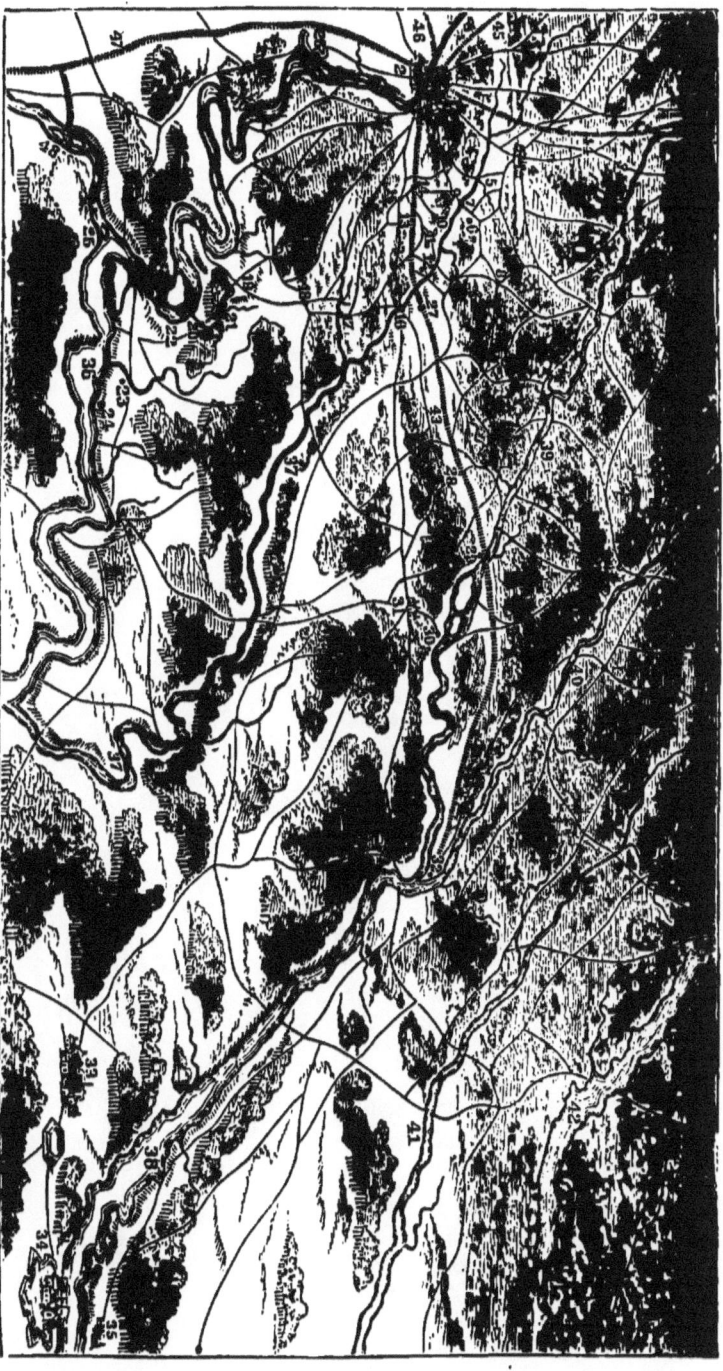

BIRD'S-EYE VIEW OF THE COUNTRY FROM RICHMOND TO YORKTOWN.

1. Richmond.—2. Manchester.—3. Hanover C. H.—4. Mechanicsville.—5. Beaver Dam.—6. Gaines Mills.—7. New Bridge.—8. Cold Harbor.—9. Garnett's.—10. Golding.—11. Trent.—12. Couch.—13. Savage's Station.—14. Fair Oaks.—15. Seven Oaks.—16. Bottoms Bridge.—17. White Oaks Bridge and Swamp.—18. Charles City Roads.—19. Malvern Hills.—20. Turkey Bridge.—21. Turkey Creek.—22. Turkey Island Bend.—23. Berkeley.—24. Harrison's Landing.—25. City Point.—26. Fort Darling.—27. Dispatch Station.—28. Summit.—29. White House.—30. Cumberland Landing.—31. New Kent C. H.—32. West Point.—33. Williamsburg.—34. Yorktown.—35. Gloucester Point.—36. James River.—37. Chickahominy River.—38. York River.—39. Pamunkey River.—40. Mattapony River.—41. Rappahannock River.—42. Pipponax River.—43. Richmond and York Railroad.—44. Richmond and Fredericksburg Railroad.—45. Richmond and Danville Railroad.—46. Petersburg and Richmond Railroad.—47. Virginia Central Railroad.—48. Appomatox.

other works of a similar character, commanding the approaches on that side. Here the woods came closer up to the road, and for a space of some twenty or thirty acres lying along the James river road, the trees had been cut down, and the ground in part had been filled with rifle-pits.

As soon as the evacuation of Yorktown was ascertained, on Sunday morning, General Stoneman, with several regiments of cavalry, followed by light field batteries, including horse artillery, started in pursuit of the enemy. About noon General Hooker's division left the camp in front of Yorktown, followed by General Kearney's division, both belonging to General Heintzelman's corps, and marched towards Williamsburg, to support General Stoneman, and assist him in cutting off the enemy's retreat. The cavalry followed close upon the rear guard of the enemy, and during the day there was occasional skirmishing between them. After having advanced about six miles the cavalry halted to await the arrival of the infantry. The divisions of Generals Smith and Hooker met at a crossing of the roads, and continued on their routes, and met again at the junction below Fort Page. It was now late in the day, and General Sumner, who desired to engage the enemy, was compelled to defer an attack until the morning.

The troops bivouacked at night in the best positions they could secure. General Hooker's division was in front of the centre of the enemy's works. General Smith's infantry, and General Stoneman's artillery and cavalry were on the right. Generals Kearney and Couch had also come up, and halted in the rear, while other divisions took position where they could be disposed to the best advantage. Rain had fallen almost constantly during the day, and now a stormy night drew its dark mantle over them, while the wearied army lay upon the wet earth, and sought repose.

Early on the following morning, the 5th, the troops commenced their march, and soon came up to the point where the road passes out of the woods into the open plain before the fort. The first who came up formed a part of General Hooker's division. As they advanced from the James river road to the opening, they were greeted with a storm of balls and grape from the bastion; and as the men were deployed in the woods, and attempted to pass over the fallen timber, they were met by a heavy fire from the rebel infantry, close in front, concealed in their rifle-pits or behind the trees.

General Hooker ordered up Bramhall's battery, but just as it left the woods and was coming out into the open ground, the wheels stuck fast in the deep clay mire, in which the horses vainly floundered in the effort to draw them out. The rebels had pushed their infantry into the woods on their right, and were pouring deadly volleys into the ranks of the

Federal troops, which compelled them to retire. One gun was abandoned. General Hooker's men struggled nobly against the terrible disadvantages under which they were fighting,—for the rebels, seeing the progress they were making, sent back for reinforcements, and they increased during the day until not less than twenty-five thousand of their troops turned back from their retreat.

As the enemy gradually augmented in number, the fight became more severe, and was hotly contested on both sides. General Hooker had resolved to maintain his position. General Grover's brigade, (the First, Eleventh and Sixteenth Massachusetts, and Second New Hampshire,) was on the left; General Sickles' brigade, (the First, Second, Third, Fourth and Fifth Excelsior of New York,) and General Patterson's New Jersey brigade, (the Fifth, Sixth, Seventh and Eighth,) occupied positions nearer the right of the column. Near these were company "H," United States First Artillery, Captain Bramhall, and company "O," New York Volunteer Artillery, Captain Smith. These regiments took positions along the edge of the woods, and the artillery opened on the forts, when the struggle became general nearly along the whole line.

At an early period of the battle it was perceived that the enemy was endeavoring to turn the left of the Federal line, when a part of the First and the Eleventh Massachusetts were ordered forward to anticipate and prevent the movement. While the Eleventh was engaged at a point about fifty yards from the enemy, a rebel officer displayed a white flag, and shouted, "Don't fire on your friends!" Colonel Blaisdell immediately ordered his men to cease firing, and Michael Doherty, a private of company A, stepped forward to meet the flag, upon which the officer called out to his men, "Now, give it to them!" The command was immediately obeyed, and a heavy fire was poured into the regiment, by which a number of men were cut down. Doherty fell among the rest, but he fired his piece at the dastardly officer, who fell dead upon the spot.

The First Massachusetts remained at its post, doing severe execution among the enemy until all its ammunition had been expended, when it was relieved by the Seventy-second New York, Lieutenant-Colonel Moses, which was in turn relieved by the Seventieth New York, Colonel Dwight, who was also aided by a portion of the Second New Hampshire.

The reinforcements of the enemy were pouring in, and adding continually to the severity of the struggle. Colonel Moses was ordered to the front, for the purpose of silencing a battery on the left. He was soon confronted with a most murderous fire, when he was relieved by the Seventieth New York. The rebel regiments in front were reinforced by another, and soon successfully engaged. Colonel Dwight was slightly wounded in the leg, and Colonel Farnum, being severely wounded, was carried to the rear. The regiment fought with determined bravery, against superior numbers, when Colonel Dwight ordered a charge through the fallen timber. The soldiers, with invigorating cheers, advanced upon the rebels, and with irresistible ardor put them to flight. The regiment held its position till its ammunition was exhausted, and then supplied themselves from the cartridge-boxes of their dead and wounded comrades.

On came the rebel reinforcements. Massive and determined columns pressed forward, and at last the helpless regiment, which had expended all its ammunition, was pressed vigorously by the enemy, and Colonel Dwight and many of his men were taken prisoners. They were carried to Williamsburg, where they were rescued the next day, when the Federal army reached that city. The heroism of this regiment may be seen from the fact that out of thirty-three commissioned officers who went into the action, no less than twenty-two were killed or wounded.

BATTLE OF WILLIAMSBURG.

The engagement had now become one of grand proportions. Two regiments of the New Jersey brigade were conducted by General Patterson to the front, to assist in repelling another attempt of the enemy to turn the Federal left. They occupied the heavy timber which interrupted the view of the enemy's works. When they advanced they were also met by fresh regiments of the enemy, and for a time the advantage alternated between the contending forces, and the tide of battle was seen to ebb and flow on either side, uncertain as to the issue. The forces of the enemy suffered severely as well as the Federals, who delivered their fire while lying upon the ground. Just then, Colonel Johnson came up with the Eighth New Jersey, in time to check the flanking movement of the enemy, which was rapidly reaching round to the left. Again the orders of the rebel officers, to the front and rear were heard, and again the surging columns of the foe were met and driven back. In this position for nearly five hours the New Jersey brigade stood the fire of superior numbers, and with all the coolness and determination of veterans resisted the advance of the enemy. At a late hour in the day the arrival of fresh troops relieved them from the ground they had disputed with such undaunted courage.

Generals Heintzelman and Sumner united their commands toward the right, on the line of the Yorktown road. General Hooker, finding himself so severely pressed, sent to General Heintzelman for reinforcements, but he was away, and the message was read and returned to General Hooker by General Sumner, who endorsed it, "opened and read by the senior officer on the field." After some time spent in painful suspense by General Hooker, he was cheered by the arrival of General Peck with his brigade, forming the advance of General Couch's division, which arrived on the ground at one o'clock, having marched up from Lee's Mills, ten or twelve miles, that morning, in the midst of a pouring rain, and through mud ankle deep. General Hooker being sorely pressed, the men were marched at once into the field, taking a position on his right, in the centre of the army, where they were at once exposed to the full force of the enemy's fire. For two hours they held their position against terrible odds. Twice they were driven back, and twice they rallied again, and recovered their ground.

When the brigade first reached the field, the One Hundred and Second Pennsylvania advanced to the front, delivered its fire, and fell back, giving place to the Ninety-eighth Pennsylvania, which held the ground until the One Hundred and Second rallied, and the two maintained the position. The Fifty-fifth New York, De Trobrian's Zouaves, came up on the left and then retired, while the Sixty-second New York held the rebels in check, and the One Hundred and Second and Ninety-eighth Pennsylvania delivered a cross-fire. The Fifty-fifth then formed a new line of battle, and advanced to the support of the Sixty-second, and the Ninety-third Pennsylvania came up and opened fire on a battery commanding the road, until the rebels were driven back at all points.

The Federal reinforcements were at last coming up to the scene of action. Urgent requests for aid had been sent to the rear, and Governor Sprague rode back from the field to Yorktown, to report the facts to General McClellan and urge forward the requisite assistance. In the mean time General Kearney, with his division, a part of General Heintzelman's corps, had received orders from him to press on with the utmost haste, which was done. He arrived, closely followed by General Berry, with his brigade, when they took a position on the extreme left, in order to prevent flanking by the enemy. The Third Michigan was ordered to the left as a support, while General Berry moved forward with the remaining regiments, arriving on the ground at about half-past two o'clock, P. M. The Fifth Michigan, Colonel Terry, proceeded to the left of the road, in front of some fallen timber and the rifle-pits, while the Thirty-seventh New York, Colonel Hayman, went still further to the left. The Second Michigan occupied a position on the right of the road. As soon as these arrangements were completed, an order was given for the troops under General Berry to advance and charge, which they did in a splendid manner, driving the enemy entirely out of the timber. At this charge the enemy lost sixty-three men killed. The rebels, being posted in the rifle-pits, caused the Federal troops much annoyance. The Fifth Michigan, however, soon compelled them to retreat, although it lost a great many of its men in the effort.

The enemy had the advantage of protection, while the Union men were obliged to expose themselves in bold relief. The Federal bullets could not penetrate the earth-works around the rifle-pits, and the only way to drive the enemy out was to make a bayonet charge. This charge was made in splendid style by the Fifth Michigan in front, and the Thirty-seventh New York at the left, the men pushing up to the pits near enough to bayonet the riflemen behind them. By this charge considerable loss was occasioned on both sides.

When General Kearney's troops were coming into action, they met the lengthened files of General Hooker's wounded being carried to the rear. The shrieks of the lacerated and bleeding soldiers, who had been fighting so long and so well, pierced the air, and this, joined to the mud and rain, and the exhaustion of those who had come several miles on a forced march, was not calculated to produce a favorable impression on them as they were going into action. General Heintzelman, however, ordered several of the bands to strike up national and martial airs; and, when the strains of these familiar tunes reached the ears of the wounded, their cheers mingled with those of the soldiers who were just rushing into the battle. The effect was wonderful on the other side; for some of the prisoners state that when they heard the bands strike up the Star-Spangled Banner, followed by that enthusiastic cheer, they knew that the victory would be ours.

The Third and Fourth Maine regiments having been detached from General Birney's brigade, and temporarily assigned to General Emory, General Birney came forward with the two remaining regiments,—the Thirty-eighth New York, Colonel J. H. Ward, and the Fortieth New York, Colonel Reilly. These were deployed to the right of the Hampton road, and, like those under General Berry on the left, relieved fragments of regiments which had borne the brunt of the battle since its commencement. All this time the rebel artillery was sending a rapid fire into the Federal ranks.

The Thirty-eighth New York regiment was ordered to charge down the road and take the enemy's rifle pits in front by the flank. Colonel Ward led seven companies of his regiment in this most brilliant and successful charge. The other three companies, under Lieutenant-Colonel Strong, were doing efficient service in an adjacent portion of the field.

The battle had now been raging uninterruptedly from an early hour in the morning, and seemed at last to be checked by the heroic conduct and successful charge of General Kearney's troops. The extreme left was still heavily pressed, however, by the obstinate force of the rebels in that part of the line.

To General Hancock was intrusted the most dangerous, because the boldest manœuvre of the day. He passed with his brigade—the Fifth Wisconsin, Colonel Cobb; the Sixth Maine, Colonel Burnham; the Forty-ninth Pennsylvania, Colonel Lowrie; the seventh Maine, Colonel Mason, and the Thirty-third New York, Colonel R. F. Taylor, supported by Lieutenant Cowan's and Captain Wheeler's batteries—to the right, for a mile parallel to the front, but completely hidden by the forest. Thence across a fifty-acre heath edged with timber, north to the extreme left of the enemy's line of works. At this point the rebels had dammed a creek which empties into York river, and straight across the narrow causeway frowned an earthwork, which looked imposing as a castle from its commanding position on the opposite hill.

General Hancock found this singular defence deserted, but it was with caution his skirmishers ventured across the dam and planted the Federal flag on the parapet, fifty feet above water mark. Then the whole force went over at double-quick, turned to the left, and followed a narrow, dangerous road, a gorge cut in the hill-side by the pond, till it emerged in turn, from the east, on the open battle-field.

A splendid picture met the eye. Two miles distant Hooker was fighting the rebels on the other side of Fort Page. From the latter point the rebel artillery was playing upon his lines. Between Hancock and the fort were two lesser works, at intervals of half a mile. Their garrisons quickly retreated on seeing him, and retired on the main force—the movement before practiced on the left, and one which plainly indicated that the rebel force was too small to hold the line. But it was also evident, from the determined stand made in and near Fort Page, that the rear guard was under orders to make a desperate maintenance of its position.

Although Hancock had a regiment with him besides his own, yet his force was scarcely five thousand, all told, and totally separated from the main body. If overpowered in front, retreat would be utterly impossible through the narrow gorge behind them. General Keyes appeared on the field at this moment, and told General Hancock that he did not visit him to assume the command as ranking-officer, but to see him, Hancock, "carry the left." General Keyes at once sent back for a support of cavalry and artillery. This was about one o'clock in the afternoon. For some reason, General Sumner omitted ordering the reinforcements forward.

A regiment was soon in the enemy's deserted works (No. 3 from York river). The old flag was raised with wild cheers from its parapet; and eight cannon were quickly unlimbered in the field beyond. A smaller, intermediate outwork was still held between this and Fort Magruder. In front of it a line of rebel skirmishers deployed, but were quickly dispersed and forced to retire. In five minutes the Union guns were playing, some on the great fort at six hundred yards distance, the rest on the woods to the north, through which the rebels were retreating on their main body.

Just then the clouds broke away in the west, and a flood of light came in upon the whole panorama. Nothing could be more beautiful and inspiring. The deserted rebel forts, surmounted with Federal colors; Hancock's infantry awaiting orders in battle line; a signal officer waving to the centre his flag-signals from the parapet of work No. 3; the long fire-belching, smoke-canopied curve of Fort Page in the distance; still further beyond, white flashes, and huge clouds of smoke appearing from Hooker's battle-ground on the left, of whose desperate contest the stunning roll of musketry and roar of cannon gave true token —all these combined formed a broad battle-picture worthy of Varney.

Wheeler's artillery fired with precision and rapidity for an hour, the fort answering gun for gun. But the rebel infantry seemed to have their hands full in managing Hooker, and as it was not yet practicable to storm the fort, the Union forces found little to do, and stood under fire of the artillery with small loss, awaiting a share in the business. It was not long in coming, and came in the shape which more than one observer had feared from the outset. It was preceded at four o'clock by one of those dead, ominous half-hour pauses which so often make the decisive turn of an engagement. Many thought the enemy were retreating. Others, who have had occasion to dread these still and awful lapses from the bloody work of a field-day, prognosticated an unknown danger impending close at hand.

Suddenly there burst from the woods on the right flank a battalion of rebel cavalry! Then, to the right and left of the horse, three regiments of infantry supporting it!

But General Hancock was equal to the crisis. Forming his infantry against this sudden attack, he held them in magnificent order, while the rebel foot and horse came on, cheering, firing, and charging in gallant and imposing style. Wheeler's battery turned and poured hot volleys into them as they came, and over five thousand muskets riddled them through and through. But they kept on—nearer—nearer—closing up, cheering, and sure of their power to sweep the Federals before them.

Thus they came, swifter than it can be told, until their line, now broken and irregular, was within two hundred yards of the unwavering columns. Then Hancock showed himself the coolest and bravest of the brave. Taking off his hat, and using the courtly prefix of the olden time, he said: "*Ready, now! Gentlemen,* CHARGE!" The whole line swept forward, as the reaper's sickle rushes through the grain. Its keen edge had not yet touched the enemy, when his ranks broke simultaneously, fled in confusion to the rear, and the field of Williamsburg was won.

About five o'clock P. M. some excitement was caused in the rear, and soon an officer, with his staff, rode to the opening in the woods where he could get a view of the field. It was General McClellan. The moment he was seen, loud and deafening cheers rose up along the lines of the centre, and rolled away to the right and left, imparting a new enthusiasm to the forces. The chief officers were quickly consulted, and reinforcements were sent to the aid of Hancock and Hooker. Hancock's brilliant and successful charge had already won the day on the right, and the effect of it in the panic and rout of the rebels was becoming sensibly felt in front of Hooker's division, when the long-looked for assistance came to his side. The rebels promptly retired, and the desperate struggle of the day closed on a splendidly contested field. The men were compelled to bivouack on the ground, with the rain still falling, in proud anticipation of a renewal of the conflict in the morning.

The rebels had been reinforced as late as five o'clock, and it was expected that General Johnston would command them in the morning in person, but the opportune appearance of the Federal reinforcements, together with the successful movements of General Hancock, created a panic among them, and they fell back on Williamsburg, and commenced their hasty retreat from that place. At two o'clock on Tuesday morning the Federal forces began to move. As they approached Williamsburg they found the way clear, and on coming up to the city the rear guard of the foe were flying on the road toward Richmond, leaving the town to be occupied by the Federal troops. General McClellan appointed General Jameson Military Governor of the place, and the troops marched through the main street of the city to the homely, but glorious and soul-stirring strains of "Yankee Doodle."

The houses, churches, barns and stables were found filled with the wounded of the rebel army, as well as the Federals whom they had taken prisoners. It was a sad, heart-rending scene, those brave soldiers mangled, dying and dead. The Federal troops immediately commenced the work of burial, while the surgeons found incessant occupation in the discharge of their duties. The battle field presented a frightful scene of carnage, and several days passed before all the dead and wounded stragglers were found in the woods and among the underbrush where they had fallen.

The loss of the Federals was about 500 killed, 1,600 wounded, and 623 prisoners. That of the rebels was somewhat greater in killed and wounded. Five hundred prisoners fell into Federal hands. Some hundred of the rebel dead were buried on the day following the battle. Lieutenant-Colonel Irwin, of the Eighth Alabama, formerly United States Senator, was found dead on the field.

Thirty-five regiments of the rebels were engaged in the action, that number being represented by the wounded men left after the battle.

BATTLE OF WEST POINT, VA.
May 7, 1862.

West Point is the name given to the landing-place at the head of the York river, which is formed by the junction of the Pamunkey and Mattapony rivers, and is thirty miles above Yorktown.

After the evacuation of that place, and the entrance of the Federal troops, the Union army proceeded in its advance toward Richmond by different routes, as already detailed. One column marched by the land route, under Heintzelman, Sumner, Hooker, Kearney and Keyes, while General Franklin led his corps by transports up the York river to West Point, leaving Yorktown at nine o'clock, on Tuesday morning, May 6th. The banks of the river presented a fine appearance, and white flags were displayed from many of the houses. The house of Mr. Bigler, a firm loyalist, was almost covered with an immense flag, bearing the stars and stripes, while one of the ladies of the house waved the beautiful emblem of peace along its folds, from one of the windows. The rebels had set fire to a valuable mill belonging to Mr. Bigler, and its ruins were still sending up great clouds of smoke into the air, a lurid witness of the destruction which had marked their progress. The army arrived at West Point about two o'clock, P. M., and commenced its disembarkation.

In consequence of the shallowness of the approach by water, it became necessary to use pontoon boats and scows to facilitate the landing. Operations were therefore slow; but the troops were landed by midnight. The rebels did not dispute the landing. Pickets were immediately thrown out into the woods in front, the roads leading to the landing-place examined, and trees were thrown across the roads. The pickets were occasionally engaged during the night, but only two or three of the Federals were lost in these irregular skirmishes. The night was spent in active labors and in jealously watching the movements of the foe.

At half-past three o'clock the next morning, the whole division was under arms. At six o'clock information that the enemy was approaching was received, and the troops prepared at once to meet him. The Gosline Zouaves, (Pennsylvania,) New York Sixteenth, Eighteenth, Thirty-first and Thirty-second, and Maine Fifth were ordered to take the advance; the New Jersey brigade following them up as a reserve. The Fourth New Jersey having in its front a marsh, and immediately on its far side a piece of woods, from which the enemy could fire upon it with advantage, Colonel Simpson ordered his fine body of pioneers to throw a bridge over the creek. This was the work of a few moments, and his regiment, by direction of Colonel Taylor, took possession of the woods, and were strongly posted behind a ravine, ready to deliver a telling fire upon the rebels, in the contingency of the Fifth Maine, immediately in front, being driven back. This contingency, however, did not occur.

The Thirty-second New York, Colonel Matteson, of Newton's brigade, was directed to clear the wood of rebels, who had made their presence known to the pickets. The Sixteenth New York was ordered to the same work in other portions of the wood. The Thirty-second proceeded to execute their duty. Entering the wood they came upon a ravine, at the bottom of which they were fired upon by the rebel skirmishers. They charged at once, delivering a galling fire upon the enemy's position. The enemy retired, the troops following until a second ravine appeared in view. In attempting to cross this the rebels from the other side again poured a volley into them with considerable effect. They had not, however, the power to drive back the Federal troops, who gallantly pursued the rebels, delivering their fire upon them, or rather upon their position, for they kept themselves adroitly concealed by the woods. At a third and last ravine, the rebels had erected a breastwork on the opposite side, from which they opened on the Federals with small arms, and grape and canister from mountain howitzers. The Thirty-second charged gallantly up to within a few feet of the work, but were forced to fall back from the superior force of the enemy. They retired in admirable order. There were only seven companies of the Thirty-second regiment engaged against Alabama, Texas, South Carolina and Tennessee troops.

At two o'clock, P. M., the gunboats, three in number, opened fire upon the enemy from their large guns, the shells apparently taking effect in the right quarter, for the enemy soon afterwards retired, their battery being silenced on the first shot from the boats. The enemy's retreat could be traced by the line of smoke in his rear. The retreating rebels were evidently attempting to destroy every thing on their route. The Sixteenth and Thirty-first regiments, New York Volunteers, were also engaged with the enemy in the woods. The loss of the Thirty-second regiment New York Volunteers was nearly one hundred in killed and wounded. Three officers,—Captain Young, of company D; Captain Brown, of company C, and Lieutenant Wallace, of company G—were killed, and Lieutenant Stone, of company B, and Lieutenant Twaddle, of company F, wounded severely, and thirteen privates were killed. The total loss in the different regiments of Newton's brigade was about two hundred in killed, wounded and missing. The loss of the rebels was heavy, as was presumed from the fact that they were seen from the transports carrying off their dead and wounded in great numbers.

Most of the Federal regiments that took part in this engagement suffered severely, and many prisoners were taken by the rebels. The timely service rendered by the gunboats was mainly instrumental in defeating the enemy.

Captain Montgomery, of General Newton's staff, had a most extraordinary escape from the Hampton Legion, into whose picket lines he became entrapped. Captain Montgomery knew that only the utmost self-possession could extricate him from his difficulty, and he coolly saluted them. They supposed he was a rebel officer, and asked him how far General Hampton was from them. Montgomery told them he had left him about ten rods distant, and said, "Now, boys, the General expects you to do your duty to-day!" and turned his horse slowly around to retire. But the rebels saw the "U. S." on his cap, and immediately sprang to their feet, while the Captain was dashing with all the speed of his horse down the road. But too late. A volley of minie rifle balls whistled round him, and his horse fell dead, pierced by seven balls. He fell upon Captain Montgomery's leg, giving him several severe bruises. The Captain fell back, with his head in a ditch, where he lay some ten minutes, pretending to be dead. The rebels came up to him, talking, swearing, and making their comments on the Yankee, while they rifled his pockets.

The brave fellow lay perfectly still, holding his breath, while these rude men were searching his person; but a sense of his ludicrous position came upon him too strongly, and he burst into a hearty fit of laughter, much to the astonishment of those who believed themselves to be pillaging a dead body.

Of course, there was no avoiding his fate now, and he surrendered himself a prisoner of war, with the merry laughter still bright upon his face. His captors were greatly annoyed by his coolness and his "shamming," and were leading him off to headquarters, when a couple of shells came whizzing through the air and exploding in their midst, dispersed them. Captain Montgomery seized the opportunity, and plunging into the woods found his way to the Federal lines, where, after a little rest, he mounted another horse and joined the fight again.

CHRONOLOGY.

1860.

Nov. 8. The election of Abraham Lincoln and Hannibal Hamlin, as President and Vice President of the United States, was announced at Washington.

9–11. James Chesnut, Jr., and James H. Hammond, U. S. Senators from South Carolina, resigned their seats in the Senate.

Dec. 3. The Second Session of the 36th Congress opened at Washington.

10. U. S. House of Representatives appointed a Committee of 33 on the State of the Union.

10. Howell Cobb, of Georgia, Secretary of the U. S. Treasury, resigned his office. John A. Dix, of New York, was appointed his successor.

14. Lewis Cass, of Michigan, Secretary of State, resigned.

17. Meeting of the South Carolina State Convention at Columbus, and adjournment to Charleston.

20. The South Carolina "Ordinance of Secession" passed.

23. Discovery of a large embezzlement of the Indian Trust Funds, in charge of Jacob Thompson, Secretary of the Department of the Interior.

24. Resignation of the South Carolina Representatives in Congress.

25. Intervention of citizens of Pittsburgh, Pa., to prevent the removal to the South of ordnance in Alleghany Arsenal.

26. Major Anderson removed his command from Fort Moultrie to Fort Sumter.

26. Messrs. Barnwell, Orr, and Adams, Commissioners appointed by South Carolina to treat with the Federal Government, arrived at Washington.

27. Captain N. L. Coste, U.S.R. service, in command of the cutter William Aiken, betrayed his vessel into the hands of the State authorities of South Carolina.

28. The palmetto flag was raised over the custom-house and post-office in Charleston, S. C., and Castle Pinckney and Fort Moultrie were occupied by the South Carolina military.

28. Enthusiastic Union meeting at Memphis, Tenn.

28. Twenty-one guns were fired at Wilmington, Del., in honor of Major Anderson and his men.

29. John B. Floyd resigned his position as Secretary of War.

30. South Carolina troops took possession of the U.S. Arsenal at Charleston, containing many thousand stand of arms and valuable military stores.

1861.

Jan. 2. Gov. Ellis, of North Carolina, dispatched troops to seize Fort Macon, the forts at Wilmington, and the U.S. Arsenal at Fayetteville.

3. Fort Pulaski, at Savannah, Ga., taken possession of by Georgia troops, by order of the Governor.

3. South Carolina Commissioners left Washington for Charleston, the President declining to receive any official communication from them.

4. United States Arsenal at Mobile seized by secessionists. No defence.

4. Fast day, by proclamation of President Buchanan.

4. Fort Morgan, at the entrance of Mobile Bay, taken and garrisoned by 200 Alabama troops.

5. Steamship Star of the West sailed from New York with troops and provisions for Fort Sumter.

7. Meeting of Alabama State Convention.

7. Meeting of Mississippi State Convention.

7. Meeting of Virginia Legislature.

7. Meeting of Tennessee Legislature.

8. Jacob Thompson resigned his place in the Cabinet, as Secretary of the Interior.

8. United States sub-Treasury at Charleston seized.

9. Mississippi Ordinance of Secession passed.

9. Steamship Star of the West, with supplies for Fort Sumter, fired into from Morris' Island and Fort Moultrie, and driven from Charleston harbor.

11. Louisiana State troops, under Captain Bradford, took possession of the U.S. marine hospital, two miles below New Orleans, and ordered the removal of the patients, 216 in number.

Jan. 11. Florida Convention adopted an Ordinance of Secession by a vote of 62 to 7.

11. Alabama Convention adopted an Ordinance of Secession by a vote of 61 to 39.

11. Abolition meeting at Rochester, N. Y., broken up by a mob.

12. Senator Seward's great Union speech in the U.S. Senate.

12. Fort Barrancas and the Navy Yard at Pensacola, Fla., seized by rebel troops.

15. Col. Hayne, Commissioner from South Carolina to Washington, demanded the withdrawal of the garrison of Fort Sumter.

15. U. S. coast survey-schooner Dana seized by Florida State authorities.

18. Massachusetts Legislature unanimously tendered to the President of the U.S. such aid in men and money as he might request to maintain the authority of the general government.

19. Convention of Georgia adopted a secession ordinance by a vote of 208 to 89.

21. Jefferson Davis, of Mississippi, withdrew from U.S. Senate.

24. U. S. arsenal at Augusta, Ga., surrendered to the State authorities.

26. Louisiana Convention passed an ordinance of secession by a vote of 113 to 17. The popular vote afterwards taken was 20,448 for; 17,296 against.

29. U. S. revenue cutter Robert McClelland, Captain Breshwood, surrendered to State of Louisiana.

29. Secretary Dix's dispatch to Hemphill Jones at New Orleans, "If any one attempts to haul down the American flag, shoot him on the spot."

31. South Carolina authorities offered to buy Fort Sumter.

31. U. S. branch mint and custom-house at New Orleans seized by State authorities.

Feb. 1. Texas Convention at Galveston passed an ordinance of secession, to be voted on by the people on the 23d of February, and to take effect March 2.

1. U. S. revenue cutter Lewis Cass, Capt. Morrison, surrendered to the State of Louisiana.

4. A convention of delegates from the seceded States organized at Montgomery, Alabama; Howell Cobb, President, J. F. Hooper, Secretary.

5. Peace Convention at Washington organized; John Tyler, of Va., Chairman, J. C. Wright, of Ohio, Secretary.

8. Congress at Montgomery adopted a Constitution for a provisional government, to go into immediate operation; Jefferson Davis, President, Alex. H. Stephens, Vice President.

8 U. S. arsenal at Little Rock, Ark., with 9,000 stand of arms and 40 cannon, &c., was surrendered to State authorities.

13. The election of Lincoln and Hamlin, as President and V. President of the U. S., formally declared in the Senate by John C. Breckinridge, V. President.

18. Jefferson Davis inaugurated as President of the Southern Confederacy.

22. John Ross, principal Cherokee Chief, rejected a proposition of Gov. H. M. Rector, of Ark., to entice his nation to take part in the rebellion.

23. Hon. Abraham Lincoln, President elect, arrived in Washington.

23. U. S. property to a great amount, together with the various army posts in Texas, surrendered to the rebels by General Twiggs. Property valued at $1,500,000, besides buildings.

27. Peace Convention, at Washington, submitted to the Senate a plan of adjustment of the national difficulties, involving seven amendments to the Constitution.

March 1. General Twiggs expelled from the army of the United States.

2. Revenue cutter Dodge seized in Galveston Bay by Texas authorities.

4. Abraham Lincoln inaugurated 16th President of the U. S, at Washington.

4. A State Convention declared Texas out of the Union.

5. Gen. P. T. Beauregard took command of the forces investing Fort Sumter, S. C.

6. Fort Brown, Texas, surrendered to State troops.

18. Supplies cut off from Fort Pickens and the Federal fleet in the Gulf of Mexico, by rebel authorities at Pensacola.

20. Sloop Isabel, at Pensacola, with provision for the Federal fleet, was seized by the rebels.

21. Great speech of A. H. Stephens, V. President of the Southern Confederacy, at Savannah, Ga.

30. Mississippi State Convention ratified the Constitution of the C. S., by a vote of 78 to 7.

April 3. South Carolina Convention ratified the Constitution of the C. S. by a vote of 114 to 16.

10. Militia organized in District of Columbia for defence of the capital.

11. Steamship Coatzacoalcos arrived in N. York, bringing Federal troops from Texas.

11. Confederate States Commissioners left Washington.

12. Attack on Fort Sumter.

12. Reinforcement of Fort Pickens.

14. Evacuation of Fort Sumter.

15. Seventeen vessels from Southern ports, without U. S. clearances, were seized at New York and fined $100 each.

15. President's proclamation, calling for 75,000 volunteers to suppress insurrection, and also calling an extra session of U. S. Congress on July 4.
16. The government of the Southern Confederacy called for 32,000 men.
16. New York Legislature appropriated $3,000,000 for war purposes.
16. At New York, Philadelphia, Trenton and other places, journals were compelled to display the American flag.
17. State Convention of Va., in secret session, passed an ordinance of secession.
18. 500 volunteers from Pennsylvania, and 300 regulars, arrived at Washington.
18. Lieut. Jones, in charge of Harper's Ferry arsenal, hearing of the advance of a large Virginia force to seize the establishment, set fire to it, and retreated to Carlisle, Pa.
18. Great Union meeting at Wheeling, Va.
19. Seizure of the U. S. transport Star of the West, at Indianola, by Texas troops under Col. Van Dorn.
19. Sixth Massachusetts regiment on its way to Washington, attacked by a mob in Baltimore, and 3 killed and 7 wounded. In defending themselves, 7 rebels were killed and 8 wounded.
19. The N. Y. 7th militia, Mass. 4th and 8th militia, and R. I. Providence Artillery left New York on their way to Washington.
19. Clearances refused to vessels in northern ports to ports south of Maryland.
20. Eighth Mass. regiment reached Annapolis, Md.
20. Great Union mass meeting of citizens in Union Square, N. Y.
20. 600 kegs of gunpowder, destined for New Orleans, seized by the U. S. Marshal at New York.
20. Fourth Mass. regiment landed at Fortress Monroe.
20. U. S. arsenal at Liberty, Mo., seized.
20. Steamship Star of the West, having been seized by secessionists, was taken into New Orleans.
20. The ports of South Carolina, Georgia, Alabama, Florida, Mississippi, Louisiana, and Texas, ordered to be blockaded by the President, as those States were in a state of insurrection against the government.
20. Bridges on Pennsylvania Northern and Philadelphia railway, near Baltimore, burned by a mob from that city.
21. Gosport Navy Yard, opposite Norfolk, Va., set on fire, and vessels scuttled and sunk, by U. S. officers in charge, to prevent their seizure by the rebels.
21. Branch Mint of the U. S. at Charlotte, N. C., seized by order of the Governor of that State.
21. Philadelphia and Baltimore railway taken possession of by U.S. government.
21. The N. Y. 6th, 12th, and 71st, and one R. I. and one Mass. regiment, with a battery, left New York on transports for the Chesapeake.
21. Fourth Mass. regiment arrived at Fortress Monroe.
21. Andrew Johnson, U. S. Senator from Tennessee, mobbed at Lynchburg, Va.
22. U. S. arsenal at Fayetteville, N. C., containing 37,000 stand of arms, 3,000 kegs of powder, and a large quantity of shot and shell, seized by State authority.
22. Depot of U. S. stores at Napoleon, Ark., seized under orders of Henry M. Rector, Governor of that State.
22. 3,200 Pennsylvania troops at Cockeysville, 14 miles from Baltimore.
22. Seventh N. Y. regiment land at Annapolis, Md.
23. N. Y. 8th, 13th, 28th, and 69th regiments embarked for Washington.
22. Embargo laid, by the Mayor and Police Board of Baltimore, on provisions and steamboats, thus withholding the government stores in that city.
23. First South Carolina regiment left Charleston for the Potomac.
24. Fort Smith, Ark., seized by a rebel force under Col. Borland.
24. N. Y. 7th and Mass. 8th arrived in Washington.
" 25. A large amount of arms removed to Alton, Ill., from St. Louis arsenal, by Illinois volunteers, to prevent their seizure by rebels.
25. Col. Van Dorn, of Texas State troops, captured 450 U. S. troops at Saluria.
25. Transport Empire City, from Texas, arrived in N.Y.with 600 men of the 3d Infantry and 2d Cavalry, U.S.A., from that State.
25. Gov. Letcher, of Va., by proclamation, transferred that Commonwealth to the Southern Confederacy.
26. Gov. Brown, of Georgia, by proclamation, prohibited the payment of all debts to Northern creditors till the end of hostilities.
26. Bridges over Gunpowder Creek, on Philadelphia and Baltimore railway, and bridge over Bush river, on the same route, destroyed by the rebels.
26. Gov. Burton, of Delaware, issued a proclamation calling for volunteers to defend the Union.
27. Military Department of Washington assigned to Col. Mansfield; Department of Annapolis to Gen. Butler; Department of Pennsylvania to Maj-Gen. Patterson.

April 27. Five men arrested at the Navy Yard, Washington, for filling bomb-shells with sand and sawdust.

27. A number of Southerners employed in the Departments at Washington, refused the oath of allegiance prescribed by the Government, and resigned.

27. The ports of Virginia and North Carolina were included in the blockade by the President.

28. U. S. frigate Constitution arrived at New York from Annapolis.

29. Secession defeated in Maryland House of Delegates by a vote of 53 to 13.

29. Ellsworth's Fire Zouaves left New York for Annapolis.

29. Daily communication between Baltimore and Philadelphia re-established.

May 1. Brig.-Gen. Harney addressed a strong Union letter to his friends in Missouri.

2. N. Y. 69th (Irish) regiment arrived at Washington.

2. Col. F. P. Blair, Jr., announced that the four regiments called for from the State of Missouri, by the President, were enrolled, armed, and mustered into the service within one week from the call.

3. Gov. Jackson, of Missouri, in a message to the Legislature, recommended arming the State, and a union of sympathy and destiny with the slaveholding States.

3. Four New Jersey regiments, fully equipped, under General Runyon, started for the seat of war.

3. President Lincoln issued a proclamation calling into service 42,000 volunteers for three years, and directing the increase of the regular army and navy of the United States.

3. Privateer Savannah captured by the U. S. brig Perry.

4. Steamship Star of the West was put into commission as the receiving ship of the Confederate navy, at New Orleans.

5. Brig.-Gen. Butler, with 6th Massachusetts and 8th New York regiments, took possession of the Relay House, at the junction of the Baltimore, Washington and Ohio railways, nine miles south of Baltimore.

6. The six regiments called for from Indiana, were mustered into service in one week from date of the call.

6. Virginia admitted into the Southern Confederacy in secret session of Confederate Congress.

6. Police Commissioners of St. Louis, Mo., demanded of Capt. Lyon the removal of U. S. troops from all places and buildings occupied by them in that city outside the Arsenal grounds.

6. City military of Baltimore disbanded by order of Major Trimble, commander.

6. Confederate States Congress recognized war with United States, and authorized issue of letters of marque and reprisal.

6. Legislature of Arkansas passed an unconditional ordinance of secession, 69 to 1.

7. Major Anderson, with consent of Sec.-of-War, accepted command of Kentucky state military.

7. Serious riot at Knoxville, Tenn., caused by hoisting a Union flag.

7. League between Tennessee authorities and Confederate States.

7. The late U. S. garrison of Fort Davis, Texas, consisting of 11 officers and 300 men, made prisoners of war by a force of 1,800 rebels near Eastonville. They all refused to enlist in the rebel army.

9. U. S. troops landed at Locust Point, in Baltimore, and were conveyed by the Balt. and Ohio branch railroad through the city.

9. The Confederate Congress authorized President Davis to raise such force for the war as he should deem expedient.

9. U. S. ships Cumberland, Pawnee, Monticello and Yankee enforcing the blockade off Fortress Monroe.

9. Steamers Philadelphia, Baltimore, Powhatan and Mount Vernon, armed by U. S. Government, and cruising on the Potomac.

9. Virginians have batteries in Norfolk harbor, at Craney Island, Sandy Point, the Hospital, Fort Norfolk, and the Bluffs, three miles from the Hospital.

10. Maj.-Gen. R. E. Lee appointed to command the rebel forces in Virginia.

10. Maj.-Gen. McClellan appointed to command the Department of Ohio.

10. The President directed that all officers in the army should take anew the oath of allegiance to the United States.

10. The secession military, under Gen. Frost, at St. Louis, Mo., surrendered to Capt. Lyon, commanding U. S. forces. A mob assailed the U. S. military after the surrender, and were fired on by them, and many killed and wounded.

10. The Winans steam gun captured by Gen. Butler, three miles from the Relay House, Md.

10. The Maryland Legislature passed a resolution imploring the President of the United States to cease the present war.

11. U. S. steam frigate Niagara off Charleston, S. C., and began the blockade of that port.

11. Gen. Harney issued a proclamation exhorting the people of Missouri, to maintain peace, and announced his determination

to use the authority of the Government for that purpose.

11. A company of Home Guards, at St. Louis, Mo., mostly German, were fired on by a mob, and returned the fire. Three of the Guards and 4 of the citizens were killed.

13. The 6th Mass. and 8th N. Y. regiments, under Gen. Butler, occupied Federal Hill, near Baltimore.

13. Convention of Union delegates from 35 counties in W. Virginia, met in Wheeling.

13. A lady from New Haven, Conn., teacher of a Grammar School in New Orleans, denuded, tarred and feathered in Lafayette Square, amid an immense crowd of people, being accused of expressing abolition sentiments.

14. Gov. Hicks, of Maryland, issued a proclamation, calling for four regiments of troops, to serve within Maryland, or for the defence of the capital of the United States.

14. Gen. Butler seized a large quantity of arms stored in Baltimore, and a schooner loaded with arms.

15. A proclamation of neutrality with respect to the civil war in the U. S. was issued by Queen Victoria, in which the subjects of Great Britain were forbidden to take part in the contest, or endeavor to break a blockade "lawfully and effectually established."

15. The town of Potosi, Washington co., Mo., taken possession of by U. S. troops, and rebel prisoners and munitions of war taken to St. Louis.

16. Gen. Butler appointed Maj.-Gen. of Volunteers.

18. Arkansas admitted to the Southern Confederacy.

18. Military Department of Virginia organized, embracing E. Virginia, N. Carolina and Tennessee, Maj.-Gen. Butler in command.

18. John Ross, principal Cherokee Chief, in two admirable letters rejects the efforts of the rebels in Arkansas to draw his nation into rebellion.

19. Shots exchanged between U. S. steamers Freeborn and Monticello, and the rebel battery at Sewall's Point, Va.

19. Eight thousand rebel troops at Harper's Ferry.

20. Death of Col. Vosburgh, N. Y. 71st, at Washington.

20. Seizure by the Government of principal telegraph offices throughout the free States, and of the accumulated dispatches for twelve months.

20. Ordinance of secession, and ordinance assenting to the Confederate Constitution passed by North Carolina State Convention.

20. Seizure of 1,600 muskets and 4,000 pikes by Federal troops in Baltimore.

20. Gen. Cadwallader, successor to Gen. Butler, occupied Federal Hill, Baltimore.

20. Fort McHenry reinforced.

20. Prize ship Gen. Parkhill, of Liverpool, arrived at Philadelphia, with a crew from the frigate Niagara.

21. Confederate Congress at Montgomery adjourned to meet at Richmond, July 20.

22. Erection of rebel batteries at Aquia Creek.

22. Maj. Gen. Butler arrived at Fortress Monroe.

22. Fort at Ship Island, Miss., destroyed to prevent its falling into rebel hands.

22. Steamer J. C. Swan, 30 miles below St. Louis, seized by order of Gen. Lyon.

22. Five thousand pounds of lead seized at Ironton, Mo., en route for the South.

23. Strong secession speech by A. H. Stephens, at Atlanta, Ga.

23. A battery of Whitworth guns, 12-pounders, arrived in N. Y. city, a present to the Government from patriotic Americans abroad.

23. At Clarksburgh, Harrison co., Va., two companies of secession troops surrendered their arms and dispersed at the demand of Union companies under Capts. Moore and Vance.

24. All vessels from the Northern States at New Orleans, which arrived after the 6th inst., were seized by the Confederate States Marshal.

24. Jeff. Davis appointed the 13th of June to be observed as a day of fasting and prayer.

24. Thirteen thousand Union troops crossed the Potomac and entered Virginia, occupying Alexandria and Arlington Heights.

24. Assassination of Col. Ellsworth, at Alexandria, Va.

25. Destruction of seven bridges and five miles of rails from Alexandria to Leesburg, Va., by the 69th N. Y. S. M.

26. Confederate privateer Calhoun arrived at New Orleans with three whaling vessels and cargoes as prizes.

26. Arrival of 600 U. S. troops at Havana, from Texas.

27. A writ of *habeas corpus* was issued at Baltimore, Md., by Chief Justice Taney, in the case of John Merryman. Gen. Cadwallader declined surrendering him, and an attachment was issued for the General's arrest, which was not served.

27. U. S. steamer Brooklyn commenced the blockade of the Mississippi river.

May 27. Brig.-Gen. McDowell took command of the Federal forces in Virginia.
27. The blockade of Mobile, Ala., commenced.
28. Blockade of Savannah initiated by U. S. gunboat Union.
28. The rebels erected barricades at Harper's Ferry and Point of Rocks; Manassas Junction fortified.
28. Strength of the Rebels in Virginia reported at 90,000 men.
28. Jeff. Davis arrived at Richmond.
28. Services of Miss D. L. Dix accepted by the War Department, for organizing military hospitals, and procuring nurses.
29. Advance of Ohio and Pennsylvania troops through Maryland, towards Harper's Ferry; rebels fall back to Martinsburg.
29. Federal troops occupied Grafton, Va.
30. Concentration of Federal troops at Chambersburg, Pa.
31. Steamers Freeborn and Anacosta attacked rebel batteries at Aquia Creek, Va.
31. Gen. Harney superseded by Gen. Lyon in Missouri.
31. Gens. Banks and Fremont commissioned as Major-Generals.
Ex-Gov. Pratt of Maryland, arrested and taken to Washington Navy Yard.
June 1. British Government prohibited U. S. and rebel armed vessels from bringing any prizes to British ports.
1. Charge of U. S. cavalry at Fairfax Court House, Va., Lieut. Tompkins, commanding.
2. Federal batteries erected at the Rip Raps, near Fortress Monroe.
2. Gen. Twiggs appointed Maj.-Gen. Confederate army.
3. Gen. Beauregard took command of the rebel forces at Manassas Junction.
3. Surprise of rebel troops at Philippi, Va., by U. S. forces under Cols. Dumont, Kelly and Lander. Col. Kelly was severely wounded.
3. Hon. Stephen A. Douglas died at Chicago. His dying message to his sons was, "Tell them to obey the laws and support the Constitution of the United States."
3. Border State Convention met at Frankfort, Ky.
4. Chief-Justice Taney's protest published against the suspension of the *habeas corpus* by the President.
5. Gun factory and arms of Merrill and Thomas, Baltimore, seized by U. S. Government.
6. Gov. Pickens, of S. C., forbade the remittance of funds to Northern creditors.
6. Thirty-five Virginia cavalry were captured at Alexandria. They took the oath of allegiance and were released.

6. Treasonable dispatches to the rebel Government discovered in the telegraph office at Washington, from Jas. E. Harvey, appointed minister to Portugal.
6. Secession camp at Ellicott's Mills, Ky., ten miles from Cairo, broken up by troops sent from latter station by Gen. Prentiss.
8. Bridges at Point of Rocks and Berlin, on the Potomac river, burned by order of rebel Gen. Johnston.
8. Sanitary Commission authorized and appointed by the Government.
8. Four bridges on the Alexandria and Hampshire railway, Va., burned by disunion troops.
8. Gen. Patterson's troops marched from Chambersburg towards Harper's Ferry.
8. Seizure of arms at Easton, Md., by U. S. troops from Annapolis.
8. Vote of Tennessee reported in favor of secession.
10. Gen. Banks assumed command in Baltimore.
10. Gov. Harris, of Tenn., authorized the raising of troops for the rebel army.
10. Repulse of Federal troops at Great Bethel, near Fortress Monroe.
11. Surprise and rout of armed rebels at Romney, Va., by Col. Wallace's Indiana regiment.
12. Gov. Jackson, of Missouri, issued a proclamation calling 50,000 State militia into service, to protect the "lives, liberty and property of the citizens of the State."
12. Meeting of W. Virginia State Convention at Wheeling. They resolved to elect loyal State officers.
13. Fast day in seceded States, by order of Pres. Davis.
13. Skirmish at Seneca Mills, on the Potomac, 28 miles above Washington, between U. S. District Volunteers and rebel cavalry.
14. Gen. J. A. Dix, of New York, appointed Maj.-Gen. of U. S. Volunteers.
14. Harper's Ferry evacuated by the rebel forces, who destroyed all the available property.
14. Flight of Gov. Jackson and Gen. Price from Jefferson City, capital of Missouri. The telegraph lines and bridges destroyed by them on their route to Booneville.
14. The great Union gun arrived at Fortress Monroe.
14. Miss Dix and a number of nurses arrived at Fortress Monroe.
14. Maryland election resulted in the triumph of all the Union candidates but Winter Davis.
15. Mr. Woodall, of Baltimore, hung by rebels at Harper's Ferry.

15. Jefferson City, Mo., occupied by U.S. troops, under Gen. Lyon.

16. Skirmish at Seneca Mills, Md. Rebel captain and 2 men killed by Major Everett's command.

17. Skirmish at Edward's Ferry, on the Potomac, between the 1st Pennsylvania regiment and a body of rebels.

17. Six persons killed in St. Louis, by soldiers of Col. Kallman's regiment discharging a volley at the Recorder's Court-building, in retaliation of a shot fired into their ranks.

17. Surprise at Vienna, Va. First Ohio regiment fired into by a masked battery, 8 killed, 6 wounded.

17. Western Virginia Convention unanimously declared their independence of the eastern section of the State.

17. Rebel forces at Booneville, Mo., defeated by Gen. Lyon. 35 rebels killed or wounded, and 30 prisoners. Federal loss, 2 killed and 8 wounded. A large quantity of arms and camp equipage captured.

17. Gov. Hicks, of Md., in a message repelled the attempt of the Legislature to search his executive records for supposed correspondence with the Government.

18. U.S. troops at Hagerstown and Williamsport, Md., crossed the Potomac, under command of Gen. Patterson.

18. First balloon ascension for U.S. military purposes, by Prof. Lowe, at Washington.

18. Surprise of 800 Union Home Guards under Capt. Cook, at Camp Cole, Mo., by rebels from Warsaw. 25 killed, 52 wounded, 23 prisoners: 45 of the enemy killed or wounded.

18. Thirty-five rebels, with arms and ammunition, captured at Liberty, Mo., by U.S. regulars from Kansas City.

18. Railway bridge over New Creek, Va., burned by rebels from Romney.

20. Senator Lane, of Kansas, appointed brigadier-general.

20. Gen. McClellan took command of the Federal army in Western Virginia.

20. Cornelius Vanderbilt offered all the steamships of the Atlantic and Pacific Steamship Company, for the service of the Government.

21. East Tennessee Union Convention held at Greenville.

22. The exequatur of Mr. Trappman, Prussian Consul at Charleston, revoked by the President, for complicity with the rebels.

23. Balloon observations by Prof. Lowe, at Falls Church, Va.

23. Forty-eight locomotives, and a large quantity of other railway property of the Baltimore and Ohio railway, destroyed by rebels at Martinsburgh, Va.

24. Great fire in Richmond, Va.

24. Riot in Milwaukee, Wis., occasioned by the banks refusing to receive on deposit certain bills comprising an important part of the currency, and their consequent depreciation.

24. Rebel batteries at Mathias Point, Va., shelled by U. S. steamers Pawnee and Freeborn.

24. Engagement of U. S. steamer Monticello, with rebels, at Carter's Creek, Va.

24. Secession of Tennessee proclaimed by Gov. Harris. Vote, 104,913 for, to 47,238 against.

25. Virginia vote announced to be 128,884 for, and 32,134 against secession.

25. Western Virginia government recognized by the President.

26. Address of the Sanitary Commission to the citizens of the United States.

26. Brilliant skirmish of Corp. Hayes and 12 men of Col. Wallace's Indiana regiment, scouting on Patterson Creek, Md.

27. John C. Fremont arrived at Boston from Liverpool, bringing a large quantity of arms for the government.

27. Marshal Kane, of Baltimore, arrested by order of Gen. Banks, and John R. Kenly appointed provost-marshal.

27. Engagement between gunboat Freeborn and rebel batteries at Mathias Point. Captain Ward of the Freeborn killed.

27. Cols. Magruder and Hardee appointed brigadier-generals in Confederate army.

27. East Tennessee Union Convention meet at Nashville. Hon. Thomas A. R. Nelson presiding.

28. Skirmish at Shorter's Hill, Virginia. Union loss, 1 killed and 1 wounded; rebel loss, 2 killed.

29. Steamer St. Nicholas and three brigs captured by secessionists on the Chesapeake.

July 1. Gen. Banks arrested Messrs. Howard, Getchell, Hincks, and Davis, late members of Police Board, Baltimore.

1. Skirmish at Farmington, Mo. A large body of rebels routed by 50 Home Guards, under Capt. Cooke.

2. Rebels driven from Martinsburgh, Va., by Abercrombie's brigade, Gen. Patterson's division. Union loss, 3 killed and 10 wounded; rebel loss, 30 killed and wounded, 20 prisoners.

2. Organization of Virginia Legislature, at Wheeling.

3. Gen. Lyon, with 2,000 Federal troops, left Booneville, Mo., for the southwest.

3. Arkansas Military Board called out 10,000 men to repel invasion.

July 4. U. S. Congress met in special session.

4. Passenger trains on Louisville and Nashville railway seized by rebels.

4. Skirmish at Harper's Ferry between N.Y. 9th and rebels. Federal loss, 2 killed and 3 wounded.

4. Rebel battery erected at Mathias Point, Va.

4. Great Union meeting at San Francisco.

5. Battle at Carthage, Mo. Union forces, under Col. Sigel, 1,500; rebels, 4,000. Union loss, 13 killed and 31 wounded; rebel loss, 250 killed and wounded. Successful retreat of Sigel.

5. Skirmish at Newport News, Va., between a detachment of Hawkins' Zouaves and rebels.

4–7. U. S. steamer South Carolina captured or destroyed 11 vessels off Galveston.

6. Western Military Department constituted: Illinois, and the States and Territories west of the Mississippi to the Rocky Mountains, including New Mexico. Maj.-Gen. Fremont commanding.

6. Skirmish of 45 men, 3d Ohio, at Middle Fork Bridge, 12 miles east of Buckhannon, Va. 1 killed and 3 wounded of the Federals, and 7 rebels killed and wounded.

7. "Infernal" machines detected floating in the Potomac.

7. Skirmish at Great Falls, Va. Major Gerhardt's 8th German battalion have 2 men killed. Several rebels killed.

7. Congressman Vallandigham assaulted in the camp of 2d Ohio regiment.

8. Telegraphic dispatches of military operations placed under censorship.

8. Skirmish at Bealington, Western Va., 14th Ohio, and 7th and 9th Indiana, and Col. Barnett's 1st Ohio battery. Rebels defeated with loss of 20 killed, 40 wounded; Union loss, 2 killed, 6 wounded.

10. Loan bill passed by House of Representatives, authorizing the Secretary of the Treasury to borrow $250,000,000, redeemable in 20 years.

10. Postal service discontinued in Middle and West Tennessee.

10. Bill authorizing $500,000,000 and 500,000 volunteers, to suppress the rebellion passed the Senate.

10. Gen. Banks appointed George R. Dodge police marshal of Baltimore, *vice* Col. Kenly, and removed all the military to positions in the suburbs.

10. House of Representatives empowered the President to close the ports of seceded States.

10. Skirmish at Monroe Station, Mo., between Federal troops, under Col. Smith, and rebels, commanded by Gen. Harris.

Rebels routed on the following day, after they had burned 25 railway cars and station house, by Union forces sent to relieve Col. Smith. Several Federals wounded; rebel loss, 30 killed and wounded, and 70 prisoners.

10. Rebel General Wise issued a proclamation to citizens of Western Va., calling for volunteers, and offering pardon for past offences.

10. Skirmish at Laurel Hill, Va. Federal troops under Cols. McCook and Andrews, rebels under Col. Pegram. Rebels defeated. Union loss 1 killed 3 wounded.

11. Alex. H. Stephens' speech, at Augusta, Ga., defending secession, and soliciting contributions to aid the Confederacy.

11. The *State Journal*, at St. Louis, Mo., suppressed by Gen. Lyon for disloyal sentiments.

11. Battle of Rich Mountain, Va. Defeat of the rebels under Col. Pegram, 60 killed, 150 wounded, and 150 prisoners. Capture of 200 tents, 60 wagons, 6 cannon, and other stores. Union loss 11 killed and 35 wounded.

12. Fight at Barboursville, Va. Six companies of Col. Woodruff's 2d Kentucky attack and defeat 600 rebels. 1 Kentuckian and 10 or 12 rebels killed.

12. 600 rebels, under Col. Pegram, surrendered to Gen. McClellan, at Beverly, Va.

12. Twelve of Col. Bendix's N. Y. regiment captured at Newport News.

13. John B. Clark, of Mo., expelled from the House of Representatives, having been found in arms against the Government.

13. Great Union speech of Joseph Holt, at Louisville, Ky.

13. Battle of Carrick's Ford, Va., and death of Gen. Garnett, rebel commander. Defeat and rout of the rebels, with a loss of 150 killed and wounded, and 800 prisoners. Federal loss 13 killed, 40 wounded.

15. Skirmish at Bunker Hill, Va. Rout of rebel cavalry by fire of R. I. battery. The rebels pursued by 2d U S. cavalry.

15. Peace meeting at Nyack, N. Y.

16. Railway cars, containing Union troops, fired into at Millsville, Mo. 3 soldiers killed, 7 wounded; 7 rebels killed.

16. Federal army under Gen. McDowell marched toward Manassas.

16. Bill authorizing the President to call out militia to suppress the rebellion, passed the House of Representatives, and the bill to accept services of 500,000 volunteers.

16. Speech of J. C. Breckinridge in the Senate in opposition to the Union Defence Bill

16. Tilghman, a negro, killed 3 of a rebel prize crew on the schooner S. J. Wa-

July, 1861.   CHRONOLOGY.   473

ring, and brought the vessel into N. York on the 22d.

17. Advance column of national army occupied Fairfax Court House, Va.

17. Battle at Scarytown, Va. Repulse of Federals with loss of 9 killed; 38 wounded, 9 missing. Rebel loss less. 3 Federal colonels and 2 captains captured.

17. Gen. Patterson's army marched from Bunker Hill, Va., to Charlestown.

17. Skirmish at Fulton, Mo. Rebels driven back with loss.

18. Kansas City, Mo., Home Guards, under Major Van Horn, attacked near Harrisonville by a superior force of rebels, whom they defeated, killing and wounding 20. Union loss 1 killed.

18. Battle at Blackburn's Ford. Attack on the rebel entrenchments at Bull Run by a portion of Gen. Tyler's Division, who were repulsed with a loss of 83 men killed, wounded and missing. Rebel loss 68 killed and wounded.

19. Six Federal officers, near Hampton, Va., fired on by rebels in ambush. Major Rawlings killed, and Lieut. Johnson and Mr. Shurtliffe wounded and captured.

19. By Gen. Order No. 46 of War Department, Maj.-Gen. Patterson was honorably discharged, and Maj.-Gen. Banks appointed his successor in the Department of the "Shenandoah," and Gen. Dix appointed to succeed Gen. Banks in the Department of Maryland.

19. The Captain-General of Cuba liberated all the vessels brought into Cuban ports by privateer Sumter as prizes.

20. Rebel Congress met at Richmond, Va.

21. Battle of Bull Run.

22. Brig.-Gen. Beauregard promoted to the rank of "General" in the rebel army, the highest grade.

22. Rebel Congress appointed a day of thanksgiving for the victory at Manassas.

22. Maj. Gen. McClellan assigned to command the Department of the Potomac.

22. Missouri State Convention met at Jefferson City.

22. Rebels attacked and dispersed at Forsythe, Mo., by Federal troops under Gen. Sweeny, with loss of two wounded. Rebel loss, 5 killed, 10 wounded.

24. Naval expedition from Fortress Monroe to Black river, by Lieut. Crosby and 300 men. Nine sloops and schooners of the rebels burnt, and one schooner with bacon and corn captured.

25. U. S. steamer Resolute, Lieut. Budd, brought two schooners and one sloop prizes to Washington.

25. Gen. McClellan arrived at Washington, and Gen. Fremont at St. Louis, and Gen. Banks at Harper's Ferry, to take charge of their respective departments.

25. Robert Toombs resigned the Secretaryship of State of the Confederacy, to take office in the army, and R. M. T. Hunter, of Va., was appointed to succeed him.

26. Fifteen Home Guards from Rolla, Mo., were attacked at Lane's Prairie by a superior force of rebels, who were repulsed with the loss of 1 lieutenant killed and 3 men wounded. Two guards were slightly wounded.

26. Three rebels captured by Col. McLeod Murphy, of New York, in Virginia, scouting alone.

28. Flight of Gen. Wise's army from Gauley Bridge, Va., pursued by Gen. Cox, who captured 1000 muskets and a quantity of powder.

28. A detachment of Col. Mulligan's Chicago regiment, aided by Home Guards, captured 28 rebels, 40 horses and 2 teams, at Hickory Hill, Mo.

29. A rebel battery at Aquia Creek, Va., engaged by four U. S. steamers for three hours, with slight damage.

30. Six Government clerks at Washington resigned, owing to a Virginia ordinance of disfranchisement.

30. Three hundred kegs of powder and 6 cannon were captured from the rebels near Warsaw, Mo.

30. The Confederate forces occupied and fortified New Madrid, Mo.

30-31. Missouri State Convention abolished the State Legislature, declared the offices of Governor, Lieut.-Gov. and Sec.-of State vacant, appointed special State officers, and provided for a special election by the people in Aug. 1862.

Aug. 1. Rebel privateer Petrel, formerly U. S. revenue cutter Aiken, sunk by U. S. frigate St. Lawrence, near Charleston. Thirty-six out of 40 of her crew were rescued by the frigate's boats.

1. Gov. Gamble, of Mo., delivered his inaugural to the State Convention.

1. Departure of Gen. Fremont's expedition from St. Louis to Cairo and Bird's Point.

2. Fort Fillmore, New Mexico, with 750 men, traitorously surrendered by Major Lynde, U. S. A.

2. Schooner Enchantress, with a valuable cargo, recaptured by U. S. steamer Albatross, Capt. Prentiss, off Charleston, S. C.

2. Defeat of rebel forces at Dug Spring, Mo., by Gen. Lyon. Federal loss, 9 killed, 30 wounded. Rebel loss, 40 killed, 50 wounded.

3. Lieut.-Col. Baylor, commanding the

rebel forces in Arizona, issued a proclamation taking possession of New Mexico, in the name of the Confederate States, declaring all Federal offices vacant, and appointing a secretary, attorney-general and other officers.

Aug. 3. Engagement at Mesilla, N. M., between Federal troops and 700 rebels. Capt. McNeely and Lieut. Brooks, of Federal army, were wounded, and 12 rebels killed.

5. The bark Alvarado, having a rebel prize crew, chased ashore near Fernandina, Fla., and burned by sailors from U. S. ship Vincennes.

5. Skirmish at Point of Rocks, Md. Sixty men of New York 28th attacked rebel cavalry, killing 3, wounding 2 and capturing 7 men and 20 horses, without loss themselves.

5. Skirmish at Athens, Mo. 300 Home Guards, under Col. Moore, defeated a force of 1000 rebels, killing 23 and wounding 50. 10 Federals killed and 10 wounded. 5 wagon loads of supplies and 40 horses were captured by the Guards.

5. Election in Kentucky for members of the Legislature, the returns showing a large Union majority.

6. Adjournment *sine die* of Special Congress at Washington.

7. The village of Hampton, Va., was burned by rebel forces under Gen. Magruder. They were prevented from burning the bridge by skirmishers of Max Weber's New York regiment.

7. The privateer York was burned by gunboat Union, which also recaptured the schooner G. V. Baker.

8. Rebel cavalry routed at Lorrettsville, Va., with loss of 1 killed and 5 wounded, by 100 men of 19th N. Y., under Capt. Kennedy.

8. Messrs. Breckinridge and Vallandigham partook of a banquet at the Eutaw House, Baltimore. Mr. Breckinridge, in an attempt to address the people, was prevented by popular clamor.

9. Skirmish at Potosi, Mo. Rebels driven off with loss of 2 killed, 3 wounded.

10. Battle of Wilson's Creek, Mo. The Federal army under Gen. Lyon, 5,200 men, was defeated by the combined forces of Gens. Price and McCulloch, 20,000. Gen. Lyon was killed. Federal loss, 223 killed, 721 wounded, 292 missing. Rebel loss, (McCulloch's report,) 265 killed, 800 wounded, 30 missing; Price's report of Missouri troops, 156 killed, 517 wounded.

12. "Bangor (Me.) Democrat" office destroyed by a mob.

12. C. J. Faulkener, ex-minister of U. S. to France, arrested on a charge of treason.

13. Skirmish near Grafton, Va. 200 rebels routed, 21 killed and wounded, by Capt. Dayton's company of 4th Virginia, without loss.

14. Mutiny in New York 79th regiment, near Washington.

14 Gen. Fremont declares martial law in St. Louis, Mo.

14. "War Bulletin" and "Missourian" journals suppressed at St. Louis.

14. Mutiny of 60 men of 2d Maine at Arlington, Va.; who were arrested and sentenced to be sent to the Dry Tortugas.

14. All loyal men notified by Jeff. Davis to leave the Confederate States in 40 days.

15. Two Federal sailors killed and 2 wounded, of the U. S. steamer Resolute, in a skirmish at Mathias Point, Va.

16. Col. Hecker's regiment surprised 400 rebels at Fredericktown, Mo., capturing 12 men and all the camp equipage.

16. Five New York newspapers were presented by the Grand Jury as hostile to the Government.

16. A "Peace" meeting at Saybrook, Conn., broken up.

16. $58,000 seized by U. S. troops at Genevieve, Mo., and taken to St. Louis.

16. Proclamation of Pres. Lincoln, declaring commercial intercourse with the eleven States in rebellion unlawful, excepting such parts thereof as have or may become restored to loyal government, and forfeiting all vessels therefrom or bound to the same, after 15 days.

17. Railway train near Palmyra, Mo., fired into by rebels. One soldier was killed, and several wounded.

18. Privateer Jeff. Davis wrecked on the bar at St. Augustine, Fla.

18. Gen. Wool assumed command at Fortress Monroe.

19. Capt. Haleman with 50 mounted men left Bird's Point for Charleston, Mo., and encountered a body of rebels, killing 2 and capturing 33 men and 35 horses, without any casualty themselves.

19. Skirmish at Charleston, Mo. Two hundred and fifty of 22d Illinois under Col. Dongherty, and Lieut.-Col. Ransom of 11th Illinois defeated 300 rebels under Col. Hunter of Jeff. Thompson's army. 20 rebels were killed and wounded, and 17 prisoners taken. The Union loss was 1 killed and 6 wounded.

19. Two hundred and forty Union fugitives from E. Tenn. arrived at Danville, Ky., and were fed in the Seminary yard.

19. Office of the "Sentinel," Easton, Pa., destroyed by a Union mob.

19. A. L. Kimball, editor of the "Essex Co, Democrat," Haverhill, Mass., was tarred

and feathered, and ridden on a rail by a Union mob.

19. "Passports" required, by notice from the Department of State, from all persons leaving or arriving within the United States.

19. Office of the "Jeffersonian," Westchester, Pa., destroyed by a Union mob.

19. Office of "The People's Friend," at Covington, Ind., destroyed by a Union mob.

20. Skirmish at Hawk's Nest, in the Kanawha Valley, Va. A body of rebels attacked the 11th Ohio, but were driven back with loss. Union loss, 2 wounded and 1 missing.

20. The Wheeling (Va.,) Convention passed an ordinance to erect a new State, to be called Kanawha.

20. A railway train from Jefferson City, Mo., when near Lookout Station, was fired into by rebels, and 1 soldier killed and 6 wounded. 2 rebels were killed, several wounded, and 5 prisoners taken.

20. Gen. McClellan assumed command of the army of the Potomac.

20. Gen. Butler assumed command of U.S. Volunteer forces near Fortress Monroe.

21. Surprise of part of company K, Ohio 7th, near Cross Lane, W. Virginia, 2 killed and 9 wounded, 5 of whom were taken prisoners, including Capt. Shutte.

22. Disloyal papers were rejected from the U. S. mails. Large bundles of papers were seized by the U. S. Marshals in Philadelphia and other cities.

22. The "Stark County Democrat" office, in Canton, Ohio, was destroyed by a Union mob.

22. The steamer "Samuel Orr" was seized at Paducah, Ky., by rebels, and taken up the Tennessee river.

24. A portion of the Cherokee Indians made an alliance with the "Southern Confederacy." The Cherokees and Creeks raised 2,000 men for the rebel army, and were promised payment of their annuities by the Confed. Commissioners.

24. Arrest of Mayor Berret, of Washington.

24. The office of the Bridgeport (Conn.,) "Farmer" was destroyed by a Union mob.

24. Office of the "Alleghanian," Cumberland, Md., was destroyed by a Union mob.

25. A band of rebels at Wayne Court-House, Va., was routed by 53 Federals under Capt. Smith, from Camp Pierpont, Ceredo, Wayne co., Va. 4 rebels were killed, and 8 taken prisoners.

25. All vessels and boats on the Potomac seized by Government authorities.

25. Gov. H. R. Gamble, of Mo., issued a call for 42,000 State militia, to serve six months, unless sooner discharged.

26. Surprise of 7th Ohio, Col. Tyler, at Cross Lanes, near Summersville, W. Virginia, by a large force of rebels. 15 killed, 40 wounded, and 30 prisoners. Rebel loss not known.

26. The War Department prohibited the transmission or publication of any intelligence of army or naval movements calculated to give information to the enemy.

26. The Postmaster-General directed postal agents to arrest express agents or others engaged in transmitting letters to seceded States in violation of the President's proclamation of 16th inst.

26. Com. Foote ordered to the command of U. S. naval forces on the Western waters.

26. A naval and military expedition to N. Carolina coast sailed from Hampton Roads, Va., under command of Com. Stringham and Maj.-Gen. Butler.

26. Skirmish of two companies of N. Y. 23d, with a large force of rebels at Ball's Cross Roads, Va. One Federal killed, and one wounded.

28. A party of Federal troops under Capt. Smith attacked and dispersed a force of rebels at Wayne Court-House, W. Virginia, and returned to Ceredo without loss. Five or 6 of the rebels were killed or wounded, and 8 captured.

28–29. Bombardment and capture of Forts Hatteras and Clark, at Hatteras Inlet, N. C. 30 pieces of cannon, 1,000 stand of arms, 3 vessels with valuable cargoes, and 750 prisoners were taken.

29. Fight at Lexington, Mo. The rebels, under Col. Reed, were driven off with loss of 8 killed and several wounded. The Federals had 5 or 6 wounded, and several loyal citizens were captured.

30. Martial law was proclaimed throughout Missouri, by Gen. Fremont, and the slaves of all persons found in arms against the U. S. declared free.

Sept. 1. Skirmish at Bennett's Mills, Mo. Attack on Home Guards commanded by Lieut. Chandler, by a large force of rebels. Federal loss, 3 killed, 6 wounded. Rebel loss unknown.

1. Fight at Boone Court-House, Va. Rebels defeated, with a loss of 30. Six Federal soldiers wounded.

2. Fight near Fort Scott, Mo. 600 rebels under Gen. Rains, were attacked and pursued by 500 Federals under Col. Montgomery. The rebels falling back on reinforcements, Montgomery retreated.

2. The Mass. 13th captured 20 Charleston, S. C., cavalry, after killing 3 and wounding 5, 2½ miles from Harper's Ferry.

2. Col. Crossman, of Gen. Kelly's staff, with two companies, attacked 400 rebels,

at Worthington, Marion co.; Va., by whom he was repulsed with the loss of two men.

Sept. 3. Passenger train on the Hannibal and St. Joseph railway, Mo., was thrown into the Platte river, by the giving way of a bridge, partly burned by the rebels. 17 persons were killed, and 60 wounded.

4. An engagement on the Mississippi river occurred, near Hickman, Ky., between national gunboats Tyler and Lexington and the rebel gunboat Yankee and shore batteries.

6. Paducah, Ky., was occupied by Federal forces under Gen. Grant.

7. Gens. Pillow and Polk occupied Columbus, Ky., with 7,000 rebels.

7. Five schooners were captured by Federal officers at Hatteras Inlet.

8. Gen. Pope broke up a camp of 3,000 rebels near Hunneville, Mo., under Gen. Green, and captured a large quantity of stores.

9. A revolt occurred among the N. Y. Rifles, at Willett's Point, N. Y. Two men were killed and 5 wounded.

9. A government steamer conveying prisoners from Lexington, Mo., to Fort Leavenworth, broke her rudder, and being obliged to land, the vessel was seized by the rebels, the prisoners liberated, and 40 Federal soldiers captured.

10. 156 Union prisoners, among them all the principal officers held captive by the rebels at Richmond, were sent to Castle Pinckney, in Charleston harbor.

10. Battle of Carnifex Ferry, near Summersville, Va. Federal commander, Rosecranz, rebel, Floyd, who retreated with small loss. Federal loss, 16 killed, 102 wounded.

11. Skirmish at Lewinsville, Va. Federal loss, 6 killed, 10 wounded.

11. The President modified Gen. Fremont's emancipation proclamation.

11. The Kentucky Legislature, by a vote of 71 to 26, ordered the Confederate troops to leave the State.

12. A rebel camp at Petersburg, Hardy co., Va., was broken up by Capt. Kid's cavalry, and large amount of stores captured.

12. Skirmish at Black river, near Ironton, Mo. A detachment of Indiana cavalry, under Major Gavitt, defeated a body of rebels, under Ben. Talbot, killing 5, capturing 4, and 25 horses and a quantity of arms.

12. The Legislature of Kentucky authorized the Governor to call out the State military to repel the Southern invaders.

12. Two slaves, the property of T. L. Snead, a secessionist of St. Louis, were manumitted by Gen. Fremont.

13. A large body of rebels, under Col. Brown, were repulsed from Booneville, Mo., with a loss of 12 killed and 30 wounded, by Home Guards under Capt. Eppstein, who lost 1 killed and 4 wounded.

12-14. Two engagements occurred on Cheat Mountain, Western Va., in which the rebels, under Gen. R. E. Lee, were defeated with a loss of 100 killed and wounded, among the former, Col. J. A. Washington, and 20 prisoners. The Federal forces, under Gen. J. J. Reynolds, lost 13 killed, 20 wounded, and 60 prisoners.

13-18. The provost marshal of Baltimore, Md., arrested Mayor Brown, Ross Winans, and Messrs. Pitts, Sangster, Wallis, Scott, Dennison, Quinlan, Lynch, Warfield, Hanson, and J. C. Brune, of the Legislature, also editors Howard and Hall, by order of the War Department.

13. An expedition from the U.S. frigate Colorado, under Lieut. J. H. Russell, cut out and destroyed the privateer Judah, under the rebel guns at Pensacola. The Federal loss was 3 killed and 15 wounded.

14. A rebel camp near Kansas City, Mo., was broken up; 7 men killed and 6 taken prisoners.

18. Col. F. P. Blair, Jr., was arrested at St. Louis for disrespectful language when alluding to superior officers.

15. A body of rebels attacked Col. Geary's 28th Pennsylvania regiment, stationed on the Potomac, three miles above Harper's Ferry, and were repulsed with severe loss. One of Col. Geary's men was killed, and several slightly wounded.

16. A naval expedition from Hatteras Inlet under command of Lieut. J. Y. Maxwell, destroyed Fort Ocracoke, on Beacon Island, N. C.

16. The Federal gunboat Conestoga captured the steamers V. R. Stephenson and Gazelle, on Cumberland river, Ky.

16. Ship Island, near the mouth of the Mississippi river, was occupied by Federal forces from the steamer Massachusetts.

17. A fight took place at Mariatown, Mo., between 600 Federals, under Cols. Montgomery and Johnson, and 400 rebels, who were defeated with a loss of 7 killed, and 100 horses and their tents and supplies captured. Col. Johnson and 2 Federal privates were killed, and 6 wounded.

17. A train on the Ohio and Mississippi railway, with a part of the 19th Illinois regiment, broke through a bridge near Huron, Ind., by which 26 soldiers were killed and 112 wounded.

17. 500 of the 3d Iowa, under Lieut.-Col. Scott, attacked and were repulsed by 3,000 rebels, under Gen. D. R. Atchison, at

Sept. 1861.   CHRONOLOGY.   477

Blue Mills Landing, Mo. The Federal loss was over 100 in killed and wounded.

18. Skirmish at Barboursville, Ky., between the Home Guard and Zollicoffer's men. 7 rebels were killed, and 1 guard wounded and another taken prisoner.

18. Eighteen secession members of the Maryland Legislature were arrested and lodged in Fort McHenry.

19. Ex-Governor Morehead and others, of Louisville, Ky., were arrested by the U. S. marshal on charges of treason, or complicity with treason.

20. Surrender of Col. Mulligan's command, at Lexington, Mo., to the rebel Gen. Price, after 4 days' siege.

21. Gen. Lane's command surprised a superior force of rebels at Papinsville, Mo., routing them with a Union loss of 17 killed and 40 wounded; rebel loss, 40 killed, 100 prisoners, and all their tents and supplies.

21. Two detachments of troops from Union gunboats, near Glasgow, Mo., encountered each other, while reconnoitering at night, and by mistake four were killed and several wounded.

21. Gen. Robert Anderson assumed command of Federal and State troops in Ky.

21. J. C. Breckinridge fled from Frankfort, Ky., and openly joined the rebels.

22. Skirmish of the 7th Iowa, at Elliott's Mills, Ky., with rebel cavalry, who were defeated with the loss of three of their number.

23. Ross Winans, of Md., took the oath of allegiance.

23. Capt. Goldsborough succeeded Com. Stringham in command of the Chesapeake blockading fleet.

23. Detachments of 8th and 4th Ohio, and Ringgold's cavalry, under Cols. Parke and Cantwell, advancing from New Creek toward Romney, Va., attacked and drove out 700 rebels from Mechanicsville Gap, and pursued their combined forces of 1,400 from Romney to the mountains. Federal loss 3 killed, 10 wounded; rebel loss 15 killed, 30 wounded.

24. The Comte de Paris and the Duc de Chartres, grandsons of Louis Philippe of France, were attached as aids to Gen. McClellan's staff, and commissioned as captains.

25. Successful expedition of 3,000 men, under Gen. W. F. Smith, for reconnoitering and forage, from Chain Bridge to Lewinsville, Va. A large quantity of stores were captured.

25. Engagement at Chapmansville, Western Va. Col. Pratt, with 560 of the 34th Ohio, defeated a body of rebels under Col. J. W. Davis, killing 29, including their commander, and wounding a large number. Col. Pratt's loss was 4 killed, 8 wounded.

25. A body of rebels were defeated near Osceola, Mo., by Federal troops under Col. Montgomery, who set fire to the town. 10 rebels killed; 1 Federal killed, 4 wounded.

25. James B. Clay (son of the illustrious Henry,) and 16 other rebels were captured near Danville, Ky., while on their way to Zollicoffer's camp.

26. At Lucas Bend, Ky., 75 of Captain Stewart's cavalry attacked and routed 40 rebel cavalry, killing 4 and capturing 5, without loss themselves.

26. By Presidential proclamation of August 12, this day was observed as a day of fasting and prayer throughout the loyal States.

27. A body of Kansas troops, under Montgomery and Jamison, engaged the advance guard of McCulloch's rebel army near Shanghai, in Benton co., Mo., and drove them back with loss.

27. Gen. Fremont, with 15 steamers and 15,000 men, sailed from St. Louis up the Missouri river.

27. The rebels evacuated Munson's Hill, Va., which was occupied by Federal troops.

28. Baker's California regiment, and Baxter's Philadelphia volunteers mistook each other for rebels, at Fall's Church, Va., and fired, killing 15 and wounding 30.

Oct. 1. The U. S. steamer Fanny, with 35 men of the 9th N. Y. volunteers, was captured by the rebels on the north coast of Hatteras Inlet. She was loaded with government stores.

2. A secessionist camp at Charleston, Mo., was broken up, and 40 rebels captured.

2. $33,000, deposited in the St. Louis Building and Savings Association, for the part payment of a U. S. annuity to the Cherokee Indians, declared confiscated to the Government in consequence of the secession of that tribe.

3. Attack on an entrenched camp commanded by Gen. H. A. Jackson, at Greenbrier, Western Va., by Union forces under Gen. J. J. Reynolds. Union loss 8 killed, 32 wounded; rebel loss greater. A drawn battle.

3. Gen. Price, and the rebel army under his command, withdrew from Lexington, Mo., leaving a brigade as a guard.

3. Gustavus Smith, formerly Street Commissioner of New York, was appointed a Major-General in the rebel army.

4. Commander Alden, U. S. steamer South Carolina, captured two schooners off the S.W. Pass of the Mississippi, with four to five thousand stand of arms.

4. A company of 110 Texas rangers were

defeated by 100 U. S. troops from Fort Craig, at Alimosa, N. M. 10 Texans and their captain killed, and 30 wounded.

Oct. 4. Two boats from U. S. steamer Louisiana, Lieut. A. Murray, destroyed a rebel schooner, being fitted out for a privateer, at Chincoteague Inlet, Va. They engaged and repulsed the rebels with a loss of 4 U. S. seamen wounded.

4. A large force of rebels, under Col. Wright, attacked the 20th Indiana, Col. Brown, at Chicamacomico, near Hatteras Inlet. Federals retreated, leaving their pickets, wounded, and camp equipage in the hands of the enemy.

4. Gen. Butler, commanding the Military Department of New England, had his headquarters at Boston.

5. The rebel forces under Col. Wright were driven from the Chicamacomico with severe loss, by U.S. steamer Monticello.

7. John Ross, principal Chief of the Cherokee Indians, negotiated a treaty of alliance on behalf of that people with the Confederate Government.

7. 57 released prisoners, taken by the rebels at the battle of Bull Run, arrived at Fortress Monroe from Richmond.

7. U. S. gunboats Tyler and Lexington exchanged shots with rebel batteries at Iron Bend, 3 miles above Columbus, Ky.

8. Brig.-Gen. William T. Sherman appointed to command the Department of the Cumberland (Kentucky), in place of Brig.-Gen. R. Anderson, retired from ill-health.

8. 200 rebels under Capt. Holliday, encamped two miles from Hillsboro', Ky., were attacked and defeated by a body of Home Guards, under Lieut. Sadler. Rebel loss 11 killed, 29 wounded, 22 prisoners; also 127 rifles and other arms. Federal loss 3 killed, 8 wounded.

9. Attack upon Wilson's N. Y. Zouaves, at Santa Rosa Island, four miles from Fort Pickens, at 2 A. M., by 1,500 rebels under Gen. Anderson. The regulars from Fort Pickens, and the Zouaves, defeated the rebels, killing and wounding about 100, and taking 35 prisoners. Federal loss 13 killed, 21 wounded.

9. Federal troops under Gen. Smith advanced from Chain Bridge, and occupied Lewinsville, Va.

10. Cavalry skirmish 4 miles from Paducah, Ky. 2 of the 4th U. S. cavalry mortally wounded, and 2 taken prisoners.

11. The rebel steamer Nashville, commanded by Lieut. R. B. Pegram, escaped from Charleston, S. C.

11. Lieut. Harrell, of U. S. steamer Union, with three boats' crews, cut out and burnt a rebel schooner in Dumfries Creek, on the Potomac, and escaped without loss.

11. Missouri State Convention met at St. Louis.

11. Marshal Kane was transferred from Fort McHenry to Fort Lafayette.

12. Rebel steamer Theodora ran the blockade at Charleston, S. C., having on board Messrs. Mason and Slidell, Commissioners to England and France, with their secretaries.

12. Capt. P. G. Morton captured a train of 21 wagons, 425 cattle, and 35 prisoners, with stores for hostile Cherokees, at Chelsea, Kansas.

12. Cavalry skirmish south of Cameron, Ray co., Mo. A company of Major James' cavalry routed a large body of rebels, who lost 8 killed and 5 prisoners. One Federal was killed and 4 wounded.

12. Six rebel gunboats, the ram Manassas, and a fleet of fireships, attacked the U. S. fleet at the mouth of the Mississippi, and were repulsed by them with slight loss on either side.

12. A party of 12 of a N.Y. Zouave regiment, under Lieut. Zeller, were captured by the rebels near Newport News, Va.

12. Forty men of the 39th Indiana attacked and defeated a superior force of rebels, 8 miles from Green river, Western Va., without loss themselves, killing 5 and wounding 3 of the enemy.

12. Night skirmish near the residence of Cy. Hutchinson, Barren co., Ky. Ten Federal horsemen, under Cols. Hobson and Pennebraker, and Capt. S. Taylor, encountered 100 rebel cavalry, of whom 4 were killed and several wounded. Federal loss, 3 killed.

12. 500 men of the Piatt (Cincinnati) Zouaves, under Lient.-Col. Toland, and two companies of the 4th Va., drove out a large body of rebels from Winfield, 20 miles below Charleston, on the Kanawha, Western Va., who had been committing depredations. The Federals captured a large quantity of military stores.

12. Skirmish between a detachment of the 39th Indiana, under Lieut.-Col. Jones, and 58 rebel cavalry, near Upton's, 14 miles below Camp Nevin, Ky. The rebels were repulsed with a loss of 5 killed and 3 wounded.

12. A woman and five children, from families of U. S. soldiers from Utah, were drowned while attempting to cross the Platte river on a raft, near St. Josephs, Mo., the rope having been cut by an enemy.

13. Eighteen miles N.E. of Lebanon, Mo., Major Wright, with two companies of U.S. cavalry, routed 300 mounted rebels, under Capts. Lorrels and Wright. 62 of the reb-

els were killed and wounded, and 30 taken prisoners. One Federal trooper was killed.

13. Skirmish at Beckweth's farm, 12 miles S.E. of Bird's Point, Mo. 20 men under Lieut. Tufts, encountered a superior force of rebels, and after engaging them retired. 2 were killed, 5 wounded, and 3 missing, of the national force: 12 were killed and wounded of the rebels.

13. Brig Grenada, of New York, was captured by the privateer "Sallie," of Charleston, which ran the blockade on the 10th instant.

14. 150 voters of Chincoteague Island, Accomac co., Va., took the oath of allegiance to the U. S., in the presence of Lieut. Murray, of U. S. ship Louisiana. The inhabitants of the island, 1,000 in number, were loyal; no other flag than the national had thus far been allowed to float on the island.

14. Major White, with one company of Missouri Scouts, captured 45 rebels at Linn Creek, Mo., commanded by Capt. Roberts.

14. The U. S. Secretary of State, Wm. H. Seward, issued a circular to the Governors of all States bordering on the ocean and the lakes, recommending that their defences should be put in effective condition to meet the contingency of foreign war, instigated by rebel emissaries.

15. U. S. steamer Roanoke, off Charleston, captured and burnt the ship Thomas Watson, which ran on Stono reef while attempting to evade the blockade.

15. Ten of the N. Y. 14th killed 2 rebels in a skirmish near Lewinsville, Va.

15. Gen. Wool, at Fortress Monroe, declined to receive a flag of truce from Norfolk.

15. 600 rebels, under Gen. Jeff. Thompson, attacked and captured 40 U. S. soldiers guarding the Big river bridge, near Potosi, Mo. Federal loss 1 killed, 6 wounded; rebel loss 5 killed, 4 wounded. The rebels paroled the U. S. soldiers and burnt the bridge.

15. The rebel batteries at Aquia creek and Shipping Point, on the Potomac, fired on all vessels passing, but inflicted no serious damage.

15. Three U. S. steamers sailed from New York in pursuit of the privateer Nashville.

16. Col. J. W. Geary, of the Penn. 28th, with 400 men from his own, the 13th Mass. and 3d Wis., crossed the Potomac at Harper's Ferry, and captured 21,000 bushels of wheat, stored in a mill near Bolivar Heights. A severe skirmish occurred with a body of rebels who disputed the ground, from whom the Federals captured a 32-pounder, and made good their retreat, accomplishing the object of the expedition. Federal loss, 4 killed, 8 wounded.

16. Major F. J. White, with 220 Missouri scouts, surprised the rebels at Lexington, Mo., and without loss, captured 60 or 70 prisoners, released Cols. White and Grover, and 12 other captives, and seized 2 steamboats, with arms, ammunition and stores.

16. 1,000 rebels under Gen. Thompson and Col. Lowe, near Ironton, Mo., were defeated with a loss of 36 killed and wounded, by Maj. Gavitt's Indiana cavalry, and 5 companies of Col. Alexander's 21st Illinois. Union loss, 11.

19. Col. Morgan, with 220 men of the 18th Missouri regiment, and two pieces of artillery, defeated 400 rebels on Big Hurricane Creek, Carroll co., Mo., killing 14, and taking 8 prisoners. Col. Morgan had 14 men wounded—two mortally.

19. Twenty rebel N. C. prisoners were sent to Fortress Monroe, to be released on taking an oath not to bear arms against the Government.

21. Battle of Edward's Ferry, Va. 1,900 men from Gen. C. P. Stone's division, under command of Col. E. D. Baker, U. S. senator from Oregon, were ordered to cross the Potomac at Harrison's Island, or Ball's Bluff, to support reconnoissances above and below that point. At 4 P. M. they were attacked by 3,000 rebels under Gen. Evans, and driven to the river bank, where, there being no adequate provision for crossing, they suffered severe loss, by the enemy's fire, and by drowning. Killed, 223, wounded, 250, taken prisoners, 500. Rebel loss about 200 in killed and wounded.

21. About 2,500 rebels, near Fredericktown, Mo., under Jeff. Thompson and Col. Lowe, were attacked by 3,500 Federal troops, commanded by Col. J. B. Plummer, of 11th Missouri, with Missouri, Illinois, Wisconsin and Indiana troops, under Cols. Ross, Marsh, Hovey, Baker, Lieut-.Col. Pennabaker, Maj. Schofield, Capt. Stewart and Lieut. White. The rebels were defeated with great loss, and Col. Lowe was killed. They left 175 bodies on the field, and had a large number wounded. Eighty were taken prisoners, and 4 heavy guns were captured. The Federal loss was 7 killed and 60 wounded.

21. A portion of the rebel General Zollicoffer's command was repulsed from an advanced position of General Schoepf's brigade, near Camp Wild Cat, Laurel co., Ky.. The Federal loss was 4 killed and 21 wounded.

22. Flag-officer Craven, of the Potomac flotilla, reported the Potomac river com-

manded by rebel batteries, at all important points below Alexandria.

Oct. 22. A detachment of U. S. cavalry broke up a rebel camp at Buffalo Mills, Benton co., Mo., killing and wounding 20, taking 60 prisoners, 22 wagons and a number of horses.

23. Col. Len. Harris, with the 2d Ohio, two guns of Capt. Konkle's Ohio battery and Capt. Laughlin's cavalry, drove out a body of 200 rebels from West Liberty, Morgan co., Ky., after a skirmish in which 10 were killed, 5 wounded, and 6 made prisoners, of the rebels, with no loss on the part of the Federals. A small quantity of stores was captured.

23. Fifty men of the 6th Indiana while skirmishing near Hodgesville, Ky., were attacked by a superior force of rebels, whom they repulsed, killing 3 and wounding 5. Three of the Federals were severely wounded, including Lieut. Grayson, their commander.

23. Gen. Fred. W. Lander was appointed to command the brigade of the late Col. Baker.

24. President Lincoln suspended the writ of *habeas corpus*, so far as related to military arrests, in the District of Columbia.

24. The steamer Salvor was captured while attempting to run the blockade at Tampa Bay, Fla.

24. Western Virginia voted almost unanimously in favor of a division of the State.

24. The western section of the California telegraph was completed to Salt Lake City, connecting the wires from the Pacific to the Atlantic ocean.

24. Skirmish between the pickets of Gen. Wm. T. Ward and a scouting party of rebels near Campbellsville, Ky. Several of the rebels were killed and wounded, and their captain taken prisoner.

25. 160 of Gen. Fremont's Body-guard, under command of Major Zagonyi, charged 2,000 rebels, drawn up to receive them, near Springfield, Mo., routed them, and occupied the town. Rebel loss, 106 killed, many wounded, and 27 prisoners. Zagonyi's loss, 15 killed, 27 wounded, 10 missing. The Missouri "Prairie Scouts," under Maj. F. J. White, attacked the rear of the rebel force, at the same time, making three successful charges, and inflicting severe loss on the enemy. The loss of the "Scouts" was 33 in killed, wounded and missing.

26. An artillery fight across the Potomac, at Edward's Ferry, for several hours. Two killed in Gen. Banks' encampment, and 3 wounded. Both parties were compelled to move back their encampments.

26. Gen. B. F. Kelly, with 2,500 Virginia and Ohio Volunteers, from New Creek, Va., attacked an inferior rebel force near Romney, who were routed and pursued through that town with severe loss. Col. Thos. Johns, of 2d regiment, Potomac Home Brigade, made a diversion of the enemy's force, by marching to the rear of Romney, by way of Frankfort, and engaged and held in check a regiment of the rebels. The expedition was successful in capturing a large supply of military stores and provisions. Federal loss, 2 killed, 14 wounded. Rebel loss, 10 killed, 15 wounded, and a number of prisoners, including Col. Angus McDonald, their commander; their artillery wagons, camps, etc., were captured.

26. Parson Brownlow was forced to suspend the publication of the Knoxville (Tenn.) *Whig*.

26. A wagon train was established between Baltimore and Washington, for want of sufficient railway facilities, consequent on the danger from rebel batteries in navigating the Potomac.

26. Major Phillips, with 300 of the 9th Illinois, from Paducah, sailed on the steamer Conestoga to West Eddyville, Ky., on the Cumberland river, where they landed and marched 6 miles to Saratoga, and surprised a detachment of rebel cavalry, under Capt. Wilcox. After a brief resistance the enemy fled, losing 13 killed, many wounded, 24 prisoners, and 52 horses. Four of the Illinois men were wounded.

26. Surprise of a rebel encampment at Plattsburg, Clinton co., Mo., by a superior force of Federals. Rebel loss, 8 killed, 12 prisoners, one cannon, and a quantity of small arms.

28. Three rebel vessels were surprised and burnt at Chincoteague Inlet, Va., by a portion of the crew of U. S. gunboat Louisiana, under Lieut. A. Hopkins.

28. D. Davis, of Ill., J. Holt, of Ky., and H. Campbell, of Mo., were appointed Commissioners by Pres. Lincoln to audit all unsettled military claims in Missouri.

29. 250 U.S. Kentucky volunteers, under Col. Burbridge, marched from Owensboro' to Morgantown, Ky., crossed the river at that point, defeated a superior rebel force and destroyed their camp. Federal loss, 2 wounded.

28. Gen. J. B. Henderson, with a superior force, surrounded and captured 400 rebels at Dyer's Mills, near Concord, Mo. They were allowed to lay down their arms and return home.

29. Nearly 100 "contrabands" arrived at Fortress Monroe in two days.

29. Rebel State "Conference" at Russellville, Ky.

20. The great naval expedition sailed from Fortress Monroe, under the command of Flag-officer Com. Samuel F. Dupont, comprising 77 vessels of all classes. The land forces, numbering 20,000 men, were commanded by Brig.-Gen. Thos. W. Sherman.

31. Skirmish at Morgantown, Green River, Ky. Col. McHeury's command drove a party of rebels attached to Buckner's camp across the river, with loss.

31. At N. York, the jury empaneled for the trial of the sailors captured on the privateer Savannah, the first rebel armed vessel that was commissioned, failed to agree.

Nov. 1. Lieut.-Gen. Winfield Scott, at his own request, was retired from active service, and Maj.-Gen. George B. McClellan was appointed to succeed him as Commander-in-chief of the U. S. army.

1. Lieut.-Col. Morse, with 450 cavalry and infantry, surprised and routed a rebel force 800 strong, under Col. Sweeny, in camp near Renick, Randolph co., Mo.

1. Rebels from Gen. Floyd's command attacked a Federal camp at Gauley Bridge, Va., by cannonading from the opposite shore. They were driven into the hills by 3 companies from Gen. Benham's camp, at Hawk's Nest.

1. A violent storm overtook the naval expedition off the N. C. coast. 3 vessels were disabled and returned, 2 were driven ashore, and 2 foundered. Seven lives lost.

2. Gen. Fremont, at Springfield, received an order from Washington, relieving him from command of the Department of Missouri. Gen. Hunter was appointed temporarily to the command.

2. An address was issued by Gov. Harris, of Tenn., calling upon the people to furnish every shot-gun and rifle to defend the soil.

2. Major Joseph's Missouri militia, numbering 129, were attacked at Platte City, Mo., by Silas Gordon with 300 rebels, who were repulsed with a loss of 13 killed and wounded. 30 prisoners, many guns, and all their equipments.

2. The English steamer Bermuda ran the blockade at Charleston, S. C., with 2,000 bales of cotton.

2. Prestonburg, Ky., was occupied by Union troops under Gen. Nelson, without opposition.

3. et seq. Rising of Union men in E. Tenn., who burned or broke down several important railroad bridges.

3. Five rebel boats made an attack on Fort Hatteras. N. C., but were repulsed by the U. S. gunboat National, and the Fort.

3. Col. Greensle drove rebel troops from Houston, Mo., and returned to Rolla with several prisoners and a large amount of property.

4. Enthusiastic Union meeting in Baltimore Co., Md., addressed by Reverdy Johnson.

4. Barboursville, Ky., was occupied by 1,500 Federals without opposition.

6. Extra session of South Carolina Legislature adjourned, after choosing Presidential electors and ordering the banks to loan the State $300,000.

5. Colonel Corcoran and 15 other national officers who were prisoners, were selected by lot by the rebels, as hostages, to be hung in the event of that punishment being awarded to the privateers held by the national government.

6. Two parties of rebel troops met above Newport News, Va., and by mistake fired on each other, killing and wounding a number. Among the killed was Major Bailey, of Mobile.

6. The grand jury at Frankfort, Ky., found indictments for treason against 32 prominent citizens, among whom were R. J. Breckinridge, Jr., J. C. Breckinridge, Humphrey Marshall, and Benj. Desha.

6. Electors for President and V. President were chosen throughout the revolted States, and also members of Congress.

6. 120 Federals, under Capt. Shields, were captured by 500 rebels near Little Santa Fé, Mo. They were on their way to join Gen. Fremont's column.

6. The 13th Indiana regiment, Col. J. J. Sullivan, and Capt. Robinson's Ohio cavalry, returned to Huttonsville, Va., from an extensive march through Webster Co. Several rebels were killed and wounded in scouting, and 13 prisoners taken.

7. Battle of Belmont, Mo., Gens. Grant and McClernand with 2,850 men, landed at Belmont at 8 A.M., drove in the rebel pickets and captured their camp, which was burnt. A battery of 12 guns was taken, and about 200 prisoners. Meantime, a large reinforcement of rebels was landed from Columbus, on the opposite side of the river, which intercepted Gen. Grant's army in their return to their boats. The Federals cut their way through a much superior force of the enemy, losing 150 of their number prisoners, together with their killed and wounded, who fell into the hands of the rebels. Federal loss, 89 killed, 150 wounded, 150 missing. The rebel loss was greater, 155 were taken prisoners.

7. Gen. Hunter, Fremont's successor in Missouri, repudiated the agreement just made between Gens. Fremont and Price, the rebel commander, concerning the privi-

leges of unarmed citizens, and the disarming of unrecognized bodies of men.

Nov. 7. Skirmishing on New river, near Gauley Bridge, Va. Federal forces under Gen. Rosecrans, drove off a body of rebels who had besieged his camp for several days. Several rebels and one private of 13th Ohio killed.

7. The Federal fleet under Com. Dupont captured Forts Warren and Beauregard at Port Royal entrance, and took the town of Beaufort, S. C., with a loss of 8 killed, 6 badly wounded, and 17 slightly. None of the national vessels seriously damaged. Rebel loss unknown, but not large.

7. Two launches and 40 men, commanded by Lieut. Jas. E. Jouett, from the U.S. frigate Santee, off Galveston, Texas, surprised and burnt the rebel privateer Royal Yacht, by night, after a sharp conflict, killing several of the rebels, and capturing 13. Federal loss 2 killed and 7 wounded.

8. U. S. gunboat Rescue shelled out a rebel battery at Urbana Creek, on the Rappahannock, Va., and captured a large schooner with stores.

8. Five railway bridges were burned in E. Tennessee by Unionists.

8. Capt. Wilkes, with the U. S. steam sloop-of-war San Jacinto, overhauled the English mail-steamer Trent in the Bahama channel, and took from her the rebel emissaries Mason and Slidell, with their secretaries, who had taken passage for England.

8. Col. Grensle returned with his command to Rolla, Mo., from an expedition against the rebels in Texas co., bringing 9 prisoners, 500 head of cattle and 40 horses and mules.

8. A portion of Gen. Nelson's Ky. brigade were ambuscaded while on their way to Piketon, Ky., by 200 rebels in a strong position. The rebels were dispersed with the loss of 10 killed, 15 wounded. Gen. Nelson had 6 killed and 24 wounded. Another portion of Gen. Nelson's brigade under command of Col. Sill, reached Piketon by a circuitous route, and attacked a body of rebels, defeating them with a small loss, and having one Federal soldier killed.

8. A bridge on the E. Tenn. railway, 200 feet span, was destroyed by Unionists. Also 4 on the line N. of Knoxville, and a heavy wooden bridge at Charleston, Bradley co., Tenn.

9. Maj.-Gen. Henry W. Halleck, of Cal., was ordered to take command of the Department of Missouri, in place of Gen. Fremont: Brig.-Gen. Don Carlos Buell, of Ind., was appointed to command the Department of Kentucky: Maj.-Gen. Hunter to command the Department of Kansas:

Col. E. R. S. Canley, the Department of N. Mexico.

10. A band of rebel marauders was captured by Lieut. Shriver, with a squad of 1st Iowa cavalry, near Clark's Station, Mo.

10. A portion of Gen. Cox's brigade crossed the New river near Gauley, Va., and attacked Floyd's forces posted there, who retreated after a severe skirmish, in which the 11th Ohio regiment lost 8 killed and 10 wounded.

10. 150 of the 9th Virginia regiment, Col. K. V. Whaley, were surprised at Guyandotte, Va., on the Ohio river, by a superior force of rebels, and after a sharp skirmish, in which 8 of the Federals were killed and 12 wounded, and nearly the same loss sustained by the rebels, Col. Whaley and 45 of his men were captured, and the rest escaped. About two-thirds of the town was burned next day by the Union Virginia and Ohio troops who arrived there, in retaliation for the treachery and cruelty of the rebel inhabitants evinced in the scenes of the engagement.

11. At Columbus, Ky., two rebel lieutenants and six privates were killed by the explosion of a Dahlgren gun. Rev. Maj.-Gen. Polk narrowly escaped.

11. 110 of Col. Anthony's regiment attacked a rebel camp on the Little Blue river, near Kansas City, Mo., which proved too strong for them, and after severe fight, Col. Anthony's men were drawn off in good order, losing 8 killed and 8 wounded.

12. Reconnoissance in force by Gen. Heintzelman, with 6,000 men, to Occoquan Creek, Va., 18 miles from Alexandria. Capt. Todd's company of Lincoln cavalry were surprised by a superior force of rebels, 3 killed, 1 wounded and 3 taken prisoners, including the captain.

12. Attack on the U.S. fleet at the Passes of the Mississippi, by the Manassas Ram, 5 gunboats and several fire ships, under command of Capt. Hollins. U. S. ship Vincennes grounded, and the Richmond was damaged by the ram and also grounded: but the enemy were driven off without obtaining any advantage.

12. The privateer Beauregard, of Charleston, S. C., with 27 men, was captured 100 miles E. N. E. of Abaco, by the U. S. sloop-of-war W. G. Anderson, Lieut. W. C. Rogers, commanding.

12. Skirmish on Laurel Creek by portions of Gen. Benham's with Gen. Floyd's forces, in which the rebels retreated after small loss.

12. Skirmish of Gen. Kelly's pickets near Romney, Va., losing 2 killed and several wounded. 12 rebels taken prisoners.

Nov. 1861. CHRONOLOGY. 483

13. Rebel Gen. Zollicoffer retreated from Cumberland Ford to Cumberland Gap, Tenn.

14. The privateer schooner Neva, from China, was seized at San Francisco, Cal., by Capt. l'ease, of U. S. cutter Mary.

14. Lieut. J. H. Rigby, with 20 men of the Gist Artillery, on an expedition from Salisbury, Md., to Wilmington and Newcastle, Md., seized 3 brass 6-pounders and 100 muskets, in possession of secessionists in those places.

14. The Gov. of Florida, by proclamation, forbade the enlistment of citizens of that State to serve in any other portion of the Confederacy.

14. $30,000 had been raised by Southern people for the widow of "the martyr Jackson," who killed Col. Ellsworth, at Alexandria, Va.

14. Gen. Benham, in pursuit of the army of Gen. Floyd, in W. Va., overtook the rear guard near McCoy's Mills, and defeated it, killing 15 rebels, among them Col. Croghan. Floyd, in his retreat, destroyed 200 of his tents, and lost 10 wagon-loads of ammunition and arms.

14. Fast-day was observed in the rebel States.

14. Steamship Champion arrived at New York from Aspinwall, bringing Gen. Sumner and several companies of regular soldiers from San Francisco, having under arrest ex-Senators Gwin and Brent, and C. Benham, late Attorney-General of California, charged with complicity with the rebels.

16. A party of 57 of the N. Y. 30th, attached to Gen. Keyes' brigade on the Potomac, while out foraging west of Upton's Hill, Va., were betrayed and surrounded by 200 rebel cavalry, and one half their number, with the teams and wagons, captured.

16. 50 wagons and 500 oxen, with the teamsters and stores, were captured near Pleasant Hill, Cass co., Mo., by the rebels.

16. 68 Federal prisoners, the crews of fishing smacks captured off the Florida coast, were taken to Tallahassee, Fla.

17. Union troops under Col. Alcorn, defeated Hawkins' regiment at Cypress Bridge, McClean co., Ky., routing them with severe loss, and taking 25 prisoners, 300 horses, etc. Federal loss, 10 killed, 15 wounded.

17. A party of Union troops recaptured nearly all the wagons and cattle seized the day before near Pleasant Hill, Mo.

17. U. S. gunboat Connecticut captured British schooner Adelaide, with military stores and supplies for rebels, near Cape Carnaveral, and took her into Key West.

17. Lieut. G. W. Snyder, U. S. A., a valuable engineer officer, died at Washington, of typhoid fever.

17. The 3d Missouri cavalry routed a large number of rebels near Palmyra, Mo., while on their way to join Price's army, killing 3, wounding 5, taking 16 prisoners.

18. The rebel Congress met at Richmond, V., Howell Cobb, of Ga., in the chair.

18. Capt. A. H. Foote was appointed Flag-officer of the fleet of the Western Military Department.

18. Gen. Halleck assumed charge of the Missouri Department, vice Gen. Hunter.

18. Information was received at Washington of the imposition practised upon the Indians west of Arkansas, by Albert Pike, rebel Commissioner.

18. Rebel troops in Accomac and Northampton cos., Va., disbanded, and Union troops, under Gen. Lockwood, seized their arms and took possession of the peninsula.

18. 150 rebels were taken prisoners by Federal cavalry, near Warrensburg, Mo.

19. Missouri rebel legislature, at Neosha, Newton co., passed an ordinance of secession.

19. N. Y. ship Harvey Birch was captured and burnt in the British channel by the rebel steamer Nashville.

19. The principal part of Warsaw, capital of Benton co., Mo., was burnt by rebels.

19. Lieut. Worden, U.S.N., held prisoner by the rebels, was exchanged for Lieut. Short, of the Confederate army.

19. U. S. gunboat Conestoga engaged rebel batteries on the Tennessee river, and silenced them, receiving but slight damage herself.

19. First flotilla of the "Stone Fleet" sailed for the South, from Conn. and Mass.

20. Col. Burchard, with Lieut. Gregg and 24 men, attacked a large company of rebels under Capts. Hays and Gregg, near Kansas City, Mo., and defeated them, killing 5 and wounding 8. The Col. and Lieut. were slightly wounded.

20. A special Committee from the Virginia State Convention to consider proposed amendments to the State Constitution, reported in opposition to free schools and free suffrage for poor whites.

20. Secession State Convention at Russelville, Ky., adopted an ordinance of secession, and appointed Commissions to the rebel government.

22. Two U. S. gunboats, Cambridge and Hertzel, from Fortress Monroe, shelled out the camps of the 2d Louisiana and 10th Georgia regiments, at the junction of James and Warwick rivers.

22. Fort Pickens opened fire on the rebel encampments and forts, near Pensacola, Fla.,

which was replied to by them, and a severe cannonade ensued for two days. Much damage was experienced by Fort McRae, the Navy Yard, and town of Warrington—loss of life slight on either side. The U. S. fleet in the harbor took part. The Richmond was badly damaged by a shot. 1 killed, 6 wounded at Fort Pickens: 1 killed, 7 wounded on the Richmond.

Nov. 23. The Confederate gunboat Tuscorora accidentally took fire and was destroyed on the Mississippi, near Helena, Ark.

24. An explosion took place at Fort Pickens, Fla., by the careless handling of a shell, by which 5 men were killed, and 7 wounded.

24. A skirmish in Lancaster, Mo., between 450 Federals under Col. Moore, and 420 rebels commanded by Lieut. Col. Blanton. The rebels were routed with the loss of 13 killed, and many wounded and prisoners. Union loss, 1 killed and 2 wounded.

24. Tybee Island, in Savannah harbor, was occupied by U. S. forces under Flag-officer Dupont.

24. Rebel Commissioners Mason and Slidell were imprisoned in Fort Warren, Mass.

25. Col. Bayard with the 1st Pa. Cavalry made a reconnoissance from Langley to Dranesville, Va., and, in a skirmish killed 2 and captured 4 rebels. 3 or 4 were wounded. 6 secessionists were also arrested. 2 of the Cavalry were wounded.

25. Com. Tatnall, with 3 steamers and a gunboat, attacked the Federal fleet in Cockspur Roads, Ga., but withdrew without injury, after 40 or 50 shots were exchanged.

25. The State of Missouri, as represented by the late Governor Jackson and the Commissioners from the rebel members of the Legislature, was unanimously received by the Richmond Congress as a member of the Confederacy.

26. The house of Mr. Bell, near Franklin, Tenn., was attacked by an armed party of rebels, the building fired, and the inmates, some 10 or 12, all killed or burned but two, who escaped.

26. Skirmish at Black Oak Point, Hickory co., Mo. Capt. Cosgrove and Lieut. Bobbitt, with 25 men, surprised a rebel camp, killed 5, captured 8, and took 75 tents, 6 wagons, 10 horses, 35 guns, and other property, and released 6 loyal prisoners.

26. A squadron of the 3d Pa. Cavalry, near Vienna, Va., were attacked on three sides by a superior force of cavalry and infantry, and retreated after a short engagement. 29 of their men were missing.

26. The Convention to form a new State in W. Va., met at Wheeling.

27. Federal troops, from Gen. Sherman's command, visited Bear Island and Edisto Island, near the mouth of the Ashepoo river, S. C.

27. Henry R. Jackson was appointed a Maj.-Gen. in the Georgia army.

27. Gen. McClellan appointed the hour of 11 each Sabbath for religious worship throughout the U. S. army, and directed that all officers and men off duty should have opportunity to attend.

27. Transport Constitution sailed from Fortress Monroe to Ship Island, Mississippi Sound, with a portion of Gen. Butler's expedition, under Brig. Gen. Phelps.

28. Capts. Robb and White, and Lieut. Moonlight, three U. S. officers, were captured from the railway train at Weston, Mo., by Sy. Gordon.

28. S. C. planters on the seaboard burnt their cotton, to prevent its capture by the Federal forces or the coast.

29. The English Government forbade temporarily the exportation of cotton.

29. Major Hough, with 4 companies of Missouri cavalry, in defence of the Sedalia railway train, had an engagement at Black Walnut Creek, Mo., in which 17 rebels were killed and wounded, and 5 taken prisoners. 5 of the cavalry, including the Major, were wounded.

29. Col. De Kay, Maj. Sharpf and other Federal officers, and 40 men, had a skirmish about a mile beyond New Market, Va., in which the rebels were routed, leaving 2 dead, and carrying off their wounded.

Dec. 1. The U. S. steamer Penguin arrived at Brooklyn with the prize "Albion," captured while attempting to run the blockade at Charleston, S. C., with arms, ammunition, provisions, &c., worth $100,000.

1. A party of Federals attacked the rebel pickets at Morristown, E. Tenn., killing a large number and putting the rest to flight.

1. Skirmish near Hunter's Chapel, Va., between a squadron of Gen. Blenker's horsemen and a squadron of rebel cavalry, who were defeated, losing 3 or 4 killed and wounded, and 2 prisoners. 1 Federal killed.

2. The first regular session of the 37th Congress commenced at Washington.

2. A party of citizens in Mo., near Dunksburg, 20 miles west of Sedalia, attacked a body of rebels under Capts. Young and Wheatley, killing 7 and wounding 10 of them. Several citizens slightly wounded.

3. Skirmish at Salem, Dent co., Mo. A party of Federal soldiers, commanded by Maj. Bowen, were surprised and fired on, while sleeping in a house near headquarters, by 300 rebels under Cols. Freeman and Turner, and 15 killed and wounded. The

main body of the Federals were drawn out by Maj. Bowen, who attacked the rebels in turn and drove them from the town. 1 Federal killed and 4 wounded. Rebel loss unknown.

3. H. C. Burnett of Ky. and J. W. Reed of Mo. were expelled from U. S. House of Representatives as traitors.

4. Col. Taylor with 30 men of the 3d New Jersey had a skirmish with a number of rebel cavalry near Annandale, Va., three or four of whom were captured, and several killed and wounded without Federal loss.

4. Gen. Phelps, with 2,000 men, attached to Gen. Butler's expedition, occupied Ship Island, Mississippi Sound.

4. A detachment of Federal cavalry surprised the rebel guard at Whip-poor-will Bridge, on the Memphis Branch railway, Ky., taking 11 prisoners. 5 or 6 Confederates were killed or wounded. 4 Federals were wounded.

4. J. C. Breckinridge was expelled from the U. S. Senate.

5. Reports of the Secs. of War and Navy show the Government had in service for the war 682,971 men.

5. Skirmish at Brownsville, Ky. 100 Home Guards defeated a superior rebel force under Gen. T. C. Hindman, of Ark. Rebel loss, 3 killed, 5 wounded; the Guards sustaining no loss.

5. Successful foray of the 13th Mass., Col. Leonard, from the Potomac to Berkley Springs, Va., capturing a large quantity of provisions.

5. Riot at Nashville. Tenn., occasioned by the attempt of the rebel authorities to enforce the the endraftment of the militia. Two persons were killed and several wounded.

7. At Sedalia, Mo., 106 mule teams and the teamsters were seized by rebels.

7. Capt. Sweeney, with 35 rebel guerrillas, were captured near Glasgow, Mo., by Capt. Merrill's cavalry.

7. Skirmish near Dam No. 5 on the Potomac. Rebels driven off, losing 12 men.

7. Skirmish near Olathe, Mo. 2 Federals killed. 3 rebels killed and 5 wounded.

8. Capt. McGuire's company of 27th Mo., captured 14 rebels at Sedalia, Mo.

8. U. S. steamer Augusta captured schr. E. Waterman, loaded with provisions, coal and war munitions, off Savannah, Ga.

9. Gen. Halleck required all municipal officers at St. Louis, Mo., as well as State officials, to subscribe to the oath of allegiance prescribed by the State Convention in October previous.

9. The U. S. steamer Harriet Lane, and 6 steamers attached to the upper Potomac flotilla, shelled the woods at Budd's Ferry, and exchanged shots with the rebel batteries opposite, at Shipping Point. Some large buildings, containing rebel stores, were burnt, by boatmen from the Jacob Bell and Anacosta.

9. Gov. Pickens of S. C. proclaimed the State invaded, by land and sea, and called for 12,000 twelve-month volunteers.

9. A detachment of the "Stone Fleet" left New Bedford, Mass., for a southern port.

9. Garret Davis was elected a senator from Ky., in place of J. C. Breckinridge.

9. The rebel Congress "admitted" Kentucky to the Confederacy.

11. Federal troops, under Lieut.-Col. Rhodes, had a skirmish near Bertrand, Mo., losing 1 man. They took 16 prisoners and a number of horses and fire-arms.

11. Five vessels of the Stone Fleet, and the ships George Green and Bullion, of Gen. Butler's expedition, sailed from Boston, Mass.

11. Skirmish at Dam No. 4, on the Potomac, near Sharpsburg, Md. Seven rebels on the Virginia shore were killed, and many wounded. Capt. Williams and 6 men having crossed the river were captured by the rebels.

11. Great fire at Charleston, S. C. 600 houses destroyed.

12. A squad of men from Col. Whitaker's regiment were defeated in an attempt to arrest secessionists near Bagdad, Shelby co., Ky., and retreated with one wounded.

12. Col. Merrill's cavalry regiment returned to Sedalia, Mo., from Waverley, bringing as prisoners 4 rebel capts., 2 lieuts. and 40 men, a mortar, and many horses.

12. Co. I, of 15th Ohio, were attacked on the banks of the Green river, Ky., by a superior force of rebel cavalry, whom they repulsed, wounding several of the cavalry, without loss themselves.

13. Villages of Papinsville and Butler, Bates co., Mo., rebel rendezvous, were burned by Maj. Williams of the 3d Kansas.

13. Wm. H. Johnson, of the Lincoln Cavalry, a deserter, who was captured, under military order was shot.

13. The British ship Admiral was captured off Savannah, Ga., while attempting to run in, by the Augusta.

13. Rebel Gov. Jackson, of Mo., issued a proclamation, from New Madrid, praising the valor, fortitude and success of the rebel army, and calling for more volunteers.

13. Battle of Camp Alleghany, Va. 2,000 Federal troops, under Brig.-Gen. R. H. Milroy, marched from Cheat Mountain Summit to attack a rebel camp on Alleghany Summit, of 2,000 troops, under Col. E. Johnson. The Federals approached in 2 divisions, of

750 each, from different directions, but did not arrive simultaneously, and alternately attacked the whole rebel force. They retired after a well contested fight of 8 hours, losing 20 killed, 107 wounded, and 10 missing. The rebels reported about the same loss.

Dec. 14. Ex-minister Faulkner was released on parole, to be exchanged for Congressman Ely.

14. Reconnoissance by Federal troops, within 28 miles of Charleston, S. C. The rebels, as they retreated, burnt their cotton.

15. Skirmish on the Virginia shore, opposite Berlin, Md. A detachment from the 28th Penn. were attacked by 120 rebels in ambush, but cut their way through to their boat, and escaped, having 1 wounded, and 2 taken prisoners. 2 of the enemy were killed and 5 wounded.

15. Many Union refugees escaped from Arkansas. Capt. Ware, late of the Ark. Legislature, organized a military company of Ark. Union men at Rolla, Mo.

16. Platte City, Mo., was fired by rebels, and the principal public buildings destroyed.

16. The *Europa* arrived from England, with news of the excitement among the British people occasioned by the arrest of Messrs. Mason and Slidell, and also the ultimatum of the British Government, demanding a surrender of the rebel commissioners, and an apology for their seizure. Mr. Seward's dispatch to Mr. Adams, dated Nov. 30, having settled the matter in anticipation, there was but little excitement in the public mind.

16. Gen. Zollicoffer established a camp on the banks of the Cumberland river, six miles from Somerset, Ky.

16. A party of 8 men from the 2d and 4th N. J. advanced to Annandale, on the south bank of the Potomac. They were surprised by the enemy and 3 of them captured.

17. Battle at Munfordsville, Green river, Ky. The rebels defeated; 33 killed and 60 wounded. Federal loss, 10 killed and 17 wounded.

17. Gen. Pope captured 300 rebels near Osceola, Mo.

17. Entrance to the harbor at Savannah, Ga., blockaded by sinking 7 vessels laden with stone.

18. A part of Gen. Pope's forces under Col. J. C. Davis and Col. F. Steele, surprised a rebel camp near Milford, north of Warrensburg, Mo., and captured nearly 1300 men, 70 wagons loaded with stores, and all their camp equipage and arms. Federal loss, 2 killed, 17 wounded.

18. Gen. Barnard, Chief-engineer of the U. S. army, reported to Congress that the defences around Washington consisted of 48 works, the perimeter of which was 48 miles, mounting above 300 guns.

18. The Island City sailed from Boston for Fortress Monroe with 240 rebel prisoners, to be exchanged.

18. Rebel Gen. Jackson attempted a movement against Williamsport, Md., but Gen. Williams being on the alert, the rebel force retired.

18. News from Ky., that Gen. McCook, was at Munfordsville, Gen. Mitchell at Bacon Creek, and Gen. Zollicoffer, (rebel) at Cumberland river, near Mill Springs.

19. Skirmishing at Point of Rocks, Md. Rebels from Va. shore commenced shelling the encampment of Col. Geary's Pennsylvania regiment, but were repulsed after half an hour's fight, without loss on the Federal side.

19. A band of 25 rebels visited the town of Ripley, Jackson Co., Va., and seized all the arms in the place, some ammunition and clothing. They also robbed the postoffice and the principal store in the place.

20. George W. Jones, late U. S. Minister to Bogota, was arrested in New York on a charge of treason.

20. Battle of Dranesville, Va. Federal forces, under Gen. E. O. C. Ord, defeated about 2,800 Confederates from South Carolina, Alabama, and Virginia. Federal force about 4,000 men, of whom 7 were killed and 61 wounded. Rebel loss, 75 killed 150 wounded and 30 prisoners, together with a large supply of forage.

20. A scouting party under Capt. Wood, captured 100 rebels near Springfield, Mo., who were released upon taking the oath of allegiance.

20. A party of rebels from Gen. Price's army committed extensive ravages on the N. Missouri railway, between Hudson and Warrenton. The bridges, wood-piles, water tanks, ties and rails were destroyed along the route for 80 miles.

20. 103 Federal soldiers, under Major McKee, repulsed a superior force of rebels four miles S. of Hudson, Mo., killing 10 and capturing 17 prisoners and 30 horses, at the same time rescuing a stock train which had just been seized by the rebels.

20. The main ship channel at Charleston harbor, was obstructed by sinking 16 vessels of the "stone fleet."

22. Reconnoissance in the vicinity of Tybee Island and Broad river, Ga., from Gen. Sherman's command.

22. Skirmish near New Market bridge, Newport News, Va. Two companies of

Dec. 1861. 'CHRONOLOGY. 487

20th N. Y. regiment, under Major Schoepf, were attacked by 700 rebel cavalry and infantry, and escaped with loss of 6 wounded. Ten of the enemy were killed and a number wounded, when they retreated.

23. Gen. Pope sent an expedition to Lexington, Mo. Two boats of the rebels were captured and burnt.

26. A skirmish took place at Camp Boyle, Columbia, Ky. A body of rebels were attacked by a detachment of Col. Hazzard's regiment, under Major Ousley, who dispersed them, killing 5 and wounding others, without loss themselves.

26. Gen. McCall sent a reconnoitering party towards Drancsville, Va., which was driven back by the rebels, who had a force of 10,000 men there.

26. A Cabinet Council at Washington, decided to give up Mason and Slidell, on the ground that they could not be held consistently with the doctrine of neutral rights always maintained by the U. S. Government.

26. Gen. Scott arrived at New York, in the Arago, from France.

26. Bluffton, S. C., was occupied by Federal troops under Gen. Stevens.

26. The Lighthouse on Morris Island, Charleston, S. C. harbor, was blown up by order of rebel authorities.

26. Major Gower, with a squadron of 1st Iowa cavalry, arrived at Jefferson City, Mo., bringing as prisoners, 1 capt., 13 men, and 10 wagon loads of stores.

26. Philip St. George Cook, a Brig.-Gen. in the rebel army, shot himself, at his residence in Powhatan Co., Va.

26. A fire occurred in the government stables at Washington, D. C., in which nearly 200 horses were burned.

27. Lord Lyons, the British minister at Washington, was notified that Mason and Slidell awaited his disposal.

27. Alfred Ely, U. S. representative from Rochester, N. Y., taken prisoner at Manassas Plains, was released in exchange for C. J. Faulkner.

27. The rebel privateer Isabel, ran the blockade off Charleston, S. C.

27. The bridges over Fabias river on the Palmyra railway, Mo., destroyed by rebels.

28. Gen. Buell's army in Ky., was reported by the War Department to number 60,000 men.

28. The rebels at Bowling Green, Ky., were reported to number 30,000, under Gens. A. S. Johnston, Buckner, and Hindman.

28. Gen. Prentiss, with 5 companies 3rd Missouri cavalry, under Col. John Glover, and 5 companies of Col. Birge's sharpshooters, 470 in all, attacked a rebel camp at Mount Zion, in Boone Co., Mo., numbering nearly 900 men. The rebels were routed, losing 25 killed, 150 wounded, and 40 prisoners. 90 of their horses and 105 stand of arms were captured. The Federal loss was 3 killed and 45 wounded.

28. A squadron of Federal cavalry, from Col. Jackson's regiment, commanded by Major Murray, left their camp near Calhoun, Ky., on a scouting expedition across Green river. They were attacked near Sacramento, by a large force of rebels under Col. De Forrest, and after a short engagement compelled to retire. Capt. A. G. Bacon was killed, and Lieut. R. H. King, of Frankfort, and 8 privates wounded. Capt. Merriweather and two privates of the rebels were killed, and a number wounded.

30. The rebel Gen. H. H. Sibley having entered New Mexico with a military force without opposition, took possession of it, and annexed it to the Southern Confederacy by proclamation.

30. Messrs. Thomas and Burnett, of Ky., were "qualified" and took their seats in the rebel Congress at Richmond, Va.

31. Two boats under Acting-Masters A. Allen, and H. L. Sturges, from the U. S. steamer, Mount Vernon, destroyed a light ship off Wilmington, N.C., which the rebels had fitted up for a gunboat. The expedition was at night, and the boats were under fire from Fort Caswell; but escaped injury.

31. Capt. Shillinglaw and Mason, N. Y. 79th, and Lieutenants Dickinson, 3rd U. S. infantry, J. W. Hart, 20th Indiana, and other officers and men were released by the rebels from Richmond, Va.

31. Capture of the town of Biloxi, Miss. by U. S. gunboats Lewis, Water Witch, and New London, with national forces from Ship Island. The town and fort surrendered without a fight. The guns were removed by Commander Smith, and the Federals retired.

1862.

Jan. 1. The rebel Commissioners Mason and Slidell, with their Secretaries, left Boston for England, via Provincetown, Mass., where the British war steamer Rinaldo received them.

1. Col. H. Brown opened fire from Fort Pickens on the rebel vessels and fortifications within range of his guns, which was returned by the enemy.

1. The British bark Empress arrived at New York as a prize, with 6,500 bags of coffee, captured by the U. S. sloop-of-war Vincennes, off New Orleans bar.

Jan .1. Part of the Louisville and Nashville railway was destroyed by order of the rebel Gen. Buckner.

1. Skirmish at Port Royal Ferry, S. C. Federal troops under Gen. Stevens, with the assistance of five gunboats, crossed from Beaufort to the mainland and attacked batteries erected by the rebels, who retreated towards Grahamville. Federal loss, 3 killed, 11 wounded. Rebels, 6 killed, 12 wounded.

1. Jeff. Owens, Col. Jones, and 50 rebel bridge-burners were captured near Martinsburg, Adrian Co., Mo., by State militia under General Schofield.

1. Four Federal soldiers were captured, 1 killed, and 10 guns taken by a party of rebels on Green river, Ky., near Morgantown.

2. The U. S. gunboats Yankee and Anncosta, exchanged shots with the rebel batteries at Cockpit Point, on the Potomac.

2. Daniel P. White of Ky., qualified and took his seat in the Confederate Congress.

3. Col. Glover, with 300 Federal troops, attacked a rebel camp 9 miles N. of Hunnewell, Mo., taking 8 prisoners, putting the rest to flight, and capturing a quantity of arms, &c.

3. 240 released Federal prisoners arrived at Fortress Monroe from Richmond.

4. The 84th Pa., 39th Ill., 500 cavalry and other troops were driven from Bath, Va., by a superior rebel force under Gen. Jackson, who took 30 Federals prisoners. The Federals retreated to Hancock, Md. 7 rebels were killed and a number wounded. 3 of the Federals were killed, several wounded.

4. Skirmish at Huntersville, W. Va. A portion of the 25th Ohio, 2d Va., and Bracken's Ind. cavalry, all under Major Webster, attacked a rebel force of 400 cavalry and 350 infantry who were guarding the rebel supplies at that depot. They were routed with a loss of 2 killed and 7 wounded, leaving $50,000 worth of army stores which were destroyed by Unionists.

5. Skirmish on the mainland near Port Royal, S. C. 7 rebels were captured.

5. Rebel army under Gen. Jackson bombarded Hancock, Md. from the opposite Va. shore, but were driven away by artillery forces under Gen. Lander without a close engagement.

5. Five Federal soldiers were killed by rebels in ambush in Johnson Co., Kansas.

6. 4,000 Cherokee Indians were driven from their homes by Texas rebels.

7. Destruction of bridges and culverts on the Balt. and Ohio railway, near the Cacapon river, by rebel Gen. Jackson.

7. Engagement at Blue's Gap, near Romney, W. Va. Federal troops under Col. Dunning, of the 5th Ohio, attacked 2,000 of the enemy, routing them with the loss of 15 killed, 20 prisoners, 2 pieces of cannon, their wagons, &c. No Federal loss.

7. 300 of the 32d Ohio, under Capt. Lacey, were sent by Gen. Milroy into Tucker Co., Va., where they dispersed 400 rebels, capturing 2 officers and a private, and a large quantity of stores. 4 rebels were found dead and many were wounded.

7. Three brigades of Gen. Smith's division, S. side of the Potomac, proceeded toward Peacock Hill, Lewinsville, Fairfax Court House and Vienna, and captured an immense quantity of hay, oats, corn, &c.

7. A band of rebels having seized a quantity of army stores from the depot at Sutton, Braxton Co., W. Va., information was sent to Col. H. Anisansel, commanding 1st Virginia Cavalry, at Clarksburg. The Col. overtook the rebels 30 miles E. of Sutton, and, attacking them, killed or wounded 22, took 15 horses and 56 head of cattle, and recaptured the greater part of the stores.

7. Skirmish at Paintsville, near Prestonburg, Ky. Col. Garfield dispersed 2,500 rebels under Humphrey Marshall, killing 8, wounding a large number, and capturing 15. Federal loss 2 killed and 1 wounded.

8. The newspapers of Missouri were put under military censorship, and their editors ordered to send two copies of each issue to the Provost Marshal.

8. Riot at Warsaw, Mo. Two secessionists were shot.

8. Reconnoissance of gunboats towards Savannah, Ga., under command of Capt. Davis.

8. Capt. Latham and 17 men of 2d Virginia regiment, encountered about 30 rebel guerrillas on the Dry Fork of Chent river, W. Va., and after a severe fight of an hour's duration, the rebels were driven from the field with the loss of 6 killed and several wounded. Federal loss 6 wounded. Capt. Latham destroyed the rebel tents and provisions.

8. The 1st Kansas regiment, on its march from Sedalia to Lexington, Mo., was fired upon from ambush, and a sergeant and 2 horses killed.

8. A. W. Bradford was inaugurated as Governor of Maryland, and made an eloquent address, expressing in the strongest terms devotion to the Union and the Constitution.

8. Major W. M. G. Torrence of the 1st Iowa cavalry, assisted by detachments of the 1st Missouri cavalry, Major Hubbard, 4th Ohio and Merrill's Horse, in all 500

Jan. 1862. CHRONOLOGY. 489

mounted men, attacked a rebel camp at Silver Creek, Howard Co., Mo., where six or eight hundred men were stationed, under Col. Poindexter. The enemy were routed with a loss of 12 killed, 22 wounded, and 15 prisoners, leaving their horses, guns, and camp and garrison equipage. The material was destroyed by Major Torrence. Federal loss 3 killed and 10 wounded.

9. A division of the Chamber of Commerce at St. Louis, Mo., was occasioned by disloyal sentiments. A new and loyal Chamber was formed.

10. A reconnoitering force of 5,000 men under the command of Brig. Gen. McClernand, left Cairo. Ill., and proceeded toward Columbus and Mayfield.

10. Waldo P. Johnson and Trusten Polk, U. S. Senators from Missouri, were expelled from the Senate for disloyalty.

10. Skirmish at Pohick Church, Va. The 5th Michigan dispersed a body of rebels.

10. Skirmish at Bath, Va., between a detachment of Federals under Capt. Russell and rebels from Gen. Jackson's division.

10. Battle near Prestonburg, Ky. Gen. Garfield, with 1,500 Federal troops, overtook Humphrey Marshall with 3,000 rebels, compelling him to destroy his stores and putting him to flight. Rebel loss 50 killed many wounded and 25 prisoners. Federal loss, 2 killed, 25 wounded.

11. The 1st Kansas regiment arrived at Lexington, Mo., and arrested several prominent rebels. They also seized a large quantity of stores designed for the use of Gen. Price.

11. Fifty rebels belonging to Col. Alexander's regiment were captured 6 miles from Sedalia, Mo.

12. The Burnside Expedition sailed from Fortress Monroe, under command of Com. Goldsborough and Gen. Burnside, for Albemarle Sound, N. C.

12. Secretary Seward telegraphed the British Consul at Portland, Me., that British troops might pass through U. S. territory on their way to Canada.

12. The rebels in Kentucky burned the houses, and carried off or destroyed the property of loyal men at Horse Cave and in Cave City and vicinity, and the people sought refuge at Munfordsville.

13. Hon. Simeon Cameron, Secretary-of-War, resigned his position, and Edwin F. Stanton was appointed in his stead on the 15th inst.

13. The steamship Constitution, with the Maine 12th regiment, and the Bay State regiment, sailed from Boston for Ship Island, Miss., via. Fortress Monroe.

15. Gen. McClernand's column advanced to Mayfield, Ky., and Gen. Grant to Fort Jefferson. 20,000 rebels reported at Columbus, Ky., under Gen. Polk.

16. Hon. Edwin B. Stanton, the new Secretary-of-War, assumed the duties of his office.

17. 150 wounded Federal prisoners arrived at Fortress Monroe from Richmond, Va. Eight rebel officers were released from the Fortress the same day.

17. Capture of British schooner Stephen Hart, loaded with arms, ammunition and stores for the rebels, by the U. S. storeship Supply.

17. Ex-President John Tyler died at Richmond Va.

17. Skirmish near Ironton, Mo. Rebels under Jeff. Thompson were defeated by Col. Miles.

17. Two companies of the 1st Kansas cavalry, under Major Halderman, arrested Capt. Whitney, Joe Shelby and several other rebel officers, and also recovered a number of horses, mules, wagons, etc., taken from Col. Mulligan's command at Lexington, Mo.

17. The Fortification Bill passed the U. S. House of Representatives, appropriating $5,960,000 for fort and harbor defences.

18. Gen. Grant made a reconnoissance in force towards Columbus, Ky.

18. Gen. Halleck levied an assessment on the wealthy secessionists of St. Louis, Mo., to provide for the wants of loyal refugees in the city who had been driven from their homes in the S. W. section of the State by rebels.

18. Capts. Murdock and Webster, with their commands, returned to Cairo from an expedition to Bloomfield, Mo. They captured Lieut. Col. Farmer and 11 other rebel officers and 68 privates, with a quantity of army stores.

19. Battle of Mill Spring. Ky. The rebels completely routed, with loss of 192 killed, and 140 prisoners. Gen. Zollicoffer, their commander, was killed. The Federal troops were under Gen. Thomas. 1,200 horses and mules, over 100 large wagons, and 14 cannon, 2,000 muskets, etc., were captured. Federal loss 39 killed, 207 wounded.

19. The U. S. gunboat Itasca captured the rebel schooner Lizzie Weston, off Florida, laden with 293 bales of cotton, 152,500 pounds, for Jamaica.

23. The property of several wealthy secessionists at St. Louis was seized under execution by Gen. Halleck, and sold to pay the assessment to support Union refugees.

23. The second stone fleet was sunk in Maffit's Channel, Charleston, S. C., harbor

Jan. 24. The Federal light boat off Cape Henry, at the mouth of the Chesapeake, went ashore and was captured by the rebels, with its crew of 7 men.

24. Two rebel vessels laden with cotton, while attempting to pass the blockade at the mouth of the Mississippi, ran aground, were deserted and burned. The fire was extinguished on board the Calhoun and that vessel captured.

26. The Burnside Expedition reached Pamlico Sound.

26. A military Commission at Palmyra, Mo., sentenced 7 bridge-burners to be shot.

28. Federal troops occupied Lebanon, Mo.

28. Rev. Bishop Ames and H m. Hamilton Fish, of N. Y., were appointed by Secretary-of-War Stanton to visit the U. S. prisoners in captivity at Richmond, Va., to devise means for providing for their comfort. The Commissioners were not allowed to visit Richmond, but they opened negotiations for the exchange of prisoners.

28. Skirmish between 50 men of the 37th N. Y. regiment under Lieut.-Col. Burke, and a body of Texas rangers near Colchester, on the Occoquan river, Va., in which 9 rebels were killed. Two Federals were killed, and 2 wounded.

29. The iron-clad battery Monitor was launched at Greenpoint, N. Y.

29. Reconnoissance on either side of the Savannah river from the Federal fleet at Port Royal, through the Wilmington Narrows and Wall's Cut, by which the feasibility of cutting off Fort Pulaski from communication with Savannah was demonstrated.

30. Gen. Beauregard took command of rebel troops in Tennessee.

30. The rebel commissioners, Mason and Slidell, arrived at Southampton, England.

30. Rebels under Capt. John Morgan, seized six Union men at a church near Lebanon, Ky. They set fire to the church, and attempted to burn one of the prisoners in the flames, who effected his escape.

31. An order from the Secretary-of State released all civilians who were captured on board vessels attempting to violate the blockade.

31. Five telegraph operators were captured by the rebels near Campbellsville, Ky.

31. Queen Victoria declared her determination to observe strict neutrality during the American contest, and to prevent the use of English vessels and harbors to aid the belligerents.

Feb. 1. The 2d Cavalry, 41st Indiana, had a skirmish near Bowling Green, Ky., in which 3 rebels were killed and 2 wounded. No loss on the Federal side.

1. The Spanish steamer Duero arrived at Liverpool, England, from Cadiz, bringing as passengers Captains Minott, of the Vigilant; Smith of the Arcade, and Hoxie, of the Eben Dodge—three American vessels which had been burned by the privateer Sumter.

1. An octavo volume of 1,100 pages was published as a report by a Committee from the U. S. House of Representatives, appointed July, 1861, to investigate frauds in Government contracts.

1. The President of the U. S. was empowered by act of Congress to take possession of all the railway and telegraphic lines throughout the country, whenever requisite for military purposes, till the close of the rebellion.

1. An interesting conference was held by U. S. Commissioner Dole with the loyal chiefs of the Seminole, Creek, Iowa, and Delaware Indians, in which the warriors pledged themselves to conquer the rebel Indians who had driven them from their homes.

2. A skirmish occurred in Morgan county, Penn., between a body of rebel cavalry, under Lieut.-Col. White, and a company of Federal infantry, under Captain Duncan, in which the Federals were defeated, with a loss of seven men.

2. 386 rank and file and 11 officers, rebel prisoners, were sent to Fortress Monroe, from Boston harbor, to be exchanged for an equal number of Federal prisoners.

3. The privateersmen confined in the City Prison, N. Y., were transferred to Fort Lafayette, and there held as political prisoners.

3. In conformity with the decision of the British Ministry, the privateer Nashville was sent off from Southampton, England, and the U. S. gunboat Tuscarora detained from pursuing her for the space of 24 hours.

3. A flag of truce from the rebels to Gen. McDowell, brought a document from Jeff. Davis to President Lincoln, threatening to hang Cols. Corcoran, Lee, and others, prisoners in their hands, in retaliation, should the punishment of death be inflicted on the bridge-burners who had been convicted in Missouri.

3. The Federal army under Gen. Grant were within 3 miles of Fort Henry, on the Tennessee river.

4. Capt. Lowing, with 80 men from Cos. F and H, Third Michigan, encountered a body of rebels near Occoquan, Va., whom they dispersed. 4 of the rebels were shot. No loss sustained by the Federals.

4. A scouting party under Capt. Hark-

Feb. 1862. CHRONOLOGY. 401

ness, of Col. Miles' 81st Pa. regiment, returned from the vicinity of Fairfax Court House, Va., bringing several rebel prisoners.

4. Steamship Constitution, with the Mass. Bay State, and the Maine 12th regiments, and other troops, under Gen. Phelps, left Fortress Monroe for Ship Island, Miss.

5. Attack on Fort Henry, Tenn. commenced by Federal gunboats under Com. Foote.

5. Queen Victoria, of England, removed the prohibitions relating to the export of material of war from the British dominions declared on the 30th Nov. and 4th Dec., 1861.

6. Jesse D. Bright, of Indiana, was expelled from the U. S. Senate, for complicity with treason.

7. A band of rebels concealed near the landing at Harper's Ferry, Va., having, by means of a flag of truce, decoyed a boat from the Maryland shore, and then fired on its occupants, by order of Col. Geary, the block of large buildings facing the landing were burned. But seven families, 40 persons in all, then resided in the town.

7. Unconditional surrender of Fort Henry to Com. Foote, with Gen. Tilghman and staff, one colonel, two captains, and 80 privates. Com. Foote transferred the fort to Gen. Grant.

7. Federal troops took possession of the Memphis and Ohio railway.

7. The rebels driven from Romney, Va., by Gen. Lander, who occupied the town.

7. Successful skirmish with rebel cavalry near Fairfax Court House, Va., by Col. Friedman, with the Cameron Dragoons; 1 rebel killed, and 12 captured, with 12 horses, &c. 2 Federals wounded.

8. Portions of Gen. Butler's expedition sailed from Boston and from Fortress Monroe, for Ship Island, Miss.

8. Capture of rebel forts and garrisons on Roanoke Island. N. C., by the Federal forces under Com. Goldsborough and Gen. Burnside. 2.500 prisoners, 6 forts, 40 guns, 3,000 small arms. Federal loss, 50 killed, 150 wounded.

8. Capt. Smith, of the 5th Virginia (loyal) with 21 men, surprised 32 of Jenkins' cavalry on Linn Creek, Logan County, Va., killing 8, wounding 7, and capturing the remainder, with 32 horses. One Federal was killed and 1 wounded.

9. Skirmish of a body of Federal cavalry with rebels near Fort Henry, Tenn. 5 rebels killed, and 30 taken prisoners.

9. Edenton, N. C., occupied by Federal troops.

10. Destruction of rebel gunboats in the Pasquotank river, N. C., also of the rebel battery at Cobb's Point, and the occupation of Elizabeth City by Federal forces from 14 gunboats, commanded by Capt. Rowan.

10. Gen. Charles P. Stone, U. S. A., was arrested by Gov't. order, and imprisoned in Fort Lafayette.

10. Arrest of several male and female secessionists in Washington. Also, of Dr. Ives, N. Y. *Herald* correspondent.

10. Capt. Phelps, of Com. Foote's squadron, commanding the gunboats Conestoga, Taylor and Lexington, captured a new rebel gunboat, and destroyed all the rebel craft between Fort Henry and Florence, Ala.

11. Bursting of the "Sawyer" gun at Newport News, Va., by which 2 Federal soldiers were killed and 2 wounded.

12. An expedition under the command of Col. Reggin returned to Fort Henry, Tenn., from up the Tennessee river, having captured $75,000 worth of contraband goods at Paris, Tenn., and also the tents and camp equipage of the rebel troops that retreated from Fort Henry.

13. Evacuation of Springfield, Mo., by the rebel army under Gen. Price. Occupation of the town by Federal troops of Gen. Curtis' army. 600 of the rebel sick, and many forage wagons were left behind.

14. The rebel camp at Blooming Gap, Va., was surprised by forces under Gen. Lander. 65 prisoners were taken, including 17 officers, and 13 killed and 20 wounded. Federal loss, 7 in killed and wounded.

14. Fort Donelson was invested and attacked by the Federal army under Gen. Grant.

14. E. M. Stanton, Sec.-of-War, issued an order releasing all political prisoners upon their taking an oath of allegiance.

14. A skirmish took place near Flat Lick Ford, on the Cumberland river, Ky., between two companies of cavalry, under Col. Munday, two companies of the 49th Indiana, and some rebel pickets, in which the latter lost 4 killed, 4 wounded, and 3 taken prisoners. There was no Federal loss.

14. Com. Foote, with 6 gunboats, attacked Fort Donelson, but was repulsed, the Commodore being severely wounded. Federal loss 60 in killed and wounded.

14. The rear guard of Gen. Price's army in S. W. Missouri was attacked by Gen. Curtis' command, and many prisoners taken.

14. Bowling Green, Ky., was evacuated by rebel troops, who destroyed most of the available property in the town that could not be removed.

Feb. 14. Three rebel schooners and one sloop, laden with rice, were destroyed by the crews of armed boats from the U. S. bark Restless, Lieut. E. Conroy, in Bull's Bay, S. C.

15. The national batteries at Venus Point, on the Savannah river, were attacked by 4 rebel gunboats, which were repulsed, one of them being severely injured.

15. The railway bridge crossing the Tennessee river at Decatur, Ala., was destroyed by Union men.

15. Gen. Burnside administered the oath of allegiance to the inhabitants of Roanoke Island.

15. The iron-clad steam gunboat Galena was launched at Mystic, Conn.

16. Gen. Price was driven from Missouri by Gen. Curtis, who followed him into Arkansas, capturing many prisoners.

16. Gen. Mitchell's troops occupied Bowling-Green, Ky.

16. Fort Donelson surrendered to the Federal army, under Gen. Grant, after three days' desperate resistance. 15,000 prisoners were captured, including Brig.-Gen. Buckner, and an immense quantity of war material. Gens. Floyd and Pillow escaped, with a portion of the garrison.

16. Destruction of the "Tennessee Iron works," owned by John Bell and Messrs. Lewis & Wood, on the Cumberland river, six miles above Dover, by order of Com. Foote.

17. The First Missouri cavalry fell into an ambush of rebels at Sugar Creek, Ark., by which 13 of their number were killed and wounded.

18. Gov. Rector of Arkansas, by proclamation, called every man subject to military duty into service within 20 days.

18. First session of the Congress of the "permanent" Government of the Confederate States opened at Richmond, Va.

18. The wire and suspension bridges over the Cumberland river at Nashville, Tenn., were destroyed by Gen. Floyd, despite the remonstrances of the citizens.

18. A skirmish at Independence, Mo., between a detachment of Ohio cavalry and a band of rebels under Quantrel and Parker. 3 rebels killed, several wounded and taken prisoners. 1 Federal killed, 3 wounded.

19. 1,000 additional rebel prisoners were taken at Fort Donelson, they having come down the river to reinforce Gen. Buckner.

19. Evacuation of Clarksville, Tenn., by the rebels. The Federal forces, under Com. Foote, took possession of the town, and captured a large quantity of army stores.

19. Bentonville, Ark., was captured by Gen. Curtis, after a short engagement with the rebels, in which more prisoners and supplies were taken.

20. The rebel steamer Magnolia, with 1,050 bales of cotton, was captured in the Gulf of Mexico, by the U. S. steamers Brooklyn and South Carolina. An attempt to fire the vessel was frustrated by the Federal seamen.

20. The town of Winton, N. C., was partially burned by the national forces.

20. The track of the Memphis and Ohio railway was torn up, and the bridges burned in many places, by order of rebel Gen. Polk.

21. Battle of Valverde, N. M. 1,500 Federals, under Col. Canby, were defeated by an equal force of rebels, under Col. Steele. Federal loss, 55 killed, 140 wounded. Rebel loss, about the same.

22. Inauguration of Jefferson Davis, of Miss., as President of the "Confederate States," at Richmond, Va., and Alex. H. Stevens, of Ga., as Vice-President, they having received the unanimous vote of 109 delegates representing 11 States, viz.: Ala., Ark., Fla., Ga., La., Miss., N. C., S. C., Tenn., Texas, Va., for the permanent organization of the Confederate States.

22. The U. S. sloop-of-war Adironac was launched at Brooklyn, N. Y.

23. 347 released Federal prisoners arrived at Fortress Monroe, among them Cols. Lee, Wood and Cogswell.

23. Lieut. Guin, of Com. Foote's command, made a reconnoissance up the Tenn. river as high as Eastport, Miss., being well received by the inhabitants. At Clifton, Tenn., he took possession of 1500 sacks and barrels of flour and 6,000 bush. of wheat.

23. Gallatin, Tenn., occupied by Gen. Buell's forces.

23. A skirmish at Mason's Neck, near Occoquan, Va., between Texas rangers, and part of the N. Y. 37th, in which 2 of the latter were killed and 1 wounded.

24. Harpers' Ferry, Va., occupied by the 28th Pa. regiment.

25. Nashville, Tenn., was occupied by Federal forces of Gen. Buell's command.

25. The 9th Ohio and 2d Minnesota regiments received handsome flags from ladies of Louisville, Ky., in compliment of their valor at Mill Spring, Jan. 19.

25. The remainder of Gen. Bank's division crossed the Potomac and occupied Bolivar and Charlestown, Va.

25. All the telegraphic lines that could be used by government were taken under military control, and the transmission of reports of military operations forbidden, without permission of the military censor.

26. Cotton and tobacco planters of Va.,

at a meeting held at Richmond, refused to consent to the destruction of their crops.

26. The command of Capt. Montgomery, was surprised by a large force of rebels at Keittsville, Barry Co., Mo. 2 Federals were killed, 1 wounded, and 40 of their horses captured.

26. The U. S. gunboat R. B. Forbes ran ashore near Nag's Head, N. C., was set on fire and destroyed.

27. Fayetteville, Ark., was occupied by Gen. Curtis, who captured a number of prisoners, stores, &c. The rebels retreated across the Boston Mountains.

27. 42 Federal soldiers were poisoned at Mud Town, Ark., by eating food which had been left for them by rebels.

27. Col. Wood's cavalry drove rebels out of Dent, Texas and Howell Cos., Mo., capturing 60 prisoners.

27. U. S. iron clad battery Monitor, Lieut. Worden, sailed from N. York for Fortress Monroe.

28. The British ship Labuan, with a valuable cargo, arrived at N. York, captured by the U. S. sloop-of-war Portsmouth off Rio Grande river.

28. The rebel steamer Nashville ran the blockade of Beaufort, N. C., and reached the town.

28. Capt. Nolen with 64 of the 7th Ill. cavalry attacked 90 of Jeff. Thompson's cavalry and a battery, west of Charlestown, Mo., and captured 4 guns, losing 1 man.

March 1. The U. S. gunboats Tyler, Lieut. Gwin, commanding, and Lexington, Lieut. Shirk, on an expedition up the Tenn. river, engaged and silenced a rebel battery at Pittsburg, Tenn., 7 miles above Savannah.

1. Evacuation of Columbus Ky., by rebel troops, leaving their heavy guns, and a large quantity of war material. 400 of the 2d Illinois cavalry occupied the town next day, and troops from Com. Foote's flotilla the day after.

1. U. S. steamer Mount Vernon, captured the schooner British Queen, at the blockade of Wilmington, N. C.

1. John Minor Botts, Valentine Hecker, Franklin Stearns, and others were arrested at Richmond Va., on a charge of "treason."

2. Death of Brig.-Gen. Lander, at Camp Chase, on the Upper Potomac, from a wound received at Edwards' Ferry Va., Oct. 22. 1861.

3. Brig.-Gens. S. B. Buckner and Lloyd Tilghman, rebel prisoners, arrived at Fort Warren, Boston, Mass.

3. U.S.Senate confirmed Gens. McDowell, Buell Burnside, McClernand, C. F. Smith, Lew. Wallace and Sigel as Maj.-Gens.; and Cols. Speed, of Tenn., Logan of Ill., McArthur of Iowa, Lauman of Iowa, Wallace of Ind., McCook of Ohio, Berry of Maine, and Terry of Conn., as Brigadiers.

4. Occupation of Fort Clinch and Fernandina, Fla., and St. Mary's and Brunswick, Ga., by Federal forces under Com. Dupont and Gen. Wright.

4. A squadron of 1st Michigan cavalry surprised and defeated a party of rebel cavalry at Berryville, Va., killing 3 and capturing 9 horses without loss.

4. Two bridges on the Nashville and Decatur railway, Tenn., destroyed by rebels.

5. Bunker Hill, Va., was occupied by rebel forces.

6. Two rebel officers were captured at Vienna, Va., by a detachment of Col. Averill's cavalry.

6 A rebel picket of 5 was captured by Van Alen's cavalry near Bunker Hill, Va.

7. Capt. Cole's Maryland cavalry encountered a few of Ashby's rebel cavalry, near Winchester, Va., 6 rebels were killed and 5 wounded. Capt. Cole had 3 men wounded.

6, 7, 8. Battle of Pea Ridge, Ark. The combined rebel forces under Gens. Van Dorn, Price, McCulloch and Pike, were defeated by the Federal army under Gens. Curtis, Sigel, Asboth and Davis. Federal loss in killed, wounded and missing, 1351. The rebel loss about 2000. Gens. McCulloch, McIntosh and Slack, were killed.

8. Destruction of the U. S. sloop-of-war Cumberland, and the frigate Congress, in action with the rebel iron battery Merrimac, in Hampton Roads, Va. 100 men were killed or drowned on the Cumberland.

8. By order of the President, Maj.-Gen. McClellan was directed to organize and command the army of the Potomac, divided into 5 army corps, under Maj.Gens. McDowell, Brig.-Gens. E. V. Sumner. S. P. Heintzelman, E. L. Keyes and N. P. Banks.

8. Col. Geary entered Leesburg, Va., capturing many prisoners, stores, &c.

8. Manassas, Va., was evacuated by the rebels.

9. Combat of the U. S. iron battery Monitor, and the rebel iron battery Merrimac, in Hampton Roads, Va. After a desperate combat of 3 hours, the Merrimac was compelled to retire, having received severe injuries.

9. The rebel battery at Cockpit Point, on the Potomac captured by Federal troops.

9. Brilliant charge of 14 of the Lincoln cavalry at Burk's station, near Fairfax

Court House, Va., against 100 infantry, 3 of whom were killed, 5 wounded and 11 captured. Lieut. Hidden was killed.

March 10. Lieut. O. Houston and 8 men of 2d Ohio battery was captured in S. W. Mo. by Texas rangers.

10. Centreville, Va., was occupied by national forces, the bridges, railway track, depot, &c. having been destroyed by rebels.

11. Gen. Pope's troops occupied Point Pleasant, Mo., 8 miles below New Madrid.

11. Berryville, Va., was occupied by Gen. Gorman, of Gen. Bank's division.

11. The country intervening between the Department of the Potomac and that of the Mississippi, was organized as the "Mountain Department," and assigned to Gen. Fremont.

11. The "Department of the Miss.," was organized and assigned to Gen. Halleck, which included his previous department, and that of Gen. Hunter's in Kansas; also all of Gen. Buell's west of Knoxville, Tenn.

11. Occupation of St. Augustine, Fla., by Federal naval forces under Com Rogers.

12. Winchester, Va., was occupied by national troops, who captured rebel stores.

12. Curtis's Iowa cavalry and a battalion of the 1st Nebraska, defeated 600 rebels and occupied Paris, Ky.

12. Occupation of Jacksonville, Fla., by Federal forces from the U. S. gunboats Ottawa, Seneca, and Pembina, under command of Lieut. T. F. Stevens.

13. Brunswick, Ga., was occupied by Federal forces under Flag-officer Dupont.

14. The rebels driven from New Madrid, Mo., which was occupied by Gens. Pope and Hamilton's forces, who captured military stores valued at $100,000. Federal loss during the siege 51 killed and wounded.

14. Battle of Newbern, N. C. Gen. Burnside's forces attacked and carried a continuous line of redoubts of half a mile in extent, after 4 hours' engagement. The rebels in their retreat set fire to the town, which was extinguished by the Federals with slight damage. 200 prisoners and 6 forts were taken, mounting 40 heavy guns. Federal loss, 39 killed, 150 wounded. Rebel loss, 50 killed, 200 wounded.

14. A detachment of Ohio and Indiana troops, under Col. Carter and Lieut. Col. Keigwin, from their camp at Cumberland Ford, Ky., attacked 300 rebels on the Cumberland Mountains, and defeated them, killing 3, wounding 6, and capturing 3 officers and 15 privates, 59 horses, 100 guns, 100 sabres and other material.

15. The Federal gunboats and mortars, under Com. Foote, began the investment and assault of Island No. 10, on the Miss.

16. Two rebel captains and 17 privates were captured on Indian Creek, Arkansas.

17. Federal forces in Va., under Gen. Shields, advanced from Winchester and drove the enemy toward Strasburg.

18. The rebel fleet on the Mississippi at Island No. 10, attacked Com. Foote's flotilla, but retired after slight loss on either side, the rebels crippling two of the Federal gunboats with their rams.

20. 67 citizens of Loudon co., Va., were sent to Richmond on the Central cars, and committed to one of the military prisons.

21. Santa Fé, N. M., was seized by 100 rebel Texans, under Major C. L. Pyron.

21. Washington, N. C., occupied by Federal troops under Col. Stevenson.

22. Rebel forces. under Gens. Jackson, Smith and Longstreet, advanced upon Winchester, Va., where Gen. Shields' forces engaged them successfully until night.

22. A skirmish occurred between a detachment of the 6th Kansas and Quantrall's band, near Independence, Mo. The latter was routed with 7 killed. The Federals lost 1 killed, and captured 11 prisoners and 20 horses.

22. Lieut. T. A. Budd and Acting Master Mather, attached to Flag-officer Dupont's squadron, having imprudently ventured on shore, with a portion of their men, to examine a rebel earthwork, near Mosquito Inlet, Fla., were fired upon by a party of rebels in ambush. Both officers and 5 men were killed, and several wounded.

23. Morehead City, N. C., was occupied by Federal troops under Gen. Parke.

23. Battle of Winchester, Va. The fight of yesterday was renewed, and after a desperate engagement, the rebels were driven from the ground in disorder, with a loss of 600 killed and wounded, and 300 prisoners. Federal loss, 100 killed, 400 wounded.

25. Maj. Pyron's Texans were defeated at Apache Cañon, between Santa Fé and Fort Union, by Federal troops under Maj. Chirington.

26. A band of rebels attacked 4 companies of State militia at Humansville, Polk co., Mo., and were defeated by them with a loss of 15 killed and many wounded.

27. Big Bethel, Va., was occupied by the Federal forces.

28. The Federal gunboats and mortars, under Coms. Farragut and Porter, attacked Forts Jackson and St. Philip, La.

28. Gen. Beauregard concentrated a large force at Corinth, Miss.

28. Morgan's rebel cavalry captured a train on the Louisville and Nashville railway. The locomotive was run into a ditch and the cars destroyed. Col. Currin Pope,

of Ky., and several other Federal officers were taken prisoners.

28. 1,200 U. S. troops, under Col. Slough, engaged the united rebel forces of Col. Scurry and Maj. Pyron at Vallo's Ranch, N. M., from 10 A. M. to 5 P. M., when an armistice was agreed on. A flank movement the next day by Maj. Chivington, with 400 men, threw the rebels into confusion, and after burning their train, they sought safety in flight. Rebel loss, 80 killed, 100 wounded, 93 prisoners. Federal loss, 38 killed, 54 wounded, 17 prisoners. The Texans retired to Santa Fé and the Federals to Fort Union.

29. A detachment of the 1st Iowa cavalry, under Capt. Thompson, overtook the guerrilla band of Col. Parker, 10 miles west of Warrensburg, Mo. 15 rebels were killed and 25 taken prisoners, among the latter Col. Parker and Captain Walton. 2 Federals were killed and several wounded.

30. Maj.-Gen Hunter arrived at Hilton Head, S. C., and assumed command of the Department of the South, comprising South Carolina, Georgia and Florida.

31. 220 rebels, captured at Winchester, Va., arrived at Fort Delaware, Del. Bay.

Apr. 1. During a storm at night, Col. Roberts with 50 picked men of the 42d Illinois, and as many seamen under First Master Johnson, of the gunboat St. Louis, surprised the rebels at the upper battery of Island No. 10, and spiked 6 large guns.

1. Col. Carline, commanding the advance of Gen. Steele's brigade in Arkansas, had a skirmish at Putnam's Ferry, in which a rebel lieutenant and several privates were wounded, and 5 prisoners taken.

4. All of Maryland and Virginia lying between the Mountain Department and the Blue Ridge, was constituted the military Department of the Shenandoah, and assigned to Maj. Gen. Banks; and that portion of Virginia east of the Blue Ridge and west of the Potomac constituted the Department of the Rappahannock, and was assigned to Maj. Gen. McDowell.

1. Gen. Banks advanced from Strasburg, Va., to Woodstock, and thence to Edenburg, driving the enemy with slight skirmishing. The railway bridge at Edenburg was burnt by rebels under Gen. Jackson.

1. Heavy bombardment at Island No. 10.

2. Manassas Gap, Va., was occupied by Col. Geary's troops by strategy, frustrating a similar attempt by the rebels.

3. U. S. Senate passed a bill for the abolition of slavery in the District of Columbia, by a vote of 29 yeas, 14 nays.

3. Gen. Steele's forces in the advance of Gen. Curtis' army, reached Putnam, Ark.

4. A schooner containing 24 recruits *en route* for the rebel army, was captured on Black creek, near the Potomac river, Va.

4. The Federal gunboat Carondelet ran past the rebel batteries at Island No. 10, at night, without damage, and arrived at New Madrid.

5. Gen. McClellan's army advanced through a severe storm from Camp Misery, and after a tedious march arrived in front of the rebel works, and commenced the siege of Yorktown, Va. Heavy firing throughout the day resulted in a loss to the Federals of 3 killed, 22 wounded.

5. Federal transports and barges arrived at New Madrid, Mo., through the inland channel, cut by Col Bissol's engineer corps, thus avoiding the rebel batteries at No. 10.

6-7. Battle of Pittsburg Landing, Tenn. The combined rebel army, under Gens. Johnston and Beauregard, attacked Gen. Grant's army on the morning of the 6th. Federal loss, 1,614 killed, 7,721 wounded, 3,963 missing—total, 13,508; rebel loss, (Beauregard's report,) 1,728 killed, 8,012 wounded, 959 missing—total, 10,699.

7. Gen. Pope, with the assistance of the gunboats Pittsburg and Carondelet, landed his forces on the Tennessee shore, opposite New Madrid, and took position in rear of Island No. 10, at Tiptonville.

7. Island No. 10 on the Mississippi, and the adjacent works on the Tenn. shore, were abandoned by the rebels and taken possession of by Col Buford's brigade.

7. Apalachicola, Fla., was captured by the Federal gunboats Mercedita and Sagamore.

8. Surrender of the rebel army of 5,200 men and all their stores, under Gens. Mackall and Gantt, to the Federal forces under Gen. Paine, of Gen. Pope's division, at Tiptonville, Tenn.

8. Gen. W. T. Sherman was dispatched by Gen. Grant with a large reconnoitering force on the Corinth, Miss., road. A portion of his force was routed by a charge of rebel cavalry, and 15 killed and 25 wounded of the 77th Ohio regiment.

10. Huntsville, Ala., was occupied by Gen. Mitchel's forces. 200 prisoners, 15 locomotives, and many cars captured.

10. Batteries on Tybee Island commenced the attack of Fort Pulaski, Ga.

10. President Lincoln, by proclamation, recommended the people throughout the United States on the Sabbath succeeding the receipt of his Proclamation to return thanks to Almighty God for having vouchsafed signal victories over rebellious enemies, and also for having averted the dangers of foreign interference and invasion.

11. Surrender of Fort Pulaski, Ga., after

a bombardment of two days. Federal loss, 1 killed, 1 wounded; rebels, 3 wounded 360 prisoners, 47 guns, 40,000 lbs. powder.

April 11. The rebel steamers Merrimac, Jamestown and Yorktown, came down between Newport News and Sewall's Point, on the Chesapeake, and captured 3 vessels.

11. Severe skirmishing in front of Yorktown, Va., by General Jameson's brigade. 20 of the Federals were killed or wounded.

11. Gen. Halleck assumed command of the Federal army at Pittsburg, Tenn.

12. Gen. Milroy, at Monterey, Va., was attacked by a large force of rebels, whom he repulsed with slight loss.

12. The Charleston and Memphis railway at Chattanooga Junction was seized by Gen. Mitchel's forces, and 2,000 rebels and much property were captured.

12. 4,000 men on five transports, accompanied by the gunboats Lexington and Tyler, left Pittsburg Landing, Tenn., and proceeded up the Tennessee river to Eastport, Miss., where they landed, and destroyed two bridges on the Ohio and Mobile railway, intercepting the rebel communication with Alabama. A body of Confederate cavalry were met on their return, who were routed, and four killed.

14. The U. S. forces were withdrawn from Jacksonville, Fla., and the rebels soon after returning the loyal inhabitants suffered severely, and many were driven away.

14. The Potomac flotilla ascended the Rappahannock river, Va., destroying several batteries. Three vessels were captured.

14. Com. Foote's mortar boats opened fire on Fort Wright, on the Mississippi.

15. M. Mercier, French Muister at Washington, paid an official visit to the rebel authorities at Richmond.

15. Ex-Sec. of War Cameron was arrested at Philadelphia, Pa., on the suit of Pierce Butler, for alleged illegal arrest.

16. Engagement at Lee's Mill, near Yorktown, Va. Federal loss, 32 killed and 100 wounded. Rebels, 25 killed, and 75 w.

17. Mount Jackson, in Shenandoah Co., Va., was occupied by Gen. Williams' troops, who captured 50 of Ashby's rebel cavalry.

17. A large boat was swamped at Castleman's Ferry, on the Shenandoah river, Va., by which between 40 and 50 of the 75th Penn. were drowned, among them Adj. Teatman, Capts. Wilson and Ward.

17. New Market, Va., occupied by Bank's army, and Fredericksburg by McDowell's.

17. Bombardment of Forts Wright, on the Mississippi, by the national flotilla.

17—24. Bombardment of Fort Jackson and St. Philip, on the Mississippi.

20. Battle of Camden or South Mills,

N. C. Gen. Reno's forces drove the rebels from their batteries and entrenchments. Federal loss in killed and wounded, 90.

22. Rebel steamer J. Robb was captured on the Tenn. river by gunboat Tyler.

24. Yorktown, Va., was shelled by the Federal gunboats.

24. Federal fleet passed Forts Jackson and St. Philip, destroying 13 rebel gunboats, the ram Manassas, and 3 transports.

25. New Orleans captured. Rebel batteries on both sides of the river destroyed.

25. Maj.-Gen. C. F. Smith died at Savannah, Tenn.

26. Rebel schooner Arctic was captured by U. S. steamer Flambeau.

26. Rebel schooner Belle was captured by U. S. steamer Uncas.

26. Skirmish at Neosho, Mo., between 1st Missouri volunteers, under Major Hubbard, and rebels and Indians under Cols. Coffee and Sternwright. Rebels defeated.

26. An advance lunette of the rebels at Yorktown was carried by the 1st Mass.

26. Capture of Fort Macon, N. C., with its garrison of 450 men under Col. White, after a bombardment of 11 hours. Rebel loss, 7 killed, 18 wounded. Federal loss, 1 killed, 3 wounded.

28. Forts St. Philip and Jackson, La., surrendered; forts Livingston and Pike abandoned, and the rebel iron battery Louisiana blown up.

30. Skirmish of Gen. Mitchel's forces with the rebels near Bridgeport, Ala.

May 2. The U. S. steamer Brooklyn and several gunboats, left New Orleans, ascending the Mississippi, to open the river and connect with Commodore Davis' fleet.

3. A reconnoissance in force under Gen. Paine from Pope's division encountered rebel cavalry pickets near Farmington, Miss., in which 8 of the latter were killed.

4. Gen. Stoneman's advance of McClellan's army encountered a rebel force near Williamsburg, Va., seven of whom were killed and 25 captured. 2 Feds. killed, 20 w.

5. Battle of Williamsburg, Va. Gen. Kearney's and Hooker's divisions engaged the rebel army under Gen. Longstreet from dawn till dark, when the Federals were reinforced and rebels defeated. Fed. loss 2,073 in killed and wounded, and 623 prisoners. Reb. loss heavier, 500 prisoners.

6. Skirmish near Harrisonburg, Va., by Federal troops under Major Vought.

7. Westpoint, Va. Gen. Franklin's division of McClellan's army having been conveyed by transports to the head of York river, effected a landing, where he was attacked by a force of rebels, and with the aid of gunboats defeated the enemy.

www.ingramcontent.com/pod-product-compliance
Lightning Source LLC
Chambersburg PA
CBHW021422300426
44114CB00010B/608